THE LAST MINSTRELS

THE LAST MINSTRELS

YEATS AND THE REVIVAL OF THE BARDIC ARTS

RONALD SCHUCHARD

OXFORD
UNIVERSITY PRESS

OXFORD
UNIVERSITY PRESS

Great Clarendon Street, Oxford OX2 6DP

Oxford University Press is a department of the University of Oxford.
It furthers the University's objective of excellence in research, scholarship,
and education by publishing worldwide in

Oxford New York

Auckland Cape Town Dar es Salaam Hong Kong Karachi
Kuala Lumpur Madrid Melbourne Mexico City Nairobi
New Delhi Shanghai Taipei Toronto

With offices in

Argentina Austria Brazil Chile Czech Republic France Greece
Guatemala Hungary Italy Japan Poland Portugal Singapore
South Korea Switzerland Thailand Turkey Ukraine Vietnam

Oxford is a registered trade mark of Oxford University Press
in the UK and in certain other countries

Published in the United States
by Oxford University Press Inc., New York

First published 2008

British Library Cataloguing in Publication Data

Data available

Library of Congress Cataloging in Publication Data

Data available

Typeset by SPI Publisher Services, Pondicherry, India
Printed in Great Britain
on acid-free paper by
Biddles Ltd., King's Lynn, Norfolk

ISBN 978–0–19–923000–6

1 3 5 7 9 10 8 6 4 2

For Warwick Gould and Deirdre Toomey
such friends

Acknowledgments

The late Anne Yeats and the late Michael Yeats were generous and selfless stewards of their father's estate, and I am one among scores of students and scholars of W. B. Yeats grateful to them and Gráinne Yeats for their interest, assistance, and permissions over several decades. They brought many of us together in Yeats and in friendship, and this is yet another book that has benefitted immeasurably from their hospitable furtherance of Yeats scholarship.

This study would have been unimaginable without my access to *The Collected Letters of W. B. Yeats,* under the general editorship of John S. Kelly. In addition to the four edited and annotated volumes in print (1865–1907), the *Collected Letters* includes the comprehensive database of Professor Kelly's InteLex Electronic Edition (Oxford University Press, 2002).

Special dedicatory thanks are due to Warwick Gould and Deirdre Toomey, who assisted me with this study from its inception and read the manuscript at various stages to completion. I am also grateful to Anthony Cuda for reading and providing helpful suggestions for each chapter. I prize the dogged research skills of Declan Kiely, who selflessly tracked down numerous fugitive items on my behalf.

I am indebted to the following librarians and libraries for assistance and permissions: Liz Baird, Taylor Institution Library; Stephen Crook, Declan Kiely, and Philip Milito, Berg Collection, New York Public Library; Stephen Enniss, Linda Matthews, and staff of the Manuscript, Archives, and Rare Book Library, Emory University; Cathy Henderson, the Harry Ransom Humanities Research Center, University of Texas–Austin; Claire Hudson, Theatre Museum, London; Michelle Lefevre, Local Studies Library, Leeds; Alexandra Mason, Kenneth Spencer Research Library, University of Kansas; Leslie A. Morris, Houghton Library, Harvard University; Eric R. Nitschke, Robert W. Woodruff Library, Emory University; Kristen Parker, Isabella Stewart Gardner Museum, Boston; Sarah Powell, Central Library, Bradford; Patricia Woodard, Hunter College Library; Patricia

Willis, Beinecke Rare Book and Manuscript Library, Yale University; the staff of Rare Books and Manuscripts, British Library; the staff of the Firestone Library, Princeton University; the staff of the Manuscripts Room, National Library of Ireland; the staff of Trinity College Library, Dublin; and special thanks to the staff of the British Newspaper Library, Colindale: without the extraordinary resources of its newspaper collections the history of Yeats's experiments in poetry and music could never have been reconstructed.

Versions of some sections of this book first appeared in *The Review of English Studies*, *Yeats Annual*, *Yeats: An Annual of Critical and Textual Studies*, *The South Carolina Review*, and *Princeton University Library Chronicle*, and I am grateful to the respective editors for permission to reprint the material, all of which has been revised and expanded as archival and other research materials have become accessible, piece by piece, year by year. Chapters 1, 3, 5, 7, 9, and most of 10 have not been published previously in any form.

I am grateful to the following individuals for assistance of various kinds: Jonathan Allison, University of Kentucky; Jacqueline Baker, Oxford University Press; Jewel Spears Brooker, Eckerd College; Terence Brown, Trinity College, Dublin; Chris Buttram, Winona State University; Deborah Byrd, Lafayette College; Margaret Campbell, London; Wayne K. Chapman, Clemson University; Liz Butler Cullingford, University of Texas–Austin; Tara Christie Kinsey, Princeton University; Brian Cliff, Trinity College, Dublin; Brendan Corcoran, Indiana State University, Terre Haute; Robert Cunningham, Atlanta; Anne Margaret Daniel, New School, NY; the late Carl Dolmetsch; the late Richard Finneran; the late Mary Fitzgerald; James Flannery, Emory University; Anne Fogarty, University College, Dublin; R. F. Foster, Hertford College, Oxford; the late George Mills Harper; Meg Harper, Georgia State University; Geraldine Higgins, Emory University; Sam Hynes, Princeton University; the late A. Norman Jeffares; Colton Johnson, Vassar College; Mary M. Lago; A. Walton Litz, Princeton University; Andrew McNeillie, Oxford University Press; William M. Murphy, Schenectady, NY; James Pethica, Williams College; Omar Pound, Princeton University; Elaine Gradman Rose, Stanford University; Ann Saddlemyer, University of Toronto; Bart Schultz, University of Chicago; Maggie Shade, and Fiona Smith, Oxford University Press; Colin Smythe, Gerrards Cross; Jon Stallworthy, Wolfson College, Oxford; the late Riette Sturge Moore; George Watson, University of Aberdeen;

Frances Whistler, Boston University; Deborah White, Emory University; and many students of Emory University and of the Yeats International Summer School, Sligo.

Research assistance for this study has been provided by the American Council for Learned Societies; Emory University; the Institute of English Studies, School of Advanced Study, University of London; the Institute of Irish Studies, Queen's University, Belfast; the National Endowment for the Humanities; and Trinity College, Dublin.

My wife, Keith Schuchard, has been my most discerning reader and constructive critic; she and my daughters Ashley, Caitlin, and Justine kept their good humor during my late-night chanting of "Impetuous Heart," "Sailing to Byzantium," and numerous other passionate poems and ballads.

Contents

Abbreviations

Aut	*Autobiographies*, ed. William H. O'Donnell and Douglas N. Archibald (New York: Scribner, 1999).
Bax	*Florence Farr, Bernard Shaw and W. B. Yeats*, ed. Clifford Bax (Dublin: Cuala Press, 1941).
Berg	The Berg Collection, New York Public Library (Astor, Lenox, and Tilden Foundations).
BIV1,2	*A Book of Irish Verse* (London: Methuen, 1895; 1900).
BL Add. MS	Additional Manuscript, The British Library, London (followed by number).
Bodleian	The Bodleian Library, Oxford University.
CL1,2,3,4	*The Collected Letters of W. B. Yeats: Vol. I, 1865–1895*, ed. John Kelly and Eric Domville; *Vol. II, 1896–1900*, ed. Warwick Gould, John Kelly, and Deirdre Toomey; *Vol. III, 1901–1904*, ed. John Kelly and Ronald Schuchard; and *Vol. IV, 1905–1907*, ed. John Kelly and Ronald Schuchard (Oxford: Clarendon Press, 1986, 1997, 1994, 2005).
CL InteLex	*The Collected Letters of W. B. Yeats*, Gen. Ed. John Kelly, (Oxford: Oxford University Press (InteLex Electronic Edition), 2002). Letters cited by accession number.
CW1–8	*The Collected Works in Verse and Prose of William Butler Yeats* (Stratford-on-Avon: The Shakespeare Head Press, 1908, 8 vols.).
CWTEH	*The Complete Works of T. E. Hulme*, ed. Karen Csengeri (Oxford: Clarendon Press, 1994).
Diaries	*Lady Gregory's Diaries 1892-1902,* ed. James Pethica (Gerrards Cross: Colin Smythe, 1996).
E&I	*Essays and Introductions* (London and New York: Macmillan, 1961).
Expl	*Explorations*, sel. Mrs W. B. Yeats (London: Macmillan, 1962; New York: Macmillan, 1963).
EP/DS	*Ezra Pound and Dorothy Shakespear: Their Letters 1909-1914*, ed. Omar Pound and A. Walton Litz (London: Faber and Faber, 1985).

EPPP	*Ezra Pound's Poetry and Prose: Contributions to Periodicals*, ed. Lee Baechler, A. Walton Litz, and James Longenbach (New York and London: Garland Publishing, 1991, 11 vols.).
G-YL	*The Gonne–Yeats Letters 1893-1938: Always Your Friend*, ed. Anna MacBride White and A. Norman Jeffares (London: Hutchinson, 1992).
Haslemere	Dolmetsch Library, Haslemere, Surrey.
Holloway	Joseph Holloway's unpublished theatre journals, National Library of Ireland.
Houghton	Houghton Library, Harvard University.
HRHRC	Books and Manuscripts, Harry Ransom Humanities Research Center, University of Texas–Austin.
Huntington	Henry E. Huntington Library, San Marino.
JHAT	*Joseph Holloway's Abbey Theatre: A Selection from His Unpublished Journal: Impressions of a Dublin Playgoer*, ed. Robert Hogan and Michael J. O'Neill (Carbondale and Edwardsville: Southern Illinois University Press; London and Amsterdam: Feffer and Sessions, 1967).
JBYL	*Letters to His Son W. B. Yeats and Others 1869–1922,* by J. B. Yeats, edited with a Memoir by Joseph Hone and a Preface by Oliver Elton (London: Faber and Faber, 1944).
L	*The Letters of W. B. Yeats*, ed. Allan Wade (London: Rupert Hart-Davis, 1954; New York: Macmillan, 1955.
LAR	*Later Articles and Reviews*: *Uncollected Articles, Reviews, and Radio Broadcasts Written after 1900*, ed. Colton Johnson (New York: Scribner, 2000).
LE	*Later Essays*, ed. William H. O'Donnell (New York: Scribner, 1994).
LBP	*Letters from Bedford Park: A Selection from the Correspondence (1890-1901) of John Butler Yeats*, ed. with an introduction and notes by William M. Murphy (Dublin: Cuala Press, 1972).
Life 1	*W. B. Yeats: A Life, I: The Apprentice Mage,* by R. F. Foster (Oxford and New York: Oxford University Press, 1997).
Life 2	*W. B. Yeats: A Life, II: The Arch-Poet*, by R. F. Foster (Oxford and New York: Oxford University Press, 2003).
LJQ	*The Letters of John Quinn to W. B. Yeats*, ed. Alan B. Himber, with the assistance of George Mills Harper (Ann Arbor: UMI Research Press, 1983).
LNI	*Letters to the New Island,* ed. George Bornstein and Hugh Witemeyer (London: Macmillan, 1989).

LTWBY1,2	*Letters to W. B. Yeats*, ed. Richard J. Finneran, George Mills Harper, and William M. Murphy, with the assistance of Alan B. Himber (London: Macmillan; New York: Columbia University Press, 1977, 2 vols.).
MBY	Manuscripts in the collection of the late Michael Butler Yeats.
Mem	*Memoirs: Autobiography–First Draft: Journal*, transcribed and edited by Denis Donoghue (London: Macmillan, 1972: New York: Macmillan, 1973).
Myth	*Mythologies* (London and New York: Macmillan, 1959).
NLI	Department of Manuscripts, National Library of Ireland, Dublin.
NYPL	Manuscripts Division, New York Public Library.
OBMV	*The Oxford Book of Modern Verse 1895–1935*, chosen by W. B. Yeats (Oxford: Clarendon Press, 1936).
P&I	*Prefaces and Introductions: Uncollected Prefaces and Introductions by Yeats to Works by Other Authors and to Anthologies edited by Yeats*, ed. William H. O'Donnell (London: Macmillan, 1988).
UP1	*Uncollected Prose by W. B. Yeats*, Vol. 1, ed. John P. Frayne (London: Macmillan; New York: Columbia University Press, 1970).
UP2	*Uncollected Prose by W. B. Yeats*, Vol. 2, ed. John P. Frayne and Colton Johnson (London: Macmillan, 1975; New York: Columbia University Press, 1976).
VMP	T. S. Eliot, *The Varieties of Metaphysical Poetry*, ed. Ronald Schuchard (London: Faber and Faber, 1993; New York: Harcourt Brace, 1994).
VP	*The Variorum Edition of the Poems of W. B. Yeats*, ed. Peter Allt and Russell K. Alspach (New York: Macmillan, 1957); cited from the corrected third printing of 1966.
VPl	*The Variorum Edition of the Plays of W. B. Yeats*, ed. Russell K. Alspach (London and New York: Macmillan, 1966); cited from the corrected second printing of 1966.
YA	*Yeats Annual* (London: Macmillan, 1982–); cited by no.
YAACTS	*Yeats: An Annual of Critical and Textual Studies*, ed. Richard J. Finneran (publishers vary, 1983–99); cited by no.
YL	Edward O'Shea, *A Descriptive Catalog of W. B. Yeats's Library* (New York and London: Garland Publishing, 1985).
YT	*Yeats and the Theatre*, ed. Robert O'Driscoll and Lorna Reynolds (Toronto: Macmillan of Canada; Niagra Falls, NY: Maclean-Hunter Press, 1975).

List of Illustrations

PLATES

TEXTUAL ILLUSTRATIONS

Chapter 2

Preface

The living voice is ever living in its inmost joy.

—William Blake, *Vala*

"What I am hoping for," wrote Yeats the month before his death, "is a small book dealing with the relations between speech and song."[1] Rekindled by his BBC broadcast experiments and by the revival of *Broadsides* between 1935 and 1937, Yeats's last hope was the final expression of one of his oldest, most frustrated desires. The recipient of the letter, Victor Clinton-Baddeley, who had worked closely with Yeats on the broadcasts, partially honored his request with *Words for Music* (1941), which contains a final chapter on Yeats's later theory of speaking verse. But Clinton-Baddeley was largely unaware that his subject's preoccupation with words for music at the end of his life had also been the passion of earlier days, and that the broadcast-broadside experiments in the late 1930s were but the last in a lifelong effort to revive the lost bardic arts of chanting and musical speech.

Yeats's turn-of-the-century experiments with Florence Farr and Arnold Dolmetsch, as briefly described in "Speaking to the Psaltery" (1902), have been perfunctorily summarized by generations of incredulous observers. His expressed desire to unite poetry and music has been continuously dismissed as the amusing aberration of a notoriously tone-deaf poet whose self-declared ignorance of music made the seriousness of his avowed interests highly dubious and subject to parody. Even Richard Ellmann, the first chronicler of Yeats's intellectual biography, saw Yeats's essay as a tongue-in-cheek treatment of "a beguiling fancy" and stated that "No one need wonder that shortly after writing the essay he gave up the psaltery."[2] Subsequent

1. *CL InteLex, 7352.*
2. Richard Ellmann, *Yeats: The Man and the Masks* (Oxford: Oxford University Press, 1979), 150. In his analysis of Yeats's "noncommittal expressions" in "Speaking to the Psaltery," Ellmann states that Yeats "does not exactly advocate or predict the use of the psaltery; he merely is 'not certain' that he will not see a psaltery movement arise. Then too, he smiles slightly at us, and perhaps the smile means that we should not take this urbane man too seriously. He writes with the confidence of the author who is making no assertions to which the reader will not consent; he seems to say, if you do not believe in the psaltery, and indeed, perhaps you are

biographers have followed Ellmann's lead, ignoring Yeats's musical claims as absurd and glossing the early experiments in little more than a paragraph and with similar skepticism and dismissal. But Yeats's curious essay was not, as Ellmann suggested, merely a devious way of deploring badly spoken verse. It was meant to be a major poetic and dramatic manifesto, and the failure to read and follow it as such has affected our understanding of his intellectual activities, his poetics and prosody, his dramaturgy, his aims for the Abbey Theatre, his cultural nationalism, his role in the development of Imagism, and his place in a complex of interrelated arts in London and Dublin.

Moreover, the failure to give credence to his declarations has left an extraordinary dimension of biography and literary history unwritten. This is not exactly the book that Yeats hoped for in 1939, but it aims to present a biographical, historical, and critical reconstruction of his lifelong preoccupation with the music and magic of speech. It also chronicles his heroic attempt, as one of the last minstrels, to resurrect the ancient art of chanting and to restore a spiritual democracy of art in Ireland particularly and in the modern world generally.

There is a conventional, almost calcified perception that Yeats adopted an affected bardic pose during the "Celtic twilight" of the 1890s, reciting poems such as "The Lake Isle of Innisfree" and "The Song of the Old Mother" in a strange, chant-like delivery, a pose that he wisely put off after the publication of *The Wind Among the Reeds* (1899), despite the lingering anomaly of "Speaking to the Psaltery." According to most critics, after Maud Gonne darkened the twilight by her precipitous marriage to John MacBride, thereby fostering "The Folly of Being Comforted" and other anguished poems of *In the Seven Woods* (1903), Yeats began to redirect much of his energy into poetic drama and to write non-visionary poems with rhythms no longer suitable for chanting. Certainly, one often hears that the poems from *The Green Helmet and Other Poems* (1910) to *Last Poems and Plays* (1940) were not written to be chanted.

To initiate a correction of this prevailing view of Yeats's rhythmic career, the first chapter, "Bardic Forefathers," traces Yeats's instinctive inheritance of the bardic tradition in his early intellectual and creative life: his intuitive awareness of the bardic poet's responsibility to the imaginative and aesthetic

right, you will certainly not deny that verse today is badly spoken. No one need wonder that shortly after writing the essay he gave up the psaltery."

life of his culture and of his essential role in creating the images, shaping the values, and restoring the dignity of a beleaguered nation. At a time when materialistic societies were pushing their counter-cultural poets to the periphery or into exile, Yeats made a bardic compact to return the poetic voice to the center of culture—on its platforms, stages, and street corners, in a poetry and drama that speak to all classes of the reading and non-reading citizenry. The development of his poetic/cultural consciousness and his attempt to define the distinctive nature of the Irish poetic voice are placed in the context of his study of the demise of the bardic tradition in the seventeenth century, the ballad and folk-song traditions that arose in Ireland and England in the eighteenth century, and their decline in the nineteenth century. As background to the onset of Yeats's own exuberant chanting in the 1880s, the chapter traces the persistence of bardic chanting in nineteenth-century poets—from Blake, Wordsworth, and Coleridge to Tennyson, Swinburne, and Morris—and shows how Yeats as inheritor was determined to take the living voices of a chanting tradition that had retreated into solitary walkways and private quarters back into the public realm. His vision of a revived oral tradition for a new century demanded not only a reaction against the moral fervor and rhetoric of Victorian poetry, but an equal reaction against the sentimental patriotism and lack of craft in nineteenth-century Irish poetry. For the bardic contrarian, only highly crafted poetry of personal, passionate utterance would be worthy of Ireland in the coming times.

Coincident with this developing vision, Yeats encountered and was entranced by the musical, incantatory voice of the actress Florence Farr, who became his companion in magical studies and his partner in developing the chanting of lyrics for his early poems and plays in London and Dublin. By 1901 they were ready to take their planned revival of romantic drama and chanted poetry to public platforms, aided by the musical expertise and craftsmanship of Arnold Dolmetsch, who began making psalteries for their expanding retinue. Chapters 2 and 3 thus delineate the efforts of this minstrel threesome to educate the public with illustrated lectures, to form a romantic theatre society, and to train chanters and psaltery players, first in London and then in Dublin. At this point the study becomes in part the biography of a vision, of what Yeats called "my chief obsession."

The neglected life of Yeats's obsessive vision manifests itself in forgotten societies, slowly surfacing correspondence and archives, fugitive newspaper reports and reviews, surviving scripts of radio broadcasts, and in the diaries and memoirs of friendly and unfriendly observers who witnessed events in Woburn Buildings, private drawing rooms, and lecture halls in several countries. Although Yeats created a public life for his public vision, it quickly disappeared from public view, glossed over by literary histories and reduced to a paragraph or two in successive biographies. Driven to narrate the contours of a whole life, biographers could not adequately accommodate a seemingly insignificant activity with so few facts and details, most of which had sunk to the bottom of the sea of print. Given time to resurface and coalesce, however, the widely dispersed materials document a lost literary movement that was the most consuming preoccupation of Yeats's literary life, and the most integral to his art. The reconstructed chanting movement provides for significant interventions in literary history, biography, and criticism; it reanimates the daily interrelation of the arts and artists that sustained the movement; and it restores the color, passion, and humor drained from literary relationships by the relentless process of historical synthesis.

Determined to find a home or stable venue for romantic drama whether in Dublin or London or both, Yeats, Farr, and friends expended tremendous energy in organizing dramatic societies and training actors and actresses in chanting. Chapters 4 and 5 trace their activities in such societies, from the Masquers Society, which came close to denying the establishment of the Abbey Theatre in Dublin, to the Dancers, which Farr and Dolmetsch organized to teach sixteenth-century dances for his concerts and dramatic arts for romantic plays, to the Court Theatre, where Farr's choral chanting for Gilbert Murray's translations of Euripides' plays came into conflict with the realistic dramaturgy of Harley Granville-Barker. Out of the romantic/realistic conflicts that accompanied the rise of Attic drama in London, however, Yeats and Farr developed the three-musician choruses that would chant the lyrics of *Deirdre* and those of subsequent plays. The experiments and techniques that were worked out in London societies, theatres, and lecture halls were subsequently transferred to the Irish National Dramatic Company in Dublin. Dolmetsch psalteries were delivered to George Russell and then Frank Fay, who began to train Sara Allgood and others for chanting Yeats's verse and choral lyrics. When the Abbey Theatre finally became a reality in 1904, it was from the outset envisioned as a theatre of musical speech and chanted verse, a theatre in which actors on the stage would also serve as reciters in the streets, taking imaginative life to the populace through the applied arts of literature.

Yeats's neglected essay, "Literature and the Living Voice," written as a foundation document for his vision of the Abbey Theatre, also served as the basis for scores of illustrated lectures by Yeats, Farr, and their ardent pupils on the "new art" of chanting. In1906, after five years of lecturing in London and Dublin (and once very successfully in Manchester), Yeats and Farr took their new art into provincial cities and universities, thrilling large audiences in Leeds, Liverpool, Edinburgh, Aberdeen, and Dundee, as they sought to displace the cultural elitism of the printed book with a poetic orality that would redress the cultural imbalance of literacy and illiteracy. They would restore a lost spiritual democracy that valued the unwritten tradition as much as the written, that provided an enhanced perception of life for all classes, the noble and the beggar-man alike. Chapters 6 and 7 record the electrifying effects of their touring performances on provincial audiences as Yeats spread his vision throughout Great Britain and as Farr took it to America and the south of France. By 1908 Yeats and Farr had made their controversial enterprise the most visible poetic movement in the country, and Yeats took steps to preserve the psaltery settings of his lyrics and choruses in his eight-volume *Collected Works*.

Literary history has excluded Yeats from any presence or role in the Imagist movement, even though Farr was a member of the first Imagist group that came together in 1908 through the Poets' Club, lecturing to them on the psaltery and chanted verse. The Imagist movement was effectively energized when she provoked T. E. Hulme into formulating his own anti-romantic, anti-chanting reaction to the Yeats–Farr movement, pitting his visual paradigm for modern poetry against their aural paradigm. Chapter 8 portrays the dynamics of this early conflict in the development of modern literature, showing how Yeats and Farr, co-opting Ezra Pound as an ally, prevailed in leading the Imagists to "compose in sequence of the musical phrase, not in sequence of the metronome," and to declare publicly that "Poetry is a spoken and not a written art." The subsequent arrival of the Bengali poet Rabindranath Tagore in the Imagist complex further invigorated Yeats's cultural imagination, especially when Tagore, whose poetry was sung to the people by modern troubadours in Bengal, enforced his belief that an oral tradition and a spiritual democracy were still possible in the West.

Yeats and Farr continued to give chanting recitals and to train actors and actresses in chanting until Farr unexpectedly left England for Ceylon in 1912. Chapter 9 follows the ways in which Yeats redirected the chanting movement after her departure and during the war. His collaboration with Pound in studying and adapting the Noh drama allowed him to assimilate its chanting and symbolic dramaturgy into his new dance plays. Just as Dolmetsch had assisted Yeats with chanting and regulated declamation earlier in the century, he now reappeared to assist Pound with evidence of free verse in seventeenth- and eighteenth-century music, giving new energy to the free verse movement, to which Yeats remained an alien observer. T. S. Eliot was brought into their company, friendship, and influence, but the collective forces of modernism and the antithetical aesthetic temperaments of the younger poets made their break with Yeats inevitable by the end of the war. Yeats's new life in marriage and in the construction of *A Vision* removed him not only from Woburn Buildings, for twenty years the headquarters of the chanting movement, but from the ability to provide for the training of verse speakers and choruses for his plays at the Abbey. Resigned to the rise of "slum plays," Yeats withdrew into his senatorship; the "unfashionable art" of his chanting movement was seemingly over.

During the 1920s the senator and Nobel laureate gave several readings before huge Dublin audiences, chanting old and new poems from "The Lake Isle of Innisfree" to "An Irish Airman Foresees His Death," but his poetic and dramatic ideals had become the dormant subjects of his memoirs. He had ignored and resisted the rise of broadcasting during the decade, but when in 1931 he was invited by the BBC to read his poems and to introduce a radio production of his *Sophocles' King Oedipus*, he saw the opportunity to resurrect and give voice to his old obsession. Chapter 10 reconstructs Yeats's compelling attempt to reunite poetry and music and reconstitute his dream of a spiritual democracy through the medium of public broadcasting. With a contemporary cast of characters playing roles similar to their earlier counterparts, he began an active program of broadcasting his own and other poems and ballads, training Margot Ruddock as his new Florence Farr and drawing on a number of actors and musicians to help effect his vision. He made Victor Clinton-Baddeley, his chief male reciter, training him to chant "An Irish Airman Foresees His Death," "Mad as the Mist and Snow," "Sailing to Byzantium," and other late poems. While realistic directors at the Abbey were actively betraying the Abbey tradition of rhythmical speech in producing his plays, he founded a new Poets' Theatre in London and began revising plays for their proper production. He initiated a series of illustrated *Broadsides* to place Irish and English poets who worked in his poetic tradition prominently before the public, and he began editing the *Oxford Book of Modern Verse*, similarly selecting poets to set against the younger school of Eliot, Pound, and Auden, determined to make his tradition prevail over their modern ways.

All of these activities over fifty years were part of an undying effort to keep poetry in the public imagination, to keep poetry in drama, and to keep essential bardic arts and responsibilities alive in the modern world. Resisting realism and modernism in all their forms to the end, Yeats is to be seen not only as a disciplined magician who transmuted ordinary reality in the visionary imagination, and not only as a poet who continually remade himself for his art, but as a modern bard dedicated to transmuting and remaking a utilitarian world whose citizenry could not thrive so long as the life of the imagination was not an integral part of national life.

Readers will be disappointed by the fact that there exist no early discs or recordings of Yeats chanting or Farr speaking to the psaltery, only the familiar recordings in the 1930s of Yeats chanting "The Lake Isle of Innisfree," "The Song of the Old Mother," "The Fiddler of Dooney," and two stanzas of "Coole Park and Ballylee, 1931."[3] After Yeats's death, Victor Clinton-Baddeley searched the archives of the BBC, only to discover that other recordings had been destroyed or "accidentally thrown away during the turmoil of the war years."[4] According to L. A. G. Strong, the late recordings that exist do not convey the combined richness, emotional power, and musicality of Yeats's earlier voice. "There was a vibrant singing note," wrote Strong, "a virility in the diction which, by the time the records were taken . . . had become unsteady and the tone itself had worn thin."[5] In contrast, when Strong first heard Yeats read at Oxford in the 1920s, "he could make almost anything sound magnificent." Even so, the late recordings are valuable in showing the way he would have his poems recited. Throughout this narrative, many witnesses are brought forward to

3. Yeats's recitations of these poems were reproduced on a commercial recording, *The Poems of William Butler Yeats/Read by William Butler Yeats, Siobhan McKenna and Michael MacLiammoir*, Spoken Arts 753 (New Rochelle, NY, 1959). The two recordings of "The Lake Isle of Innisfree" were made by the BBC on October 4, 1932, and October 28, 1937; "The Song of the Old Mother" was recorded on March 14, 1934, the stanza from "Coole Park and Ballylee, 1931" on October 28, 1937. The Spoken Arts recording also includes Yeats's broadcast of "Modern Poetry" on October 11, 1936, in which Yeats reads from C. Day Lewis's "Two Songs," Edith Sitwell's "Ass-Face," and T. S. Eliot's "Preludes."

4. V. C. Clinton-Baddeley, "The Written and the Spoken Word," *Essays and Studies 1965* (London: John Murray, 1965), 80. Subsequent attempts to locate discs and recordings have been unsuccessful.

5. L. A. G. Strong, "Remembrance of W. B. Yeats," BBC Third Programme, April 15, 1954.

describe in their own words the nature and effect of his and Farr's readings, in public and in private, over many years. The appendices provide Farr's own descriptions of her methods in "The Chanting of Poems" (1905) and her short essay on "Music in Words" (1906), as well as Edmund Dulac's later essay on "Music and Poetry" (1937), written in response to Yeats's later method of chanting.

I

Bardic Forefathers

I

The bardic instincts that drove Yeats to revive the lost art of speaking and chanting to musical notes are first apparent in his fragmented reveries over childhood and youth: "Since I was a boy," he wrote in "Speaking to the Psaltery," "I have always longed to hear verse spoken to a harp, as I imagined Homer to have spoken his, for it is not natural to enjoy an art when one is by oneself. Images used to rise up before me . . . of wild-eyed men speaking harmoniously to murmuring wires while audiences in many-coloured robes listened, hushed and excited" (*E&I* 14). His father, who read with great intensity and subtlety, had like many a Victorian father carefully superintended the growth of his son's artistic sensibility. Among the works of imaginative literature that he first read aloud to his son was Sir Walter Scott's *The Lay of the Last Minstrel* (1805), a vividly remembered work that gave Yeats "a wish to turn magician that competed for years with the dream of being killed upon the sea-shore" (*Aut* 68). By his late teens, his bardic reveries had begun to affect his creative process; his father then wrote patiently of his "youth of eighteen" to Edward Dowden: "His bad metres arise very much from his composing in a loud voice, manipulating of course the quantities to his own taste" (*JBYL* 53). Yeats was certain that he composed to a manner of music, and in the bardic manner he had already begun to dwell on the vowels, placing strong emphasis on the rhythm, which he hummed over and over for hours in the process of composing. "Like every other poet," he modestly confessed, "I spoke verses in a kind of chant when I was making them; and sometimes, when I was alone on a country road, I would speak them in a loud chanting voice, and feel that if I dared I would speak them in that way to other people" (*E&I* 14). One of the first companions to whom he dared chant was the poet Katharine

Tynan, who occasionally stayed at the Yeats home in the mid-1880s. "He would read his poetry for hours if you would allow it," she wrote. "If you brought him a new poem he would chant it over to himself with his head on one side. . . . I used to be awakened in the night by a steady, monotonous sound rising and falling. It was Willie chanting to himself in the watches of the night."[1]

By his twenty-first year Yeats had identified himself with the third-century Irish chieftan, King Goll, who was suddenly possessed by madness in battle and disappeared into a forest. In "The Madness of King Goll," Yeats's warrior-king turned poet, "Murmuring, to a fitful tune," discovers an old tympan, an ancient Irish stringed instrument, which he uses to summon the muse Orchil, who gives him poetic release from his divine, impulsive rhythm (*VP* 85). For Yeats, the poem was a metaphorical idealization of his own creative life, and so closely did his father identify him with Goll that he etched a portrait of his bearded son as Goll tearing the strings out of the tympan in a moment of creative intensity (Plate 2).[2] Yeats included the poem among those he contributed to *Poems and Ballads of Young Ireland* (1888). In his review of the volume, as he aligned himself with poets of an Irish bardic tradition, he stated admiringly and enviously that when reading certain poems of Samuel Ferguson "one seems to be listening to some old half-savage bard chanting to his companions at a forest fire. If we long, while listening, for the more elaborate music of modern days, the fault is in us and in our time" (*UP1* 159). His vision of himself as a modern manifestation of the ancient bard came gradually and instinctively to life.

In *The Trembling of the Veil* (1922), Yeats recounted how in the four-year period beginning in 1887 he was obsessed with his conviction that the world had become "a bundle of fragments"; in his longing for a lost "Unity of Being," he delighted in reading about those historical ages "where poet and artist confined themselves gladly to some inherited subject-matter known to the whole people" (*Aut* 164). He took great pleasure in remembering that the works of Homer, Dante, Ariosto, and Wolfram of

1. Katharine Tynan, *Twenty-Five Years* (London: Smith, Elder, 1913), 190.
2. The portrait appeared as an illustration for Yeats's "King Goll. An Irish Legend" in the *Leisure Hour*, September 1887 (Plate 2). Yeats wrote with some embarrassment to John McGrath about the illustration on January 19, 1893: "The picture you speak of was done from me & is probably like though it was not intended as a portrait. Be sure I would never have had myself painted as the mad 'King Goll' of my own poem had I thought it was going to turn out the portrait it has. I was merely the cheapest & handiest modle [*sic*] to be found" (*CL4* 939). The initial sketch (MBY), recently discovered, is reproduced as Plate 1.

Eschenbach were sung by both poets and the common man. Although he still preferred Shakespeare to Chaucer, he begrudged his preference because of the dissociation that had occurred between them:

> Had not Europe shared one mind and heart, until both mind and heart began to break into fragments a little before Shakespeare's birth? Music and verse began to fall apart when Chaucer robbed verse of its speed that he might give it greater meditation, though for another generation or so minstrels were to sing his lengthy elaborated *Troilus and Criseyde*.
>
> (*Aut* 165)

Yeats knew that the fractured harmony between poetry and musical speech had scarcely held together beyond the seventeenth century. Nonetheless, as the poet's relation to his culture and the common man was one of his abiding interests as a young poet, he had become a student of bardic traditions wherever he found them: the Irish *File*, the English bards, the rhapsodists of ancient Greece, the minstrels of Europe and India. He was no less interested in how the bardic gave way to the ballad tradition in Ireland and England, the Gaelic to the Anglo-Irish, and he began to exercise his knowledge of both traditions in his early critical writings. In 1887 he published "Popular Ballad Poetry of Ireland," claiming in his nationalist mode that while England had allowed "the true ballad—the poem of the populace—" to perish, Ireland had preserved what was necessary for a popular ballad literature to arise, "national traditions not hidden in libraries, but living in the minds of the populace" (*UP1* 147).

Identifying Clarence Mangan, Thomas Davis, and Ferguson among the best of the Irish ballad writers, he was particularly attracted to the latter for his bardic subjects and overtones. Ferguson had been a student of James Hardiman's two-volume *Irish Minstrelsy; or, Bardic Remains of Ireland* (1831), and Yeats had studied Ferguson's "Appendix to Articles on Hardiman's Minstrelsy," describing how "Ferguson's articles on Hardiman's minstrelsy, with their translations from the Gaelic, had sown a harvest of song and ballad" (*P&I* 27).[3] The young Fenian poet appears to have been struck by

3. See Yeats's "William Carleton" in his edition of *Stories from Carleton* (1889), *P&I* 23–8. Ferguson's four-part review-essay and "Appendix" had appeared in the *Dublin University Magazine* between April and November 1834: iii. 456–78; iv. 152–67, 447–67, 514–42. In his commentary on the Appendix, composed of songs from the original Irish and Hardiman's annotations thereof, the more ameliorative Ferguson observed: "That the spirit of petty anti-Anglicism sought to be imparted by Mr. Hardiman throughout these annotations, is highly prejudicial to the best interests of the country, we should think will not be disputed by even the most enthusiastic advocates of Irish independence. . . . He certainly holds out no very alluring prospect of reconciliation" (515).

Hardiman's ringing declaration that "no men were ever more deserving of national honour than the ancient bards of Ireland."[4] In recounting the passing away of the bards and their ancient music, Hardiman made an urgent appeal to modern Irish poets:

> The few who inherit their spirit are gradually disappearing, and thus Irish poetry, with all its charms, may be left to linger awhile, and then sink into oblivion, unless rescued by the timely interposition of those who still retain some respect for the ancient honour of their country.[5]

Stirred by the irresistible challenge, and steeped in the histories and legends of ancient Ireland recently provided in Standish O'Grady's *History of Ireland, Heroic Period* (1878), Lady Wilde's *Ancient Legends of Ireland* (1887), and others, Yeats began to characterize bardic life and lives in his writings, especially when they enhanced the conception of his poetic self. In one of his first reviews, "The Poetry of R. D. Joyce" (1886), he described Joyce as "essentially a bard" among contemporary Irish poets, one who "sought to give us whole men, apart from all that limits," and expressed his desire to be identified not with the coterie poets but with the "bardic class" that runs from Homer to Burns, Scott, and Joyce, poets "who sing of the universal emotions, our loves and angers, our delight in stories and heroes, our delight in things beautiful and gallant" (*UP1* 105).

In his introduction to *Fairy and Folk Tales of the Irish Peasantry* (1888), he described with awe how Carolan, "the last of the Irish bards, slept on a rath, and ever after the fairy tunes ran in his head, and made him the great man he was" (*P&I* 12). He then seized the opportunity to write "Bardic Ireland," a review-essay of Sophie Bryant's *Celtic Ireland* (1889). His descriptions of bardic activities recounted there were to reverberate in his life and work for years to come: how the bards "rode hither and thither gathering up the dim feelings of the time, making them conscious"; how to them "A poem and an incantation were almost the same"; how as mythmakers "the whole ancient world of Erin may well have been sung out of the void by the harps of the great bardic order"; how their Ireland "was above all things democratic and communistic—all lands belonging to the tribe" (*UP1* 163–5).

In his study of eighteenth- and nineteenth-century collections of Irish ballads and songs, Yeats became increasingly grateful to the Gaelic

4. James Hardiman, *Irish Minstrelsy, or Bardic Remains of Ireland*, Vol. i (London: Joseph Robins, 1831), p. xxi.

5. Ibid. p. x.

translators for bringing them into English-speaking Ireland, particularly Jeremiah Callanan, "the first fine translator of old Irish songs, and himself author of some good and well-prized verses" (*P&I* 50), and Edward Walsh, whose *Popular Irish Songs* (1847) was to become an important resource for Yeats's own work.[6] He soon collaborated with Katharine Tynan and other contributors in compiling *Poems and Ballads of Young Ireland* (1888), which he described as "another link, however small," in "the long chain of Irish song that unites decade to decade" (*LNI* 42). He was convinced, as he observed in his introduction to *Representative Irish Tales* (1891), that in Ireland "the ballad age has not yet gone by" (*P&I* 71).

Seeing himself as the inheritor of the Irish bardic and ballad traditions, he set out to reconcile in his work the ancient Gaelic tradition with the younger Anglo-Irish tradition. To this end, he advocated the building up of an Irish literature in both languages, proudly recognizing his Gaelic-speaking contemporary, Douglas Hyde, as "the last of the ballad-writers in the school of Walsh and Callanan—men whose work seems fragrant with turf smoke" (*P&I* 8). In his earliest personal attempt to effect a synthesis, Yeats wrote "*Love Song*. From the Gaelic" (*VP* 717),[7] followed by the ballads that appear in his first two volumes of poetry—"The Ballad of Moll Magee" (1887), "The Ballad of Father O'Hart" (1888), "The Ballad of the Old Foxhunter" (1889), and "The Ballad of Father Gilligan" (1890), ballads meant to link him to the bardic tradition and the populace of the nation.[8]

Yeats had simultaneously become attuned to the distant bardic orders in England through Blake and those Romantic poets who had not relinquished

6. Yeats was to include two of Walsh's poems and two of his translations in *BIV1*; he later adapted words from a traditional Irish song in Walsh's collection, "Ben-Eirinn I," for the Tramp's song in *A Pot of Broth* (see *CL3* 223).

7. Yeats adapted the poem from Walsh's translation of a stanza from Edmund O'Ryan's "Edmund of the Hill," which was included in the 1883 edition of Walsh's *Irish Popular Songs*. Yeats included his adaptation in his review of *Popular Ballad Poetry of Ireland*, where he said of O'Ryan's "pastoral aspiration" that he knew "nothing more impossibly romantic and Celtic" (*UP1* 153).

8. Yeats's "*Love Song*. From the Gaelic" ["My love, we will go, we will go, I and you"] appeared in *Poems and Ballads of Young Ireland*, 8. "The Ballad of Father O'Hart,"originally titled "The Priest of Coloony," appeared in *Irish Minstrelsy* (London: Walter Scott, 1888), edited by Henry Halliday Sparling, who was soon to be the son-in-law of William Morris. Sparling had lectured on Irish minstrelsy to the Southwark Club in 1888 during the period of Yeats's first lectures there. In his introduction, Sparling writes of handing down poems, songs, and ballads from fireside to fireside of peasants: "Their ears attuned to the old music; their memories replete with traditionary lore; their thought and speech coloured and formed by the 'olden golden tongue;' it is to the peasantry is due the continuity and development of ethnic life and feeling in Ireland" (p. xvi).

the power of the voice to the printed page. "Hear the voice of the bard," Blake had proclaimed, "Who Present, Past, and Future sees," and, as Yeats immersed himself in Blake and the English bardic tradition, he delighted in Gilchrist's accounts of Blake singing and chanting his poems, sometimes for a music professor who wrote musical notations for his voice. Even on his deathbed, Gilchrist reports,

> he lay chaunting Songs to Melodies, both the inspiration of the moment, but no longer as of old to be noted down. To the pious Songs followed, about six in the summer evening, a calm and painless withdrawal of breath; the exact moment almost unperceived by his wife who sat by his side.[9]

Blake had been drawn to the cult of ancient minstrelsy that developed in the mid-eighteenth century following Thomas Gray's pindaric ode, *The Bard* (1757), in which a venerable bard, perched on a rock on Mount Snowdon, stops the marching army of Edward I and with his lyre reproaches the King for all the misery he has brought upon the country. He laments the slaughter of his bardic brothers ("Dear lost companions of my tuneful art"), and lauds the spiritual power and poetic genius that the King's barbarity can never extinguish, before plunging to his death in the roaring tide below. The poem inspired Blake's painting *The Bard, from Gray* (1785), which Yeats himself would come to admire.[10] As Blake wrote in the *Descriptive Catalogue*, quoting from Gray's description of the bard on a rock,

> Weaving the winding sheet of Edward's race by means of sounds of spiritual music and its accompanying expressions of articulate speech is a bold, and daring, and most masterly conception, that the public have embraced and approved with avidity. Poetry consists in these conceptions.[11]

Yeats had early perceived David Erdman's later assertion that what Blake's painting does "is to assert the moral and social power of the inspired bard, a power to overwhelm evil rulers and summon together patriots."[12]

9. *Life of William Blake* (1880; New York: Phaeton Press, 1969), i. 405.
10. Yeats includes Blake's description of the painting in the *Descriptive Catalogue*, with an identifying note, in the second edition of *The Poems of William Blake* (London: George Routledge and Sons, 1905), 254, 277.
11. *The Complete Poetry and Prose of William Blake*, newly rev. edn (New York: Doubleday, 1988), 541.
12. In *Blake: Prophet Against Empire*, rev. edn (Princeton: Princeton University Press, 1969), Erdman argues, "In Blake's elevated conception of bardic power we can see the influence of Percy's thesis . . . that Saxon minstrels and other ancient poets enjoyed tremendous political and moral eminence" (33). This thesis informs Yeats's *The King's Threshold* (1903), in which Seanchan starves himself to death on King Guaire's threshold to make him restore the ancient right of the poet to sit at the center of courtly power.

Upholding the bardic strain in support of reviving the suppressed cultures of Europe, Blake would staunchly defend the authenticity of James Macpherson's highly popular *Poems of Ossian* (1790), and he was no less defensive of Thomas Chatterton's fabrication of the medieval minstrelsy of Thomas Rowley. Even Blake's bête noir in painting, Sir Joshua Reynolds, upheld in his "Thirteenth Discourse" (1786) the desirability of uniting poetry and music and the necessity of deviating from natural speech in poetic recitation. Reynolds declared that

> the manner in which poetry is offered to the ear, the tone in which it is recited, should be as far removed from the tone of conversation, as the words of which that Poetry is composed. This naturally suggests the idea of modulating the voice by art, which I suppose may be considered as accomplished to the highest degree of excellence in the recitation of the Italian Opera; as we may conjecture it was in the chorus that attended the ancient drama. And though the most violent passions, the highest distress, even death itself, are expressed in singing or recitative, I would not admit as sound criticism the condemnation of such exhibitions on account of their being unnatural.

Macpherson's *Fragments of Ancient Poetry Collected in the Highlands of Scotland* (1760) had preceded his Ossianic poems and prepared the way for Bishop Thomas Percy's three-volume *Reliques of Ancient English Poetry* (1765), which greatly increased the popularity of and appetite for early English ballads. Aside from its influence on Blake's early "Songs," Percy's *Reliques* set in motion numerous collections of English, Scots, Welsh, and Irish ballads well into the nineteenth century, highlighted in England by Walter Scott's three-volume *Minstrelsy of the Scottish Border* (1802–3), the antiquarian work that inspired his *Lay of the Last Minstrel*, and William Motherwell's *Minstrelsy, Ancient and Modern* (1827). Percy included as an appendix to the first volume of *Reliques* his highly influential "Essay on the Ancient Minstrels in England." There he describes the popularity and heroic exploits of English minstrels, successors of the ancient bards, from the Norman Conquest to the end of Elizabeth's reign, when the minstrels were gradually succeeded by "a new race of ballad-writers, an inferior sort of minor poets, who wrote narrative songs merely for the press."[13] He shows that the admired and revered minstrel, in addition to singing and chanting verses at community festivals and in great houses, was "a regular

13. Thomas Percy, *Reliques of Ancient English Poetry*, ed. Henry B. Wheatley (London: George Allen and Unwin, 1885; rpt. 1927), i. 380.

and stated officer in the court." Percy's description of the minstrels' position in the populace would further strike home with the young Yeats: "Their skill was considered as something divine; their persons were deemed sacred; their attendance was solicited by kings; and they were everywhere loaded with honours and rewards."[14]

Percy's *Reliques* was the immediate inspiration for James Beattie's *The Minstrel* (1771–4), a two-volume personal history of the poetic mind that would uniformly attract the Romantic poets, particularly Wordsworth. Indeed, Wordsworth and Coleridge were so drawn to the wistfully fading tradition that they habitually chanted their poems and poetic dramas in a bardic manner. Many of the accounts by their contemporaries uncannily prefigure descriptions of Yeats a century later. "Whatever might be thought of the poem," wrote Hazlitt of Wordsworth chanting "Peter Bell,"

> 'his face was as a book where men might read strange matters,' and he announced the fate of his hero in prophetic tones. There is a *chaunt* in the recitation both of Coleridge and Wordsworth, which acts as a spell upon the hearer, and disarms the judgment. Perhaps they have deceived themselves by making habitual use of this ambiguous accompaniment. Coleridge's manner is more full, animated, and varied; Wordsworth's more equable, sustained, and internal. The one might be termed more *dramatic*, the other more *lyrical*.[15]

In his youth, Wordsworth identified himself with the protagonist of Beattie's *The Minstrel* and was frequently observed reciting and chanting aloud passages of his own poems and those of other admired poets, particularly Thomson's *Seasons*.[16] But his bardic consciousness was more deeply stimulated in 1803 by his first visit to Scott, who read to William and Dorothy from the first four cantos of *The Lay of the Last Minstrel*. As Kenneth Johnston succinctly describes the signifcance of their convergence,

> both [Scott] and Wordsworth, young men aged thirty-three and thirty-two, respectively, were already casting themselves as "last" minstrels, poets

14. Ibid. 353, 346.
15. William Hazlitt, "My first acquaintance with poets," in *The Liberal: Verse and more from the South*, 2 (1823), 41; rpt. in *The Complete Prose of William Hazlitt*, ed. P. P. Howe, (London and Toronto: J. M. Dent and Sons, 1932), xvii. 118–19. Hazlitt continues: "Coleridge has told me that he himself liked to compose in walking over uneven ground, or breaking through the straggling branches of a copse-wood; whereas Wordsworth wrote (if he could) walking up and down a straight gravel-walk, or in some spot where the continuity of his verse met with no collateral interruption" (119).
16. "Memoir of William Wordsworth, Esq.," *The New Monthly Magazine and Universal Register*, 11 (1819), 48.

> of older cultural orders destroyed by present politics. Scott's revolutionary disappointment was 150 years old, but Wordsworth's was still active. Scott took refuge in poeticized history; Wordsworth constructed his refuge, for public consumption, in a poeticized nature. But his private retreat in *The Prelude* was more like a personalized history.[17]

In *The Prelude*, taken up again after the visit, Wordsworth recounted how, when he first discovered "words in tuneful order," he often strolled with a friend by a lakeside, "Repeating favorite verses with one voice, | Or conning more, as happy as birds | That round us chanted" (v. 564–6). After hearing Wordsworth's "recitation" of *The Prelude* over a two-week period, the astonished and deeply moved Coleridge was inspired to write "To William Wordsworth: Composed on the Night after His Recitation of a Poem on the Growth of an Individual Mind" (1807), characterizing the poem as a "prophetic lay" and emphasizing that the "deep voice" of the poet chanting in a state of passionate intensity literally lifted the poem into the realm of supernatural song:

> An Orphic song indeed,
> A song divine of high and passionate thoughts
> To their own music chanted!
> O great Bard!
> Ere yet that last strain dying awed the air,
> With steadfast eyes I viewed thee in the choir
> Of ever-enduring men. (ll. 45–50)

To Coleridge, Wordsworth's poem took its place among the "archives" of great poetic works as the poet's voice "Makes audible a linkèd lay of truth," and at the end of his tribute Coleridge remained "hanging still upon the sound" of the chanting voice.

James Gostwick, the English poet, essayist, and critic of German literature who paid a visit to Wordsworth and his environs in the summer of 1844, described his additional meeting with John Wilson, Wordsworth's earliest disciple and lifelong friend, who filled Gostwick's ears with his imitations of Wordsworth's chanting. "It was a rare privilege," wrote Gostwick fresh from the occasion, "to walk beside this man of genius along the shore of Windermere, and listen to his expressive chanting of

17. Kenneth R. Johnston, *The Hidden Wordsworth* (New York and London: W. W. Norton, 1998), 803.

Wordsworth's poetry, of which his memory seems full to overflowing."[18] As Gostwick traveled through Wordsworth country, he came to lament the noticeable displacement of chanting by solitary composition and reading, except for those minor poets whose inner voices had no living connection to their printed verse.

> You can easily discover [in Wordsworth's lyrics] the mode of their composition; not in the silence of the study, but chanted forth in concert with the sounds of winds, and woods, and streams.... In these days, when memory, self-cultivation, and oral delivery, are sacrificed to the habit of almost continual reading, it is forgotten that poetry is, at least, intended to be read *aloud*, if not to be sung: and well it is that this rule is forgotten, for the sake of many minor poets; their verses would make but a miserable sound if chanted in the open air. By the by, while I speak of chanting, I remember that Coleridge... attacked the dogma, that all reading should be in conversational tones; and with regard to poetry, I am sure he was right.[19]

Coleridge also believed that he was right about the chanting of dramatic verse, evident in the actor James Wallack's account of him reading to the cast of his tragedy, *Remorse*, and giving specific directions as to how certain passages were to be delivered: "His reading was a sort of high musical chant: and his ideas of stage-effect were so exquisitely ridiculous, that the actors had great difficulty in listening to him without bursting out in laughter."[20] As will be seen, the scene is remarkably similar to ridiculing accounts by Joseph Holloway and others of Yeats's instructions to actors at rehearsals in the Abbey Theatre.

Yeats was aware, through his own readings and his conversations with mentors such as William Morris and John Todhunter, that the chanting

18. James Gostick, later Gostwick (1814–87), wrote under the pseudonym of Oswald Herbst two letters from Penrith and Ambleside to his Dresden friend Carl Frühling for publication in *Tait's Edinburgh Magazine*, n.s. 11 (August and October 1844), 521–4, 641–5, here 641–2.

    John Wilson (1785–1854), who wrote under the pseudonym Christopher North, was then Professor of Moral Philosophy at Edinburgh University. Although at this time Wilson had become a severe critic of Wordsworth's poetry, Gostick reported to Frühling: "Of Wordsworth he spoke with the utmost veneration, and, as I thought, almost exceeded the bounds of due praise" (642).

19. "Letter from England," *Tait's Edinburgh Magazine*, n.s. 11 (October 1844), 642. Gostwick evidently recalls Coleridge's note to a discussion of the difference between "metrical composition and prose" in Vol. ii, Chap. 18, of the *Biographia Literaria*, in which Coleridge asserts that "it is no less an error in teachers, than a torment to the poor children, to inforce the necessity of reading as they would talk. In order to cure them of *singing* as it is called: that is, of too great a difference, the child is made to repeat the words with his eyes off the book; and then indeed his tones resemble talking."

20. See *The Reminiscences of Alexander Dyce*, ed. Richard J. Schrader (Columbus: Ohio State University Press, 1972), 179.

tradition had survived not only in these major Romantic poets but in Victorian poets of his own time, particularly Tennyson, as witnessed by William Allingham and F. T. Palgrave. "You don't say it properly," Tennyson said to Allingham after he recited a line (431) from "Passing of Arthur" ("And bowery hollows crown'd with summer sea"). Tennyson proceeded to chant it "in his own sonorous manner, lingering with solemn sweetness of every vowel sound,—a peculiar *incomplete* cadence at the end. He modulates his cadences with notable subtlety."[21] In his "Personal Recollections," Palgrave says that "none of [Tennyson's] friends, and few even among occasional visitors," failed to hear him recite. Noting that casual listeners often found Tennyson's method of chanting "too little varied or emphatic, his voice and delivery monotonous," Palgrave attempted to characterize his impression of Tennyson's method, beginning with his "grand range and 'timbre' of voice":

> his power of modulation; his great *sostenuto* power; the *portamento* so justly dear to Italian vocalists, might be the truer word; the ample resonant utterance: all was simply no deliberate art of recital but the direct outward representative, the effluence at once of his own deepest sentiment as to what Poetry should be, and of the intention, the aspiration, of his own poems. Such had they sung themselves to him, as he thought them out, often keeping them, even when of considerable length, in memory before a syllable was placed on paper: and in strict accordance with that inner music was the audible rendering of it. Whether this conformed to common practice or not, he "could no otherwise."[22]

Like Coleridge listening to Wordsworth, Palgrave remembered "the entrancement, the intoxication (I hope I may be allowed the word), with which we listened for the first time, from the author's lips . . . to those passionate lyrics." After listing all the major poems that he heard Tennyson chant in this way, he asserted that "these can never be heard again, no, nor

21. *William Allingham: A Diary*, ed. H. Allingham and D. Kradford (London: Macmillan, 1907), 158.

22. "Personal Recollections by F. T. Palgrave," in *The Life and Works of Alfred Lord Tennyson*, (London: Macmillan, 1899), iv. 299. Further descriptions of Tennyson's chanting may be found in Hallam Tennyson's *Tennyson and His Friends* (London: Macmillan, 1911), notably for this study by Sir James Knowles: "Then came a great surprise and delight, for it was not reading as usually understood, but intoning on a note, almost chanting, which I heard, and which brought the instant conviction that this was the proper vehicle for poetry as distinguished from prose. I was so enchanted that I begged for more and more" (246–7). For a full discussion of "The Voice of Tennyson," see Francis Berry, *Poetry and the Physical Voice* (London: Routledge and Kegan Paul, 1962), 47–65.

read, to similar advantage. Something of their music, some part of their very essence, has passed with the Maker."[23]

Yeats had heard stories of Swinburne's chanting from his youth, when his father recited for him "Tristram and Iseult," the Prelude to *Trystram of Lyonesse*, and Yeats would eventually bring the choruses of *Atalanta in Calydon* into his own chanting canon. His father later recalled for Yeats how in the 1870s he "heard many stories of Swinburne—amongst others of his reciting his ode to [Guiseppe] Mazzini himself, and often bursting into floods of tears. A capacity for nervous weeping is exactly what I should expect from his kind of lyrism" (*LJBY* 93).[24] The semi-deaf Swinburne, always referred to as "the Bard" by his long-time companion Theodore Watts-Dunton, was known for the often unnerving effect of his histrionic, sonorous declamations, sometimes accompanied by nervous, Corybantic movements of his body. "It is true," Clara Watts-Dunton attested, "that he was so carried away by excitement that he seemed unable to keep his feet or legs still when he recited either tragic or purely humorous sentences. In fact his whole body vibrated on these occasions."[25]

Swinburne's biographer, Edmund Gosse, who gathered testimonials from witnesses, affirmed that he was a great declaimer and reciter of his own verse and that of others: "His voice was a strange but extremely agreeable one, when he did not allow it to get beyond his control."[26] Though his physical movements distracted numerous listeners, most were compelled to admit to the unexpected cadences and the mesmeric power of his bardic voice. After hearing him chant "The Two Noble Kinsmen," Clara Watts-Dunton

23. The two-minute, twenty-seven-second wax cylinder recording made in May 1890 of Tennyson reciting the opening of "The Charge of the Light Brigade" can be heard on CD (*The Spoken Word / Poets: Historic Recordings of Poets Born in the 19th Century*, The British Library Board, 2003) and on the internet at http://charon.sfsu.edu/tennyson/lightbrigadewax.html.

24. By 1886 Yeats was sufficiently steeped in Swinburne's poetry to observe in his review of R. D. Joyce's poetry, "There is a slight hint of Swinburne in the rhythm of one or two of the lyrics that is startling after the originality of all the rest of Joyce's work" (*UP1* 113). "When I was a young man," Yeats later reflected, "poetry had become eloquent and elaborate. Swinburne was the reigning influence and he was very eloquent. A generation came that wanted to be simple, I think I wanted that more than anybody else." See "The Growth of a Poet," *Listener* (April 4, 1934), 591–2; rpt. *LAR* 249–53.

25. Clara Watts-Dunton, *The Home Life of Swinburne* (London: A. M. Philpot, 1922), 242.

26. Edmund Gosse, *The Life of Algernon Charles Swinburne* (London: Macmillan, 1917), 306–7. As George Trevelyan wrote to Gosse about Swinburne's distinctive manner of recitation, "My sole recollection is of hearing him, more than once, reciting poetry to the ladies in the Italian saloon at Wallington. He sat in the middle of the room, with one foot curled on the seat of the chair beneath him, declaiming verse with a very different intonation and emphasis with which our set of young Cantabs read Byron and Keats to each other in our college rooms at Trinity" (325).

found a "weird and subtle charm about Swinburne's delivery of poetry that he loved.... His methods may have been 'unsound'; they were certainly effective. When I took leave of him after that memorable recital, it was with the sensation of one who had been hypnotised." When the actress Lillah McCarthy visited the Pines in preparation for playing Gwendoline in Swinburne's *Locrine*, the poet said to her, "You cannot be this part—you are too young":

> Then he read, with a voice like a choric chant. The voice sounded strange and wonderful to me. It told me of the loveliness of the words and the beauty of the cadence of the language which poets use. Swinburne handed me the manuscript, after choosing a difficult passage for me to read. My ear had caught the cadence of the lines and I chanted as he had done. Imagine my delight when I heard Swinburne exclaim: 'That is right, you have a fine vibrating voice; appealing in its heroic quality.' [27]

Another occasional visitor to the Pines, the Dutch novelist Maarten Maartens, would invariably insist upon a recitation from Swinburne, who in obliging "would read aloud with a mannered outpour of tumultuous utterance, and then sink back, exhausted and radiant."[28] One evening Maartens heard him chant from the long *Tale of Balen* (1896) in a "wearisomely impassioned" manner, but admitted nonetheless that it was "an appropriate utterance of his own creation":

> You felt the immediate concord betweeen the travail and the bringing forth. At the first moment, however, when he ceased, I felt a poignant grief that it was over, a past experience in my life, an emotion of poetic sympathy that I shall never feel again. It had been very beautiful. Gloriously, and to me quite newly, direct; all the difference between seeing a beautiful woman and feeling her embrace.[29]

There is at least one account of Yeats's own visit to the Pines. "I cannot now remember whether Yeats knew Swinburne," recalled John Masefield; "he must, I suppose, have met him at odd times":

27. Lillah McCarthy, *Myself and My Friends* (London: Thornton Butterworth, 1933), 34–5.
28. Gosse, *The Life of Algernon Charles Swinburne*, 279–80.
29. Ibid. 308. As late as September 1904, when Yeats's friends Sydney Cockerell and Emery Walker visited Swinburne at the Pines, Cockerell wrote in his diary that after dinner "we went up into his room and he delighted us by reading out two fine scenes from his new unfinished play on the Borgias. He read in a loud and dramatic manner, with much nervous movement, enforcing every sentence." See Wilfrid Blunt, *Cockerell* (New York: Alfred A. Knopf, 1964), 101.

> I know that early in our acquaintance, he called at the Pines to consult Mr. Watts-Dunton about some matter. While there, he asked Watts-Dunton how Mr. Swinburne was? He was told, 'Very well. He is now composing a poem. If you open the door you will hear him.'
>
> Yeats opened the door, and heard, as it were, the murmur of many bees on a hot summer day. This was Mr. Swinburne trying over his measures in a musical chant.[30]

Swinburne and his predecessors from Blake to Tennyson were loathe to give up the voice of poetry to the eye of the solitary reader, but it is evident that any thought of chanting before a public audience was gone. The chanting of poems had retreated into drawing-rooms, parlors, and walking paths, reserved for a few privileged companions, friends, and visitors—some inspired, some discomfited, by the unfamiliar intensity of resounding voice and bodily movement. Yeats was keenly aware that the experience of poetry had become a private experience for a literate and educated elite, no longer accessible to or part of the imaginative life of the common man. Undaunted, he was committed to reversing the modern shift of poetry from the ear to the eye; it was essential to his vision of cultural revival in Ireland.

That a bardic sense of the poetic voice had been audibly but privately carried through the nineteenth century by some major English poets would have become even more evident to Yeats when in March 1888 his father moved the family to the London suburb of Bedford Park, a veritable commune of artists, writers, scholars, and amateur actors who would in various ways enhance his developing theories of chanting lyric and dramatic verse. There he met Edwin Elllis, with whom he began editing their three-volume edition of *The Works of William Blake* (1893). As he worked on the edition, Yeats found further authority for chanting and musical speech, not only in Gilchrist's biographical account of Blake singing and chanting his verse but in his own immersion in the symbolic poems. In studying Blake's "Samson," Yeats discovered anew what he thought to be a great rarity in blank verse, the essence of his own poetic rhythm, "cadence—the first and last of poetic virtues, within whose realm is ample room for all

30. John Masefield, *So Long to Learn* (New York: Macmillan, 1952), 97. Yeats later forgot the occasion that he had recounted to Masefield, writing to the American professor Samuel C. Chew on April 9, 1918, "I never met Swinburne, but have never seen any special significance in the fact that he never commented so far as I know either publicly or privately on my work or the work of my school. He was occupied with the thoughts of a different age, with a difficult order of ideas. I think Mr. Arthur Symons was the only one amongst my friends who knew him personally" (*CL Intelex* 3425).

the rest to slap, sing, or march, or dance, or weep—its value to literature cannot be disputed."[31] He would soon incorporate the principle of cadence into his critical criteria, observing that Ferguson "had not the subtlety of feeling, the variety of cadence of a great lyric poet" (*BIV1* xix). Nor did the cadences of Ferguson's verse possess another necessary quality discovered in Blake, those "minutely Appropriate Words" which allow the chanting poet "to embody those fine changes of feeling which enthral the attention."[32]

Yeats soon carried his strange cadences to meetings of the Rhymers' Club, where he exercised and gained public confidence in his chanting and became, as Ernest Rhys attested, "by far the best" reader among them, intoning his verse "with a musical voice and very haunting cadence."[33] Rhys further recalled how Yeats read, "in a curious sing-song, that haunted my ears for days, the *Ballad of Father John O'Hart*. His voice gave a strange resonance to the lines: 'There was no human keening; | The birds from Knocknarea | And the world round Knocknashee | Came keening in that day.' "[34] Indeed, most of the Rhymers were moved to record their indelible memories of Yeats's readings, including Victor Plarr, who remembered that Ernest Dowson refused to read, leaving the task "to Lionel Johnson, perchance, who read marvelously . . . or to Mr. W. B. Yeats, whose half-chant is incomparable."[35] Edgar Jepson also portrayed Yeats as the central figure of their readings, "wearing in those days the air of a Byronic hero, long-haired and gaunt, and delivering his poems in a harsh and high and chanting voice." All except Yeats, wrote Jepson, "read their verse in hushed voices."[36]

Yeats, however, contradicted Plarr and Jepson, declaring that he loved to hear Dowson read "O Mors" and "Villanelle of Sunset," and he was especially moved by Johnson's recitation of "Te Martyrum Candidatus"; he

31. *The Works of William Blake*, ed. Edwin J. Ellis and W. B. Yeats (London: Bernard Quaritch, 1893), i. 182–3. Yeats wrote in his own copy of this section, "The Symbolic System," on May 3, 1900, "The greater part of the 'symbolic system' is my writing." See Allan Wade, *A Bibliography of the Writings of W. B. Yeats* (London: Rubert Hart-Davis, 1958), 224.
32. Blake had written in his "[Public Address]" (1809–10), "I have heard many People say Give me the Ideas. It is no matter what Words you put them into & others say Give me the Design it is no matter for the Execution. These People know <Enough of artifice but> Nothing of Art. Ideas cannot be given but in their minutely Appropriate Words nor Can a Design be made without its minutely Appropriate Execution." See *The Complete Poetry and Prose of William Blake*, ed. David V. Erdman (New York: Doubleday, 1988), 576.
33. Ernest Rhys, *Everyman Remembers* (London: J. M. Dent & Sons, 1931), 105.
34. Ernest Rhys, *Wales and England Wed* (London: J. M. Dent & Sons, 1940), 93; *VP* 93.
35. Victor Plarr, *Ernest Dowson 1888–1897* (London: Elkin Mathews, 1914), 66.
36. Edgar Jepson, *Memories of a Victorian* (London: Victor Gollancz, 1933), i. 235–6.

later told an audience that he wished he "could but read it to you as he himself would have read it with that clear, that crystal line monotone in which every consonant had its full weight without taking from the music of the whole" (*YT* 68). After hearing Johnson read "The Church of a Dream," Yeats was never able to read the poem naturally again, "for a very vivid recollection of his curious impressive reading always comes to me. He read with great expression and yet with very slight variation of note" (*YT* 75).[37] Johnson's modulation of the voice to give variety within a "crystal line monotone" was instructive to Yeats and influenced the character of his own practiced chant. Thus, Yeats's desire to hold in his hands the recited poems of his friends led him to suggest the first *Book of the Rhymers' Club* (1892).[38] The poems in that volume, he recalled,

> were not speech but perfect song, though song for the speaking voice. It was perhaps our delight in poetry that was, before all else, speech or song and could hold the attention of a fitting audience like a good play or good conversation, that made Francis Thompson . . . come but once and refuse to contribute to our book.
>
> (*Aut* 234)

II

On January 29, 1889, in Bedford Park, the chanting bard had met and soon fallen in love with Maud Gonne, and in the early glow of their romance she told him of her wish for a play that she could act in Dublin. Yeats thus threw himself into the composition of *The Countess Kathleen* (later *Cathleen*), reading the earliest drafts to his friend the actress Florence Farr and chanting to her Oona's lyric, "Who will go drive with Fergus now." On August 3, 1891, with three acts completed, he summoned the courage to ask Gonne to marry him for the first time. "No," she replied, "she could

37. In a later version of Johnson's reading, Yeats wrote that he would "remember all my life that evening when Lionel Johnson read or spoke aloud in his musical monotone, where meaning and cadence found the most precise elocution, his poem suggested 'by the Statue of King Charles at Charing Cross.' It was as though I listened to a great speech. Nor will that poem be to me again what it was that first night" (*Aut* 234).

38. Yeats inscribed his presentation copy (private) of *The Book of the Rhymers' Club* to Lady Gregory, "This little work was put together at my suggestion. I suggested it because I wanted to have copies of Dowsons poems. He had read them to us at the Cheshire Cheese." The inscription is reproduced in facsimile in Sotheby's *Catalogue of Valuable Autograph Letters, Literary Manuscripts and Historical Documents* (July 23/24, 1979), lot 404, p. 289.

not marry—there were reasons—she would never marry; but in words that had no conventional ring she asked for my friendship" (*Mem* 46). Yeats continued to see her day after day, reading from his unfinished play, and the last two acts began to show not only the effect of her crushing refusal but the infusion of his minstrel imagination. In the fourth act appears the soul-weary Kevin, a young bard "who carries a harp with torn wires," a reimagined King Goll who offers his soul in place of Cathleen's: "The face of Countess Kathleen dwells with me," Kevin tells the merchants. "The sadness of the world upon her brow— | The crying of these strings grew burdensome, | Therefore I tore them—see—now take my soul." When the First Merchant refuses his offer, Kevin asks in despair, before he is led away, "Is your power so small, | Must I bear it with me all my days?" (*VPl* 136). Indeed, prophetically, the poet would carry his wounded soul and his torn harp with him all his days, but he now told Gonne that he had a new understanding of the play, that he

> had come to understand the tale of a woman selling her soul to buy food for a starving people as a symbol of all souls who lose their peace, or their fineness, or any beauty of the spirit in political service, but chiefly of her soul that had seemed so incapable of rest.

When she suddenly left for Paris, he stayed on in Ireland, as he says, "finishing *The Countess Cathleen* that had become but the symbolical song of my pity" (*Mem* 47).

The theatre community in Bedford Park had organized and supported an Amateur Dramatic Club, and, in the midst of writing his own play, Yeats saw the Club as a place to initiate a revival of poetic drama. On one of his frequent visits to William Morris's home in nearby Hammersmith, he lost no time in asking Morris to write a verse play. "I once asked Mr. William Morris if he had thought of writing a play," Yeats recalled, "and he answered that he had, but would not write one, because actors did not know how to speak poetry with the half-chant men spoke it with in old times" (*E&I* 168). Yeats later informed John Masefield that when Morris's talk turned upon poetic drama he always declared that "the verse ought to be chanted."[39] Masefield, curious about the influence of Morris and Swinburne on Yeats's chanting, asked Sydney Cockerell if they chanted their verse. "I heard Morris read on many occasions," Cockerell replied, "Swinburne only once":

39. Masefield, *So Long to Learn*, 96.

> They both chanted their verse, but they did not go to such lengths as Yeats, who when "cantilating" with Florence Farr seemed to me to emphasize the rhythm at the expense of the meaning. Morris's reading was very impressive, and so was Swinburne's. Morris was a fine reader of prose also. He did not chant it.[40]

Masefield concluded that Morris and Swinburne as chanters of verse "were the two most eminent poets likely to have influenced Yeats in his young manhood," but he confessed that he could not determine the weight of their influence. It is evident, however, that in his readings and literary conversations with the younger poet, Morris impressed upon Yeats the communal nature of poetry and the aural quality of all great writing. "I owe to him many truths," Yeats later wrote, "but I would add to those truths the certainty that all the old writers, the masculine writers of the world, wrote to be spoken or sung, and in a later age to be read aloud for hearers who had to understand swiftly or not at all and who gave up nothing of life to listen, but sat, the day's work over, friend by friend, lover by lover" (*Expl* 221).

Although Yeats could not persuade Morris to write a verse play for him, he was successful in enticing John Todhunter, a Bedford Park poet and playwright who also intoned his verse in a sonorous chant, to write his second poetic drama, *A Sicilian Idyll.* The play was produced at the Beford Park Clubhouse in June 1890 with Florence Farr in the role of Amaryllis. The aspiring actress, recently separated from her husband, the actor Edward Emery, had been drawn into Bedford Park activities by her resident sister, Henrietta Paget, wife of the artist and amateur actor Henry Marriott Paget. Yeats met Farr there or at the Morris home in Hammersmith, where she took embroidery lessons from May Morris, and they quickly became close friends. By May 1889 he had asked her to read first drafts of *The Countess Kathleen*, and his sisters believed that he may have been in love with her before he met Maud Gonne. Her tranquil beauty was permanently associated in his mind with the sculpted image of Demeter that then rested near the doors of the British Museum library. When he first heard her speak verse in Todhunter's play, however, he was stunned by the beauty of her speech.

From that moment, Yeats's abiding dream quickened into a possible reality: her rhythmical acting and incomparable delivery of verse, he wrote,

40. Cockerell's letter of February 27, 1950 to Masefield is printed in *So Long to Learn*, 97.

"confirmed a passion" for reviving the art of minstrelsy (*LNI* 3). When he reviewed the play for the *Boston Pilot,* he told his American readers that Farr "won universal praise with her striking beauty and subtle gesture and fine delivery of verse. Indeed her acting was the feature of the whole performance that struck one most... I do not know that I have any word too strong to express my admiration for its grace and power" (*LNI* 39). While the play was in rehearsal, Yeats had joined the Golden Dawn, and to bring Farr into the magical fold he introduced her for membership shortly after the production. Together they advanced as active adepts, absorbing the rituals of ceremonial magic into their vision of symbolic drama, making their chanting voices an integral part of magical enchantment. "If I had not made magic my constant study," Yeats would write to his mentor John O'Leary, "I could not have written a single word of my Blake book nor would 'The Countess Kathleen' have ever come to exist. The mystical life is the centre of all that I do & all that I think & all that I write" (*CL1* 303).

Yeats's poetic and esoteric relationship with Farr was complicated by the fact that she also enjoyed an intimate friendship with George Bernard Shaw, who had turned his fictional and musical interests to Ibsen and the realistic drama. The storming of the London scene by Ibsen's plays had unsettled Yeats; after receiving a free ticket to see *A Doll's House,* he hated the play, "resented being invited to admire dialogue so close to modern educated speech that music and style were impossible" (*Aut* 219). It thus pained Yeats greatly when, in February 1891, Farr, with Shaw's encouragement, put down her great poetical voice to play Rebecca in Ibsen's *Rosmersholm,* a play, as Yeats said disparagingly, "where there is symbolism and a stale odour of spilt poetry" (*Aut* 219). Thus, when Todhunter's *A Sicilian Idyll* was revived in July, Yeats, fearful that he might lose her to the Ibsen siege, was quick to note her recent success in the role but quicker to declare, mainly for her wandering eyes, that "She is an almost perfect poetic actress," exhibiting a mastery of symbolic acting. "All her gestures are rhythmic and charming, and she gives to every line its full volume of sound" (*LNI* 115).[41] He was doubly pleased to have an opportunity to reiterate the *Rosmersholm / Sicilian Idyll* contrast for readers of the *Providence Sunday Journal* in America: "She will always, however, be best, I believe in poetic drama, her exquisite

41. In his review for *United Ireland* (July 11, 1891), Yeats emphasized her incantatory power for his Irish audience: "There is one scene of incantation which was delivered the other day at the Vaudeville by Miss Florence Farr with astonishing power and effect—a scene that has the very stateliest qualities of dramatic verse" (5; *UP1* 192).

recitation being no small part of her charm" (*LNI* 137).[42] Nonetheless, her success in *Rosmersholm* was rewarded in the following year with the role of Blanche Sartoris in the production of Shaw's first play, *Widowers' Houses.*

Yeats would learn to live with the fact that she was not to be restrained in her allegiances or drives; the multiplicity of her temperament was evident in the necessity and ease with which she moved from the roles of Todhunter to those of Ibsen, from those of Shaw to those of Yeats. She would become Yeats's Aleel, but she also maintained an abiding interest in Ibsen's women and became the embodiment of Shaw's New Woman as she took further roles in his plays and began to write novels and esoteric monographs. "She set no bounds to her relations with men whom she liked," wrote Shaw of their affair,

> and already had a sort of Leporello list of a dozen adventures . . . She was in violent reaction from Victorian morals, especially sexual and domestic morals; and when the impact of Ibsen was felt in this country, and I wrote somewhere that "home is the girl's prison and the woman's workhouse" I became *persona grata* with her; and for some years we saw a great deal of one another.
>
> (Bax vi–vii)

Shaw was most astute, however, in observing that "She found the friend she really needed in Yeats." Yeats, too, was strongly aware of how important to his future plans was the special friendship that evolved out of her verse speaking at Bedford Park: "I made through these performances," he wrote, "a close friend and a discovery that was to influence my life" (*Aut* 118).

Indeed, as this book aims to recount, for the next twenty years Yeats and Farr would collaborate in their efforts to return musical speech to lyrical, narrative, and dramatic verse in a modern revival of the minstrel tradition. In February 1894 Yeats used his review of Villiers de L'Isle Adam's *Axël* to assert his first dramatic principle, that "the actor should be a reverent reciter of majestic words" (*UP1* 325). The following month they began their first experiments with the chanting of lyrics in dramatic verse for Farr's production of Yeats's *The Land of Heart's Desire*, a curtain-raiser for Shaw's *Arms and the Man*, in which Farr played Louka. Their moderate success led Yeats to revise *The Countess Kathleen* for the first edition of his *Poems* (1895).

42. Not uncritical of her performance, Yeats had already observed the fault that many subsequent critics would note: "Her one fault is a slight tendency to underact. She has shown by one magnificent rendering of the incantation scene in the *Idyll* that she has power enough for anything, but does not seem as yet quite sure of herself. On Friday . . . she gave the incantation with a force that added vehemence and beauty, whereas on Tuesday she underacted it sadly" (*LNI* 115).

"Yeats called and read his play . . . in a haunting recitative," wrote Rhys. "His ruling belief at that time was that of an Ireland personified in the Countess Cathleen."[43] In the play's transitional state, Yeats changed the name of Kevin to Aleel; he expanded the role of the bard, giving him a "small square harp" and surrounding him with "fantastically dressed musicians," his first version of troubadours who would form the musical chorus of later plays. And he added the chanted lyric "Impetuous Heart"[44]—all in anticipation of launching a theatre for poetic drama and musical speech. The bardic additions not only enhanced the performative mode of the play; they become an integral part of its theme.

At this propitious time, Lady Augusta Gregory, the widow of Sir William Gregory of Coole Park, came into his life under the offices of her neighbour in Co. Galway, Edward Martyn, who aspired to write Irish plays in the Ibsen manner. In August 1896 Martyn took Yeats from his Tillyra Castle to visit Lady Gregory, and when they met again the following winter in London he told her of his plans to establish a Dublin-based "Celtic Theatre." The plans were discussed more seriously with Lady Gregory and Martyn in the summer of 1897, when Yeats spent two months at Coole collecting folklore. They set about raising subscriptions for the venture, and for the next year Martyn was instrumental in dealing with the difficult matter of patents, theatrical licensing, and inspection of suitable halls.

In the uncertainty of the undertaking, however, Yeats was compelled to continue pursuing his dramatic ideals in London with Farr. The plays of Maurice Maeterlinck and Villiers de L'Isle Adam provided a European context for his efforts there and confirmed his belief that the symbolic or romantic drama would soon displace the drama of social realism. In the spring of 1897 he discovered Robert Bridges's *Return of Ulysses*, which he described in his review as "perfect after its kind, the kind of our new drama of wisdom" (*E&I* 199). He became even more determined to establish a theatre in London, beginning with a production of his much-revised early play, *The Shadowy Waters*, which the London publisher Leonard Smithers

43. Rhys, *Wales England Wed*, 104.

44. The manuscripts of Yeats's transformation of the lyric, originally entitled "The Lover to his heart" (dated November 19, 1894) and subsequently incorporated into the 1895 revision of *The Countess Cathleen* as "The Wind that blows by Cummen Strand," are included in *The Countess Cathleen Manuscript Materials*, ed. Michael J. Sidnell and Wayne K. Chapman (Ithaca, NY: Cornell University Press, 1999), 359–65.

proposed to publish with illustrations by Aubrey Beardsley.[45] Facing difficult licensing obstacles and a lack of funds in Ireland, Yeats and Farr expressed to Lady Gregory their desire of "taking or building a little theatre somewhere in the suburbs" of London in order to produce both Irish and non-Irish plays. As Lady Gregory recorded in her diary, Yeats had in mind "his own plays, Edward Martyn's, one of Bridges', and he is trying to stir up Standish O'Grady and Fiona Macleod to write some. He believes there will be a reaction after the realism of Ibsen, and romance will have its turn."[46]

Fearful that he would abandon his dream of an Irish theatre, Lady Gregory redoubled her efforts to find funding for him. At the time, however, Yeats was not to be deterred from the idea of a subscription theatre in London because he knew, he later said, "If I wrote well, my plays would reach Ireland in the end" (*Mem* 117). The subsequent collapse of his plans to publish *The Shadowy Waters* and open a suburban theatre in London in 1898 temporarily halted the revival of romantic drama, but not the development of a dramaturgy based primarily on musical speech.

III

Like the Romantics before him, Yeats had immersed himself in Percy's *Reliques*, and the appended "Essay on the Ancient Minstrels in England" had become the source for many of his observations on the minstrel tradition. He was the proud owner of the three-volume Wheatley edition (*YL* 1556), which had become a touchstone for his assessment of nineteenth-century Irish poets and ballad writers. By the time he wrote "Nationality and Literature" (1893), he was confident that "The future will put some of our ballads with 'Percy's Reliques' " (*UP1* 273), and it is evident that Percy's collection was a partial inspiration for his own *A Book of Irish Verse* (1895).[47]

45. *The Shadowy Waters*, conceived when Yeats was eighteen in 1883, passed through many drafts and transformations before it was first published in *The North American Review* in May 1900. Yeats was to announce the completion of the play in the second issue of *Beltaine* (February 1900), but declared that "I rather shrink from producing another verse play unless I get some opportunity for private experiment with my actors in the speaking of verse. The acting of the poetical drama should be as much oratory as acting, and oratory is a lost art upon the stage."

46. Augusta Gregory, *Our Irish Theatre* (New York: Capricorn Books, 1965; for 1913), 2–3.

47. Two such ballads, he believed, were Mangan's "Dark Rosaleen" and "O'Hussey's Ode to the Maguire," the latter an adaptation from the Gaelic of O'Hussey, the last hereditary bard of the Maguires, who laments the fate of his outcast warrior-chief, Hugh Maguire. In his

Although he had often expressed his appreciation of peasant verse-makers, he made it clear in the Preface that the collection was compiled "not at all for Irish peasants" but "for the small beginning of that educated and national public, which is our greatest need and perhaps our vainest hope" (*BIV1* xxvii).

Yeats obviously hoped that the anthology would become a vital addition to his "Library of Ireland," a scheme that he had been developing through the National Literary Society to distribute books by the best contemporary writers to Irish towns. In addition to the obligatory Thomas Moore, he included some eighteenth- and nineteenth-century ballad-makers and translators (Callanan, Walsh, Doheny), the more literary writers of the Fenian movement (Ferguson, Allingham, De Vere), the major figures of the Young Ireland movement (Davis, Mangan), and a generous selection of contemporary poets (Todhunter, Hyde, Tynan, George Russell, and Lionel Johnson, among others). But his earlier uncritical praise of his predecessors now gave way to his belief that they must be judged in relation to the greatest poetry, implicitly symbolist poetry, and he used his introduction to begin that critique. In developing his symbolist aesthetic, Yeats began to reassess Irish poets in terms of imaginative energy, spiritual passion, organic rhythm, and the evocative power of their images and symbols. No less important to him was the poet's relation to the people and his ability to shape emotions; above all, he judged the extent to which the poet was a slave or master of life, and thereby the extent to which he was a master of the poetic craft. Many of the poets and ballad writers, he observed, "never understood that though a poet may govern his life by his enthusiasms, he must, when he sits down at his desk, but use them as the potter the clay" (*BIV1* xiv).

Yeats began his introductory essay with a brief but appreciative recognition of the eighteenth-century Irish poets, such as Red O'Sullivan and William O'Heffernan, whose songs "had made the people, crushed by the disasters of the Boyne and Aughrim, remember their ancient greatness"

introduction to the *Book of Irish Verse*, Yeats described it as a poem that "must live for generations through sheer passion" (xvii), and much later in *Dramatis Personae* he described Mangan and these two poems as "our one poet raised to the first rank by intensity, and only that in these or perhaps in the second of these poems" (*Aut* 296). Other Irish ballads that Yeats thought worthy of comparison with the best of those in Percy's *Reliques* include Callahan's translations from the Gaelic of "Shule Aroon" and "Kathleen O'More," Michael Doheny's "A Cushla Gal Mo Chree" ("Bright Vein of My Heart"), Allingham's "The Winding Banks of Erne," and Ferguson's "The Welshmen of Tirawley" and "Conary," the latter being "the most perfect equivalent for the manner of the ancient Celtic bards in modern literature" (*UP1* 159).

(*BIV1* xii). For all the beauty of their songs and the web that they wove around the hearts of the people, however, there had crept into their lyrics a "flitting incoherence, a fitful dying out of the sense, as though the passion had become too great for the words," as though the severity of life disallowed the luxury of craft to contain them. "The great bardic order," Yeats lamented, "with its perfect artifice and imperfect art, had gone down in the wars of the seventeenth century, and poetry had found shelter amid the turf-smoke of the cabins." Outside the cabins, meanwhile, the Fenian and Young Ireland movements had begun to write poetry driven more by nationalist than literary values. As an inheritor, Yeats was determined that the continuance of the written and the renewal of the oral traditions in Ireland at the end of the nineteenth century would no longer be diverted from craft and high art in the service of nationalist politics and sentimental patriotism.

The contrarian poet who was writing and chanting the symbolist lyrics that would make up *The Wind Among the Reeds* declared that now and in the next century "he who does not strive to be a perfect craftsman achieves nothing":

> The poor peasant of the eighteenth century could make fine ballads by abandoning himself to the joy or sorrow of the moment, as the reeds abandon themselves to the wind which sighs through them, because he had about him a world where all was old enough to be steeped in emotion. But we cannot take to ourselves, by merely thrusting out our hands, all we need of pomp and symbol, and if we have not the desire of artistic perfection for an ark, the deluge of incoherence, vulgarity, and triviality will pass over our heads.
>
> (*BIV1* xxii)

Thus, while he strove to recognize individual and comparative strengths among the poets, Yeats criticized the mechanical rhythms, conventional metaphors, weak architecture, and insincere motives of much modern Irish poetry. He resumed his relentless criticism of the lyrics of Thomas Moore's *Irish Melodies* as being "too often artificial and mechanical in their style when separated from the music that gave them wings." He had never been able to accommodate the highly popular Moore in the received tradition, holding that he was never a poet of the people: "Moore lived in the drawing-rooms," Yeats had written earlier, "and still finds his audience therein" (*UP1* 62). His exclusion of Moore had been reinforced by William Morris, who told Yeats that while Moore might be a great song writer, "He is not a poet, he has not the poet's rhythm" (*P&I* 178–9).

When Mangan was not inspired by ancient song, Yeats observed, and when Ferguson had no subject of the bardic age to move him, the two poets lost their passion and "fell into rhetoric." Yeats knowingly risked crossing sacred ground when he concluded that "in the main the poets who gathered about Thomas Davis, and whose work has come down to us in 'The Spirit of the Nation,' were of practical and political, not of literary importance" (*BIV1* xviii). In his poem, "To Ireland in the Coming Times" (1892), Yeats had earlier affirmed that his magical and symbolic pursuit of intellectual beauty made him no less "one" with Davis, Mangan, Ferguson, but his introduction to *A Book of Irish Verse* required him not to reaffirm their nationalist bond but to qualify their poetic association. It was the beginning of a bold but necessary surgical procedure on modern Irish verse, one that anticipated and inspired Ezra Pound's similar procedure on modern English verse when the Imagist movement got underway a decade later.[48] Still, Yeats had not yet identified and articulated, beyond the vitality instilled by the Celtic element of "natural magic," ancient legends, and heroic ideals, the particular quality of Irish verse that distinguished it from English verse.

Shortly after *A Book of Irish Verse* appeared, Yeats had a revelation while reading "some bad Irish verses," verses that he would have withheld from the volume but that nonetheless intrigued him. "I found that they were moving me greatly, moving me as dozens of bad Irish verses used to move me when I was a boy; and I laid the paper down to think why. I lit suddenly upon their secret, and upon the secret of much Irish poetry."[49] Yeats recounted the moment of revelation in introducing his review of George Sigerson's *Bards of the Gael and Gall Examples of the Poetic Literature of Erinn done into English after the Metres and Modes of the Gael* (1897):

> Their emotion was the actual emotion of their writer, and they moved me just as commonplace, sincere words of grief would move me in life. The same verses written by a writer of a country where the literary habit is impersonal, as it is in England, would have wearied me from the first. The love-poems are almost all the utterances of some actual love and hate, and we know whom they praised and whom they cursed. They are the work of a people who are

48. Yeats continued the criticism of contemporary poets and prose writers in four articles written for *The Bookman* from July to October 1895, articles that he wanted his publisher T. Fisher Unwin to preserve in pamphlet form, to be titled *What to Read in Ireland*, with an introduction "on the relation of Irish literature to general literature & culture & to contemporary movements" (*CL1* 475), but the project did not materialize. See *UP1* 359–64, 366–73, 375–87.

49. See Deirdre Toomey, "Bards of the Gael and Gall: An Uncollected Review by Yeats in *The Illustrated London News*," *YA* 5 (1987), 203–11; here 208.

> intensely personal in all the affairs of life, and who utter in verse the things that others hide in their hearts.
>
> (*YA5* 208–9)

What had suddenly come clear to him in reading the verses in Sigerson's collection was the common characteristic of peasant poets, ancient bards, and generations of Irish exiles—they all wrote out of "a most tumultuous life." It was, as Deirdre Toomey asserts, the first published statement of Yeats's doctrine of personal utterance, a doctrine that would further energize his aural poetics. "Here are hymns," he wrote in a passionate, nationalist outpouring of personal emotion suddenly realized,

> made by men famous for their austerities, dirges that wives have sung over their husbands and that bards have sung over their kings, and the lamentations over great men driven into exile sung by men who had fought at their side, and the lamentations sung by exiles over the land they have been driven from, and love-poems made by poets whose love sorrows are still tales by the hearth-side. . . . Englishmen will never understand us until they understand our opinions are often for opinion's sake, but that our emotions are almost always the results or precedents of action; and that sentiment, which is emotion not seeking an utterance in action, is commoner with them than with us.
>
> (*YA5* 209)

To Yeats, the distinctive, impassioned emotion of the imperfect art of the Irish bardic, ballad, and peasant traditions was to be preserved and enriched in the new century by poets (and actors) who possessed "a passion for artistic perfection," who once again could heighten personal utterance and give it communal life with the chanting voice, which, as Coleridge and others had witnessed, lifts intense poetic emotion out of the temporal and into an Orphic realm of sacred rite or mysterious ritual. In his own poetry, chanted with incantatory power of voice and accompanied by priestly, hieratic gestures of arm and hand, Yeats—like Blake, Wordsworth, Coleridge, Tennyson, and Swinburne before him—appeared to become a medium of the supernatural, conducting symbols and rhythms in a visionary trance, "Where only body's laid asleep" (*VP* 138).

If Yeats's criticism of the Irish poets for surrendering their poems to politics, patriotism, and rhetoric seemed harsh to his contemporaries, he was even more severe with English poets from Wordsworth to Swinburne who had left the procession of symbolist poets and surrendered their increasingly discursive and prosaic poems to Victorian morals, scientific speculation, humanitarian ideas, and theological arguments. Yeats had admired the early poetry of Wordsworth and Tennyson until they became moralists. He credited the early Wordsworth with speaking directly and powerfully as a man to men, admired such poems as "The Solitary Reaper," whose persona sings of "old, unhappy, far-off things, | And battles long ago," and praised the mood achieved in poems like "Resolution and Independence," which he described as an example of "great lyric poetry" (*UP2* 430). His view of the early Tennyson was strongly shaped by Arthur Henry Hallam's essay on Tennyson's lyrics, and he lauded the "vivid personal exaltation" evident in poems such as "The Silent Voices" and "The Wanderer" (*UP1* 252).[50] But in gradually relinquishing their interior lives to the heterogenous concerns of the external world, Wordsworth and Tennyson had, for Yeats, obscured the passionate personality that they had revealed in chanting to small numbers of enthralled witnesses.

"It seems to me that the imagination has . . . been laid in a great tomb of criticism" (*E&I* 196), Yeats wrote obliquely of Matthew Arnold and his Victorian contemporaries in 1895, before turning to direct criticism in subsequent essays, describing Tennyson's "In Memoriam" as an Arnoldian "criticism of life." "The poetry which found its expression in the poems of writers like Browning and Tennyson," he wrote in "The Autumn of the Body" (1898), "and even of writers who are seldom classed with them, like Swinburne, and Shelley in his earlier years, pushed its limits as far as possible, and tried to absorb into itself the science and politics, the philosopy and morality of its time" (*E&I* 190). In Yeats's eyes, each poet had paid dearly: Wordsworth became consummately dull with the ecclesiastical sonnets, and the dreary brooding over scientific opinion "so often extinguished the central flame in Tennyson" (*E&I* 163). It was only with the modern poets, Yeats declared in 1898, "with Goethe, Wordsworth, and Browning, that poetry gave up the right to consider all things in the

50. In his essay "On Some of the Characteristics of Modern Poetry, and on the Lyrical Poems of Alfred Tennyson" (1893), reviewed by Yeats, Hallam named Tennyson the living representative of "the aesthetic school of poetry" founded by Keats and Shelley, a school of poets whose "fine organs trembled into emotions at colours, and sounds, and movements, unperceived or unregarded by duller temperaments," whose poems manifest "a sort of magic producing a number of impressions too multiplied . . . to allow of our tracing them to their causes, because just such was the effect, even so boundless and so bewildering, produced on their imaginations by the real appearance of nature" (*The Poems of Arthur Henry Hallam, Together with His Essay on the Lyrical Poems of Alfred Tennyson*, ed. Richard Le Gallienne [London, 1893], 93–4). Throughout the 1890s Yeats invoked the principles of Hallam's essay, which he described as "one of the most profound criticisms in the English language" (*UP2* 130), in his critique of those nineteenth-century poets whose poetry had become mixed up with politics, morals, and rhetoric.

world as a dictionary of types and symbols and began to call itself a critic of life and an interpreter of things as they are" (*E&I* 192).[51]

In leaving the symbolist procession for the matters of the world, in writing more for the reader than the singer and listener, they had further removed themselves from the bardic succession. As Yeats described Tennyson's departure:

> We can at least speak as men to men, out of our own experience, out of our own passions, though we may have to change the circumstance. If Tennyson had written "Locksley Hall" for a troubadour to sing, he would never have made his hero rail against the woman he had once loved and against the man she had chosen instead of him. He would have known that his audience, in which there would be so much normal human nature, would have thought all that ignoble, for when we are reading a book we are quite in the snare of the words, and if they are beautiful one forgets the rest. The human side of it is not thrust before us as it would be if a living man spoke to us, with a voice trembling with passion or quivering with gayety.
>
> (*YA8* 90)

Yeats believed that restoring the passionate personality and voice to Irish poetry and poetic drama would set them above an English poetry and drama mired in modern problems, Victorian rhetoric, and abstract personalities. "Personal utterance," he later reflected on his discovery, "which had almost ceased in English literature, could be as fine an escape from rhetoric and abstraction as drama itself" (*Aut* 105). In the process, he would learn that a price was to be paid for his countercultural assault on the modern moral

51. Yeats distinguished clearly between the "old" rhetorical and the "new" symbolist traditions in his review of Ernest Rhys's *Welsh Ballads* (1898): "The movement that found a typical expression in the consolations of 'In Memoriam,' in the speculations of 'Locksley Hall,' in the dialectics of 'Bishop Blougram's Apology,' in the invective of [Hugo's] 'Les Châtiments,' and found its explanation when Matthew Arnold called art a criticism of life, has been followed by a movement that has found a typical expression in the contentment of [Morris's] 'The Well at the World's End,' in the ecstasy of [Wagner's] 'Parsifal,' in the humility of [Maeterlinck's] 'Aglavaine and Selysette,' in the pride of [Villers de L'Isle Adam's] 'Axel,' and might find its explanation in the saying of William Blake that art is a labour to bring again the golden age. The old movement was scientific and sought to interpret the world, and the new movement is religious, and seeks to bring into the world dreams and passions, which the poet can but believe to have been born before the world, and for a longer day than the world's day" (*UP2*, 91–2). Despite identifying Goethe as a "critic of life" here, Yeats thought him the greatest of the nineteenth-century European poets, and having read deeply in Eckermann's *Conversations with Goethe* he would have delighted in Eckermann's description on the opening page, in an entry dated December 3, 1822, of Goethe's declamatory recitation: "Goethe, to our great delight, read us the poem of 'Charon.' I could not but admire the clear, distinct, and energetic manner in which Goethe read the poem. I never heard so beautiful a declamation. What fire! What a glance! And what a voice! Alternately like thunder, and then soft and mild. Perhaps, in some parts, he displayed too much force for the small room in which we were assembled; but yet there was nothing in his delivery which we could wish otherwise."

and social distractions of Irish and English poetry. "One thing I had not foreseen when I accepted so joyfully the doctrine of personal utterance," he later wrote, "was that it involved the man that lived it [in] a tumultuous life" (*YT* 73).

At the beginning of 1899 the visonary bard was on the threshold of that tumultuous life. After criticizing his nineteenth-century predecessors in *A Book of Irish Verse,* Yeats had received bitter and unforgiving criticism for his views of Davis and others; to the Dublin barrister and orator John F. Taylor, it was as though Yeats had attacked the nation itself.[52] In the Preface to the second edition of the volume (1900), he steadfastly reaffirmed his literary values in the face of that criticism: "I have endeavoured in this book, to separate what has literary value from what has only a patriotic and political value, no matter how sacred it has become to us" (*BIV2* xv; *P&I* 223–4).[53]

As he began to voice his views about the subjects of a new national drama based on ancient Irish legends, he found himself drawn into public controversy by John Eglinton, who in refuting Yeats declared that "a national drama or literature must spring from a native interest in life and its problems and a strong capacity for life among the people."[54] In defending the artistic use of legendary material, Yeats responded in "John Eglinton and Spiritual Art" that "the difference between good and bad poetry is not in its preference for legendary, or for unlegendary subjects . . . but in the volume and intensity of its passion for beauty, and in the perfection of its

52. In his final revision of "Modern Irish Poetry" for his *Collected Works* in 1908, Yeats recalled that "Taylor, the orator, a man of genius and of great learning, never forgave me what I have said of Davis here and elsewhere, and it is easier for me to understand his anger in this year than thirteen years ago when the lofty thought of men like Taylor and O'Leary was the strength of Irish nationality" (*CW8* 130; *P&I* 110). Despite Taylor's hostility towards him, Yeats always recognized the exceptional power of Taylor's oratorical voice and the influence of his delivery on his own recitation: "When Taylor spoke, it was a great event, and his delivery in the course of a speech or lecture of some political verse by Thomas Davis gave me a conviction of how great might be the effect of verse, spoken by a man almost rhythm-drunk, at some moment of intensity, the apex of long-mounting thought. Verses that seemed when one saw them upon the page flat and empty caught from that voice, whose beauty was half in its harsh strangeness, nobility and style. My father had always read verse with an equal intensity and a greater subtlety, but this art was public and his private, and it is Taylor's voice that has rung in my ears and awakens my longing when I have heard some player speak lines, 'so naturally', as a famous player said to me, 'that nobody can find out that it is verse at all' " (*Aut* 103).

53. In his postscript for the 1908 revision of "Modern Irish Poetry," Yeats stated that "if I rewrote it now I should take more pleasure in the temper of our writers and deal more sternly with their achievement" (*CW8* 129–30; *P&I* 110).

54. The articles by John Eglinton, Yeats, AE and William Larminie in the Saturday issues of the *Dublin Daily Express* were collected in *Literary Ideals in Ireland* (London: T. Fisher Unwin, 1899; rpt. New York: Lemma Publishing, 1973); here, 12–13.

workmanship."[55] In spirited defense of his vision of art, he entered into a high prophetic mode, affirming his conviction "that all men will more and more reject the opinion that poetry is 'a criticism of life,' and be more and more convinced that it is a revelation of a hidden life."[56] And in his further contribution to the volume, "The Autumn of the Flesh," he was moved to announce, in his belief that the age of criticism was about to pass, that the arts are "about to take upon their shoulders the burdens that have lain upon the shoulders of priests, and to lead us back upon our journey by filling our thoughts with the essences of things, and not with things."[57] He was to be a priest of what he called a poetry of essences, "separated from one another in little and intense poems," written for the ear, their full intensity and passion sounded by the essential voice.

Yeats had now assimilated the residual spirit of the Irish and English minstrel traditions into his symbolist aesthetic, magical practice, and cultural nationalism, and in revising his earlier Introduction for *A Book of Irish Verse* as "Modern Irish Poetry," he was intent to define the communal role of the modern bardic poet in Ireland by presenting as an exemplar Douglas Hyde, not only as the translator of *The Love Songs of Connacht* (1893), which Yeats had reviewed,[58] and from which he frequently chanted to friends, but as a poet who

> has written Gaelic poems which pass from mouth to mouth in the west of Ireland. The country people have themselves fitted them to ancient airs, and many that can neither read nor write, sing them in Donegal and Connemara and Galway. I have, indeed, but little doubt that Ireland, communing with herself in Gaelic more and more, but speaking to foreign countries in English, will lead many that are sick with theories and with trivial emotion to some sweet well-waters of primeval poetry. [59]
>
> (*BIV2* xxxi; *P&I* 110)

55. Ibid. 37. 56. Ibid. 36. 57. Ibid. 74.
58. When Yeats reviewed the bilingual volume in October 1893, he described the poems, in one of the earliest expressions of his symbolist aesthetic, as growing out of a world where everything "was so old that it was steeped in the heart, and every powerful emotion found at once noble types and symbols for its expression" (*UP1* 295).
59. Yeats's interest in the revival of primitive peasant poetry was stimulated by his reading of the Finnish *Kalevala*, the Welsh *Mabinogion*, and the Icelandic Sagas as evidence of the widespread attempt of European countries to find cultural identity in ancient folklore and oral poetry. He was particularly intrigued by the *Kalevala*, the epic constructed by Elias Lönnrot (1802–84), who sought out the most accomplished singers of ancient poetry, or "runo," and notated the songs by numbering the strings of his kantele, the five-stringed zither that is the national musical instrument of Finland. These works were, as he wrote in "The Celtic Element in Literature" (1898), part of "the ancient religion of the world," stating comparatively that the "old Irish and the old Welsh, though they had less of the old way than the makers of the

The multifarious efforts of a decade had begun to coalesce in 1899, and when Edward Martyn finally agreed to provide personally the financial backing for an Irish Literary Theatre, Yeats went into revision mode once again with *The Countess Cathleen.* On February 24 he signed and dated the Preface for the new edition of his *Poems*, which contained his latest changes for the play. After mailing the manuscript, he requested his publisher T. Fisher Unwin to run special proofs of the play and print copies for rehearsal purposes, alerting Farr in London that it was time to begin rehearsals, train reciters, and educate the public with lectures on chanting for a May production.

In the midst of all the turmoil that was to follow, what was most at stake for Yeats in founding the theatre and staging his play was the recovery of the lost arts of rhythmical speech, the chanting of "those wavering, meditative, organic rhythms, which are the embodiment of the imagination" (*E&I* 163). The history of this recovery is inextricably intertwined with the twenty-year drama of *The Countess Cathleen*, which was to become an evolving and lasting medium for realizing his dream of a revivified oral culture that would take the imaginative arts to the "sick children of the world," as he had described them in one of his earliest poems, too long deprived of dreaming, reverie, and the "certain good" of words chanted by the poet's magical voice.[60] For the rest of his life, the driving force of his work was to restore that voice in the public domain.

Kalevala, had more of it than the makers of the Sagas" (*E&I* 175). He was further impressed at this time by Carmen Sylva's collection of Romanian poems and folk songs collected from peasants, *The Bard of the Dimbovitza* (1892, 1894), praising the poems in a review for their "superhuman preoccupations and extravagant beauty" (*UP1* 411).

60. Published under various titles from 1885, "The Song of the Happy Shepherd" (*VP* 64–7) had appeared as "Song of the Last Arcadian" in *The Wanderings of Oisin* (1889) and as the first poem under the descriptive heading "Crossways" in *Poems* (1895).

2

London Minstrels

I

While the Dublin papers had favorably anticipated the promise of an Irish Literary Theatre for months, Yeats's astrological charts forecast days fraught with nationalist and religious friction. Although versions of *The Countess Cathleen* had been in print for seven years, exciting no previous controversy, its religious heterodoxy now attracted the scrutiny of Edward Martyn's religious adviser, who warned of blasphemous content. Martyn, the primary financial supporter of the Irish theatre, was a pious and scrupulous Catholic who had always been suspicious of Yeats's unorthodox religious beliefs, and he threatened to withdraw all support for the enterprise. Yeats was not in the least pleased with this unexpected irritation, anymore than he was with Maud Gonne's double refusal in Paris of marriage and the role of Cathleen, before he returned to London to begin rehearsals. He was equally frustrated by having to employ English actors and to place Martyn's Ibsenite play *The Heather Field* on the bill with his poetic drama. To forestall a premature end to the theatrical venture, Yeats had to scurry about for sympathetic Catholic clerics to assuage Martyn's fear of public association with a blasphemer. No sooner was the day saved than one of Yeats's bitter antagonists, Frank Hugh O'Donnell, chafing over being rebuked by nationalist groups (at Yeats's insistence) for an unwarranted attack on Michael Davitt, began distributing his notorious pamphlet *Souls for Gold! A Pseudo-Celtic Drama in Dublin*. O'Donnell accused Yeats not only of being anti-Catholic but anti-Irish as well: "He has no right to outrage reason and conscience alike by bringing his degraded idiots to receive the kiss of the Mother of God before the whole host of Heaven as reward for having preferred the gold of the devil to the providence of the All-Father" (*CL2* 677). The pamphlet provoked a barrage of letters to the press from patriotic Catholics, and the pressure of protest led to a condemnation of the play by Archbishop Logue, who, having read extracts from O'Donnell's pamphlet but not Yeats's play, wrote that "an Irish Catholic audience which could patiently sit out such a play must have sadly degenerated, both in religion and patriotism" (*CL2* 410). In this climate of nationalist and Catholic hostility, Yeats was forced to hire and advertise the presence of thirty policemen for the opening night. Despite all this turmoil, he remained focused on the primary principle of the production, writing in the program notes that "the chief endeavour with Mr. Yeats' play has been to get it spoken with some sense of rhythm."[1]

It had indeed been a difficult endeavor, more taxing to Yeats than the accompanying theological crisis. He had invited Florence Farr, who directed his *Land of Heart's Desire* five years earlier, to stage *The Countess Cathleen* for him. Her now sixteen-year-old niece, Dorothy Paget, who had played the Faery Child, chanting under Farr's direction her "strange and dreamy" lines, was tapped to play Cathleen; Farr's friend, the English actress and elocutionist Anna Mather, agreed to play Oona, Cathleen's nurse; Farr took the part of the bard Aleel herself and began rehearsals in London, training the principals in rhythmical speech and chanting. In April, she journeyed to Dublin to begin stage preparations, give press interviews, and prepare Dubliners for the romantic dramaturgy of the play. "One of the greatest difficulties we have had," she told the *Daily Express*,

> is to find actors who can recite verse properly. Since the introduction of prose plays and the natural style of acting that art has almost disappeared. When poetic drama was the inevitable form, actors were as much orators as actors. It is not, of course, the old style of declamation that we want, but when verse is spoken as prose it is intolerable. . . . But when verse, I mean, of course, blank verse, is properly spoken, it has a charm altogether independent of its meaning.[2]

Yeats himself wrote letters to the press and gave lectures in London and Dublin on their method, asserting that "our actors must become rhapsodists again and keep the rhythm of the verse as the first of their endeavours.The music of a voice should seem more important than the expression of face or the movement of hands, for poetry spoken as prose, without music, as the performance of Mr. Swinburne's 'Loch Rhyne' the

1. *Beltaine: The Organ of the Irish Literary Theatre,* ed. W. B. Yeats, Number One to Number Three (May 1899–April 1900) rpt. in one volume (London: Frank Cass and Company, 1970), 7.
2. *The Daily Express* (Dublin), April 5, 1899, 5.

other day, sounded like bad, florid prose."[3] In the midst of these public preparations, however, the Ibsenite George Moore, a founding director of the Irish Literary Theatre, descended upon the London rehearsals. When Moore saw Dorothy Paget and heard Farr's verse-speaking instructions, a vision of financial disaster led Moore and Martyn to depose Farr as stage manager and remove Paget from the role of Cathleen. Moore replaced her with the English actress May Whitty, who also had the lead in *The Heather Field,* and turned over the stage management to her husband Ben Webster. Yeats, powerless and submissive before this *coup de réalisme*, wrote apologetically to Paget, who was demoted to reciting Lionel Johnson's opening prologue and playing the minimal roles of the Sheogue and a peasant woman:

> I am very sorry but, although you would please me better as the Countess Cathleen than any body else will, I have been forced to give the part to Miss Whitty. . . . You act exactly as I think verse should be acted but you act according to a quite new way, according to a theory of acting which Mrs Emery & myself alone as yet have accepted. Miss Whitty acts in the old way & will be quite sure of succeeding up to a certain point. . . . She will make her audience cry by the usual stage methods of pathos of manner & expression, but you brought tears to both Mrs Emery's eyes & mine not by pathos but by beauty [of speech.]'
>
> (*CL2* 395–6)

Yeats and Farr did what they could to influence Miss Whitty's delivery, even changing her lines as necessary. "She acts admirably & has no sense of rhythm what ever & talks of throwing up her part when ever I make any criticism on her way of speaking," Yeats wrote to Lady Gregory. "She enrages me every moment. . . . I am getting the others to speak with a little, a very little music. Mrs Emery alone satisfies my ear" (*CL2* 398). In a

3. *The Irish Literary Society Gazette* (London), 1 (June 1899), 6. Swinburne's *Locrine: A Tragedy* (1887) was produced at St. George's Hall, Langham Place, on March 20, 1899, under the auspices of the Elizabethan Stage Society. Yeats lectured to the Irish Literary Society on April 23, speaking "on the 'Ideal Theatre,' with special reference to the Irish Literary Theatre." The lecture and title were revised as "Dramatic Ideals and the Irish Literary Theatre" for delivery to the National Literary Society (Dublin) on May 6. That spring he took every opportunity to find public and private venues for the chanting in London and Dublin, and at a dinner party held by Edward Marsh on April 23 he chanted poems from *The Wind Among the Reeds*. As Marsh recounted to Victor Lytton, "they seemed most beautiful in sound, tho' I can never understand poetry read out. He read them in an extremely monotonous voice, with very strong emphasis on all the accents—it was rather effective, but I think it's possible to read in a more natural way without sacrificing the music of the verse" (Christopher Hassall, *Edward Marsh, Patron of the Arts: A Biography* [London: Longmans, 1959], 96).

last-minute attempt to forewarn his uninstructed audience, Yeats printed the two lyrics from the play separately in the program, explaining that they

> are not sung, but spoken, or rather chanted, to music, as the old poems were probably chanted by bards and rhapsodists. Even when the words of a song, sung in the ordinary way, are heard at all, their own proper rhythm and emphasis are lost . . . in the rhythm and emphasis of the music. A lyric which is spoken or chanted to music should upon the other hand, reveal its meaning, and its rhythm so become indissoluble in the memory. The speaking of words, whether to music or not, is, however, so perfectly among the lost arts that it will take a long time before our actors, no matter how willing, will be able to forget the ordinary methods of the stage or to perfect a new method.[4]

After the curtain went up on *The Countess Cathleen* in the Antient Concert Rooms on May 8, the performance met with milder disturbances than anticipated. However, a loud interruption came from a group of middle-class Catholic students from Royal University, described by Joseph Holloway, Dublin's inveterate theatregoer and journal keeper, as "an organised claque of about twenty brainless, beardless, idiotic-looking youths" who "did all they knew to interfere with the progress of the play by their meaningless automatic hissing & senseless comments, & succeeded (happily) in showing what poor things mortals can become when the seat of reason is knocked awry by animus, spite & bigotry."[5] But among this group of students was Yeats's one ideal member of the audience, James Joyce, who applauded vigorously and remembered indelibly in *A Portrait of the Artist as a Young Man* the catcalls and hissing of his fellow students:

> —A libel on Ireland!
> —Made in Germany!
> —Blasphemy!
> —We never sold our faith!

4. *Beltaine*, 7–8.
5. Joseph Holloway, unpublished journal, "Impressions of a Dublin Playgoer," this entry included but mistranscribed in *Joseph Holloway's Abbey Theatre: A Selection from his Unpublished Journal*, ed. Robert Hogan and Michael J. O'Neill (Carbondale and Edwardsville: Southern Illinois University Press, 1967), 6. When Holloway's entries appear in one of the four editions of the edited selections, they are so cited; however, since many entries related to this study are highly elided or not included in the published selections, quotations from unpublished or elided passages are from the original journals. The 221 volumes (1895–1944) of Holloway's journals are in the National Library of Ireland. They were issued on microfilm in 1988 as *The Diaries of Joseph Holloway: From the National Library of Ireland, Dublin, 1895–1944. Manuscripts of the Irish Literary Renaissance, Series 1* (Reading: Berkshire Research Publications, 1988, 105 reels).

—No Irish woman ever did it!
—We want no amateur atheists.
—We want no budding buddhists.[6]

The next day these same students sent a letter to the press, condemning Yeats for representing the Irish peasant "as a crooning barbarian, crazed with morbid superstition, who, having added the Catholic faith to his store of superstitions, sells that faith for gold or bread in the proving of famine."[7] Joyce, enraptured as he was by a play that reflected his own internal drama, refused to sign the letter. He was deeply impressed by the chanting of the lyrics, "Impetuous Heart" by Farr as Aleel, and especially "Who will go drive with Fergus now," chanted "with the thin voice of age" by Anna Mather as Oona:

> Who will go drive with Fergus now
> And pierce the deep wood's woven shade,
> And dance upon the level shore?
> Young man, lift up your russet brow,
> And lift your tender eyelids, maid,
> And brood on hopes and fears no more. (*VPl* 65)

As Richard Ellmann describes the effect of the lyric on Joyce, "its feverish discontent and promise of carefree exile were to enter his own thought, and not long afterwards he set the poem to music and praised it as the best lyric in the world."[8] In March 1902, when his fourteen-year-old brother George, sick and dying, asked Joyce to sing the lyric to him, "Jim went downstairs to the parlour," their brother Stanislaus attests, "and, leaving the doors open, sat down at the piano and sang the melancholy chant to which he had set the verses":[9]

6. *James Joyce, A Portrait of the Artist as a Young Man*, ed. Seamus Deane (New York: Penguin Books, 1992), 246.
7. The letter, dated May 8, 1899, appeared in the *Freeman's Journal* on May 10. Most of the letter is reprinted in Richard Ellmann's *James Joyce*, new and rev. edn. (New York: Oxford University Press, 1982), 753–4. The remainder of the letter and the names of the students are given in Wayne K. Chapman, "The '*Countess Cathleen* Row' of 1899 and the Revisions of 1901 and 1911," *YA11* (1995) 108, 119 n.10.
8. Ellmann, *James Joyce*, 67.
9. Stanislaus Joyce, *My Brother's Keeper*, ed. Richard Ellmann (New York: Viking Press, 1958), 134. See *The James Joyce Songbook*, ed. Ruth Bauerle (New York and London: Garland Publishing, 1982), 117. The editor notes that the following music "was supplied by Anthony Burgess, who states it was given him as being Joyce's composition for the Yeats poem. Although Maria Jolas and Ada MacLeish, who were friends of Joyce in the middle years, do not recognize the melody as ever sung by him, it is our best approximation of Joyce's early composition" (116).

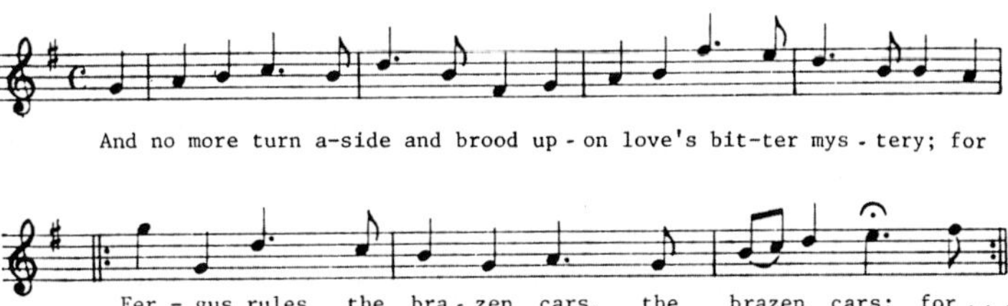
Who Goes With Fergus?
And no more turn a-side and brood up - on love's bit-ter mys - tery; for
Fer - gus rules the bra - zen cars, the brazen cars; for . . .

The play and its lyrics had become, as Yeats desired, "indissoluble" in Joyce's memory, and when at the close of *Portrait* Stephen looks up at the wheeling swallows as a long-awaited symbol of departure, he recalls the Countess Cathleen's dying words and becomes suffused with a "soft liquid joy" as the verses "crooned in the ear of his memory composed slowly before his remembering eyes the scene of the hall on the night of the opening of the national theatre":

> Bend down your faces, Oona and Aleel,
> I gaze upon them as the swallow gazes
> Upon the nest under the eave before
> He wander the loud waters.[10]

And when in the opening episode of *Ulysses* Buck Mulligan impatiently admonishes Stephen to give up his moody brooding, he mocks Stephen's chanting of Yeats's lyric as he descends the Martello stairs, booming out in a droning voice, "And no more turn aside and brood | Upon love's bitter mystery | For Fergus rules the brazen cars," setting off in Stephen's mind the besetting memory of his mother. "Fergus' song," he recalls. "I sang it alone in the house, holding down the long dark chords. Her door was open: she wanted to hear my music."[11] He repeats a line, carrying the haunting lyric with him from Martello tower to Night Town as he begins his personal odyssey.

Joseph Holloway was also enraptured by the performance, recounting how, as he followed the play's progress, "a spiritual, half-mystic, visionary sensation crept over my senses... as if I were in fairy land." Although Yeats thought May Whitty's performance "effective and commonplace"

10. *A Portrait of the Artist*, 245; *VPl 163*.
11. James Joyce, *Ulysses* (New York: Vintage Books, 1990), 9. At the end of the Circe episode, Stephen "*murmurs thickly with prolonged vowels*" broken lines from the lyric when Bloom awakens him from his drunken sleep (608–9).

(*Aut* 310), Holloway praised her "sympathetic and lovable" manner and recorded that she spoke Cathleen's lines "with a delicious, natural, sweet-musical cadence expressively and most distinctly." He further observed that Farr "declaimed all her lines in majestic, beautiful, rhythmic manner grand to listen to—most impressive if occasionally indistinct." The indistinctness of Farr's and Mather's chanted tones led him to express his only reservation about their otherwise "laudable attempt 'to lend to the beauty of the poet's rhyme the music of the voice.' " "The chanting is difficult to follow," he wrote, "until the ear grows accustomed to listening to measured rhythm. Many of the artists failed to allow those in front to clearly understand what they spoke" (*JHAT* 7–8).

Although George Moore eventually, haltingly, allowed that the performance was "not in vain," in that it awakened in him and the audience "a sense of beauty," he was characteristically more forthright in his expressed dislike of the chanting:

> The theories of the author regarding the speaking of verse I hold to be mistaken; I do not think they are capable to realization even by trained actors and actresses, but the attempt of our "poor mummers of a time-worn spring," was, indeed, lamentable. Many times I prayed during the last act that the curtain might come down at once.[12]

After all the reviews and opinions, it was Yeats's father, John Butler Yeats, who revealed even within the family how mixed were the reactions to Yeats's verse experiments. "I hope Willie will go on writing dramas and that some time he will prove he can write dramas which are to be *acted* as well as chaunted," he wrote to Lady Gregory after the final performance. "A lyric or any other outpouring of musical passion is all the more penetrating if the personality uttering it is already familiar to you in a story or drama. *The Countess Cathleen* in itself is such a drama, and I cannot agree with Willie in all his ideas as to the rendering of it" (*LBP* 47).

In their public production of *The Countess Cathleen*, Yeats and Farr struggled valiantly in a skeptical, even hostile atmosphere to launch their theory of chanting poetic drama and lyric poetry. But at this point some readers familiar with conventional accounts may well ask why there was

12. George Moore, "The Irish Literary Theatre," in *Samhain*, ed. W. B. Yeats (Dublin: Sealy Bryers and Walker, 1901), 12. In a footnote to Moore's criticism, Yeats responded: "I do not want dramatic blank verse to be chanted, as people understand that word, but I do not want actors to speak as prose what I have taken much trouble to write as verse. Lyrical verse is another matter, and that I hope to hear spoken to musical notes in some theatre some day."

no mention of Farr's use of the psaltery in the production. The hard fact is that there was no psaltery as yet; Farr and Mather chanted to musical notes provided by a harp and violin in Herr Bast's string quartet, which provided the incidental music for the lyrics and, as Holloway notes, at other "odd times" during the play. George Moore's notorious account in *Hail and Farewell* of Farr plucking the wires of the psaltery at rehearsals and muttering lines from "Impetuous Heart" is a mocking fabrication and a disingenuous conflation of events that took place over several years.[13] In 1899 the psaltery was still an unstrung image in Yeats's mind; for the past fifteen years the ancient instruments of bards and minstrels had existed only as symbols of evocation in his poems and plays. By the time his tympans, harps, lutes, and lyres became a stringed reality in the psaltery in 1901, Yeats's verse-speaking theories would become the unifying matrix for his lyric, dramatic, and magical practice, and for the next eleven years the arts of musical speech would consume more of his energy and interest than any single aspect of his poetic and dramatic art.

Yeats and Farr did not allow the crises and criticisms of that historic production to deflate in the slightest their convictions about chanted verse, and one late review by Max Beerbohm, who came from London on behalf of the *Saturday Review*, gave them great encouragement. Yeats's verses, wrote Beerbohm, "more than the verses of any other modern poet, seem made to be chanted; and it is, I fancy, this peculiar vocal quality of his work, rather than any keen sense of drama, that has drawn him into writing for the stage. It is this peculiar quality, also, which differentiates *The Countess Cathleen* from that intolerable thing, the ordinary 'poet's play.' "[14]

13. In *Ave* (1914), the first volume of *Hail and Farewell*, ed. Richard Cave (Washington, DC: Catholic University of America Press, 1985), Moore states that Edward Martyn "had come to tell me that Yeats had that morning turned up at rehearsal, and was now explaining his method of speaking verse to the actors, while the lady in the green cloak [Farr] gave illustration of it on a psaltery. At such news as this a man cries Great God! and pales. For sure I paled, and besought Edward not to rack my nerves with a description of the instrument or the lady's execution upon it." Moore says that he subsequently "found Yeats behind some scenery in the act of explanation to the mummers, while the lady in the green cloak, seated on the ground, plucked the wires, muttering the line, Cover it up with a lonely tune" (103). Moore wrote to Rev. James O. Hannay ("George A. Birmingham") on October 27, 1911, about the fictionalization of *Ave:* "The reviewers look upon my book as a book of reminiscences, whereas I took so much material and moulded it just as if I were writing a novel, and the people in my book are not personalities but human types" (NLI MS 8271).
14. Max Beerbohm, "In Dublin," *Saturday Review* (13 May 1899); rpt. in *More Theatres* (London: Rubert Hart-Davis, 1969), 140–4. Beerbohm went on to say that Whitty, Farr, and Mather "all delivered the verses well, giving to them the full measure of their music; and I know not

In early summer, Farr engaged one of her artistic friends, Pamela ("Pixie") Colman Smith, to design for *The Countess Cathleen* new scenes for future productions,[15] and in October Yeats wrote to Maud Gonne that the play was "likely to be acted in New York" (*G-YL* 113).[16] By the end of the following year, after numerous experiments with technique and notation, Yeats and Farr were ready to take their "new art," as they called it, before London audiences. On December 8, 1900, Yeats introduced Farr and their method to the Irish Literary Society, where she chanted several poems, including Aleel's lyric from *The Countess Cathleen*. "She and the chanting were a great success," Yeats wrote to Lady Gregory. "I heard people saying 'how beautiful' all about me" (*CL2* 597). The enthusiastic response was greatly encouraging, and four days later he wrote again to Lady Gregory that he was beginning, "you will be sorry to hear, some slight revisions of Countess Cathleen" (*CL2* 602). The revisions, which included a new love scene for Aleel and the Countess at the beginning of Act III, were for his new edition of *Poems* (1901). The text of the play would remain undisturbed for ten years.

At the beginning of 1901, as the Irish Literary Theatre entered the final year of its three-year trial period, Yeats had been continually frustrated by a schism in the Golden Dawn and by the conflict with Edward Martyn and George Moore over dramatic principles and the future direction of the theatre. Beneath the surface disillusionment, however, a concealed current of energy invigorated Yeats as he renewed his plans to establish a theatre in London. He wrote to Florence Farr that he and some unnamed friends were planning a "theatrical project" which offered great opportunities. "We can," he told her in the heat of a Golden Dawn controversy, "make a great movement & in more than magical things" (*CL3* 26–7). Yeats's companions in the new undertaking were Laurence Binyon and Thomas Sturge Moore, who in the last two years had become ardent disciples of Yeats's dramatic

when I have found in a theatre more aesthetic pleasure than I found in listening to them" (144).

15. On July 16, 1899, Yeats's father wrote to him: "Of course I shall be delighted to see Miss Pamela Smith, and shall be most keen to see her designs from The Countess Kathleen" (*LBP* 54).

16. Margaret Wycherly's company eventually produced the play at the Madison Square Theatre in New York on March 28, 1905, followed by further performances in May. The critic for the *New York Times* credited Miss Wycherly, who played the Countess Cathleen, with "a painstaking effort" but observed that although she "has a pleasing and sympathetic voice" she possessed "no such variety of expression as needed to convey the melodious color of Mr. Yeats's richly imaginative verse" (March 29, 1905, 4).

theories and were anxious to establish in London the equivalent of the theatre in Dublin. Just before the opening of the Irish Literary Theatre in May 1899, Binyon had espoused Yeats's theatrical ideals in the March issue of *The Dome,*[17] and in succeeding months he sought the active interest of friends in setting up a suburban theatre. In June, Binyon introduced Sturge Moore to his close friend, William A. Pye, a wine merchant and collector of books and paintings who lived in Limpsfield, Richmond. Binyon and Sturge Moore soon became friends with Pye's daughters, Sybil and Ethel, with whom they first planned the Literary Theatre Club. As Sybil Pye recalled, "Father was to be a 'business member', Tom to direct the elocution, Binyon to be a 'dining-out missionary'!"[18] Binyon and Sturge Moore began writing poetic dramas based on Greek rather than Irish heroic plays. They set up a movable stage in the Pye's drawing room and began rehearsing scenes from *Henry IV, Part II* and Binyon's *Paris and Oenone*. When Yeats learned of the group's existence late in 1900, he saw it as the nucleus for his long-planned suburban theatre, as a group that could be trained to produce *The Countess Cathleen* and *The Shadowy Waters* in London. Acting as a catalyst, Yeats united with Binyon and Sturge Moore to turn their dramatic club into a society for the performance of romantic drama; at his instigation they began summoning the support of authors and artists in their circle. On January 27, 1901, Sturge Moore called on Charles Ricketts to discuss "the possibility of the foundation of a Theatre society for Romantic Drama." Ricketts, intrigued by their plans, noted in his diary that the scenery of the new society "would be done on a new decorative, almost symbolic principle. I have half a mind to write a pamphlet on this subject which has haunted me for years."[19] Yeats was delighted by his interest in the project, for Ricketts had been in his mind as his scene designer since 1899, when Yeats first wrote in *The Dome* of the difficulties

17. See Binyon's "Mr. Bridges' 'Prometheus' and Poetic Drama," *The Dome*, 2 (March 1899), 199–206. Binyon makes reference to Yeats's letter of January 27 to the editor of the *Daily Chronicle*, in which he delineates his dramaturgy and claims that "We have forgotten that the Drama began in the chanted ode, and that whenever it has been great it has been written certainly to delight our eyes, but to delight our ears more than our eyes" (*CL2* 349). In support of Yeats, Binyon states that "it is merely common sense to speak poetry in the tone of poetry, and not in the tone of one who politely but frigidly accepts an uncongenial invitation. As long as verse is spoken like this, it is idle to blame the audience for disliking verse" (206).

18. Sturge Moore Papers, Box 5/19d (ii), Sterling Library, University of London.

19. *Self-Portrait: Taken from the Letters and Journals of Charles Ricketts, R.A.*, comp. T. Sturge Moore, ed. Cecil Lewis (London: Peter Davies, 1939), 52.

of restoring the "theatre of art."[20] In the following weeks a variety of essential artists would be brought into the fold. Yeats and Farr, meanwhile, began the difficult task of educating their potential London audience in the "lost" arts of musical speech, symbolic scenery, and rhythmical acting.

Their developing dramaturgy drew heavily upon the ceremonial rituals of the Golden Dawn, magical rituals that were conducted like symbolic scenes. As the chanting experiments progressed, Yeats and Farr vigorously pursued public forums for their esoteric interests. In October 1900 Yeats began writing his lecture on "Magic," a public manifesto first delivered before the Fellowship of the Three Kings on May 4, 1901, prior to publication in the September issue of the *Monthly Review.* Yeats, for years a student of Cabalistic visionary techniques, opened his lecture by declaring, "I believe in the practice and philosophy of what we have agreed to call magic, in what I must call the evocation of spirits, though I do not know what they are, in the power of creating magical illusions, in the visions of truth in the depths of the mind when the eyes are closed" (*E&I* 28). Meanwhile, members of Farr's private "Sphere" or Egypt group, since 1896 a secret society within the Golden Dawn devoted to the study of Egyptian symbolism and invocation, had created the more public Egyptian Society, whose object was to illustrate the life and thought of ancient Egypt by plays and lectures. On February 9, 1901, her friend York Powell wrote to Oliver Elton from Christ Church, Oxford: "Mrs. Emery was here last night. She is now an *Égyptologiste*, and she has also been experimenting in the harmonizing of the saying of verse with a background of music. It is pretty and effective. I thought that it was a curious and happy success. You get a kind of Greek effect. It is only good verse that is worth doing this way."[21] Yeats and Farr knew that the development of the chanting movement depended in part on making its esoteric contexts comprehensible to a public audience.

The two adepts took the new art before a semi-public audience for the first time on Saturday evening, February 16, in the Hall of Clifford's Inn, off Fleet Street. They again commandeered the actress-elocutionist Anna

20. Yeats wrote in "The Theatre," first published in the *Dome*, 4 (April 1899), "I know some painters, who have never painted scenery, who could paint the scenery I want, but they have their own work to do," later adding a note to this sentence, "I had Charles Ricketts in my mind" (*E&I* 170).

21. See Oliver Elton, *Frederick York Powell: A Life* (Oxford: Clarendon Press, 1906), i. 315–16. Farr had published books on *Esoteric Egyptology* (1896) and *Egyptian Magic* (1896).

Mather, who had played Oona to Farr's Aleel in *The Countess Cathleen,* for a lecture-demonstration entitled "Some New Methods of Speaking Verse" at an open meeting of the Fellowship of the Three Kings, an event that attracted the curiosity of the London press. As J. R. Runciman of the *Saturday Review* described the lecture, "Having superfluously stated that he knew nothing of music, [Mr. Yeats] proceeded to reveal his new musical art."[22] Several critics amusedly saw the lecture as part of a widespread "cantillating epidemic" originating in America, but Yeats's friend and admirer, the war correspondent Henry Nevinson, reported faithfully in the *Daily Chronicle* that

> the poet's purpose is really to revive the old chanting of ballads and lyrics as it was done by the bards of Ireland and most European countries—certainly by the Homeric rhapsodists of Greece, where Mr. Yeats maintains even the drama was chanted or intoned. Admirable examples of the poet's meaning were given by Miss Florence Farr and Miss Anna Mather, with the accompaniment of a harp and even so familiar an instrument as the piano, where one felt the lyre, the tympan, and the Pan-pipe alone would have been in place. The effect, especially in some of Mr. Yeats's own lyrics, was peculiarly beautiful.[23]

Another journalist was impressed by Farr's chanting of Yeats's "The Lake Isle of Innisfree" to the accompaniment of a small Irish harp, "played beautifully" by Miss Georgina Macdonald. But the most successful efforts, he reported, were Farr's rendering of Dante Gabriel Rossetti's "The Blessed Damozel" and Mather's recitation of John Todhunter's "The Banshee." In the latter poem, "the word 'keening' was drawn out in a very weird and impressive manner":

> Green, in the wizard arms,
> Of the foam-bearded Atlantic,
> An isle of old enchantment,
> A melancholy isle,
> enchanted and dreaming lies;
> And there, by Shannon's flowing,

22. J. F. Runciman, "At the Alhambra and Elsewhere," *Saturday Review*, February 22, 1901, 237. As Runciman summarized Yeats's lecture, "Poetry, when spoken, [Yeats] said, lost its rhythm; when sung, he said, one could not catch the words. Therefore he proposed something between singing and speaking: a kind of free chant with no fixed time and in no fixed scale. We were given some specimens of this, and I have scarcely yet recovered from my extreme surprise. . . . Of course the ladies who recited the poems for Mr. Yeats did their work (I presume) as Mr. Yeats wanted it done; but it seems to me that the thing should not be done."

23. Henry Nevinson, "Daily Chronicle Office," *Daily Chronicle*, February 18, 1901, 5.

In the moonlight, spectre thin,
The spectre Erin sits.

An aged desolation
She sits by old Shannon's flowing,
A mother of many children,
Of children exiled and dead,
In her home, with bent head, homeless,
Clasping her knees she sits,
Keening, keening![24]

Todhunter was among the "many well-known people present," but also included in the crowd was an unknown poet named John Masefield, who had met Yeats the previous November after moving to London.[25] Masefield, who was deeply and permanently moved by the event, was particularly struck by Mather's chanting of Keats's "Bacchic Ode" from *Endymion*, rendered, he recalled, "with a fresh delight that would have charmed Keats"[26]:

24. Yeats had included Todhunter's "The Banshee" (1888), Maud Gonne's favorite poem, in *BIV1* 83–6. W. P. Ryan, in his early study, *The Irish Literary Revival* (London: 1894), asserts that Todhunter's "Banshee" and his "The Fate of the Children of Lir" "have set him in the first rank of Irish poets of our century. It has been justly said that he sings or chaunts his story in the style of one of the olden bards. He possesses the spirit and energy of the bards, and gives example very often of the wild, rough strength they possessed" (98).

25. As Masefield recalled of their first meeting in Woburn Buildings on November 5, 1900, Yeats read aloud Dora Sigerson's poem, *Can Doov Deelish* (*Dear Black Head*), which he had included in *BIV1* 226–7:

Can doov deelish, I cry to thee
Beyond the world, beneath the sea,
Thou being dead.
Where hast thou hidden from the beat
Of crushing hoofs and tearing feet
Thy dear black head?

"His reading was unlike that of any other man. He stressed the rhythm until it almost became a chant; he went with speed, marking every beat and dwelling on his vowels. That wavering ecstatic song, then heard by me for the first time, was to remain with me for years" (*Some Memories of W. B. Yeats* [Dublin: Cuala Press, 1940], 13).

26. John Masefield, *So Long to Learn* (New York: Macmillan, 1952), 100. Masefield further recalled "the extraordinary beauty of the ending, as an unusual thing (at that time a startling thing).... By that lecture, a great change was wrought in the methods of speaking verse.... Before many years had passed, I was to be made truly thankful that I had heard the beginning of a movement that was to mean very much to me" (101). Masefield was to credit Yeats's "kindling experiments" in 1901 as the inspiration for the Oxford Recitations, which he conducted from 1923 to 1930.

For wine we follow Bacchus through the earth;
Great God of breathless cups and chirping mirth!—
Come hither, lady fair, and joined be
  To our mad minstrelsy![27]

Masefield wrote to a friend that apart from Yeats's followers much of the audience was comprised of people who held "established ideals" and remained "rather unsympathetic" to his verse-speaking methods."[28] Indeed, the aged Shakespearean actor and elocutionist Hermann Vezin made a "fierce onslaught" against Yeats's methods, arguing vehemently that rhythm must be subservient to sense in poetry. Even Lady Gregory was skeptical. She wrote in her diary the next morning that it was

> amusing enough—but only a "fad"—Mrs. Emery's voice is better in ordinary reciting, and Miss Mather hasn't much voice at all. Yeats didn't give a regular lecture but warmed up after criticism by Todhunter and Vezin & said, in answer to one [critic] that all lyrics were sad, & that all the finest poetry was the fruit of an austere sadness.
>
> (*Diaries* 303)

Masefield confirmed in his letter that in the heated debate following the lecture "two old fogeys made genuine asses of themselves. Dr. Todhunter . . . made a splendid speech to refute their arguments and then we all had tea and so home to bed by lamplight."[29] Several days later Yeats wrote to the novelist and socialite Violet Hunt:

> I wish you had heard our chanting on Saturday. It roused the indignation of <all> a large part of an audience consisting almost wholly of teachers of elocution for far as I could make out, & woke a real enthusiasm in some few.

27. Keats's description of the triumphal progress of Bacchus appears in Book IV of *Endymion*, lines 193–272. As "Michael Field" recorded in her journal after a dinner party in the spring of 1902, "Yeats intoned as if to the psaltery Keats' *Bacchic Ode*" (*Works and Days*, ed. T. and D. C. Sturge Moore [London: John Murray, 1933], 263). Yeats had written to Robert Bridges about their experiments with Keats's lyrics: "Miss Farr has found your verse & mine <&> a little modern lyric verse to be vocal, but when one gets back a few generations lyric verse ceases to be vocal until it gets vocal as song not as speach is, as one approaches the Elizabethans. We had great difficulty even with Keats & though we got a passage which is splendidly vocal we had to transpose a line because of a construction, which could only be clear to the eye which can see several words at once" (*CL3* 91).
28. Quoted in Constance Babington Smith, *John Masefield: A Life* (New York: Macmillan, 1978), 64. According to one reporter, Hermann Vezin "gave many humorous illustrations of good and bad recitation, including a most amusing imitation of his own voice as heard through the phonograph. The Rev. E. Taylor dealt with the advantages which a somewhat chanting style of recitation might import into a great poem, such as 'Paradise Lost,' and he recited a fragment of it very finely." Unidentified article in press-cutting book, NLI MS 12145.
29. *John Masefield: A Life*, 64.

> To me it was the first quite musical speach of any verse in our time, with the exception of our Irish experiments. I am going on to elaborate the thing much more highly. It is the rudiments of music—music as it was in early Greece.
>
> (*CL3* 41–2)

Yeats had become increasingly romantic about the future of his experiments since the production of *The Countess Cathleen* in Dublin, and one aim of the lecture was to prepare an audience for a proposed production of the play in London, as revealed shortly afterward in a letter by Pixie Smith. She wrote to the American author Albert Bigelow Paine about meeting Yeats at a studio tea hosted by Beatrice Erskine ("Mrs. Steuart Erskine"), co-editor of the *Kensington* magazine:

> W.B.Y. was there and he is a *rummy critter!* . . . *Then* W.B. began to talk! folk lore—songs—plays—Irish language—and lots more—reciting a sort of folk song which was splendid! And not stopping for interruptions made by Mrs. E[rskine] *pig*——who made silly remarks: it *was* fun! . . . He most excited about Countess Cathleen [in] my theatre! And wants me to give a performance of it to the "Brotherhood of the Three Kings" a crazy Irish sort of literary society! Won't it be fun?!!!!!"[30]

In late May Pixie Smith and Edith Craig, who had a costumery in Henrietta Street, did indeed stage scenes from *The Countess Cathleen* in their new theatre, the Henrietta Theatre, evidently using her earlier designs. "Yeats came & saw part of 'The Countess Cathleen,' "she wrote to Paine, "and seems much pleased with the theatre!"[31]

Most of their experimentation had been with short lyric poems and lyrics from his plays, and, although he was on uncertain ground with dramatic verse, he believed that the Greeks chanted at least the choruses of their plays. As he took his chanting experiments before the public, Yeats was helpless to prevent the formation of a comic gap between the seriousness of his efforts and the tongue-in-cheek responses of London journalists, but the public launching of the new art was a crucial first step for establishing a society for romantic drama in London.

Just as he and fellow members of the Romantic Theatre Society launched their efforts to reform verse speaking in the theatre, Yeats encountered

30. Letter of March 17, 1901 to Albert Bigelow Paine (Huntington). The short-lived *Kensington: A Magazine of Art, Literature and the Drama* (seven numbers, March–September 1901), published Yeats's story "The Fool of Faery" in the June number.
31. Letter of May 28, 1901, to Albert Bigelow Paine (Huntington).

Gordon Craig's stage scenery for the Purcell Operatic Society's production of *A Masque of Love.* Stunned by the symbolic setting, he wrote immediately to Norah Dryhurst, secretary of the Society, describing "the only good scenery I ever saw" and expressing his desire to contact Craig and write an essay as "a eulogy of that wonderful purple that was like the edge of eternity, & endeed of all the rest of his arrangements" (*CL3* 52–3). He saw the production as an historical moment in the theatre, for Craig had visibly resurrected an art that Yeats thought only Ricketts might recover. When Yeats left for the Stratford Shakespeare Festival in April, his imagination was stirred by Craig's perfect scenic complement to musical speech and symbolic movement. As he wrote about the Shakespearean productions, he recalled how Craig had "created an ideal country where everything was possible, even speaking in verse, or speaking in music, or the expression of the whole life in a dance, and I would like to see Stratford-on-Avon decorate its Shakespeare with like scenery" (*E&I* 100–1). Yeats's enthusiasm, however, was dampened by the plans of Martyn and Moore to let the Irish Literary Theatre become a stock company under the control of F. R. Benson, the English actor-manager who would stage their autumn production of *Diarmuid and Grania* in 1901.[32] Knowing that their ideas of realistic stage management would prevail, and desperate to preserve artistic integrity for Irish romantic and heroic plays, Yeats futilely urged them to employ Craig. Dismayed over the bleak prospects of the Irish Literary Theatre, he turned to his new artistic relationships in London.

Ricketts had remained on the periphery of the group until April 18, when Sturge Moore called again to discuss their progress and the adaptability of certain plays. "The idea of the Art Theatre revived," Ricketts noted. "We discussed 'Prometheus Bound' and 'Hippolytus.'"[33] Several plays were under consideration, but Yeats was determined that they would learn the arts that would enable them to stage *The Countess Cathleen.* Ricketts, who had a reputation as a discerning and demanding drama critic among his literary friends, had read none of Yeats's plays at this time. He often found Yeats "vague" and "diffuse" in their discussions, and for months

32. Yeats had arranged for Mrs. Patrick Campbell to produce the play in London, but when he and George Moore insisted that she also produce the play in Dublin as the final production of the Irish Literary Theatre, she broke the agreement.

33. Charles Ricketts, unpublished diary for 1901 (BL Add. MS 58099). Numerous entries in Ricketts's diaries were not included in Sturge Moore's compilation for *Self-Portrait.*

he remained privately skeptical of his ability as a playwright. On July 21, however, he finally sat down to read *The Countess Cathleen*,

> and to my astonishment and against all my suspicions I was greatly impressed with its effectiveness. As an artist his work is melodious, and greatly heightened by naif and forcible images, sparks of Irish thought and diction that in emotional scenes and homely scenes have a great and refreshing quality. There is a directness of thought and diction that conveys an impression of character in the persons which I do not think quite intentional. This work is free from the nagging tone one finds in all modern plays excepting Atalanta, and the Tragic Mary.[34]

Thus, Ricketts joined the succession of English artists—including his lifelong companion, the artist and lithographer, Charles Shannon—who in the following months became avid supporters of Yeats and the London theatre project.

Sturge Moore had meanwhile confided their still secret plans for a new theatre to other friends, including Robert Trevelyan, who was inspired to write his own poetic drama, *Polyphemus*, and A. H. Fisher, the artist, who wrote to Sturge Moore on May 9: "I hope your theatre schemes prosper though I am sure they will entail much work and anxiety over countless petty and irritating things."[35] Trevelyan and Fisher would become important observers and promoters of the group in the months ahead. By July 30 Sturge Moore's new play, *Aphrodite Against Artemis*, was scheduled for a copyright reading at the Dalston Theatre, an event that formally marked the establishment of the Literary Theatre Club.[36] The parts were read, according to Ricketts, "by a set of amateurs and friends," with May Morris taking the part of Phaedra. Ricketts, newly interested in scenes and costumes for Yeats's play, afterward bantered with Farr about the design of her symbolic costume:

> I spoke to Miss Farr about her part in Yeats's *Countess Cathleen* in Dublin, where she had taken a man's part: had she found her clothes trying? Yes, she had; "You see Yeats had insisted on my wearing mauve—a most trying

34. Ricketts's diary for 1901; Ricketts refers to Swinburne's *Atalanta in Calydon* (1865) and Michael Field's *The Tragic Mary* (1890).
35. Sturge Moore Papers, Box 23/94.
36. When asked by *The Academy* to list the two works that had pleased and interested him most in 1901, Yeats listed Binyon's *Odes* and Sturge Moore's *Aphrodite Against Artemis*, "which is powerful with a beautiful constrained passion" (*CL3* 131).

colour—a mauve tunic just down below the knees, you know, and over that a great common purple cloak."[37]

Ever since that first production of the play in Dublin, Yeats had been reluctant to produce his plays until he found artists who could design symbolic scenery and costumes and players who could be trained to speak the verse to his satisfaction. Accordingly, in recent months there had been much practice and experimentation at his Monday evenings. Moreover, it had become clear to Yeats and Farr (and their friends) that they had to move beyond the harp and piano as accompaniments to the chanting. When Lady Gregory returned in May from a two-month trip toYugoslavia, she found Yeats "still interested in his chanting" (*Diaries* 305) and presented him with a one-stringed Montenegrin lute, which was employed immediately at chanting sessions during his regular Monday evenings in Woburn Buildings. "I am delighted about the one stringed lute," he wrote to her on news of its purchase. "One string should do much to restrain the irrelevant activities of the musician" (*CL3* 59).

Farr began to bring to these evenings several young actresses who would soon be trained in the new art as members of what Yeats called "some Order naming itself from the Golden Violet of the Troubadours" (*E&I* 19). The two began to train as chanters several poets—Sturge Moore, Laurence Binyon, Robert Bridges, and even Roger Fry, the art critic. "I had my second lesson in voice production this afternoon," Sturge Moore wrote to Sybil Pye, "and fancy I am really going to be improved by them and rendered capable of reading out loud. Mrs. Emery is certainly very good though I don't follow her taste everywhere.... You must now write some short and sweet poems to let me chant them when I become a master bard."[38] William Rothenstein, who was a regular at Yeats's chanting sessions, described the atmosphere: 'When Yeats came down, candle in hand, to guide one up the long flight of stairs to his rooms, one never knew what company one would find there. There were ladies who sat on the floor and chanted stories, or crooned poems to the accompaniment of a one-stringed instrument.'[39] It was in the midst of these bizarre activities that the musician and instrument-maker Arnold Dolmetsch came to their rescue.

37. Ricketts diary, BL Add. MS 58099; also printed in *Self-Portrait*, but with emendations by Sturge Moore.
38. Sturge Moore Papers, Box 16/466.
39. "Three Impressions," *The Arrow: W. B. Yeats Commemoration Number* (Summer 1939), 16.

Yeats had known Dolmetsch since he played before the Rhymers Club at Herbert Horne's Hobby Horse House, Fitzroy Square, in 1891–2; had seen George Moore make him the model for the musician Evelyn Innes (as Yeats was the model for Ulick Dean) in *Evelyn Innes* (1898); had witnessed his setting of Swinburne's *Locrine*;[40] and had followed him in other productions of William Poel's Elizabethan Stage Society, most recently in the historic production of *Samson Agonistes* in April 1900.[41] Toward the end of the 1890s more of the bohemian world gathered in Dolmetsch's rooms at 7 Bayley Street than in Yeats's rooms at 18 Woburn Buildings. William Morris, who frequented the concerts, had summoned Dolmetsch to play for him at his death bed, and some of Yeats's friends had written poems to Dolmetsch, including Arthur Symons's "On an Air of Rameau / To Arnold Dolmetsch" and John Todhunter's "A Chest of Viols."[42] On February 26, 1901, less than two weeks after their first lecture on chanting before the Three Kings, Yeats and Farr attended Dolmetsch's first concert at his new

40. For the production of Swinburne's *Locrine: A Tragedy* on March 20, 1899 (see n. 3 above), Dolmetsch had set "Had I wist quoth Spring to the Swallow" for soprano voice with lute and viol accompaniment (the setting is printed in Mabel Dolmetsch, *Personal Recollections of Arnold Dolmetsch* [New York: Macmillan, 1958], 165–6). Yeats wrote of the production in "The Theatre" (1899), "Mr. Swinburne's *Locrine* was acted a month ago, and it was not badly acted, but nobody could tell whether it was fit for the stage or not, for not one rhythm, not one cry of passion, was spoken with a musical emphasis, and verse spoken without a musical emphasis seems but an artificial and cumbersome way of saying what might be said naturally and simply in prose" (*E&I* 168–9). He did not comment upon the chanting of Lillah McCarthy, who wrote of Yeats in *Myself and My Friends* that "Of all the poets I have heard reading their own poetry, Yeats stands out as pre-eminent. His voice is beautiful and his diction supple. His restrained use of emphasis never interrupts the rhythm of the lines, and yet, so consummate is his art, that the emotions which the words themselves call forth are intensified and clarified by his speaking of the verse" (38).
41. In *William Poel and the Elizabethan Revival* (London: Heinemann, 1954), Robert Speaight states that "The performance had, quite rightly, the effect of recitation rather than acting. The choruses, which are the greatest thing in *Samson Agonistes*, were generally spoken or intoned; but occasionally they were chanted to a very simple sequence of notes which Poel believed had been in use for thousands of years" (12). Yeats later told Speaight "that he had never agreed with Poel's method of verse speaking. This is not surprising since for Yeats, when his poet's blood was really up, every syllable was a key word and every tune was an incantation" (75).
42. Dolmetsch played for Morris on September 20, 1896, before Morris's death on October 3. Morris presented him with an inscribed copy of the Kelmscott Coleridge (1896), "Arnold Dolmetsch from William Morris in memory of Sep. 20, 1896" (Haslemere). Symons' "On an Air of Rameau" appeared in his *Images of Good and Evil* (London: William Heinemann, 1899), Todhunter's "A Chest of Viols" in the *Londoner* of March 31, 1900. Symons was grateful to Dolmetsch for composing the music for a song ("We the leafy trees and flowers") in his translation of Kalidasa's *Sakuntula*, produced at the Botanical Gardens on July 6, 1899.

rooms in Charlotte Street. Afterward, they persuaded him to help them with the theory and problems of musical speech; they would soon make him a central figure in the development of the new art and the slowly surfacing dramatic movement.

Dolmetsch had strongly advised them to educate their potential audience through lectures and demonstrations, much as he had done in the 1890s for the old music and instruments, and thus they began to search for a second presentation. On their behalf, Henry Nevinson arranged for his friend Norah Dryhurst, who reviewed for the *Daily Chronicle,* to invite them to perform for her drama class in the Highbury group of Evening Continuation Schools on March 23. Nevinson arrived early to help arrange the rooms and shift the piano and harp for an evening of dramatic scenes and chanting. "Yeats spoke charmingly & with humour," he noted. "Florence Farr recited three of his best lyrics & the harper played. As delighted as Nevinson was with the evening, however, one of Dryhurst's students was so thoroughly repulsed that he wrote an article for the local paper, mockingly addressing Yeats's theme "that lyrical poetry should be chanted, as in the olden time." In its early days, the new art had come face to face with a Highbury utilitarian: "He [Yeats] thought that actors moved about too much," wrote the Continuation student,

> and that they ought to be kept up to their chins in barrels until they were able to speak a poet's lines and give every shade of meaning in them. This was very nice of Mr Yates. But there are people who think that minor poets ought to be put into barrels which come not merely up to their chins but above their poetic brows and hyacynthine locks and are full of water. There is another form of barrel with spikes inside which is generally rolled downhill with the poet inside. This was popular in the middle ages.[43]

Before Yeats and Farr approached Dolmetsch, they had tried speaking through music, using a harp, organ, or piano, "until," says Yeats, "we got to hate the two competing tunes and rhythms that were so often at discord with one another, the tune and the rhythm of the verse and the tune and

43. "Patchwork," *The Holloway & Hornsey Press*, April 12, 1901, 5. Yeats's critic took the further liberty of asserting his belief that poetry was better and more original if read from the bottom of the page up, but he looked forward to the day when "humanity will rise up and have its revenge on the whole of the poetaster race by making its members work at some useful prosaic trade or other instead of wasting time and spoiling good honest paper with things called lyrics. Language was not given to man to use as a rattle."

rhythm of the music" (*E&I* 16). They were seeking a musical method of recording their personal declamations, and they wanted a musical accompaniment that would enhance but remain subservient to the poetic rhythm. Dolmetsch, who thought quarter-tones and less intervals the especial mark of speech as distinct from singing, first persuaded them to write out what they did in wavy lines:[44]

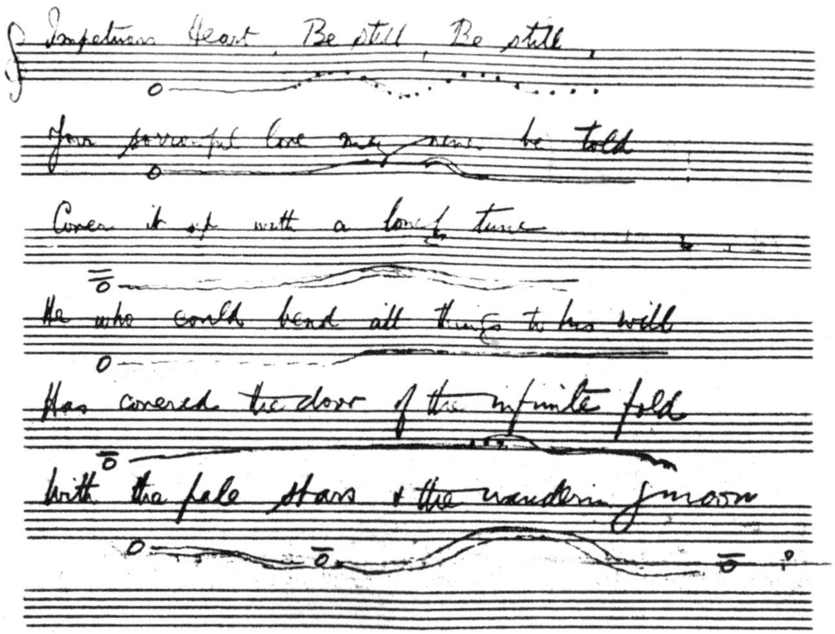

As they practiced this method, Dolmetsch began experimenting with various stringed instruments. Keeping in mind the symbolic as well as practical aspects of their needs, his first designs were similar to a small harp. He then spent several evenings listening to Yeats chant his poems in his strange, trance-like states—not to set the poems to music, but to record the "absolute rhythm," as Ezra Pound would later call it, of the poet reading in a moment of passionate intensity, or as Yeats described it, "in the way he recites when alone, or unconscious of an audience" (*E&I* 21). Dolmetsch subsequently taught Farr to regulate and record her speech with ordinary

44. The "wavy line" transcription of "Impetuous Heart," courtesy of the Department of Special Collections, SUNY Library, Stony Brook, NY.

musical notes. "Dolmetsch is interesting himself in the 'chanting,'" Yeats wrote to Lady Gregory on 7 May, "& has taught Mrs. Emery to write out the notes she speaks to" (*CL3* 68):[45]

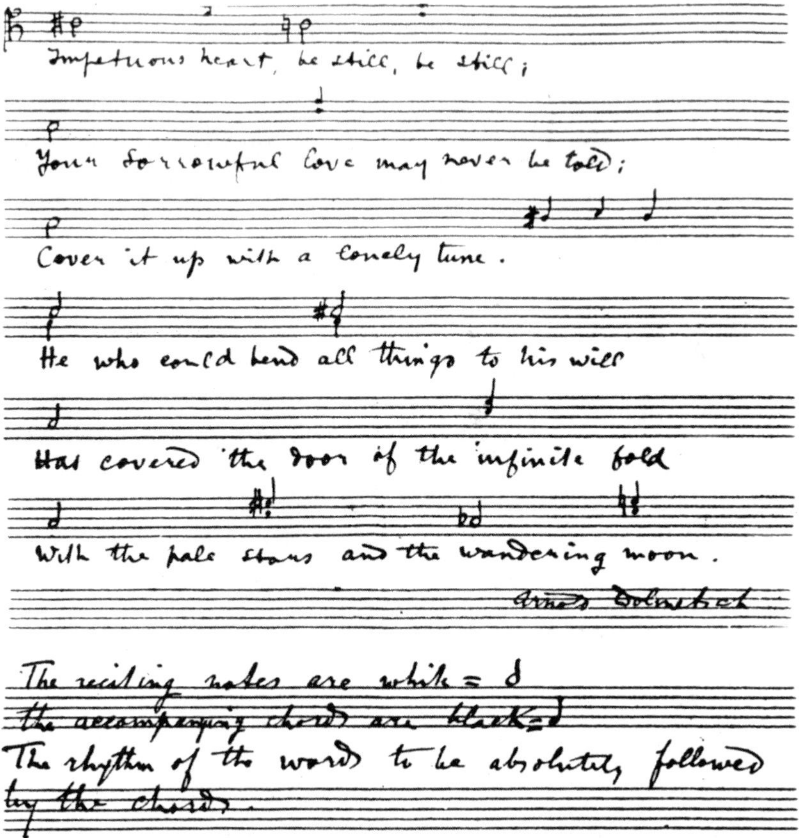

By midsummer, Dolmetsch, the consummate craftsman of old English instruments, had completed a prototype of the psaltery. On July 20 Yeats wrote to Robert Bridges, two of whose poems ("Nightingales" and "Will love again awake") were in Farr's rapidly growing repertoire: "Dolmetsch

45. The following manuscript, signed by Dolmetsch, shows markings of "reciting notes" and "accompanying chords," the "rhythm of the words to be absolutely followed by the chords." Courtesy of the Department of Special Collections, SUNY Library, Stony Brook, NY.

has interested himself in the chanting—about which you ask me—and has made a psaltery for Miss Farr. It has 12 strings, one for each note in her voice. She will speak to it, speaking an octave lower than she sings" (*CL3* 91).[46] Dolmetsch worked closely with Farr over the summer to perfect both the method and the instrument. The completed psaltery-cum-lyre, made of satinwood, has not twelve but twenty-six strings of fine steel and twisted brass, tuned from G to -G (thirteen notes with their octaves in juxtaposition), and contains all the chromatic intervals within the range of the speaking voice. On October 6 Dolmetsch wrote to Farr: "The psaltery is finished. It has gone through many tribulations, but it is now perfectly satisfactory, and, I think, very pleasant to see. I must have a good long talk with you about it."[47]

Over the summer Farr had also been collaborating with Olivia Shakespear on the first of two Egyptian plays, *The Beloved of Hathor*, reciting much of it to Nevinson, who was overtly encouraging but privately "not very hopeful." By late September she had become "quite serious about her Egyptian play," and when Dolmetsch wrote to say that the psaltery was finished she hired the Victoria Hall in Archer Street. On November 16, within a day or two of Yeats's return from Dublin, she produced the play for the inaugural meeting of the Egyptian Society, presided over by the president, Marcus Worsley Blackden of the Egyptian Archaeological Survey, and the secretary Robert Palmer Thomas, both members of the Golden Dawn and its Egypt Group. Nevinson was there to recordthe presence of

46. Bridges wrote in reply to Yeats's description of the new art on July 24: "I agree about the recitation, I think. Setting *song* aside . . . the mere reading of poetry, if well read, is full of melodious devices, which it is the art of a good reader to conceal, so that he gets his effects without calling attention to them. The word recitation—and the presence of an instrument—makes open confession of his art, and without becoming a singer he ceases to be a reader. The hearer has his attention called to the method itself—and as I have never had any experience of good chanting or recitation I do not know how I should like it. There was a kind of recitation fashionable some years ago in London drawing rooms—satirised by Anstie [Thomas Anstey Guthrie]—and it even crept into the churches. I have heard the Old Testament 'recited' in Westminster Abbey. This used to draw tears from me—tears of laughter. I shook as at a French farce. This is the only sort that I ever heard. I can't really imagine a recitation which I shd myself like as well as good reading (in which the same art wd be disguised) but I think there must be such a thing—and I hope you and the lady will discover it" (*LTWBY1* 83).

47. Letter of October 6, 1901, to Florence Farr, Sterling Library, University of London. This psaltery (MBY) is signed and dated on the underside of the top string bar, "Arnold Dolmetsch/London June 1901." The top and bottom string boards are inlaid with strips of ivory; the tuning plugs are woodburnt G to -G (12 tones plus two).

Yeats, Shaw, Todhunter, "and many others interested in art and letters." Farr played the Priestess of Hathor and cast her niece Dorothy Paget as Nouferou, an attendant at the temple, "played with such sweetness by a young girl novice to the stage." Nevinson, who knew what to emphasize, filed his review for the *Daily Chronicle*:

> The reproductions of the Egyptian costume made a singularly beautiful effect against a plain white background such as we see on many of the ancient frescoes, and the music of the battle-chants and other verses, finely sung behind the scene to a psaltery made by Mr. Arnold Dolmetsch, was rendered with the grand severity of early recitative, such as we may imagine Homeric singers to have borrowed from Egypt or Chaldea. The action of the play, the contest between the warrior's earthly passion and the service of Hathor and Egypt on the field, turns upon the use of ancient magic. . . . Those who know Miss Florence Farr's powers of solemn or sweet recitation will not need to be told with what rare skill she rendered the lines she had put into the mouth of the Priestess. The whole performance was followed with the utmost interest and attention.[48]

This was Yeats's first occasion to hear Farr chant publicly to Dolmetsch's psaltery. Suddenly their earlier experiments with piano and harp took on enormous possibilities, and Yeats wrote immediately to Dolmetsch about perfecting the art of chanting with the new instrument. For the next month the threesome worked diligently at the new enterprise. On December 14 Yeats informed Lady Gregory that he was "working every week with Dolmetsch at the chanting" (*CL3* 137), and a few days later he wrote with delight to say that Dolmetsch had assured him " 'the chanting' is now quite perfect in theory & only requires a little practice. He says it is 'a new art.' We can now make a perfect record of everything" (*CL3* 139). Farr kept Nevinson apprised of their progress, and even of their antics, telling him that Dolmetsch "was like a cross between an organ grinder and his monkey."

A month later, in the new year, Farr and Shakespear staged a return engagement for the Egyptian Society with their double bill of *The Beloved of Hathor* and *The Shrine of the Golden Hawk*. Yeats was there to review the plays for *The Star*, seizing the opportunity to emphasize to his London readership how important were the principles of symbolic drama to the dramatic effects achieved in the production. "The plays themselves are

48. "An Egyptian Play," *Daily Chronicle*, November 18, 1901, 6.

less than fragments of a ritual," he explained, "—the ritual of a beautiful forgotten worship. The characters are priests and priestesses of Ancient Egypt, and the names and mysteries of a religion that was one with magic are perpetually in their mouths."[49] While he experienced some irritation over "the chaos of motives and of motiveless incidents" and the absence of "a strictly dramatic interest," he found the real merit of the plays to lie in the "unearthly" effect created: "it came, I think, more from the scenic arrangements, which did not grossen the imagination with realism, and from the symbolic costumes and from the half-chanting recitation, than from anything especially dramatic." But Yeats's real pleasure was in hearing Farr and Paget chanting to Dolmetsch's psaltery, and the various imperfections visible in the plays were minimized by their beauty of voice, "which becomes perhaps the essential thing in a player when lyrical significance has become the essential thing in a play." To Yeats, transported by the scene and sound, they were more than actresses; they were priestesses, magicians: "They spoke their sentences in adoration of Heru, or Hathor, copied or imitated from old Egyptian poems, as one thinks the Egyptian priestesses must have spoken them. They spoke with so much religious fervor, with so high an ecstasy, that one could not but doubt at times their Christian orthodoxy." In these Egyptian plays, the new art of speaking and chanting dramatic verse to the psaltery had made its stage debut.

II

Farr had originally commissioned a £4 psaltery, but Dolmetsch got carried away and spent £10 on it: in addition to using fine steel and twisted brass for the strings, he inlaid strips of ivory over the string bars and carved an exquisite Yeatsian rose for the sound box. Only part of the extra cost could be covered by Farr's proceeds from the Egyptian plays. Inadvertently, Dolmetsch's extravagance quickened the pace of the movement: to get Farr out of the financial difficulty Yeats began to write his chanting essay, "Speaking to the Psaltery." It was also designed to become, as he explained to Lady Gregory on January 13, a "considerable addition" to his first volume of critical essays, *Ideas of Good and Evil*, and "in any case a necessity that I

49. "Egyptian Plays," *The Star*, January 23, 1902, 1; *UP1*, 266–7.

may launch Mrs Emery" (*CL3* 147). More immediately, it was meant to be a public prologue to a proposed lecture in which he would proclaim the revival of an ancient poetic practice. In the essay he strongly affirmed his unswerving belief in the multiple values of this bardic art—its heightening of a poem's unique lyric rhythm, its accuracy through fixed notation in unfolding the personal emotional tone of the poet within the poem, its ultimate power of bringing poetry and rhythm "nearer to common life" (*E&I* 19). On February 24 Yeats invited to his Monday evening a large group that included Standish O'Grady, Laurence Binyon, and Nevinson to hear Farr speak to the psaltery. Yeats himself chanted Blake's "The Sick Rose" and Nashe's "A Litany in Time of Plague," impressing on Nevinson's memory the chanting of "Dust hath closed Helen's eye." Yeats then talked out the theory that he was formulating for his essay: "He was very sublime all through," Nevinson wrote in his diary that night, "chiefly on this theory of art as indefinitely delicate variety under the appearance of monotony in form.... The whole evening was of immense interest."[50]

While Yeats worked on his chanting essay, Sturge Moore joined the publicity effort with a new essay, "A Plea for an Endowed Stage," published in the January issue of *The Monthly Review*. Sturge Moore wanted a national theatre in England as determinedly as Yeats wanted one in Ireland, and with the financing and future of their societies uncertain he did not want its interests to become separated from those of the national movement. Sturge Moore's essay, while underscoring Yeats's dramatic principles, was therefore cautious not to exclude other repertory interests:

> Toward reform of the theatre every year we witness some effort or other: we are told that verse must be chanted, that scenery must be decorative or symbolical, that acting must be rhythmic or realistic. There are occasions... when each of these demands must be satisfied, as now this beauty, now that, is sought out in the play chosen for performance; but to restrict the stage to any one would be to set the history of drama at defiance and to neglect the boundless variety of human moods.[51]

50. Nevinson, 1902 diary, Bodleian. Yeats had quoted Nashe's line as an example of symbolical writing in "The Symbolism of Poetry" (1900, *E&I* 156). Yeats's story, "Dust Hath Closed Helen's Eye," which originally appeared in *The Dome* in October 1899, was included in *The Celtic Twilight* (1902).
51. Thomas Sturge Moore, "A Plea for an Endowed Stage," *Monthly Review*, 6 (January 1902), 119–20.

Sturge Moore doubtless hoped that their society would become part of the new body of a national company. He wrote to W. A. Pye after the essay appeared: "There is a possibility of the ideas put forward being acted upon—if you support and sympathize, I'd be grateful if you'd join the list of supporters."[52] Their list included "Michael Field"—the poets Katharine Bradley (Michael) and her niece, Edith Cooper (Field)—who discussed Sturge Moore's ("Tommy's") article with Ricketts ("Fay"), who was from the outset an avid but qualified supporter:

> Tommy's emphasis is on elocution: Fay is inimical to any specialised training of the voice. Poetry is now for the eye. It deals with words that expresss enhanced thought—it ought not to be chanted or made subordinate to music. He believes that a sensitive intelligence is what is desirable in the reciter of poetry or the actor of a poetic drama.[53]

The growing list of supporters would not be publicized until a more definite dramatic strategy was in place. However wise Sturge Moore may have been in wanting to identify the society with the future of literary drama more generally, Yeats succeeded in keeping the focus on his particular breed of romantic drama.

On March 24, as he worked on "Speaking to the Psaltery," Yeats called Dolmetsch in for his Monday evening to write the musical notation for his chanting of "Impetuous Heart,"[54] which would be used as a textual illustration of the new art of regulated declamation. Yeats quoted Dolmetsch's musical explanation of the notation in his essay: "It is written in the old C clef, which is, I am told, the most reasonable way to write it, for it would be 'below the stave on the treble clef or above it on the bass clef.' The central line of the stave 'corresponds to the middle C of the piano; the first note of the poem is therefore D.' The marks of long and short over the syllables are not marks of scansion, but show the syllables one makes the voice hurry or linger over" (*E&I* 17):

52. Struge Moore Papers, Box 21/262.
53. Michael Field, 1902 Journal, BL Add. MS 46791.
54. "Speaking to the Psaltery" appeared in the *Monthly Review*, 7 (May 1902), where the following musical illustration (SUNY–Stony Brook) is identified and attributed to Dolmetsch opposite p. 96: "Lines from *The Countess Cathleen* with Mr. A. Dolmetsch's notes for musical reading to the psaltery." The essay was reprinted in *Ideas of Good and Evil* (1903) and expanded in 1907 for inclusion in *CW3* and later in *Essays and Introductions*.

The next day Yeats wrote to Lady Gregory: "Dolmetsch was here last night & was enthusiastic over 'the chanting.' He kept saying 'beautiful, beautiful' " (*CL3* 166).[55]

Yeats then invited Henry Newbolt, editor of *The Monthly Review,* to his next Monday evening, when he and Sturge Moore further elucidated the dramaturgy for the romantic theatre. Newbolt had already accepted for the April number Sturge Moore's latest essay, "The Renovation of the Theatre,"

55. Not long after Yeats's death, and shortly before his own in February 1940, Dolmetsch recalled this evening for Joseph Hone: "The point was to find the 'tune' to which the poet recited his own verse. I once spent a whole night listening to Yeats reciting; but I came to the conclusion that he did not realize the inflexions of his own voice. In fact, he had a short phrase of fairly indistinct tones which he employed to recite any of his poems. This did not interfere with the expression of his readings, which was very beautiful; but it was useless from my point of view.

"I then tried Florence Farr, whose golden voice harmonized perfectly with the notes of the instrument. I taught her to play."

"In my own room, with nobody but Yeats and myself present, it was delightful" (NLI MS 5919; the typescript was edited and emended in Joseph Hone, *W. B. Yeats, 1865–1939*, 191).

and he apparently agreed that Yeats's essay was a logical follow-up to Sturge Moore's argument that no renovation could take place without first finding a cure for "our present deplorable mania for speaking verse absurdly."[56] On April 5 Yeats wrote to Newbolt: "I enclose the article of 'Speaking to the Psaltery' . . . & I would be greatly obliged if you put it in the May number. If it is not out then I shall not be able to give my lecture until Autumn" (*CL3* 169). Yeats looked upon the lecture as a crucial event for the future of his oral and dramatic movements; he wanted to give it in June, with as much public preparation as possible, before his annual departure for Ireland and Coole Park.

Newbolt was sympathetic: he enjoyed hearing his own verse set to music by Elsie Fogerty, who was soon to found the Central School of Speech and Drama (1906) specifically to teach "poetic speech." When he obliged to print the essay in May, Yeats was not only able to settle the debt to Dolmetsch for the original psaltery but to commission him to make several additional, less elaborate psalteries at £2.10 each. Further, he immediately booked Clifford's Inn for his lecture in June and arranged for a publicity rehearsal there on the afternoon of May 15. He filled the room with critics and columnists, including William Archer, London's well-known drama critic and leader of the national theatre movement; Harley Granville-Barker, the actor-director who was assisting Archer in the preparation of a "Blue Book" on the national theatre; George Bernard Shaw, who, as music critic for *The World* and drama critic for *The Saturday Review*, had in the 1890s witnessed the launching of every important musical and dramatic experiment in London; and Arthur Symons, Yeats's old friend, representing *The Academy*; Ricketts, accompanied by Shannon, was there as a still-skeptical observer. While Yeats, Sturge Moore, Binyon, and Dolmetsch explained the theory, Farr and her two nieces, Dorothy and Gladys Paget, provided illustrations on the psaltery. Sturge Moore noted in his diary that Farr, a precursor of T. S. Eliot's Madame Sosostris, unfortunately "had a bad cold no voice. Her nieces did a part of Atalanta in unison effect very fine."[57] Shaw, with a different ear, advised Farr afterwards, "keep your head; and don't let your nieces cantilate or atalantilate anything in public

56. T. Sturge Moore, "The Renovation of the Theatre," *Monthly Review*, 7 (April 1902), 109. Yeats had been preparing Newbolt for his essay since he began it in January, writing to Lady Gregory on January 22: "Monday night I have to be at my rooms as usual for Mrs Emery is to chant in the new Dolmetsch way to Newbolt & others" (*CL3* 150).

57. Sturge Moore Papers, 1901 diary, Box 10, Sterling Library, University of London. See T. S. Eliot, *The Waste Land* (1922): "Madame Sosostris, famous clairvoyante, | Had a bad cold" (lines 43–4).

until they can first *say* the piece interestingly and articulate it delicately and penetratingly" (Bax 20–1).

Yeats's aim on this occasion was only to demonstrate the logic, beauty, and effectiveness of the method for both lyric and dramatic verse to friendly ears. Archer, declaring himself a "hopeless ignoramus" in the techniques of music, gave the most sympathetic and discerning account of what his untrained ear had heard. Yeats, Sturge Moore, and Binyon, he reported, began vying with each other "in proclaiming their total ignorance of music and inability to distinguish one tune from another," but with the assistance of Dolmetsch, and the occasional concurrence of Symons, the only other poet present, they agreed on three procedural points: "first, that poetry ought to be recited in such a way as throw into relief its metrical structure; and, second, that the musician ought not to be allowed to smother it, so to speak, in melody, perverting its natural phrasing and accent. A third point was emphasised by Mr. Dolmetsch: namely that the system of 'speaking through music' (know in Germany as melodrame) led to horrible dissonances and was wholly inartistic."[58] Yeats was emphatic in stating that their musical notations represent the ways in which a poet speaks or chants, not sings, his poems, and the ways in which he wishes them to be spoken or chanted by others. As Farr and Dolmetsch joined in, Archer synthesized their theoretical explanations:

> Proceeding on these principles, Mr. Yeats desires to revive what he believes to have been the method of the old rhapsodists and bards, of chanting or lilting their measures—not singing them (that he expressly repudiates) but speaking them with such insistence on the rhythm, and such clear transitions from note to note, as can be recorded by anyone who knows what these symbols signify. The psaltery, meanwhile, is to be used as a sort of tuning fork, striking the new note at each transition. Harmony, I take it, is not to be attempted. The instrument is to be in unison with the voice and is to be silent at the points of transition, which are not very frequent, as Mr. Yeats would have phrases of considerable length spoken on one note. This is his theory as I understand it; and he would apply it to the delivery not only of lyric but more especially of dramatic verse.

After the theoretical presentation, Farr began to illustrate the different modes of speaking to notes and chords, reciting some poems to Dolmetsch's notations, some to her own. According to the nature and rhythm of the lyric, she varied both the manner and mode of her voice. Some poems she actually spoke, "with very strong rhythmical emphasis," to a single note of

58. William Archer, "Sing-Songing and Song-Singing," *The Morning Leader*, June 7, 1902, 4.

the psaltery: "other pieces," wrote Archer, for lack of an accurate term, "she intoned, very much as the Psalms are intoned in church," but Yeats and Farr themselves considered intoning an inferior and inartistic form of recitation. Archer was enchanted when she began to chant and lilt to the psaltery Shelley's "Hymn of Pan":[59]

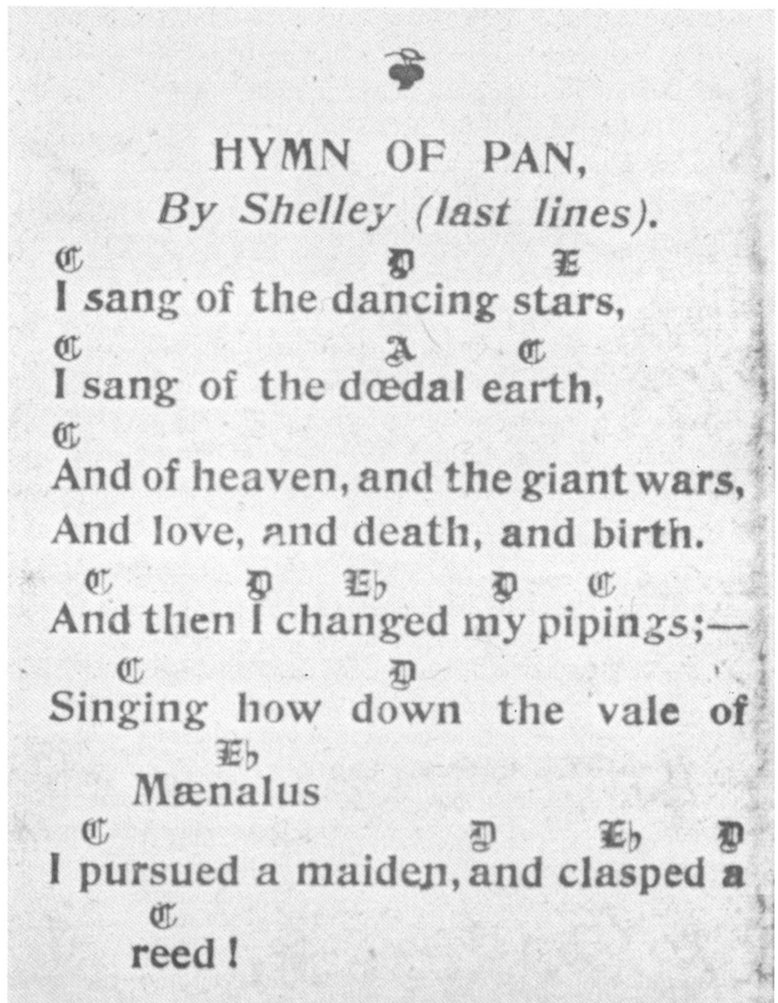

HYMN OF PAN,

By Shelley (last lines).

C D E
I sang of the dancing stars,
C A C
I sang of the dœdal earth,
C
And of heaven, and the giant wars,
And love, and death, and birth.
C D Eb D C
And then I changed my pipings;—
C D
Singing how down the vale of
Eb
Mænalus
C D Eb D
I pursued a maiden, and clasped a
C
reed!

59. Farr's setting for the last lines of "Hymn of Pan," as printed in her *The Music of Speech, Containing the Words of Some Poets, Thinkers and Music-Makers Regarding the Practice of the Bardic Art Together with Fragments of Verse Set to Its Own Melody* (London: Elkin Mathews, 1909), 23.

She followed the Shelley with Arthur O'Shaughnessy's "Ode."[60]

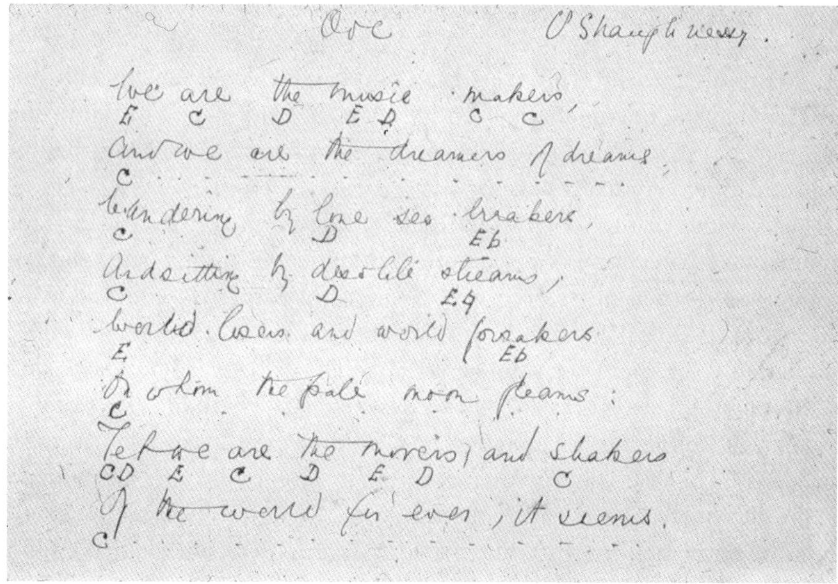

Ode O'Shaughnessy.

We are the music makers,
E C D E D C C
And we are the dreamers of dreams,
C
Wandering by lone sea breakers,
C D Eb
And sitting by desolate streams;
C D E4
World losers and world forsakers
E Eb
On whom the pale moon gleams:
C
Yet we are the movers and shakers
CD E C D E D C
Of the world for ever, it seems.
C

Though Yeats insisted that lilting was not singing, Archer believed that she kept her voice at the tension of song rather than speech:

> Miss Farr chanted to what seemed to me distinct musical phrases, very beautifully adapted to the poetic phrases they accompanied. It could scarcely be said that she had set them to 'tunes,' for there was no structure, no symmetry, no definite melodic scheme in the settings. The musical phrases did not, so to

60. Farr's holograph setting appears on a single page in NLI MS 13573; on the same page she wrote out the lines of the poem beneath musical staves and additional notation, treble clef, with the instruction "To be lilted an octave lower." Arthur W. E. O'Shaughnessy (1844–81), born and raised in London by his Galway father and English mother, was a prolific Victorian poet before his death at age thirty-six. Employed as an ichthyologist in the British Museum, he was a regular member of the Ford Madox Brown–Rossetti circle. His popular "Ode," in nine stanzas, appeared as the opening poem in *Music and Moonlight* (London: Chatto and Windus, 1874). Yeats had alluded to the third stanza of the poem in "The Symbolism of Poetry" (1900): "This is maybe what Arthur O'Shaughnessy meant when he made his poets say they had built Nineveh with their sighing" (*E&I* 158): "We, in the ages lying | In the buried past of the earth, | Built Nineveh with our sighing, | And Babal itself in our mirth". Yeats had included O'Shaughnessy's "Song" ("I made another garden, yea, | For my new Love") in the first two editions (1895, 1900) of *A Book of Irish Verse*; on the contents page of his own copy of the second edition he made notes for a new edition that never appeared, indicating that he would replace "Song" with "Music Makers" (*YL* 2450, 376).

> speak, rhyme with each other. There was no regular musical pattern to distort or overlay the poet's rhythmic pattern. Nevertheless, each phrase, taken by itself, was a fragment of a melody.

Archer thought that the lilts were both novel and effective, greatly enhancing for him the poetic effect of both poems. "I am inclined to think," he concluded, "that in this system of 'lilting' Miss Farr, or Mr. Yeats, has hit on something very like a new art."

Yeats wrote to Archer that his article had given them "a great lift," for his recorded perception of the unique relation between the poetry and the music had escaped other observers. Symons, in particular, annoyed Yeats with a more critical appraisal of his "mechanical method" in *The Academy*. To Symons' ear, there was a fundamental difference between Yeats's reading of his own lyric and Farr's attempt to reproduce the rhythmic effect of that reading by following the notation and striking the shifting pitch on the psaltery: "The one was a spontaneous thing, profoundly felt; the other, a deliberate imitation, in which the fixing of the notes made any personal interpretation, good or bad, impossible."[61] Symons was especially doubtful of any method of regulating the speech of actors in dramatic verse. The actor, he concluded, might benefit from studying the notation of one of Yeats's readings, but if he is not to become a human phonograph, and if he is to make verse live on the stage, "let him forget his notes and Mr. Yeats's method."[62]

Yeats sent a lively rejoinder immediately, challenging Symons to borrow one of his psalteries and arguing by analogy that the notation of a song, which is much more elaborate than any notation made for a poem by Dolmetsch or Farr, still allows the singer room for personal interpretation.

61. "The Speaking of Verse," *The Academy and Literature*, May 31, 1902, 559; rpt. in *Plays, Acting, and Music* (London: Duckworth, 1903), 23–6.

62. Ibid. An article by the critic for the New York *Nation*, written in support of Symon's article, was reprinted in *The Academy* of July 12: "Like many other well-intentioned movements, this revival of 'speaking to music' is merely an amusing bit of archaism, which cavalierly disregards the reasons for things as they are.... Now that poetry has become an individual enjoyment—a matter chiefly for the closet—it has largely dispensed with melody. Meanwhile long generations of refined social intercourse have probably greatly improved the speaking voice; and in our own time...in Bernhardt before her mannerisms overtook her, we have heard a declamation so varied, so subtle and harmonious, that beside it any form of intonation—anything, in fact, but the most perfect melody—must have seemed crude and inartistic. We are no longer a singing people, and the fact is to be deplored; but our regeneration lies along the lines of perfected music and of intelligent declamation, not along those of an archaistic return to outworn musical modes. Cantilation, at least, will not win us back from prose to poetry."

"Indeed, I am persuaded that the fixing of the pitch gives more delicacy and beauty to the 'personal interpretation,' for it leaves the speaker free to preoccupy himself with the subtlest modulations." To Yeats, everything in any artist's work that can be recorded and taught should be recorded and taught, "for by doing so we take a burden from the imagination, which climbs higher in light armour than in heavy" (*CL3* 196).

Despite Farr's request, Shaw refused to have anything to do with these "cantilationary polemics," writing severely to her on June 6:

> The fact is there is no new art in the business at all. Yeats thinks so only because he does not go to church. Half the curates in the kingdom cantilate like mad all the time. . . . Sarah Bernhardt's "golden voice", which has always made me sick, is cantilation, or, to use the customary word, intoning. It is no use for Yeats to try to make a distinction: there is no distinction, no novelty, no nothing but nonsense.
>
> (Bax 19–20)

Shaw's reaction was vividly characteristic of those that accused Yeats of doing what he was struggling against—cantilating, intoning, neglecting the words for the music, evading the meaning and feeling of the author. Earlier Yeats had berated J. F. Runciman of *The Saturday Review* for inventing the report that he called his method "Cantilation": "you will perhaps permit me to say that Mr. Runciman invented the word. I never used it, and I don't mean to, and I don't like it, and I don't think it means anything" (*CL3* 51).[63] Cantilation and intoning, to Yeats and Farr, were merely lifeless forms of chanting for the sake of sound, or for the sake of exhausted religious ritual, and involved little emotional ecstasy, less imaginative absorption in the work, almost no attention to the individual power, meaning, and music of the words themselves—all requisite demands of the new art. But many in the press were unrelenting, seeing his lecture as another vagary of the Celtic Renaissance. "This prospect sounds somewhat alarming," wrote J. Ashby-Sterry of *The Graphic*. "The recitation nuisance in private life is bad enough, but if we are likely to have poets with psalteries turned on unexpectedly to declaim their own poems another terror will be added to social life."[64] Yeats's essay and the psaltery proceedings inspired much

63. In a note printed immediately under Yeats's letter, printed in the *Saturday Review* of March 16, 1901, Runciman replied that "Mr. Yeats himself gave me the word some months ago. I have never heard it used by anyone save Mr. Yeats."

64. "The Bystander," J. Ashby-Sterry's column in *The Graphic*, June 14, 1902, 794.

journalistic doggerel: Ashby-Sterry was moved to wile away a Don Juan mood by penning six stanzas of "Tramping Troubadours":

> Don't publish your poems! Cried bold Mr. Yeats,
> His host of bard brothers addressing,
> For as sure as you do,
> You the process will rue
> When your "sales" you find sadly depressing.
> Don't pour out your souls in inanimate books,
> For we've learn'd that the public won't heed them,
> No! no! Keep your lays,
> For more vocal displays—
> Go about with a psaltery, and read them!
> This is no little joke, please to understand that,
> On the part of the Poet in question;
> 'Tis a plan of his own,
> And in no flippant tone
> Has he made this astounding suggestion.
> So, since business is meant on the side of the Bards,
> We on ours should require no persuasion
> Hearth and home to defend
> To the bitterest end
> From this terrible bardic invasion.[65]

The publicity campaign and its spin-offs effectively generated much interest in Yeats's public lecture, and Dolmetsch contributed further by putting Farr on the program to recite to the psaltery at his next concert on May 28: "Yeats, Crane, Marsh, Trevelyan, and a better audience than usual," noted Cockerell as he closed the evening in his diary.[66] One critic noticed Yeats as he reported on Dolmetsch's performance of Bach's "Goldberg Variations" on the harpsichord: "Bach wrote them, I believe, to help a patron to sleep. Bach knew what he was doing. Even Mr. Yeats was hard put to it to keep awake."[67] As the notices appeared, Yeats wrote in gratitude to Dolmetsch for his assistance and expertise: "You are the only one, I suppose, in the World now, who knows anything about the old music that was half speech, and I need hardly say, that neither Miss Farr nor myself could have done anything in this matter of speaking to notes, without your help" (*CL3* 194).

65. *Truth*, July 3, 1902, 6. 66. Sydney Cockerell, 1902 diary, BL Add. MS 52639.
67. "Aria, with Variations," *Sunday Sun*, June 1, 1902, 2.

Yeats could not yet foresee the future course of the new art, but, as if to underscore the fulness of his commitment to it, he made an astounding declaration in his new essay: "I, at any rate, from this out mean to write all my longer poems for the stage, and all my shorter ones for the psaltery, if only some strong angel keep me to my good resolutions" (*E&I* 19–20). To seal the resolution with his angels, he began writing for the lecture a poem originally entitled "Prayer to the Seven Archangels to Bless the Seven Notes." That version, for two musician's voices, drew upon the symbols of his earliest lyrics, in which he demonstrates his conviction that "the great passions are angels of God" (*E&I* 197). It looked back to "The Rose of the World," in which the poet commands the archangels in their "dim abode" to bow down to the Rose of Intellectual Beauty, and to "The Countess Cathleen in Paradise," in which Cathleen is envisaged "'Mong the feet of angels seven | What a dancer glimmering!" (*VP* 112, 125). On June 5, five days before Yeats's lecture, Sturge Moore took him to meet and dine with Michael Field, who found Yeats "fearfully shy at first, doctrinaire and 'causy,' but gradually he became warm and vivid in his monologuing." After dinner, Yeats, his eyes "abstract and fervid," chanted for the first time what Edith described as "a little prayer to the Psaltery—a most charming poem. All the Archangels appear in it with shoes of the seven metals."[68] Within days the archangels had been transformed into "kinsmen of the Three in One," the title into "The Players Ask for a Blessing on the Psalteries and on Themselves," the prayer into an invocation, the two voices into three. In the revised poem the three chanting musicians employ the psalteries to musically and magically summon before them the supernatural "masters of the glittering town." As in the earlier poem, "The Travail of Passion," where the descent of immortal passions is seen to be a painful "scourge" that they must endure (*VP* 172), one player perceives that a purple-gowned master "dreads the weight of mortal hours," but a second player reverses the illusion: "O no, O no! They hurry down | Like plovers that have heard the call." In the visionary moment, the third musician asks for a blessing from their masters, who have the power to release immortal music from the players' mortal hands: "The notes they waken shall live on | When all this heavy history's done; | Our hands, our hands must ebb away" (VP

68. Michael Field, 1902 Journal, BL Add. MS 46791. Most of this entry is included undated in *Works and Days*, 263. On this occasion Yeats also "intoned as if to the psaltery Keats' *Bacchic Ode*."

213).[69] Most of Yeats's friends were of course unaware of the magical and symbolical associations of the psaltery for him at this point in its "heavy history," but his poetic consecration of the psaltery in the poem made sacred for him the instrument that had gradually become the central symbol of his bardic, priestly art. "The Players ask for a Blessing on the Psalteries and on Themselves" would take its place in the volume *In the Seven Woods* (1903) and remain permanently in the oeuvre as one of his most puzzling poems for later readers.

III

It was a colossal poetic event: on June 10, 1902, in the hall of Clifford's Inn, Yeats, Dolmetsch, Farr, and the Misses Dorothy and Gladys Paget gathered to formally launch the new art. A specially printed and widely circulated handbill (Plate 3) had been received with great curiosity by the press, which, describing the program as "so unlike the age," gave it unusual notice.[70] In a fashion paper for ladies, Yeats was portrayed as a Don Quixote wandering about in London drawing rooms with a band of troubadours giving recitations entitled "The Psaltery by the Hearth": "I shall not be surprised if the idea were successful. If it curtailed Bridge it would prove something more than Quixotic."[71] "If Mr. Yeats can popularise his psaltery and invent a notation for his quarter-tones," wrote the *Daily Graphic*, "it is possible that he may be able to do a memorable service to music as well as to poetry. Meanwhile, if he wants to realise his dream of 'wild-eyed men speaking harmoniously to murmuring wires, while audiences in many-colored robes listen, hushed and excited,' he has only to go to a smart recital at Steinway Hall on a summer afternoon."[72] Not since Verlaine's celebrated lecture and reading at Barnard's Inn nine years earlier had so many members of London's literary family assembled. Admission was strictly for ticket holders: outside the overflowing Hall, former home of William Morris's Art-Worker's Guild, disappointed latecomers were

69. Although the poem was presented under the new title at the lecture, Yeats continued to work on the last lines, writing to Lady Gregory on June 16, "I don't think the last two or three lines are quite right yet" (*CL3* 203).
70. "Literary Gossip," *The Globe and Traveller* (London), May 31, 1902, 8. A copy of the handbill (Plate 3) is in NLI, bound in MS 12145.
71. *Lady's Pictorial*, June 7, 1902, 1029.
72. "The 'Monthly Review,'" *The Daily Graphic*, May 10, 1902, 12.

being turned away. Earlier in the day, Sturge Moore and Shannon had bicycled to Michael Field for tea: "Shannon stops Michael from going to Hammersmith after the ticket—" Edith wrote in the diary; "all tickets have been taken up." Sturge Moore offered his and Ricketts' tickets to Katharine Bradley and Dora Sanger. "Michael has heard the psaltery," she continued. "(Ricketts was relieved to find we take it only as an amusement added to life)."[73] Inside the Hall, Dolmetsch rose out of the chattering crowd to take the chair, dressed in his Elizabethan concert costume, his white lace jabot cascading out of his black velvet doublet. Now, at forty-four, he had scarcely changed since George Moore fixed his magnetic portrait in the opening of *Evelyn Innes:*

> Iron-grey hair hung in thick locks over his forehead, and, shining through their shadows, his eyes drew attention from the rest of the face, so that none noticed at first the small and firmly cut nose, nor the scanty growth of beard twisted to a point by a movement habitual to the weak, white hand. His face was in his eyes: they reflected the flame of faith and of mission; they were the eyes of one whom fate had thrown on an obscure wayside of dreams, the face of a dreamer and propagandist of old time music and its instruments.[74]

The roar hushed to dead silence as a beautiful woman and two younger ladies dressed in green and purple classical robes flowed onto the platform. They stood stately, solemnly, as if members of a Greek chorus, adjusting the psalteries against their waists like Grecian lyres. They were followed by the poet, dressed in a black velvet frock coat, his tie an enormous purple bow of silk falling uncontrolled to the waist. He stepped to the podium, brushing from his forehead a returning forelock of raven-black hair. He had summoned the crowd, it was reported, "with a view to restoring the ancient and well-nigh lost art of regulated rhythmic declamation,"[75] and at precisely 8:45 p.m., his monocle deftly secured, Mr. W. B. Yeats publicly launched his new art with a lecture entitled "Speaking to Musical Notes."

The evening proved to be as extraordinary as it was meant to be. "Beardsley's sister was there," observed Katherine Bradley, "looking like a lovely, flowery cavern belched up from the shades. . . . But what an audience." Behind her was Dolmetch's French wife, Élodie, known to

73. "Works and Days," Journal of Katherine Bradley and Edith Cooper, 1902, BL Add. MS 46791.

74. George Moore, *Evelyn Innes* (London: T. Fisher Unwin, 1898), 1.

75. Clement Shorter, "Mr. Yeats's Method of Reciting," *The Sphere*, June 21, 1902, 278.

Dolmetsch and friends as "Melodie": "She held with great distinction a root of pansies in her hand."[76] Yeats began his lecture, reported the hostile critic from the *Musical Standard*, "by dwelling on the point that he knew nothing about music, a fact that was patent to everyone as the evening advanced. He then referred his listeners to a German authority whose name he had unfortunately forgotten. Presuming thus on the good nature of his audience, he went on to expound his scheme."[77] To Clement Shorter, however, Yeats gave a "fascinating lecture," pausing at intervals for Farr to illustrate his theme, "the idea being that the voice should be sustained and enriched—in union with the rhythm of the verse—by the murmuring of the strings."[78] To the Manchester critic, Yeats began by pleading "the cause of rhythm and the value of sustained tones" and by asserting that the glory of speech's manhood "was the day when poets spoke their verses to regular musical tones." "Since the Garden of Eden," he declared, "the world has been labouring to bring forth the photographic camera, and now that the monstrous birth is accomplished we may be left in peace to recover beautiful arts."[79] To Nevinson, Yeats set out to prove that there was no necessary feud between the poet and the reciter. "Tennyson's sonorous voice, rising and falling, has been noted by all who have listened to him, and Mr. Yeats has heard Mr. Swinburne composing aloud. So in order to prove then and there that poetry and the chant were one Mr. Yeats introduced Mr. Dolmetsch with his 'psaltery' and Miss Florence Farr with her voice, and the audience heard . . . poems with the proper cadence."[80] Farr chanted to the psaltery Yeats's "Impetuous Heart," Shelley's "Ode to a Skylark," and Blake's "The Voice of the Ancient Bard." Yeats called the audience's attention to the frequent habit of poets, in composing their poems, to speak them to the simplest tunes, or folk music, thus regulating the rise and fall of pitch and rhythm. Without disclosing the name of George Russell (AE), he described how an anonymous Irish friend, who had his own musician and was experimenting with Yeats's methods in Ireland, always wrote his poems to two tunes, one for long lines, the other for short lines, as Farr illustrated in chanting AE's "The Gates of Dreamland." Before the break for discussion, Lionel Johnson, now in the last months

76. "Works and Days," BL Add. MS 46791.
77. "Speaking to Musical Notes. / A Criticism of Mr. W.B. Yeats's Lecture," *Musical Standard*, June 21, 1902, 389–90.
78. Shorter, "Mr. Yeats's Method of Reciting," 278.
79. "Our London Correspondence," *Manchester Guardian*, June 11, 1902, 6.
80. Henry Nevinson, "Daily Chronicle Office," *Daily Chronicle*, June 11, 1902, 7.

1. John Butler Yeats: initial study of W. B. Yeats as "King Goll"

2. Published illustration of Yeats as "King Goll"

CLIFFORD'S INN HALL

(30 yards east of "The Griffin," Fleet Street.)

ON TUESDAY, 10th JUNE, AT 8.45,

Mr. W. B. YEATS

Will give a Lecture upon "Speaking to Musical Notes;" it will be illustrated by Lyrics, spoken by Miss Florence Farr to a Psaltery made for the purpose by Mr. Arnold Dolmetsch.

A short Scene from "Atalanta in Calydon," by A. C Swinburne, will follow the Lyrics.

Althœa, Miss FARR. *Chorus*, The Misses PAGET.

Speaking to musical notes is not to be confounded with the ordinary method of speaking through a melody. When that is done the rhythm of the words and the rhythm of the melody compete with one another, and are often at discord. But in speaking to the musical notes and chords, which arise from the feeling and the rhythm of the verse itself, the voice is sustained and enriched by the murmuring of the strings. The most ancient poets of the world in all likelihood regulated their declamation by no very different method, and only when declamation is regulated and recorded can it become an art perfecting itself from generation to generation.

"I am not certain that I shall not see some order naming itself from "the Golden Violet of the Troubadours, or the like, and having among its "members none but well-taught and well-mannered speakers who will "keep the new art from disrepute. They will go here and there speaking "their verses and their little stories wherever they can find a score or two "of poetical-minded people in a big room, or a couple of poetical-"minded friends sitting by the hearth, and poets will write them "poems and little stories to the confounding of print and paper."—*See the Article on "Speaking to the Psaltery," by W. B. Yeats, "Monthly Review," May, 1902.*

The Lecture will be given in order to start a fund for the making of Psalteries for these purposes.

Tickets can be taken beforehand from Mrs. Emery, 67 The Grove, Hammersmith, W.

Reserved, 7/6 and 5/-; Unreserved, 2/-

NO MONEY CAN BE TAKEN AT THE DOORS.

3. Handbill for lecture on "Speaking to Musical Notes"

4. Arnold Dolmetsch playing the lute

5. Florence Farr with the Dolmetsch psaltery

Samhain : An occasional review edited by W. B. Yeats.

Published in October 1902 by Sealy Bryers & Walker and by T. Fisher Unwin.

6. Florence Farr chanting to the psaltery in Dublin

What is the right thing for me to do in regard to the I. N. Th. now? Oct. 9th/03.

Some change is directed by the Highest
Irresolution as to the course of action
Anger in the mind
Most solid materiality needed.

19 cards bad.

5 Trumps - within my own Will.

5 W
2 C
3 S
4 P
Energy must prevail.

Three 3s - deceit - I think something now which is not fact.

I am in a happy friendly successful current, which will carry me on if I decide with a certain amount of self-assertion. That will restore peace & be well for a youngish man. All will change for the better & quarrels will pass away. Some gift will cause quarrels & anger but it will bring good fortune & gain whilst away from home — self-assertion is absolutely necessary.

7. Annie Horniman's Tarot reading in favor of the Irish National Theatre Company

8. “Willy lecturing on Speaking to the Psaltery in the wild and woolly West”

9. Actors and psaltery chorus in the *Hippolytus* of Euripides

10. Yeats and Florence Farr in "A Celtic Solo"

11. Florence Farr in America

12. Charles Shannon's portrait of Yeats with psaltery

of his life, heard her speak to chords on the psaltery his "Te Martyrum Candidatus."[81]

During the question-and-answer intermission the Manchester critic was delighted with Dolmetsch, "whose tentative English and sudden smiles gave a very engaging air to his little explanations." The *Musical Standard* critic, however, complained that "It is a pity that Mr. Yeats respected so little the intelligence of his audience as to ask them to accept his school boy parodies as gospel, for during an interval some rather pertinent questions from the audience showed that of all the speakers he was the least qualified to discuss the subject, and even Mr. Dolmetsch ... was obliged to acknowledge the instability of many of the lecturer's claims."[82] Yeats, however, kept the session light-hearted, asserting that "one of the uses of the psaltery is to give a proper deep-toned power to curses, cursing being, in the lecturer's opinion, a much-neglected form of speech, of which, again, the world may not be quite aware."[83] He even read out Shaw's anti-cantilating letter to Farr: "Mr. Yeats concealed the authorship of a letter which he read denying that this melodious speech is a new art, but he spoke of it as from a distinguished dramatist, and it must surely have been that dramatist of Mr. Yeats's own country whose work Manchester has been seeing, who wrote: 'The curates of the kingdom cantonate [*sic*] like mad all the time, toastmasters cantonate, and Sarah Bernhardt has cantonated me sick with her "golden voice".' "[84] It was further noted by Shorter that Yeats, under questioning, "gave due credit to the Church for having preserved something of the traditional method of speaking to musical notes."[85]

After the interval Yeats introduced Swinburne's "Atalanta in Calydon" and characterized Swinburne's method of chanting his verse. In presenting a choral scene from the work, Farr used the full compass of her speaking

81. In James A. Healey's copy of Yeats's selection of Johnson's *Twenty-One Poems* (1904), which included this poem, Yeats inscribed in May 1905: "The greater number of these poems have been read to me by Lionel Johnson himself & some of them bring the sound of his voice into my ears. He read his verse better than any man I have ever heard read. He had a very subtle and yet very stately way of speaking it & this quality—this distinction in voice and manner he had not less in public speaking. He had this imagination of personality very strongly & all his personal relations with this world were studied and skilful beyond those of other men. I shall not again meet courtesy like his" (*YA8* [1990], 259–60).

82. W. W., "Speaking to Musical Notes. / A Criticism of Mr. W. B. Yeats's Lecture," *Musical Standard*, June 21, 1902, 389.

83. "Our London Correspondence," 6.

84. Ibid.

85. "Mr. Yeats's Method of Reciting," 278.

voice while the Pagets used two or three notes of their singing voices, occasionally striking a note on the psaltery to "keep them right."[86] "Miss Farr spoke with a clear ringing voice," wrote the *Musical Standard* critic, "and fully brought out the music of Swinburne's lines, in marked contrast with the uninteresting and at times unintelligible intoning of the chorus, who robbed their part of all the music this most musical of poets had put into it. For it is clear that all the inflexion of verse must be destroyed when the 'speaker' (as Mr. Yeats would have it) is restricted to the use of three or four notes in close relationship to one another in the scale." The program concluded with their chanting of "The Players ask for a Blessing on the Psalteries and on Themselves."

As the colorful assemblage disbanded, the journalists poured back into Fleet Street to file their reports, and Yeats's friends went home to record their impressions and verdicts in letters and diaries. "The lecture on the Psaltary [*sic*] was a great success," Pixie Smith wrote to Lady Gregory: "people *packed* like herrings in a box!"[87] "As an entertainment it was excellent," wrote Wilfrid Blunt. "Yeats, however, was far from convincing me that the method was either new or good as a way of reading poetry, indeed it reduced the verse to the position it holds in an opera libretto. It was impossible to distinguish whether the words were sense or only sound, and the whole effect depended on the reciter."[88] Perhaps no one was more critical than Edith Cooper, whose supercilious view of Farr could not have been more objectionable to Yeats:

> In Speaking to the Psaltery there is nothing of further accomplishing in speech. Music trifles a little that is all. I did not like hearing Florence Farr taking Shelley's Pan on her lips. Her voice has been trained; but there is no ancestry in it, not that quality that comes from one's own people having laughed rightly, & let loose or guarded their mirth prudently, & never having sneered—that quality that is like fine manners to an ugly face.

86. Dorothy Paget's six-page typescript of a "Scene from [Swinburne's] Atalanta in Calydon," extensively annotated with "details of harmonic progression of the choruses, as well as some stage directions and deletions," was described and offered for auction as part of lot 173, a "collection of papers of Florence Farr, Dorothy Paget and their family," in Sotheby's London Catalogue of December 15, 1988. Some parts of lot 173 were reoffered in lot 262 of the Sotheby's auction of July 15–16, 1998 (now in the Sterling Library, University of London), but other items not offered, including Paget's annotated typescript of "Atalanta in Calydon" (evidently with notes and chords for the psaltery), appear to have been dispersed elsewhere and are untraced.
87. Letter of June 12, 1902 (Berg).
88. Wilfrid Scawen Blunt, *My Diaries, Part Two* (New York: Knopf, 1923), 28.

To twist the knife, she concluded her entry by pitying the figure of Yeats, "doomed to lecture & strive artificially to recall the figure of the poet with his lyre. It was ghostly as wax works are ghostly—too solid for the *real* ghost."[89]

Yeats was jubilant after the lecture and wrote to Lady Gregory on his thirty-seventh birthday:

> My lecture was a great success. People were standing up and many could not get in. We sold £22 worth of tickets and if we had had the courage to take a big hall could have sold many more. We have spent the money on new psalteries and on charming dresses for our troubadours to speak in. Dolmetsch is now making little tunes for my Wandering Aengus and some of my other things to be spoken to. I am taking two psalteries to Dublin & think of leaving one with Russell.
>
> (*CL3* 200–1)[90]

Yeats was not in the least discouraged or deterred by the criticism; he paid no mind to the mockery as Lady Gregory pasted the clippings. Indeed, the lecture had been an event of enormous practical and symbolic import for him. Here, at the mid-point of his life, his public launch of a cultural dream formed the hourglass nexus through which all of his past poetic, dramatic, and critical experiments in chanted verse and musical speech would flow into the future.

To celebrate his birthday, Yeats went off to Newbuildings Place, Wilfrid Blunt's Jacobean manor house in Southwater, Sussex, for a weekend "Poets' Party." Yeats and Cockerell went down together on the Saturday afternoon train. Blunt met them at Christ's Hospital driving a four-horse carriage, which also took away Lord and Lady Alfred Douglas, who had come down on the same train. Lady Douglas was Olive Custance, a poetess with whom he had eloped three months earlier. Lord Douglas (Oscar Wilde's "Bosie") was the cousin of Blunt, who had paid for the elopement and was trying to help reclaim his nephew's lost reputation. Blunt's wife was Lady Anne Isabella Noel, daughter of William Noel, Earl of Lovelace, and Ada Augusta Byron, only child of Lord Byron. After tea, Cockerell went for a long stroll with Yeats and Blunt, "then interesting talk until midnight."[91] Their many

89. "Works and Days," BL Add. MS 46791.

90. Dolmetsch's notations for "The Song of Wandering Aengus' " and other lyrics were included in the expanded version of "Speaking to the Psaltery" (*E&I* 23–7).

91. Cockerell diary, BL Add. MS 52639.

shared political interests would have ensured discussion of the recent Boer peace in the Transvaal.

The next morning Neville Lytton (grandson of Bulwer Lytton and son of the viceroy of India when Blunt began his anti-imperialist rage there), his wife Judith (Blunt's daughter), and Edward Marsh came over from Guildford, and the group devoted the afternoon to "talk about the psaltery and the best method of reciting poetry."[92] After lunch, there were readings: Yeats read "When You Are Old" and his new "Blessings on the Psaltery." Blunt read "The Wind and the Whirlwind," his long poem on the British intervention in Egypt. As Cockerell recorded in his diary, Douglas then read his "Ballad of Perkin Warbeck," written in 1895 and based on the story in Holinshead's Chronicles of a fourteen-year-old boy who, despite his lowly social position, is raised to be king because of his beauty. Douglas later vehemently denied having read the poem:

> I was appalled on the first night of my stay . . . when, after listening with growing feelings of dismay and embarrassment to Mr. Yeats' reading in a wailing monotone of his own poems for at least an hour after dinner, I was called on by Wilfrid to read my own 'Ballad of Perkin Warbeck.' I utterly declined to do this. I utterly loathe reading my poems aloud. . . . I was firmly resolved that I would rather die in great agony than read any of my poems to the poets assembled.
>
> I am not proud of this. I think it was rather foolish of me, and on this occasion I paid a severe penalty for my folly, for Wilfrid said . . . 'Never mind, Alfred, I will read the ballad myself.' This he proceeded to do, and as he was without exception the worst reader of poetry I have ever encountered, my sufferings were terrible. I sat and listened to my poor ballad being murdered in a mumbling voice, with about three 'ers' in every line, and as soon as it was over I hastily left the room, and did not return till the poetry-reading was quite finished.[93]

After the readings, Yeats, Douglas, and Cockerell "sat on again till midnight discussing poetry and philosophy. A very memorable day." Even so, Cockerell found himself "not much in favour" of Yeats's regulated declamation and chanting, and Blunt wrote in his diary that "all agreed that Yeats' theories of recitation were wrong, useful for concealing indifferent verse. When he recites it is impossible to follow the meaning, or judge whether the verse is good or bad. All the same he is a true poet, more

92. Ibid. 93. Lord Alfred Douglas, *Without Apology* (London: Martin Secker, 1938), 24–5.

than his work reveals him to be, and he is full of ideas, original and true, with wit into the bargain. We all like him."[94] They did not, however, as yet comprehend the uncompromising force of his determination to effect a poetical, theatrical, and cultural transformation with the psaltery.

Cockerell and Yeats returned to London on the Monday morning train as Yeats began to prepare for a busy week with the chanting and the romantic theatre society before departing for Ireland. That night, Shannon confirms, he and Ricketts went to Woburn Buildings to join others in the dramatic circle "to hear chanting."[95] Yeats spent Wednesday evening in Dolmetsch's company, writing excitedly to Archer about their new discovery: "I have been round at Dolmetsch's this evening and have found to my very great surprise that I have made the poems of mine which have most 'folk' feeling, to actual little tunes, much like those A.E. writes to. What's most astonishing of all," he continued, apparently convinced that the voices of ancient bards had spoken through him, "my little tune 'The Song of the Old Mother' is in the Irish gaped scale' " (*CL3* 204).[96] He would never forget what was for him an ecstatic revelation: it was as though he had received final confirmation of what he had believed all along, that his own ear and rhythmical imagination were tuned to an ancient scale.[97] It was as though he and Dolmetsch were the reincarnation

94. Blunt, *My Diaries*, 29.

95. Charles Shannon, 1902 Diary, BL Add. MS 58114. Yeats had invited William Sharp, who missed the public lecture, to join this psaltery session: "Come round on Monday evening as Mrs. Emery is going to speak to the psaltery. I go away on Thursday morning" (*CL4* 993).

96. The Irish "gapped scale" was a pentatonic scale containing two intervals greater than a whole tone, leading those used to the heptatonic scale to erroneously suppose that two notes were missing and thus to describe it misleadingly as a gapped scale. The scale was being explored by members of the Irish Folk Song Society: on November 26, 1904, at a meeting of the Irish Literary Society in London, Miss Rowe, accompanied by Georgina Macdonald (Yeats's harpist in 1901) on a small bardic harp, "gave examples of bardic recitation in the ancient 'gapped' scales" (*Journal of the Irish Folk Song Society*, 2 [1904], 44). In "Anglo-Irish Ballads," the preface to *Broadsides* (Dublin: Cuala Press, 1935), Yeats wrote, "If what is called the gapped scale, if the wide space left unmeasured by the mathematical ear where the voice can rise wavering, quivering, through its quarter-tones, is necessary if we are to preserve in song the natural rhythm of words, one understands why the Greeks murdered the man who added a fourth string to the lyre" (*P&I* 179).

97. John Eglinton attests in *Irish Literary Portraits* (London: Macmillan, 1935) that "few have been, like the whole Yeats family, entirely without ear for music. I have heard Yeats claim that this insensibility to the great art of the moderns has been an advantage to him, in helping him to preserve an 'antiquity of mind' " (19).

of Blake and the musician who took down the notation of his lyric songs. Again, Dolmetsch recorded the notes on the old C clef (*E&I* 26–7):

On Friday, Yeats and Sturge Moore went to Ricketts and Shannon for tea "to discuss the Romantic Stage idea."[98] Their aim was to prepare for a

98. Shannon diary, BL Add. MS 58114.

public launch when Yeats returned from Ireland in the autumn. Yeats had learned that Gordon Craig was "very anxious" to stage some of his plays, possibly involving Craig's famous mother, Ellen Terry: "But for divination I should believe that something will come of it," he wrote to Lady Gregory (*CL3* 201). Accordingly, he put Sturge Moore in charge of recruiting and training verse speakers in his absence. They plotted a schedule of chanting lessons for members of the theatre club, discussed possible plays for production, particularly *The Countess Cathleen*, and the all-important matter of funding, which Ricketts would undertake to provide with proceeds from his Vale Press edition of Marlowe's *Faustus.*[99] Everything was in order. Thus, the next day, on June 21, with the streets of London gaily decorated for the Coronation of Prince Edward and the streets of the procession barricaded, Yeats set out for Dublin and Coole, confident of the future of his bardic art and armed with new psalteries for George Russell and Frank Fay.

IV

Yeats was hardly on the boat before members of the Literary Theatre Club and new would-be troubadours gathered around Sturge Moore, Farr, and Dolmetsch for a summer of chanting to the new psalteries that were ready for distribution. Several new actresses were brought in, including Mary Price Owen (a friend of Annie Horniman), Gwendolyn Bishop and Flora Mayor (Farr's friends), and an American actress from California, Miss Eleanor Calhoun, who had collaborated with William Poel and had invited Dolmetsch to join her for a Shakespearean tour in America. From the Golden Dawn came John Hugh Armstrong Elliott and his wife, Eleanor Blanche Elliott. They were joined by Sturge Moore's friend, the Rossetti-like beauty and social reformer, Mona Wilson. Her cousin, Frank Sidgwick, an aspiring poet just down from Cambridge, expressed his desire to take

99. True to his word, Ricketts began work on Christopher Marlowe, *The Tragical History of Doctor Faustus* (London: Hacon and Ricketts, 1903). The binding, colophon, and title-page design were done by Ricketts at his Vale Press: "This edition [of 310 copies] has been seen through the Press by John Masefield. Decorated by Charles Ricketts under whose Supervision the Book has been Printed for the benefit of the Romantic Stage Players."

chanting lessons.[100] Miss Wilson recalled that Sturge Moore bribed them while he instructed them in verse speaking:

> It was part of his system, and of his own practice, that the verse must never be ruffled by involuntary breath, and I was told to do breathing exercises as well as reading passages from *Paradise Lost* before dressing in the morning. The bribe was the possibility of being chosen for Countess Kathleen, as he was hoping to produce Yeats's play.[101]

Several of Dolmetsch's students joined in, including Helen Coombe, the wife of Roger Fry; Fry's sister, Isabel; and Trevelyan's wife, Elizabeth, who was taking clavichord lessons. Dolmetsch gave freely of his time and was of course essential to the group's progress. When recruiting the Trevelyans into the chanting group, Sturge Moore revealed his own enthusiasm for Dolmetsch's presence and instruction:

> You know I have Dolmetsch here every week now for us to continue Yeats's chanting. It is very interesting and I like him very much. He is so enthusiastic and alive.
>
> He thinks I could learn to chant myself and Binyon also as we can both distinguish notes he says and usually in reading keep the musical intervals with correction. There is a Miss Owen who does it far better than Mrs. Emery who comes here. You should try to come once and bring your wife and then she might be able to teach you to chant. I dare say she could write it down. That is the most difficult part. Dolmetsch does it.[102]

100. Mona Wilson (1872–1954), a graduate of Newnham College, Cambridge, went on to become a prominent scholar and biographer, writing *The Life of William Blake* (1927), and other works. Her father, James Maurice Wilson (1836–1931), the former headmaster of Clifton College, Bristol, and now Archdeacon of Manchester, was the half-brother of Arthur and Henry Sidgwick. Frank Sidgwick (1879–1939), was the son of Arthur Sidgwick, a classicist and don at Corpus Christi, Oxford, where he delighted generations of undergraduates with his enthusiasm for and beautiful readings of Greek poetry. Arthur's brother Henry (1838–1900), professor of Moral Philosophy at Cambridge, had founded Newnham College with his wife, Eleanor; his prominence in the family led to Frank being misidentified in the psaltery company as "Henry." After coming down from Trinity College, Cambridge, Frank had joined A. H. Bullen's publishing firm in October 1901 and was now his junior partner. Three years later he mocked Yeats's "Innisfree" and chanting in a poem entitled "When My Ship Comes In, "proclaiming that he would "follow no poet to Innisfree, | For I don't much care for the honey-bee's hum, | And a clay-wattled cabin is not for me: | But I'll bid farewell to the life of a clerk | And third-floor lodging in Battersea Park' " (*Cornhill Magazine* [January 1905], 53).
101. Sturge Moore Papers, Box 25/126B.
102. [July 1902], ibid., Box 16/480. In "Music For Lyrics" included in the third volume of his *Collected Works* (1908), Yeats stated that "Mr. Arnold Dolmetsch, when he took up the subject at my persuasion, wrote down the recitation of another lyric poet [Laurence Binyon], who like myself knows nothing of music, and found little tunes that delighted him"

By the end of July, Sturge Moore's rooms in St. James's Square had become known as the "Chantry," as Roger Fry described it to Trevelyan, his long-time friend. (Fry had recently illustrated Trevelyan's poetic drama, *Polyphemus.*)[103] "Fry was much impressed by the chanting," Sturge Moore wrote to Trevelyan, urging his attendance. "Could you perhaps come next Tuesday evening Dolmetsch will be here though neither Miss Owen or Mrs. Bishop, I fear, still Miss Fry does it very well."[104] "Fry told me of his visit to the Chantry," replied Trevelyan on August 2, accepting the invitation.[105] The Trevelyans evidently returned on several occasions as the summer wore on, for on September 26 Sturge Moore sent them a reminder that "Dolmetsch is coming here this evening again."[106]

A full ten years after the publication of *The Countess Kathleen and Various Legends and Lyrics,* Yeats had really begun to fulfill his boyhood dream of seeing and hearing lyric and dramatic poetry chanted in an ancient mode that was rooted, he believed, in Greek, Egyptian, and European bardic practices as old as their religions. He and Farr had now taken the new art from the suburbs to the heart of the London artistic world, making a significant impact in that limited public sphere. If a few mocking journalists and skeptical friends frankly disagreed with their efforts, the resistance could not dampen their determination or halt their momentum. They had succeeded in stirring the interest and beginning the education of an intrigued literary public and press. Moreover, they had established a cult of fervent followers who, equipped with a small armory of psalteries, were motivated to develop their chanting skills without Yeats's presence. Only three years after the production of *The Countess Cathleen* at the opening of the now defunct Irish Literary Theatre, Yeats was flush with his London success and his discovery of the Irish bardic wellspring of his own lyric voice. Returning to Dublin to prepare his company for an autumn revival of *Cathleen ni Houlihan*, he was driven to the sea like Cuchulain to fight the invulnerable tide.

(234–5). In the manuscript, "another lyric poet" is preceded by "Laurence Binyon," crossed out (Spencer Research Library, MS 25Wb.2:1[proofs], 2 [MS]).

103. Sturge Moore Papers, Box 16/69. 104. Ibid., Box 16/481.
105. Ibid., Box 16/69. 106. Ibid., Box 16/488.

3
Dublin Minstrels

On arrival in Dublin, Yeats was greeted with the distressing news that members of the Anglo-Israelite sect, who believed that the English had descended from the lost tribes of Israel, had resumed destructive excavations on the Hill of Tara in search of the Ark of the Covenant. He was prevailed upon by Arthur Griffith, George Moore, and Douglas Hyde to visit the site for a confrontation with the landlord, and his involvement in the lively protest led him to write to the editor of the *Times* "to draw the attention of the public to this desecration. Tara is, because of its associations, probably the most consecrated spot in Ireland, and its destruction will leave many bitter memories behind it" (*CL3* 209). The matter also made him miss his appointment to meet Frank Fay at rehearsals of James Cousins's plays; in his letter of apology he said he "should have especially liked to know how you were getting on with the Psaltery. I think you would do better to begin with 'regulated declamation' rather than with the lilts" (*CL3* 210). With the other psaltery safely in AE's hands, he was finally free to retreat from the distracting demands of London and Dublin to the Seven Woods of Coole, where he would soon find a poetic way to confront "Tara uprooted, and new commonness | Upon the throne and crying about the streets | And hanging its paper flowers from post to post" (*VP* 198). At Coole he would continue to make strategy for his double theatrical front and to press AE on conducting the new art in Dublin.

Yeats's friendship with AE had been moving toward this collaboration since they discovered each other as bardic chanters at the Metropolitan School of Art in 1884. As Joseph Hone describes the fast friends in those days, "When all the rest of the family had retired to bed, Willie and [AE] would sit in the kitchen . . . and then chant their verses to each other. It was supposed upstairs that they were trying to disincarnate themselves."[1] As the two poets moved from one Dublin literary or occult society to another, AE's reputation for chanting rivaled that of Yeats. At meetings of the Dublin Hermetic Society, which they joined in 1885, Ella Young describes how fellow members would persuade AE to recite his own poetry "in a rich chanting voice," for sound, he insisted, was "one of the great things in poetry."[2] John Eglinton, who had met AE through Yeats at the art school, recounts an occasion on which AE hailed him as he got off a train, "breaking at once into a sonorous chant" as they walked to a cemetery, where "on the slab of a certain tomb we would sit till midnight, while he narrated his visions."[3] Yeats made the first of several dedications—"To My Mystic Friend | George Russell"—in *Fairy and Folk Tales of the Irish Peasantry* (1888), the year in which they joined the Theosophical Society. AE did not approve of Yeats joining the magical order of the Golden Dawn two years later. When he learned that his friend had become a student of Cabalistic meditation techniques, the mystic and the magician soon diverged into different visionary pathways. In the introduction to his *A Book of Irish Verse* (1895), Yeats distanced himself from AE in describing him as a member of a "little mystical movement" and as "an exquisite though still imperfect craftsman, who has put a distinctive mood of the little group into haunting stanzas" (*BIV1* xxiv).[4] However, as Yeats became increasingly prophetic of a magical revolution, he never excluded the mystic AE from his large cultural vision. When Yeats rejected the word "decadence," preferring "the autumn of the body" in his belief that "the arts lie dreaming of things to come," he drew on AE's poem "The Gates of Dreamland" to define his meaning: "An Irish poet whose rhythms are like the cry of a sea-bird in autumn twilight has told its meaning in the line, 'The very sunlight's weary, and it's time to quit the plough' " (*E&I* 191). It was one of the first poems that Yeats had Farr arrange for the psaltery:

1. Joseph Hone, *W. B. Yeats 1865–1939* (London: Macmillan, 1942), 46.
2. Ella Young, *Flowering Dusk* (London: Dennis Dobson, 1947), 35.
3. John Eglinton, *Irish Literary Portraits* (London: Macmillan, 1935), 45.
4. In the second edition of *A Book of Irish Verse* (1899), where the revised introduction is entitled "Modern Irish Poetry," Yeats expanded his earlier description of AE as "the chief poet of the school of Irish mystics." In characterizing his poetry as having a "more disembodied ecstasy than any poetry of our time," Yeats implied that AE's mystic practice had exacted a price in his art: he placed AE among those poets who think "the labours that bring the mystic vision more important than the labours of any craft" (*P&I* 108).

E D C D E A
"Come away," the red lips whisper, "All the world is weary now:
E D C D E A
'Tis the twilight of the ages and it's time to quit the plow.
E D C D E A
Oh, the very sunlight's weary ere it lightens up the dew!
(B ♭ E) (A F) (B ♭ E) (A E)
And its gold is changed and faded before it falls to you."[5]

Their mutual, habitual, and increasingly public chanting of poems actually led Yeats and AE to their first experiments with Edward Martyn, who was an accomplished organist of liturgical and Palestrina music as well as an amateur playwright. "One day I was walking through a Dublin street with Mr. George Russell ('A.E.')," Yeats recounted,

> and he began speaking his verses out loud with the confidence of those who have the inner light. He did not mind that people stopped and looked after him even on the far side of the road, but went on through poem after poem. Like myself, he knew nothing of music, but was certain that he had written them to a manner of music, and he had once asked somebody who played on a wind instrument of some kind, and then a violinist, to write out the music and play it.
>
> (*E&I* 15)

When they were informed that the music could not be played "because it contained quarter-tones and would be out of tune," they were unconvinced. Shortly thereafter, when they were both guests at Martyn's Tillyra Castle, Co. Galway, they asked him to listen to the musical phrases of their verses. Martyn's response was a revelation to them, especially to Yeats:

> Mr. Russell found to his surprise that he did not make every poem to a different tune, and to the surprise of the musician that he did make them all to two quite definite tunes, which are, it seems, like very simple Arabic music. It was, perhaps, to some such music, I thought, that Blake sang his *Songs of Innocence* in Mrs. Williams' drawing room, and perhaps he, too, spoke rather than sang. I, on the other hand, did not often compose to a tune, though I sometimes did, yet always to notes that could be written down and played on

5. Text and music from Florence Farr's *The Music of Speech* (London: Elkin Mathews, 1909), 26. It was evidently this poem that Farr chanted at Lady Gregory's dinner party in London on February 19, 1899. See Pethica, *Diaries*, 204: "Pleasant talk, & Mrs. Emery read E. Bronte's 'Remembrances' & a poem of AE's—& Yeats read from the 'Love Songs of Connaught.' "

my friend's organ, or turned into something like a Gregorian hymn if one sang them in the ordinary way.[6]

Yeats subsequently took Martyn's notation of his poem to Florence Farr in London, and when she spoke it to him, "giving my words a new quality by the beauty of her voice," their experiments in speaking to musical notes and regulated declamation got underway. Even as they pursued the new art in London, however, Yeats never forgot AE's potential role in the development of chanted verse for platform and stage in Ireland. Six months after the production of *The Countess Cathleen*, Yeats wrote to AE about his continuing difficulty with George Moore over chanted verse in the Irish Literary Theatre: "Moore does not much like my ideas of the proper way of speaking verse; but he is wrong & I want to do a little play which can be acted & half chanted & so help the return of bigger poetical plays to the stage. This is really a magical revolution for the magical word is the chanted word" (*CL2* 463–4). Much to Moore's disgust, AE frequently chanted Yeats's poems before him. "I'll never forget one night at George Moore's—not for the first time—," recalled Richard Best, "AE quoting some verses of Yeats." When AE intoned "The Falling of the Leaves," which he much admired, Moore asked petulantly why neither he nor Yeats could recite it in a natural voice. Russell replied, "It's the only way I can repeat it that's quite natural."[7] When he began to chant "The Lake Isle of Innisfree" Moore became exasperated: "Oh, if you go on with that," said

6. Yeats confuses Mrs. Williams' for Mrs. Mathew's drawing room in one of his favorite passages in vol. i of Alexander Gilchrist's *Life of William Blake* (London: Macmillan, 1880). In 1784 John Thomas (Nollehens) Smith " 'heard Blake read and sing several of his poems'—'often heard him.' Yes! *sing* them; for Blake had composed airs to his verses. Wholly ignorant of the art of music, he was unable to note down these spontaneous melodies, and repeated them by ear. Smith reports that his tunes were sometimes 'most singularly beautiful,' and 'were noted down by musical professors;' Mrs. Mathew's being a musical house. I wish one of these musical professors or his executors would produce a sample. Airs simple and ethereal to match the designs and poems of William Blake would be a novelty in music. One would fain hear the melody invented for / How sweet I roam'd from field to field—/ or for some of the *Songs of Innocence*. 'He was listened to by the company,' adds Smith, 'with profound silence, and allowed by most of the visitors to possess original and extraordinary merit.' Phoenix and an admiring circle of cocks and hens is alone a spectacle to compare mentally with this" (47–8). This passage may have prompted Yeats to have Farr set Blake's "Lyric" ("How sweet I roamed") to the psaltery. See Farr's *The Music of Speech*, 24.
7. Yeats was to write in a note for the music to the lyrics in his *Collected Works* (1908): "I wrote and I still speak the verses that begin 'Autumn is over the long leaves that love us' ["The Falling of the Leaves"] to some traditional air, though I could not tell that air or any other on another's lips . . . When, however, the rhythm is more personal than it is in these simple verses, the tune will always be original and personal, alike in the poet and in the reader who has the right ear; and these tunes will now and again have great beauty" (*CW3* 235).

Moore, "I'll throw myself from the window, because I can't stand it, I've heard it too often."[8]

Into the chanting lives of Yeats and AE at this time appeared the young poet and scholar Thomas MacDonagh, who dedicated his first volume of poems, *Through the Ivory Gates* (1903) to Yeats. He became a close listener and follower of their chanting and began to practice the chanting of his own poems. Developing a scholarly interest in the history of English prosody, he eventually wrote and published his master's thesis at University College Dublin on *Thomas Campion and the Art of English Poetry*. There he extended his study of Campion's prosody in *Observations in the Art of English Poesie* (1602) into a treatise on the derivation of English metrics and rhyme from Campion's work, and in developing his overarching thesis that English verse could be divided into song-verse and speech-verse, he included Yeats and AE as exceptional modern examples of tone-deaf poets in whose chanting the elements of song and speech meet and combine. While the negative response of Moore to their chanting is balanced by other admiring, impressionistic accounts, no friendly or unfriendly observer ever gave them the sustained study of MacDonagh, who had each poet chant for him on numerous controlled occasions.

MacDonagh's studies had led him to believe that chanting owed its origin "either to chanting to the harp or lyre, or to the invention of tone-deaf poets and of poets who, though high-musicial, compose their verse through chanting rather than through song."[9] He had further come to observe that "A person with a musical ear cannot chant a poem set to a tune, while that

8. W. R. Rodgers papers, HRHRC. Monk Gibbon's comparison of the chanting theory and style of AE and Yeats later in their lives may reflect generally on these earlier years: "It was not a theory for general consumption and was chiefly successful because the manner so obviously fitted the man. A.E. chanted in long rolling periods with an occasional unexpected stress in an unmistakable Armagh brogue. He would beat time with a barely perceptible motion of his plump right hand, holding his pipe in his left, and fixing you with his penetrating eyes behind their steel-rimmed glasses, as though he wished you to realise that the recitation of poetry is always an act of ritual. Yeats might recite standing, coming down with bold emphasis upon every stressed phrase as well as emphasising the metre. He had no wish to speak poetry apologetically as though it were prose; poetry was in lines and the listener was entitled to have this brought home to him. His voice was more deliberate and more resonant than A.E.'s, and there was a challenge in it, in contrast with A.E.'s Brahminical detachment. If they had been anyone but themselves their audience would probably have burst into loud laughter; but because they were themselves the necessary reverence was forthcoming and one ended by finding the chanting a most moving experience" (*The Masterpiece and the Man: Yeats as I Knew Him* [London: Rupert Hart-Davis, 1959], 86).

9. Thomas MacDonagh, *Thomas Campion and the Art of English Poetry* (Dublin: Talbot Press, 1913), 50.

tune is being played on an instrument."[10] Testing this assertion with a lyre and a variety of old songs, such as Campion's "What if a day or a month and a year" and Shakespeare's "It was a lover and his lass," he stated that "I have then, while playing the tune, tried to chant, as I understand chanting and as I usually chant verse. I have found that my voice always broke into the melody."[11] For a tone-deaf poet like Yeats, however, the chanting is not disrupted or taken over by the tune. Yeats, he observed,

> being quite tone-deaf—or perhaps, I should say, tune-deaf—though of fine ear for all sound values other than pitch, could, I am sure, continue his chanting, not only undisturbed, but probably aided by the rhythm of the tune on the lyre. It is this chanting quality in his verse and in the verse of some others, joined to a wandering rhythm caught from Irish traditional music, that has informed a new species of verse. It is chant-verse, overflowing both song-verse and speech-verse. For not only does something of the word reverence of chanted speech unstress the lyric beat of this poetry, but something of the musical quality of chant lightens and changes the weight of its speech-verse.

"I read every word of it," Yeats wrote in thanking MacDonagh for a copy of the book, much excited by its discoveries. "Your distinction between song-verse and speech-verse is thoroughly sound & I shall look forward to what you write on chant-verse. I find it extraordinarily difficult to explain to any, my own system of scansion for I have very little but instinct."[12] Yeats deeply trusted the driving inner rhythms of his creative "instinct," rhythms that would occasionally reveal recognizable, recurring "tunes" to the ears of musicians when Yeats chanted for them. Moreover, he was intrigued by what was to him the mystery of the phenomenon, which he took as an inexplicable attribute of his lyric gift. He would declare publicly and unapologetically that he and other poets "speak certain kinds of poetry to distinct and simple tunes, though the speakers may be, perhaps generally are, deaf to ordinary music, even what we call tone deaf."[13] The instinct or gift had thus led him to declare proudly, "I hear with older ears than the musicians" (*Expl* 218), to assert ironically that his so-called "monotonous chant" was "only monotonous to an ear that was deaf to poetic rhythm" (*Expl* 173–4), and to state frequently that though he had a poor sense of

10. Ibid. 51. 11. Ibid. 52.

12. Undated letter [?March 1913], printed in *Thomas MacDonagh*, ed. W. Parks and Aideen W. Parks (Athens: University of Georgia Press, 1967), 120. On February 12, 1913, MacDonagh had inscribed a presentation copy to Yeats, who made marginal strokes in the chapter on "Music and Metre—Quantitative Verse and Accentual Verse" (*YL* 1182).

13. "Music for Lyrics" (see Appendix 2), *CW3* 234.

pitch he had a perfect sense of rhythm.[14] In sanctifying his poetic rhythms, creatively conducted in magical meditation, and in safeguarding himself from the word-warping tunes of "ordinary" popular music, he cultivated his tone-deafness as part of his public aspect, willingly providing astonished friends with the many tone-deaf anecdotes (i.e., that he could not recognize the tune of "God Save the Queen") recorded in memoirs.[15]

MacDonagh continued his study of the tunes and rhythms of Yeats's chanting in *Literature in Ireland* (1916), published posthumously shortly after he was executed in the aftermath of the Easter Rising. In his characterization of the distinctive "Irish Mode" of Anglo-Irish poetry, he distinguished the different stress patterns of English and Irish accentual verse, the former underemphasizing or slurring the unstressed syllables in order to emphasize the stressed, the latter allowing for the clear articulation of several syllables between stresses, thereby providing a more even intonation, saved from monotony by the musical rise and fall of the voice, with wavering rather than uniform rhythms. "Mr. Yeats," he argues, "for all his want of musical ear, owes, I believe, this peculiar musical quality of his early verse to that Irish chant which at once saves Irish speech from too definite a stress and from an utterance too monotonous and harsh."[16] MacDonagh believed that the failure to recognize this essential difference led English readers to misunderstand the rhythms of Yeats. He further believed that Yeats's greatest poems were syllabic, like old Irish verse, and in examining the musical quality of Yeats's chant-verse he was not surprised to discover a form of Irish *debhidhe* in the chanted choral lyrics of *Deirdre* (" 'Why is it,' Queen Edain said"): "This poem is really syllabic, seven syllables to the line, like one species of Debhidhe poems in Irish—without, of course, the arrangements of assonance. I do not know if Mr. Yeats is aware of this syllabic measure; but again and again in his poems . . . I find this tendency."[17] Conscious or unconscious of the measure, Yeats was deeply aware that he

14. As Yeats declared it in his "Commentary on 'The Great Clock Tower,' " "I am not musical; I have the poet's exact time sense, only the vaguest sense of pitch" (*VPl* 1008).

15. See also Padraic Colum's account of how "absolutely tone deaf" was Yeats: "I had heard him say that he liked a harp because it looked well-shaped. Now as we heard the music from outside the drawing room, he said to me, 'What are they playing? Fiddle or piano?' " (*The Yeats We Knew*, ed. Francis MacManus [Cork: Mercier Press, 1965], 23).

16. Thomas MacDonagh, *Literature in Ireland: Studies Irish and Anglo-Irish* (New York: Frederick A. Stokes, 1916), 71.

17. Ibid. 72. For a recent study of the influence on Yeats's poetry of Gaelic and Anglo-Irish speech rhythms through the traditions of amhrán (Irish song meter) and the ancient method of singing known as sean-nós, see Brian Devine, *Yeats, the Master of Sound* (Gerrards Cross: Colin Smythe, 2006).

wrote his poems to "wavering, meditative, organic rhythms," and it greatly pleased him to think that his mind was instinctively attuned to ancient Irish folk rhythms. He would discover that the difficulty in putting his chanted lyrics on the stage, of hearing the precise rhythms of his verse lost in singing, was exactly the difficulty that MacDonagh described, of finding, in Yeats's own words, a player of musical ear "who did not sing too much the moment the notes were written down" (*CW3* 233). The problem of musically trained players moving irresistibly from chant into song when the psaltery or another instrument sounded the tune, a problem that he did not have in his protective tune-deafness, would plague him for years and make him so restless, impatient, and corrective in rehearsals of his verse plays.

When the demise of the Irish Literary Theatre enabled Yeats to extricate himself from Moore's mockery of the chanting and their contentious collaboration on *Diarmuid and Grania* in the autumn of 1901, AE took Yeats to the newly formed National Dramatic Company of William and Frank Fay in April 1902. As a nationalist drama critic for the *United Irishman*, Frank Fay, himself a student of stage history and dramatic recitation, had recognized Yeats as a "gifted word musician" but criticized the aims of his Irish Literary Theatre and its reliance on English actors."[18] But in publicly challenging Yeats to move beyond his "undoubtedly charming" plays—*The Land of Heart's Desire* and *The Countess Cathleen*—with plays that inspire men to action, Fay seemed from the beginning to be challenging him to cooperate with his own amateur company: "Let Mr. Yeats give us a play in verse or prose that will rouse this sleeping land," he had written in May 1901. "There is a herd of Saxon and other swine fattening on us. . . . This land is ours, but we have ceased to realise the fact. We want a drama that will make us realise it." Two months later, while Yeats and Lady Gregory responded by collaborating on *Cathleen ni Houlihan,* Fay asserted more forcibly that Yeats's plays must be acted by Irish actors if they were to be of use to Irishmen, extending his challenge to Yeats to "get together a company of amateurs and train them in the way he wants them to go."[19]

When Yeats saw the Fays' production of Alice Milligan's *The Deliverance of Red Hugh* in August, he was stirred to meet the challenge. "I came away with my head on fire," he wrote. "I wanted to hear my own unfinished

18. *The United Irishman*, May 4, 1901; rpt. in Frank J. Fay, *Towards a National Theatre*, ed. Robert Hogan (Dublin: Dolmen Press, 1970), 53.
19. *The United Irishman*, July 27, 1901; rpt. in Fay, *Towards a National Theatre*, 71.

On Baile's Strand, to hear Greek tragedy, spoken with a Dublin accent" (*Aut* 331). AE had meanwhile written his *Deirdre* in reaction to the Yeats–Moore *Diarmuid and Grania,* which he felt was divested of heroism, and when the Fays put AE's play into rehearsal in November, Yeats consulted Lady Gregory about giving them *Cathleen ni Houlihan*, with the suggestion that it would be "the first attempt at a permanent Irish company" (*CL3* 126). Even so, he was doubtful about Fay's verse-speaking without Farr's intervention: "He might even try Cuchullain, though I should prefer he did not, 'The Shadowy Waters' would be beyond him—unless Mrs Emery came over & worked with him" (*CL3* 126). Although AE requested that the Fays be allowed to produce the play with his *Deirdre*, Lady Gregory held out, believing that it should be staged first by the Irish Literary Theatre if Martyn continued to fund it. But by the end of January 1902 it was clear to her that Fay's company, working with actors from Inghinidhe na hÉireann ("Daughters of Ireland"), should have it. It was to Yeats's great advantage that Maud Gonne served as president, producer, and stage manager of Inghinidhe na hÉireann; whereas she had turned down his Countess Cathleen three years earlier, she now agreed to play his Cathleen ni Houlihan. On February 17 Frank Fay wrote to say that "Your little play reached us safely through Mr Russell, and it is now in rehearsal. We are all delighted that Miss Gonne is to act Kathleen and I look for a great success for all of us. . . . There are some verses which the old woman sings. Could you send Miss Gonne the airs to which you wish them sung or do you wish them spoken" (*LTWBY1* 93–4). As Fay would discover, Yeats wanted them chanted.

The historic production of AE's *Deirdre* and Yeats's *Cathleen ni Houlihan* in the Hall of St. Teresa's Total Abstinence Association from April 2 to 4 was, in its popular success, a spectacle of chanting. As Holloway characterized the standing-room-only evening, "Most of the performers chanted their lines after the monotonous method of the Ghost in *Hamlet*, & a few, having very marked accents, the effect produced at times was not impressive to put it mildly." Maire Quinn, he recorded, "chanted her lines in agreeable, if monotonous, monotone as the beautiful Deirdre, and Mr J. Dudley Digges made an admirable Naisi, realising the role with excellent dramatic impressiveness, or telling declamatory effects, as the text demanded." "At the end of the first act," wrote Ella Young for the *All-Ireland Review*, "a man turned to his neighbour and said wearily, 'How am I to sit through three acts of this sing-song thing!' At the end of the third act, a bright-eyed old man, who had been listening intently all the time, bent forward to say to a friend enthusiastically, 'That's something like a play; that's the play for me!' "[20] To Padraic Colum, who played Buinne in AE's *Deirdre*, the most memorable and dramatic moment came when AE, wearing the robe of the Druid Cathvah, appeared behind a gauze veil to renew the heroic appeal. "Tall, bearded, commanding, he chanted the verse that had the very rhythm of sorcery":

Let the Faed Fia fall;
Mananaun Mac Lir.
Take back the days
Amid days unremembered.
Over the warring mind
Let the Faed Fia fall,
Mananaun Mac Lir![21]

Maud Gonne was no less impressive as Kathleen in Yeats's play: her friend Ella Young was taken by "the wild, strange songs Kathleen chants to herself." Yeats reported at once to Lady Gregory that she played the part "magnificently, & with wierd [*sic*] power" (*CL3* 167); in his memory, "her height made Cathleen seem a divine being fallen into our mortal infirmity" (*CW4* 241). As Yeats later revealed, two of her songs in the play, "Do not make a great keening" and "They shall be remembered for ever," were chanted to an air that she heard in a dream.[22] Holloway, too, was greatly impressed by "the creepy realism of the tall & willowy Miss Maud Gonne"; she played a wonderfully "mysterious" Kathleen who "chanted her lines with rare musical effect, & crooned fascinatingly, if somewhat indistinctly,

20. Ella Young, "The Irish Plays," *All-Ireland Review*, April 19, 1902, 101.
21. "Foreword," *Printed Writings by George W. Russell (AE): A Bibliography*, comp. Alan Denson (Evanston, IL: Northwestern University Press, 1961), 13.
22. See Yeats's "Note on the Music" for vol. ii of *Plays for an Irish Theatre* (*The Hour Glass, Cathleen Ni Houlihan, The Pot of Broth*) (London: A. H. Bullen, 1904), [84]; (*VPl* 234; also *CW4* 242). While the volume was in preparation Yeats had written to Lady Gregory from America that he wanted Farr "to write a note on the way to speak those poems in 'Kathleen-ni-Hoolihan' " and to get Fay to "give you the music Mrs MacBride used for the lines 'They shall be remembered for ever.' That might go in too (as well as Mrs Emerys)—it was a tune heard by clairvoyance" (*CL3* 482–3). Lady Gregory informed Yeats that she had "got the Cathleen chant from Mrs. Emery" (*CL3* 483n); Yeats did exclude Farr's note: "it is too meager to mean anything; but I thought her notation was to go in as well as the Dublin notations. I suppose Bullen objected, but it is a great mistake to humour him by giving in to him" (*CL3* 529). In the end, Farr's notations were copied out in another hand and included, unattributed, in the volume, but when the identical notations were reprinted in the *Collected Works* they were duly attributed to her *(CW3* 233)

some lyrics" (Holloway). "She was the veritable Shan Van Vocht," added Young,

> and when she entered the little fire-lit room there came with her a sense of tragedy and the passion of deathless endeavour. When she drew herself proudly to her full height as Kathleen Ni Houlihan, old age fell away from her, and for one short moment she was Kathleen of the poets, "star-crowned, victory-compelling, girt, with a beauty immortal."

"I have never seen an audience so moved," testified James Starkey (Seamus O'Sullivan), as when Maud Gonne "spoke the closing words as she turned away from the cottage door. I was with Arthur Griffith, and I can still see his face as he stood up at the fall of the final curtain to join in the singing of what was then our national anthem—'A Nation Once Again.' "[23]

Yeats and AE sensed at once that a national theatre had been born. The day after the performances closed, Yeats began negotiations with the Fays about the future of their newly named Irish National Dramatic Society. He raced back to London to take strategic actions: first he sent the text of "Speaking to the Psaltery" to Newbolt for the *Monthly Review*, together with news of the Dublin success; he then approached Annie Horniman about possible financial support for the new company; and finally, he wrote to the *United Irishman* regarding his own sentiments about the production and its import:

> Perhaps I was stirred so deeply because my imagination ignored, half-unconsciously, errors of execution, and saw this art of decorative acting as it will be when long experience may have changed a method into a tradition, and made Mr Fay's company, in very truth, a National company, a chief expression of Irish imagination. The Norwegian drama . . . began at a semi-amateur theatre in Bergen, and I cannot see any reason in the nature of things why Mr. Fay's company should not do for Ireland what the little theatre at Bergen did for Europe.
>
> (*CL3* 171)

Yeats also wrote to Fay about "our theories of the stage" and of the need to give members of the company more instruction and practice in musical speech before their autumn productions, for which he would write a new *Samhain*. "You had better start formally with a proper blast of trumpets" (*CL3* 173), advised Yeats, who was clearly moving to co-opt and train the

23. Seamus O'Sullivan, *The Rose and Bottle* (Dublin: Talbot Press, 1946), 120. Thomas Davis's ballad, "A Nation Once Again," appeared in *The Spirit of the Nation* (1843), which collected the best ballads and songs of *The Nation*, of which Davis had been a founding editor in 1842. The ballad contains the ringing refrain, "And Ireland, long a province, be | A Nation Once Again."

company of amateurs in the direction he wanted it to go, just as Fay had challenged him to do.[24]

For his part, AE immediately announced his plan to write a new play on the Children of Lir as a sequel to *Deirdre*. He further advised Yeats that he was defending their plays against an attack by Standish O'Grady in the *All Ireland Review*, to the effect that by bringing plays on the Red Branch cycle into the public domain they would only succeed in "degrading the ideals of Ireland and in banishing the soul from the land."[25] He also delighted in informing Yeats that in the aftermath of the production an hysterical lady had been raving and accusing him "of practising the *Black Art* on the audience when I chanted!! She saw three black waves of darkness rolling down over the stage and audience and it made her ill. . . . I feel filled with the pride of wickedness, almost a demon. Isn't it a delightful audience we get in Dublin. If I write another play I'll work in more magic."[26] Yeats did not take up the invitation to join the fray against O'Grady, but he did importune AE to begin working with a musician to take down the chants of his poems, just as Dolmetsch was taking down his in London, and send them over to Farr. "I will try and get some musical person to take down the chants," he replied on April 19. "But when I get them taken down as they have been before and repeated to me from the notes I do not recognise my chant, and there would be no use in forwarding it. However, someone may succeed in doing it right. I will want several chants for the Children of Lir and choruses and I am going to do the music myself in my own way, if I can get a few girls to understand."[27]

O'Grady's stern admonishment about further productions of heroic plays—to "drop this thing at your peril"—came as a surprise and shock to AE and Yeats, both of whom had greatly admired O'Grady and had been deeply inspired by his resurrection of the Red Branch cycle and other tales of heroic and bardic literature in his *History of Ireland: The Heroic Period* (1878) and *Early Bardic Literature* (1879). The former, said Yeats, "started us all; it stirred others too."[28] "When I read O'Grady," wrote AE, "I was

24. This is confirmed by James Cousins in *We Two Together* (Madras: Ganesh, 1950): "There were stirrings of jealousy over a play of mine [*The Sword of Dermot*] being given precedence to others; also discontented gossip concerning what was described as the scheming of Yeats to pocket the company and establish a dramatic dictatorship which certain of the members resented" (91).
25. Standish O'Grady, *All Ireland Review*, April 12, 1902, 84.
26. George Russell, *Letters from AE*, ed. Alan Denson (London: Abelard-Schuman, 1961), 41.
27. Ibid. 41–2.
28. *Samhain: An Occasional Review*, ed. W. B. Yeats (Dublin: Sealy, Bryers and Walker, October 1902), 12.

as such a man who suddenly feels ancient memories rushing at him, and knows he was born in a noble house . . . It was the memory of race which rose up within me as I read, and I felt exalted as one who learns he is among the children of kings. That is what O'Grady did for me and others who were my contemporaries."[29] O'Grady had fashioned his translations of the heroic cycles, which contain sexual customs and passions that were to him unfit for popular consumption, for the reading luxury of the Irish aristocracy, not for edification of the Christian crowd. He had since become the voice of conscience for that class in imploring Yeats and AE to desist from bringing dramatic versions of the tales onto the stage and thereby "degrading Irish ideals." AE, in the midst of his chanting and dramatic experiments, and with measured respect for O'Grady, wrote an impassioned reply entitled "The Dramatic Treatment of Heroic Literature." "The drama in its mystical beginning," he wrote,

> was the vehicle through which divine ideas, which are beyond the sphere even of heroic life and passion, were expressed; and if Mr. Yeats and myself fail of such greatness, it is not for that reason that the soul of Ireland will depart. I can hardly believe Mr. O'Grady to be serious when he fears that many forbidden subjects will be themes for dramatic art, that Maeve with her many husbands will walk the stage, and the lusts of an earlier age be revived to please the lusts of to-day.[30]

AE wrote for himself and for Yeats, proclaiming the power of the chanting voice over the written page, the predominance of the dramatic poet over those writers who have lost "that power of the bards on whom tongues of fire had descended, who were masters of the magic of utterance, whose thoughts were not meant to be silently read from the lifeless page." Yeats was thrilled by AE's eloquent characterization of the power of drama, and particularly of the living voice, which Yeats would quote and make his own; it was a manifesto for the new art and the new dramatic movement:

> For there never can be, while man lives in a body, a greater means of expression for him than the voice of man affords, and no instrument of music will ever rival in power the flowing of the music of the spheres through his lips. In all its tones, from the chanting of the Magi, which compelled the

29. George Russell, "Introduction" to O'Grady's *The Coming of Cuchulain* (Dublin: Talbot Press, 1920), pp. x–xi.
30. AE's "The Dramatic Treatment of Heroic Literature" first appeared in the *United Irishman*, May 3, 1902, p. 3, and was reprinted by Yeats in *Samhain*, 11–13.

> elements, to those gentle voices which guide the dying into peace, there is a power which will never be stricken from tympan or harp, for in all speech there is life, and with the greatest speech the deep tones of another Voice may mingle.... It is through drama alone that the writer can summon ... so great a power to his aid; and it is possible we yet may hear on the stage ... the old forgotten music which was heard in the duns of kings, which made the revellers grow silent and great warriors to bow low their faces in their hands.[31]

Summoning musical friends to his aid, AE returned anew to his chants and notations for Yeats, but his assistants could not relieve his growing frustration over the notations.[32] "I cannot get the notation of chants done so that I can recognise any likeness," he complained to Yeats on May 24, "and I don't think I would care to send them over otherwise. The whole feeling is in the semitones and if these are left out there is nothing to care about, no spirit or charm. I wish you would come and live in Ireland. All these things you are trying to do could be much better done over here."[33] As Yeats and Farr were preparing for their lecture at Clifford's Inn on June 10 they wanted more than "Dreamland" to illustrate the folk tunes of AE's chants, but none was forthcoming. On June 1 AE complained to Lady Gregory of the burden that he had brought upon himself:

31. Four years later, in evidence of how fast and far he was to move away from these dramatic ideals, AE wrote in the preface to *Some Irish Essays* (Dublin: Maunsel, 1906): "I cannot let *The Dramatic Treatment of Heroic Literature* be reprinted without saying that I feel now O'Grady was right, and I retain the essay only because of some compliment implied to the finest personality in contemporary Irish literature" (7).

32. The Dublin musicians who helped AE have never been identified, but in all likelihood they were his friend and fellow playwright James Cousins, who had played Ainle in *Deirdre*, and James' fiancée, Margaret (Gretta), a pianist who occasionally accompanied James Joyce's singing in her drawing room. She was completing a degree in music at the Royal University and was a member of a circle that regularly met with AE at a Dublin vegetarian restaurant. Cousins, himself a good musician, was at present training a choir of children in voice production for the "Fairy Chorus" in his new one-act verse play, *The Sleep of the King*, which the Fays would include in the Samhain festival on October 29. As Stephen Gwynn observed, the play "gave the troupe their one opportunity of showing how they spoke what was written in metre. They spoke verse not as actors generally do, but as poets speak it, in a kind of chant, which I confess seems to me the natural and proper manner." See Stephen Gwynn, "An Uncommercial Theatre," *Fortnightly Review*, ns 72 (December 1, 1902), 1044–54; here 1047.

    AE may also have called upon Violet Mervyn (Elizabeth Young, Ella Young's elder sister). She was known to Dublin playgoers as the creator of the role of Deirdre in AE's play when it was first performed in January 1902; moreover, she was at present playing the part of Priest of the Floods in the revival of the Farr-Shakespear *Shrine of the Golden Hawk* and had thereby become familiar with chanting to the psaltery. Yeats wrote to AE on April 21 about the performances and told him that he planned to see Miss Young for him (*CL3* 177).

33. *Passages from the Letters of AE to W.B. Yeats* (Dublin: Cuala Press, 1936), 31; complete letter in NLI MS 9967.

> He brings over two psalteries and is going, he says, to start the new art in Ireland if he can. I am sorry I ever turned his mind on the subject for I foresee he looks upon me as the proper person to use the psaltery in Ireland. I am like Willie in not knowing one note from another, and I am less adventurous and dread going out of my depth in strange arts. He has been worrying me to send him over "chants."[34]

AE's temporary gloom appears to have been lifted by the enthusiasm and readiness of Frank Fay to receive a psaltery and be instructed in regulated declamation. Yeats had also informed AE of the success of the London lecture, particularly of his "discovery" that actors could chant in unison, as demonstrated by Farr and her neices chanting scenes and choruses from Swinburne's *Atalanta in Calydon* to the Clifford's Inn audience. "I am much interested in the chanting," AE replied on June 16, "but the speaking in unison is done in every church and is no discovery. I do not suppose you or any of your audience ever were in church, but it is done there constantly to a fixed notation and is very impressive as a mere piece of sound." In anticipation of Yeats's arrival in Dublin, he wanted him to know that he would find Frank Fay "ready to absorb everything. He is the most enthusiastic devotee of methods of speech I ever came across and will get his folk to learn it if he thinks it could be applied to drama."[35]

AE went directly to work with his new psaltery as Yeats headed for Coole. After a week of practice he was ready to hold a Sunday evening for musical friends to try their hand, writing to Yeats to send his scores of music for the instrument. Meanwhile, he had come to some strong conclusions of his own and felt that Dolmetsch had "side-tracked" Yeats by saying that it was not necessary to include quarter-tones in the notation. He had finally discovered how his own chants could be noted down successfully—with semitones and quarter-tones:

> The whole modern system of singing which ignores everything but full tones and half tones is bad. The old Arabic notation went into twenty-fourths, and all these tremulous fragile tones between the full tones are lost in the modern system which always seemed to me wanting in sublety [*sic*], and now hardly any musician has got an ear to recognise the gentler sounds and when they occur they seem discords to him.

Further, he did not think that music was necessary for the chanting voice in any case; the psaltery, he felt, was too limited in its range, causing a loss

34. Berg Collection; quoted in Foster, *Life 1* 266.
35. *Passages from the Letters of AE to W. B. Yeats*, 32.

of emotion when the voice was forced to adjust to its tone. "If you do not agree with this," he concluded, "I will brand you as a heretic to the doctrine of poetic speech."[36]

On July 7 AE returned the scores to Yeats with his verdict for the musical evening: those who tried to speak to the psaltery did not do so very successfully because they began singing rather than speaking musically when they saw the notes. He forcefully reiterated his strong disagreement with Dolmetsch's view of quarter-tones in regulated notation: "They are absolutely necessary if the speaking is at all to be a rendering of the original chant or speech, and nobody should be allowed to vary them at their own sweet wills. I remember to the smallest inflection of a tone any air to which I composed a verse after ten years, and never vary a tone. I am getting two of them taken down for the violin and will let you have copies of them."[37] Yeats was prepared to let AE find his own way in the matter, but hereafter the record of any further experimentation by him disappears. There is a hint of half-hearted interest in a letter of August 25 to Susan Mitchell in which he describes to her an old hermit, "the Dark Man," who sat next a dun near Rosses Point playing the harp and chanting: "(I'm thinking he played it as well as I play the psaltery)."[38] His interest may have waned with the loss of inspiration for completing his play on the Children of Lir: in late August he declared toYeats that he had "escaped from my brief folly of playwriting."[39] When Yeats sat down to write the text for a new issue of *Samhain*, drawing heavily upon AE's "The Dramatic Treatment of Heroic Literature," his summary of their progress together did not go beyond this point.

> "The old, forgotten music" he writes about . . . is, I think, that regulated music of speech at which both he and I have been working, though on somewhat different principles. I have been working with Miss Farr and Mr. Arnold Dolmetsch, who has made a psaltery for the purpose, to perfect a music of speech which can be recorded in something like ordinary musical notes; while AE has got a musician to record little chants with intervals much smaller than those of modern music.
>
> (*Expl* 89)

Fay was much slower to take up the psaltery, deferring to AE as he and his brother reorganized the National Dramatic Society, moved into the Camden Street Hall, and prepared for the Samhain performances. Yeats

36. Ibid. 32–3. 37. Ibid. 33. These notations have not survived.
38. NLI MS 9967. 39. *Letters from AE*, 43.

was elected President of the Society (after AE had declined), with AE, Maud Gonne, and Douglas Hyde as Vice-Presidents. He had meanwhile completed and sent to the Fays the manuscripts of *The Hour-Glass* and *A Pot of Broth* and was busily revising *Cathleen ni Houlihan* for rehearsals. Fay wrote to Yeats on August 28 to request the airs of the songs in *A Pot of Broth* and to ask, with greater awareness of Yeats's penchant for chanting, "Will you let me know whether you can do the verses I suggested and if you wish them chanted would you send the notation."[40] In the midst of rehearsals, the Fays decided to withdraw *The Hour-Glass* from their Samhain program, reserving the play for the later opening of the National Dramatic Society. More distracting to Yeats was Fay's plan to have dedicatory verses recited by the actors at the opening performances; Yeats argued that it would give an amateur air to the project, but he privately objected to verse speaking by actors as yet untrained in his methods. He even declined to write and chant his own dedicatory verses, claiming that "Such things are never done well & give the air of a penny reading entertainment" (*CL3* 223). Fay was also frustrated by the difficulty of finding appropriate music and musicians for the plays ("We must not have the whiskey-stained Irish music we had to put up with at St. Teresa's," he wrote on September 16), and these matters led him to lament, wearily, "What a pity there is not here someone, like Dolmetsch, who would do for our old music what he has done for other old music."[41]

Upon the scene at Coole in August 1902 there arrived as guests two Americans with a keen interest in meeting Yeats—Cornelius Weygandt, an English professor at the University of Pennsylvania, and John Quinn, a New York lawyer and collector of books and paintings, both of whom were deeply impressed by their first experience there and carefully recorded their impressions of Yeats's mind and talk. Weygandt, who had occasionally corresponded with Yeats about his work during the previous six years, arrived in Coole to find that Yeats was only one member of a large house party, but they had time alone to walk in the Seven Woods and talk in the library. As they strolled in the woods Yeats "chanted snatches of the verses he was making," beginning with lines from "The Old Men Admiring themselves in the Water," composed the day before ("All that's beautiful drifts away | Like the waters"), lines that he "could no more get out of his

40. NLI MS 13068.

41. NLI MS 13068 (13). This letter, removed from the folder for an exhibition, has since been mislaid.

head than had it been an old tune."[42] These were followed by a single line, "quiet wanders eating her wild heart," from his poem-in-progress, "In the Seven Woods."[43] "Mr. Yeats had none of his poems by heart," Weygandt observed, "but he could and did tell me folk-tales with the detail of incident of their peasant repeaters. These old stories, told in his haunting voice by that gray lakeside, carried me all but past the portals of this world to the very verge of that eerie land into which he is so often wrapt away." On their walk they talked of "The Other People" and the conviction of neighboring peasants in the reality of visions that had appeared to them. Yeats admitted that he could not believe that some of the visions they described were pure imaginings. "Strange visions had come to him, he said, after walking in these woods, visions of 'immortal, mild, proud shadows,' but always as dreams, and not as objective realities. At times, however, he had seen visions in waking dreams, and he felt the border of the unseen so near that no man should say that no man had crossed it."

When they returned to the library to join other guests, Yeats read his new morality play, *The Hour-Glass*, and an earlier poem "The Rose of the World." "The presence of many people took away not one jot of the effect of the play," wrote Weygandt, "but the poem, read where many were, fell short of the snatches of its fellows chanted from memory as their maker walked between the woods and the water."[44] Yeats had been reading Spenser when Weygandt arrived, and when they were later alone in the library he frequently reverted to Spenser's verse, in which he had discerned a measureable rhythmical loss between Spenser and Shelley. "Old writers gave men four temperaments," wrote Yeats,

> and they gave the sanguineous temperament to men of active life, and it is precisely the sanguineous temperament that is fading out of poetry and most obviously out of what is most subtle and living in poetry—its pulse and breath, its rhythm."
>
> (*E&I* 379–80)

42. "With Mr. W. B. Yeats in the Woods of Coole," *Lippincott's Magazine*, 73 (April 1904), 484–7; rpt.with additional passages in *Tuesdays at Ten* (Philadelphia: University of Philadelphia Press, 1928), and in *W. B. Yeats: Interviews and Recollections*, ed. E. H. Mikhail (New York: Barnes and Noble, 1977), i. 15–19.
43. This version of the lines, "I am contented, for I know that Quiet | Wanders laughing and eating her wild heart" (*VP* 208), was never published and may have been an early version spoken by Yeats or misremembered by Weygandt.
44. *Tuesdays at Ten*, 183.

Yeats also discussed Mangan, Ferguson, and Aubrey De Vere, but what most impressed Weygandt was the nationalist context to which Yeats brought all topics round, including the psaltery: "But always the talk turned again to the many phases of the movement that is striving to give Ireland a national life—to the Celtic art in Loughrea Cathedral; to Irish painting; to Irish music and to Mr. Yeats's own theories of the chanting of verse to the psaltery," and finally to the forthcoming productions of the new Irish National Theatre Society. Weygandt was much moved by the visit; he would return the generosity of Coole the following year by becoming one of Yeats's most hospitable and accommodating hosts when John Quinn arranged his first American tour.

Quinn, like Weygandt, had also looked in on the Fay company's rehearsals before leaving Dublin, where he was sketched with AE and William Fay by Jack Yeats in the Camden Street Hall.[45] On Sunday August 31 he and Jack set out for Coole in a sidecar, breaking the journey at Killeeneen, where they met and joined Yeats, Lady Gregory, Edward Martyn, and Douglas Hyde and his wife, all of whom were among six hundred spectators attending the Feis in honor of Raftery, the blind Connacht poet.[46] Quinn was enthralled by the recitations in Gaelic of old poems and stories and by the competitions in Irish music and dancing. The party, less Martyn, went on to Coole in two sidecars that evening, and from the moment of his arrival Quinn wished that he "could picture something of the charm that hangs around Coole, of its tangled woods, its stately trees, the lake, the winding paths, the two beautiful old gardens, and the view of the distant Burren hills. There seemed to be magic in the air, enchantment in the woods and the beauty of the place, and the best talk and stories I ever found anywhere."[47] Quinn, too, was witness to the reading of scenarios, plays, and poems; to Lady Gregory reading in English; to Hyde reading in Gaelic from *The Love Songs of Connacht* and from his new play, *An Naomh ar Iarraid*, translated by Lady Gregory as *The Lost Saint*.[48] Yeats, wrote Quinn, "had just finished a poem on 'The Seven Woods of Coole,' and he kept

45. Jack Yeats's sketch of Quinn and AE at the Camden Street rehearsals is included as plate 4 in *CL3*, facing p. 362.
46. Quinn's copy of the program for the Killeeneen *feis*, with autographs and Jack Yeats's sketches of Yeats, Lady Gregory, Hyde, Quinn, and himself, is reproduced in Foster, *Life* 1 271.
47. John Quinn, "Lady Gregory and the Abbey Theatre," *The Outlook* (New York), 99 (December 16, 1911), 917; partially reprinted in *The Abbey Theatre: Interviews and Recollections*, ed. E. H. Mikhail (London: Macmillan, 1988), 104–8.
48. Yeats would include the Irish and English versions of *The Lost Saint* for publication in *Samhain* (October 1902), together with *Cathleeen ni Houlihan*.

murmuring it over and over again," lines which Quinn held in memory for years: "I am contented, for I know that Quiet | Wanders laughing and eating her wild heart | Among pigeons and bees." Quinn, Yeats, and Hyde sat up every night until one or two in the morning, talking about many people and topics related to Ireland, but chiefly about Yeats's plans for the development of the theatre. What struck Quinn, who was interested more in Yeats's lyrical than in his dramatic poetry, was that Yeats himself "was more interested in the poetry that moves masses of people in a theatre."[49] Quinn may not have understood how Yeats's plans for a national theatre involved moving a people to an heroic and aesthetic perception of life with dramatic verse and musical speech, but Yeats was certain of his aim. Before he left Coole he was making plans to educate Dubliners in the new art at Samhain.

As these two American friendships got underway, Yeats lost one of his closest English friends, Lionel Johnson. On the night of September 29, Henry Nevinson received word in his office at the *Daily Chronicle* that a man had been found dying in Fleet Street and that his only piece of identification was an unsigned letter addressed to Nevinson. "I went to St. Bartholomew's Hospital," he wrote, "and was there shown Lionel Johnson . . . quite unconscious, the skull being fractured. It appeared that while bringing me his 'copy' he had fallen down at the corner of Whitefriars Street and knocked his head against the curb. The doctors told me his skull was thin as paper."[50] Johnson died on October 4, and Nevinson was one of the few who attended the burial service at Kensal Green on October 8:

> We met the coffin just coming out of the chapel & marched in procession to the grave. No one of note there, a few Irishmen, an old lady in black and white petticoat and duck's feet, his sister terribly overcome, & a few others. . . . We walked on to Willesden. Found Mrs. Emery reciting various things to the lyre, & reading Yeats's letters from Ireland.

49. "Lady Gregory and the Abbey Theatre," 918. Quinn's memory of the conversation is echoed in Yeats's essay on Spenser, which was still in progress during his visit: "Every generation has more and more loosened the rhythm, more and more broken up and disorganised, for the sake of subtlety of detail, those great rhythms which move, as it were, in masses of sound. Poetry has become more spiritual, for the soul is of all things the most delicately organised, but it has lost in weight and measure and in its power of telling long stories and dealing with great and complicated events" (*E&I* 380).
50. Henry Nevinson, *Changes and Chances* (New York: Harcourt, Brace, 1923), 192. For another account of Lionel Johnson's death see *YA8* 122 n. 97: "His death from a ruptured blood vessel following several strokes was quickly mythologised as having been occasioned by a fall from a bar-stool."

Yeats's letters, now lost, would have addressed Johnson's death, but they would also have anticipated Mrs. Emery's forthcoming visit to Dublin, where she and Yeats would give interviews, lectures, and performances on "Speaking to Musical Notes" during the Samhain festival. Yeats had written to AE to secure a hall for the lecture, doubtless disappointed that AE would not be on the stage with them to chant his poems to the psaltery. Fred Ryan, secretary of the Fays' National Dramatic Society, wrote to Yeats on August 11 that it would be "better to have the lecture just before [the Society's] performances. But in our own hall, for it is necessary to make that known."[51] As the Antient Concert Rooms were booked every night, Yeats arranged to include Farr on the musical program for the opening night of the festival. In anticipation of her arrival and performances, he completed the new *Samhain* and urged the publisher to get copies to the Dublin papers ten days before the festival began on October 27.

Yeats wrote with a great sense of liberation as he informed his Dublin audience that the Irish Literary Theatre had "given place to a company of Irish actors." He dissociated the new Irish company from Edward Martyn's Ibsenite declaration the previous spring that Irish actors should be training themselves for "the modern drama of society" and that AE's *Deirdre* and Yeats's *Cathleen ni Houlihan* were not part of that preparation. "It is not," Yeats happily agreed, "but that is as it should be. Our movement is a return to the people." The new Irish theatre, he announced, would provide plays not of the middle classes in cities but plays of countrypeople and heroic characters, plays that would "ennoble the man of the roads," that would be based not on the theatre of realism but on a school of "imaginative acting." He wrote prophetically that the dramatic conjoining of poetry and countryman would eventually lead to the recovery of a "lost art" that would bring fame and livelihood to the Irish theatre. The essential aspect of this lost art of imaginative acting was the new art of poetic and musical speech:

> The habit of writing for the stage, even when it is not countrypeople who are the speakers, and of considering what good dialogue is, will help to increase our feeling for style. Let us get back in everything to the spoken word, even though we have to speak our lyrics to the psaltery or the harp, for, as A.E. says, we have begun to forget that literature is but recorded speech, and even

51. NLI MS 13068 (13).

> when we write with care we have begun "to write with elaboration what could never be spoken". But when we go back to speech let us see that it is the idiom either of those who have rejected, or of those who have never learned, the base idioms of the newspapers.
>
> (*Expl* 95)

Even as he wrote, however, he had not wholly extricated himself from the persistent legacies of his association with Martyn and Moore in the Irish Literary Theatre. He was now caught up, as he described the situation to Sydney Cockerell, in "a strange sort of spider's web of George Moore's spinning" (*CL3* 236). In the summer of 1901, in the middle of their difficult collaboration on *Diarmuid and Grania*, Moore and Yeats began yet another collaboration when it seemed that the Irish Literary Theatre might continue. After Yeats described the plot, Moore sent him a scenario, but when Moore resigned from the Literary Theatre Society Yeats found it a welcome excuse to withdraw from further collaboration. When Moore subsequently informed him by telegram that he was writing a novel on the scenario and that he would take out an injunction against Yeats if he used it, Yeats replied that he would use nothing of Moore's but would use his own plot. At Coole, he immediately began drafting *Where There Is Nothing*, and in response to Moore's legal threats he sought the advice and assistance of John Quinn, who had just returned to America. On September 27 Quinn replied that he would arrange for the private printing of the play for American copyright but recommended that "the copyright performance should be had in England" (*LJQ* 39). The urgent copyrighting of *Where There Is Nothing*, together with *The Hour-Glass*, was certainly one of the topics of the lost letters that Yeats wrote to Farr while she practiced lyrics on the psaltery; during Nevinson's visit after Johnson's funeral she enlisted him on the spot as a reader, hired a licensed hall, and contacted Sturge Moore and other members of the Literary Theatre Club for a copyright reading. On October 18 Nevinson finished reading *Where There is Nothing,* "which is fine," he wrote in his diary, "but too Fabian or anarchist in doctrine, too preachy, much too undramatic and obvious. Some of the satire excellent, some too obvious & common, as of a man who approached social questions for the first time." Two days later he met Farr at the Victoria Hall for the reading: "A number of men came. Sturge Moore the only one of importance, & he not of great importance but all friendly & cleverish." Nevinson took the part of Paul Ruttledge for the first play, and for the second "had to take the wise man by Mrs. Emery's order & I saw Sturge

Moore turn suddenly green—very absurd." Yeats would soon discover some of the tensions that had developed around Farr in the London group, but as he arranged for the publication of *Where There Is Nothing* in a supplement to the *United Irishman*, Farr set out for Dublin with her psaltery, and with Pixie Smith in tow.

The Samhain festival got under way with a progam of Irish music, dance, and recitation in the large hall of the Antient Concert Rooms, with Yeats, Lady Gregory, Pixie Smith, Sarah Purser, Maud Gonne, Douglas Hyde, AE, and probably James Joyce in attendance. AE had written to Yeats at Coole about meeting this "extremely clever boy" of twenty-one, and when Yeats arrived in Dublin for Samhain AE wrote immediately to Joyce: "Yeats will be in Dublin all this week and will be at the Antient Concert Rooms every night. He would like to meet you, and if you could come here on Tuesday at 5 o'c I will bring you to his hotel."[52] Joyce would have been attracted by the Irish songs at the beginning of program, including Miss Naylor's "The Blind Girl to Her Harp," John C. Doyle's "My Dark Rosaleen," and the Misses Wheatley's "Silent, O Moyle," among others, but he would not have missed the return of Aleel to Dublin. "A novel and interesting feature of the entertainment," reported the *Freeman's Journal*, "was the chanting by Miss Florence Farr of lyrics . . . to the accompaniment of the psaltery, invented and made by Mr. Arnold Dolmetsch, the famous musician."[53] When Farr came out in her flowing Greek robe with the psaltery, Yeats arose from the audience to join her and describe briefly his theory of chanted verse:

> He said that which they to-day called music was a modern invention. A very great scholar told him recently that singing was unknown in Scandanavia until the twelfth century. Before that it was all a kind of regulated recitation. Greek music, which was once very famous, was certainly simply regulated declamation which had no meaning apart from the words.

Yeats told the audience of their earliest experiments with "Impetuous Heart" and of their eventual collaboration with Dolmetsch, who had "assured them that they had truly got the old art of the troubadour and the old art of the bard. The audience would be privileged to hear that night a modern equivalent for the old recitation of the bard; they would hear the recitation of the bard revived again after centuries of oblivion." Farr began by chanting "Impetuous Heart," which was followed with

52. NLI MS 9967. 53. "Samhain Festival," *Freeman's Journal*, October 28, 1902, 6.

"breathless interest" as the words "were partly spoken, partly chanted by her, the musical notes drawn from the psaltery merely serving the subordinate purpose of emphasising the meaning of the poem." She then "lilted" O'Shaughnessy's "A Plea for the Idealist" to a rudimentary tune. To conclude the program, she recited, in his memory, the "Te Martyrum Candidatus" of Lionel Johnson, "of whom Mr. Yeats spoke most eulogistically."[54] The first-night presentation of the new art in Dublin, a prelude to the full-scale program which would conclude the week, was greeted with "enthusiastic applause" by the audience, which was, according to the *Daily Express,* "of only very moderate dimensions, considering the interesting character of the experiment, which, it is only fair to say, is not yet fully worked out."

The following evening brought the greatly awaited revival of AE's *Deirdre* and Yeats's *Cathleen ni Houlihan*, highlighted again by the stunning presence and chanting of Maud Gonne. "Miss Maud Gonne was a tragic and poetic figure as Kathleen, and chanted the beautiful lines allotted to her most musically and with infinite pathos," wrote the *Freeman's Journal*, whose reporter had an unusual if not instructed sense of the symbolic importance of the production:

> It marks ... a new departure in dramatic representation in this country. The company ... is entirely independent of all outside influences. It is independent of the English trained actor; the motive springs of its art, as well as its sympathies, are Irish, and it is also, and to a very remarkable degree, free from the conventional stage tricks and time-honoured "traditions" with which we are all too familiar. ... But when all defects and shortcoming are allowed for ... the fact remains that we had there, by a group of young and inexperienced Irish actors, a representation of two plays, widely different in character, which stirred the emotions by its sincerity, which pleased the eye by its beauty, and which touched the imagination by its fervour.[55]

54. "The Samhain Festival," *Daily Express*, October 28, 1902, 5. This is the only recorded occasion on which Yeats gave a public eulogy for Lionel Johnson. He had written to York Powell on October 22, that he intended to write in memory of Johnson, but he did not do so until he recalled him in an essay, "Poetry and Tradition" (1907), a lecture, "Friends of My Youth" (1910), a poem, "In Memory of Major Robert Gregory" (1918), and in *The Trembling of the Veil* (1922).
55. "Irish Drama at the Antient Concert Rooms," *Freeman's Journal*, October 29, 1902, 6. Holloway wrote in his diary that there was a general problem with the audibility of Yeats's actors and that "some of the intoning of Miss Maud Gonne as the weird old woman Kathleen ni Houlihan was lost through indistinctness of utterance also" (Holloway).

Yeats and the Fays could not have been more pleased with the reception and reviews of plays throughout the week, and particularly with Stephen Gwynn's extensive review of the week's dramatic activities in the *Fortnightly Review*.[56] The next night AE's *Deirdre* played again with the first performance of Yeats's comedy *A Pot of Broth*. William Fay's extraordinary acting in the latter removed all lingering doubts that Yeats had about his association with the Fay company. At the end of the week, as he took the stage to bestow bouquets and baskets of flowers on the company, he said that "it would be difficult, and perhaps invidious, to single out any for especial praise, where all were so admirable; yet he might be allowed to say that Mr. W. G. Fay's comedy parts, at once so restrained and so humourous, reached the highest point of comic acting."[57] Yeats never forgot that performance, describing its import years later in *Dramatis Personae*: "When *The Pot of Broth* was played in the Antient Concert Rooms in October, that trivial, unambitious retelling of an old folk-tale showed William Fay for the first time as a most lovable comedian. He could play dirty tramp, stupid countryman, legendary fool, insist on dirt and imbecility, yet play—paradox of the stage—with indescribable personal distinction" (*Aut* 333).

The next day was given over to lengthy interviews, first with a music critic from the *Freeman's Journal* who "recalled with pleasure" Farr's rhythmic declamation of the bard Aleel three years earlier. When he asked them what they were attempting to achieve with this new art of "Speaking to Musical Notes," Yeats replied that they were trying to get back to primitive folk music:

> "You must always go back to folk art if you want to get any real art at all," said he; "then you must bring your folk art into sympathy with the thought of the age. The greatest of all the arts I hold to be the art of speech; and its secret has been lost for centuries. Greeks understood it; and we are trying to

56. Gwynn was particularly impressed with the effect of Maud Gonne's "chanting an uncanny chant," and he concluded his review with a general assessment of Yeats's verse-speaking experiments. Though he was unable to attend their performance in Dublin, he wrote that he had "heard his views before, and have heard Miss Farr speak or chant verse on his method, accompanying herself on a queer stringed instrument. The important thing is the deliberate attempt to re-establish what has never died out among Irish speakers—a tradition of poetry with a traditional manner of speaking it. . . . What Mr. Yeats and his friends have done is to kindle in Ireland the desire for an art which is an art of ideas. No matter in how small a part of Ireland the desire is kindled, nothing spreads so quick as fire" (Gwynn, "An Uncommercial Theatre," 1054).

57. "Samhain," *Freeman's Journal*, November 3, 1902, 6. "Of Miss Gonne's acting there was no necessity to speak," he said, "it would do credit to any stage in the world."

> go back to the regulated declamation of the Greeks, when the Greek orator was accompanied by a little boy who blew on a pitch pipe to give him the note. In modern music the words are so overlaid by sound that their beauty is lost. We want to make the words live, and restore the art of impassioned speech."[58]

The interviewer was particularly intrigued by the psaltery itself, "a pleasant little instument—graceful in form, and combining lightness of construction with depth of tone." Despite its lyre shape, he thought it resembled the ancient Greek lute or cithara in having a finger board behind the strings, but it also recalled to him some of the primitive harps to be seeen on Assyrian bas reliefs. "Indeed," he remarked, "it is not unlike the clar-seth, or tealogy, which was brought to Ireland by the Celto-Phoenicians, and which afterward passed over to Wales, and was the original of the Welsh Crwth."

Yeats doubtless relished the critic's association of the psaltery with ancient Irish instruments,[59] just as Farr appreciated his recognition of her ability to vary her method according to the character of the verse. In some cases, the critic reported,

> she uses simple musical declamation on two or three notes, with a contrasting accompaniment designed to bring out the colour of the poetry; in others the accompaniment is in unison with the voice; and in yet other poems use is made of the reiteration of a musical phrase of a very simple character, called by Mr. Yeats and Miss Farr a "lilt." . . . The result is a very charming "speech song," or rhythmic musical oratory, somewhat resembling the plain song of Church music, but with more emotional intensity and greater dramatic possibilities.

Farr showed him a leather-bound book in which she had copied a number of poems, the musical notes to be used carefully marked over each phrase. "I first speak the words as if declaiming," she said; "then I find out what the

58. "Speaking to Musical Notes / Interview with Miss Florence Farr," *Freeman's Journal*, October 31, 1902, 4.

59. In the succeeding interview that day, Yeats told the reporter that "a distinguished Irish antiquarian" had informed him that the psaltery resembled "the cruit, which was an early form of the Irish harp." This statement, and the assertions about the psaltery by the *Freeman's* critic, led to a corrective commentary in a column, "By the Way": "Originally, a small harp, or lyre, plucked with the fingers . . . the old Irish *cruit* was subsequently played with a bow . . . Nor must the cruit be confounded with the psaltery. It is the timpan, originally of three strings (hence called the trigonon) which is really the matrix of the psaltery or nabla, and which, being developed to eight strings—being called the ocht-tidach—is identical with the early Christian psaltery or lyre of the ninth century" (*Freeman's Journal*, November 1, 1902, 5).

notes are upon which the voice naturally falls; and finally I write out the sounds. But I often have to try again and again before I am satisfied with the result." When asked about the future of her art, she replied that she was longing to employ it for productions of Shelley's *Prometheus Unbound* and Swinburne's *Atalanta in Calydon*, as she knew of no successful method of presenting such works at present. "My idea in producing 'Prometheus Unbound' would be to have the lyrics 'lilted,' and the choruses chanted either in unison or in harmony. The dialogue would be given possibly in regulated declamation, or, perhaps, in the usual way, giving proper value to the rhythm." As he listened to her speak and chant, the critic thought that the method strongly resembled the *Aria parlante* of the sixteenth-century Italian musicians—Giulio Caccini, Jacopo Peri, Claudio Monteverde—artists who attempted to revive the ancient recitation of poetry by restoring music to "the function which it had among the Greeks of being a just vehicle for the ever-varying emotions which poetry calls forth." The variations of the form that had come down to us, he believed, through Wagner's "melos" (the latent melody of the spoken language) to Farr's declamation, were all based on something between common speech and singing. "Miss Farr's chant," he concluded with satisfaction, "like the 'Aria parlante,' fulfills Plato's requirement, and consists of speech, music, and rhythm."[60]

In the second interview, Yeats finally revealed the musical authority for his assertions about the Greeks and regulated declamation, William Chappell's *The History of Music* (1874), which had superseded the general histories of music by John Hawkins and Charles Burney nearly a century earlier (1776) and the subsequent minor, derivative histories of Thomas Busby (1819), W. C. Stafford (1830), George Hogarth (1835), and others.[61]

60. Plato, *Republic*, iii. 398c–d. In dialogue with Adeimantus, Glaucon says that "you can tell that song or ode has three parts—the words, the melody, and the rhythm ... And as for the words, there will surely be no difference between words which are and which are not set to music; both will conform to the same laws, and these have already been determined by us?" When Adeimantus agrees, Glaucon asks, "And the melody and rhythm will depend upon the words?" "Certainly," he replies (*The Republic of Plato*, vol. ii, trans. Benjamin Jowett, third edn (Oxford: Clarendon, 1908)).

61. Sir John Hawkins (1719–89), authored the first history of music, *General History of Music* (1776), in five volumes; Charles Burney (1726–1814), musical historian and father of author Fanny Burney, published his four-volume *History of Music* from 1776 to 1789; Thomas Busby (1754–1838) published his two-volume *A General History of Music from the Earliest Times to the Present* in 1819; later popular histories were written by W. C. Stafford (1793–1876), *History of Music* (1830), and George Hogarth (1783–1870), *Musical History, Biography and Criticism* (1835), enlarged to two volumes in 1838.

"Generally, she spoke to a little tune," the reporter observed of Farr's chanting of several lyrics, "but the tune never became important in itself."[62] In this instance, the reporter was under Yeats's tutelage as he described what he heard: "Yet no word was given an intonation that an orator would not have given it in some impassioned moment." He soon confessed, "Mr. Yeats pointed this out to me and said":

> Chapell [*sic*] says in his history of music that Greek music was simply regulated declamation. Indeed, it is extremely doubtful if anything except an incantation was ever sung, as we understand singing, in ancient times. It is quite certain, for instance, that the old Irish would not have listened with patience to a bard who was singing the genealogies of the clan if they could not have heard the names of their own fathers. The great art of ancient times was certainly a regulated declamation which made poetry an impressive speech, the most powerful of all emotional influences in life. Even to this day barbaric peoples everywhere speak verses either to little tunes or to some instrument they use as a pitch pipe.[63]

Yeats went on to give one of his favorite examples of the effect the ancient poets had on their listeners: "Petrarch certainly was accustomed to speak or sing his sonnets to the lute, and his hearers used to go away murmuring. Not the phrases of the music as it would be in the tone over highly developed art, but the cadences of the poet."[64]

When the interviewer wanted to know whether anyone had ever revived an art that the world had left for dead, Yeats immediately turned to the romantic movement and to the modern arts and crafts movement for

62. "A Poet's Discovery / Speaking to the Psaltery / Mr. Yeats Interviewed," *Irish Daily Independent and Nation*, October 31, 1902, 5.
63. Yeats appears to have read carefully in Chappell's *History of Music*, vol. i, *From the Earliest Records to the Fall of the Roman Empire* (London: Chappell, 1874), for Chappell bears him out on many points: "While the number of strings was limited to four, the lyre must have been used rather as the substitute for a pitch-pipe to guide in the recitation of epic poetry, than as a musical instrument. Nothing like tune could be played upon it, but still there would have been music in the Greek sense of the word, since there was a combination of recitation, metre, and rhythm. In the Odyssey we read of a skilled singer and player on the lyre, (*Phorminx*,) as having changed his chant 'to a new string upon a new peg.' That was the entire musical change, and it was evidently to raise or lower the pitch of his voice in recitation, to suit a new sentiment in the poem. We may imagine his chant to have been something like what is now called 'intoning' or 'monotone.' . . . The custom, that an orator should have a lyre or a pipe by him to regulate the rise and fall of his voice, endured for many centuries after the time of Homer" (26–7).
64. In a one-page fragment from a draft (Berg) of "Literature and the Living Voice," Yeats wrote: "I remember reading somewhere that when Petrarch sang one of his sonnets to a lute the hearers murmured after him not the tune but the *cadences* of the poem." The anecdote was deleted in the final version of the essay.

examples. "The romantic revival in English literature began when Coleridge and Wordsworth imitated the ballads in Percy's Reliques, which seemed barbarous to their time." He then credited Ruskin and Morris with the recovery of a taste that had been lost for two or three hundred years, so that decorative artists finally understood that they must not polish, varnish, and stain their material to make it look like something else. "They laid down the principle that a wooden chair must always look like wood, that a stone statue should always look like stone, that glass must always look like a thing that was once fluid, and not like a stone that you cut." "But, Mr. Yeats," the interviewer objected, "that is a rather different thing. You want us to give up a fine modern art which has just come to perfection, and go back to the rudiments." "Not so different," Yeats insisted:

> Ruskin and Morris objected to decorative artists disguising the material in which they worked. I object to the words of a poem being sung in such a way that one forgets that they are words at all. To pronounce "love," for instance, "lo-o-ove" is just as much against the principles of the modern art movement, as to cut glass or to polish a table until it looks like dark marble. Besides, after all, I am a poet, and I speak in the interests of poetry, and I cannot see its music subordinate to any other music without a sore heart.[65]

Farr broke in to say that she had "a good many" pupils who had taken up their new art: "Some of them are doing very well," she said. "People had already learned to value and make the most of their singing voice, but I am teaching them to value and make the most of their speaking voice."

As the session concluded, the interviewer asked her to speak a piece of prose in what she believed to be the method of the Greek orators. "She took up the psalter," he wrote, "and spoke a passage of simple prose on one note, and then changed the note for a somewhat more elaborate passage. The effect of the piece, spoken upon two notes, was extraordinarily impressive. The monotone greatly heightened the dramatic effect. One was able to attempt to minute changes of emphasis which would have been lost in ordinary recitation."

The Dublin public was thus primed for the illustrated lecture on "Speaking to Musical Notes" at 2:30 on Saturday afternoon, November 1,

65. In October 1890 Yeats had reviewed for an American newspaper the third annual exhibition of the Arts and Crafts Exhibition Society at the New Gallery in Regent Street, London. Yeats concluded his review, misleadingly entitled "An Exhibition at William Morris's," by declaring that "we have in this exhibition . . . the long-waited-for deliverance of the decorative arts" (*UP1* 186).

the last day of the Samhain festival. Presented under the auspices of the Celtic Literary Society, the event attracted only a modest audience to the Antient Concert Rooms, where Holloway noticed "many interesting people," including Maud Gonne, Standish O'Grady, Edward Martyn, and Douglas Hyde among them. Pixie Smith sketched Farr chanting to the psaltery on the cover of Lady Gregory's copy of *Samhain*, which was signed by friends as a memento of the occasion (Plate 6). A reporter from the *Independent* captured Yeats's opening remarks:

> A poem was a thing made of meaning and music, and which of the two was the more essential to it was impossible to say. It was like body and soul—when they were separated it meant death. The essence of all fine literature was music—style was chiefly verbal music. If in the speaking or reading of a poem the verbal music were destroyed it ceased to be a poem, and became instead bad, florid prose.[66]

He went on to quote Goethe, "Art is art because it is not nature," and then to declare, as Holloway recorded, that "Poetry being a thing apart from nature must have a law of interpretation all its own":

> At least, that is Yeats' idea, hence all this pother about speaking it to musical notes which the lecturer endeavoured to instill into the minds of his hearers in his own enthusiastic, excitable, impressionable way, with continuous hand action (though he sneered at the over-gesticulation of trained elocutionists in reciting verse, though he himself in speaking is the most extravagant wind-milled actioned I ever saw!) & fidgety movements.
>
> (Holloway)

Farr spoke and chanted to the psaltery a program that included Shakespeare's song from *As You Like It* (V, iii), "It was a lover and his lass"; Shelley's "Hymn of Pan"; Lady Gregory's translation of "Emer's Lament"; O'Shaughnessy's "Ode" and "A Plea for the Idealist," which Holloway described as "A pretty lyric about the purusit of the Ideal—in which the horn played an important part was made impressive." She also added some new lyrics for the first time—Yeats's "He gives His Beloved Certain Rhymes" and Alice Mary Buckton's "Old Yule Night."[67] She concluded

66. "Celtic Literary Society / 'Speaking to Musical Notes,'" *Irish Daily Independent and Nation*, November 3, 1902, 2. The *Irish Times* did not cover the lecture, though on November 1 it published an article entitled "Speaking to the Psaltery" (9) that briefly summarized Yeats's essay and the interviews in the *Freeman's Journal* and *Irish Daily Independent*, and announced the afternoon lecture.

67. Alice Mary Buckton's poem had appeared in her first volume of verse, *Through Human Eyes* (London: Elkin Mathews, 1901), with an introductory poem by Yeats's friend Robert Bridges.

with a new feature of the presentation—imitations of well-known actors and actresses, in which she demonstrated on the psaltery that each spoke to a certain limited number of notes. She began by giving the "grosser tones" of Henry Irving in a passage from *The Merchant of Venice.* She first repeated the passage to be mimicked, then played the notes to be mimicked, and finally gave the imitation unaccompanied, to Holloway's ear "a perfect vocal imitation be it said." She then did Sarah Bernhardt in a passage from Racine's *Phèdre,* Ellen Terry as Portia in "The Quality of Mercy" speech ("two lifelike echoes of the artists"), and Mrs. Patrick Campbell as Ophelia ("not quite so good"). Holloway had been a critical witness to the chanting in the opening week of the Irish Literary Theatre three years earlier, but he was now struck with amusement by the bizarre event. "There is an air of unconventionality about Yeats' lectures that entertains me, & his method of announcing each of Miss Farr's selections as the lady glided in & out, attired in Greek flowing robes had a touch of comedy in it that amused me 'internally' at all events. Visible laughter would have been a sacrilege!" Holloway, in his own way, like others who would succeed him in theirs, sensed that he was looking through the ridiculous to the heart of the sublime.

"I have been asked to write about the chanting of the psaltery," wrote Frank Fay in opening his review of the event. "I would rather not, but the Editor of the *United Irishman* [Arthur Griffith] is not a man whom one may refuse."[68] Fay was a reluctant reviewer because he had not heard Yeats chant frequently enough to write with justice on the basis of one performance with Farr. But as a long-time student of rhythmical recitation who had heard several poets (including AE) and elocutionists (including Clifford Harrison) declaim, he had come to the conclusion "that the

Subtitled "On Hearing a Distant Horn," the poem portrays the son of Odin and other heroes riding through the night to a horn that summons them to greet the dawn; it is based on the Scandanavian association of Yuletide "with the rising of the sun at the Winter Solstice: celebrating the return of the Bright-haired Sun-God with fires and festivities" (5). The poem concludes: "The Horn! again! again! . . . | It faints, it fails, it dies away, | To join the far, the bright affray, | Leaving the heart forlorn | For the faded light and the vanished dawn | Of that immortal Day!" There is no poem in O'Shaughnessy's published volumes, or in the archive of his writings at Queen's University, Belfast, entitled "A Plea for the Idealist." The title was evidently adapted from a partially recited poem such as "Song of a Shrine," which ends with a plea that "not a height | Of love's imagination fond and bright, | Be less than perfected in her, divine— | The pure Ideal of his soul's pure shine."

68. "Mr. Yeats' Lecture on the Psaltery," *United Irishman*, November 8, 1902, 3; rpt. in Frank Fay, *Towards a National Theatre*, ed. Robert Hogan (Dublin: Dolmen Press, 1970), 95–7.

elocution-books are all wrong, and that no reciter will ever speak verse so well as the man who wrote it." Although Yeats placed great emphasis in the lecture on the importance of speaking or chanting with "a wise monotony," Fay found that when Farr spoke too long on one note the sound prevailed over the sense, "birth" becoming "bir," "mirth" becoming "mir," the very quality that Yeats objected to in singing. Moreover, he thought that the only poem in Farr's program that gave the effect of *speaking* was "He Gives His Beloved Certain Rhymes"; the other poems, including "Impetuous Heart," struck him as *singing*, the very effect that Yeats deplored in describing musical speech. "The notes to which Miss Farr sings 'Impetuous Heart,' " he felt bound to say, "are, doubtless, an approximation to the sound of Mr. Yeats's voice when he recites that poem, and while I quite recognise the importance of reciting a poem with the rhythm that gave it birth, anything less than that seems to me but an improvisation and as of questionable value." Though Fay could not yet reconcile the gap in his own mind between poet and singer, speech and song, he insisted that "No one must take me as being a hostile critic of Mr. Yeats or Miss Farr. I merely state my impressions; I am not quite convinced yet."[69]

In the week following his lecture, Yeats did everything in his power to remove the doubts in Fay's mind and persuade him to experiment diligently with the psaltery. To Yeats, Fay's cooperation had become crucial for the successful establishment of a romantic, heroic, symbolic theatre in Ireland. Over the summer Fay had deferred to AE's judgment, such that he closed his review by calling on AE's assistance: "I have written in the hope that AE, who, I think, the one person competent to criticize what Mr. Yeats has done, will give his views on the subject to those readers of the *United Irishman* who are interested in it." But AE had now recused himself from the experiment and would offer no public response. Fay was Yeats's last hope, but one, for the new art in Dublin. In the afterglow of

69. Fay's review prompted an antagonistic response from an anonymous writer (signed "X.Y.Z") who criticized Fay for letting his loyalty to Yeats prevent him from reaching an objective conclusion about the performance: "To some who were present, Mr. Yeats' address and the chanting of Miss Farr may have been interesting; but to anyone who had not come within the glamour of Mr. Yeats' personality, both speech and song, bordered perilously on the ludicrous. . . . Mr. Yeats' own poetry, I should think, would be especially unsuited to musical treatment. For music is essentially concerned with human emotions and passions; and these are but dimly reflected in Mr. Yeats' beautiful verse" ("Mr. Yeats' Lecture on the Psaltery," *United Irishman*, November 15, 1902, 3).

the Samhain festival, exhilarated by Maud Gonne's moving performance and chanting in *Cathleen ni Houlihan,* Yeats retrieved the psaltery from AE and bestowed it on Gonne, who promised him that she would experiment with it. Thus, in high hopes that Maud Gonne would become his Florence Farr in Ireland, and having done all that he could do in a summer's work to develop the Irish side of his theatrical dream, Yeats took the boat for England.

4

Minstrels and Masquers

When Yeats returned to London on November 12, he immediately joined Sturge Moore for a gathering at the Pye home in Limpsfield to discuss the progress of their theatrical project over the summer. He quickly discovered that the members of the Literary Theatre Club had been squabbling with Florence Farr: "Poor Mrs Emery is out of favour with all my psaltery people," he wrote to Lady Gregory. "Dolmetsch I hear is angry because she takes money for lessens as he taught her for nothing. Sturge Moore is angry because she wont work & doesnt keep tune & he says his own pupils are better & Pixie Smith says I hear that Mrs Emery gossiped scandal about Mrs Dolmetsch" (*CL3* 253). The general dissension refuelled Annie Horniman's long-standing animosity toward Farr, but she had generously ordered six new psalteries for the group. Yeats diplomatically tried to calm the conflicts by meeting personally with various members; he was thus grateful to Wilfrid Blunt for sending some pheasants to greet his return: "they come in good time to entertain a musician and a troubadour, but alas you do not like my troubadours" (*CL3* 259–60). Keeping one eye on the pace of activity in Dublin, he wrote to encourage Frank Fay in his experiments with speaking to the psaltery. A disappointing letter arrived from Maud Gonne in Paris, regretful to report to him that because of a bad cold "I have done little or nothing at the Psaltery since I came home" (*G-YL* 160). He was as yet unaware of her greater distraction from the psaltery—the presence in Paris of John MacBride, to whom she was secretly affianced.

Yeats's return to London had been eagerly awaited: plans had been made for him to hear Miss Owen, whom Dolmetsch now preferred to Farr. Knowing her to be a trained singer, Yeats let his prejudice be known to Lady Gregory: "I cant see how any body is likely to speak well who has been a bagpipes for years" (*CL3* 253). The audition was to Yeats's ear a self-fulfilling prophecy: "Miss Owen spoke to the Psaltery for me last week," he reported,

> but one felt always that she was a singer. She had learnt what I believe they call voice production, which seems to upset everybody's power of speaking in an impressive way. You felt that she had learnt to take words as musical notes, and not as things having a meaning. However she did very much better when I tried her with a lilt. There is a Mrs. Elliott who is working at it. She has a fine musical ear but has never learnt voice production, and she does it almost as well as Mrs. Emery. She makes her own little lilts and is extraordinarily impressive and poetical. She is a really beautiful person too and that helps things.
>
> (*CL3* 264)

In the following weeks both Miss Owen and Mrs. Elliott worked diligently to master Yeats's theories and please his ear, so that by January he could say that "Miss Owen is beginning to be a comfort. She has nothing like Mrs. Emery's gift but she is immensely painstaking" (*CL3* 298). When Nevinson sat next to the "very sweet and charming" Eleanor Elliott at a Yeats–Farr lecture later that month, he bemusedly recorded in his diary that she had practiced chanting Yeats's lyrics so avidly that her husband cried out in his sleep at night, "Impetuous heart, be still, be still."[1] As the various actresses became more proficient with the psaltery and chanting, Yeats became more confident about staging *The Countess Cathleen* in London, and in the late autumn of 1902 he began directing the Literary Theatre Club toward that end. Gwendolyn Bishop, who was also in rehearsal for the December production of Laurence Housman's *Bethlehem*, was designated to play the Countess Cathleen, and so it seemed that the romantic drama might establish a London foothold at last.

Gordon Craig was in charge of the stage production for Housman's play, and through that production Yeats obtained first-hand information about Craig's methods, primarily through the intervention of Craig's sister, Edith, who suddenly emerged as the most instrumental member of her family in supporting Yeats's London fortunes. Edith, who had herself taken up stage and costume design, had by chance received in September a copy of Yeats's new play, *Where There Is Nothing*, and, as a member of the Committee of the Stage Society, strongly recommended it for production. In November, after much disputation, the Society sent him a message saying that they would like to produce the play in January 1903. Yeats was of two minds: he

1. Nevinson diary, January 30, 1903 (Bodleian).

was ambitous to create a London audience for his plays and knew that the advertisement and production would help to establish his reputation, but he feared losing the independence he enjoyed in his own theatre groups. On the advice of his London agent, A. P. Watt, he finally gave them the play, with Edith Craig responsible for securing performers and preparing stage designs with Pixie Smith. The following week Miss Craig introduced Yeats to several members of the Stage Society, and he took advantage of the meeting to tell them of his theatrical plans.

Gordon Craig and Ellen Terry had meanwhile advanced their plans to form a partnership in stage production, and Yeats, eager for them to include his plays in the venture, wanted their friends to support and applaud his principles. Thus on January 5, 1903, Yeats invited several of their friends to his Monday evening to hear Farr speak to the psaltery. He was therefore furious when she drifted into a lackluster performance, "the worst performance on the Psaltery I have ever heard," he told Lady Gregory. "There are times when she makes me despair of the whole thing" (*CL3* 298). Nothing was lost, however, at least for Yeats and the Literary Theatre Club. That same evening, Sturge Moore, who was scheming to get the Club prominently on stage after two years of planning, made on behalf of Ricketts a proposal to Gordon Craig: that Ricketts use his Vale Press to raise £600, which Craig should use to stage for them *The Countess Cathleen*. "All the speaking of verse," Yeats reported to Lady Gregory, "to be left entirely in the hands of Sturge Moore and of course the author" (*CL3* 298). Yeats was caught off guard by the revised proposal and its acceptance, and it made him regret his arrangements with the Stage Society, to which he would have to sacrifice control over the actors, acting, and scenery in getting his play produced. "I need hardly say," he went on to confide, "that this performance which is evidently going to be a much bigger thing that I had foreseen will enormously strengthen my position. It makes me a little anxious about the performance of 'Where There Is Nothing'. I have left the securing of the caste entirely to Miss Craig, and I have no way of judging whether she will be able to get good performers."

Important as the Literary Theatre Club was to establishing a theatre of romantic drama, Yeats was forced to look beyond the Club to the Stage Society and the Craig–Terry partnership—even if it meant compromising some of his ideals—whenever he saw the possibility of getting his plays staged. Prior to the proposal, the Club had the ideals but not the resources or experience to mount a production, but Ricketts's offer to Craig created the ideal situation. Thus, plans to stage *The Countess Cathleen* were delayed until the autumn, when funds from the Vale Press edition of Marlowe's *Faustus* might be in hand. *Where There Is Nothing* suffered the first of several delays, probably at the instigation of Yeats, who seems to have realized that the future of his plays and the Literary Theatre Club lay hand in hand. Nonetheless, his recent association with Craig–Terry and members of the Stage Society convinced him that the Club needed an infusion of more professionally experienced and influential members, and he evidently suggested to Sturge Moore that their aims might best be realized by forming a more highly organized group with selected members of the Stage Society and other theatrical groups. Coincidentally, events were already under way to make that suggestion a reality.

In November 1902 Robert Trevelyan had discussed Sturge Moore's dramatic theories with Gilbert Murray, who in 1899, because of ill health, had resigned his professorship in Greek at Glasgow and moved to Surrey, where he had since resumed writing, joined the Committee of the Stage Society, and renewed his efforts to help William Archer in the national theatre movement. On November 11 he wrote to Archer: "Have you read articles by one Moore in the Monthly Review? Robert Trevelyan (whose opinion is of very moderate value) assures me that Moore is the one dramatic genius of the last two centuries but that his conceptions of what the Theatre should be are even greater than his dramatic achievements."[2] Archer, of course, was thoroughly familiar with Sturge Moore's and Yeats's ideas, and he subsequently sent Murray copies of *The Countess Cathleeen* and *The Land of Heart's Desire*. "I am in a state of enthusiasm about Yeats," Murray wrote to Archer on January 10, 1903:

> It is a litle milder now, but a few days ago it was dangerous. I had read many poems of his before, and liked them, but the Countess Cathleen and the Land of Heart's Desire quite took my breath away. . . . Of course I am haunted by an uncomfortable dread that I may wake up and find the element of make-believe and fairydom too unsatisfying.[3]

Murray wrote to Yeats at once, praising the poetic beauty of his two plays and, as he read deeply in Yeats during the following week, he defended

2. William Archer Letters, Theatre Museum: National Museum of the Performing Arts, London. Sturge Moore's articles in the *Monthly Review* for 1902 were "A Plea for an Endowed Stage" (January) and "The Renovation of the Theatre" (April).
3. Theatre Museum, London; quoted in Charles Archer, *William Archer* (London, 1931), 271.

The Shadowy Waters, which Archer disliked, as possessing "great beauty—wonderful beauty in its way!"[4]

Yeats was flattered by the praise, as he had reason to be, and he quickly availed himself of Murray's interest and influence. Murray had long been an inconspicuous but important figure in London dramatic circles. He had been on the Committee of J. T. Grein's Independent Theatre, of which the Stage Society was direct heir, and had himself attempted to revive the poetic drama through modern interpretations of Greek drama. The Stage Society had produced his *Andromache* in February 1901, his last play before immersing himself in verse translations of the *Bacchae* and *Hippolytus* of Euripides. When Yeats replied to Murray on January 22, he included copies of *The Hour-Glass* and *Where There Is Nothing*, writing mainly to sound Murray's future dramatic interests in London:

> We have founded a little company lately in Ireland & I have written these plays for it. I wonder if you yourself are going on writing plays & if you are, whether you have thought of carrying out any plan like ours? To me [it] seems as if one must get a homogenious audience somewhere, even if it is only some thirty of one's friends & then get a little company who will do just what they are told out of sheer enthusiasm. When one has got that one can begin the business which is the building up of the whole dramatic art afresh from the foundations.
>
> (*CL3* 309)

Yeats then had Farr send tickets to Murray for a series of three chanting recitals that she was giving at Mrs. Jopling-Rowe's art studio beginning January 30.[5] "We notice Miss Farr's recitals have attracted a great gathering of poets," observed the *St. James Gazette*, "and indeed one can imagine poets competing for the honour of having their lyrics spoken in this way."[6] Murray attended the first recital, with Yeats, Todhunter, Nevinson, and about thirty others present. Murray, in the midst of his translations, was deeply impressed by the chanting and wrote to Farr two days later to ask for additional tickets for J. W. Mackail, the classical scholar and biographer of William Morris, and to thank her for "the pleasure and the

4. Letter of January 16, 1903, to William Archer, Theatre Museum, London.
5. Farr's three recitals were scheduled for January 30 and February 3 and 12 in the studio of the Art School, 3, Logan Place, Pembroke Rd., 1 guinea the course. The circular stated that she would speak or chant to the psaltery poems by Shakespeare, Shelley, Keats, Blake, Rossetti, Walt Whitman, Lionel Johnson, Robert Louis Stevenson, and others. On the verso of the circular sent to Murray (Bodleian) Farr wrote, "Dear Sir, Mr. WB Yeats has asked me to send you enclosed tickets as he thinks you would like to hear the chanting."
6. "With Psaltery and Verse," *St. James's Gazette*, February 9, 1903, 15.

food for reflection which you have given me."[7] Nevinson thought that her chanting of Rossetti's "Sister Helen" was "the greatest success." After the performance, the two dined at the Globe, where she talked

> chiefly on Yeats and her husband. She says Yeats is not personally attractive to her, not as a lover, nor she thinks to other women. How Lady Gregory & Miss Horniman write of him as "our poor poet"—that is bad.[8]

Yeats and Farr were no less enthusiastic over their discovery of Murray's translations, especially of the *Hippolytus*, which Yeats added to his list of poetic plays. Farr began learning the chants of the Chorus, "Could I take me to some cavern for my hiding," spoken as Phaedra, planning to die, flees to the castle.

Yeats had meanwhile kept up his correspondence with Frank Fay, encouraging him to continue his experiments with the psaltery and offering to send him some of Farr's lilts for recitation. Fay, who was preparing a dramatic reading for the Celtic Literary Society, replied on December 12: "I got your former note about the lilts and shall be glad to study any you send me. But I can only read pieces by Irishmen or women at the Celtic and consequently I would prefer any lilts of *yours* that have been recorded." He had been experimenting with Yeats's own poems since the Dublin lecture, at which he had made notes for specific poems. "In you lecture you said the whole effect of 'O sweet Everlasting Voices' ['The Everlasting Voices'] would be missed unless. . . . I missed what followed. Would you supply it for me as I wish to read this poem."[9] Yeats's reply does not survive, but he was interested in Fay's recitation techniques and wondered if he used quarter-tones. "Yes I use quarter and other vague tones," Fay replied. "I am trying the psaltery and find that at worst it would be an excellent voice

7. Letter of February 1, 1903, University of London (203/8). Murray was unable to attend the second recital but attended the third with the MacKails, with whom he was staying in London.
8. Nevinson's diary (Bodleian). Farr had married the actor Edward Emery on December 31, 1884, but after four years of marriage Emery emigrated to America. "She attached so little importance to the incident," wrote Shaw, "being apparently quite content to forget him, that I had some difficulty in persuading her to divorce him for desertion by pointing out that as long as their marriage remained undissolved, he might turn up at any moment with very serious legal claims on her" (Bax v–vi). As John Butler Yeats wrote to his daughter Lily on August 1, 1894, "Mrs. Emery has got her divorce the day before yesterday. Paget [Henry Mariott, her brother-in-law, who had witnessed the marriage] was in court with her, and says the event about which there were so many misgivings just took 7 minutes. The doubt was as regards the desertion, since in reality Emery had not deserted exactly, he was *sent* away. I think her sister paid him money to depart" (*LBP* 13).
9. Letters of Frank Fay, NLI MS 13068.

producer.... There is no getting over the fact that the quarter tones are the distinction between the speaking and the singing voice and that if you systematically suppress them you are chanting as they do in churches which you object to. I wish I could have had a longer time with Miss Farr when she was here.... I am unconvinced but thoroughly interested and will go on making my experiments." Fay subsequently wanted to see examples of regulated declamation, which seemed to him "more feasible than the lilts which contain too many notes."[10]

Yeats also informed Fay that he was planning to bring out a primer of the new art, evidently in association with Dolmetsch. He wanted to draw on Fay's knowledge of the French stage—did French actors practice on one note or use quarter-tones in recitation?—not only for the primer but to answer Shaw's criticism that the Comédie actress Sarah Bernhardt was guilty of intoning.[11] Fay was "glad to hear of the primer," but he advised Yeats to talk to some of the present actors of the Comédie-Française, either Eugène Sylvain or Paul Mounet;[12] referred him to Jules Edmond Got's "The Making of an Actor" (1879) and Constant-Benôit Coquelin's *L'Art de dire le monologue* (1884); and even suggested arranging an interview with English-speaking Coquelin himself, before publishing the primer. Moreover, he was critical of Yeats for placing the primer in the hands of a musician. "I don't think the musician is the person to be associated with you. It is a master of speech whose aid you will need not a master

10. Ibid.
11. Yeats was also seeking specific information to support the general statements about the French stage and the Comédie that he would make in his American lectures: "When the French drama began in the seventeenth century it imitated the Greek far enough to create a rhythmical chanting manner of speech, which is still the chief glory of the French stage.... In every country indeed where strong and noble sentiments have been the substance of drama, the stage has been the place of perhaps the most perfect of all oratory. But everywhere as modern life began with its weaker emotions... oratory has perished. Even in France the great tradition keeps its place not quite unassailed" (*YA8* 99).
12. Sylvain had visited London toward the end of May to lecture on "L'Art de Dire." The London *Globe and Traveller* of May 31 reported that the lecture, "given last week, interested some of its hearers immensely, but the audience was sparse and not very intelligent" (8). In his article, Arthur Symons had described in detail the method of Sylvain, who "with his large, round, vibrating voice" spoke verse "in the spirit of rhetoric, that is to say, to over-emphasise it consistently and for effect," and compared it to the method of Yeats in "The Speaking of Verse": "Many actors treat verse as a slightly more stilted kind of prose, and their main aim in saying it is to conceal from the audience the fact that it is not prose. They think of nothing but what they take to be the expression, and when they come to a passage of purely lyrical quality they give it as if it were a quotation, having nothing to do with the rest of the speech. Anything is better than this haphazard way of misdoing things, either M. Sylvain's oratory or the intoning into which Mr. Yeats' method would almost certainly drift" (*The Academy and Literature*, 62 [May 31, 1902], 599).

of music however eminent. . . . To the musician music is all important. To the man who will write this primer *speech* must be all important. Think this over."

Fay then took it upon himself to send Yeats a copy of Coquelin's *L'Art du Comédien* (1894), a monograph on the acting tradition of the Comédie-Française and the Conservatoire de Musique et de Déclamation. He wrote to Yeats on January 21, 1903, in reinforcement of his belief that Shaw was wrong on Bernhardt, attributing Shaw's opinion to a limitation or prejudice of the English ear: "I hope you got Coquelin's book all right. . . . I don't know how far the remarks in his book refer to tragic verse, but, while to English ears and to the ears of men like Shaw who have lived long in England, French declamation is always chanting, which some like and some abominate according to temperament." But whatever satisfaction this afforded Yeats, Fay was obliged to inform him that "Coquelin strongly objects to Chanting and Got, while impressing on his pupils that Molière (in spite of Arthur Symons) was very fine French verse, was always careful to warn them against singing. There is one consolation however, none, except themselves, will think the English speaking voice very musical."[13] Otherwise, Fay could not have been more obliging to Yeats: he determined to work through his reservations and please him in the speaking and chanting of his dramatic verse and in the training of actors and actresses in the young amateur company.

The Fays had been working with Yeats since August to restructure the loosely knit Irish National Dramatic Company, and on February 1, 1903 it was officially reorganized as the Irish National Theatre Society, with Yeats as president. As his London productions were temporarily delayed, he now turned much of his energy to staging *The Hour-Glass* in Dublin and to working his often repeated theories of speech, acting, and scenery into a new lecture, "Reform of the Theatre," which he delivered to the Dublin audience after the opening performance of the play on March 14. During this period of increased dramatic activity, Yeats was distraught over Maud Gonne's decision to marry John MacBride, and many of the poems that made up *In the Seven Woods* (1903) reflected his grief: "O heart! Oh heart!

13. Fay alludes to Symons's essay on "Coquelin and Molière," originally published in the *Academy* in July 1902 and reprinted in *Plays, Acting and Music* (London: Duckworth, 1903). After seeing Coquelin in Molière's plays at the Garrick Theatre, Symons wrote that he "could not help wishing that the fashion of Molière's day had allowed him to write all his plays in prose. Molière was not a poet, and he knew that he was not a poet. . . . Molière was a great prose writer, but I do not remember a line of poetry in the whole of his work in verse" (39).

If she'd but turn her head | You'd know the folly of being comforted." In his personal suffering, Yeats remained true to his resolution to write his shorter lyrics for the psaltery. Ricketts, in the midst of preparing the Vale Press *Faustus*, wrote heartlessly to Michael Field on February 14: "Have you heard the news that Maud Gonne has gone and left Yeats and the future of Ireland for matrimony and comfortable Catholicism? Yeats is inconsolable in sonnets of the Oh thou! type to various little lilts and tunes."[14] On February 23, two days after the wedding in Paris, Nevinson went to see Farr, finding Yeats there with several other women. "But I was occupied mainly with Yeats," he wrote,

> talking to him on Ireland & then on poetry. He said he had been trying Wordsworth & Tennyson again lately & found them thin & feminine after the ancient singers who put their own life into their work & did not consciously look around for poems. All great poetry, he said, is concerned with "the normal", the few central truths of man, a saying which surprised me remembering his own work. Tennyson he thought fake & posing always, Wordsworth generally; Browning "a mere sage" putting himself outside the world. He read (very badly) the ballad of Walsingham for its truth and deep reality. Mrs Emery read badly except for one comedy from the Connaught Love Songs.[15]

Nevinson tactfully refrained from broaching the tender subject of Maud Gonne's marriage; he did not hear directly of Yeats's suffering until he was alone with Farr again on March 2: "Talked recitations & heard of Yeats's grief about Maud Gonne, who had not even told him about the engagement until the day before it became public as she hates marriage & all sex. They had a sort of understanding to be together in old age. Now he contemplates an onslaught on the Church."

As Yeats worked on the reorganization and expansion of the Literary Theatre Club, Sturge Moore continued to work with the actresses on verse speaking and on preparing his own plays for possible production. Binyon

14. Letter of February 14, 1903, BL Add. MS 58088; printed in *Letters from Charles Ricketts to "Michael Field" (1903–1913)*, ed. J. G. Paul Delaney (Edinburgh: Tragara Press, 1981), 9.

15. Farr made the anonymous sixteenth-century ballad, sometimes attributed to Sir Walter Ralegh, part of her repertoire with the psaltery, and she used the first line as an example of a descending melodic phrase in *The Music of Speech* (London: Elkin Mathews, 1909), 16:

-G F♯ E C B
As ye came from the Holy Land of Walsingham.

The "comedy" from Douglas Hyde's *The Love Songs of Connacht* (1893) was probably Hyde's translation of "The Roman Earl," a morose old man's counsel against women.

and A. H. Fisher were usually present for the chanting sessions, as was John Masefield, who was seeing *Faustus* through the Vale Press for Ricketts. On February 18, Fisher, ever critical of the new art, had written to Sturge Moore after receiving a copy of his newly published *Absalom*:

> Thanks very much for your splendid play—I read it with delight the night it came and have just read it again with no less enjoyment than when you lent me the manuscript years ago. It is so good that I do not think even the twanging of the psaltery could quite spoil the richness of the lines.[16]

Miss Owen had become the model chanter in Sturge Moore's circle, which featured her at their weekly Wednesday evening meetings. Out of a growing amorous attraction, Sturge Moore encouraged a resistant Sybil Pye to rejoin the group, hoping to forward his suit by making her a chanter, but she politely declined his invitations for February 25 and March 4.[17] Not to be denied, he invited her again later in March: "I will write tonight to ask Miss Owen and to get some other people.... I should so like you to hear the chanting as I believe you would do it better than anybody. The delicacy of your taste is just what nobody has, and I think you would soon get over the slight coldness."[18] When Miss Pye reluctantly arrived on April 3, she found that "Miss Owen was there... and Miss Horniman, and Tom asked me to read Matthew Arnold's 'Dover Beach'. I felt very shy with these ladies; but Fisher's kind deep voice, saying how much he had enjoyed my reading, and Tom's commendation of it, made me happy again."[19] Sturge Moore then sent her a formal proposal of marriage, which she painfully declined in a letter of April 9, leaving him in mutual commiseration with Yeats over love's bitter mysteries.[20]

As soon as *The Hour-Glass* productions ended Yeats went to Coole to proceed with plans for his English theatre, which he envisaged as a counterpart to the Irish National Theatre Society. On March 17 he wrote to Murray, asking him to join "Arthur Symons, Sturge Moore, Edith Craig, myself, and others who agree in wanting plays that have some beauty," to form the Committee of "a new sort of Stage Society" (*CL3* 329).[21] The

16. Letter of February 18, 1903, Sturge Moore Papers, Box 23/103.
17. Letters of February 19 and March 4, 1903, Sturge Moore Papers, Box 22/5/6iii.
18. Sturge Moore Papers, Box 21.
19. Letter of July 24, 1945, to Marie Sturge Moore, Sturge Moore Papers, Box 5/19c.
20. Sturge Moore Papers, Box 21/29, Box 22/14.
21. Other members of the Managing Committee included Walter Crane, Penelope Wheeler, Pixie Smith (Librarian), John Hugh Elliott (Honorary Treasurer), and Lina Marston (Honorary Secretary).

constitution, Yeats explained, was to be much like that of the Stage Society, but the new group would "have little dealing with the problem plays & shall try to bring back beauty and beautiful speech—." A working list of plays for posssible production had been drawn up, including, in addition to Yeats's plays, Murray's translation of *Hippolytus*, a translation of *Oedipus Tyrannus,* Marlowe's *Faustus*, an unnamed play by Congreve, and Robert Bridges' *Return of Ulysses*. "We have a notion too," Yeats added, "of doing some ballets and masques" (*CL3* 329).

While Yeats waited for Murray's reply, he and Sturge Moore continued their correspondence on revised stage designs for a London performance of *The Hour-Glass*. He insisted that Sturge Moore adhere to specific color principles "until we have got our people to understand simplicity."[22] Craig had been delighted with the scenario of the play when he read it the previous summer, and there seemed to be a chance that Craig and Terry might stage it at the Imperial Theatre. In any event, it could be performed by the new theatre society, to which his thoughts returned: "I hope all goes well at the meeting on Saturday. I have written a letter to be read out. Nothing yet from Gilbert Murray. I had not got his address so wrote C/o Lord Carlisle—" (*CL3* 339).

Murray was in Naples reading *Hippolytus* scholia when the letter reached him. Yeats informed him that the new society would be called the "Theatre of Beauty," a name which momentarily infuriated him: "A preposterous name," Murray wrote to his wife. "Even an offensive name. I shall decline to be on the Committee."[23] But in his absence his name was added to the Committee. Symon's *Plays, Acting, and Music* had just been published, and Yeats explained to Murray that Symons, literary editor of *The Academy*, "will I suppose be our critical voice" (*CL3* 345). Yeats wanted to put Ricketts on the Committee, but Edith Craig objected on grounds that he would be too extravagant. Moreover, Ricketts had left for a three-month visit to Rome and Spain just as the Committee organized, and his departure marked the first of several untimely absences among the group between March and November 1903.

22. *W. B. Yeats and T. Sturge Moore: Their Correspondence 1901–1937*, ed. Ursula Bridge (London, 1953), 6. The editor dates the letter "after March 1903"; however, as the next quotation from the letter reveals, it was written prior to the meeting on Saturday, March 28.

23. Letter of March 1903 to Mary Murray, quoted in *Gilbert Murray: An Unfinished Autobiography*, ed. Jean Smith and Arnold Toynbee (London: George Allen and Unwin, 1960), 109.

The proposed "Theatre of Beauty" held its organizational meeting on Saturday, March 28, at Edith Craig's new costumery, 13 Henrietta Street, Covent Garden, with Walter Crane, who was also on the Committee of the Stage Society, in the chair.[24] One item of business was to find a more suitable name. Yeats insisted to Murray that, though he supported the name when he heard it, the "Theatre of Beauty" was not his; indeed, Yeats sent to the meeting his own choice, "The Order of the Rose," but both were summarily rejected in favor of Walter Crane's less esoteric, "more business-like" proposition, "The Masquers."[25] Yeats wrote resignedly to Murray: "The name of the society has been changed to "The Masquers" which is at any rate harmless" (*CL3* 345). Even so, it was a likely name, given the collective experience and interest of the group in masques. In June 1899 Crane had proposed and directed the Art Workers' Guild production of "Beauty's Awakening: A Masque of Winter and Spring," for which Dolmetsch supplied the music and which marked Arthur Symons's first appearance on stage.[26] Then Gordon Craig's staging of Purcell's *Masque of Love* in March 1901 represented for Yeats "a new art" and for Crane "a new note in the Theatre."[27] To Yeats's delight, Craig produced the masque again in March 1902, and in that year Craig began writing two more masques, *A Masque of London*, and, with Martin Shaw, *A Masque: The Harvest Home*. At the time of the Masquers meeting, the latter masque was in press for the third number of Pixie Smith's periodical, *The Green Sheaf*.[28] Craig and Martin Shaw were also circulating a prospectus in hopes of performing *A Masque of Love* in the gardens and drawing rooms of large country houses. The Masquers Society thus planned to stage the Purcell masque for Craig, who had received no response from the circular. Further, it must have seemed to the group that all the elements were present for

24. See Joseph Hone, *W. B. Yeats* (London: Macmillan, 1942), 192.
25. *Black and White*, April 4, 1903, 10.
26. See H. J. L. J. Massé, *The Art-Workers' Guild, 1883–1934* (Oxford: Shakespeare Head, 1935), 55, and Roger Lhombreaud, *Arthur Symons* (London: Unicorn Press, 1963), 143.
27. See Edward Gordon Craig, *Index to the Story of My Days* (New York: Viking, 1957), 238–9.
28. *The Green Sheaf* (1903–4), originally to be titled *The Hour-Glass*, after Yeats's new play, was Pixie Smith's personal elaboration and enlargement of the format of Jack B. Yeats's *A Broad Sheet*, to which she contributed regularly in 1902. W. B. Yeats consecrated the magazine to "The Art of Happy Desire," after Lady Gregory's translation from Irish of Raftery's "The Hill of Heart's Desire," which appeared in the first number. "It is," Yeats wrote, "to be quite unlike gloomy magazines like the Yellow Book and the Savoy. . . . Ricketts and Shannon are going to do them pictures and I think they will make quite a stir in the world for a little time at any rate" (*CL3* 271–2). In the sixth number (1903) L. C. Duncombe Jewell published "The Mermaid of Zennor," "Written for the Psaltery, 10 Mîs Merh, 1903."

a revival of the masque tradition, for individuals such as Dolmetsch and Craig and societies such as the Elizabethan Stage Society were absorbed in recovering lost Renaissance traditions in music and acting. Masques were also particularly appropriate for the new society, for the form would allow them to demonstrate and highlight the various elements of the "Art of the Theatre." Yeats would soon attempt to write his own masque.

During the Masquers' organizational period Gordon Craig and Ellen Terry inaugurated their partnership with a production of Ibsen's *The Vikings* (*Hærmændene Paa Helgeland*), which opened at the Imperial Theatre on April 15. Since January, Yeats had convinced Craig of the importance of "speaking" verse properly, and Craig had allowed Yeats to bring the new art to bear upon the production in hopes of giving it a poetic beauty to match the scenic beauty. Yeats wrote some verse for a song that Craig was to speak to "a kind of lyre," and Edith Craig was put in charge of verse speaking. But when Craig began to speak, the orchestra drowned out the lyre and the words so completely that Yeats was unaware that William Archer's translation of the song had at the last moment been substituted for his own as being more like Ibsen. "The poor verses I made for them are spoken with great energy but are quite inaudible," wrote Yeats, who did notice that Craig's "amazing" scenery "rather distracts one's thoughts from the words" (*CL3* 352).

Yeats was under no illusion of finding anything but distracting scenery, music, and speech from the professional theatre companies. While Farr, Dolmetsch, and Sturge Moore trained the London group in the several arts of the romantic drama, Yeats advised Murray of the difficulty of beginning a literary theatre, again echoing his pronouncements at the beginning of the Irish Literary Theatre four years earlier: "[The Masquers] will have to accept actors trained by the existing theatre, & the right way is to get a little company as Antoine did, and to train them in one's own way from the beginning" (*CL3* 345). Craig was of the same mind, and in May he announced that he would open a "School for the Art of the Theatre," a school which would revive, teach, and harmonize the components of the symbolic drama. Yeats strongly encourged and may have partially inspired Craig's school, for the development of an "Art of the Theatre" would be essential to the continuation of a "Theatre of Beauty." Yeats also pointed with pride to the achievements of the "school" of the Fay brothers, who were already arranging to bring the arts of the Irish National Theatre Society to London. "Our little Irish Theatre," Yeats told Murray, "which is being trained in the right way from the beginning will bring to London some of the plays it has been acting here & play them for the Irish Literary Society on May 2nd" (*CL3* 345). The favorable reception of the Irish players on their first visit to London for performances at the Queen's Gate Hall gave new impetus not only to the Irish National Theatre Society but to the Masquers Society as well. The occasion brought some of the young Irish actors and actresses into contact with Yeats's theatrical friends in London for the first time. "I remember my first visit to London," wrote Sara Allgood, "on one of those, to us, exciting weekends.... I well remember Miss Florence Farr, sitting on a low stool, and chanting to the psalterie [*sic*], Yeats's poems, it was all too beautiful."[29] Yeats wrote to Lady Gregory: "The success of the plays here will help the chanting & all the more practical side of my work emmensely" (*CL3* 363). Although Sydney Cockerell wrote to congratulate Yeats on the "unqualified success" of the performances, he nonetheless qualified his appreciation of *Cathleen ni Houlihan*: "the intonation seemed to me a litle overdone—but this may be because I am not in sympathy with the attitude that you & Mrs Emery wish us to adopt when anything poetical has to be read or declaimed. I am no poet & in these matters I remain a Philistine" (*LTWBY* I 123).

The success of the Irish plays marked the beginning of a momentous month, as Yeats and Farr redoubled their efforts to school the London public in the applied arts of literature. On May 5 they returned once again to Clifford's Inn to speak on "Recording the Music of Speech," the first of a series of three lectures announced by circular. Although the music of speech was the dominant theme in each of the lectures, Yeats varied their titles to expand his vision of how theatre, culture, and the new art were interrelated. Importantly, the influential drama critic E. K. Chambers, author of *The Medieval Stage* (1903), placed a major review of both the Irish plays and the verse-speaking lecture in *The Academy,* praising the freshness of "the company of clever amateurs" and delineating the relation between the two experiments. Chambers interpreted Yeats to say "that the drama of the future, for Ireland at least, will not only be founded on national

29. Unpublished memoirs, Berg Collection, NYPL. When the *Freeman's Journal* received the circular of the Masquers, the paper observed that "it is something for Ireland to boast of that the literary Londoners are evidently following the lead of the Irish literary theatre. We miss from the list of the masquers the names of Mr. George Moore and Mr. Edward Martyn, who were identified with Mr. Yeats in the Dublin productions, and of Dr. John Todhunter, who years ago was the moving spirit in a Greek play performance" (July 16, 1903, 5).

sentiment, but will also be a folk-art, making its appeal to a society which has either never attained to or has discarded the printed book":

> Herein it is to take rank with Mr. Yeats's other "new art," that of spoken poetry, about which he lectured in Clifford's Inn on Tuesday, while Miss Florence Farr illustrated the lecture by speaking and chanting beautiful ditties to the accompaniment of one of Mr. Arnold Dolmetsch's psalteries. It was a very charming performance, and if the dramatic recitation would give way to the musical recitation one would have reason to be grateful, even if one did not altogether give up the printed book. In insisting that the musical accompaniment of verse must bring out and not obscure the expressiveness of the words Mr. Yeats is on thoroughly firm ground.[30]

Yeats and Farr had now begun to attract the attention of the major critics and papers as word of the new art spread more widely among the London literati: they were being taken more seriously, both sympathetically and skeptically, and less facetiously. The critic from the *Times* credited Yeats with being "too modest a lecturer" for not providing sufficient details, but he nonetheless attempted to represent the theory to London readers:

> You take the most expressive, the best possible, reading or recitation of a poem (which, in the case of modern poets, seems usually to be their own), and listen carefully for the music, the "lilt," which the voice makes from the natural intonation of the words. You write it down in so many notes of music, and ever after adapt, and teach other people to adapt, the recitation of that poem to that tune. But mark, it is not precisely a tune, in the sense of a musical composition with an independent... existence of its own. It grows out of the words, and is one with them; and the voice is not tied to any particular note at any particular moment. The natural intonation of the words, in fact, is the important thing, and the tune is no more than the embodiment of the spirit of unity which runs through a poem, and holds together the subtle varieties of separate lines or phrases. The office of the music, as Gluck said, is to enforce the expression of the sentiment without weakening it by superfluous ornament; and the art of chanting is the invention or the revival of a conscious attempt to systematize in poetry the natural music which should exist in every sentence of ordinary conversation, and does, as Hazlitt noted, in moments of exaltation and excitement.[31]

In the course of the lecture, Yeats confessed "that he hoped for a golden age when civilization should be destroyed and forgotten, and speech be once more the poet's medium instead of the printed page." Explaining that

30. "The Experiments of Mr. Yeats," *The Academy and Literature*, May 9, 1903, 465–6.
31. "Clifford's Inn-Hall," *The Times*, May 7, 1903, 15.

passionate declamation "was one of the things which had been lost from the wisdom of past ages and the youth of the race," he deeply lamented that poetry

> is now the recreation only of the leisured, for they only have time to read poetry in books. It is only the recreation of the intellectually educated, for they only have the power to read it in books. But if the spoken voice were the poet's medium he could appeal to the workers who had no leisure to read, and the illiterate, who are not the less spiritually educated. In the old days we know the spoken voice was not neglected.[32]

The second lecture on May 12 was entitled "Heroic and Folk Literature," with Farr and Pixie Smith chanting lyrics from writers in the heroic or folk traditions. Yeats had requested and received from Lady Gregory in time for the lecture "that story about the favourite music of the Fianna, & about Finn liking best 'what happens' " (*CL3* 363). "Very excellent & true & fresh he was," wrote Nevinson; "he has only to shake himself & beautiful things fall out." Yeats, who had joined Farr in immersing himself in Nietzsche in recent months, applied Nietzsche's Apollonian and Dionysian principles to his own thought for the first time in this lecture, as reported by Nevinson in the *Daily Chronicle*:

> Mr. W. B. Yeats followed out the distinction which Nietzsche drew between the Dionysic and the Apollonic moods of poetry, which went to make up the pefection of the Greek drama. The folk poetry, corresponding to some extent to the Greek chorus, is the extravagant cry, the utterance of the greatest emotions possible, the heartfelt lyric of an ancient people's soul. With the heroic poetry comes the sense of form, the dramatic or epic portion of the work of art, the heroic discipline, which, of course, has no relation to morality as generally understood or to service to the State and mankind. In romance Mr. Yeats saw the beautiful beginning of decline from the true heroic age, as we find it in the epics of Finn, to whom the sweetest music was "the thing that happened."[33]

Farr had been ill the day before and feared she could not perform, but Yeats wrote to urge her presence: "If the lecture goes well," he wrote, "it will help towards other lectures. I have an invitation for instance, from Edinburgh and if only we can get a little credit for this double

32. "The Speaking of Verse," Unidentified clipping, dated May 7, 1903 [MBY clippings book 1]. Yeats had evidently written an outline of this lecture on the verso of a page of a letter sent to Lady Gregory on May 8, including the point that "Poetry will recover power | All but few too busy to read" (*CL3* 364).
33. "Daily Chronicle Office," *Daily Chronicle*, May 13, 1903, 7.

performance of ours it may enable me to get the Edinburgh people to invite us both. In some ways the Theatre is a more taking subject than the New Art itself. I have much more to say about it and can group all our activities under this one title" (*CL3* 367–8). Farr obligingly recovered and chanted to the psaltery some anonymous English ballads, a piece from Morris's translation of the Odyssey, and, "best of all," thought Nevinson, "the splendid lament of Queen Emer over Cuchullain, which Mr. Yeats described as the best poem that ever came out of Ireland." Clement Shorter, who favored Farr's chanting of the ballad "William and Margaret" and Pixie Smith's "charming lilting" of "The Song of Wandering Aengus," thought the quality of the chanting uneven, perhaps due to Farr's illness, "but there can be no doubt," he wrote, "that, by Mr. Yeats's method, a speaker can give moving and complete expression to rhythmic changes too subtle, and too delicate, for the ordinary speaking voice."[34] The lecture and chants led G. K. Chesterton to declare that "No one assuredly had done so much for the right appreciation of primitive literature in the modern intellectual world as Mr. Yeats." In praising Farr's chanting as illustrating Yeats's meaning "almost to perfection," he related a new expression of Yeats's expanding theory: "it is Mr. Yeats's theory that the remedy—at least the only feasible remedy at present, for this reign of vulgarity and cynical inattention which now, as he said in a fine phrase, 'has made all the arts outlawed'—is to draw yet closer the circle of culture, and to go on performing as specialities the things which were once universal habits of men, singing, telling stories, and celebrating festivals."[35]

Three days later, on May 15, Yeats gave an out-of-series lecture at Caxton Hall, Westminster, on "What The Theatre Might Be," illustrating his point with Craig's model theatre and addressing "the possibility of reverting to the original simplicity of the theatre, in scenery, acting and elocution."[36] In addition to Farr, who chanted Greek choruses, Miss Owen was on the platform with him. He had written to her on short notice only five days earlier, pleading with her to join him in a duologue: "I shall have to touch lightly on 'Chanting in relation to the stage.' Would you come & do the

34. *The Speaker*, May 16, 1903, 152.

35. "Mr. Yeats and Popularity," *Daily News*, May 16, 1903, 8. Chesterton's review was based on his observations at this lecture and at the succeeding lecture on "What the Theatre Might Be."

36. As reported in an advance announcement for the lecture in the *Daily News*, May 13, 1903, 8. Yeats's notes for this lecture are probably those printed in Joseph Hone's *W.B. Yeats: 1865–1939*, 190.

Angel's part for me out of the 'Hour Glass'? I will read the Wise Man's part, I mean that we will do just that one scene" (*CL3* 364–5). He would soon describe in *Samhain* the effect he hoped to achieve with the lyrical passages of the Angel's part—"to make a voice sound like the voice of an Immortal . . . spoken upon pure notes which are carefully recorded and learned as if they were the notes of a song" (*Expl* 108–9). The Dublin and Welsh papers were now beginning to carry news of Yeats's London lectures, and the Irish correspondent who witnessed the Yeats–Owen duologue sent word that

> Mr. Yeats pleaded for a return to the elemental staging of the primitive, unelaborate stage of Aeschylus and Shakespeare. One of the great conflicts of our day, he said, was between the country and the towns, and the country would lead the way in the matter of a simple stage, with natural actors, as opposed to the elaborate illusion, artifice, and over-acting of the modern stage, which only defeated the true purposes of the art of the poet and dramatist.[37]

"He has it," wrote the amused and delighted Welsh reporter, "that the average English man goes to the theatre, firstly, to digest his dinner; and, secondly, in order that he may have something to talk about the next time he dines out. The theatre manager, knowing this, gives him something by Shakespeare, and acknowledges that it is by Shakespeare, but at the same time promises him a fine forest scene."[38]

The next night Yeats and Farr lectured on "Chanting" to the Irish Literary Society in Hanover Square. Nevinson, who accompanied them, found the room "full of delightful, simple-hearted Irish." Prior to his lecture, Yeats had to endure musical settings of his poems, sung so unintelligibly, Nevinson noted, that "even he couldn't follow the words. 'The only thing I heard was "twitter'" said one to him. 'There wasn't a twitter in it', he replied." When called upon to respond, Yeats politely disguised his dislike of the settings in an anecdote, telling the story of

> a king who had had a palace built over him till at last one day he came out & sat on the grass where his voice could be heard & the palace remained just as beautiful as before. "All music is miraculous to me—the best and the worst the same." His little address was admirable—Mrs. Emery was good, but

37. *Weekly Freeman* (Dublin), May 23, 1903, 9.
38. "What the Theatre Might Be," *South Wales Daily News*, May 18, 1903, 6.

> felt the few scoffers in the audience. People didn't understand his "Song of Kali".[39]

Scoffers aside, Yeats and Farr were now ready to take the psaltery to the provinces, and on the following morning they set out for Manchester, where they were to perform in the Whitworth Hall of Owens College. Yeats wrote to Sydney Cockerell that they were "getting £20 for it so the New Art is beginning to march" (*CL3* 374). Nevinson, their greatest admirer, dutifully scurried over from Fleet Street to witness their departure:

> Went between violent storms to see Yeats and Mrs. Emery off to Manchester in a 2nd class dining saloon—a good caravan for strolling minstrels. Envied them very much—that freedom and absolute devotion to art.

Their arrival in Manchester had been prepared for by C. H. Herford, Professor of English Literature and Language at Manchester University, who had come down for the first London lecture and had written an article in the *Manchester Guardian*. As his friend Ernest Rhys described him, Herford was "one of the most brilliant and scholarly critics of his day, one of the men who *knew*, as apart from the men who made up their knowledge as they went on. He had a philosophy of literature and never temporized or adapted his pen to the hour; a word from him counted."[40] Certainly Herford's generous appraisal of the Yeats-Farr chanting on May 9 helped to fill the Whitworth Hall on May 18. The result of their experiments over the past two years, wrote Herford,

> might be described as a subtly modulated monotone—the monotone which in the hands of a great artist can often thrill us with a more potent magic than all the bright play of contrasts—the monotone of Rembrandt's shadows, of twilight, of the tolling bell. The faint undertone of the psaltery does for the poetry which it accompanies something of what is done for a landscape by far-off notes of music exquisitely fitted to sustain the mood it excites.... Mr. Yeats, himself a master of subtly modulated monotone, of glimmering twilights and lustrous glooms, has unusual title to be heard when he claims as the true principle of vocal expresion in poetry "a monotony in external things

39. Yeats probably read one of Sarojini Naidu's song-offerings to Kali, the Hindu Great Mother. In "Kali the Mother," eventually collected in *The Broken Wing* (London: William Heinemann, 1917), among the alternating voices—similar to those in Yeats's "The Players Ask for a Blessing on the Psalteries and on Themselves"—are those of the "Poets," who bring to her "the subtle music of our hearts" (41). Yeats had known Sarojini Naidu from 1896, when she contributed to *The Savoy*. In July of that year John Butler Yeats did a pencil drawing of her. A fuller account of Yeats's telling of the parable can be found in Stephen Gwynn's *Experiences of a Literary Man* (London: Thornton Butterworth, 1926), 212.
40. Ernest Rhys, *Letters from Limbo* (London: Dent & Sons, 1936), 106.

for the sake of internal variety, a sacrifice of gross effects to subtle effects, an asceticism of the imagination."[41]

Herford pulled all strings in encouraging his fellow Mancunians to attend Yeats's illustrated lecture: "It is thought that, apart from the larger public which might be attracted by a musical recitation of this somewhat novel kind, the numerous teachers in the neighbourhood who have to struggle unaided with the problem of how poetry ought to be 'said' will welcome this opportunity of gathering at least some stimulus and suggestion."

And indeed they did come, packing the large Whitworth Hall by the hundreds.[42] Yeats told his first provincial audience of his experiments with Farr and Dolmetsch, describing how the music of speaking to notes "must be very simple, and should only be a murmur in the background of the words." He went on to speak eloquently of what was lost in culture by the death of spoken arts. In England, he said, "we only read poetry, and as a nation we are without taste." Quoted directly by his reporter, he asserted that wherever poetry was still spoken, as in the East, "it entered into the life of the people and cultivated taste in art and literature":

> "It may be possible some day by this restored bardic art, for poetry to return to its old position in the world. The poets created all the values. The crown of the king glitters because the poets of antiquity called gold beautiful. I don't think there is any golden money that would purchase if the poets of antiquity had not called gold precious. It seems to me, then, that we are living upon values created by long-silent lips, and I would wish, however feebly, to bid those lips again to open and to speak to us, and not merely to write for us dead words upon dead paper."[43]

Farr chanted poems of O'Shaughnessy, Keats, and others in her repertoire, but to their enthralled reporter "it appeared that 'speaking to the psaltery' might have been specially invented for the proper delivery of the poetry of Walt Whitman and Shelley—particularly that of Walt Whitman. Miss Farr

41. "Speaking to the Psaltery," *Manchester Guardian*, May 9, 1903, 8. Herford quotes from Yeats's "Speaking to the Psaltery" (*E&I* 18).

42. The Whitworth Hall was by far their largest venue to date, and later this year Yeats told his American audiences, perhaps with some exaggeration, that he had "heard Miss Florence Farr recite to a great audience—an audience of eight or nine hundred people—and make every word heard to the end of the house, every phrase and rhythm, every single word of the poem heard to the farthest corner, and all perfectly expressible" (*YA8* 89).

43. "Speaking to the Psaltery" / "Mr. W. B. Yeats in Manchester," *Manchester Guardian*, May 19, 1903, 7.

gave Whitman's 'Out of the cradle endlessly rocking' and Shelley's 'Hymn to Pan,' and her recital of the former was remarkably impressive."[44]

At this point the paper's music critic, Arthur Johnstone, intervened in the article to offer a professional commentary. They could not have hoped for more, as approval by the expert of an influential paper marked an important shift in press response to the seriousness of their art. Johnstone first described technically what he heard in Farr's musical speech: "The first three notes of the ordinary scale, major where the words are confident, but converted to the minor the moment there is any hint of faltering or sadness, furnish the material for most of the tunes." He was not uncritical of their limited musical resources, but he moved beyond them to a larger declaration that "Mr. Yeats's idea is an important one—I believe, a sound one." He pointed to analogies in modern musicians who had arrived at similar notions by totally different pathways—the work of Hugo Wolf, of Richard Strauss in "Morgen!", and of Peter Cornelius in "Ein Ton" ("The Monotone")—and he caught the spirited revolutionary fervor of Yeats's "confession of faith":

> If we are ever to find a way back to a true harmony between music and poetry it will almost certainly be by some such way as Mr. Yeats's—that is to say, by consulting the poet, who has hitherto not been allowed to exercise the slightest influence over the musician, except in the very rare cases where poet and musician have been identical, as with Wagner and Cornelius. Such cases are too exceptional to be of much interest for Mr. Yeats, who desires to alter the entire attitude of the public towards poetry and make them regard it essentially as something to be heard rather than something to be read in silence. For such a purpose nothing depending on the extremely elaborate and difficult *technique* of modern music will serve, and it is, therefore, possible that Mr. Yeats may be on the track of an important discovery.[45]

On this ringing confirmation, the exhilarated partners returned to London to prepare for the third lecture in the series on May 29, "Poetry and the Living Voice." On the 23rd Yeats went to Gilbert Murray as a house guest for two days, evidently to discuss the Masquers. Shaw, who

44. Farr had been developing her repertoire of Whitman's poems: on April 24 she had recited "The Wound-Dresser" before the Humanitarian League.

45. Arthur Johnstone (1861–1904), music critic of the *Manchester Guardian* from 1896 until his untimely death in 1904, was himself an avid student of the relation of words and music. He had read before the Manchester College of Music his paper, "Relation of Music to the Words in Songs," extracts from which were included in his posthumous *Musical Criticisms*, with a memoir by Henry Reece and Oliver Elton (Manchester: At the University Press, 1905), pp. xxxiv–xxxviii.

frequently depended on Farr's assistance, had to accept the fact that she was "too busy psalterying" to copyright for him his new play, *Man and Superman* (Bax 22). The enchanted reporter from Manchester reappeared; he was to be rewarded for his diligent fascination, a public witness to minstrels becoming magicians.

Perhaps emboldened by their success, perhaps because members of the Fellowship of the Three Kings were in attendance, the two adepts of the Golden Dawn and students of magic concluded their lecture series by bringing to the new art the magical and symbolical context of their esoteric arts. Yeats now drew upon his earlier essays on "The Autumn of the Body" (1898), "The Symbolism of Poetry" (1900), and "Magic" (1901) to set up his lecture on "Poetry and the Living Voice." Where in the earliest essay he had accused some of his nineteenth-century predecessors—the early Shelley, Browning, Tennyson, and Swinburne among them—for hastening the process of "externality" in literature by absorbing into their poetry "the science and politics, the philosophy and morality of its time" (*E&I* 190), he now accused them of the enervation of language in a poetry that was without passion or personality. "Putting Byron as the last man who tried to express his simple passions, albeit in the worst language," the Manchester correspondent reported, "Mr. Yeats believes the poetry of the nineteenth century to have grown more full of inversions, of interruptions, of insincerity, of all things which devitalise the spoken word. A convention of morality has been substituted for the utterances of the ancient passionate man. The language of poetry has become separated from the language of daily life, and we speak with no conscious joy in our words as symbols of our thoughts."[46] "He says that poetry is ecstasy," wrote "Observer" for the *Christian Commonwealth*, "that it must be passionate, that it ought now, as in olden times, to express the man who writes it; and that it has a tendency to hypnotise the hearer save that the variety of thought breaks the monotone."[47] Yeats was alluding to the magical process of meditation, trance, evocation, and the ecstatic vision of images that are symbols of "the great memory," the divine imagination, which the poet attempts to embody in symbolic poetry, as set forth in his essay on "Magic." To Yeats and Farr, the psaltery was at once an instrument and a symbol of evocation, the living voice of the poet-reciter an expression of the emotion and ecstasy of

46. "Our London Correspondence," *Manchester Guardian*, May 30, 1903, 6.
47. "Poetry and the Living Voice / An Hour With Mr. W. B. Yeats," *Christian Commonwealth*, June 4, 1903, 608.

vision. As he had stated in "The Symbolism of Poetry," where he makes the creative process analogous to the magical process, "in the making and in the understanding of a work of art, and the more easily if it is full of patterns and symbols and music, we are lured to the threshold of sleep, and it may be far beyond it" (*E&I* 160). Crucial to the efficacy of the symbolic poem in representing the magical contemplation of eternal beauty, is the poetic rhythm, which helps explain why Yeats wanted his own rhythms regulated. "The purpose of rhythm," he wrote in his essay, "is to prolong the moment of contemplation, the moment when we are both asleep and awake, which is the one moment of creation, by hushing us with an alluring monotony, while it holds us waking by variety, to keep us in that state of perhaps real trance, in which the mind liberated from the pressure of the will is unfolded in symbols" (*E&I* 159). The mind of the poet is communicated to the mind of the listener through both the symbolic patterns of the poem *and* the living voice. And thereby, as he says, does the poet "make and unmake mankind" (*E&I* 159). In chanting a poem, Yeats withdrew into an approximation of the magical process in which he created the poem, into the visionary trance in which its images and rhythms arose—recreating the rhythmic breathing and pauses, recovering the cadence achieved through many subtle repetitions of line, conducting the living voice with the hieratic movement of arm and hand, affording the listener some sensual access to the achieved poetic ecstasy of his imaginative world.

Yeats was now making it daringly clear that the psaltery experiments were related to his earlier prophecy that "certainly belief in a supersensual world is at hand again" (*E&I* 197), and to all the rites, rituals, and esoteric practices that he had pursued to that end in the past decade. He told his audience, the Manchester reporter recorded in awe, that he

> looks forward to the day when the utterances of passionate man and the inspired priest will be informed with the ecstasy which is the very life of poetry. And the way back to simplicity of direct thought lies in the magic effects of spoken verse. Nothing but a pure burning impulse passionately expressed will serve when the thought is to be wedded to the spoken word. The magic is in the monotony of the rhythm, the five beats in a line of blank verse, for example, which can produce a trance-like condition of mind during which the spiritual part of a man is influenced and informed.

To deepen and strengthen the monotony of the poet's rhythm, Farr, in illustration, "added the monotony of chanting in order that the trance might be prolonged and sure. It is to be the beginning of better things."

The striking program of magical revelations was not over. Farr then brought out her retinue of chanters and lilters, including Pixie Smith and Eleanor Elliott, but she was not to be upstaged:

> She rendered a poem ["Out of the Cradle Endlessly Rocking"] by Walt Whitman, in which a bird is represented as calling on its dead mate, that left a powerful impression, and when she repeated the psalm with great tenderness: "By the rivers of Babylon we sat down; yea, we wept when we remembered Zion," one felt how the Jews' lament could almost break one's heartstrings. It was in bright contrast that there came some rousing passages from Ulysses' travels.

The critic, "Observer," who had also attended the previous lecture, gave due credit to her pupils: "Several other ladies, who have studied with Miss Farr, attempted similar renderings, and with considerable success." He was particularly struck by Pixie Smith: "a quaint litle lady, rich in Indian jewels, and girlish shyness, sat on a chair and quietly said or sang two of Mr. Yeats' dreamy Irish poems to the very 'lilt' to which he composed them."[48] A devoted witness to all this was Sydney Cockerell, who had earlier attended Shaw's lecture on "The Confessions of a Municipal Councillor" at Caxton Hall before coming over to Clifford's Inn for the Yeats: "two of the most gifted Irishmen of the day," he wrote in his diary that evening, "and a great contrast between them. Yeats has more wisdom, Shaw of course more cleverness. Lady Margaret [Sackville] and Lady Delwarr [*sic*] were there."[49]

Another member of the packed audience that Friday afternoon was a young poet-dramatist who had come down to London for the first time from Yorkshire, Gordon Bottomley, who had recently published his first play, *The Crier By Night*. Yeats had written to inform him of the lecture and to correct his misunderstanding of a criticism Yeats had made of the play:

48. Ibid. Farr's handwritten notations and instructions for lines to be lilted and spoken in "The Song of Wandering Aengus" were included in a letter of May 9 to Mary Price Owen and are reproduced in *CL3* 365–6. Nevinson noted that Pixie Smith also chanted Yeats's "The Happy Townland" (originally "The Rider from the North" but often cited by its familiar refrain, "The Little Red Fox") and that Eleanor Elliott was "hardly up to the mark." He was especially pleased to hear Yeats quote his own favorite saying of the Greek pirate who said "I am a servant of the god of war & I worship the Muses." On December 16 Pixie Smith wrote to Yeats about her recitations and "The Little Red Fox": I had an amusing argument the other day with John Sargent about the meaning of the little Red Fox! . . . I think the sale of your books should go up—! For the numbers of people who have asked where the Red Fox comes from—& The dream of the Wandering Angus—& then they dash out to get the book!" (*LTWBY1* 132).

49. Cockerell, diary for 1903, BL Add. MS 52640. Lady Margaret (1881–1963), who was with her mother, was the daughter of the 7th Earl De La Warr.

"When I said that dramatic verse should be vocal, should have the accent of speech, I did not necessarily mean that it should be conversational. Oratory & song are also speech, I merely meant that it should be really written with that feeling for the natural order of the words & for the cadence of speech that makes easy speaking & easy hearing" (*CL3* 379). Bottomley could hardly wait to meet the master: "the first thing I did when I set foot in London for the first time," he later wrote, "was to go to Clifford's Inn and hear its author give an address on Speaking to Musical Notes, illustrated by Florence Farr with a psaltery . . . and by Pamela Colman Smith without a psaltery." Like Masefield two years before him, Bottomley was wholly mesmerized by the lecture, and Yeats's theories of speaking and poetic drama were to have an immediate and lasting impact on his own verse drama. "[S]ince I heard that music of words in 1903," he attested,

> (and his words were the most musical of all) I have been increasingly concerned in that re-exploration of the nature and possibilties of spoken poetry which he initiated then. . . . [T]hose two days established for me certain foundation principles with regard to the performance of poetry and the pre-eminence of its rhythmic nature in the theatre that the experiences of succeeding years have only amplified in testing and justifying them.[50]

For Yeats, it had been a spectacular month of performances and reviews. But other Masquers, too, had been in a flurry of creative activity during May. Gordon Craig began making designs for *A Masque of London* and drawings for two new masques, *A Masque of Lunatics* and *A Masque of Hunger*.[51] Craig, Sturge Moore, and Ricketts were further bound together by being elected to the Society of Twelve. Arthur Symons began writing his own plays on heroic legends, including *Tristan and Iseult*, which he "chanted in expressive and rhythmic tones," won over by Yeats at last.[52] Yeats, meanwhile, had on May 10 gone to Dolmetsch for the evening and persuaded him to write a "Primer on the New Art," which Yeats wanted his sisters to publish as one of the first books from their new Dun Emer Press. "Dolmetsch is ready to write an Essay," he wrote to Cockerell, "and to go through Mrs. Emery's notations. To touch them up here and there

50. "His Legacy to the Theatre," *The Arrow*, Commemoration Number (summer 1939), 11.

51. Craig, *Index*, 248.

52. As witnessed by James Huneker: "He read, rather he chanted, in rhythmic and expressive tones, for me, several acts of his new tragedy, 'Tristan and Isolde,' which Duse has elected to play next year." See "About Arthur Symons and His New Book," *Book Buyer*, 28 (June 1904), 375. In 1903 Symons wrote *Otho and Poppaea*, a dramatic scene; *The Death of Agrippina*, a one-act play; and *Tristan and Iseult*, a four-act play.

and pick the best. I have been discussing with Dolmetsch the problem of music printing" (*CL3* 375). Dolmetsch had already begun his introduction to the primer:

> Speech and Music can be combined in any proportion and the result be beautiful. It is almost all speech if one recites on a single note, but in a fugue where all the voices say "A" for five or ten minutes and say "men" on the last note, it is practically all music. Between these two extremes there is a world of beauty, the existence of which has been almost forgotten. Poetry and music were parts of the same art long ago. As late as the middle of the 17th century, there were poets who could set their songs to music so as to show off all their beauty. Once there were musicians with such feeling for poetry that they could in their settings bring out the very tune hidden in the words.[53]

At the end of the month, Yeats gathered and excerpted the numerous reviews of his lectures and published them in a four-page circular entitled "Lectures by Mr. W. B. Yeats On Poetry and the Living Voice / Illustrated by Miss Farr" (*CL4* 885–9), to be sent to prospective venues for future lectures. Also published in May was Yeats's first volume of critical prose, *Ideas of Good and Evil*, containing "Speaking to the Psaltery," "The Theatre," and other essays that made up his dramatic manifesto. With their organized publicity program under way, the Masquers were ready to expand.

By early June the Committee of the Masquers Society began soliciting subscriptions with a circular that announced their aim of producing "plays, masques, ballets, and ceremonies" and "only those which convey a sentiment of beauty." Symons made sure the Society's announcement was

53. The short manuscript continues: "But for a long time there has been no poet musician, nor any musician regarding poetry otherwise than as a vague source of inspiration for music. The fact that of late years some musicians have taken to write their own words is no argument to the contrary, but the reverse; for their only object in so doing is to render the words still more subservient to the music; and certainly they have not proved themselves to be poets.

"Therefore, since poetry and music have become separated, musicians have had things practically their own way and poets have been driven into speaking their verses rather than letting them be ruthlessly destroyed by music. Nay, more, they have to a great extent fallen into composing for the eye, for feeling ordinary speaking to be unsatisfactory they lose sight of the real aim of poetry, which should be a music of words."

"This state of things is due in great measure to the extraordinary developments, whether in the right direction is not decided, of the art of music, and the consequent specialised training, thought to be necessary to a musician, which renders him unable to understand anything besides the particular narrow corner of his art he is devoted to."

"They had better therefore be left out of consideration at present, and the poet try to" [the manuscript breaks off at this point]. From undated notebook entitled "Workshop material," Dolmetsch library, Haslemere.

noticed in *The Academy:* "One of its chief endeavours will be to bring the stage back again to that beauty of appropriate simplicity in the presentation of a play which will liberate the attention of an audience for the words of a writer and the movements of an actor."[54] On June 29 he wrote to Gilbert Murray to urge his articulate presence at the next meeting: "I cannot speak at all, & Sturge Moore is no better, while Crane is really damaging by his irresolution."[55] W. A. Pye promised to join, as did Fisher and Trevelyan, all of whom were urged to contact their friends. It seemed as though the new society was destined for success, but suddenly there were troubled, ominous letters. On July 4 Trevelyan wrote to Sturge Moore:

> The "Masquers" sound interesting, but I want to hear more about it. Perhaps I may on Monday. I hope they will do one of your plays: I should think the Orpheus would be possible, if they could be got to give the verse properly. I wonder why they chose Sunday for the performances. For most people it is surely the very worst day . . . bad trains . . . restaurants shut . . . Of course I have subscribed and will do my best to get others, but I fear the Sunday performances may prove a stumbling block . . . to many who would naturally be most interested in the scheme.[56]

As Sturge Moore explained, Sunday was "not a choice but a necessity because of the difficulty of getting theatres for single performances."[57] Until the Stage Society challenged a two-hundred-year-old "Sunday Law" with a production of Shaw's *You Never Can Tell* in November 1899, there had been no Sunday performances in London theatres. That "victory" subsequently gave rise to numerous "side-show" dramatic societies, and for them, as for the Masquers, Sunday was the only day that a theatre could be hired, or the only day on which theatres would hire out for single performances or "meetings." These conditions served to doom independent societies to a nomadic, short-lived existence—hence Archer's relentless movement for a national repertory theatre.

By the beginning of July the Committee were faced with a disappointing response to their appeal for subscriptions. Sunday inconveniences notwithstanding, many of those sympathetic to Yeats's aims were already members of the Stage Society, which also held its meetings on Sundays. When Yeats returned from Coole, where he had been since early June, only forty subscriptions had been received. Murray, downcast, pessimistically asserted

54. *The Academy and Literature*, June 27, 1903, 624.
55. Gilbert Murray Papers, Bodleian.
56. Struge Moore Papers, Box 16/80.
57. Letter of July 9, 1903, to Robert Trevelyan, Sturge Moore Papers, Box 16/212.

that 500 subscriptions (the number of the Stage Society) were necessary to run a half season. Edith Craig realistically compromised with an estimate of 300. Yeats, however, appears to have been undaunted, as he had always felt that "thirty of one's friends" made a sufficient audience for romantic drama.

Thus, on July 6, 1903, their ideals mired in practicalities, the Masquers assembled in Clifford's Inn for their first formal meeting. Yeats had determined to attend in person, explaining to Lady Gregory that "they had a very disastrous time last meeting for lack of some articulate person" (*CL3* 371). Nevinson was in the chair, more aware than anyone that without Yeats's leadership things fall apart. That evening he noted in his diary:

> Took chair at Masquers' first meeting in Clifford's Inn. Yeats, Sturge Moore, Gilbert Murray, Mrs. E[mery], Mabel [Beardsley], Miss Craig and thirty others there. Much difficulty in getting the rules through and amended. . . . Yeats alone spoke with any real light and definite intention.[58]

The Masquers agreed to give eight performances a year, expanding and clarifying Yeats's original list of plays to include Marlowe's *The Tragical History of Dr. Faustus*; Congreve's *The Way of the World*; Sir Richard Jebb's translation of Sophocles' *Oedipus Tyrannus*; Alfred de Musset's *Fantasio*; Villiers de L'Isle Adam's *La Révolté*; Ibsen's *Peer Gynt*; Maeterlinck's *Les Aveugles*; Purcell's *Masque of Love*; and Jonson's *Masque of Queens*.[59] They agreed to include in future productions a ballet by Rameau and unnamed plays and masques by Gabriele d'Annunzio, Robert Bridges, Yeats, Gordon Craig, Laurence Irving, and Douglas Hyde.[60] For their opening performance they chose Yeats's new play, *The King's Threshold*, to be followed by Murray's translation of *Hippolytus*. Yeats believed that *The King's Threshold* contained his best verse for dramatic recitation, and though it was written for the Irish National Theatre Society, particularly the part of Seanchan for Frank Fay, it was "constructed rather like a Greek play" (*CL3* 413), under the influence of Murray and the Greek heroic dramas of his London contemporaries. Yeats wanted the Masquers to open with the play, and

58. Nevinson diary (Bodleian MS. Eng. Misc.e.612/1).
59. Although Jonson's masque was not named, Symons wrote to Murray on July 22: "We decided on Ben Jonson masque ('The Two Queens') at Crane's suggestion, and at mine, 'La Révolté', for the second performance." Gilbert Murray Papers, Bodleian.
60. The Irving play was probably his translation from the French of *Griselda*, which Ellen Terry had considered before choosing *The Vikings* to begin the Craig–Terry partnership. Hyde's play was probably Lady Gregory's translation from the Irish of his *The Twisting of the Rope*.

in August he revised the opening speech of King Guaire in honor of his troubadours and the new art:

> I welcome you that have the mastery
> Of the two kinds of Music: the one kind
> Being like a woman, the other like a man.
> Both you that understand stringed instruments,
> And how to mingle words and notes together
> So artfully that all the Art's but Speech
> Delighted with its own music [61] (*VPl* 257)

Members of the Society readily agreed on their opening plays, but they could not agree on a starting date. Most of the members of the Committee were not immediately available for a production, and this unfortunate diffusion of energies proved to be the Society's undoing. Yeats was to spend the greatest part of the sumer at Coole, with a lecture tour of American impending for the autumn. Murray was in frail health and could not undertake strenuous work. Edith Craig was committed to a tour of the provinces with Ellen Terry until mid-November. Arthur and Rhoda Symons had planned their second six-month tour of the Continent for September. Nor was Gordon Craig of any help in keeping the Society inact. By the end of June he had become disillusioned with the poor response to his "school" and left London temporarily to explore new opportunities in Germany. Moreover, while Craig was a rebel against the commercial theatre, he continually maintained his independence from the London theatre societies. He had not joined the Stage Society—though of course he worked for it, accepting and rejecting plays at whim—and while he worked closely with the Masquers, he refused to become formally associated with them. His departure left a hole in the Masquers' plans, and though Ricketts had returned from Spain in May he had not yet been approached to do the scenery for the first production. Further, the Vale Press *Faustus* had brought only £150 of the projected £600, probably because the edition was uniform with the Vale Press Shakespeare, which was being boycotted by the libraries.[62]

61. As Yeats revised the play, he was intent on inserting more chanted lyrics. In two typed fragments of the text, he wrote in the margin next to a speech by the Youngest Pupil ("O no, we have not forgotten, here is the story"), "note a poem in rhyme to be spoken or sung to notes will take the place of this." See *The King's Threshold: Manuscript Materials*, ed. Declan Kiely (Ithaca: Cornell University Press, 2005), 326
62. See Charles Ricketts, *Self-Portrait: Taken from the Letters and Journals of Charles Ricketts*, R. A., Comp. T. Surge Moore, ed Cecil Lewis (London: Peter Davies, 1939), 105.

The personal circumstances of the Committee evidently surfaced at the meeting, for Sturge Moore came away with deflated spirits. Three days later he wrote to Trevelyan, who had missed the meeting:

> I was at the Masquers meeting on Monday night and made a speech, my maiden speech. It made people laugh but whether at me or what I said I cannot feel sure. Murray was there and I shook hands with him. . . . I have no very great hope of the Masquers doing much but still something will be attempted and some experience gained.[63]

After the meeting Yeats returned to Coole. Murray, having assessed their situation, wrote to him on July 17: "The charms of suicide, from the point of view of the Masquers, seem to me greater every day."[64] Murray pointed to the poor subscription, the unavailability of the Committee, and the inadequate schedule of productions beyond *The King's Threshold* and the *Hippolytus*. He was especially upset by the possibility that they would produce plays by members of the Committee and then "relapse into chaos." "But, the real point is—," Murray asked,

> what do we have to offer that the Stage Society has not? We have less money; less experience; the same field to choose actors from, or a worse one; we have no special Manager; even no special scenic Artist, since Gordon Craig will have nothing to do with us.

Murray seemed to be suggesting that the Society let itself fall back into the hands of the stronger, more solvent Stage Society, but in effect he was trying to force Yeats to take decisive action:

> Of course I won't resign while the Society is struggling for life but I don't see any gleam of a prospect for our attaining a good artistic end. Our only real asset consists in your plays; and I think they would have a better prospect acted by themselves to a paying public, unhampered by an intermortuate "society."

Yeats replied to Murray on July 21, and their correspondence reveals the suspicion and mistrust that had spread among members of the fragmenting Society. Murray had pointed to what he thought was Sturge Moore's fear of success, and Yeats agreed that though Sturge Moore was a fine poet and dramatist he was "hopelessly impracticable." Furthermore, Yeats was no longer keen to stage *The Countess Cathleen* in London, not only because of the unsuccessful Vale Press project and the precipitous departure of Craig,

63. Letter of July 9, 1903, Sturge Moore Papers, Box 16/212.
64. Gilbert Murray Papers, Bodleian.

but because he did not believe that Sturge Moore had been successful in training the young actresses to speak verse as well as he had hoped or in attracting male actors to their company. Yeats was prepared to step over Sturge Moore and, in the absence of Craig, rest the fortunes of the Society on Ricketts's designing talent and on the resources of his "treasure chest," the Vale Press:

> Now if Ricketts, who could also raise more money, could be put to stage the Hippolitus . . . we would get a beautiful series of dresses & stage pictures & might if we were lucky get tolerable speech. With Ricketts behind us I have not the smallest doubt that we could get a good many subscribers.
>
> (*CL3* 402)

Yeats was unaware that Murray himself had become anxious about the Masquers performing the *Hippolytus* under Edith Craig, as a subsequent letter from Murray to Archer reveals: "As you know, I have rather shirked the notion of having it done, especially by the Masquers, because I felt that I should have no control when once Miss Craig's poodle [Martin Shaw] got the bit between his teeth, and I did not know what might happen."[65] Though Yeats wanted the Society to continue, it was difficult to dismiss the problems pointed out by Murray, to whom he offered an escape: "I don't think the Masquers should go on unless you & Miss Craig & <the few practical ones> Symons see your way perfectly clearly" (*CL3* 403).[66] Yeats was testing their commitment, but he knew that the real difficulty lay in his own absence from London. "If I were living in London," he confessed, "I should not have the slightest doubt about making the Masquers a success, but I feel I cannot urge anybody to go on with what seems to be a very troublesome business." Murray clearly wanted to dissolve the Society, but Edith Craig, fighting suggestions of dissolution to the end, attempted to strengthen the management of the Masquers by putting Acton Bond on the Committee as an experienced theatrical person. Murray's impatience, meanwhile, was beginning to leak out to his wider circle of friends. As Bertrand Russell heard from his wife, Alys, sister of Mary Berenson, at whose Florence villa she was a guest with José Blomfield, "Gilbert gave the

65. Letter of January 20, 1904, Theatre Museum, London. The music director Martin Shaw, a close friend of Gordon Craig, had recently proposed to Edith Craig and was briefly associated with members of the theatre group. See Martin Shaw, *Up to Now* (London, 1929), 37–8.

66. Symons wrote to Murray on July 18, after receiving a similar recommendation for dissolution: "I am desperately afraid I agree with everything you say . . . Miss Craig will evidently not give up. Can we, in any case, desert in a body if she insists on going on?" (Bodleian).

most killing description of the Masquers, which shocked Mary and sent Miss Blomfield into fits."[67]

Murray had one more card to play—an invitation to Mrs. Patrick Campbell, who had only returned in June from a long tour of America with Charles Frohman's company, to take the lead in the Masquers' production of *Hippolytus*. Symons was delighted to hear of the prospect and, his own gloom lifted, informed Murray of the encouraging news that "Subscriptions are coming in and £68 is actually in hand. I feel more hopeful."[68] On August 3, however, she wrote to Murray with the deflating news that she "must decline your proposition." Murray evidently begged her to reconsider, for she wrote back to request "the altered version" of *Hippolytus*:

> I wonder how the Masquers propose producing the play without any scenery! I didn't see Yeats play. I wish I knew more about it all. I even still seek to do their beautiful things but I have taken out two years in America to pay my debts and I am very tired—if only we could join and work faithfully together! In the end the public might come.[69]

In the end she agreed to play *Hippolytus* for the Masquers if the Society would mount experimental productions of plays that she was interested in producing commercially. Yeats, long an admirer of Mrs. Campbell, wrote to Murray and Edith Craig on August 14 that her offer should be accepted:

> I dont think it will injure our artistic aim if we keep our influence which should be easy, and it will certainly save us a great deal of trouble. I dont care so long as we have the arrangement of a few performances, and so long as the plays performed keep fairly within the definitions of our prospectus.
>
> (*CL3* 418)

However, even with Mrs. Campbell tentatively on board, Murray remained difficult and cantankerous, deeply bothered by how their announcements would appear in the public eye. He sent a memo to the Masquers:

> As to announcing only two definite performances, and those two Senachan and Hippolytus: I think this looks rather fatuous. Our only two plays, plays by members of the Committee. It suggests a ludicrous conception of our coming into existence in order to run our own things. I therefore do definitely object to Hippolytus as the second play, though I will write to Mrs. Campbell to

67. Letter of July 1903, Hannah Whitall Smith Papers, Lilly Library, Indiana University; quoted in Duncan Wilson, *Gilbert Murray OM* (Oxford: Clarendon Press, 1987), 104.

68. Letter of July 22, 1903, Gilbert Murray Papers, Bodleian.

69. Undated letter, Gilbert Murray Papers, Bodleian.

get the ground clear for its being done as fourth or eighth, suppose [*sic*] this world shall subsist to witness our eighth performance.[70]

As long as neither the Masquers Society nor the Irish National Theatre Society had a secure future, Yeats wanted to continue juggling both while journeying back and forth between London and Dublin. While working on the text of *Samhain* for 1903, he anticipated his return to London by beginning work on a masque. "I will see you shortly in London about poems, etc.," he wrote to his publisher, A. H. Bullen, "I propose to keep back the narrative & lyrical part of my sisters book until I have finished a Masque I am working at" (*CL3* 426). The fugitive manuscript of this unpublished, evidently abandoned masque, originally entitled "The Marriage of Sun and Moon"—a new form for his old theme—may have incorporated the surviving synopsis of his "Opening Ceremony for the Masquers":[71]

A man comes to one of the galleries of Theatre and blows a horn. The curtains part and a veiled figure comes out.

She asks who seeks her, speaking in rhymed verse. He answers that many people have come from afar to see her face and that they are there gathered together. She replies that she can only unveil her face to her servants and they have wandered away from her, she does not know where they are gone. He replies that they are straying here and there, because they have been blindfolded by her enemies. But now some have been sent for them, who are two [*sic*] young to have been blindfolded by the world, and they are bringing them to her.

In her presence innocence will be able to take the bandages from their eyes, for in her presence no enchantment can endure.

She asks have they mirrors with them; he says, yes, they have kept their mirrors through all their wanderings.

He says I will call them in. He blows the horn again. Many blindfolded people come in, carrying mirrors and led by children. If performed in a hall with a passage down the centre they should come down through the hall, and go up on the stage by steps. If in an ordinary theatre they will have to come in by the wings.

They express their joy at hearing beauty's voice again, and wish that they could see her. She bids the children to take the hoodwinks off, for in her presence the enchantment is ended. The children take off the hoodwinks. The servants cry out that alas she is veiled, they want to see her face. She says there are many there who can only see her face in the mirror of her servants

70. Undated carbon typescript, Bodleian.

71. TS (carbon) signed "WBY" in Lady Gregory's hand, undated, 2 pp. (Berg).

> the artists, but that her servants can see it. She kneels to God who has made her beautiful. She kneels down with her back to the audience. They say let us hold our mirrors that all who are worthy may see her face in the mirror.
>
> They hold their mirrors so that the reflection can be seen by the audience. The children stand at the two sides of the stage singing the praises of beauty.

The Masquers appear to have been active and hopeful of surviving in the early autumn of 1903. Gordon Craig returned from Germany in the autumn and was available, while he continued work on his *Masque of Hunger* and *Masque of Lunatics*. Annie Horniman was working up costume designs for *The King's Threshold*. Florence Farr, who had her own masque in mind, was preparing on the psaltery choruses and lyrics from Murray's translation of the *Bacchae*. On September 11 Murray wrote to his wife: "I have to see Miss Farr, who wants to chant *Bacchae* choruses to me before performing them in public. And also the Masquers."[72] William Fay, hoping to arrange a return engagement for the Irish players beginning on Boxing Night, asked Yeats if he had any objection to their performing *The King's Threshold* for the Irish Literary Society, "for I think you said something about the Masquers going to do it."[73] But as the autumn advanced it became apparent that the stars were crossed for the Masquers. Most of the Committee were away; Yeats's lecture tour of America had materialized for early November; and Sturge Moore, who had recovered from his rejection by Sybil Pye, now planned a November wedding with his cousin, Marie Appia, followed by a lengthy period of Continental travel. At the end of August he had gone to France to visit her, leaving Hugh Fisher to look after his rooms in St. James's Square. While waiting for the maid to arrive, Fisher wrote a description of the rooms, recording his sense of uncertainty for the nucleus of Yeats's group:

> There is a little air of austerity about the whole room but with a group of people and a lady chanting poems to the twanging of one of Dolmetsch's psalteries you forget the chilliness and enjoy the music of the verse though not of the psaltery. Lady Gregory, Yeats, Binyon, the Miss Pyes, Smiths, Miss Wilson, Mrs. Emery and the rest—will they gather here again when Marie Appia comes?[74]

Another member of the group, Annie Horniman, must have sensed the change as well. When the Society's plans to produce *The King's Threshold*

72. Gilbert Murray Papers, Bodleian.
73. Undated letter [Autumn 1903], NLI MS 13068.
74. Manuscript "Notes" dated August 29, 1903, 4 pp. (Sturge Moore Papers, Box 23).

remained indefinite, she took her designs and financial support to Dublin for the Irish National Theatre Society's production of the play from October 8 to 10, a production auspiciously accompanied by John Millington Synge's first play, *In the Shadow of the Glen*. It was an extraordinary evening of acting and verse speaking, with Maire Nic Shiubhlaigh (Maire Walker) playing Synge's Nora Burke, Frank Fay playing Yeats's Seanchan. Holloway was rhapsodic, especially over Fay's musical speech:

> Truly he lent the beauty of the voice of the poet's words and his delivery of the final speeches was as musical as the song of birds and fascinated the senses quite in the same indescribable manner. This "creation" places the young actor in a very enviable position as a player of rare poetic achievement and there is no knowing what flight in poetic drama he may yet attain.
>
> (Holloway)

Annie Horniman was transported by the magical evening as well. The day after the first performance she cast her tarot cards and horoscope: "What is the right thing for me to do in regard to the I. N. Th. now? Oct. 9th/03? . . . Some gift will cause quarrels and anger but it will bring good fortune and gain whilst away from home—self-assertion is absolutely necessary" (Plate 7).[75]

The quarrels and anger lay further in the future, but with Annie Horniman's gift, good fortune came quickly to the Irish side of Yeats's dramatic movement. By planetary circumstance Annie Horniman gave Yeats his "Theatre of Beauty" in Ireland when, had the London group remained cohesive, she might well have supported the Masquers Society. As an avid Londoner, she would have been particularly pleased to lend her support to a theatrical invasion of the West End.

Yeats was of course greatly relieved to secure the future of his Irish theatre, but he could now do little to avoid the rapid deterioration of the Masquers. As soon as Yeats sailed for America, Acton Bond moved that the society should become inactive until members of the Committee were available for work, and on November 12 Murray wrote to Archer:

> My hands are red with the lifeblood of the Masquers. Miss Craig held out, one throbbing and painful nerve when the rest of the body was at peace. But Acton Bond and I overcame her (at the cost of missing a train) and we

75. Reproduced in James W. Flannery, *Miss Annie Horniman and the Abbey Theatre* (Dublin, 1970), facing p. 8.

> parted not in anger. I never saw the Masquers Committee look so happy and self-contented.[76]

For five months Murray's sense of responsibility to the society's subscribers, and his sense of futility over continued struggle, had become a mounting personal burden. He finally wrote with relief and regret to Yeats:

> You will hear with mixed feelings that the Masquers Society is no more! . . . We are returning subscriptions, and explaining that, though we had enough money and members to justify us in starting, we found other circumstances unfavourable and thought that the attempt at a "Theatre of Beauty" should be postponed, though we will keep our faith in it.
>
> It is a great weight off my mind! We shall actually end our life without having swindled anybody, and I shall no longer shrink from the eye of a policemen. But what bad luck we have had, in the way of marriages and foreign travels.
>
> (*LTWBY*1 131)

Edith Craig finally accepted the demise of the Masquers Society, but only with a determination to keep Yeats's plays alive in London. She was not long in insisting that the Stage Society resume plans to stage *Where There Is Nothing*, and by December it was scheduled for early spring. As Yeats justified the agreement to the Duchess of Sutherland, the play "has too large a cast for my own company" (*CL3* 481). Still, the Irish National Theatre Society was looking to pick up some of the pieces of the Masquers. Padraic Colum, whose *Broken Soil* had in its December production given even further promise to the flourishing company, asked Yeats to allow them to produce Murray's *Hippolytus*. Yeats had plans for his Irish society to produce eventually both "Irish work and foreign masterpieces," but he thought it premature for them to stage non-Irish plays at that time. Nor did he want them to produce the play in his absence or before he had an opportunity to get Ricketts to stage it. "Now that The Masquers has come to and end," he wrote to Lady Gregory from New York, where he was enjoying a new year's rest before departing for St. Louis, "I must see if I cannot get hold of that £170 [i.e., £150] Ricketts has for theatrical adventure. As soon as we feel strong enough to play non-Irish work, we should, I think, approach Ricketts and see if he will work for us. This is really important, so do try and restrain them over The Hypolitus, if you agree with me" (*CL3* 507).

76. Theatre Museum, London.

Yeats would eventually get Ricketts to work for him, but he would not get the £150.

As he attempted to direct theatre activities from abroad, Yeats informed Lady Gregory that he was preparing for "my big lecture, the most important of the whole lot" (*CL3* 505). His lecture on "The Intellectual Revival in Ireland" to a large Irish-American audience at Carnegie Hall was preceded by careful rehearsals; twice he went to the empty Hall to practice oratorical passages and voice projection. "This is necessary," he continued, his success as an orator now much on his mind,

> because I have found out that the larger the audience the more formal, rhythmical, oratorical must one's delivery be. My ordinary conversational, happy-go-lucky, inspiration-of-the-moment kind of speaking gets all wrong when I get away from the small audiences I am accustomed to. Oratory does not exist, in any real sense, until one's got a crowd.... After all, I don't feel it would have been worth coming here unless I was to get full advantage out of the practice of speaking. And I can only get that advantage by working over and over my words. One does not want to speak as badly as a clergyman or a lawyer, and I have found to my surprise that, while they speak badly, they get too idle and easy. In a way, I think I spoke better years ago when I had to make more effort; and now I am making an effort again and hope to come back with a far better style.[77]
>
> (*CL3* 506, 508)

Even with snow and sub-zero temperatures, Yeats drew an audience of between five and six hundred people, and thus he was pleased to hear from Quinn that he had been "perfectly audible throughout the whole large hall and the speech delighted everyone, Gaelic Leaguers and Catholics alike."[78] Quinn passed on news of Yeats's success to AE, who replied that he was "glad Yeats is improving as a speaker. I always held he had the material for a great orator in him if he would let himself go and not try to emulate the solemnity of a funeral service."[79]

When Yeats boarded the train the next day to begin his western itinerary, AE was writing to him about the company's rehearsals for the first production of *The Shadowy Waters*, scheduled for performance in the Molesworth

77. After returning to Dublin, Yeats wrote in *Samhain* (1904): "Everybody who has spoken to large audiences knows that he must speak difficult passages, in which there is some delicacy of sound or of thought, upon one or two notes. The larger his audience, the more he must get away, except in trivial passages, from the methods of conversation. Where one requires the full attention of the mind, one must not weary it with any but the most needful changes of pitch and note, or by an irrelevant or obtrusive gesture" (*Expl* 172).

78. Letter of January 7, 1904, NLI MS 18564.

79. NLI MS 9967.

Hall from January 14 to 16, with Frank Fay as Forgael and Maire Walker as Dectora. "The Company are hard at work on *Shadowy Waters*," he reported.

> I think Frank Fay has got sonorous verse as a disease. I hear him roll off the beautiful words and could not gather a glimmer of their meaning because he was thinking of sound and not sense. I gave him a warning and I think he will not try to chant without care for anything else but melody. He has communicated the sonorous microbe to all except Miss Walker whose beautiful voice is always perfect in verse-speaking.[80]

Although Fay may have needed to modulate the sound of his voice, the fact that he was producing the play with chanted verse was music to Yeats's ears. However long his belief and practice might last, Fay had loyally convinced himself of the rightness of Yeats's chanting and was faithfully instructing the company in musical speech. Thus, in Yeats's absence, he created the poetic atmosphere that Yeats desired in chanting the melancholy lines of Forgael. To Holloway, "the piece fairly mystified the audience by the uncanny monotony of its strange incomprehensibleness, until a peculiar, not wholly disagreeable dreariness filled the minds of all who listened to the strange music of the chanted words" (Holloway). Though Yeats's London project had failed, his Irish theatre was on the right track, and as the train carried him over the long miles from the Mid-West to California he could now drift into a reverie over his Irish theatre of speech and return in March to receive Annie Horniman's offer of a permanent theatre.

80. *Passages from the Letters of AE to W. B. Yeats*, 41–2. When AE wrote to Quinn on January 24 to say that though the verse was "lovely" the play "ought never to have been staged at all," on the grounds that it was not effective as a play, he reiterated his opinion: "I think Fay is getting obsessed with too much sound in his speaking" (NLI MS 9967).

5

Dancers and Choruses

I

Florence Farr sensed doom for the Masquers Society when Annie Horniman gave her full support to the Irish National Theatre Society. It was a bitter pill for her to swallow, given the energy and expectation invested over two years. Instinctively, as she had often done within the Golden Dawn, she made plans to form yet another society to keep the core of her London dramatic group intact, and by October 20, 1903, her old friend York Powell had promised to put up her circular for a society to be known as "The Dancers." With the Masquers dissolving and Yeats going to America, she was determined to keep her friends and "pupils" together as a fun-loving but serious group that would serve as a standing company for societies performing poetic drama. She recorded in her spiritual diary the sequence of associations that generated her new action: "1 Dolmetsch hearing the noise of the church army suggesting Religion of Dancing. 2 I having read Neitsche's [*sic*] Dance Song, brought about the idea of the Dancers when 3 Miss Thomson wrote wanting to join some society. Three impulses from different directions caused the idea to germinate in the soil of my mind already full of bitterness against Committee [Masquers] & waste of time generally."[1] The Michael Fields had expressed their sentiments about the managing committee of the Masquers exactly: "Stubble to be burnt!"[2] The organization of the new society would be decidedly anti-establishment, anti-Masquers. With Yeats leaving for America, her first step in getting the Dancers on the right footing and in readiness for his return had been to strengthen her alliance with Arnold Dolmetsch.

1. Farr's spiritual diary is in a private collection.
2. Journal entry for June 26, 1903, BL Add. MS 46792.

It had taken Dolmetsch most of 1902 to recover his losses from an untoward bankruptcy. When he moved from Bayley Street to larger rooms in Charlotte Street in February 1901, he subleased the former to an Italian tenant who converted the house into a gambling saloon and brothel in the guise of a nightclub. After a raid by the police, the landlord sued for breach of convenant, and at the trial Dolmetsch was cited as a foreign accomplice. His vociferous anger over the injustice resulted in the confiscation of the lease, the seizure of his effects by the bailiffs, and a heavy fine that forced him to petition for bankruptcy. As the proceedings ensued, his extensive collection of musical instruments and books were sold at auction, most of it fortunately acquired by Herbert Horne's sister, Beatrice, a musician who regularly played in the Dolmetsch consort.[3] A wealthy pupil of Dolmetsch's French wife Élodie relieved their distress somewhat by providing them with three cottages at Boveny, near Windsor, and it was at Boveny that Dolmetsch had finished the psaltery for Farr.

At the beginning of 1902 Dolmetsch returned to London, taking a house in Seymour Place and resuming concerts at Clifford's Inn. After working with Yeats's troubadours over the summer, he made plans to improve his financial situation with his first American tour. Immediately after Christmas, Dolmetsch, Élodie, and Mabel Johnston, a pupil-member of their consort, sailed for New York. While the tour was an artistic and monetary success, there was discord in the ménage, and when they returned in February 1903 Dolmetsch began divorce proceedings, with plans to marry Miss Johnston. "What is the use of going to all that trouble?" asked Shaw, who had seen Dolmetsch through his first divorce. "In another month you will be snapped up again: and the chances are that the new one will be possessed of seven devils for every one that possessed the other. Much better marry Élodie again: she was no worse than any other woman."[4] Despite Shaw's consternation, Dolmetsch married Mabel Johnston four days after the divorce decree was granted, and he set about the difficult task of finding a harpsichordist to replace Élodie, who eventually returned to France.

On October 14 Dolmetsch distributed the program for his fall series of concerts at Clifford's Inn, announcing that Farr had promised to recite. At

3. Financial details of the bankruptcy were reported in the *Westminster Gazette* on November 21, 1901. After a hearing of indebtedness paid to date, "Mr. Registrar Hope said that the case was undoubtedly one of misfortune, and granted the discharge subject to a judgment for £25" (4). See also Margaret Campbell, *Dolmetsch: The Man and His Work* (London: Hamish Hamilton, 1975), 139–41.

4. Quoted in Campbell, *Dolmetsch: The Man and His Work*, 150.

the opening concert on November 4, she sang and recited to the psaltery five songs and the connecting story from the early-thirteenth-century fable *Aucassin et Nicolette*, accompanied by the Dolmetsch consort on lute, treble, and bass viols. This performance had been set in motion the previous May, when E. K. Chambers wrote in reaction to the Yeats–Farr concert in Clifford's Inn, "If Mr. Yeats will look at the musical notation printed in Mr. Bourdillon's edition of 'Aucassin et Nicolete' he will find that the *viel caitif* who tells that story did precisely the sort of thing which Miss Farr does."[5] Yeats had urged her to try to recreate for such ancient poems the regulated declamations that had died out when musical elaboration began. He heard her rendition immediately before leaving for America, noting later his opinion that "even the music of *Aucassin and Nicolette*, with its definite tune, its recurring pattern of sound, is something more than declamation" (*Expl* 219). In Yeats's absence, Farr's renewed association with Dolmetsch allowed her to develop the choral and dancing elements of the romantic drama independently of Yeats. For his part, Dolmetsch found in Farr's newly formed society an opportunity to give his concerts a new dimension.

When Dolmetsch began giving concerts of Renaissance music in the early 1890s, he often tried to explain to his audiences the construction of the old dances. Shaw attended most of these concerts as a music critic and praised them in *The World*, but he was continually frustrated by the incompleteness of Dolmetsch's dance explanations. "I know that Mr. Dolmetsch cannot get up the dances for us," Shaw wrote in 1893, noting ironically that the "old hall of the Art Workers, Guild in Clifford's Inn would be the very place for a Masque." While he was delighted that Dolmetsch could immediately illustrate with music when asked about a pavan or a galliard, he lamented that "What we are left in the dark about is the dance."[6] Now, ten years later, Dolmetsch had a willing company of former Masquers who might be trained to illustrate the dances at his concerts.

In her prospectus for the Dancers, Farr described the society as "A Fellowship united 'to fight the High and Powerful Devil, Solemnity'—called

5. "The Experiments of Mr. Yeats," *The Academy and Literature*, May 9, 1903, 466. "He [the *viel caitif*]," Chambers continued, "chanted his metrical passages to two simple musical phrases, which he repeated over and over again, and brought in a third phrase, slightly more cadenced, for the concluding line of each passage, before he went back to his prose." Farr did use F. W. Bourdillon's translation of *Aucassin and Nicolette* (London: Macmillan, 1897).

6. *The World* (February 22, 1893), as collected in Shaw's *Music in London 1890–94* (New York: Vienna House, 1973), ii. 266–7.

by some 'the Master of the World.'"[7] To counter the solemnity surrounding the disbanding of the Masquers, she summoned the Nietzschean themes of laughter and dancing. She had first become a devotee of Nietzsche through Shaw, then Yeats, whose serious interest in Nietzsche's work was piqued by John Quinn almost a year earlier, and she made her own translations of passages from *Thus Spake Zarathustra* for chanting to the psaltery. By the autumn of 1903, Nietzsche was a constant subject of discussion in her circle, as confirmed by Henry Nevinson, who cycled to Farr's flat in Hammersmith on September 20 to hear "a play by one Synge, an Irish scene, and some very beautiful stuff from Nietzsche about Life and Wisdom." Thus, for the preliminary meeting of the Dancers on December 5, the circular promised the dancing of a farandole and the chanting of their Zarathustran theme song from *The Higher Man*:

> Pray you unlearn the hornblowing of affliction, and the melancholy of the masses, and the jests of their buffoons. Be like the wind when it rushes out of mountain crevasses, and so dances to its own pipings that the seas tremble and leap under its feet. Praise the good lawless spirit, that gives wings to the ass, and draws milk from the lioness; which blows like the storm upon to-day, and upon the flocking together of the people. . . . None of you greater men have learned to dance as we must dance to dance beyond ourselves. . . . I pray you to laugh more—to laugh beyond yourselves—raise your hearts, dance high and higher, never forget how good laughter is. I throw you this crown, this crown of laughter, this crown of roses; I proclaim the holiness of laughter. Learn how to laugh you solemn ones.[8]

To reduce "drudgery," the Fellowship was—unlike the Masquers—to have no elected committee, no minutes, and no stodgy officers: "The most courageous and enthusiastic person in the Fellowship will be Governor as long as he can retain his pre-eminence." Monthly meetings were planned, the group to assemble "in beautiful and simple dresses, to dance, sing, chant, talk, and dedicate its members to lightheartedness." Fifty members of a desired hundred had subscribed before the first meeting, each paying five shillings to meet the initial costs of stationery, printing, and the hiring of halls. The requisites for membership were laced with Nietzschean quotations:

7. Gilbert Murray Papers, Bodleian.
8. *Thus Spake Zarathustra*, Part Four, "The Higher Man," extracted from paragraphs 19–20, Farr's ellipses, probably adapted from Alexander Tille's translation in 1896.

> Members must submit to the discipline of the Muses, either by taking part in the dances that in old times "made the great dance beyond themselves, until they can become greater than mortality can understand," or they must fight the battles of the Fellowship in speech and song; or if they are artists, musicians, or poets, they will restore or design beautiful dances, music, and poems, which will inspire the indifferent with "the enthusiasm and courage which gives a lasting rapture to existence."

Farr had learned from Nietzsche that the dancing, singing satyrs of the Dionysiac chorus were the seers of the visionary world, dramatizing that vision through the medium of dance, music, and the spoken word. She planned to conclude the inaugural meeting by chanting a chorus from Gilbert Murray's translation of the *Bacchae*, "Will they ever come to me, ever, again, the long long dances." She wrote to Murray beforehand: "I am going to chant your chorus 'Shall we ever' at the Sesame Club on 30th Nov. . . . I shall also chant it at the dancers on 5th Dec. My dream for them is to some day do scenes from your 'Bacchae' and I shall try to stir them up to it by giving them that as an example."[9] "I feel rather bound to go," Murray wrote to Archer, reluctant to get involved in the activities of yet another society, even more reluctant to give them the *Bacchae*.[10] Part of his hesitation to let the Masquers do the *Hippolytus* arose from his feeling that she did the choral chants "badly and wrong," when he first heard her attempt them during the summer, but he was now pleased with her chanting of the *Bacchae*.

Several journalists were curious about the new society, which inspired A. A. Sykes of *Punch* to preserve the first meeting in doggerel entitled "L'Allegro To Date":

> But come, thou Mistress FLORENCE FARR,
> So buxom, blithe, and debo*narr,*
> Haste thee, nymph, and bring with thee
> Care-dispelling jollity . . .
> The old forgotten dancing-lore,
> The steps we cannot understand,
> DOLMETSCH agrees to take in hand.
> These on the well-trod stage anon,
> When next our learned sock is on,
> We'll show, while ARNOLD, Fancy's child,

9. Undated letter [*c*. November 23, 1903], Gilbert Murray Papers, Bodleian. Unless otherwise indicated, the letters quoted from Farr to Murray are in the Murray Papers.
10. Letter of November 25, 1903, Theatre Museum; copy in Murray Papers.

Tootles his native wood-wind wild.
These delights if thous canst give,
Miss Farr, within thy Club I'll live.[11]

Nevinson, who had been away covering the Balkan War during October and November, was at Farr's flat when a reporter from the *Daily Mail* arrived for an interview. The reporter, Nevinson observed in amusement, came under the illusion that the purpose of the society was "to reform balls," but after entering into the proper spirit he succeeded in getting Farr to state their real aims. "As you can see," said Farr, "we are going to revive old dances, folk dances that have been long forgotten, or are in danger of being lost, and those that we don't understand will be taught by Mr. Arnold Dolmetsch. Our idea is to assist various societies devoting themselves to uncommercial, beautiful, or ancient drama, dances, and pageants."[12] Farr was, in effect, keeping alive the aims and spirit of both the Masquers and Craig's school for the "Art of the Theatre." She did not, however, keep the infeuding nucleus of the Masquers intact, as Pixie Smith revealed in a letter to Yeats in America: "I am lilting and storytelling at a great rate," she wrote on December 16. "*The Masquers* is dead—at least for the present—The Dancers—came out with a flourish of newspaper notices—and Edy Craig & I think of getting up a *grand* mock dance & offer to do it for them!—" (*LTWBY1* 132). Farr frequently antagonized Yeats's "psaltery people," enough for many of them not to follow her without Yeats's generalship, but the split between members of the Dancers and the Masquers grew in part out of the long-standing antagonism between Farr and Horniman, originating in Golden Dawn conflicts and animosities and lately refueled by the latter's gift to the Irish National Theatre at the expense of the Masquers. Farr later told Murray indifferently that "Miss Horniman . . . dislikes me for some reason Yeats can explain but which I have forgotten."[13]

The first performance by the Dancers was Yeats's *Cathleen ni Houlihan* on January 2, 1904. The ubiquitous Nevinson noted that after the play they performed "all manner of dances, some excellent. A Mrs. [Gwendolyn] Bishop bounded about with splendid abandon." Lady Gregory peeped in on a mission to Farr and reported to Yeats in America:

11. *Punch*, 124–5 (December 16, 1903), 424.
12. " 'The Dancers.' / A Society to Fight the 'Devil Solemnity,' " *Daily Mail*, December 7, 1903, 5.
13. Undated letter [January 1907].

> I looked in at Mrs Emery's 'Dancers' as I wanted to see her about music for Shadowy Waters. She had a good many people, and if she keeps them together it may be quite a useful society. Walter Crane dancing the Sarabande was a fine sight, his face wooden all the time. He is rather disgusted at the collapse of the Masquers. Mr. Elliott who I met at the Sesame was sorry for your sake, you would be so disappointed! but I told him you would not take it to heart.[14]

At the monthly meeting on March 5, Nevinson again "looked on at the revel. . . . A Champion O'Brien & his pupil Barry did fine Irish dances to a flute." The dances were interspersed with story-telling of uneven quality, and members had to endure "a terrible long Welsh story about a curate & a girl & a harper with no point at all, not even in the grave." On April 9 the Dancers were joined by Helen Laird (Honor Lavell), an actress for the Fay company, and a young Irish poet, Maurice Joy, who came in "robes of an Irish sea-god." "I told the story of the Magic Snake," wrote Nevinson, "which was well received. A young man got up and told a stupid pseudo-Irish story about a drunkard & his wife & the rat & the cat. Scant applause & some hissing. Nearly a row between him & Joy." But as the dances, stories, revels, and rows went apace, Farr received her first commission from Murray, who obviously knew little of the highly animated activities of the Dancers.

Aware that Murray was now under pressure from Mrs. Patrick Campbell and others to relinquish the *Hippolytus*, William Archer offered to have the play staged by his dormant New Century Theatre, an offer that greatly pleased and relieved Murray. "Would you really contemplate tackling the Hippolytus?" he replied on January 20. "I should be delighted. The Chorus could be worked by Miss Farr and a few of her pupils (if that is the name for them!). As to scenery, both G Craig and Rickets [*sic*] have expressed a wish to do it. . . . The chief difficulty that I see is about the enunciation of the verse, and the getting of some ascetic and poetic looking person for Hippolytus."[15] Neither Craig nor Ricketts was enlisted to do the scenery, but Farr was asked to compose the choral music and to select, train, and lead the Chorus. Archer engaged Harley Granville-Barker to produce the play, and Ben Webster was cast as Hippolytus. When rehearsals began in March, Murray recruited the critical eye of Jane Harrison, the classical

14. Undated fragment (Berg); quoted in Foster, *Life1* 587 n. 38.
15. Theatre Museum, London; copy in Gilbert Murray Papers, Bodleian.

scholar, whom he thought would be "useful both as an archeologist and as an *amicus curiae* in Cambridge."[16]

By April 18, Farr had finished her masque, *The Mystery of Time*, infused with Nietzschean overtones and intended for the Dancers. Nevinson read it and suggested revisions, but most of the evening they "talked Hippolytus." Although the Dancers had convened monthly through April, Farr, Dorothy Paget, Gwendolyn Bishop, and others chosen for the chorus now gave over their interests and energies to the new enterprise, so that at their final meeting in April, Nevinson observed, the dances "were not very good." Dolmetsch had become absorbed in composing and playing the music for the Elizabethan Stage Society's production of *Much Ado About Nothing*, and though he and Farr met frequently in the spring, it was to have psalteries made, tuned, and re-strung for her Chorus. Yet another society for poetic drama had thus to give way to stronger theatrical forces. Farr's adaptation of the new art to the choruses of classical drama was to have a far-reaching impact, but not before colliding with the realistic stage management of Harley Granville-Barker.

II

The scene for the conflict between Farr and Barker over the several productions of Murray's translations of Euripides had been long in the making. Barker had been a member of the stage crew when Farr produced Yeats's *The Land of Heart's Desire* and Shaw's *Arms and the Man* in 1894, and he had played in Mrs. Patrick Campbell's production of Murray's *Carlyon Sahib* in 1899, the beginning of Barker's lifelong friendship with Murray. Since then, while Yeats and Farr fostered the romantic drama, Barker's talent as playwright–actor had been nurtured on the realism of the Independent and New Century theatres, and the Stage Society. Dismayed by the artificial methods of the actor–manager system and the "well-made play,' he followed the spirit of Antoine in urging actuality in gesture, speech, and sentiment. Above all, he was impatient with the snail-pace movement toward a National Theatre, and when Archer approached him with Murray's *Hippolytus* he was unilaterally in the midst of important negotiations with J. E. Vedrenne, manager of the Court Theatre. In exchange for Barker

16. Letter to William Archer of March 21, 1904, Theatre Museum.

superintending a production of *Two Gentlemen of Verona* during a series of Shakespearean revivals, Vedrenne would cooperate with Barker in giving six matinees of *Candida*. Contingent upon the success of these matinees, Barker hoped to establish at the Court a repertory company that would prepare for a National Theatre by performing literary drama on a regular basis, with new productions every fortnight, an ideal beyond the means of the independent societies. "Without doubt the National Theatre will come—," he wrote to Archer, seeking support for his scheme, "but as Ibsen has leavened the whole English Theatre during the past fifteen years—so we ought to be getting some more leaven ready for the National Theatre when it does come."[17] To Barker, this leaven included classical and Continental as well as English drama, and so he was delighted to anticipate his plans at the Court by producing Murray's translation of the *Hippolytus* through Archer's New Century Theatre.

Barker and Farr immediately came into conflict over the Chorus, for she set out to arrange it much as if she and Yeats were producing the play for the Masquers, with musical speech, rhythmical movement, and symbolic gestures. Barker patiently addressed most of his complaints to Murray, who acted uncomfortably as arbiter for their disagreements over the music, the dresses, and the entrances and movements of the Chorus. Although Murray declared to Barker from the beginning that "she really *is* indispensable, unless we can find someone else who knows her method," even he was at times apprehensive about her arrangements.[18] "Mrs. Emery is here doing choruses in Dorian modes and what not!" he exclaimed to Archer as rehearsals began. "I cannot judge of the music a bit, of course. She sometimes seems to me very good, and sometimes not."[19] And when Archer felt compelled to explain the methods and origins of the Chorus in a preliminary circular, his misleading statements led to further complaints by Farr to Murray, who wrote to Archer on Whitsunday: "I have a note from Miss Farr saying (1) she does not *cantilate*, she *chants*: (2) neither Dolmetsch nor Yeats have had anything to do with her music, except that D[olmetsch] made the psalteries."[20] Archer quickly apologized and made corrections for the official circular, and though he congratulated her on the "strikingly beautiful" choruses, he also voiced the reservations of Barker

17. Letter of April 21, 1903; quoted in Charles Archer, *William Archer* (London, 1931), 273.
18. Letter of March 3, 1904, Theatre Museum.
19. Letter of April 2, 1904, Theatre Museum.
20. [May 22, 1904], Theatre Museum.

and himself over the passivity of the chorus, seeing Farr's studied reveries as inattention:

> I have attended too few rehearsals to speak with any authority . . . but I would wish here and there a little more firmness or crispness of attack in your pupils. Your own voice comes out beautifully in the solo passages. Once or twice it seemed to me, when you were not doing anything, as if you let your attention wander and were not *in* the scene. I have no doubt this was merely due to the hundred distractions of a dress rehearsal and will be "all right at night." It was merely an almost indefinable matter of expression.
>
> Let me thank you for the inspiring work you have put into this thing, and wish you all success on Thursday.[21]

Archer desired a more aggressive chorus, while Farr was following Yeats's principles of speech and movement, aiming to create a magical effect. "Where one requires the full attention of the mind," Yeats would soon write in *Samhain,* "one must not weary it with any but the most needful changes of pitch and note, or by an irrelevant or obtrusive gesture" (*Expl* 172).

When the *Hippolytus* opened at the Lyric Theatre on May 26, the general praise was accompanied by responses to the chorus as varied among critics as among friends of the production. J. T. Grein was overwhelmed by the performance, writing that "For once the sound of tragedy unalloyed by modernity rang through a London playhouse," and he lauded the "impassioned elocution" of Edyth Olive as Phaedra, Ben Webster as Hippolytus, Alfred Brydon as Theseus, Granville-Barker as the Messenger, and the "sweet cadence" of Farr's chanting as leader of the Chorus. "It cannot be uged with sufficient emphasis," he concluded, "that diction is the soil, the basis, and the backbone of the histrionic art. The whole aspect of the production . . . its delicately-attuned intercalations of the chorus, was one of dignity and refinement."[22] Grein's review in the *Illustrated London News* was accompanied by sketches (Plate 9) of the chorus holding psalteries and the actors wearing, in Ricketts's words, "their own naked legs and feet in sandals, which I liked. The dresses were ugly, the scenery hideous."[23] Farr was herself upset over the spartan dresses forced on the Chorus, preferring robes that she had designed for Yeats's troubadours. When plans were made

21. Letter of May 24, 1904, HRHRC.
22. "Euripides' 'Hippolytus' at the Lyric," *The Illustrated London News*, 124 (June 4, 1904), 833; an illustrative sketch (Plate 9) by Ralph Cleaver is on p. 840.
23. Letter of June 4, 1904, to Michael Field, Ricketts diary, BL Add. MS 58088.

to revive the production in the autumn she wrote conditionally to Murray, "Will you make them let me provide my own dress this time?"[24] Where Yeats played down the scenery for the words, Barker played it down for the idea. To Ricketts, the scenery was the barest aspect of the production, "hardly worth looking at."

As Ricketts wrote to Michael Field, he was "on the whole favourably impressed by the Phaedra," but he could not restrain his ridicule of the Chorus.

> The chorus drove one mad, or made one laugh—"the laughter of the madman," even Phaedra could not stand it, and at one moment said, "Cease women!" Imagine 6 limp English women half chanting, half speaking in the chorus, each waiting upon the other to commence, the nerve racking hesitation of the opening lines and flat endings! Just like the row the middle classes make in church; curiously enough Miss Farr was quite decent, a little languid or desponding, but then she was answerable for the others and the choruses in Euripides are too monstrous and too frequent.[25]

Farr was perhaps not altogether answerable, for she had complained to Barker about the lack of a conductor for the Chorus, and she complained to Murray that Barker's directions for entrances made her look like a "chorus girl."[26] During the performance Ricketts sat next to Arthur Symons, who admitted that he was "fairly sympathetic" to the Chorus, and at intermission they had tea together. Symons expressed his hatred of any mock music added to verse, which is speech refined by intensity of mood and emotion: "Verse should be spoken as simply, that is more simply, than prose. Its beauty lies in its structure, texture, and substance; to add a tremolo to it is as if you played music with a tremolo obbligato."[27]

Murray's translation was part of the focus of Jane Harrison, who in writing for the *Cambridge Review* proclaimed that "London has had a great awakening . . . to the consciousness that Euripides ia a great dramatist—the town rings with it—and Mr. Murray poet as well as scholar."[28] She recalled

24. Letter of September 22, 1904.
25. Letter of June 4, 1904, to Michael Field, as above.
26. Letter of Harley Granville-Barker to Gilbert Murray of September 16, 1904.
27. See Charles Ricketts, *Self-Portrait: Taken from the Letters and Journals of Charles Ricketts, R. A.*, comp. T. Sturge Moore, ed. Cecil Lewis (London: Peter Davies, 1939), 107–8, and his letter of June 4, 1904, to Michael Field, above.
28. "Hippolytus Crowned in London," *Cambridge Review*, June 15, 1904, 372; partially rpt. in Florence Farr's *The Music of Speech* (London: Elkin Mathews, 1909), 14–15. Harrison wrote of Farr's performance: "Miss Florence Farr led the chorus; she is an artist with a beautiful way of her own, strange sometimes, often very beautiful. Her voice is *saisissante* mesmeric. She

that Cambridge had been "troubled and a little dazed" by Murray's verse translation when he read it there three years earlier, "so the comfortable theory was started that perhaps all that beauty was not in the original." As most reviewers sensed, the production of the *Hippolytus* signaled the revival of Attic drama in England, but the mixed reactions to Murray's translations into English rhyming verse continued as they were published and produced during the next decade, especially after the Imagist movement got underway. The increasing feeling that Murray was turning Euripides into a nineteenth-century English poet-dramatist culminated in the publication of T. S. Eliot's "Euripides and Professor Murray" (1920). The modern idiom having taken hold, Eliot, describing Murray as a "very insignificant follower of the Pre-Raphaelite movement" as a poet, said of Murray's translations: "Greek poetry will never have the slightest vitalizing effect upon English poetry if it can only appear masquerading as a vulgar debasement of the eminently personal idiom of Swinburne."[29]

For the moment, however, the majority of English critics celebrated the translations for revealing the "modernity" of Euripides. "Mr. Gilbert Murray's rare and beautiful translations of Euripides," wrote Desmond MacCarthy, "proved that, in the hands of a poet and a scholar, the old Greek dramas could be refashioned into plays, which the English reader might enjoy and understand with the same close, effortless sympathy with which he might follow the work of a modern imagination."[30] "I liked the Chorus," wrote the classical scholar S. H. Butcher to Murray. "It was a bold experiment but well justified. The chant or whatever it sd be called has great capabilities. And in this case it had the special merit of making the beautiful words of the translator audible and articulate."[31] Wilfrid Blunt had expected the performance to be dull and vulgar, but he wrote with delight in his diary that

> it was all the contrary.... Everybody enunciated well... and the chaunting chorus seemed to me in its place.... The climax of Hippolytus is trememdous,

monotones most of the lines, shifting her note now and again by simple intervals; occasionally she lapses rather than breaks into rather rudimentary tunes. Her voice, 'is it speech half asleep or song half awake?' This leader was a revelation and a delight, but where she led, alas, the chorus could not follow; she dreams and wavers with lovely hesitations over the stage, they fumble and blunder in sheer ineptitude, and when the male chorus tried to waver and moan, they were ridiculous."

29. T. S. Eliot, *Selected Essays*, new edn (New York: Harcourt Brace & World, 1950), 48–9.
30. Desmond MacCarthy, *The Court Theatre, 1904–1907* (London: A. H. Bullen, 1907), 10.
31. Letter of June 2, 1904, Gilbert Murray Papers, Bodleian.

> the catastrophe the most powerful thing in dramatic literature. At the end of it we were all moved to tears, and I got up and did what I never did before in a theatre, shouted for the author, whether for Euripides or Gilbert Murray I hardly knew.[32]

Yeats had attended the opening performance of the *Hippolytus* on May 26 and accompanied Lady Gregory to the final matinee on June 3. Farr's performance made an impression on him as lasting as any on record: "I . . . keep among my most vivid memories," he wrote thirty years later, "a moment when, during the performance of a Greek play translated by Gilbert Murray, Florence Farr and her one pupil sang or spoke about 'the daughters of the sunset' with alternating voices; so I thought, so I still think, did the ancient world . . . hear poetry."[33] In Farr's arrangement, two members of the Chorus chant the song after Phaedra goes off wildly and painfully into the Castle, planning to die. Murray's own textual comment defines the appeal to Yeats's artistic temperament: "the one thing that can heal the pain without spoiling the interest is an outburst of pure poetry. And the sentiment of this song, the longing to escape to a realm, if not of happiness, at least of beautiful sadness, is so magically right."

> Could I take me to some cavern for my hiding,
> In the hill-tops where the Sun scarce hath trod;
> Or a cloud make the home of mine abiding,
> As a bird among the bird-droves of God!
>
> . . . .
>
> To the strand of the Daughters of the Sunset,
> The Apple-tree, the singing and the gold;
> Where the mariner must stay him from his onset,
> And the red wave is tranquil as of old.[34]

Yeats collected his impressions of the Chorus of *Hippolytus* for *Samhain*, proclaiming that "the expressiveness of the greater portion as mere speech, has, I believe, re-created the chorus as a dramatic method. The greater portion of the singing, as arranged by Miss Farr . . . was altogether admirable speech, and some of it was speech of extraordinary beauty" (*Expl* 176).

32. Wilfrid Scawen Blunt, *My Diaries, Part Two* (New York: Knopf, 1923), 104.
33. (*VPl* 1009) Farr's "one pupil" was Dorothy Paget. Her working copy of *The Hippolytus of Euripides* (London, 1904), "with extensive autograph annotations recording detailed stage directions, movements and (by means of letters) the harmonic progression of the choruses," was included in lot 173 (unsold on day of auction) of Sotheby's catalogue sale of December 15, 1988, 124. The item (xi) is untraced. According to a representative of Sothebys, "Nothing is known of the custodial history of the papers."
34. Gilbert Murray (trans.), *The Hippolytus of Euripides* (London: George Allen, 1902), 39.

Conscious of the opinions of London critics, he was intent to defend the new art and Farr's choral experiment to his Dublin audience, clearly to prepare it for the use of a chorus in poetic drama at the Abbey:

> When one lost the meaning, even perhaps where the whole chorus sang together, it was not because of a defective method, but because it is the misfortune of every new artistic method that we can judge of it through performers who must be for a long time unpractised and amateurish. This new art has a double difficulty, for the training of a modern singer makes articulate speech, as a poet understands it, nearly impossible, and those who are masters of speech very often, perhaps usually, are poor musicians. Fortunately, Miss Farr, who has some knowledge of music, has, it may be, the most beautiful voice on the English stage, and is, in her management of it, an exquisite artist.
>
> (*Expl* 176)

Thus, as Yeats and Farr took the new art to larger audiences in public theatres, and as Farr set out to graft the new art to Barker's modernized and naturalized Euripides, they encountered anew the old frustrations of limited means, overtrained singers, untrained actors, and sophisticated (and thereby unmoved) managers and audiences "whose ears," Yeats lamented, "are accustomed to the abstract emotion and elaboration of notes in modern music" (*Expl* 219). Indeed, he found it incredible that London managers would stage an ancient poetic drama according to the dictates of those who are deaf to poetical rhythm. Remarkably, these frustrations were never admitted as defeats or disenchantments, however cautiously Yeats prepared his audience: "It is possible, barely so, but still possible, that some day we may write musical notes as did the Greeks, it seems, for a whole play, and make our actors speak upon them—not sing, but speak" (*Expl* 174). Only in her diary would Farr confess her occasional personal weariness: "I've tried to get people to speak beautifully but not a soul does speak any the better for all my efforts = Not a soul sees the truth any clearer for all I have said and written."

III

As soon as the *Hippolytus* closed at the Lyric, Barker turned his attention to directing the Stage Society's long-delayed production of Yeats's *Where There Is Nothing*, performed at the Court Theatre from June 26 to 28 and received with mixed reviews. "I watched Yeats' play from a box," Ricketts wrote in his diary,

> with Hardy the novelist before me; he is much older than I had imagined; he seemed wizened in mind and body and never once made an intelligent remark. Yeats' play failed to strike the audience, though it seemed to me to be written for effect, with striking episodes which should tell over the footlights. It is much too long and showed halts in construction, but it could be cut down to a telling thing.[35]

After this production the theatre went into remodelling, as Barker and Vedrenne agreed during the summer to combine their managing talents to make the Court the center of experimental drama in London. They planned an autumn season of matinees around fortnightly productions of Euripides, Maeterlinck, and Shaw, reviving the *Hippolytus* for their opening production.

When Barker reluctantly recast Farr as leader of the Chorus again, she immediately took steps to improve its performance. Looking to a promising future, she corresponded with Shaw about his old notion that she should study phonetics with Henry Sweet at Oxford,[36] but for practical reasons her summer was taken up with assisting and making dresses for Mrs. Patrick Campbell. Mrs. Pat, fascinated by Farr's psaltery, had commissioned Dolmetsch to make for her three similar but gilded psalteries for use in some of her own productions.[37] Farr borrowed one of Mrs. Pat's psalteries

35. Ricketts, *Self-Portrait*, 109. Four days later Yeats went to dine with Ricketts: "We spoke about the failure of his play. He showed himself critical and shrewd. When he does not pontify he is all right" (109).

36. On June 30, 1904, Shaw had advised Farr to study with Sweet in order to "learn the science of pronunciation and become a professor of phonetics for dramatic purposes" (Bax 24), with a view to teaching in Herbert Tree's new School of Acting, but nothing came of the plan.

37. As Dolmetsch later recalled, he "tuned her Psaltery to a vague drone which did not interfere much with her voice" (NLI MS 5919; edited in Joseph Hone, *W. B. Yeats, 1865–1939*, [London: Macmillan, 1942], 191). Mrs. Pat, playing the water sprite Undine, and two other actresses used the psalteries to accompany Undine's songs in W. L. Courtney's *Undine,* initially for the playwright's performance at St. James's on February 19 and subsequently at the Shakespeare Theatre in Liverpool on September 13, 1903. The production was revived at the *Criterion* on May 23, 1906, for twenty-one performances. Yeats probably encouraged her use of the psalteries (not mentioned in reviews) for the play, an adaptation of Friedrich, Baron de la Motte-Fouqué's romance, *Undine* (1811), a work in which Yeats had an abiding interest: in his review of the Arts and Crafts Exhibition of 1890 he said that a sculpted figure of Fouqué's Undine was "perhaps, the most interesting exhibit of all" (*UP1* 185), and in 1893 he began his review of Robert Buchanan's poem *The Wandering Jew* by saying that in *Undine* Fouqué "describes the Father of Evil as having a face that no man could remember and a name that sounded 'Greek and noble,' but passed out of men's minds as soon as it was uttered" (*UP1* 264). Mabel Dolmetsch remembered that Mrs. Pat used the three psalteries with other Rhine maidens in a production of *Das Rheingold*: the psalteries "were designed to be tuned to

for experimentation, tuning it with others to octaves different from her own in order to get a greater contrast of voices. She made improvements in the music, which she arranged for two psalteries, one tuned to B♭ and one to G. She also planned to print a small edition of the music to be sold at the theatre with the paper edition of Murray's translation; however, as new restrictions and disappointments began, the Vedrenne–Barker management would not allow her the £6 printing costs.

After the opening at the Court on October 18, Jane Harrison wrote a personal letter to Farr. "It was no-wise as critic that I wanted to write! Only to tell you . . . how deeply grateful I was to you now and before for my best moments during that beautiful play. . . . Your art of speaking the natural notes of a phrase is I think so difficult and delicate as to be apparently incommunicable. As you do it you make it beautiful and poignant—when the rest attempt it I feel doubtful as to the whole technique."[38] What Harrison did not know was that Barker had excluded Farr's pupils from the Chorus, increasing the size with professional singers and making it impossible for her to make significant improvements over the earlier performance. "Granville Barker will have to see they do not tread on each other," she wrote sarcastically to Murray. "He has chosen them all himself this time, so we ought to have a bevy of beauty and talent."[39] To Yeats, such singers were "bagpipes," incapable of poetic expression, "trained by a method of teaching that professes to change a human being into a musical instrument, a creation of science, 'something other than human life' " (*Expl* 175).

When the drama critic E. K. Chambers witnessed the performance of Murray's "exquisite translation," he was also struck by "the extraordinary modernity of the piece," but he sensed more than others the tension between Barker's modern production and Farr's ancient chorus. "Of course," he qualified,

> you have to adapt yourself to the choric setting, which is quite alien to modern methods of stage presentation. . . . Miss Florence Farr's stationary maidens, speaking their melodies to Mr. Dolmetsch's psalteries, are quite charming, and quite appropriate to the spirit of Greek tragedy; but they are a free adaptation

a common chord, so that they were able to accompany their singing by sweeping their hands to and fro over the strings in a shimmer of sweet concord." See Mabel Dolmetsch, *Personal Recollections of Arnold Dolmetsch* (London: Routledge and Kegan Paul, 1962), 32.

38. Letter of October 22, 1904, Letters to Florence Farr (235/14), Sterling Library, University of London.

39. Undated letter [October 1904].

> rather than an academic reproduction of the actual Dionysiac chorus, moving in set measures round the Dionysiac altar on the wide threshing-floor.[40]

Barker, in his desire to "naturalize" the Greek plays, to produce them not with archaeological accuracy but as though they had been written for the modern stage, had no sympathy for the "free" archaic atmosphere of Farr's arrangements. But Murray did, and his lifelong support of Farr's choral principles was, in effect, a way of keeping the modernized plays anchored in antiquity.

At Coole, Yeats brooded over the treatment of poetic drama in the realist camp, but he was inspired by the *Hippolytus* to begin his *Deirdre*, which he told Quinn would be "a long one-act play with choruses, rather like a Greek play" (*CL3* 616). Yeats introduced into the legend three wandering musicians to function as a chorus and provide "a music that can mix itself | Into imagination" (*VPl* 374). Hoping to have the play ready by the following spring, he conceived the part of the First Musician, described in the stage directions as a "comely woman of about forty with a stringed instrument," for Farr, and he aimed to present her choral method in Dublin under proper stage conditions. "The first musician was written for you—," he later informed her. "I always saw your face as I wrote very curiously your face even more than your voice and built the character out of that" (*CL4* 519). By the end of the year he was deep into the play, reciting a passage over whiskies and sodas at George Moore's flat. "He has succeeded in it," Gogarty recounted to George Bell on December 12, "in giving a kind of classical heroic value to a commonplace or folk word," and he was stunned by Yeats's chanting of the three musicians' song, "But is Edain worth a song | Now the hunt begins anew?" (*VPl* 352–3):

> The effect of his reading this is not to be transmitted to you. He forgot himself and his face seemed tremulous as if an image of impalpable fire—and not red, black and white coloured Yeats. His lips are dark cherry red and his cheeks too, take colour and his eyes actually glow black and then the voice gets all vibrating as he sways like a Druid with his whole soul chanting. No wonder the mechanics in America were mesmerized! I know no more beautiful face than Yeats' when lit with song.[41]

40. E. K. Chambers, "Drama: The Modernity of Euripides," *The Outlook*, October 29, 1904, 378.
41. Oliver St. John Gogarty, *Many Lines to Thee: Letters to GKA Bell from Martello Tower... 1904–1907*, ed. James F. Carens (Dublin: Dolmen Press, 1971), 58–9.

A Dublin interviewer, asking Yeats about future productions after the opening of the Abbey Theatre on December 27, reported that the theatre company was planning a production of *Oedipus the King:* "Mr. Yeats sees his greatest difficulty in the management of the chorus, but if the Society definitely decides on the production Mr. Yeats believes that this little obstacle can be overcome."[42] The adaptation of Greek choruses to his own plays would continue to absorb him: Farr's choruses at the Court led him to revise *On Baile's Strand*, adding three singing women as choral agents to forecast the tragic action of Cuchulain killing his son: "No crying out, for there'll be need of cries | And knocking at the breast when it's all finished" (*VPl* 515). As Yeats explained in his notes for the play, the choral lyric of the three women "must be for the most part a mere murmur under the voices of the men" (*VPl* 526) as Cuchulain binds himself by an oath of obedience to Conchobar. Farr's choruses for the production of Murray's translations of Greek plays had an immediate and permanent effect on the conception and construction of Yeats's drama, leading to the recurring use of three musicians as a chorus in numerous plays from "Deirdre" (1907) to "The Death of Cuchulain" (1939).[43]

Yeats had no sooner embarked on *Deirdre* when no other than George Moore, under the pseudonym of "Paul Ruttledge," the principal character of Yeats's *Where There Is Nothing,* wrote an abusive article in *Dana* on the stage management of William Fay, suggesting that Fay and the directors of the Irish National Theatre should do well to study the realistic stage management of Antoine.[44] Such an admonition, Yeats retorted, "is like telling a good Catholic to take his theology from Luther" (*Expl* 173). Frank Fay, enraged, planned to counter, with Yeats advising him on the line of rebuttal:

> If I were you I would make your article an attack on realistic stage management.... Put Moore on the defensive and you will win. Be just to Antoine's

42. "The National Theatre Society / Its Work and Ambitions / A Chat with Mr. Yeats," *Evening Mail*, December 31, 1904, 4.
43. See also the musicians in *At the Hawk's Well* (1917), *The Only Jealousy of Emer* (1919), *The Dreaming of the Bones* (1919), *Calvary* (1920), *The Cat and the Moon* (1926), and *The Resurrection* (1931); also the musical attendants in *A Full Moon in March* (1935) and *The King of the Great Clock Tower* (1935), and the musical choruses in the translations of *Sophocles' King Oedipus* (1928) and *Sophocles' Oedipus at Colonus* (1934).
44. See "Stage Management in the Irish National Theatre," *Dana*, 1 (September 1904), 150–2. George Moore had been Yeats's collaborator on *Where There Is Nothing*; their bitter separation over the matter, recounted in Yeats's *Autobiographies,* informed Moore's decision to write as Paul Ruttledge.

> genius, but show the defects of his movement. . . . It is the art of a theatre which knows nothing of style, which knows nothing of magnificent words, nothing of the music of speech.
>
> (*CL3* 642–3)

When Fay decided against a formal reply, Yeats transformed the carefully formulated points of his letter into an essay for *Samhain.* And when he heard that Moore was audaciously scheming to rejoin the Society, Yeats decisively told Fay and his confused colleagues that such a consideration was "out of the question" (*CL3* 670).

The new essay, "The Play, the Player, and the Scene," was essentially an expanded version of "The Reform of the Theatre" (1903); it laid down the same principles of reform but aimed to repulse the threat of realism at home and abroad by attacking the vitality of the stage tradition espoused by Moore and Barker. The movement toward realism in the modern theatre, he told his Irish audience, began in England under the influence of Garrick, and every theatrical advance—the substitution of the proscenium stage for the platform, the elaboration of costume and scenery—led to "a decline in dramatic energy" (*Expl* 172). While this tradition reigns today, Yeats believed, its methods are obsolete and its spirit is rapidly approaching exhaustion. England has left in desuetude the truly vital tradition that has come down from Shakespeare, but its elements have persisted in Ireland since the Restoration. He argued that it is now incumbent upon the Irish, who are sensitive to the "unseen reality" of things, to recreate "a drama of energy, of extravagance, of fantasy, of musical and noble speech" and to revive the stage management appropriate to this drama (*Expl* 170).

Yeats characteristically ended his new manifesto by proclaiming prophetically that the age of science is ending, that "The hour of convention and decoration and ceremony is coming again" (*Expl* 180). After addressing his audience, he was as dogmatic with the directors of the Abbey as he was with the committee of the Masquers that the principles of romantic, symbolic drama be uniformly accepted as their sole stage philosophy. With Synge, who kept the Abbey informed of avant-garde movements in France, he discussed the development of his theories from the earliest experiments in *The Land of Heart's Desire* and *The Countess Cathleen*, coaxing him into line: "I know that you will be an upholder of my musical theories ere long, they follow logically from certain principles which we have all accepted. One must have a complete asthetisism [*sic*] when one is dealing with a synthetic art like that of the stage" (CL3 674). In time, the dogmatism would begin to tear the fabric of the Abbey company. "I imagine you get few people to tell you the truth," AE admonished him frankly in December 1905, "because you are all too ready to fly in a rage, they have not your vehement power of language and while they remain quiet, they go away to work against you" (*LTWBY1* 153).

Yeats had no desire to return to London for the autumn production of the *Hippolytus*. With the patent for the Abbey Theatre recently received, and with John Quinn as his guest, he threw himself into rehearsals for *On Baile's Strand*, drilling his actors in the cadences, adding and deleting words and lines as they proved difficult to speak. Joseph Holloway, who thought Yeats's demands made him the most irritating of directors, looked in on one of the rehearsals:

> He's ever flitting about and interrupting the players in the middle of their speeches, showing them by illustration how he wishes it done, droningly reading the passage and that in monotonous preachy sing-song... Anon he would rush on and erase or add a line or two to the text, but ever and always he was on the fidgets, and made each and all of the players inwardly pray backwards.
>
> (*JHAT* 45)

Annie Horniman voiced her own exasperation over Yeats's interruptions, writing to Frank Fay that members of the company know that

> Mr. Yeats cannot hear *tones*, think it polite not to make him aware of the facts of the case. Personally I consider that he is being treated as a blind man would be if he were insulted by ugly faces being pulled at him by people who spoke politely to him all the while. Quarter tones are such extremely delicate things that no amateur is to be trusted with them except in very rare cases. If you do anything with notes, do them "purely"; or else leave them alone altogether and trust to the ordinary speaking voice and its various degrees of tones. There is nothing in this letter which is not simple musical fact and I wish that you would shew it to any friend who can play any instrument or sing.[45]

For several years the Irish Literary Theatre's emphasis on peasant comedies had diverted Yeats's attention to other elements of stage management,

45. Undated fragment of letter, evidently to Frank Fay (NLI MS 10952); quoted in Gerard Fay, *The Abbey Theatre: Cradle of Genius* (New York: Macmillan, 1958), 70–1. She eventually overcame her politeness about Yeats's tone-deafness, writing to him on October 26, 1906, about his uncritical view of Arthur Darley's music for *Deirdre*: "You are so jealous & ignorant on the subject of an Art beyond words that what you say does not matter. There now! I'm not blaming you for it, I'm very sorry for you indeed, you poor dear tone-deaf Demon!" (*LTWBY*1, 173).

but now he longed to return to heroic legends and give emphasis to the "passionate speech" of their characters on the stage. To Yeats, Frank Fay's musical voice had become the masculine counterpart to Farr's, and Yeats used that voice to support his insistence that he wanted not a monotonous chant but musical speech on the stage. "An actor must so understand how to discriminate cadence from cadence," he wrote in his essay, "and so cherish the musical lineaments of verse or prose, that he delights the ear with a continually varied music. This one has to say over and over again, but one does not mean that his speaking should be a monotonous chant. Those who have heard Mr. Frank Fay speaking verse will understand me" (*Expl* 173). In the momentous performance of *On Baile's Strand* at the opening of the Abbey Theatre on December 27, Holloway had to agree that Fay, "the music of whose speech and the beauty of whose diction, together with the natural dramatic effectiveness of his acting, excited all to admiration," had indeed made Yeats's dinstinctions clear.[46]

With the successful opening of the Abbey Theatre, characterized by D. P. Moran as "this illustrated chanting movement,"[47] Yeats finally found a fortresss for symbolic drama, and to sweeten the taste of triumph he made a final raid on Barker's camp. Yeats wanted the Abbey to join the revival of Greek drama, but so complete was his theoretical dissociation of the Irish from the English theatre movement that he excluded Euripides from the repertoire. In America he had been intrigued to learn that students at the University of Notre Dame had given a performance of Sophocles' *Oedipus the King*. Remembering that the play was presently forbidden in England by the Censor, he now determined to identify the Abbey with Sophocles. Thus, on January 24, 1905, he wrote to ask Murray if he would translate *Oedipus the King* for the new theatre:

> We can offer you nothing for it but a place in heaven, but if you do, it will be a great event. . . . It is much better worth writing for us than for Granville Barker. Nothing has any effect in England, but here one never knows when one may affect the mind of a whole generation. . . . Do not ask us to play Euripides instead, for Euripides is rapidly becoming a popular English dramatist, and it is upon Sophocles that we have set our imaginations.
>
> (*CL4* 22–3)

46. Holloway, *Joseph Holloway's Abbey Theatre*, 50.
47. *The Leader*, February 11, 1905; quoted in Peter Kavanagh, *The Story of the Abbey Theatre* (New York: Devin-Adair, 1950), 49.

"O Man," Murray replied, advising Yeats not to cast his lot with the play, "I will not translate the Oedipus Rex for the Irish Theatre, because it is a play with nothing Irish about it; no religion, not one beautiful action, hardly a stroke of poetry" (*LTWBY1*, 145). Yeats would not accept Murray's Aeschylean alternatives; he invited Robert Gregory to translate Sophocles' *Antigone,* and though it was announced in October 1906 for production in 1907, it failed to appear. Yeats first attempted his own version of *Oedipus the King* in 1910–11, but not until 1926 would he complete and produce his prose translation. Meanwhile, his association of Euripides with the Court stage management and the censorious English temperament kept the Abbey's imagination closed to his plays.

After the *Hippolytus,* the Court Theatre produced Shaw's *John Bull's Other Island,* originally written at Yeats's request for the Irish players, and the production marked a significant turning point for the future of the Court and for Shaw's reputation. "Shaw's plays have been very successful of late," Cockerell noted, "and he has leapt from comparative obscurity into extraordinary fame."[48] Meanwhile, under Murray's prodding, Barker and Vedrenne cast Farr as the Nurse for the subsequent production of Maeterlinck's *Aglavaine and Selysette*, but her main interest, as she maintained her fragile relations with the Court management, was a scheme to go on tour with the choruses from Murray's translations, as *The Trojan Women* (1905), *Electra* (1905), and *Medea* (1906) appeared in rapid succession. She gathered testimonials from Yeats, Murray, Jane Harrison, and Dorothea Beal (her former principal at the Cheltenham Ladies' College, where she performed in 1903) for a circular entitled *The Chorus of Classical Plays to the Music of a Psaltery (CL4* 889–91).[49] When Yeats returned from Dublin in November, he took Farr to meet and chant for Quinn, and to discuss the possibility of an American tour. On December 22, as she waited for Vedrenne to notify her about leading the chorus for *The Trojan Women*, she wrote to Murray:

> I am waiting until after Christmas to go on with my various schemes. If Vedrenne does engage me for the Troades I think I will only go to Cambridge, Edinburgh, Glasgow, Manchester, Liverpool and Oxford, otherwise I should carry out my original scheme of starting off and going from place to place quite slowly . . . I should in fact turn myself into a wandering minstrel for the

48. Cockerell diary, BL Add. MS 52642.
49. Original copies of the circular are in the Quinn papers (NYPL) and the Murray papers (Bodleian); rpt. in *CL4* 889–91.

time being and go on all through the spring. I think it would be rather a pleasant life; with a few books I should be quite content among strangers.[50]

IV

Farr was not the only would-be minstrel planning a tour in 1904. James Joyce had written to Oliver St. John Gogarty on June 3 about his plans "to coast the south of England from Falmouth to Margate, singing old English songs."[51] He had earlier visited a rehearsal of the "Mummers," his sobriquet for the Abbey players, expecting to get from Yeats the name of his "lute maker." "Isn't Joyce delightful?" wrote Gogarty to George Bell on 26 June, "He always quotes Yeats parodied, to heal or endorse his deeds. 'And little shadows come about my eyes'—this of his black eye. Yeats won't give him the address of his lute maker so he cannot tour Margate and Falmouth as he intended."[52] When Yeats, aware of Joyce's continuous mockery, refused to disclose any information about Dolmetsch, Joyce had to secure his address from the London Academy of Music. Like Villona, the Hungarian pianist in his "After the Race," Joyce also planned to expound on "the beauties of the English madrigal, deploring the loss of old instruments." "My tour will not be a success," he told Joseph Holloway, "but it will prove the inadequacy of the English." Joyce was forced to abandon his arrogant minstrelsy, however, when Dolmetsch, one of the few lutanists in England, met the guitarist's short-notice request for a lute with a curtly formal reply on July 17. "Dear Sir," he wrote,

> Lutes are extremely rare. I have not heard of any for sale for years. You should read my articles on this subject in "The Connoisseur" for April and May. I have made one lute, some years ago, but it is doubtful whether I shall make any others. It would certainly be very expensive, and I could hardly say when it would be finished. The lute is moreover extremely difficult to play, and very troublesome to keep in order.
>
> A spinet or some simple kind of Harpsichord, or even a very early piano would be far more practicable. I could get you one of these fairly easily. £30 to £60 would get one.[53]

50. Letter of December 22, 1904.
51. *Letters of James Joyce*, ed. Stuart Gilbert (New York: Viking Press, 1957), 54.
52. Letter of June 26, 1904, Gogarty, *Many Lines to Thee*, 11.
53. Quoted in Richard Ellmann, *James Joyce* (New York: Oxford University Press, 1959), 161. Dolmetsch had written in "The Lute" that "The modern painter who wishes to introduce

Though Joyce would later incorporate brief allusions to the Dolmetsch episode into the Circe chapter of *Ulysses* ("Lynch, did I show you that letter about the lute?") and the Eumaeus chapter ("an instrument he [Stephen] was contemplating purchasing from Mr Arnold Dolmetsch, whom Bloom did not quite recall, though the name certainly sounded familiar, for sixty-five guineas"),[54] he now settled for a more modest concert at the Antient Concert Rooms on August 27. There, in connection with the Irish Revival Industries Show, Joyce excelled, in Holloway's opinion, with his rendition of Yeats's "Down By the Salley Gardens," and in singing with "artistic emotionalism" some of the Irish songs, including "The Croppy Boy," that found their way into his writing. He also sang "In her Simplicity" from the opera *Mignon* ("too high for him") and gave as an encore "My Love Was Born in the North Country" ("a short and sweet item—tenderly)."[55] It was a curious paradox that Joyce, like other of Yeats's parodists and mockers, heightened the atmosphere that Yeats had created.

Publishers and editors of magazines like *The Connoisseur* had begun to seek out Dolmetsch's expertise in early music and instruments for their pages, and he had no difficulty in arranging lectures to supplement his income, a practice he strongly recommended to Yeats. Dolmetsch certainly enjoyed a measure of professional recognition by 1904, but the public attitude toward the early music was still uneven, often capricious and patronizing, and when music critics and exhibitors did give serious attention to the movement that he had inspired, his central role and pioneering efforts were frequently, glaringly overlooked. Even the psaltery was excluded by oversight when Dolmetsch submitted one for the First Exhibition of Modern Decorative Art, arranged by Walter Crane in Turin earlier in the year. His personal difficulties during the past two years had not bolstered his flagging spirits, and the departure through divorce of Élodie, whose mastery and touch on the harpsichord had proved to be

a lute into one of his works, a fashionable thing nowadays, has every chance of reproducing some impossible model, perhaps a complete forgery." See *The Connoisseur* (April 1904), 213–17. Joyce subsequently wrote in "After the Race": "The resonant voice of the Hungarian was about to prevail in ridicule of the spurious lutes of the romantic painters when Ségouin shepherded his party into politics." See James Joyce, *Dubliners* (New York: Penguin, 1992), 39.

54. James Joyce, *Ulysses* (New York: Vintage, 1990), 518, 661–2.

55. *Joseph Holloway's Abbey Theatre*, 43. Joyce used "My Love Was Born in the North Country" in *Stephen Hero*, "The Croppy Boy" in *Ulysses*, and from the opera *Mignon*, which appeared in Dublin shortly after the London production in 1870, "Arrayed for the Betrayal," referred to as "an old song of Aunt Julia's" in "The Dead." See Zack Bowen, *Musical Allusions in the Works of James Joyce* (Dublin: Gill and Macmillan, 1975), 19, 28, 61–2,

irreplaceable, had noticably affected the quality of the ensemble performances. In frustration and uncertainty, Dolmetsch set aside his autumn concerts in favor of a second American tour. It was scheduled for November and December; when successes and invitations mounted, the tour was extended into the winter of 1905. Dolmetsch was thus absent for the opening of the Abbey Theatre, but in the distant cities he was telling American poets more about the Irish poet who had intrigued them the previous year.

By coincidence, an American dramatic group was staging Yeats's *The Hour-Glass* in Chicago while Dolmetsch was there under engagement by Ben Greet to provide the music for a Shakespeare festival. Yeats, who was planning a revival of his play for the Abbey, had earlier discussed with Miss Owen and Dolmetsch his desire to make the Angel's voice "sound like the voice of an Immortal," which he believed could be ensured through regulated declamation (*Expl* 109). Dolmetsch attended one of the Chicago performances and wrote spontaneously to Yeats on April 2: "I *should like* to make some music for such a morality play, Angelic music, introduced as you would. It would be beautiful" (*LTWBY1* 148). The planned collaboration, however, would not take place. Dolmetsch, reluctantly deciding to remain in America, signed a contract with Chickering and Sons of Boston to open a new department of keyboard instruments, lutes, and viols. "I shall not come back to England," he continued, informing Yeats of a brief return in May, "and will only stay . . . a few weeks. I shall return to America for an idefinite period alas! They are willing to support me here, whilst in England they let me starve." For a decade Dolmetsch had been, perhaps more than any other man, the embodiment of the renaissance spirit of the 1890s, and his removal to America was a great loss to the London artistic world. Within a decade, however, he would return to influence a new generation in the arts of music, poetry, and dance.

V

In August of 1904 Farr had succeeded in copyrighting her masque, *The Mystery of Time*, along with Shaw's *How He Lied to Her Husband*, and during the uncertainty about her future at the Court she delayed her tour of the provinces and arranged a production of the masque together with a psaltery recital at the Royal Albert Hall Theatre. The two parts of her program on January 17, 1905, were separated by the first performance of the masque, played by young Lewis Casson as the Present, Gwendolyn Bishop as the Future, and Archibald McLean as the Past, each performing a Bacchanal dance.[56] "The Present is evidently a student of Nietzsche and Schopenhauer," observed the critic E. A. Baughan, "and delivers himself of such aphorisms as 'The Supreme Desire is to be without the Supreme Desire,' and 'The smallest thing is the Now.'"[57] When Shaw heard that Mrs. Emery was going to chant Nietzsche, he mischievously asked, "Why not some of my maxims?" and to the bewilderment of the audience she added to a program that included "ultramystical" poems by Lady Gregory, Carmen Sylva, Rossetti, Yeats, and Nietzsche, several maxims from Shaw's *The Revolutionists's Handbook*. "But why," puzzled one critic, "some of Mr. Bernard Shaw's epigrams, which are certainly not lyrical in character, should have been treated in the same way it was hard to understand. To hear the sage reflection that 'Every man over forty is a scoundrel' solemnly delivered to the accompaniment of a psaltery was certainly a quaint experience."[58] For the next several years, whenever she felt she had a sympathetic audience, Farr introduced a mock-serious element by chanting Shavian maxims:

G F E♭ D C
Youth, which is forgiven everything,
G C
forgives itself nothing.
A♭
Age, which forgives itself everything,
E♭ D C
is forgiven nothing.
G E
If history repeats itself, and the
E♭ -G E
unexpected always happens,

56. Shortly after the production Farr submitted the masque to George Robert Mead, editor of the *Theosophical Review*. On January 26, he replied, "very pleased to give space for your Masque to the Review, and have no doubt but the T.P.S. will... have it on sale in pamphlet form" (Sterling Library, 203/9). It appeared in the *Theosophical Review*, 30 (March 1905), 9–19, and in separate wrappers as *The Mystery of Time: A Masque* (London: Theosophical Publishing Society, 1905). It was reprinted in wrappers by the *New Age* in January 1908.

57. E.A.B., "Speech and Song," *Daily News*, January 18, 1905, 12.

58. H.A.S., "The Art of the Chaunt," *Westminster Gazette*, January 18, 1905, 2.

E♭
How incapable must man be of
C G C
Learning from experience.[59]

Predictably, Farr's first lone venture into London's musical arena with the new art raised the ire of music critics, who fired off familiar questions and prejudices. "In short," wrote Baughan in a longer review-article on Farr's chanting, "the medium of modern music is much more plastic to the expression of fine shades of meaning than the monotonous chanting which Miss Farr has recently brought to the notice of the public."[60] The *Westminster* critic also took up the chanting at greater length in "Should Poetry Be Chaunted?"

> In brief, then, while there may be something in the contention that a more emotional kind of utterance than that commonly employed is appropriate in the delivery of verse, it is difficult to believe that success can ever attend any attempt to systematise the thing by the employment of a written notation and musical instruments.[61]

If the applicability of the method was not effective for poems of the "ultramystical and imaginative order," reasoned the critic, then it would be even less so for verse "of a more robust and straightforward order." "Who can imagine the beauty of such a passage as 'The quality of mercy' being increased by the adoption of a sing-song delivery and the twanging of what might pass for a feeble guitar? Yet if there be anything in the theory at all it should hold, one might suppose, not for one kind of poetry only, but for all."

The *Musical News* brought Yeats into its review, "Words and Music," quoting from his published opinions on the supposed incompatibility of language and song. By 1905 most critics had already had Yeats's theory of speaking to notes thrust upon them, and many were beginning to formulate their own views on the relation of music and speech.

> Mr. W. B. Yeats has long felt that there was something about singing which he disliked; he objected to the unavoidable lengthening of the vowels, and he was sensible of the natural music of the words being distorted thereby. Were

59. See Farr, *The Music of Speech*, 24.
60. E. A. Baughan, "The Chanting of Poems," *The Outlook*, January 21, 1905, 90.
61. H. A. S., "Should Poetry Be Chaunted?", *The Saturday Westminster Gazette*, January 21, 1905, 14.

> he a musician, probably his keener appreciation of musical rhythm would reconcile him to this.[62]

In asserting that the musician's art "reflects the sentiment and enforces the meaning of the text in a manner which no vague chanting of this archaic kind can possibly do," the critic concluded that "the style of the Rhapsodists was certainly of absorbing interest to the Greeks, but its revival in the present day would be simply an archaism serving no useful purpose."

Such utilitarian criticism, together with Baughan's longer and more considered essay, "The Chanting of Poems," led to Farr's first printed reply to her critics. She set out not to defend herself but solely to explain to interested readers the mechanism of her art, giving examples of a variety of musical phrases and chords from her collection:

> No one knows better than I do that chanting in the sense of making a monotonous singing sound on notes robs the voice of its beautiful sense-inflections. For the difference between speech and singing is just this—that in speech each word has a melody of its own, which starts from a certain keynote on which it is uttered, while in singing the melody of the separate word is sacrificed to the melody of the phrase. I do not chant myself or use the singing voice except for refrains, as in the case of "Sister Helen." I simply speak as I would without music, and having discovered the drift of my voice in the phrase, indicate that on the psaltery.[63]

Farr's measured, matter-of-fact reply belies her more spirited response to criticism from musicians; indeed, she was riled into giving a "great lark" of a talk on "The Fight Between the Poets and Musicians" before the Irish Literary Society in London. "There was a strong opposition of musicians present," she wrote to her new American acquaintance, John Quinn, "but I got rapturous applause at the end when I did a lot of imitations of the way people speak verse under the existing state of things. Goodbye. I am enclosing an autobiography of Hughes."[64]

With Dolmetsch gone, Farr had found a new associate in Herbert Hughes, a young Belfast composer whom she met through Synge and Joseph Campbell at the Irish Literary Society. Hughes, founder of the Irish Folk Song Society, had recently published his collection of Gaelic

62. "Words and Music," *Musical News*, February 11, 1905, 129–30.

63. "The Chanting of Poems," *The Outlook* (London), February 18, 1905, pp. 220–1; rpt. in *The Music of Speech*, 16–17; see Appendix 1, 404–6.

64. Letter of April 18, 1905, NYPL. Yeats had introduced Quinn to Farr during Quinn's visit to London in November 1904. On November 7 he wrote to Lady Gregory, "I brought Quinn out to Mrs Emery on Sunday to hear her speak to the Psaltery" (*CL3* 666).

airs in *Songs of Uladh* (1904), with Campbell providing the lyrics. Farr greatly admired some of the songs, and together they worked on effects with the psaltery, resulting in plans for a joint recital–lecture tour on "Folk Music of Ireland and the Bards." The scheme never materialized, but on Synge's advice Yeats asked Hughes to take over the music for the Abbey Theatre, telling Lady Gregory that he found Hughes "full of what sound like good and practical ideas as to . . . what sort of music you would have in the country and so on" (*CL4* 221). Hughes seemed ideal for the Abbey, for his singular interest in traditional folk songs would ensure a distinctive Irish quality for the music in the plays, and Yeats felt that he could therefore leave the music wholly to Hughes without the fears he would have over most professional musicians.[65]

The Court management resignedly settled on Farr as Leader of the Chorus for *The Trojan Women*, much to the apprehension of Barker, who despaired both of her "feeble" manner on stage and the "deplorable" music of her choruses. "I *dread* that she may be writing tin-pot choruses—," he wrote to Murray,

> the formal ones I'm not so afraid of but those bits with Hecuba at the last. What is to be done? Miss Farr is taking to discover on the psalter all sorts of progressives and phrases which to her simple ear are quite effective and might be to ours if the composer of the *Belle of New York*, not to mention Verdi and Wagner, had not accustomed us to them for other purposes. Now this is torture to a musical ear (so I'm told). You see, she really has a big subject to deal with this time—far bigger than *Hippolytus*—one that mustn't be wobbled or patheticized about. Would it be possible to drop a little sound musical advice on her head? I am really worried.[66]

Barker was on his own with Farr, however, for Murray went off to Crete during rehearsals, returning just before the opening. In his anxiety, Barker prevailed upon the musical sense of Shaw, whose *How She Lied to Her Husband* was currently playing at the Court. On March 5 Farr received some unsolicited Shavian advice: "By the way," he casually entered upon the

65. See Maire nic Shiubhlaigh's description in *The Splendid Years* of Hughes's music for the *caoin* in Synge's *Riders to the Sea* (Dublin: James Duffy, 1955), 56. "We gave *Riders to the Sea* in the Molesworth Hall towards the end of 1904. Herbert Hughes, the Irish composer, a friend of the society, transcribed the *caoin* as it was sung on the stage, and later presented me with a copy." Hughes also wrote "Chant for Cathleen Ni Houlihan"—the music for the song "Do not make a great keening"—with a marginal note: "rhythm to follow the verse rather than strict time" (Charles Deering McCormick Library, Northwestern University).

66. Undated letter [January 1905], Bodleian; quoted in C. B. Purdom, *Harley Granville Barker* (London: Rockcliff, 1955), 33–4.

purpose of the letter, "are you arranging choruses for the Trojan Women? If so be very discreet about using modern fashionable discords. In the Hippolytus, towards the end, you began to ramble up and down staircases of minor thirds in a deplorable manner. I strenuously advise you not to introduce deliberate figuration of discords. The effect is modern, cheap and mechanical" (Bax 26). But Farr was not to be swayed by Shaw's ironic interpretation of her "modern" arrangements, and in Murray's absence she became increasingly obstinate. Barker complained that she would not hold her tongue in rehearsals and insisted on doing things her own way.

The matinee performances of *The Trojan Women* opened on April 11, and Yeats was there for the Irish theatre as an approving witness of Farr's delivery. "She used often delicate melodies of a very simple kind," he wrote for *Samhain*, "but always when the thought became intricate and the measure grave and slow, fell back upon declamation regulated by notes" (*Expl* 219). But impatience with the "artificial" manner of the Chorus in the Court productions led Barker's friends to press the matter. To Desmond MacCarthy, who could not bear their "monotonous and lugubrious chant," the Chorus represented the first and only lapse from the management's guiding principles, and he declared that

> the Chorus on the modern stage must be represented by people who utter their comments ... like people naturally moved. ... A chorus of men would probably be more effective; for the voices of men speaking together are much more impressive, and they look and move far better than women in the Greek dress, who for some reason or other appear self-conscious.[67]

At the close of the contentious production, both Barker and Farr were ready to end their mutual dependency, Barker by excluding Farr from the subsequent production of Murray's *Electra*, Farr by finding her way back to private productions of symbolic drama.

During the long preparations for *The Trojan Women*, Farr simultaneously managed the New Stage Club's premier London performance of Oscar Wilde's *Salomé*, a production warmly praised by Symons, Sturge Moore, and Beerbohm, but cold-shouldered by Yeats, partially out of his intense dislike of the "vulgar" voice and effeminate manner of Robin Farquharson as Herod. This modest success, accompanied by a public outcry against the play's repulsiveness, inspired her to recall the members of the dormant Literary Theatre Club and wheedle them into resuming their theatrical activities. She proposed beginning her new project with Shaw's *Candida*

67. Desmond MacCarthy, *The Court Theatre, 1904–1907* (London: A. H. Bullen, 1907), 13.

and verse plays of Binyon and Symons. Shaw tried vigilantly to dissuade her. "Let me know," he ended his deflation of her scheme, "whether on sane consideration you still think the project feasible" (Bax 28). Meanwhile, she learned that Barker would have no further use for her services, news that made her even more determined to resuscitate the Club. With her provincial tours postponed and her unfashionable choruses homeless, she seized the opportunity to provide a program of mystical plays for the International Theosophical Congress, hiring the Court for a joint production of her *Shrine of the Golden Hawk* and Yeats's *The Shadowy Waters*.

When the curtain rose on July 8 the Court was "packed almost to suffocation," and Yeats, prominent in his box, must have delighted in the presence of an aging Maurice Maeterlinck, who sat in the stalls in a lounge suit and "appeared to have a more mystical—or mystified—light in his eye than usual."[68] *The Shrine of the Golden Hawk* was actually more favorably received than *The Shadowy Waters*, which Yeats reluctantly allowed her to perform so that he might make some experiments and revisions. Although Yeats was pleased with Farr's performance as Dectora, he found Farquharson's portrayal of Forgael unendurable, making him shudder at the actor's womanly gestures and movements. "You cannot play Forgael without nobility or any of my verse without pride & he has neither," Yeats wrote to Lady Gregory" (*CL4* 118). Farr had engaged Farquharson, the stage name of Spanish-born actor Robin de la Condamine (her "marionette" as she called him [Bax iv]), after his success as Herod in *Salomé*, and as he and the other players were acting without pay as a favor to her, Yeats could not put his hands on him. "I long to get him by myself," he wrote to Quinn, "and make him speak on a note day after day till he had got rid of accidental variety" (*CL4* 126).

The main experiment of the performance was Ricketts' design for Forgael's magic harp. Constructed of dim glass and electrically lighted from within, it lit up to suggest "supernatural fire" when Forgael enchanted the mutinous sailors and Queen Dectora, transfiguring her enmity to love. When the harp proved troublesome, Yeats substituted a psaltery, altering the text accordingly and taking pleasure in featuring, "in the centre of a myth, the instrument of our new art" (*VP* 816; *VPl* 341).[69] Some of Farr's

68. "A Night of Mystery. / Theosophical Plays at the Court Theatre," clipping in NLI MS 12146, misattributed to the *Evening Standard* of July 10, untraced.

69. When the play was revised after Farr's performance for inclusion in *Poems 1899–1905* (1906), Yeats hoped that when next performed at the Abbey "The play will, I hope, be acted as on its first production, with a quiet gravity and a kind of rhythmic movement, and a very scrupulous cherishing of the music of verse. The 'OOO' of the lamentation will be sung as Miss Farr

musical settings for several lines still survive. In a book of songs given to her by Yeats, she wrote over the last bars of Liszt's "Wanderer's Night Song" (*Wanderers Nachtlied)* the concluding lines from Dectora's last speech, "Bend lower, that I may cover you with my hair | For we will gaze upon this world no longer," and Forgael's concluding description of the murmuring harp, "It has begun to cry out to the eagles" (*VP* 769).[70] On another manuscript setting, below her notation for Forgael's playing of the harp while Dectora sleeps, she wrote for future players: "Don't speak on these notes but use them as a very simple accompaniment to the voice; it is the repetition of the same musical phrase that is important; any varieties introduced would spoil the magical effect."[71]

The appreciative theosophists and the sympathetic reviewers further restored her fervor, and a few weeks after the performance she asked Murray for permission to do the *Bacchae*, as she had longed to do with the Dancers—with archaic dresses, primitive symbolic scenery, and magical effects. Murray was completing his translation of *Electra*, which Barker planned to produce in the spring with revivals of the *Hippolytus* and *The Trojan Women*, excluding Farr from the choruses. "Have you any further ideas about the music—," Barker asked him, "who is to break the matter to Miss Farr? Someone must steal her psalteries for we shall want them."[72] When Murray informed Barker of her request for the *Bacchae*, Barker reacted strongly, warning Murray that her proposed "archaic—or archaotic production" would harm the Greek play cause, and yet he finally admitted that their real conflict was one of ideals: "I think she may well get a more 'beautiful' production than we do at the Court because Beauty is her sole idea . . . while I want to make the plays come as naturally to the theatre as possible, and also I have an uneasy feeling that all through—to get

sings the 'Ochone' in her recitation of 'The Lament of Emer' " (*VPl* 342). As the music critic of the *Manchester Guardian* had written on May 19, 1903, of her chanting of "The Lament of Emer," "the words were all spoken, the only musical effect being a downward harmonic scale, sung in the manner of a refrain at the end of each stanza" (7).

70. Yeats had given Farr a copy of *Fifty Mastersongs by Twenty Composers,* vol. ii, *For Lower Voice,* ed. Henry T. Fink (Boston: Oliver Ditson, 1902), inscribed "Florence Farr Emery | from W.B. Yeats, 1904". Liszt's "Wanderer's Night Song" appears on pp. 83–4. Sterling Library, University of London.

71. Farr's more detailed setting for Forgael's playing of the harp as Dectora sleeps is preserved in NLI MS 13573. The lines for Farr's settings are taken from *The Shadowy Waters* (London: Hodder and Stoughton, 1900), 36–41, from "A white bird beats upon my face" to "were but lifted up."

72. Undated letter [August 1905]; quoted in Purdom, *Harley Granville Barker*, 50.

good results—Miss Farr lowers the standard."[73] While Murray remained indecisive about giving her the *Bacchae*, Barker continued to persuade him that Farr should be excluded from the Chorus in *Electra*.

Murray had tried to be diplomatic and practical in coming to her defense, telling Barker that she should not be dropped until a suitable replacement was found and that he had no person or system in mind as good as or better than hers. Further, he let Barker know that he was "clearly against making the choruses more *musical*. . . . I mean, against sacrificing the words to the music. I would sooner get the words clear than have even a very good unintelligible song."[74] In response, Barker agreed that if someone could be found to replace her "jejune harmonies" he would let her chant to someone else's music as a member, but not Leader, of the Chorus, but he knew her mind well enough: "It seems to me that at the slightest of these proposed changes . . . Miss Farr will throw us over—I wonder!"[75] As the time for casting approached, Barker was adamant about excluding her. Murray wrote to Farr after the end of the Michaelmas term to soften the blow. After granting her permission to produce the *Bacchae*, subject to permitting his attendance at rehearsals, he broke the bad news:

> You will receive, I fear, a letter from Mr Barker which may not be pleasant reading. We are getting someone else, a man whom I do not know, to do the music for the Electra and train the Chorus. You may be sure that this was not an easy decision to come to, or one that we made without both doubts and regrets. We shall certainly get no one to speak the lines like you, and no one to bring out the romance and beauty of the lyrics in the same way. What influenced us was a wish to get, if we can, more discipline and sureness into the Chorus; and, in a secondary degree, music which they can more easily manage. I wish I could hope that you would come and lead the Chorus on the stage all the same, but I do not like to ask you.[76]

In her place a popular actress-singer, Gertrude Scott, was chosen to lead a chorus of eight professional singers, and Farr responded with detached equanimity to Murray's apologetic letter: "I knew they were doing without me for the chorus in Electra a long time ago—but it is very kind of you to explain."[77]

73. Undated letter [August 20, 1905]; quoted in ibid. 51.
74. Letter of August 19, 1905; quoted in ibid. 50–1.
75. Undated letter [August 20, 1905]; quoted in ibid. 52
76. Undated letter [late-December 1905]; Sterling Library, University of London. The man who replaced Farr was the musical director Theodore Stier.
77. Undated letter [mid-December 1905]; Bodleian.

Barker commandeered the German musical director for the Court Theatre, Theodore Stier, and commissioned him to write new choral music and direct the chorus for *Electra* with five days notice.[78] Stier's music for the chorus was closely supervised by Barker and Murray, with all three side by side on a piano bench. As Murray described the scene to Lady Carlisle, "I read each lyric; then in various ways we tried to get the same effect helped by the music. No melody. Chords here and there to emphasise important words . . . If Stier understands . . . I think the music will be better than we have ever had—better for my purpose, that is."[79] But even under Murray's tutoring Stier could not arrange the new chorus to complement the production. "As to the Chorus," wrote A. B. Walkley after the opening performance on January 16, "no doubt the ladies do their best; it is not their fault that they cannot present, either in evolution, intonation, or significance, a genuine Greek chorus."[80] "Went to see Murray's Electra," Sturge Moore wrote in his diary after the final performance, "very well put on but horribly slow as a spectacle and not once was the audience carried away." He was even more emphatic about the failure of the chorus: "The chorus is absurd. Chanting or singing makes no difference as long as they are a mere collection of languid or awkward individuals. They ought to move in unison then the mere fact of their speaking or moving would be dramatic."[81]

When Barker followed *Electra* with a revival of the *Hippolytus* at the Court on March 26, 1906, with Gertrude Scott again leading the Chorus, he had grudgingly invited Farr to play the Nurse as a concession to Murray. "Do you think that Florence Farr could do it?" Barker had asked him. "Would you like her to be asked? And what about the difficulty of having her play the nurse and listening to her own chorus. Would she remember a single line and would she hold her tongue at rehearsals?"[82] She accepted the part with a vengeance: if Barker wanted realism, he would get realism.

78. Theordore Stier's account of the production appears in his *With Pavlova Round the World* (London: Hurst and Blackett, 1927), 260–1. "The work had been in other hands before it came into mine," Stier explained, "but with a sublime disregard for the limitations of ancient musical expression and the fact that in those times music as we know it did not exist, the composer had iconoclastically written the score for an eight-part chorus and modern instruments. In addition to these urgent difficulties there were but five days in which to complete the work."

79. Letter of December 26, 1905 (Bodleian); quoted in Ducan Wilson, *Gilbert Murray OM* (Oxford: Clarendon Press, 1987), 168.

80. A. B. Walkley, *Drama and Life* (London: Methuen, 1907), 131.

81. Diary for 1906, entry for January 26; Sturge Moore Papers, Box 10.

82. Letter of February 28, 1906, Bodleian.

In Yeats's presence, however, she mischievously learned and rehearsed her lines lyrically, such that he wrote to Lady Gregory on March 29, before attending the performance that night:

> I think Mrs. Emery must be very fine in the 'Hypollitus' she is the Nurse and I have heard her do it a couple of times when she was learning the part. She has learned how to act without losing her beauty of speech, instead of trusting to the speech alone a little too much as she used to.
>
> (*CL4* 365–6)

The day after the opening, however, he wrote with some puzzlement to Lady Gregory, unprepared to discover that Farr was playing the role in its realistic extremity:

> I think I was a little disappointed with Mrs Emery's performance as the nurse in Hippolytus but this may only be that I know her so well that I cannot realise any characterisation she assumes upon the stage. She tried to play as an old woman, and I never found it convincing and the old voice robbed me of her own beautiful voice. I expect to like her a great deal better on Sunday, when there will be no characterisation, except a selection among passions, the only sort possible to the principal character of poetical drama.
>
> (*CL4* 367)

But he did not like her better on Sunday; appalled at her performance, he wrote or said to her, as he later recalled, " 'Why do you play the part with a bent back and a squeak in the voice? How can you be a character actor . . . you who belong to a life that is a vision?' But argument was no use, and some Nurse in Euripides must be played with all an old woman's infirmities and not as I would have it, with all a Sybil's majesty" (*Aut* 81).

Without her leadership, the chorus had also deteriorated. "The chorus is still quite good," Yeats had written reservedly to Lady Gregory,

> but every now and then one saw signs that she was no longer teaching them, in some one or other of the women who would sing a big round note, soft and foolish like a raw egg—the usual sort of modern singing, sounding very strange in the midst of the really articulate voices of the others. There was one big fat woman that roused one to fury, the usual mechanical wind instrument on two legs.
>
> (*CL4* 367)

When the planned revival of *The Trojan Women* was abandoned, so ended the drama of the psalteries and choruses at the Court.

VI

When the Masquers disbanded in November 1903, Ricketts gave the £150 from the Vale Press *Faustus* to Sturge Moore, who held the money in hopes of eventually putting together a new theatre project. Finally, in December 1905, under Farr's now-or-never entreaties, he agreed to form a limited liability company, reviving the Literary Theatre Club as the Literary Theatre Society, Limited. Sturge Moore asked his wife, Marie, to serve as secretary, W. A. Pye as president; he named to the committee himself, Binyon, Ricketts, Shannon, Farr, and Gwendolyn Bishop. Their working list of plays included Shelley's *The Cenci*, Swinburne's *Atalanta in Calydon*, Maeterlinck's *Monna Vanna* in English, Sturge Moore's *Judith*, and unnamed plays by Synge and Douglas Hyde. But as soon as Sturge Moore took action, Farr pressed her unresolved case with Murray, writing on December 7 to tell him of her new "Theatre of Poetry" and its plans. "Now you have had time to think it over," she asked, "will you let me produce the *Bacchae*?

> If we do the Bacchae I should . . . try to get the real archaic feeling into it and have properly designed dresses from vases and a little orchestra of pipes as well as the psalteries.
>
> The chorus would be in their proper place on the level of the audience, shadowy figures against a light background except when they were doing something very important; and I should not compete in any way with the Court productions as the spirit of the whole thing would be to get a real decorative effect.

She closed this latest request, written as the *Electra* went into rehearsal, by pulling at his dramatic allegiance, much as Yeats had done at the beginning of the year: "I think you have had so many experiments in their taste you'd be interested to try another kind of production altogether."[83]

Farr meanwhile wrote to Shaw of the Literary Theatre Society's notion to open with *The Cenci*, but when on December 27 he deprecated the choice as "ludicrously unreal to the sort of audience you want" (Bax 30), she shrewdly persudaded him to let her have the "Don Juan in Hell" scene from his *Man and Superman*, she to play Ann. "The chatter was distinctly vital and vivacious," Ricketts wrote of Shaw's and Farr's visit to discuss the staging.[84] But during the following fortnight, when Murray finally gave in to Farr with the *Bacchae*, Barker must have blocked her attempt to break

83. Letter of December 7, 1905, Bodleian.
84. Ricketts, *Self-Portrait*, 128.

the Court's hold on Shaw, for on January 16, 1906, Sturge Moore heard from her that inexplicably Shaw could not attend to the scene, "so we do 'Aphrodite Against Artemis.'"[85]

At last, on April 1, 1906, the Literary Theatre Society opened at King's Hall, Covent Garden, with a long-delayed performance of Sturge Moore's Euripides-inspired play, with Farr taking the lead as Phaedra. Todhunter wrote to her about her performance:

> You managed I think all through to convey the possession of Phedra by the Goddess very distinctly; but occasionally I felt that in the abrupt changes of intonation necessary in the lines you did not do justice to the more beautiful tones of your voice which are always delightful to hear.... But you carried the weight of the play on your shoulders with a fine audacity and made your personality felt more and more as the play went on.[86]

Shaw, who thought the play was "full of absurdities (Archer quoted several of them)," was straightforwardly brutal to his former mistress:

> There was the making of something in your Phaedra; but you really havnt [sic] any adequate idea of the work and the unrelaxing grip such a part demands. A great deal of it was inaudible, simply because you acted it to yourself confidentially without the slightest regard to the necessity for never letting go your grip of the man in the back row of the gallery.... Murray asks whether you have not a mother with a large stick to keep you awake. Barker gives you up in tragi-comic despair, and declares that you positively *like* doing things feebly.
>
> (Bax 33–4)

Her dress and the scenery were designed by Ricketts, who was "on the whole pleased with the performance; though it was bad, it was not as bad as the rehearsal led me to expect.... The audience received the play quite enthusiastically, and on the call for Author, dear Moore turned up with a long written speech which he delivered in a nervous and deliberate way."[87] William Archer, however, as Shaw had indicated to Farr, was not so kind: "How is it possible that educated men and women can be induced to recite such lines?" he asked in his scathing review. "The one excuse for the play is that it gives us... a fresh realization of the greatness of Euripides.... He knew exactly what scenes to write, and what must not be

85. Sturge Moore's 1906 Notebook, entry for Tuesday, January 16. Sturge Moore Papers, Box 10.
86. Letter of April 2, 1906, University of London (203/14).
87. Ricketts, *Self-Portrait*, 132. A photograph of Farr as Phaedra in the Ricketts dress is in the Sterling Library.

written. These he left to Mr. Sturge Moore."[88] Ricketts came to the defense of his friend against Archer, protesting "against the principles of distortion and misquotation" and asserting that what Sturge Moore achieved

> has not been done by Euripides in his fate-led "Phaedra" or by Racine in the musical sorrows of his "Phèdre"; the tangle of passion and remorse, the despair of the Phaedra of Mr. Moore touches even in its range the subconscious self, where the proprieties and limits of a common sorrow or of accident are outreached; this has been done in its degree by him only.[89]

However much Ricketts' spirited and eloquent defense of the play and production may have heartened the Society, the reality was that without Yeats's presence, energy, and personal commitment, its existence would be short-lived.

Members of the Society returned in June to stage two performances of Wilde's *Salomé* and *A Florentine Tragedy.* Ricketts then wrote to Shaw, again suggesting that the Literary Theatre Society cooperate with the Stage Society in a production of "Don Juan in Hell." When this fell through, Frederick Whelen, co-founder and president of the Stage Society, met with Ricketts and Sturge Moore on October 27 to propose amalgamation. As Sturge Moore wrote to Pye, they decided to hold off: "Whelen very much wants us to amalgamate the two Societies for good and all. That is they want to absorb us. But we have determined if possible to maintain our identity and to move slowly by way of experiment towards a final amalgamation."[90]

The final experiments of the Literary Theatre Society took place at Terry's theatre on March 23, 1907, ironically just as the Court management was preparing "Don Juan in Hell" as the last production of its two and one-half year existence. When Farr left on a tour of America with her psaltery, the Society delayed the *Bacchae*; they produced in its place a double bill: B. J. Ryan's translation of Aeschylus' *The Persians,* which Murray had recommended to Yeats as a substitute for Sophocles' *Oedipus the King*,

88. William Archer, "A Rival to Euripides," *The Tribune* (London), April 2, 1906, 4.

89. Ricketts' letter is printed in Archer's column, "About the Theatre," *The Tribune* (London), April 7, 1906, 2. "It seems to me that Mr. Ricketts' generous indignation has got the better of his urbanity," wrote Archer in introducing the letter, "but I have not infrequently observed that the differences of literary appreciation are apt to engender diverse estimates of good and bad manners." Archer wrote in response to the letter: "That Mr. Moore's intentions were laudable, subtle, perhaps even intelligent, I do not doubt; my point is that he lacks the rudimentary taste, the indispensable modicum of self-criticism, without which, in drama especially, nothing of the slightest value can be produced. His calculated crudities and frigid audacities are as remote from true realism as they are from sane idealism."

90. Sturge Moore Papers, Box 21/292.

and—the ironies of it all subsumed by a mood of reconciliation—Granville-Barker's play, *A Miracle* (Farr received the news in Boston). Soon thereafter the Literary Theatre Society merged with the Stage Society. On May 12, 1908, a disillusioned Sturge Moore wrote to Pye that he was giving up any idea of success with the theatre "as poetic drama is not enjoyed in England."[91]

Thus, the organized attempts of Yeats and Farr and their friends to establish an exclusive Theatre of Beauty in London from 1901 to 1906 ended with the dissolution of the Literary Theatre Society. Inevitably, they were caught up in a dramatic movement that was much larger than the romantic drama, as Sturge Moore earlier realized and feared. Even in Ireland Yeats could not for long withstand the pressure to produce other than peasant, folk, and heroic plays. England did not dislike poetic drama, but, as in Ireland, poetic drama could not thrive or survive there alone. The persevering Stage Society, which absorbed the Masquers, the Dancers, the Court, and the Literary Theatre Society, survived in part because it embraced all modes of literary drama. The common foe was what Wilde had embodied as "Public Opinion," and while the separate struggles for the survival of romantic and realistic drama led to antagonisms among friends, the literary theatre movement ultimately gained strength from the early diversity and conflict of ideals. The dramatic experiments first worked out in those societies continued to have a significant impact on the course of English drama, as the artists that Yeats brought into intimate contact carried their experiences into new productions and influenced new playwrights. "I wonder what deep force is turning us all so insistently to the drama nowadays?" wrote Gordon Bottomley to Robert Trevelyan in 1908. "There never was a time when serious dramatists had less hope of attention and respect, or even of loyal cooperation from the theatre brood, than now: yet the force gathers greater force, and perhaps another generation will, by us, have their desire."[92] The Stage Society continued to channel and provide outlets for that rich force until its demise in 1929. The Society's non-exclusive focus on *literary* drama had prepared the way for the eventual establishment of a National Theatre in England.

In retrospect, it is evident that the new art was a catalyst for these dramatic activities. The unflagging determination to establish, teach, and

91. Ibid.
92. Letter of December 14, 1908, Trinity College Library, Cambridge.

develop the art of speaking to musical notes led to the inception of the romantic societies and the Greek choruses, and while the societies and choruses collapsed in turn, they served to sustain the experiments as Yeats, Farr, Dolmetsch, and others experimented with its development for both lyric and dramatic verse. The scores of lecture–recitals that aimed to create an audience for both modes, and the dozens of people brought into its apprenticeship, testify to the emphasis of Yeats's and Farr's artistic and practical energies and to the magnitude of their commitment during these six years.

Certainly the new art became intimately related to the cadences of Yeats's poetry, conceptually and symbolically crucial to the construction and revisions of his plays, and, as will be seen in the next chapter, increasingly central to his concept of imaginative culture. Moreover, as Farr's chanting to the psaltery motivated Murray to turn his translations into a major revival of Attic drama, her controversial choruses launched a new interest in the choral arts, which continued to flourish until the production of T. S. Eliot's *Murder in the Cathedral* in 1935. Thirty years after the first performance of the *Hippolytus*, when Murray was asked about the staging of choruses, he continued to prefer "merely a chord struck on a 'psaltery' here and there by the Leader of the Chorus. This was Miss Farr's method." But such future ramifications were not in the minds of Yeats and Farr in the autumn of 1905, when, greatly anticipating the new year, they stood on the threshold of a major new phase of the new art.

6
A Spiritual Democracy

I

Today, when the casual conversation of scholars drifts towards Yeats's chanting, the initial smiles turn inevitably to intoned mockery and knowing laughter over his avowed disavowal of print. Even in his own day critics could not comprehend his motive. The *Pall Mall Gazette* reported as a curiosity that Yeats, in a speech before the Irish Literary Society in December 1905,

> said he was in revolt against the printed book, which made the world ignorant. In the olden days, he said, refinement was acquired by plays and by hearing of great people and great things when sitting among friends. Thus the mind was elevated. In his opinion Shakespeare could never have been Shakespeare if his father had known how to read and write. Mr. Yeats also gave it as his opinion that not more than 20,000 people in the British Empire get any good out of printed books.[1]

A century later we can begin to see that Yeats's experiments in minstrelsy, and his statements about the printing press that so bemused and baffled the public in the first five years of the twentieth century, were the recurring signs of a long-planned attempt to establish what Yeats termed in 1906, the year he fully launched his plans, a "spiritual democracy." This would be effected in part by developing the Abbey into a unique "theatre of speech," one that would not only redress the cultural imbalance brought by the book but restore personal utterance to dramatic, narrative, and lyric poetry for all the people. "Out of the written book," Yeats had said before London and American audiences, "has come our decadence, our literature, which puts the secondary things first. It is because of the written book, in which we

1. "The Irish Literary Society," *Pall Mall Gazette*, December 4, 1905, 6.

speak always to strangers and never with a living voice to friends, that we have lost personal utterance" (*YA8* 90). Yeats's attendant dream of a revived oral culture, partially inspired by the continuing existence in western Ireland of what he called the "culture of the cottage," was conceived in direct opposition to what he called Matthew Arnold's "culture of scholarship," an impossible culture for Ireland. Ironically, it was his rediscovery of Chaucer in 1905 that prompted him into action.

As a younger man, Yeats thought Arnold the only contemporary master of the essay form, and his early "twilight" poetry often echoes Arnoldian lines: "Out-worn heart, in a time out-worn, | Come clear of the nets of wrong and right" (*VP* 147). He absorbed much of Arnold's intimidating critical thought, but not so his notions of the poet and his culture. Throughout the 1890s, he labored to articulate his own vision of art and culture under Arnold's louring presence. Arnold's imprecise assessment of the Celtic sensibility troubled him, as did his concept of the poet's role in a spiritually ailing culture where scientific rationalism had displaced the "fact" of religion. Yeats agreed that culture should make prevail the best that is known and thought in the world, but he had a different view of "the best": it could not exclude or fail to presuppose the unwritten tradition, could not rely solely on print for dissemination, and could not be confused "with knowledge, with the surface of life, with the arbitrary, with mechanism" (*E&I* 288). Yeats felt that Arnold's culture, which perceived literature as a "criticism of life," was too much a flood of ideas and abstractions that dealt with "exterior law" rather than "interior life." "I cannot get it out of my mind," he had written prophetically in the face of Arnold in 1895, "that this age of criticism is about to pass, and an age of imagination, of emotion, of moods, of revelation, about to come in its place; for certainly belief in a supersensual world is at hand again" (*E&I* 197). To Yeats, poetry was not an aesthetic, ethical and philosophical substitute for Christianity, but the medium for an ancient, image-invoking religion, and the poet was not a purveyor of morality and "high seriousness" but a priest of the magical vision of life. In "The Celtic Element in Literature" (1897), he lamented Arnold's failure to understand "that our 'natural magic' is but the ancient religion of the world, the ancient worship of Nature and that troubled ecstasy before her" (*E&I* 176). Arnold and his contemporaries, Yeats believed, looked at nature "without ecstasy," in the modern way, "the way of people who have forgotten the ancient religion" (*E&I* 178).

Thus, while Arnold served as antagonist for his definition of the poet's role in culture, Yeats aligned himself with those poets in the ancient "processional order," which derived from the *priscus magi*, flowed into bardic Ireland, and re-emerged in modern times with Blake and the Symbolists. In the new manifestation of the order, Yeats would have the poet-priest employ the ancient arts of this tradition to speak through legend and symbol to all levels of culture, on the stage through players trained in passionate speech, in the countryside through minstrels trained in the arts of reciting lyrical and narrative poetry. Yeats first defined his democratic cultural vision in "Ireland and the Arts" (1901):

> I would have Ireland re-create the ancient arts, the arts as they were understood in Judaea, in India, in Scandinavia, in Greece and Rome, in every ancient land; as they were understood when they moved a whole people and not a few people who have grown up in a leisured class and made this understanding their business.
>
> (*E&I* 206)

In re-creating the old spiritual democracy, the poet, like Seanchan claiming his "ancient right" in *The King's Threshold*, resumes his bardic position at the center of culture, inciting all to "imaginative action" through art that is "a revelation, and not a criticism" of life (*E&I* 197).

Prior to 1905, Yeats's essays and lectures on the theatre and on speaking to the psaltery aimed to bring these lost romantic arts to a modern culture overburdened with realism. His theoretical emphasis was on their imaginative vitality, but establishing their practicality for a sizeable audience required, as we have seen, scores of lecture-demonstrations. The larger cultural vision that contained them had become subordinated to the practicalities of establishing a favorable critical milieu and a permanent theatre, though he had written to Gordon Craig as early as November 1902 that "Our movement is a real movement of the people" (*CL3* 258). But in 1905, with most of the toilsome groundwork laid, the piecemeal ideas of culture found cohesion in a major new lecture-essay, "Literature and the Living Voice," described to John Quinn in its untitled state as "a rather elaborate article on the necessity of having verse sung or spoken" (*CL4* 76).[2] Some of the ideas for the essay were actually put together prior to

2. Yeats told Quinn that he was writing the article for the *International Review*, but "through an accident" it was actually published in *The Contemporary Review* for October 1906 and reprinted by Yeats in *Samhain* for December 1906. Sections III, IV, and V were printed as an appendix, "The Work of the National Theatre Society at the Abbey Theatre, Dublin: A Statement of

his first American tour in 1903, in a lecture entitled "Poetry in the Old Time and in the New," and offered as one of several topics to American audiences.[3] The lecture was seldom chosen, but a reporter at the University of Toronto thought there was "a good deal to be said in favor of Mr. Yeats's ingenious theory, that real culture is the result of the interaction of the individual and the community, and is not to be secured by mere reading of books."[4] Yeats spoke in anticipation of applying the principles of the lecture to the Irish theatre after the tour. "It is," he declared sanguinely, "sometimes the impracticable movements that lift the world out of its course and place it on another track." Describing his rediscovery of the old art of the troubadours with the help of Dolmetsch and Farr, he confided that the theatre hoped "presently to send troubadours, or whatever will be the new word we will adopt, to our patriotic societies, just as one sends singers or players."[5] After his return from America in March 1904, he went to Coole to revise and enlarge the lecture, hoping to have a new version printed for the opening of the Abbey Theatre as a sort of manifesto for his concept of a full theatre of speech, but he was forced to put it aside in October under more practical demands. When completed, the new essay synthesized and placed in the context of culture several more narrowly focused lectures and essays, including "Speaking to the Psaltery." "It gives," he wrote in a prefatory note, "a better account than anything I have written of certain dreams I hope the Theatre may in some measure fulfil [*sic*],"[6] and yet it remains one of his most neglected essays on the theatre.

In June 1905, while the essay was still in composition, the Abbey players performed *The Hour-Glass*; when Yeats was called on stage with demands for a speech, he used a new idiom to place the revived play in a new context, telling his audience that "to his mind, the function of the theatre was to put before the people strong, great types, and so contribute to the evolution in Ireland of a great democracy."[7] With this fervent public utterance, he disclosed the language of his cultural vision and, in his lecture

Principles," in *The Poetical Works of William B. Yeats*, ii (1907). The essay was incorporated into "The Irish Dramatic Movement" for the *Collected Works*, iv (1908), and reprinted in *Plays and Controversies* (1925), all of which attest to the continuing centrality of the essay in Yeats's mind.

3. The texts of the lectures that Yeats offered on his American tour are printed and discussed by Richard Londraville, "Four Lectures by W. B. Yeats, 1902–4," *YA8*, 78–122.
4. "Culture, Ancient and Modern," *The Globe* (Toronto), February 16, 1904, 6.
5. From Lecture I ("Poetry in the Old Time and in the New"), *YA8*, 89.
6. "Notes," *Samhain*, ed. W.B. Yeats (Dublin: Maunsel, 1906), 3.
7. "The Irish National Theatre," *The Freeman's Journal*, June 10, 1905, 8.

version of "Literature and the Living Voice," would soon give his idea of "democracy" familiar currency on both platform and stage. Three days later, on his fortieth birthday, Yeats received from his friends, through a subscription arranged by Lady Gregory, a magnificent Kelmscott Chaucer. They could not have given him a more timely gift.

Yeats had seldom read Chaucer since he was a boy, when his father read him the *Prioress's Tale* ("the story of the little boy murdered by the Jews") and *The Tale of Sir Thopas* (*Aut* 69), and he later recalled that as a young poet in the grip of generalization he "began to pray that my imagination might somehow be rescued from abstraction and become as preoccupied with life as had been the imagination of Chaucer" (*Aut* 163).[8] In July 1905, however, he turned to Chaucer as to a great need. "Three or four years ago, I had the need of Spenser and read him right through," he wrote to Sydney Cockerell, thanking him for his share in the gift. "Now it is Chaucer, a much wiser and saner man" (*CL4* 130). Yeats placed Chaucer first on his daily schedule at Coole, reading little else, and wrote to Florence Farr of his plans for the two of them to take a bicycle tour following the route of the pilgrims from Southwark to Canterbury. At the end of the month, he declined to write an article on Shakespeare for A. H. Bullen, professing that "my imagination is getting so deep in Chaucer that I cannot get it down into any other well for the present" (*CL4* 147). Yeats admired Chaucer both as a maker and as a teller of tales, and at the well-head of his art he found the "masculine" elements he had been looking for: simplicity and variety of structure, vividness and variety of language. In these essentials Chaucer showed Yeats how to make his own art more picturesque and appealing to the common man. Further, he revealed to him an antidote for the general weakness of modern poetry, which Yeats characterized in contrast to Chaucer's verse as "monotonous in its structure and effeminate in its continual insistence upon certain moments of strained lyricism" (*Expl* 220). Where Arnold had disavowed Chaucer as a touchstone of "high seriousness," the means to culture, Yeats embraced him as the artistic paragon of his spiritual democracy.

As Yeats worked these principles into "Literature and the Living Voice," he rummaged through the storyteller's bag of tricks to find new techniques for his public recitations. Conscious of a possible monotony of mood in her

8. By 1890 Yeats had at least some sense of Chaucer's writing, evidenced in a letter of January 3, 1890, to the editor of *The Nation* regarding criticism of his edition of *Stories from Carleton*. Yeats characterizes Carleton's "Shane Fadh's Wedding" as "a story of almost Chaucerian breadth and power" (*CL1* 206).

chanting performances, he instructed Farr to bring Chaucerian variety to her repertoire. In replying to her suggestion to add a new Lionel Johnson poem, he revealed his increased concern with attending to the ear and attention of the audience:

> I doubt of the long grave poems like *Dark Angel* having enough internal movement for the Psaltery. One wants changes of voice—even different speakers at times—and choral bits for singing. The danger of the Psaltery is monotony. A thing the antiants were more alive to in all arts than we are—Chaucer for instance follows his noble *Knight's Tale* with an unspeakable tale told by a drunken miller. If Morris had done the like—everyone would have read his *Earthly Paradise* for ever. By the by Chaucer in that same unspeakable tale calls a certain young wife "white and small as a weasel". Does it not bring the physical type clearly to the minds-eye? I think one wants that sort of vivid irresistible phrase in all verse to be spoken aloud—it rests the imagination as upon the green ground.
>
> (*CL4* 151–2)

During the summer Yeats labored to inject such vivid Chaucerian language into his verse; when he revised *The Shadowy Waters* after Farr's production for the Theosophical Society, he delighted in getting "liquorice-root" and "creaky shoes" into an abstract passage (*VP* 227–8).[9]

By September the new lecture and an enlivened program were ready for the public, and the resilient twosome made ambitious plans to embark on a provincial tour of Great Britain. But Chaucer was not the only catalyst who sparked Yeats into his new enterprise, for the presence of Morris was continually evoked through the artistry of the Kelmscott masterpiece before him, the most exquisite object of Morris's arts and crafts movement. Where Chaucer led Yeats back to the art of writing for a listening audience, Morris suddenly led him back to the motives of the arts and crafts movement.

9. Yeats had written to Quinn on September 16, 1905, about "liquorice root" as an example of the common idiom he wanted to achieve (*CL4* 179). Two years later, on December 8, 1907, Quinn ironically wrote to Yeats about the improvement of *The Shadowy Waters*, "but two lines of it struck me as a little too homely for a dream play, which is what it seems to me: 'I've nothing to complain but heartburn, | And that's cured by a boiled liquorice root.' I can't make any rhythm out of these lines and they break the mood that the rest of the play brings on one. But you know and I don't" (*LJQ* 92–3). As Steve Ellis points out, Yeats had omitted the phrases from the 1906 acting edition of the play, and by *Later Poems* (1922) "the short passage relating Aibric's heartburn and its liquorice-root cure was also omitted from the revised narrative poem." See "Chaucer, Yeats and the Living Voice," *YA8* 48. Yeats periodically returned to his Kelmscott Chaucer with different interests: "I am enjoying my Chaucer reading very much," he wrote to Lady Gregory on December 19, 1910, "and am beginning to get excited by the change of method that came when poets wrote to be read out not to be sung" (*CL InteLex* 1479).

Could not the present endeavor to unite the recovered arts of musical speech to modern literature and culture be seen as a manifestation of that movement? That is the way Yeats had come to see it, and in Morris's name that is the way he would present it to his new audiences.[10] In his Blakean belief in the divinity of the imagination, Yeats had come to embrace Morris's notion that imaginative art was a vital and essential part of life itself, not the sole province of educated readers.

II

Yeats had not always voiced his curious bias against the printing press as an obstacle to culture. Indeed, when he founded the National Literary Society in June 1892, his primary aim for the society was to establish a new "Library of Ireland," comprised of books by the best contemporary writers and scholars for distribution to small Irish towns. At the inaugural meeting, Yeats "proposed a resolution declaring the Literary Society started":

> He said he had heard it said that more books were sold in a single town in England than in all Ireland. The fact was that the educated classes [in Ireland] did not take any interest in Irish things, and they did not justify that apathy by an increased interest in the literature of the world (hear, hear). They had a less interest in the literature of the world than the educated classes of most other countries (hear, hear). They were more backward from a literary point of view than they were forty years ago, and those who had considered the subject had come to the conclusion that the difficulty was one of distribution—the extraordinary difficulty of getting books distributed amongst the people of Ireland (hear, hear).[11]

Yeats went on to describe his wish for the new society to establish a distribution system similar to that of the Young Irelanders, who in 1848 had circulated nationalist books through the Repeal Reading Rooms. He

10. Yeats concluded one of his American lectures ("Poetry in the Old Time and the New") with one of his early statements about the relation of the arts and crafts movement to his speech movement: "About twenty years ago there began the modern great movement of applied art of design.... It seemed as though art had become a part of daily life, as though they must make the things of daily life beautiful. Now we have begun precisely the same movement. The written book has the same relation to the song or to the play as the picture has to applied design. We have plunged all the arts again into life. The plunge of poetry into life means first of all that we shall bring it close again to speech, that we shall make it passionate, that we shall no longer write as scholars but as men, and that, as far as possible, we shall take subjects which our audience is interested in" (*YA8*, 91–2).

11. *Irish Daily Independent*, June 10, 1892, 5.

appealed to the Society for its support in commissioning a new series of books and in requesting other literary societies in Dublin and Ireland to distribute those books to the people. In addition to social, historical, and political works, Yeats wanted the library to include folk, heroic, and imaginative literature by contemporary Irish writers. "They could," he persuaded his audience, "guarantee that the books which would be offered would be by the best scholars, and be issued at such a price as would ensure them a circulation in every part of Ireland."

Toward this goal Yeats persuaded his London publisher T. Fisher Unwin to agree to publish the series. Determined that the National Literary Society should go "straight to the people,"[12] the ardent young Fenian began lecturing in provincial towns to promote the library project. Just as it appeared that the Library of Ireland would materialize, however, Yeats received the disturbing news that Sir Charles Gavan Duffy had gone forward with his own plans for a National Publishing Company and Library of Ireland. Duffy, who had been a leader of the Young Ireland movement and an editor of *The Nation* in the 1840s, had returned to London from a political career in Australia and retirement in Nice to be appointed president of the new Irish Literary Society in London, where Yeats had initially proposed the project. Duffy wanted the new library to serve the nationalist cause by publishing the works of friends and political associates of his Young Ireland youth. To Yeats, the didactic, ill-written ballad poetry and the politically motivated literature of Duffy's past ensured the failure of any new library, and the ensuing conflict over the contents stymied all attempts to harmonize the two projects.

When Yeats saw that Duffy was gaining the upper hand through his reputation and influence, he sent an "Opinion" to the Irish papers, asking whether Duffy's National Publishing Company would "publish the right books on the right subjects" and distribute them to a sufficient number of Irish readers: "Whether it does or does not succeed in doing these things must largely depend on whether or not it keeps itself in touch with the young men of Ireland whom it wishes to influence, with those who represent them, and with the various organizations which they have formed or are forming through the country." Yeats could not restrain himself from further questioning the singular authority of his aged usurper in publishing a series of books "which would be quite unfitted for the Ireland of to-day,"

12. Ibid.

declaring that "No one man, however profound his knowledge of the Ireland of forty years ago, however eminent be his name, should have all the power thrust upon him . . . and no man, above all no man who has lived long out of Ireland, can hold the threads of all these needs and interests within his hands."[13]

Meanwhile, in what Yeats saw as an act of betrayal that he would never forgive, his friend T. W. Rolleston, with whom he had founded the London society, suggested to Duffy that the two of them go to Fisher Unwin with Duffy's proposed series of books. Unwin, believing the series presented to him to be Yeats's series, accepted their proposal and signed a contract with them, effectually killing what Yeats later called "my Irish propaganda" (*Aut* 191) and minimizing his influence on the project. The episode was a bitter personal setback to his ambition of affecting Irish culture through a critical press; it was the first in a sequence of events that led him to shift his paradigm from the distribution of an Irish print culture for a literate elite to the distribution of an ancient oral culture and imaginative life for an uncultivated populace.

What diverted Yeats from his bitterness and disillusionment over the library was the popular cultural movement generated by Hyde's Gaelic League in 1893. The League had been formed in the aftermath of Hyde's influential address before the National Literary Society in December 1892, "The Necessity of De-Anglicizing Ireland," in which he called for the displacement of English customs by Irish customs, especially the English language by the Gaelic language, including literature. Yeats, who had no Gaelic, immediately countered with a question, "Can we not build up a national tradition, a national literature, which shall be none the less Irish in spirit from being English in language?" (*UP1* 255). Yeats reviewed and was greatly moved by Hyde's English translation of the *Love Songs of Connacht* (1893), which revealed a peasant world where "everything was so old that it was steeped in the heart, and every powerful emotion found at once noble types and symbols for its expression' (*UP1* 295). The rapid spread of the

13. *Freeman's Journal*, September 6, 1892; *UP1* 240. In his 1914 lecture on Thomas Davis, Yeats reflected on his conflict with Duffy, who had opened the New Library of Ireland series with his edition of Davis's *Patriot Parliament of 1691* (1893): "it seemed then as if our new generation could not do its work unless we overcame the habit of making every Irish book, or poem, shoulder some political idea; it seemed to us that we had to escape by some great effort from the obsession of public life, and I had come to feel that our first work must be to close, not knowing how great the need of it still was, the rhymed lesson book of Davis" (*Davis, Mangan, Ferguson: Tradition and the Irish Writer*, ed. Roger McHugh [Chester, PA: Dufour Editions, 1970], 20).

cultural revival through the League—the establishment of branches where songs were sung and stories were told in Gaelic, the restoration of the local *feis*, where prizes were awarded for competitions in Gaelic recitations, music, singing, and dancing—made him determined to complement the revival of ancient tradition and heroic literature in English. It was clear to him that the oral distribution of culture to the people could succeed on a scale that his own (or Duffy's) New Library of Ireland (which soon collapsed) could never have imagined. "Irishmen who wrote in the English language," he observed, "were read by the Irish in England, by the general public there, nothing was read in Ireland except newspapers, prayer-books, popular novels; but if Ireland would not read literature it might listen to it, for politics and the Church had created listeners" (*Aut* 296).

Yeats's growing fascination with the "culture of the cottage" and the oral tradition had become heightened in 1897 through his new friendship with Lady Gregory, who made him a collaborator in the collection of folklore, fairy tales, visions, and beliefs in the west of Ireland. Through these encounters, his former vision of the library as the transforming agent of culture was rapidly displaced by a bardic notion that the poet and storyteller could restore the communal experience of literature. He worked the idea into "The Adoration of the Magi" (1897), in which he describes how the imaginative lives of three old brothers were enhanced by their love of old Gaelic storytellers who "would chant old poems to them over the poteen . . . for they would not enjoy in solitude, but as the ancients enjoyed" (*Myth* 309). Increasingly aware that the great mass of Irish people read little but listened well, his first proposal that summer for a "Celtic Theatre" was motivated by his desire to take heroic life to them visibly and audibly on the stage; thus, he defined his ideal audience:

> We hope to find in Ireland an uncorrupted and imaginative audience trained to listen by its passion for oratory, and believe that our desire to bring upon the stage the deeper thoughts and emotions of Ireland will ensure for us a tolerant welcome . . . We will show that Ireland is not the home of buffoonery and of easy sentiment, as it has been represented, but the home of an ancient idealism. We are confident of the support of all Irish people, who are weary of misrepresentation, in carrying out a work that is outside all the political questions that divide us.[14]

14. Written at Coole in the summer of 1897, the signatories, in Lady Gregory's hand, were Yeats, Standish O'Grady, Edward Martyn, George Moore, and William Sharp (for whose sake the word "Celtic" was added, though his plays were never acted by the Irish theatre).

Such were the developing attitudes, combined with his own romantic vision of the bardic past, that accompanied the opening of the Irish Literary Theatre and the chanting experiments in 1899.

At the beginning of that year, just as the Irish Literary Theatre was announced, Lady Gregory founded the Kiltartan branch of the Gaelic League and renewed her own study of the language. She had also discovered a manuscript of poems by the Connacht poet Anthony Raftery and had given them to Hyde for translation. Consequently, as Yeats later observed with some envy, "men began to know the name of the poet whose songs they had sung for years" (*Aut* 324). Hyde was now a frequent visitor to Coole, and he and Lady Gregory began their collaboration on a series of one-act Gaelic plays (Yeats contributed to the scenarios) for the proposed Irish theatre. As an active Gaelic Leaguer under Hyde's encouragement, Lady Gregory helped establish the annual *feis* in Killeeneen, the site of Raftery's grave. At the inaugural *feis* in August 1900, she erected a stone cross to mark the grave and perpetuate his memory as a poet of the people; it was at this time that Yeats inscribed in Lady Gregory's copy of *Poems* (1899) his quatrain adapted from Hyde's translation of a song from Raftery's eighteenth-century predecessor, "The Song of Heffernan the Blind: a translation."[15] At the ceremony and blessing of the cross, Yeats, a member of the platform with Lady Gregory and Hyde, spoke in support of the Gaelic language and affirmed his belief in the cultural revival, just as he did the previous February in *Beltaine*: "We are anxious to get plays in Irish, and can we do so will very possibly push our work into the western counties, where it would be an important help to that movement for the revival of the Irish language on which the life of the nation may depend."[16] Within his constant support of the League, however, he steadfastly defended his belief that a strong national tradition could also be built in English. At this time he was himself dismayed that Hyde's vision was becoming blurred by activities and causes that had begun to politicize the organization, and it may have been during or after this inaugural *feis* that he tried to refocus Hyde on what was for Yeats the primary, Raftery-inspired dream. He kept the encounter vividly in memory, recalling thirty years later that, while they were walking together, Hyde "heard haymakers sing what he recognised as

Lady Gregory published an edited version in *Our Irish Theatre* (New York: Capricorn Books, 1965), 8–9.

15. See Nancy Rutkowski Nash, "Yeats and Heffernan the Blind," *YA4*, 201–6.

16. *Beltaine: The Organ of the Irish Literary Theatre*, ed. W. B. Yeats, no. 2 (February 1900), 4.

his own words and I begged him to give up all coarse oratory that he might sing such words" (*Expl* 337).[17]

When Yeats and Farr began their lectures on the chanting of verse, he wrote "What Is 'Popular Poetry'?" (1901) to define the necessary relation of the written and unwritten traditions. He also expressed his hope that young authors writing in Gaelic might escape an illusory journalistic influence that "does not see, though it would cast out all English things, that its literary ideal belongs more to England than to other countries" (*E&I* 11). He told his cosmopolitan American audiences in 1903 that "we need not trust always to the written book. Why should we not recover again something of the old art of the troubadour?" (*YA8* 88). By 1905 Yeats's cultural vision and the role of poetry and drama in it had come into full focus, nowhere more succinctly stated than in a question he later posed in *The Trembling of the Veil*:

> We had in Ireland imaginative stories, which the uneducated classes knew and even sang, and might we not make those stories current among the educated classes, rediscovering for the work's sake what I have called "the applied arts of literature", the association of literature, that is, with music, speech, and dance; and at last, it might be, so deepen the political passion of the nation that all, artist and poet, craftsman and day-labourer would accept a common design?
>
> (*Aut* 167)

With the Abbey Theatre successfully established, Yeats knew that the time had arrived and that all was in place to take his vision of cultural unity and the gospel of chanted verse far and wide. Thus, in January 1906, he boldly launched his cultural campaign with a tour of Great Britain. Except for the one successful trip to Manchester in 1903, he and Farr had not ventured outside of London and Dublin, where they were accustomed to the mixed reactions of sophisticated audiences. Now they looked to such university towns as Dundee, Aberdeen, Edinburgh, Cork, Cambridge, Oxford, Liverpool, and Leeds, and as they sent circulars and canvassed for engagements they also made plans for a joint tour of America. Yeats had written to one of John Quinn's American agents:

> If possible, I should very much desire that Miss Florence Farr be engaged in conjunction with me, or for some Lectures in conjunction with me and for

17. In *Samhain* (1903) Yeats noted the return of Hyde the poet since that day in 1900: "he had ceased to write any verses but those Oireachtas odes that are but ingenious rhetoric. . . . But now Dr. Hyde with his cursing Hanrahan, his old saint at his prayers, is a poet again; and the Leaguers go to his plays in thousands" (*Expl* 104).

> others on her own account, to illustrate my theories by recitations of poetry to musical notes. . . . I found a constant difficulty while I was in America in making audiences understand certain things I said about recitation to a musical instrument, a constant need for Miss Farrs [*sic*] help. She has a most wonderful voice & method.
>
> (*CL4* 238–9)

While Quinn remained silent about a joint tour, engagements came in from Scotland and the north of England. Yeats told Farr at the outset:

> We shall have to make our own way in lecturing—one lecture will lead to another—we have not the advantage of the sort of popular subject which advertises a lecture by itself—our reputations are too esoteric for the general public outside certain university towns. We shall make our way by our faculty, not by our subjects or fame.
>
> (*CL4* 334)

Farr would now provide more commentary on her method as well as illustrate Yeats's theories, and to this end she wrote her own essay, "Music in Words" (1906; see Appendix 2). By mischance, the scheduling of the first lectures in Scotland conflicted with one of Farr's acting engagements: Yeats would not have missed the irony of her playing Mrs. Stockmann in Ibsen's *An Enemy of the People,* as he went off to begin their great mission alone.[18]

W. B. YEATS IN DUNDEE

THE MAN AND HIS LECTURE

> It is seldom, indeed, that Dundee, the practical and commercial, loses itself so utterly, as some hundreds of its citizens did last night, in listening to the inspired and inspiring utterances of Mr. Yeats.[19]

Yeats began his lectures on "Literature and the Living Voice" by lamenting the decline of imagination since the Renaissance and the corresponding loss of the "true aesthetic perception" of the world, "his eyes, now soft, now flashing fire, his musical voice, his whole being radiating enthusiasm and eagerness." He explained that in the old spiritual democracy, where

18. In mid-January 1906, Farr, in the midst of rehearsals, wrote to Gilbert Murray after the production of his translation of *Medea*: "I play Mrs Stockman with Tree the end of this week but am free Friday or Sunday daytime" (Bodleian). The actor-manager Herbert Tree, playing Dr. Stockmann, produced *An Enemy of the People* for three nights only, January 18–20, at His Majesty's Theatre.
19. *The Courier & Argus* (Dundee), January 12, 1906, 7.

classes of people were bound together by their imaginative possessions, the minstrel's songs and stories appealed to prince and ploughman alike, but in the modern "aristocracy of culture," where a life of imagination and thought was confined to a few thousands among millions, literature had less and less hold on the mass of the people. Such a cleavage, with the culture of an intellectual aristocracy hopelessly cut off from an emotional people, was largely created by the printing press, which gradually replaced the minstrel and the player, depriving the populace of their source of imaginative culture. If in the past the peasant had want of imagination, he at least possessed a fine memory, a vital faculty now greatly diminished by the power of print. The widespread dissemination of cheap literature, like the machine replacing the hand, had inculcated a drab uniformity of thought, a vulgarity of taste and belief. Unable to choose literature for themselves, the common people now read vulgar imitations of fine literature, even as in clothes the poorest garments, unsuited to the occupations of the wearers, are coarsely cut after the aristocratic style. As the reporter noted, "His philosophy of clothes, reminiscent of Teufelsdrockh, was delightful, and the audience chuckled appreciatively at his analogy of the raiment of a leisured gentleman and a scarecrow." The point of the analogy, stated succinctly in "The Galway Plains" (1903), grew out of his continuing dialogue with Arnold: "The poet must always prefer the community where the perfected minds express the people, to a community that is vainly seeking to copy the perfected minds" (*E&I* 214).

MR. W. B. YEATS IN ABERDEEN

INTERESTING LECTURE

> They must make the drama to be regarded as a serious art even in small communities. He had one theatre in Ireland which played Irish dramas, and though many were poor, all had a fineness to some extent which appealed to the people.... If we had produced a political democracy we had lost the spiritual democracy to which the troubadours sang.[20]

Yeats gave great urgency to the need to recapture a spirit of culture which does not regard literature from a utilitarian point of view and which nourishes the aesthetic perception of life, lest all intellectual life decay. "In Ireland to-day," he said, "the old world that sang and listened

20. *The Aberdeen Daily Journal*, January 13, 1906, 3.

is, it may be for the last time in Europe, face to face with the world that reads and writes, and their antagonism is always present under some name or other in Irish imagination and intellect" (*Expl* 206). Yeats saw Ireland as one of several small nations on a crucial cultural battleground fighting to protect "an old picturesque conception of life" from "that modern, utilitarian, commercial civilization which has been organized by a few great nations," such as England. Defeat of the former by the latter, he believed, would be a defeat for culture: "if we are to find victory," he had argued, "we must somehow or other change our arms and our formation of battle" (*YA8* 87). To counter the effects of modern culture and its printing presses, Yeats wanted the theatres to help preserve and spread folk literature, believing fervently that when there is good literature among the people there is "fine feeling, a conception of life far higher than where you have only the little weekly paper of scraps and jokes."[21] Though it might take centuries, the old culture could be made to prevail again—by deposing the printed word as the means of culture and by reviving the oral tradition, adapting it to modern needs, as the Irish theatre had begun to do. "He wished this were done in this country, and the spoken literature would come back. There were four centuries of printing against twenty of spoken literature." All national language movements, Yeats argued, including the Gaelic movement, are parallel attempts to revive a spiritual democracy for the common people. "That this is the decisive element in the attempt to revive and to preserve the Irish language I am very certain" (*Expl* 205). The Irish theatre complemented and worked in harmony with the Gaelic League, for it would be difficult to revive the oral tradition until the people had a common knowledge of legend and story.[22]

21. "Mr. W. B. Yeats in Leeds," *Yorkshire Daily Observer*, March 15, 1906, 7; also in NLI MS 12146, 55, as an unidentified clipping.

22. In December 1905 AE had chastised Yeats for offending young writers, journalists, and members of the Gaelic League, stating that "if you wish to lead a movement you can only do so by silence on points which irritate you or by kindly suggestions to the people.... Look at Hydes power compared with your own and you have twenty times his ability. Fall out of their affections and they will turn on you like Healy or Parnell.... You may lose all your present actors who are not paid, as they will probably meet continually the young men in the clubs who will say you are confessedly not a Nationalist... I am giving you the situation as it appears to me... Remember there is Martyn, Moore, Colm who is young and who may be swept from you by the tide of popular resentment & the Gaelic League which has no affection for you, and an amalgamation of all the dissenters with a Gaelic dramatic society associated with it would leave you Synge, Lady Gregory, & Boyle with yourself and none of these have drawing power in Dublin" (*LTWBY1* 153).

MR. W. B. YEATS IN LEEDS

MODERN MINSTRELSY

> In prevailing upon Mr. W. B. Yeats to give a lecture in the city, the Leeds Arts Club enabled an audience which filled the Philosophical Hall last night to enter into an intellectual region contrasting strangely with the workaday world. Mr. Alfred Orage, who presided, confessed to feeling a sense of incongruity in a lecture upon poetry in relation to the human voice being given in busy, practical Leeds, but when the time for dispersing came many who were present would gladly have lingered.[23]

If modern writers were meanwhile to reach the workingman, they must put literature more in touch with life by embodying the spoken art in the printed book. By making their work simpler, and by adapting the language to the spoken as distinguished from the printed work, "they would bring back to literature a great deal of the masculine vitality they found in writers like Chaucer, who wrote essentially for the ear, and in whose works the variety of the world flowed in on every page." Yeats told his audience that from Chaucer he had discovered the need to simplify his own work and had rewritten his plays to increase their "masculine force."[24] As he rephrased the matter for Quinn, following revision of *The Shadowy Waters*, "I believe more strongly every day that the element of strength in poetic language is common idiom, just as the element of strength in poetic construction is common passion" (*CL4* 179).

Yeats thrilled his northern audiences with descriptions of Ireland's western townlands, where the old culture still lingered and the old songs and stories still brought refinement to illiterate minds. In some villages, not yet invaded by modern life, every colleen could add a verse to a lament, and Yeats often closed his lecture by chanting Lady Gregory's translation of the deserted Aran fisher-girl's lament, the audience "listening with an enthralled silence more eloquent than the loudest applause":[25]

23. "Mr. W. B. Yeats in Leeds." A. R. Orage and Holbrook Jackson were co-founders of the Leeds Arts Club before moving to London in 1907 to become co-editors of *The New Age*.

24. On May 18, 1906, with Chaucer again firmly in mind, Yeats wrote that for him the writing of drama "has been the search for more of manful energy, more of the cheerful acceptance of whatever arises out of the logic of events, and for clean outline, instead of those outlines of lyric poetry that are blurred with desire and vague regret." See Yeats's "Preface" to *Poems, 1899–1905* (London: A. H. Bullen, 1906), p. xii (*VP* 849).

25. *The Courier & Argus*, 7.

> You have taken the east from me;
> you have taken the west from me;
> you have taken what is before me and what is behind me;
> you have taken the moon, you have taken the sun from me;
> and my fear is great you have taken God from me![26]

The poems of the folk, he asserted, contain their individual joys and sorrows and are the only "true" poems. For years he had longed to write such "popular" poetry, a term he abandoned in "What is 'Popular Poetry'?" when he realized it had come to characterize the debased poetry of the middle class, "of people who have unlearned the unwritten tradition which binds the unlettered . . . to the beginning of time and to the foundation of the world" (*E&I* 6). The poetry he and Lady Gregory had found in Galway and the Aran Islands

> was not what people understood as popular poetry, but it was what was recognised as true poetry. It was of the kind produced formerly by the art of men whose minds had doors opening out into the great assembly houses of the ages, in which all was thought and culture. . . . It was the poetry of ancient and perfect culture. It was the culture of the people which went back to ages and ages.[27]

To Yeats, the true poetry of the folk possesses genuine beauty, in contrast to most poetry of the contemporary coteries, which possesses mere prettiness. In the distant past the art of the people mingled with the art of the coteries, and true folk poetry could once again have its counterpart in written poetry that is established upon the unwritten, the tradition to which Yeats would have modern poets return:

> There is only one kind of good poetry, for the poetry of the coteries, which presupposes the written tradition, does not differ in kind from the true poetry of the people, which presupposes the unwritten tradition. Both are alike strange and obscure, and unreal to all who have not understanding, and both, instead of that manifest logic, that clear rhetoric of the "popular poetry," glimmer with thoughts and images whose "ancestors were stout and wise," "anigh to Paradise" "ere yet men knew the gift of corn."
>
> (*E&I* 8)

26. A full translation of the poem, entitled "The Grief of a Girl's Heart," was first published in Lady Gregory's "West Irish Folk Ballads," *The Monthly Review* (October 1902), 123–35, though Yeats quoted a large portion of the translation as early as 1901 in "What Is 'Popular Poetry'?" (*E&I* 9).
27. "Mr. Yeats Unbosoms Himself," *Evening Telegraph* (Dublin), February 14, 1907, 2.

And there may be a way, he hinted, turning to his own plan for the theatre, of making something like "perfect culture" and "good poetry" prevail again. As he told a group of Trinity College students, following a discussion of modern drama, they must help him close the gap between the educated class and the emotional people: "You here," he said, "who represent the educated and cultured class, should support us artists in carrying out our work, and help us to guide the wild horse of the people by putting into the saddle education and culture."[28]

VOICE AND VERSE

NEW ART OF MUSICAL RECITATION

Mr. W. B. Yeats and a Novel Experience

> The harmony between the word and the incidental music was closer than one has experienced before. Mr. Yeats and Miss Farr are clearly on the right track and should be encouraged to proceed.[29]

Florence Farr joined Yeats for Leeds and Liverpool, appearing in her striking "artistic costume" to elucidate and illustrate her attempts to recover the music and power of magical words. Whereas the songwriter took a poem and tried to express in music the emotions behind it, she tried to express the music inherent in the poet's words. The psaltery, by admitting the employment of quarter-tones, lends itself to the tune of a word and the cadence of a line. "It is only by listening very carefully to the little tunes contained in every word," she wrote, "that one comes to divine something of the real meaning of the tradition of magic words. . . . An eight-barred folk-melody has more power to create a lasting impression on the sources of emotion, if it be repeated often enough, than elaborate orchestral effects."[30]

The first part of her program included selections from Homer, Gilbert Murray's translations from Euripides, and lyrics by Yeats and Verlaine. "Then, accompanying herself, she recited the paraphrase 'By the waters of Babylon, we sat down and wept,' and Orage was visibly moved by the

28. "Trinity College Students," *Evening Telegraph* (Dublin), February 14, 1907, 2.

29. *The Leeds and Yorkshire Mercury*, March 15, 1906, 6.

30. "Music in Words," *Musical World*, 5 (September 15, 1906), 67–8 (see Appendix 2); rpt. in Farr's *The Music of Speech* (London: Elkin Matthews, 1909), 17–21.

sad strains, holding back his tears with difficulty."[31] She concluded with a variety of old Irish songs and laments. "In all of them," wrote the Leeds critic, "but more particularly in the Greek and old Irish selections, written for the ear, she amply proved that the theory held by herself and Mr. Yeats is no idle dream, but that a modern art of minstrelsy would be a welcome development."[32] Throughout the tour the audiences and the press were effusive with appreciation. Capacity crowds met every engagement, quickly dispelling their initial fears of sparse attendance. As a speaking poet in search of a richer culture, Yeats was clearly in his prime. And Farr's voice had reached such a "wondrous" peak of subtle expressiveness that he was moved to dedicate a new edition of *In the Seven Woods* "TO FLORENCE FARR | The only reciter of lyric poetry | who is always a delight, because | of the beauty of her voice and | the rightness of her method."[33]

A NEW VOCAL ART

DUAL LECTURE AT THE UNIVERSITY

> His present effort was directed to recreate the applied arts of literature, to give song and recitation their right place in the work of culture.[34]

To Yeats, only literature and the arts keep alive the great conceptions of life in men's and women's minds. In presenting his concept of the theatre's role in creating a spiritual democracy, he re-stationed the poet and his theatre at the center of culture, holding that the poet, not the government official, perpetually creates the "types" that culture desires. "Laws and education," he declared, speaking as if he were Seanchan on the king's threshold, "tried to perpetuate a type which their authors thought would be of use to the race, but the poet shaped the type which benefited the race."[35] In shaping a culture's sense of significant life, the image-making poet labors to create a whole literature, writing lyric and narrative as well as dramatic verse, and his theatre helps to transmit this literature throughout culture by training living voices for his words. As reported, "It is his aim to make modern lyricism not so much a written as a spoken art, and he

31. See Mary Gawthorpe, *Uphill to Holloway* (Penobscot, ME: Traversity Press, 1962), 196.
32. "Mr. W. B. Yeats in Leeds," 7.
33. *Poems, 1899–1905*, [140], (*VP* 850).
34. *The Liverpool Daily Post and Mercury*, March 16, 1906, 8.
35. *The Aberdeen Daily Journal*, 3.

seeks the means to do this largely through the theatre."[36] Yeats elaborated his vision of the theatre's domain in his essay:

> But if we are to delight our three or four thousand young men and women with a delight that will follow them into their own houses, and if we are to add the countryman to their number, we shall need more than the play, we shall need those other spoken arts. The player rose into importance in the town, but the minstrel is of the country. We must have narrative as well as dramatic poetry, and we are making room for it in the theatre in the first instance.
>
> (*Expl* 213)

Three years earlier, in his persistent preparation for such a theatre, Yeats had, with a sense of both neglect and expectation, turned his own interest back to narrative poetry, writing "The Old Age of Queen Maeve" and "Baile and Aillinn." Since the formulation of his initial conception, however, the Irish theatre had developed mostly on dramatic lines, particularly and most quickly along the lines of peasant comedy. "We have done nothing for the story-tellers," he explained, "but now that our country comedies, with their abundant and vivid speech, are well played and well spoken, we may try out the whole adventure."[37]

The "whole adventure" involved turning the theatre into a sort of speech guild for culture, using its workshops to restore all the spoken arts, training minstrels and reciters for the countryside as well as actors for the stage. On the dramatic side, the Abbey was already under a plan of reorganization to provide for performances in Irish towns. On the lyric and narrative side, he explained, using Morris as his analogue, the Abbey was on the threshold of a movement "which might, perhaps, be called the applied art of literature as distinguished from the applied art of design."[38] It was a modest beginning, but if other theatres began teaching the spoken arts to generations of players and reciters, an oral tradition might thrive once again. In his new theatre of speech, infused with the spirits of Chaucer and Morris, he began to answer the question he continually posed to himself: "How can I make my work mean something to vigorous and simple men whose attention is not given to art but to a shop, or teaching in a National School, or dispensing medicine?" (*E&I* 265). Farr, removed by Barker from

36. *The Leeds and Yorkshire Mercury*, 6.
37. "Notes," *Samhain*, 3.
38. *Evening Telegraph*, 2.

the chorus that exploited her music, returned to London from Liverpool to begin rehearsing her new role as the Nurse for the revival of *Hippolytus* at the Court.

III

No modern poet has had a greater sense of community than Yeats, nor a more romantic vision of becoming a poet of the people. From the time he wrote his earliest ballads and adaptations of Irish songs, he yearned to hear his poems sung as Homer had been sung. He wanted the people to recognize him in the same way that Ariosto was recognized by the sailors who captured him—by the poetry which they had not read but heard sung. Yeats would be Ireland's new Raftery, finding delight in hearing the people murmur the cadences of his poems, finding pleasure "from that tale of Dante hearing a common man sing some stanza from the *Divine Comedy*, and from Don Quixote's meeting with some common man that sang Ariosto."[39] Yeats said, in defining the extra-dramatic scope of the Abbey, "I have begun my real business. I have to find once again singers, minstrels, and players who love words more than any other thing under heaven, for without fine words there is no literature" (*Expl* 210). The minstrel and players would take the poet's words to the people, and in an Elizabethan spirit still alive and receptive in Ireland, they would create a joyful and reckless theatre of romance, extravagance, fantasy, whimsy, naiveté, and energy. "Above all," he affirmed in December 1906,

> it will be a theatre of speech; the speech of the country-side, the eloquence of poets, of rhythm, of style, of proud, living, unwasted words, and among its players there may be some who can sing like a poet of Languedoc stories and songs where the music shall be as simple as in a sailor's chanty, for I would restore the whole ancient art of passionate speech . . . The labour of

39. *Aut* 165; Yeats's story of Ariosto's capture by the sailors is recounted in *The Aberdeen Daily Journal*, 3: "If poems were to be set to music, it must be done as sailor chanteries were set, as the mediaeval epics were set. Ariosto was once captured, but released when he declared himself. His captors knew his poetry, but not by reading it. They had heard it sung as the poems of Homer were sung by the people."

> two players, Miss Florence Farr and Mr. Frank Fay, have done enough to show that all is possible, if the summer be lucky and the corn ripen.[40]

The troubadours in Yeats's dream were to be called reciters in the Abbey, after the *reacaire* of the ancient poetic colleges of the Celtic world. These colleges trained the *File,* the poetic "seer" who was second in rank only to the king and who served as the curator and re-animator of the inner life which held the people and the culture together. The *File* was dependent upon the fully trained *reacaire,* or reciter, to take his poems to the people. Yeats had first conceived his troubadours in this context in "Speaking to the Psaltery," where he described them as "well-taught and well-mannered speakers" who will know

> how to keep from singing notes and from prosaic lifeless intonations . . . and they will have by heart, like the Irish *File*, so many poems and notations that they will never have to bend their heads over the book, to the ruin of dramatic expression and of that wild air the bard had always about him in my boyish imagination. They will go here and there speaking their verses and their little stories wherever they can find a score or two of poetical-minded people in a big room, or a couple of poetical-minded friends sitting by the hearth, and poets will write them poems and little stories to the confounding of print and paper.
>
> (*E&I* 19)[41]

MR. YEATS' LECTURE ON LITERATURE AND THE LIVING VOICE

> Mr. Yeats has a mission. I am not sure how he would define it, but to me it seems to be this. He would restore what he called imaginative culture by bringing back the old art of telling and listening to stories. . . . Mr. Yeats now went on to speak of the special place of the reciter among the applied arts of literature.[42]

When Yeats first began to think about the theatre, he held the actor doubly responsible for the reciter's art, asserting as early as 1894 that "the actor should be a reverent reciter of majestic words" (*UP1* 325). By the

40. "Preface," *The Poetical Works of William B. Yeats* (New York: Macmillan, 1907), ii, pp. vii–viii (*VPl* 1294).

41. Yeats alludes to his earlier poem, "To Some I Have Talked with by the Fire," in which his heart "brims with dreams about the times | When we bent down above the fading coals, | And talked of the dark folk who live in the souls | Of passionate men" (*VP* 136).

42. *The Sphinx* (Liverpool University), March–April 1906, 147. Clipped and pasted in NLI MS 12146.

time he and Farr began their chanting experiments, and after he had some experience of actors, he had separated the two arts altogether. The struggle for a romantic theatre demanded that he distinguish the nature of the reciter and describe his special role in the theatre's applied arts movement.

Yeats aproached the "true" reciter's art by first comparing the "arts" of modern recitation and modern acting, the former being merely a "poor imitation" of the latter. "Modern recitation is not, like modern theatrical art, an over-elaboration of a true art, but an entire misunderstanding. It has no tradition at all. It is an endeavour to do what can only be done well by the player. It has no relation of its own to life" (*Expl* 214). Yeats often derided elocutionists for making a mockery of poetic meter and emotion, and in his new lecture he played anecdotally for audience agreement:

> The modern recitation, confused with acting, was ridiculous (applause). He never enjoyed but one recitation. It was tragic, and a little child, having stood thumb in mouth in amaze, suddenly ran with a scream from the room, thus expressing his (the lecturer's) feelings perfectly (laughter and applause).[43]

In his serious attempt to restore to the reciter the integrity and mysteriousness that the elocutionists now demeaned, his imagination fed on the minstrel tradition from Raftery back to Wolfram of Eschenbach. In the spirit of these predecessors, his reciters would appear on stage and in public places, where with fictitious names and appropriately extravagant costumes they would jest for the attention of an audience.

> Many costumes and persons come into my imagination. I imagine an old countryman upon the stage of the theatre or in some little country courthouse where a Gaelic society is meeting, and I can hear him say that he is Raftery or a brother, and that he has tramped through France and Spain and the whole world.
>
> (*Expl* 216)

In the summer of 1904, anticipating a reciter for the Abbey opening, he had Charles Ricketts make costume designs for a Black Jester. In thanking him, he wrote: "And so soon as I can make some little progress with the poems I have in my mind for recitation, I will have the costume made" (*CL3* 627). Neither the plan nor the costume ever materialized, but now the costume designs re-entered his imagination:

43. *The Liverpool Daily Post and Mercury*, 8.

> I can imagine, too—and now the story-teller is more serious and more naked of country circumstance—a jester with black cockscomb and black clothes. He has been in the faery hills; perhaps he is the terrible *Amadán-na-Breena* himself; or he has been so long in the world that he can tell of ancient battles. It is not as good as what we have lost, but we cannot hope to see in our time, except by some rare accident, the minstrel who differs from his audience in nothing but the exaltation of his mood, and who is yet as exciting and as romantic in their eyes as were Raftery and Wolfram to their people.
>
> (*Expl* 216–17)

"We cannot of a certainty," wrote Yeats in presenting his idea of the reciter to his Irish audience in *Samhain* (1906), "try it all at one time, and it will be easier for our audience to follow fragmentary experiments, now that the dream is there upon the paper."[44]

The reciter cannot be a player, because in his art he must possess and retain a strong and unique "personality." Unlike the actor, he dramatizes only himself in striving to re-live the story, not to act it. Most modern poems, when spoken to an audience, sounded artificial because a living voice was giving expression to impersonal and abstract words, but when poems are written to be sung of spoken they have, when spoken by a passionate reciter, a simplicity and sincerity that seem a natural expression of emotional life. Yeats thus wanted his reciter to be a "whole man," one who would have a strong personal appeal to the folk, a musical voice, and a natural impulse to express the emotions and stories felt in the depths of his mind, like some of the Gaelic storytellers Yeats had met and heard. Such men had helped lead him "to this certainty: what moves natural men in the arts is what moves them in life, and that is, intensity of personal life, intonations that show them, in a book or a play, the strength, the

44. "Notes," *Samhain*, 3. Yeats actually began to experiment with his audience in February 1906 by introducing Irish music between the acts. He enlisted the services of Herbert Hughes, founder of the Irish Folk Song Society, and of Arthur Darley, who, appropriately, "has tramped through the remotest parts of Ireland, collecting from wayfaring minstrels those legendary airs that have been handed down through generations of wandering fiddlers and harpists" (NLI MS 13068). Yeats also planned to involve the poets of the Abbey Theatre in various experiments in music and poetry, writing to Katharine Tynan on September 1 of his "plans for improving our new poets myself. I want to get them to write songs to be sung between the acts. Herbert Hughs [*sic*] will set them & we have a fine singer in Miss Allgood. I hope to begin with two groups of songs—one selected from 'The Rushlight Man' [Joseph Campbell], Colum & so on & one chosen from [Lionel] Johnson, you & myself. I will get them sung so as to make the words as expressive as possible. I am not quite sure that the time has come yet but I shall get one or two things set as a start. One has to go slowly, perfecting first one thing & then another. We have got our peasant work very good now, & are starting on our verse work" (*CL4* 490).

essential moment of a man who would be exciting in the market or at the dispensary door" (*E&I* 265). In defining the role of the player-reciter in his new theatre, Yeats found the fullest expression of his doctrine of personal utterance.

After the tour of provincial cities and universities in the spring of 1906, Yeats and Farr continued to give performances of "Literature and the Living Voice" whenever invitations came, and when Farr could not join him he lectured alone, determined as he was not to break the momentum of the cultural movement. Not even the turbulent aftermath of the *Playboy* riots diverted him from his mission in Dublin.

> MR. YEATS UNBOSOMS HIMSELF
>
> ON LITERATURE & THE STAGE
>
> *"The Living Voice."*
>
> **Poetry in the Aran Isles.**
>
> **Poetic Drama Impossible.**
>
> **Taste of the People Debased.**
>
> **Printed Book Should Be Deposed.**
>
> **Scarcely Any Intellect in Ireland.**
>
> The playhouse could only get back to its old uses by the gradual awakening and existence of
>
> **An Increasing Interest In Speech**
>
> itself. That could come by making songs, actions, and other things a part of dramatic literature. . . . To get to the second of the vocal arts—the narrative style—they were obliged to go back to the reciter.[45]

The formal training of the reciter would relate not only to the subtle techniques of the narrative style, but also to the education and development of his personality. As Yeats intimated, "The reciter must be made exciting and wonderful in himself, apart from what he has to tell, and that is more difficult than it was in the Middle Ages" (*Expl* 216). The difficulty

45. *Evening Telegraph*, 2.

notwithstanding, Yeats believed that the heightening of personality should come ideally through adeptship in a magical society. The ideal reciter, too, would have a magical vision of life that informs his being and gives him the air of excitement and mysteriousness that commands and holds attention. He is, in Yeats's term, a "messenger" of the poet, and before he recites the poet-magician's poem he must have a learned understanding of its symbol and sound. As the creative process is analogous, in Yeats's mind, to the magical process, the reciter's knowledge of ancient secrets significantly increases his interpretive power. Yeats told an interviewer that his model reciter, former adept Florence Farr, "alone among modern readers has the genius . . . to apprehend and reproduce the subtle music which haunts the poet's brain."[46] The reciter learns the art of regulated declamation to preserve this music, but in voicing the "far-off things" of the poet, he expresses the poetic emotion through his own vibrant personality, "with his own peculiar animation":

> His art is nearer to pattern than that of the player. It is always allusion, never illusion; for what he tells of, no matter how impassioned he may become, is always distant, and for this reason he may permit himself every kind of nobleness.
>
> (*Expl* 215)

The reciter and all the hieratic elements of his art—the wavering intonations, the rhythmic movements of the body, the notes sounded on the psaltery—take on "nobleness" through his attempt to make visible and audible the divine music that the poet has heard and symbolically embodied in the poem. The reciter keeps the power of the poem communal and off the solitary page; Yeats's own comment on the visibility of poetic emotion touches a motive force behind his revival of the art of speaking to musical notes:

> All circumstance that makes emotion at once dignified and visible increases the poet's power, and I think that is why I have always longed for some stringed instrument, and a listening audience, not drawn out of the hurried streets, but from a life where it would be natural to murmur over again the singer's thought.
>
> (*E&I* 295)

46. See Pelham Edgar, "The Poetry of William Butler Yeats," *The Globe* (Toronto), December 24, 1904, Saturday Magazine Section, 5.

As Florence Farr helped to explain, the reciter emphasizes the music and cadence of the words, slowly creating that magical unity of mood necessary for unleashing the poet's power, an evocative power that unlocks in the unconscious mind the universal images and rhythms perceived by the poet. The enchanted audience, having become, in Yeats's words, "a single mind, a single energy," are moved to "murmur" these shared rhythms after the poet or reciter, as did the listeners of Dante, Ariosto, Petrarch and others who wrote for the people. The murmuring of divine cadences begins with Yeats's earliest poetic wanderers—with Oisin, who hears with Niamh the continuous "low murmurs" of the enchanted Danaan land (*VP* 13), and particularly with King Goll, who, "Murmuring, to a fitful tune," tears the strings out of his tympan in his attempt to express "some inhuman misery" (*VP* 85). Later, in "The Two Trees," the poet tells his beloved that the holy tree "made my lips and music wed, | Murmuring a wizard song for thee" (*VP* 134). His more recent mythical counterpart, Seanchan, has heard "Murmurs that are the ending of all sound" (*VPl* 187), murmurs which become the music of his poetry. Seanchan's pupils, gathered by King Guaire, are described precisely as reciters, as those "that understand stringed instruments, | And how to mingle words and notes together | So artfully that all the Art's but Speech | Delighted with its own music" (*VPl* 257).

In *The King's Threshold*, Yeats manipulates the heroic myth into an expression of his own cultural struggles and ideals. Like the herdsman whose song is murmured by the children in the play, his reciters would carry the poet's magical cadences in ballad, rann, story, and song to the children of Ireland, thereby linking the mind of the people to the mind of the poet, which is itself linked to the mind of Nature. In this role they join and extend the poet in his desire to restore the aesthetic perception of life, to recreate imaginative culture, and to reconstitute a spiritual democracy. "If we accomplish this great work," Yeats concluded, "if we make it possible again for the poet to express himself, not merely through words, but through the voices of singers, of minstrels, of players, we shall certainly have changed the substance and the manner of our poetry" (*Expl* 220).

Yeats and Farr were now ready to think about taking the new art to America, but when Yeats first broached the matter with Quinn he was discouraged from accompanying Farr on a joint tour. Quinn wrote circumspectly on July 13, 1906: "This is, after all, a provincial people. . . . for you two to come would be too risky, too easily misunderstood" (*LJQ* 77).

Yeats knew that such advice meant that the new art would be received as an artistic curiosity in isolation from the great cultural and theatrical scheme that might foster its widespread future. For three years he had anticipated telling the Americans of his theatre of speech, and he was not to be put off by Quinn's moral cautions, but his plans were suddenly diverted by a new crisis that would have kept him at home in any case—the riots following the opening of Synge's *The Playboy of the Western World* in January 1907. A few days later Farr sailed for America alone, leaving Yeats in the din and debate of controversy.

7
Minstrel Abroad

I

In January 1907 Farr prepared for her first trip to America with great excitement, gathering letters of introduction, writing for engagements, printing publicity photographs, and seeking advice from friends who had preceded her abroad. Her mission was to introduce the psaltery as an instrument for chanting poems and classical choruses in preparation for a more extended tour with Yeats. In planning her programs, she wrote to Quinn on January 8 that "Mrs. Patrick Campbell thinks they would like me to give readings from Gilbert Murray's *Hippolytus* with the choruses on a psaltery. She believes in me much more *without* the psaltery than with it," adding that Yeats's friend from San Francisco, Agnes Tobin, "believes in the Nietzsche translations."[1] She took comfort in knowing that Dorothy Paget, who had signed a one-year contract with the Forbes Robertson company in America, and Pixie Smith, who was storytelling and holding an exhibition of her drawings at a Fifth Avenue gallery, would both be in New York to greet and assist her. On the London side, her friend W. L. Courtney, editor of the *Fortnightly Review,* gave her a good send-off in the *Daily Telegraph.*[2] Thus, on January 30 she sailed from Liverpool on the *Baltic*, taking the psaltery, copies of her printed circulars, and a variety of costumes, including a gown with a trailing train designed for her by Ricketts.

1. The unpublished letters from Florence Farr to John Quinn quoted in this chapter are in the Quinn Papers, Manuscripts Division, NYPL.
2. *Daily Telegraph*, January 12, 1907, 11. "She intends to give readings of Greek plays and chant the choruses to the music on the psaltery, such as she wrote for the production of 'Hippolytus' at the Court Theatre. She will also give recitations of ballads and lyrics with or without musical accompaniment." Her arrival on February 8 was noticed in the New York *Herald* of February 9, which announced in its "Theatrical Jottings" that she was "to appear here in readings of Greek plays and recitations" (12).

Her planned six-week tour would be extended to three months as she chanted her way into the drawing rooms of some of America's wealthiest patrons and enjoyed numerous public engagements in New York, Boston, Buffalo, Chicago, Philadelphia, and Toronto. Quinn had made several arrangements for her, prompting Yeats to write gratefully to him on February 18, in the aftermath of the *Playboy* turmoil: "It is good of you to take so much trouble about Mrs Emery she & Lady Gregory are my closest friends. She is a charming person, kind & gentle." He added, perhaps as a hint of their intimate relationship and as a caveat to Quinn to keep his proper distance from her, "I have seen a great deal of her of late especially, & it has been in part my urging that sent her to America" (*CL4* 630).[3]

Yeats had some hope of escaping the *Playboy* turmoil and joining her, but in the meantime he had put her in touch with some of the hostesses who had entertained him on his American tour, including Julia Ellsworth Ford, wife of the wealthy hotelier Simeon Ford, of Rye, New York, and Julia H. Worthington, a socially prominent New Yorker who had entertained Yeats at her country home on the Hudson. As Nina Wilcox Putnam described her, "Mrs. Ford collected celebrities as some people collect postage stamps."[4] Mrs. Ford had met Yeats at Yale in November 1903, arranged for his lecture at the New York Arts Club, and co-authored an article on him for *Poet-Lore.* Though she was, in Putnam's view, "ugly, overburdened with art-jewelry, nervous and all-enveloping," she was a generous hostess and the author of plays, stories, art criticism, and a privately printed book, *AE: A Note of Appreciation* (1906). "Dorothy Paget said that Mrs. Simeon Ford has asked me to stay with her 20 miles out of New York," Farr wrote to Quinn before departure, "but Mr. Yeats says I'd better keep in New York itself until I see what set will take to me best. It's all very difficult isn't it?" While she booked into the Hotel Martha Washington on East 29th

3. Quinn was apologetically six months late in answering this letter, replying on August 23, "I did what I could for Mrs. Emery and think I opened a few doors and smoothed out a few rough places. I think, all things considered, she did very well" (*LJQ* 85). Yeats had some reason to worry about Quinn's inevitable advances to Farr. As Francis King writes in *Ritual Magic in England* (London: Neville Spearman, 1970), "The surviving Golden Dawn tradition is that Florence Farr was not a nymphomaniac—that she was not really greatly interested in sex—but that she was almost incapable of saying no to any man who asked her to sleep with him. I am satisfied that, on one occasion at least, she had physical intercourse with Aleister Crowley" (202). Quinn had met Farr during his three-week vacation in London in the autumn of 1904, writing to Yeats on his return, "Please say to Mrs. Emery that I was sorry not to have the pleasure of seeing her again before I left" (*LJQ* 63).
4. Nina Wilcox Putnam, *Laughing Through* (New York, 1930), 213.

for her Manhattan base, the two hostesses gladly engaged Farr for her first performances with the psaltery in America, arranging two programs as an "entertainment" at the Barnard Club of New York.

William Archer had written to John Corbin, the dramatic critic of the New York *Sun*, urging him to attend her recitations and give her advance notices. He was thus present at the Barnard Club for the first program, delayed by a week, on February 20 to witness her reading of Greek plays and chanting of the choruses, "in reality a recital in what is supposed to be the manner of the Greeks." She then lectured briefly on "Heroic and Folk Poetry," illustrating with chants from epics and ballads by Lady Gregory, Douglas Hyde, William Morris, and others. In announcing her second program on lyric poetry at Barnard the following week, Corbin presented her to New Yorkers as the recognized exponent in England of a new art in speaking verse. "She calls it 'lilting,' " he wrote, a technique which "consists in reciting poetic numbers with an irregular, sometimes intermittent, cadence that is at once musical and quite natural to the speaking voice." He identified Yeats as "the begetter of the idea of lilting," Dolmetsch as the musician who has "furnished forth with the musicianly skill Mr. Yeats lacks," and Farr as the practitioner who "deserves the attention of all who are interested in the subtler phrases of dramatic art." Corbin was himself fascinated by Farr and would write about her again before she departed. "At the end of the month Miss Farr leaves us to go to Boston," he lamented, "but promises to return for further illustrative talks and *conférences.*"[5]

After her second lecture at the Barnard Club, the Corbins held a recitation party to introduce her to more socialites and editors. Quinn's friend Mrs. Alice Brisbane Thursby, whom Farr had met in London at a meeting of the Irish Literary Society, was there, but her brother Arthur Brisbane, the highly influential editor of the New York *Evening Journal*, failed to appear; however, Norman Hapgood, chief editor of *Collier's Weekly*, did attend, and he was so impressed by the chanting that he promised to write Mrs. Jack Gardner, the prominent hostess and art collector in Boston, to say that her recital was "unique and lovely." Mrs. Patrick Campbell's friend, Mrs. Clarence Mackay (Katherine Duer, wife of the wealthy Chicago capitalist in cable, telegraph, and telephone companies), arrived with promises of assistance, but the highlight of the evening for Farr came after her

5. *New York Sun*, February 16, 1907. This edition of the *Sun* is untraced; clipping in Robinson Locke Collection, series e, p. 3 (Newspaper Division, NYPL).

performance with the psaltery, when Corbin informed her that he would try to place an article in the phenomenally successful *Saturday Evening Post*, which then boasted a circulation of a million copies a week under the literary editorship of George Horace Lorimer.

News of her early success spread rapidly as she performed in and out of New York. Cornelius Weygandt, who had received a letter of introduction to Farr from Yeats, heard her chant the choral lyrics of Yeats's unpublished *Deirdre* at Bryn Mawr College in Philadelphia on February 18.[6] The next week she was at Mrs. Field's Club in Brooklyn, followed by a performance at a children's hospital benefit in the Waldorf-Astoria. Yeats wrote to Lady Gregory on March 2 that Percy French had turned up that afternoon with word that a friend of his "had heard from Dolmetsch that Mrs. Emery is doing very well in America" (*CL4* 633). As her Harvard lecture had been delayed, and as Wellesley College had not come through on the grounds that it was "too late in the year," her arrival in Boston and reunion with Dolmetsch was now delayed until mid-March, so she stayed in New York to give private lessons, to have a photographic sitting with Alice Boughton, and to work on piecing together a full itinerary. A letter of introduction from William Archer had put her in correspondence with Professor George Pierce Baker of Harvard, who was trying to find engagements for her in the Cambridge–Boston area. Baker's *The Development of Shakespeare as a Dramatist* (1907) was in press; the young T. S. Eliot, a freshman in Baker's class and a friend of Mrs. Gardner, may have been among the admiring Harvard students, one of whom would be selected to give Farr a tour of Harvard.[7] She was also to receive what she thought an "unsatisfactory" letter from Dolmetsch, who was busy rehearsing a new concert series; after earlier assuring her that he could secure five bookings, he had to leave

6. Cornelius Weygandt, *Irish Plays and Playwrights* (London: Constable, 1913), 25. Yeats had written to Weygandt on February 13 "may I introduce Miss Florence Farr (Mrs Emery) of whom you have heard me speak. She speaks verse more beautifully than [any]body in the world" (*CL4* 622).

7. Eliot was a student in English 28hf: English Literature: History and Development of English Literature in Outline, taught by professors Baker, Briggs, Hall, Kittredge, and Wendell. Baker was to become a strong proponent of Yeats's chanting, lilting, and cadence in the reformation of modern dramatic dialogue, urging his readers to follow the example of Yeats and the Abbey Theatre: "That is what the Irish theatre, more than anything else, has revealed to us," he wrote after describing how Yeats taught an actress to speak rhythmically, "that dialect is not a matter of the use of certain words, nor is it even certain ways of arranging words in sentences: it is the lilt and the cadence of speech. . . . It is to this importance of rhythmic flow, cadence, lilt—call it what you will—that we have been waking in our modern drama, waking slowly." See Baker's "Rhythm in Dramatic Dialogue," *Yale Review*, 9 (September 1929), 129–30.

whatever Boston arrangements could be found in Baker's hands. Shaw had sent a letter of introduction for her to his friend the critic James Gibbons Huneker, who had recently written the introduction to Shaw's *Dramatic Opinions and Essays* (1906). Huneker finally wrote to her on March 2 to apologize for not answering her letter, regretful that as he was no longer writing on music or drama for the press he could be of no service in that direction: "But I've done something more practical, I hope, than boring you with a visit—i.e.—I've written to three places that are looking for such exquisite art as yours (I've seen you, heard you in London) and I look for results. . . . But it will be *veni, vidi, vinci* with you I am sure."[8]

Each appearance led to new invitations, and as she moved from venue to venue she gained confidence in her program with American audiences. "The Nietzsche Campaign is a great success everywhere," she wrote to Quinn on March 9. "You must hear it." She wrote again the next day, evidently having heard from Yeats, informing Quinn that there was a possibility of Yeats coming, but affirming Quinn's own view that they should not lecture and travel together in such a provincial society. During the next week, however, Farr enjoyed one of the most cosmopolitan arrangements of her tour, an elegant dinner party and performance in the home of Robert J. Collier. The invitation followed Agnes Tobin's letter to him on Farr's behalf and would have been encouraged by his colleague Norman Hapgood after he heard her at Corbin's party. Robert was the son of Peter Fenelon Collier, an Irish immigrant from Co. Carlow who had established the huge Collier printing and publishing firm in New York and had made Mark Twain a family friend along the way. Robert had been an editor of *Collier's Weekly* since its inception in 1896 and was married to Sara Steward Van Alen, granddaughter of Mrs. William Astor. "You were quite right about the Colliers," she wrote to Quinn on March 17 about the evening, "and they were quite charming":

> He & I sat at one end of a long table & she & Mark Twain at the other & all the women were beautiful. Mrs. Cushing the artist's wife with red hair & black dress and white Gibson Girl face. Mrs. J. J. Astor & two other tall wonderful things in gold and black.
>
> They got me to chant a few different specimens for about 40 minutes and all filed out shaking hands & [Norman] Hapgood said he'd call here & give me

8. Letters to Florence Farr (203/21), Sterling Library, University of London. Huneker identified the Contemporary Club of New York and Bridgeport, Connecticut, as two of the places he had sent her circulars and a personal letter.

> letters to Boston and Collier was most intelligent about it all & they sent me home in an "electric"—I thought it was all over; I'd received so much praise and fervour. Lo! and behold next day a check arrived for $200.

Farr, who had informed Quinn that she needed to clear £100 on her tour, was overjoyed by the lavish windfall: "So now I've secured the £100. Isn't it lucky?"[9]

When Farr arrived at the Bartol Hotel in Boston on March 18 she was surprised and delighted to find her room full of flowers and chocolates. There she was met by Dolmetsch and his wife Mabel for a long talk to review their three-year separation. "We were delighted to see her," wrote Mabel, "and passed some merry hours listening to her amusing talk and anecdotes about our mutual acquaintances."[10] She entertained them with the psaltery, and while she was in Boston she participated in the christening of their infant son, Rudolph, holding him at the font as a proxy for his godparents.

Dolmetsch was still at Chickering and Sons piano manufactory, happily engaged in making harpsichords, clavichords, lutes, and psalteries. "Dolmetsch has a lovely time here now," she informed Quinn. "Chickerings simply let him do all he likes he is like Celini when he was patronised by the King of France. He's made a wonderful harpsichord with 8 different actions, one just like a little warbling bird." Dolmetsch, who was to include her in one of his current series of concerts at Chickering Hall, told her that he thought her art had progressed "very greatly" since he last saw her. "Dolmetsch is quite surprised that the Psaltery has not smashed up

9. Quinn Papers, Manuscripts Division, NYPL. Quoted in B. L. Reid, *John Quinn and His Friends* (New York: Oxford University Press, 1968), 45–6. Robert Joseph Collier (1876–1918) inherited $4,000,000 and the Collier firm on the death of his father in 1909. The portrait painter Howard Gardiner Cushing (1869–1916), a Harvard graduate who had studied at the Académie Julian in Paris, was married to Ethel Cochrane of Boston. The capitalist and inventor John Jacob Astor IV (1864–1912), who had built the Astoria side of the palatial Waldorf-Astoria hotel, was then married to Ava Lowle Willing of Philadelphia; he was to be lost on the *Titantic*. Norman Hapgood (1868–1937), Harvard graduate, journalist, and drama critic, was married to Emilie Bigelow, daughter of the Chicago banker Anson Bigelow. Hapgood writes of his and Robert Collier's long friendship with Mark Twain in *The Changing Years* (New York: Farrar and Rinehart, 1930): "He saw much of Robert Collier, they got on happily in their personal relations, and through the book branch of the Collier business they were of practical use to each other also. We who were a generation younger than he sometimes spoke of him as Old Mark . . . The literary group of which we were all part treated [him] as a credit to the human race, a benefactor of it; creator of the most lasting American fiction since Hawthorne and Poe; and we trusted in posterity to agree with us" (211).

10. Mabel Dolmetsch, *Personal Recollections of Arnold Dolmetsch* (New York: Macmillan, 1958), 69.

in this climate," she wrote to Quinn.[11] Professor Baker had also done right by her; the Boston papers ran preliminary notices of her concerts: "they admit the public for 50 cents to the lecture."

Farr had meanwhile received from Yeats a new typescript of *Deirdre*, with his permission to give readings from it. She sent it on to Quinn, who hoped to arrange a public reading of the play for her at the end of April. Farr may have read from *Deirdre* at Harvard and at Radcliffe College, as she did at Bryn Mawr. She was quite familiar with the play, for Yeats had sent her an earlier draft the previous October, and she had known the choral lyrics since Yeats began chanting them late in 1904. In any event, her varied programs at the two colleges were met with enthusiastic response by members of the audience. "Miss Farr has a wonderfully musical voice," reported the *Boston Evening Transcript* of her lecture on "The Music of the Spoken Word" in Agassiz House, Radcliffe College, where she was presented by one of her patronesses, Alice W. Longfellow, daughter of the poet (who portrayed her as "grave Alice" in "The Children's Hour"). "Her method of recitation is all her own," Farr's enchanted reporter continued, "it is neither spoken recitation, nor singing, nor, in the ordinary sense, intoning. It is really more natural than any of these, and is something very like a new art."[12] But there were exceptions to the general approbation: "At Radcliff after my Elocution imitation," Farr reported to Quinn, "a professor of Elocution got up & walked out muttering language unspeakable!!!! Most of 'em liked it."

Farr was taken up by figures of the Boston arts society and fêted between engagements to lunches, high teas, dinners, and concerts, and she had a photographic sitting at the studio of J. E. Purdy, who flashed pictures

11. Dolmetsch wrote to Joseph Hone many years later of Farr's visit: "But I got engagements for her in America and it came out that in public, she raised the pitch of her voice and was not capable of following it with the Psaltery as I did myself. Result, the whole thing was discordant; she did not know it and it ended in failure. I never found a reciter with a sufficiently musical ear to *listen* to the instrument and make the voice and the instrument fit together. The art of listening is almost extinct amongst the present day Singers, as witness the way they get out of tune with their accompaniments. Listeners have become hardened to this" (NLI MS 5919; partially quoted and edited in Hone, *W.B. Yeats, 1865–1939* [London: Macmillan, 1942], 191).

12. *Boston Evening Transcript*, March 23, 1907, 5. The Boston reporter was keen to mention that the psaltery was made by Dolmetsch, who was much in the news with his own concert series. "According to Miss Farr," the reporter continued, "each separate word has a little tune inherent in it, just as each line of poetry has a melody of its own. This music of words she was able to discover, not by the piano, but my means of a psaltery made by Arnold Dolmetsch, the tones of which were more sympathetic than those of the piano. . . . Among the selections that she gave were several of Yeats's beautiful poems, old seventeenth and eighteenth century songs, passages from the Odyssey and one of the Psalms."

of her in twelve positions with the psaltery (see Plate 11). "Mrs. James T. Fields has taken me up here & has introduced me to all the nice people she knows," she informed Quinn. "Her husband published for Emerson, Lowell etc. & they entertained Dickens in '67." The poet Annie Adams Fields, whose home on Charles Street, Beacon Hill, had long been a literary salon, was the colorful widow of James Thomas Fields, the former head of Ticknor & Fields, Dickens's main American publisher, and since his death in 1881 she had been the companion of the poet Sarah Orne Jewett. "I met the famous Mrs. Jack Gardner," Farr addded, "& she was gracious but has done nothing practical." Isabella Stewart Gardner, "Mrs. Jack," as she was known, was to entertain and befriend Yeats and Lady Gregory during the Abbey company's first American tour in 1911.[13] She lived in Fenway Court, the famous mock-Venetian palazzo that she had filled with Old Master and other fine paintings under the guidance of Bernard Berenson, who was about to publish his *North Italian Painters of the Renaissance* (1907) and whose *Venetian Painting in America—The Fifteenth Century* (1916) was to draw heavily upon the collection he helped her build. She had just acquired Piero Pollaiuolo's *Woman in Green and Crimson*, which may have captured Farr's aesthetic and sartorial interest. Farr was charmed by both women and wrote to Quinn about her continuing success with them and others. "I fell into the arms of Mrs James T. Fields," she wrote on March 31:

> *The* old lady that entertained Dickens & knew Emerson & we read poetry to each other by the hour. I think the trick is done. Mr Byrne the "intelligence" of Chickerings has also taken it up [speaking to the psaltery] *con amore*. . . . Mrs. Jack Gardner came to the Radcliffe College lecture & we had a long talk. I like her. I am to be motored over to Cambridge & shown Harvard tomorrow by a nice boy; so you see at last I have found a few men.[14]

13. In *Our Irish Theatre* Lady Gregory recounts (191–2) her own lecture in the music room at Fenway Court (now the Isabella Stewart Gardner Museum) in September 1911; thereafter Mrs. Jack became one of the firmest friends of Lady Gregory and the Company. "There was something of Hugh Lane in her and I wish they had met," she wrote in her journal. "She was 'a great lady,' one of the few I have known" (*Lady Gregory's Journals*, ed. Lennox Robinson [London: Putnam, 1946], 240–1). There are seven inscribed books each of Yeats and Lady Gregory in the library. Yeats wrote in her guestbook, "interview every hour of the day and night."
14. Francis Byrne was the youngest member of the Chickering firm and had hired Dolmetsch to take control of the early instruments department at the factory. Mabel Dolmetsch described him as being "of Irish extraction" and "of a romantic turn of mind. Possessed moreover of artistic tastes and keenly interested in the older music, he was able to inspire his superiors . . . with his own enthusiasm." Byrne, she added, was "much fascinated" by Farr's recitations to the psaltery. (*Personal Recollections of Arnold Dolmetsch*, 64, 69).

On April 4 she left Boston to begin her Midwestern swing to Toronto, Buffalo, and Chicago. At the University of Toronto she was hosted by James Mavor, a Scots-born professor of political economy who had entertained Yeats in 1904.[15] "I had a great time there with delighted professors also at Harvard," she wrote to Quinn, adding that "Everyone has got quite warned off introducing me to women now: so I'm getting along much more amusingly and the women I do meet are quite jolly & not hysterical."

In Buffalo, Farr was the guest of the William P. Northrups, at whose home a gift from Quinn was awaiting her arrival: volume ten of Nietzsche's Works, *The Genealogy of Morals*, together with his poems translated by John Gray—a welcome addition to her collection and more powder for her Nietzsche campaign. Her lecture on "The Chanting of the Greek Chorus," under the auspices of the Buffalo Fine Arts Academy and the Society of Artists, was prominently announced in the *Buffalo Express*, which described her as "a London favorite," as "the first woman in England to appear in the Bernard Shaw plays" and "among the first to introduce Ibsen to London."[16] She lectured and chanted in the Sculpture Court of the Albright Art Gallery, which she described to Quinn as "a wonderful Greek Temple in the middle of parks & it was in a white-marble sculpture gallery that I recited." Her host, she informed him, was a proprietor of the *Buffalo Express*: "I don't know what wonderful things are not to be said in it about me," she wrote before reading the generous coverage of her performance:

> Standing between two of the marble pillars in the sculpture court, surrounded on every side by the glories of Greece as represented by their sculptured masterpieces, Miss Farr had an ideal environment for her talk. She was clad in soft, clinging robes, suggestive of the Greek, and the accompaniment to the choruses was played upon a psaltery, much like the ancient Grecian lyre.
>
> Miss Farr has a wonderful gift in her voice, which is responsive to the speaker's every mood, every thought, now rising to the tones of anger, again softened to the cadences of love, at times joyous with the song of praise over a victory won, and then sobbing like a lost soul as Heba [*sic*] and the women mourned over the body of mighty Hector's infant son.... The effect was hauntingly beautiful and impressive, and when she finished it seemed almost like an intrusion to lose the last echo of the speaker's voice amid the noise

15. On April 6, 1907, the Toronto *Globe* announced her performance that afternoon in the Chemical Theatre, stating that she had devised "a new method of vocalization" with her Dolmetsch psaltery, "neither singing, chanting nor reading, but a modulated form of recitative that has aroused great enthusiasm among the aesthetic critics of London, Boston and New York" (18).
16. "As in the Days of Old Greece," *Buffalo Express*, April 9, 1907, 5.

> of the applause. The lecture was listened to with rapt attention by a large audience and it was one of the most interesting entertainments that has been given in the beautiful gallery.[17]

Quinn sought the assistance of the Irish journalist Francis Hackett, who wrote for the Chicago *Evening Post*, to help with engagements there. The twenty-four-year-old Hackett had emigrated from Kilkenny to New York in 1901 and had befriended Quinn before he landed a job as literary editor of the Chicago paper in March 1906. He was living and teaching English among the foreign residents at Jane Addams's Hull House, and through his efforts he got Farr booked for a lecture there, followed by a private entertainment at the Fortnightly Club.[18] Mrs. Patrick Campbell had sent letters to two Chicago hostesses, Mrs. Franklin MacVeagh and Mrs. Clarence Mackay, who, as Farr reported to Quinn, "seems to be going in for culture with a vengeance."[19] Farr pursued these ladies assiduously until Mrs. MacVeagh, who had a lingering illness, "got the other woman to have me. I asked Mrs. MacVeagh's friend for $200 but she didn't feel like it!!!" Farr nonetheless greatly enjoyed her Chicago encounters, telling Quinn afterwards that "the further west I went the better it was." Hackett, too, enjoyed her company, reporting to Quinn that "She was a delightful woman, and was personally liked very much here, as well she might. I think her work was a good deal too good to do more than flabbergast half of the Chicagoats, however." He was regretful, if not repentant, for failing to write about her, confessing to Quinn that "I did nothing for her, unfortunately, having overdone work so much, earlier in the year, that every Celtic devil; procrastination, indolence, and the genius for ineffectiveness; were holding a perennial feis on my hearth."[20] Even without Hackett's publicity

17. "Chanting the Greek Chorus/Delightful Descriptive Lecture by Miss Farr at the Albright Gallery," *Buffalo Express*, April 10, 1907, 5.
18. Hackett got Miss Ella Raymond Waite of Hull House to arrange the booking. Farr's performance for the Fortnightly Club in the Fine Arts Building was hosted by Mrs. Ralph Emerson and Mrs. Thompson of Rockford.
19. Letter of [date] 1907, NYPL. Mrs. Franklin MacVeagh, née Emily Eames, was wife of the Chicago businessman and politician who would become Taft's Secretary of the Treasury in 1909; Mrs. Clarence Mackay, née Katherine Alexander Duer, was wife of the telegraph and telephone capitalist.
20. NYPL. Hackett, who attended one of Yeats's readings at a private home in New York in 1903, later confused Farr's visit with Yeats's in his memoir, *American Rainbow* (New York: Liveright, 1971): "He was now nearly forty, his dream possessing him but his alarm for it governed. He seemed to poise on the edge of it, as an Irish elk might scan a settled valley below him, his head lifted. I cannot remember whether Florence Farr was there with her psaltery to further the work as a ritual does, but he employed ritual, less a vestige of druids than of rectories" (121).

assistance, however, she received invitations, as she did in Buffalo, to return for more performances before her departure or during her autumn tour.

Farr made her way back to Boston for a concert to aid a library fund at the Radcliffe Union on April 15. "Mrs Gardner said she'd never seen anyone 'sit in a chair' as I did. I finished with the French 'Mort de Mari.' "[21] When she apprised Quinn of her recent movements the following day, she reported the widespread interest in Yeats. "A good many people spotted here and there seem to think a lot of him. In Toronto especially. In Chicago they said 'We have had John the Baptist & now we have you!' "[22] A few days later she received a forwarded letter from Yeats, "full of wanting to come to America but he says he is off to Italy with Lady Gregory until the end of May" (*CL4* 647). Alluding to the post-*Playboy* rows and attacks in Dublin, she surmised of their departure for Italy: "I think they've made Ireland too hot to hold them for the moment. I certainly think that the best thing he can do is go for the public generally."[23]

II

Yeats had deliberately begun to close himself off from the public by retreating into a series of meditations that he called "discoveries." As he moved

21. This was Pierre de Ronsard's "Sur le Mort de Marie" (1556), his sonnet on the death of his fifteen-year-old mistress Marie Dupin. Warwick Gould and Deirdre Toomey describe the sonnet as "something of a cult-piece in the early 1890s," noting that Sturge Moore had translated it in *The Dial*, 3 (1893), 17 (*YA11* [1995], 128).
22. Yeats had lectured at the University of Toronto on February 13–14, 1904. Later that year Pelham Edgar tracked him down in London for an extensive interview in the Toronto *Globe* of December 24, 1904, when Edgar described the "profit of leading him back to the subjects which he has most at heart. You will hear much of Miss Florence Farr and that wonderful psaltery which Mr. Dolmetsch invented for her, for Mr. Yeats, as is pretty generally known, holds strong theories concerning the music of verse and the proper method of rendering it. Two things he equally abhors: modern elocution, and modern music as applied to poetry. Yet no man holds stronger views as to the essentially musical element in verse, and Miss Farr alone among modern readers has the genius . . . to apprehend and reproduce the subtle music which haunts the poet's brain. Mr. Yeats himself has a way of reading his own poems which brings out the rhythms with remarkable effect. In fact, he has two methods. He sometimes says the poems to a set tune of very original quality, but generally he gives out the lines, not in a sonorous chant as Tennyson is said to have done, but whith a sustained and plaintive lilt which he adapts as readily to the mood of pathos as to humor" ("The Poetry of William Butler Yeats," *Saturday Magazine Section*, 5).
23. Yeats had written to Farr from Florence in mid-April that he had "a great sense of peace in being out of the Dublin stress & worry—new anger there at our taking 'Play Boy' to London—just two days before I left there was an attack of extraordinary violence in the Freeman describing the play as 'obscene'—I had to get the company togeather—for they were all except Frank Fay wavering—& to win them over by speach [*sic*]" (*CL4* 650).

among cities in England, Scotland, Ireland, and Italy during the past year, he became increasingly observant of people and performers around him whose actions revealed what he perceived to be a general decline of "personality," a fragmentation of the "whole man," and a drift of culture itself into the grip of mechanism, knowledge, and the myriad surfaces of life. Many of his personal discoveries came from his attempt to explain to himself the growth of impersonality in terms of the essential personality of the new art. He pursued his discoveries by examining the antinomies between the ancient art of musical speech and the modern elabortion of music. The primary question that he posed to himself in a section entitled "Personality and Intellectual Essences" is how the artist succeeds in moving audiences and why they are unmoved in the present. He had begun to probe and posit answers to this question in discussions of nineteenth-century English poets in lectures he gave with Farr in 1903. In repeatedly asking himself over the years how he could make his work mean something to "vigorous and simple men whose attention is not given to art but to a shop," he had come to the rediscovery of an old conviction, that poets must dramatize the intensity of their inner lives in words and rhythms that move and excite the common man. "An exciting person," he asserts of the poet and reciter, "will display the greatest volume of personal energy, and this energy must be seen to come out of the body as out of the mind" (*E&I* 265–6). The loss of personality and energy in modern literature, he declared, is in part due to "the lack of that spoken word which knits us to normal man." In the absence of the spoken word, intonation, and impassioned speech, we have also displaced our old delight in the whole man with a new delight in ideas, abstractions, states of mind, "in all that comes to us most easily in elaborate music." The division between the old and the new music thus became a controlling metaphor for subsequent discoveries. "Music is the most impersonal of things," he wrote, venting his spleen against musicians and settings in "The Musician and the Orator," "and words the most personal, and that is why musicians do not like words. They masticate them for a long time, being afraid they would not be able to digest them, and when the words are so broken and softened and mixed with spittle that they are not words any longer, they swallow them" (*E&I* 268).

In the volume published as *Discoveries* (1907), Yeats presents tableaux of mostly unidentified individuals who allow him to pit personality against impersonality through the spoken word and musical speech. He becomes fascinated by a young girl playing a guitar, an instrument that allows her to "move freely and express a joy that is not of the fingers and the mind only but of the whole being."[24] In the unity of music and mind, voice and bodily expression, he discovers the nature of his delight in her: "That is the way my people, the people I see in the mind's eye, play music, and I like it because it is all personal, as personal as Villon's poetry." The unobtrusive relation of the guitar and its notes to her song leads him to compare her performance on the guitar to a performer on the modern piano: "Nearly all the old instruments were like that," he ruefully observes of her stringed instrument. "But if you sit at the piano, it is the piano, the mechanism, that is the important thing, and nothing of you means anything but your fingers and your intellect." In her singular performance he discovers anew "what sweetness, what rhythmic movement there is in those who have become the joy that is themselves" (*E&I* 268, 271).

In his next discovery, "The Looking-Glass," he juxtaposes the guitar player to "a girl with a shrill monotonous voice and an abrupt way of moving." In talking to her, Yeats discovers that she has recently completed her education, moving him to question the value of an education "that does not begin with the personality, the habitual self, and illustrate all by that." To Yeats, her voice has been brought to its harshness by "the neglect of all but external activities." What would have brought her to a greater wholeness and harmony of being, he affirms, is an education in musical speech: "Somebody should have taught her to speak for the most part on whatever note of her voice is most musical, and soften those harsh notes by speaking, not singing, to some stringed instrument, taking note after note and, as it were, caressing her words a little as if she loved the sound of them" (*E&I* 269–70).[25]

24. In an inscription in *Discoveries* (Stanford), Yeats identifies Sibell Lilian, Countess of Cromartie, as the model for "A Guitar Player" (originally entitled "The Banjo Player" in a confusion of instruments and published under that title in the *Gentleman's Magazine* in September 1906). She had attended his Monday evenings and he had been her guest in Castle Leod, Ross-shire, Scotland, in January 1906. When Yeats defined "the great lady" to Quinn as one who possesses a combination of "joyous youthfulness" with "simplicity and conscious dignity," he wrote of the rare quality that "Maud Gonne had it, especially in her young days before she grew tired out with many fools, and the little Countess of Cromartie has it more than anyone I have ever known." Quoted in Foster, *Life* 1385.
25. Yeats was to write in volume iii of his *Collected Works*, published in October 1908, regarding the teaching of verse speaking to children: "nothing but the attempting of [verse speaking] will show how far these things can be taught or developed where they exist but little. I believe that they should be a part of the teaching of all children, for the beauty of the speaking-voice is more important to our lives than that of the singing, and the rhythm of words comes more into the structure of our daily being than any abstract pattern of notes" (*CW3* 234).

In these private meditations for the public eye, Yeats seeks to justify the necessity of the poet's personal expenditure of artistic energy, and his refusal to admit that he cannot reverse the impersonal element in art and culture makes his desire to do so all possessing. He believes in the power of the poetic voice and in the universal emotions of poetry to stir and strengthen those emotions in the people. He keeps in his mind's eye the unblurred vision of ordinary people who once murmured the lines of Homer, Petrarch, Dante, Chaucer, Ariosto, and other predecessors in that poetic procession. And so in *Discoveries* he finds new conviction and self-affirmation as a modern inheritor of that procession and redoubles his search for artists—in the whole domain of performing arts—who renew his faith in it. Thus, when he hears the popular French music-hall singer Yvette Guilbert, "who has the lyre or as good," perform with wondrous personality to an impersonal audience, to "people whose life had nothing it could share with an exquisite art," he discovers anew in her individual performance the general cultural commitment behind the new art: "I longed to make all things over again, that she might sing in some great hall, where there was no one that did not love life and speak of it continually" (*E&I* 295). In America, Farr too was making her own discoveries about the personality of the new art and would soon record them for Yeats.

III

How delighted Farr must have been, deep in her tour of Midwestern cities and homes, on opening the *Saturday Evening Post* to see herself introduced by John Corbin to a broad American readership, photographed in the Ricketts gown and with a crown of laurel leaf in her hair.[26] Describing her as the "leader of a new movement" that aims to change the relationship of music and words, Corbin characterized her indebtedness to Yeats and Dolmetsch, her chanting and lilting with the psaltery, her "remarkably pure and strong" voice, and her provocative effect on American listeners: "One traveler likened her lilting to folk-songs he had heard in Finland, another to New Zealand folk-songs. There is a suggestion also of the

26. "Lilting to the Psaltery," *Saturday Evening Post*, 179 (April 20, 1907), 22–3. Among the authors publishing in the magazine in 1906–7 were Booth Tarkington, Joseph Conrad, O. Henry, Arthur Train, Brand Whitlock, Ernest Poole, Stewart Edward White, Corra Harris, Edwin Balmer, Perceval Gibbon, and Beatrix Demarest Lloyd.

Gregorian chant." Farr had explained to Corbin that she does not willingly attempt poems or songs by poets who wrote or write for conventional musical accompaniment. "But with all primitive poetry," her enthralled witness confirmed, "and modern poetry written in a primitive manner, her results are extraordinary." Having followed her from stage to drawing room, Corbin was further impresssed by the wide range of her programs. "In a single recital, lately given in a private house, she began with Yeats, Douglas Hyde, and others of the modern Irish school, passed to William Blake, then to one of Nietzsche's Zarathustra rhapsodies, a passage from the Bacchæ of Euripides, a selection from Homer, the music for which she adapted from the modern Greek manner of reciting the Iliad, and finally to a psalm of David."

The article not only put the new art before the American public; it prepared the way for an extended tour of the land. Farr immediately began to plan for an autumn return; however, basking in her personal success and adulation, she told Quinn that she preferred to come independently of Yeats. "I know Yeats wants to try his luck again," she wrote, reiterating her desire for distance: "If I do return myself I shall try to arrange a different time as I don't want to get myself mixed up with him in anyway. Mutual friendship is one thing but I don't care about mutual scandal with him." This was not to deny the intimacy of her friendship with Yeats; it was characteristic of her detached, unsentimental manner in conducting her affairs. But she and Quinn had also become fast friends during the tour, had enjoyed exchanging off-color stories, and she wanted to encourage the future of their relationship upon her return. Ironically, she had just received from Yeats a letter in which he had slipped uncharacteristically into an intimate expression: "I want you too [*sic*] understand that I am sorry you are away & I am afraid to say it, because you get cross if one says such things & yet after all I shall be very glad when you return" (*CL4* 651).[27] At the same time, Farr, in a weak moment, made an oblique overture to Quinn, writing to him on April 16: "I simply hate the thought of going back to

27. George Yeats told Richard Ellmann that Yeats's affair with Farr "came after Maud's marriage. Yeats never knew whether she had been Shaw's mistress, but remembered her saying to him <when they> when he told her that they were going to meet Shaw, 'You might have told me before, so I could put on my best dress.' The liaison with Yeats ended with her saying, 'I can do this for myself.' It began when Yeats, puzzled at her apparent loneliness and lack of lovers, decided to read ^ <books> literature ^ to her to <[?]> see what would happen." See Warwick Gould, "'Grasping on the Strand': Richard Ellmann's W. B. Yeats Notebooks," *Poems and Contexts: YA16* (London: Palgrave, 2005), 314.

England. I am sick to death of life altogether & nothing seems to have any attraction for me."

Farr continued to impress public and private audiences right up to her departure, including a farewell performance for Quinn's friends at his apartment on May 7. Quinn had solicited the reportorial presence of Frederick J. Gregg, Yeats's former classmate in secondary school, and provided him with printed material about Farr by Yeats and Shaw to encourage an article. Two days later she boarded the *Grosser Kürfurst* in Hoboken for a next-day sailing. On the eve of her departure Gregg wrote a bon voyage for her in the *Evening Sun*:

> Miss Florence Farr had the satisfaction of knowing that her speaking of quaint poetry to a not improbably ancient musical accompaniment had made a real impression on the artistic coterie of New Yorkers. . . . She gave before a number of American colleges her reading of the classics, a performance analogous, perhaps, to the dances of our Ruth St. Denis or Isadora Duncan in a poet's pantomime, but transcending these by all power of the spoken word and the low soft voice, that excellent thing in woman.[28]

Gregg relished reporting the individual responses at Quinn's party. "Florence Farr," remarked one listener after hearing her chant Rossetti's "Sister Helen," "makes your blood curdle." A no less "profound impression" was made on the audience with her chanting of Whitman's "Out of the Cradle Endlessly Rocking," with her translation from Nietzsche's "Song of Life" from *Thus Spake Zarathustra*, and finally "with the gorgeously Oriental Psalm 137, a Psalm of the Captivity, 'By the Waters of Babylon,' with the Hebrew curse, 'Happy shall he be that dasheth thy little ones against the stones,' which is as grimly horrible as the best Celtic curse that Dr. Douglas Hyde ever translated." Greatly pleased by Gregg's farewell portrait, Quinn sent copies to friends and agents in anticipation of her return in the autumn. The articles by Gregg and Corbin had framed, highlighted, and promoted Farr's American tour, and Gregg seemed to capture in the last the peculiar spirit of her enthusiastic reception: "In

28. "Music and Musicians/Upon the Psaltery and in the Poet's Guise," *Evening Sun*, May 9, 1907, 6; edited and partially rpt. in *The Music of Speech*, 6–9. Gregg's article contained a subheading in bold: "**Florence Farr's Reading of Homer and Greek Choruses in Alma Tadema Clothing Proves the Most Interesting Revival Since Miss Matheson's 'Everyman.'**" Quinn also made arrangements for Farr to be interviewed by Miss Gertrude Lynch of the Sunday *Sun*, together with the paper's artist, Miss Aspell, after she returned to New York in April but this did not take place. On June 6 Farr wrote Quinn to thank him "for the lovely notices in the New York Sun."

popular view, it is the true Athenian zest to see and to hear some new thing, yet one of the oldest things in the world, which gives this 'speaking to the psaltery' its curious interest to-day."

Farr returned to London revivified not only as a "leader" of the new art but as a New Woman as well, fortified by having cleared over $700 in America, well beyond her greatest expectation, and exhilarated by the enthusiastic reception of chanting to the psaltery. For the next six months she wrote vigorously for the *New Age,* which had just come under the new editorship of her Leeds friends A. R. Orage and Holbrook Jackson. They freed her to write on the great variety of her intellectual interests—a series of essays on Ibsen's women, on modern women and the art of womanhood, on modern man, on the wrongful degradation of prostitution in western culture, on the necessity of laughter, and on other subjects that had grown out of her recent experiences, including "G.B.S. and New York," a comical comparison of her own attitude toward New York with those expressed in Shaw's plays.[29] Yeats returned from Italy anticipating the arrival of the Abbey players in Oxford and London and longing to throw himself into his eight-volume *Collected Works*. On June 6 Farr wrote to Quinn to say that the *Playboy* had been a success in Oxford. "Yeats doesn't want to go to America until next year," she reported. "He wants his collected edition to precede him & is all right in other ways."

Yeats strongly supported Farr's solo return and the prospect of spreading the new art across America, and over the summer he would do all that he could to enhance her success there. He inscribed and sent to her the second volume of Macmillan's American edition of his *Poetical Works*, in which he dedicates *The Land of Heart's Desire* to her, praises her importance in helping him "restore the whole ancient art of passionate speech," and describes in an appendix how she had "divined" the art of regulated declamation.[30] "He says he hopes it will help in America," she wrote to Quinn. Moreover, during the summer Yeats sent her any new reading discoveries that would

29. For an account of Farr's eighteen contributions to the *New Age* from May 23, 1907, to January 4, 1908, see A. Walton Litz, "Florence Farr: A 'Transitional' Woman," in Maria DiBattista and Lucy McDiarmid (eds.), *High and Low Moderns: Literature and Culture 1889–1939* (New York and Oxford: Oxford University Press, 1996), 85–106.

30. See Yeats's "Preface" to *The Poetical Works of William B. Yeats in Two Volumes*, vol. ii, *Dramatical Poems* (New York: Macmillan, 1907), p. viii: "The labour of two players, Miss Florence Farr and Mr. Frank Fay, have done enough to show that all is possible, if the summer be lucky and the corn ripen." Appendix IV, "The Work of the National Theatre Society at the Abbey Theatre, Dublin: A Statement of Principles," was comprised of sections III, IV, and V of "Literature and the Living Voice" (513–24; here 523).

add illustrative force to her lecture. "I am reading Norths Plutarch," he wrote to her in early August,

> and I find a beautiful thing. Alcebiades refused to learn the flute because he thought it ill became a gentleman either to put his cheeks out of shape or to make music he could not speak to. He had so much influence that ever after the flute was despised. This might help you with your lectures . . . Alcebiades said the flute should be left to Thebans that did not know how to speak. He also claimed that the patrons [of] Athens, Pallas and Apollo, objected to the flute and that Apollo skinned a man for playing on it. [31]
>
> (*CL4* 703)

In return, Farr began to gather the music he wanted for his *Collected Works*.

IV

As Yeats began to put together the successive volumes of his work for publication at A. H. Bullen's Shakespeare Head Press in Stratford-upon-Avon, his foremost concern was the preservation and inclusion of the music for his plays and poems. He did not hesitate to prevail upon Farr's cooperation: he returned her original music for *The Shadowy Waters* and requested new music for the acting version; he could not find her music for the three women's song in *On Baile's Strand*; he was anxious for her to collect and preserve all the music that she had done for him. "Keep the music safe for me," he pleaded (*CL4* 701). In succeeding weeks he asked her to set for the psaltery the lyrics in *Deirdre* and *The Golden Helmet*.[32] In the end, however, she failed to provide the expected music for both the new *Shadowy Waters* and *The Golden Helmet*, but she did begin to send her earlier music for the lyrics in *Cathleeen ni Houlihan*; for the lyric ("The Four Rivers") from *The King's Threshold*; for the two Fools' songs, and the "Song of the Women" in *On Baile's Strand*; and for the three musicians' songs in *Deirdre*.

31. Yeats summarizes the account of Alcibiades in *Plutarch's Lives of the Noble Grecians and Romans, Englished by Sir Thomas North* (1579), ed. W. E. Henley (1895), ii. 93–4.

32. Yeats did not send Farr the lyrics of *The Golden Helmet* until October 29, 1907, hoping that she might "manage at your leisure to put some lyrics to them. You will remember the play is noisy and violent" (*CL4* 763). He anticipated that her music would be included when he wrote his introduction: "The degree of approach to ordinary singing depends on the context, for one desires a greater or lesser amount of contrast between the lyrics and the dialogue itself. . . . the little song of Leagerie when he seizes the 'Golden Helmet' should in its opening words be indistinguishable from the dialogue itself" (*CW3* 222).

The latter, Yeats emphasized in his note on the music, must be sung or spoken "with minute passionate understanding" (*CW3* 223). By the end of August he had also assembled Arthur Darley's music for *The Shadowy Waters* and the traditional folk-airs for *The Hour-Glass* and *The Unicorn from the Stars* (*CW3* 231–2).[33] "There is a good deal of music ready to go to print for the plays," he wrote to Bullen, emphatic about its importance: "This music is essential to the completeness of my record, even apart from its own merits it is necessary to show how I want the things set. I mean the degree of attention to the speaking voice. I don't want therefore to leave them to the last moment especially as Mrs. Emery goes to America in November" (*CL4* 712–13).

Farr had now made plans to sail on the *Lusitania* on November 2 with Mrs. Patrick Campbell; Yeats would cast her horoscope and report that the current planetary movements "should give you success in America" (*CL4* 729). She had meanwhile sent him more music, which he forwarded to Edith Lister, Bullen's secretary at the Shakespeare Head. "You will probably find yourself out of sympathy with this music," he had forewarned Miss Lister, "but it gets its meaning from the method of speaking and is a necessary record of that method. It is important to me that people whom I cannot personally teach and who may produce my work shall know my intentions" (*CL4* 721–2). A fortnight later he informed her that he was holding back some of the incidental music so as not to overburden the volume before all the musical odds and ends came in. "The only thing absolutely necessary as a record," he emphasized to forestall any deletions, "is Miss Farr's music, and some fragments of folk music for the prose plays" (*CL4* 731).

Farr did more for Yeats than send music; as she prepared her settings for the lyrics in Yeats's plays, she wrote out her own recent "discoveries" about musical speech. They were born both from her struggle to teach her pupils to chant and from her study of musical forms of the eighth and seventeenth centuries—from liturgical chant, plain-song, and melismata to the beginnings of opera, "nuove musiche" and "aria parlante." She had

33. In his prefatory note for the music, "The Music for Use in the Performance of these Plays," Yeats gave instructions for the relation of speech and song in the various lyrics, preceded by a general directive: "Some of it is old Irish music made when all songs were but heightened speech, and some of it composed by modern musicians is none the less to be associated with words that must never lose the intonation of passionate speech. No vowel must ever be prolonged unnaturally, no word of mine must ever change into a mere musical note, no singer of my words must ever cease to be a man and become an instrument" (*CW3* 222).

observed the relation of these forms to her own art, how the various musicans had attempted to add beauty to the words of the poet, and she had learned much from them about the alternation of voices in choruses, an art that she had sought to develop in choruses of lyric and dramatic poetry. "There is no more beautiful sound," she wrote, "than the alternation of carolling or keening and a voice speaking in regulated declamation. The very act of alternation has a peculiar charm" (*E&I* 22).

Suddenly the discovery came. Where Yeats saw the absence of personality as the explanation for a diminishment of impassioned speech and the poet's power to move the people, Farr saw the absence of ecstasy and the loss of belief in the magical power of words as the explanation for the death of these musical forms in the present. She had always tried, she declared, to make her speaking to the psaltery "more beautiful than the speaking by priests at High Mass, the singing of recitative in opera and the speaking through music of actors in melodrama." In studying the music of the eighth and seventeenth centuries, she posited that "one would think that the Church and the opera were united in the desire to make beautiful speech more beautiful," but her personal discovery was that such an assumption proved groundless when tested: "There is no ecstasy in the delivery of ritual, and recitative is certainly not treated by opera-singers in a way that makes us wish to imitate them."

To Farr, the presence of ecstasy was what distinguished the new art from all the forms to which it was said to be related. Not until a belief in the magical power of words and a delight in the purity of sound is restored, she asserted, will the arts of plain-chant and recitative become "the great arts they are described as being by those who first practised them." Alluding to the training of her own pupils, and simultaneously elevating the new art above the modern practice of ancient modes, she declared that not until neophytes in the arts of musical speech learn to speak with imagination and ecstasy will their separate arts ever become alive and move an audience. In effect, the reciter must become a magician:

> When beginners attempt to speak to musical notes they fall naturally into the intoning as heard throughout our lands in our various religious rituals. It is not until they have been forced to use their imaginations and express the inmost meaning of the words, not until their thought imposes itself upon all listeners and each word invokes a special mode of beauty, that the method rises once more from the dead and becomes a living art.

Yeats could not have said it more eloquently himself; Farr's "note" went right into volume iii of the *Collected Works* and later became a permanent addendum to "Speaking to the Psaltery."[34]

No sooner had Farr notified Yeats of her impending departure than two unexpected communications arrived from Harley Granville-Barker and the editors of the *New Age*. Granville-Barker had sent her an out-of-the-blue invitation to give a reading of the *Bacchae* with his wife of one year, the actress Lillah McCarthy. Simultaneously, following the initial success of her articles on Ibsen's women, Orage and Jackson had offered her further work. As only one firm booking had been made in Buffalo, and even though her Boston agent had already printed a circular for national distribution, she wrote to Quinn on September 17 that "a good offer" to write dramatic criticism for the *New Age* "at very good pay—a thing I have always longed to do in London has induced me to postpone America until the end of January." The further inducement was the opportunity of giving several readings of Greek plays with Mrs Granville-Barker. "I thought I should only be able to do one," she explained to Quinn, "but now I shall be able to do some more perhaps." It was an untoward decision; the momentum for the tour was broken. She would never visit America again, or see Quinn, and her free-wheeling contrast of the degraded status of prostitutes in Western civilization with their sacred veneration in ancient Eastern civilizations would lead to her early removal from the weekly's columns.[35] "The New Age is getting very stodgy now," she wrote to Quinn on June 18, 1908. "They are not taking any more articles by me as Shaw says . . . I am 'one of the victims of the revolutionary paper which is like a woman of bad character always trying to show she is respectable.' He says at the same time my articles 'though scandalous were extremely amusing and stimulating.' "

A more serious setback to the new art was also in the making. Even before he went to Coole to work on his *Collected Works*, there was evidence of a subterranean rift developing between Yeats and Frank Fay, an off-shoot of the larger friction created when the English director Alfred Waring was brought in over William Fay to conduct the Abbey's spring tour in 1906. As bad feelings and jealousies developed, the situation was compounded

34. The "Note by Florence Farr" and her music for the lyrics were incorporated into "Speaking to the Psaltery" in Yeats's *Essays* (London: Macmillan, 1924), the fourth volume of Macmillan's *Collected Works*, 1922–6, and subsequently into *Essays and Introductions* (London: Macmillan, 1961).

35. See Farr's "The Rites of Astaroth," *New Age* (September 5, 1907), 294–5.

by Yeats's announcement that he was bringing an English actress, Letitia Darragh, into the company for the autumn productions of his *Deirdre* and *The Shadowy Waters*. When Frank Fay learned that Miss Darragh was to receive the parts of Deirdre and Dectora over Sara Allgood, he protested to Yeats in his most remonstrative voice:

> You are not interested in acting. That is why I argue against you. The public likes acting: you want to get the public. You won't get them by my delivery of verse; you will get them for my brother and Miss Allgood. . . . You want oratory and peculiar personal qualities, what you call distinction and so forth. The public cares precious little for them. I am not admitting that Miss Allgood has not or will not develop these qualities. But it seems to me the mistake you make is judging actors not for how they can act but on their personal qualities.[36]

By the end of the year, the division between Yeats and the Fay brothers had become increasingly strained, evident in Yeats's highly critical "Plan of Reoganization" for the National Theatre Society, written out on December 2. Asserting that as the only verse writer in the theatre he should have control over the verse plays, he stated that while Frank Fay is "a born teacher of elocution up to a certain point" the actors come from his hands "without passion, without expression, either in voice or gesture" (*CL4* 531).[37] He was even more critical of Frank himself, declaring that he was no longer improving his own verse speaking. "I am not quite sure that he is as good as he was. I do not want to add acting in the sense of movement as he thinks, but I have always asked for a degree of expressiveness in voice, not less but more than that required for prose drama" (*CL4* 532). Adding insult to injury, Yeats wished to make provision for Farr to make an annual visit to Dublin for the teaching of verse speaking, and he reserved the right to bring in Farr and Darragh "or some equivalent" as needed for his plays.

The acrimonious situation was further exacerbated for both Fay brothers when, following the *Playboy* riots, yet another English stage director, Ben Iden Payne, was brought in to conduct the company's spring tour of

36. Letter of July 20, 1906, NLI MS 13068.

37. Yeats wrote unguardedly in the letter that "From the first day of the Theatre I have known that it is almost impossible for us to find a passionate woman actress in Catholic Ireland." In a letter of Decemer 22, 1908, Frank Fay confirmed to Patrick Hovey that Yeats had refused to let Sara Allgood play Deirdre in the opening performance on November 24, 1906 "because he said she had no passion. Old Lady Gregory once told me that Roman Catholic girls did not have passion and hence it became necessary to import Miss Darragh. I still think Yeats's Deirdre has merely Lust—a different thing, as I take it from Passion" (Huntington, HM 26381).

England. Not only were they to suffer the indignity of having an English director of Irish plays, but Payne cast his wife, the actress Mona Limerick, as Deirdre instead of Sara Allgood.[38] Not insensitive to the friction and ill-feelings, Payne resigned at the end of the tour. As William Fay reflected on events, "The consequence of Iden Payne's appointment that I had foreseen and of which I had warned the directors duly came to pass. Although I was nominally in full control again, the old spirit of camaraderie was gone and the company was thoroughly out of hand."[39]

In this out-of-hand atmosphere, Yeats and Frank Fay began to clash more frequently over the speaking of verse in the plays, and their mutual respect deteriorated rapidly. On April 7, 1907, just after Yeats left for Italy, Fay vented his disgruntlements to W. J. Lawrence, the Dublin drama critic who had led the attack on the *Playboy*, writing that he thought Yeats was "worse than useless" as a stage manager. [40] In a subsequent letter to Lawrence of May 24, Fay's more pointed critical dagger went straight to the heart of the matter, criticizing as he did Yeats's theory of beautiful words as "effeminate artistry": "His love of beautiful words & sounds is all right, but Ireland needs masculine thought & a human drama, not 'Shadowy Waters,' and putrid 'Deirdres,' bleating about a life they never lived." During rehearsals in November for the production of *The Unicorn from the Stars*, Yeats said of their problem to William Fay that Frank cared for nothing but beautiful speech and that he cared for nothing but beautiful words.[41] Frank

38. Payne's account of his Abbey experience includes a description of Yeats at rehearsals of *Deirdre*: "He spent most of the time walking about and intoning alternate renderings of some line or phrase in a low whisper. (Intoning, by the way, is the only word to describe Yeats's manner of speaking verse.) One, day, when we were rehearsing his *Deirdre*, he was troubled about the end of one of Naoise's speeches. In the prompt script we were using it went, 'Light torches there and drive the shadows out, For day's red end comes up.' There was a muttered accompaniment to the rehearsal from the right aisle as Yeats paced up and down. 'Day's *grey* end comes up; day's *red* end comes up.' His voice gradually grew louder and louder, and eventually I had to ask him to remember that a rehearsal was in progress. He apologized and asked which reading I preferred. He even said he would abide by my decision. I preferred red as the more dramatic coloring for sunset, and red it was for the production of the play. But later on he must have changed his mind, for in the final edition of *Deirdre* day's end was grey" (*Life in a Wooden O: Memoirs of the Theatre* [New Haven and London: Yale University Press, 1977], 72).

39. W. G. Fay and Catherine Carswell, *The Fays of the Abbey Theatre: An Autobiographical Record* (New York: Harcourt, Brace 1933), 228.

40. Fay's letters to W. J. Lawrence are in NLI MS 10952.

41. Frank Fay confirmed this in a letter of April 28, 1908, to Patrick Hovey: "Yeats's verse is often beautiful sound; but it is often pure artistry. He told my brother, when we were rehearsing the lamentable comedy of the Unicorn from the Stars that I cared for nothing but beautiful speech and he cared for nothing but beautiful words" (Huntington, HM 26374). Yeats's specific complaint is evident in his letter to Lady Gregory on May 5, 1910, when Fay

had come to believe that Yeats's verse was not dramatic, the cause of his inability to bring Cuchulain alive in *On Baile's Strand* like he did Seanchan in *The King's Threshold*. The quarrels between the two lovers of verse and drama had become irreconcilable. On January 13, 1908, in the heat of such recriminations, the Fays left the Abbey Theatre.

During the turmoil and stress of this major upheaval in the theatre, Yeats was engaged in sitting for a series of portraits to serve as frontispieces for the *Collected Works*. He had sat for Augustus John at Coole and for his father and Antonio Mancini in Dublin, and he went to his first sitting for Charles Shannon on January 8. Later that month he had a photographic sitting for the American photographer Alvin Langdon Coburn, who was now living in England. Yeats had met Coburn through William Orpen, who had sat for Coburn on January 14, and Lady Gregory invited him to a dinner party to honor Hugh Lane on the opening of his Dublin art gallery in Clonmell House. Coburn was seated directly across the table from Yeats, who was dressed in a velvet coat and flowing black tie. At the end of the meal, wrote Coburn,

> he recited one of his own poems, and it occurred to me how few people would have been able to do this. He seemed hardly conscious of the people as he spoke. What he did would have been a pose in anyone else, but with him it was quite natural, for Yeats is a real poet.

When they talked after dinner, Yeats agreed to give Coburn a photographic sitting the next morning.

> I remembered how he had looked reciting at the dinner table, and I asked him if he would do so again while I photographed him. Without any hesitation he began on some beautiful lines, while I flared a magnesium flash-light at intervals. . . . [T]his seemed the most fitting way of getting the effect of speaking in the portrait of Yeats.[42] (Plate 13)

Coburn's photograph of Yeats chanting was included on Yeats's list of portraits for Bullen in March, but it was finally excluded, to be used later as the frontispiece for Bullen's edition of *Poems: Second Series* (1910).

wanted to return to the company: "Any desire I have for Frank Fay is founded on his teaching of acting not on his verse speaking. I had sooner not have him teaching them to sing the verse & getting cross when I object" (*CL InteLex* 1347).

42. Alvin Langdon Coburn, *Men of Mark* (London: Duckworth, 1913), 24–5, with accompanying photograph, number XIX, one of a series taken that morning. Coburn later specialized in photographs with birth-charts, including his photograph and horoscope of Yeats, and bequeathed them to the Universal Brotherhood, of which he was a member, and through which they were received by the Astrological Association in London.

When it was evident that her American tour had collapsed, Farr decided to take the psaltery to Mentone, on the French Riviera, where she would also work on a novel entitled *All Sorts and Conditions of Love*.[43] There she met Harry Villiers Barnett, formerly an art critic, editor, and journalistic confrère of W. E. Henley, who had moved from London to the Riviera in 1904 and founded *The Continental Weekly*. "A new Troubadour has come chanting through Provence," Barnett wrote after interviewing Farr and attending a performance, "and I am persuaded that she is more splendid, more skilled, more subtle, more various, and far more expressive than were any of her predecessors of the Middle Ages.... Florence Farr has re-found the Troubadour's secret and some other, older and more precious, secrets as well."[44] Barnett lavished extensive praise on her voice, instrument, interpretation, and "high artistic genius." He was struck by the "cunningly simple" psaltery and the way she used it to punctuate a note, chord, or melodic phrase and occasionally to counterpoint the melody of her voice: "The wire strings are tuned to a complete chromatic scale," he observed.

> They are arranged in couples sounding a note and its octave. By this means Mr. Dolmetsch, the inventor, secured a roundness and mystery of sound which single strings could never produce. The sounds are subtle, soft, and of a peculiarly delightful, antique timbre. They provide a curious and romantic background for the voice, a non-insistent, far off, delicate horizon of significant, suggestive tone.

She could not have found in France a more enthusiastic critic or a more appreciative audience, which included the Swedish operatic prima donna Christine Nilsson (Comtesse de Miranda), who personally congratulated her. "It is a new music," Barnett declared, "a new and great addition to the world's store of beauty, and you have only to taste such an experience of it as was vouchsafed at Mentone on Monday to understand why so many of the acutest intellects of our time have welcomed it with wonder and praise." The highlight of the performance to Barnett was her rendering of a fragment of Homer. In introducing the piece, she told the audience that her recitation was based on the method used by modern Athenians in reciting Homer's poetry, as explained to her by an old Greek gentleman.

43. This manuscript, completed during her second visit to Mentone in January 1912, was eventually published as *The Solemnization of Jacklin* (London: A. C. Fifield, 1912).

44. Farr quotes from Barnett's article on her in *The Music of Speech*, 9–12; copies of *The Continental Weekly*, which she refers to as the "Green Paper," have not been located.

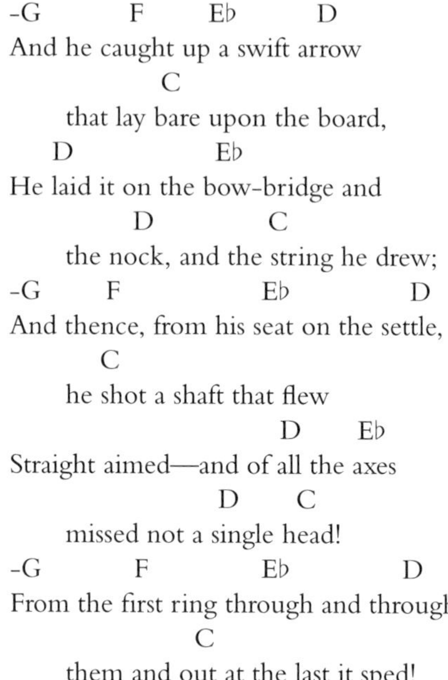

-G F E♭ D
And he caught up a swift arrow
C
that lay bare upon the board,
D E♭
He laid it on the bow-bridge and
D C
the nock, and the string he drew;
-G F E♭ D
And thence, from his seat on the settle,
C
he shot a shaft that flew
D E♭
Straight aimed—and of all the axes
D C
missed not a single head!
-G F E♭ D
From the first ring through and through
C
them and out at the last it sped!

"Thus she began on a descending scale from the dominant in a minor mode," reported Barnett,

> first enunciating the theme on the psaltery, and then uttering the noble syllables of William Morris's translation of "The Odyssey" to approximately the same notes; so the verse moved in drama and in tones whose lines of music really reproduced in sound the gravity and grace of an antique frieze until, at the close, the original theme reappeared, and with an intensity and beauty of effect that cannot be described the speaking song was replaced by the veritable singing song. Than this, nothing could be more impressive.

Farr remained in Mentone until late April, writing to Quinn that she was to give concerts in Bordighera and Monte Carlo: "I only wish you were here now!" She was herself much missed by Yeats, as he worked apace on volumes of the *Collected Works*, returned to London to resume sitting for Shannon, and began sitting for a charcoal by John Sargent and a bronze mask by Kathleen Bruce. "Yeats tells me my next birthday has a most extraordinary combination of planets," Farr had written to Quinn on March 25. "He tells me he is going to London now and wants me to return but the weather is too fine here." Yeats wanted her in London for practical as well as personal reasons, for he was now beginning to put together a section to be entitled "Poems for the Psaltery" and had drafted his introduction, "Music for Lyrics," self-consciously asserting his certainty "that all poets, even all delighted readers of poetry, speak certain kinds of poetry to distinct and simple tunes, though the speakers may be, perhaps generally are, deaf to ordinary music, even what we call tone-deaf" (*CW3* 234).[45] Sifting through the settings in his possession, he wrote to Edith Lister on April 7:

> I send you a number of lilts. The one marked 'lilt by AD' ['The Song of the Old Mother'] was taken down by A Dolmetsch from myself—at least he told me so . . . I also sent a 'Wandering Aengus' lilt which is my own & the one Pixie Smith sings. If it is any good put it in. It is quite unembellished. . . . I have written to Miss Farr for more. [46]

It was crucial that Farr come up with the musical settings for his lyrics as she did for the plays. "I am putting a great mass of Psaltery settings to my lyrics in the collected edition—," he wrote to Lady Gregory on April 17, "at least if I can get them out of Mrs. Emery."[47] Perhaps his next letter to Farr on April 21 was designed to appeal to her sympathy and hasten her return: "London is unendurable when you are not in it. I have no real friends—I have been too long away—and wander about without a soul to whom I can talk as if to myself. I go to bad plays or blind myself with reading by candle light out of bordeom."[48]

He was not so lonely in Dublin, however, where he had begun a new and intimate relationship with an aspiring actress, Mabel Dickinson. Offering her services as an exercise therapist and masseuse, she had recently moved into rooms in Nassau Street, conveniently near the Nassau Hotel, where Yeats stayed in Dublin. As they began to meet at the United Arts Club and elsewhere, he praised the "personality" of her acting as if she were one of his new "discoveries." "You can act," he wrote to her in March. "You have dignity without stiffness and emotion without insincerity and movement without artifice."[49] He also began to tell her a great deal about the psaltery. Never one to miss an opportunity of persuading an attractive actress to take it up, he used the instrument to coax her into his company, telling her that he would bring his own psaltery back from London on his next visit. On

45. The original manuscript for Yeats's introduction, originally entitled "Lyrics Set to Music for the Speaking Voice," is in the Spencer Research Library, Kansas University (MS 25Wb.2:2).
46. Letter of April 7, 1908, *CL InteLex* 850
47. Letter of April 17, 1908, *CL InteLex* 865.
48. Letter of April 21, 1908, *CL InteLex* 873.
49. Letter of [March 29, 1908], *CL InteLex* 844.

April 17 he wrote to her that "Shannon has put a Psaltery—the one I am to bring to Dublin—& a magic crystal and a rose into the background of my portrait."[50]

At the end of the month, Yeats received the disturbing news that Synge had gone into the hospital for another operation, necessitating Yeats's immediate return to Dublin to take over rehearsals. On May 11 he broke away from theatre matters to write to Miss Dickinson:

> I have brought my Psaltery to Ireland & am writing for proofs of some Psaltery music which is to make a part of my Collected edition. I have left the Psaltery at Cramers to have a new string put on it. May I come & show it to you & try what you can do with it. People born under your star have almost always acting gifts, & you may yet do beautiful things with this instrument of mine if you will try it.[51]

As their relationship deepened, she may have experimented with the psaltery and the chanting to a modest degree. In March 1909 he wanted to give her a role in *The King's Threshold*, but thereafter there is little evidence of her interest in the instrument; however, at the Irish Literary Society celebration of the Samuel Ferguson centenary on March 5, 1910, she appeared on the program with Farr and Anna Mather, taking a part in chanting Ferguson's "The Naming of Cuchullain."[52] Their five-year romance-affair ended in May 1913 after Yeats, "horror struck" by her announced pregnancy, swiftly escaped from a frightening false alarm.

Farr proved to be difficult in coming up with music for Yeats's poems, or at least Yeats thought that she had made or preserved more settings for his lyrics than was actually the case. In disappointment, Yeats had to write to Miss Lister to change the heading of "music to the psaltery" to "mainly for the psaltery," "as only a few of the lyrics I have remembered have accompaniments." On the other hand, Yeats or Bullen may have decided to limit the number, given the combined length of music for plays and lyrics in the appendix, for on June 18 Farr wrote to Quinn: "I have written out a lot of my music for the Collected Edition which will appear in vol III

50. Letter of April 17, 1908, *CL InteLex* 864. Shannon's portrait of Yeats, with the psaltery propped and resting on the left border (see Plate 12), was used as the frontispiece for volume iii; the original painting now hangs in the Houghton Library, Harvard University. Shannon decided to place the psaltery in the painting as a characteristic object in Yeats's life, but it was obscured by the reduction for the frontispiece photograph and by the poor, darkened quality of subsequent reproductions.

51. Letter of [May 11, 1908], *CL InteLex* 899.

52. "Irish Literary Society," *Irish Book Lover*, 1 (April 1910), 124. R. F. Foster says that she coached Molly Allgood in "Swedish drill" in rehearsals for her role in Synge's *Deirdre* (*Life 1* 413).

I believe. W B Yeats is very pleased about it all and has been arriving at cockcrow at Shannon's studio I'm told." She could not resist joking with Quinn about Yeats's vanity: "But that was quite necessary as it took him all the time (till Shannon was ready) to rearrange his tie and his hair." In its final form, the appendix to volume iii contained only three of her settings: "The wind blows out of the gates of the day," a lyric chanted as the Faery Child is carried away in *The Land of Heart's Desire;* "The Happy Townland," from the unpublished play "The Country of the Young" (which became *The Travelling Man*); and "I Have Drunk Ale from the Country of the Young" ("He Thinks of his Past Greatness When a Part of the Constellations of Heaven") from *The Wind Among the Reeds*, with a notation that all of the music "suits my speaking voice if played an octave lower than the notation" (*CW3* 237). The other three lyrics included were Dolmetsch's notations for Yeats's chanting of "The Song of Wandering Aengus" and "The Song of the Old Mother" and for A. H. Bullen's chanting of "The Host of the Air."[53] Missing from the record were the numerous other lyrics by Yeats that Farr had spoken to the psaltery during the past eight years.

With the main work of the *Collected Works* behind him, Yeats left London immediately to visit Maud Gonne in Paris. "Yeats has entirely disappeared for a whole month," Farr informed Quinn on July 13. "He went to Paris about that time ago to see Maud Gonne & I've not heard or seen a sign of him since. So I imagine that his long years of fidelity have been rewarded at last!" If not his fidelity, at least his steadfast devotion was by year's end to find recompense, the evidence suggests, with the consummation of his long-frustrated love for Maud Gonne. During his daily visits to Maud Gonne's house at 13 rue de Passy, he relaxed into the family life with Seán, now four, Iseult, now fourteen, and Maud's friend Ella Young, an occasional member of the household. Describing Iseult as "a beautiful dark-eyed dark-haired girl" who could hold her own in every discussion, Young witnessed the avuncular Yeats teaching her to chant to the psaltery: "She has a lovely voice," wrote Young, "and the Poet is

53. In his "Music for Lyrics," Yeats identified the first two as "taken down by Mr. Arnold Dolmetsch from myself" and the third as taken down by Dolmetsch "from a fine scholar in poetry, who hates all music but that of poetry, and knows of no instrument that does not fill him with rage and misery." The "fine scholar" is A. H. Bullen; his initials accompany the musical notation (*CW3* 238; *E&I* 26). In his letter to Edith Lister of May 24, asking her to change "Music to the Psaltery" to "Mainly for the Psaltery," Yeats stated that " 'O'Driscoll drove with a song' for instance to Mr. Bullen could hardly I suppose be helped by a psaltery" (NLI MS 13307 [4]).

teaching her to chant verse as he thinks it should be chanted. He is desirous of chanting verse to the sound of a plangent string, a note now and then for accompaniment or emphasis. He has in mind an instrument unfamiliar and strange-looking, worthy to be carried in the hand, and yielding a pleasant resonance when plucked by the finger."[54] Gonne did not object to this instruction, though having abandoned the psaltery herself she affirmed that she was "in favour of the voice alone." During that extraordinary month, the drawing room in Paris, like many another in London and Dublin, was turned into a veritable chantry. For her part, Gonne was preparing her play, *Dawn*, for a performance by the Daughters of Ireland. Young had written the two lyrics chanted by the Bride in the play, "A Lament" and "The Red Sunrise," both of which Gonne chanted, like the lyrics of *Cathleen ni Houlihan*, "to music that came to her in dream—music out of the faery world."[55]

After Yeats returned to Coole from Paris, he knew that he owed Farr a long-overdue letter: "the result of your sending me those lines—alas—to put into chantable English is that I have never written to you."[56] What moved him to write was the gnawing uncertainty of Mrs. Patrick Campbell's promised production of his *Deirdre*. "Have you seen Mrs. Campbell?" he asked her. "Do you know what she plans to do? Is she really going to come here? I have put *Deirdre* into rehearsal but I have never really believed she would play in it." The highlight of the previous year for Yeats had been her revelation to him, after the Abbey players had put on a special matinee performance for her and her company on October 25, that she would return from America to produce Yeats's *Deirdre* at the Abbey Theatre in a year's time. She allowed Yeats to make the special announcement from the Abbey stage after the matinee performances, and she announced it herself from the stage of the Gaiety Theatre in her farewell address the following night. "Mrs. Campbell has won my heart for ever," he wrote to Farr. "I am fifty times more grateful to her than I would have been if she had put the Play on in a London Theatre. It is a really beautiful thing of her to

54. Ella Young, *Flowering Dusk* (New York and Toronto: Longmans, Green, 1945), 102.

55. Ibid. Gonne's one-act *Dawn*, an imitative patriotic melodrama strongly reminiscent of *Cathleen ni Houlihan*, was published in the *United Irishman* on October 29, 1904, and in the *Gaelic American* on November 5, 1904, but no record of its performance has been traced. It was reprinted in *Lost Plays of the Irish Renaissance*, ed. Robert Hogan and James Kilroy (Proscenium Press, 1970), 73–84.

56. Letter of [late September 1908]; Wade transcribes Yeats's holograph as "chantable English" (*L* 511), John Kelly as "charitable English," *CL InteLex* 968.

come into our little Theatre and play there bringing us her great name and her great fame—A beautiful romantic thing. You do not often see me in this mood but I am really touched" (*CL4* 763). Despite the fading faith that a long year with no communication had brought, she would keep her promise to Yeats. She had returned to England with the play that had been her American success, Arthur Symons' translation of Hugo Von Hofmannsthal's *Electra,* with scenery by Ricketts, and she had engaged Farr to play Clytemnestra to her Electra. When he learned that they were to open at the Court Theatre in Liverpool on October 21, Yeats stole away on the first boat from Dublin to join them.

The play was a duologue of magnificent tragic voices that Yeats would never forget. "I remember the shudder in my spine," he wrote twenty-three years later, "when Mrs. Patrick Campbell said, speaking words Hofmannsthal put into the mouth of Electra, 'I too am of that ancient race' " (*Expl* 345). Yeats would meet there a young twenty-seven-year-old journalist from the *Liverpool Courier*, Dixon Scott, who was overwhelmed by the beauty and power of the voices. "Miss Florence Farr," he wrote of her Clytemnestra in his florid review,

> lacked (or rather she had no reason for) those rare bodily devices which Mrs. Campbell uses to sustain the dark glamour of her voice; but her speech was always full of a significant and sinister beauty. To hear the two voices in turn, leaping and retaliating, beating up into fierce contrasts, and striking out dim harmonies was to get a pleasure impossible to describe in words. The voice of Mrs. Campbell had the quality of deep waters—now running in sudden, snarling cascades of rich sound—now sliding into something secret and dim, like a still pool in the black heart of some forest. But that of Miss Farr's surged and moaned like the wind in the trees of that forest, like an old wind wandering among eternal pines; and when it fell a little, or drooped towards tenderness, it was but to provoke that strange, desirable terror which comes upon men when they hear lost winds chattering dreadfully among the last year's leaves.[57]

Scott wrote to his friend Mary McCrossan about his extraordinary fortune in meeting Yeats. "Isn't it stupendous? He was in Liverpool . . . unknown to anybody except Mrs. Patrick Campbell—he had come over with the express purpose of seeing her play 'Electra.' "[58] His awe of the poet, however, was soon displaced by the glamour of Farr, who swept him off his

57. " 'Electra' / Mrs. Patrick Campbell's Triumph," *Liverpool Courier*, October 22, 1908, 8.
58. Letter of October 24, 1908, *The Letters of W. Dixon Scott*, ed. Mary McCrossan (London: Herbert Joseph, 1932), 67.

feet with her open arms. He informed McCrossan incredulously that she had agreed to have dinner with him the next night. "I had speech with her yesterday too; for she came into the University Club . . . and publicly fell on my neck and kissed me for my notice of her 'Electra' effort ." Astonished by the attention to him of an actress almost twice his age, he sent McCrossan a vivid account of his Liverpool evening:

> Had you been in Princes Road at 10.30 on Saturday night you'd have seen an amazing spectacle: a wonderful Egyptian-looking person, habited in purples and umbers and scarlets and great hats and veils, cavaliered by a lean and hungry youth in spectacles, emerging from the recesses of Ullet Road and boarding a car in company. The Scarlet Woman was Florence Farr; the youth, your servant. 'Twas a gory and colossal time. I had to see her home; and we talked and talked; and she is very very glamorous and vivid."[59]

Yeats's primary mission in Liverpool was to prepare the way for Mrs. Campbell's performance in *Deirdre* at the Abbey for the week beginning November 9, but from their talk emerged her wholly unexpected proposal to work closely with him on his new play still in composition, *The Player Queen*, for possible production by her. "She wants me to write," Yeats wrote to Quinn, "as she phrases it, with her at my elbow."[60] She had also made plans to produce *Deirdre* in London on a double bill with *Electra* later in the month, but she would honor Yeats in Dublin first, coming for rehearsals on November 2 at her own expense. When the play opened a week later before a packed, "spellbound" audience, Mrs. Campbell, backed by Sara Allgood, Maire O'Neill, and Eileen O'Doherty as the three musicians, gave Yeats his most successful night at the Abbey since its opening. Holloway was greatly impressed with the performance of Sara Allgood:

> The beautiful speech, exquisite posing, and delicious chanting of Sara Allgood as the 'First Musician' led up to the coming of the ill-fated pair of lovers in truly poetic way. The atmosphere was perfectly created by this unusually talented young player so that when "Deirdre" in the person of Mrs. Campbell appeared, the way had been perfectly paved for her great, well-won success.
>
> (*JHAT* 120)

"Never before have the beauties of this play been brought out as they were last night with Mrs. Patrick Campbell in the principal part," wrote the critic for the *Freeman's Journal*:

59. Ibid. 69–70. The irrepressible Scott was to die of dysentery at Gallipoli in 1915.
60. Letter of [October 30–November 15, 1908], *CL InteLex* 980.

> The beautiful words were beautifully spoken, and not only in her speech, but in her every motion, Mrs. Campbell gave us a Deirdre full of life, vigour, the majestic beauty, such as would seem to have been the author's conception of the part. Mrs. Campbell has had many great triumphs in her long connection with the stage, but those who have seen her in many parts say that she surpassed herself last night.[61]

An outburst of enthusiastic and prolonged applause met the fall of the curtain, and after Mrs. Campbell came forward for three bows there were calls for Yeats to speak: "I can only say very few words," he began, flushed with emotion, "after one of the greatest experiences which can ever come to a writer, that is to hear his words perfectly spoken and perfectly acted. It is for these experiences that we write, for these that we live, and I am profoundly moved, and so you must permit me to remain silent."

The actors and directors then adjourned to the Gresham Hotel, where Mrs. Campbell hosted a dinner in their honor, with Farr and Gwendolyn Bishop included as her guests. During rehearsals, Mrs. Campbell had been so impressed with Sara Allgood's chanting of the lyrics of the First Musician that she summoned her daughter Stella and Farr to hear her. Farr, listening to Allgood chant in a role that Yeats had created in her image, was enviously disconcerted at being merely an onlooker of the play in which she was heavily invested. Holloway was sensitive to such reactions: "Miss Farr was finding fault with everyone [Arthur] Sinclair told me." Not to be upstaged or excluded from the proceedings, Farr determined that she and Bishop would perform after the dinner, as if to assert her preeminence as a performer of chanted verse. "Miss Farr recited a little poem by Arthur O'Shaughnessy—," reported Holloway, "a gem in its way [J. M.] Kerrigan thought. A Miss Bishop danced a Salome dance." After the second-night performance, the company held a dinner in the same venue in Mrs. Campbell's honor, with Holloway present to record that "Miss Florence Farr repeated one of Yeats's shorter lyrics ['He Gives His Beloved Certain Rhymes']—the one composed to Maud Gonne years ago in which the poet bids her brush her hair with a golden brush—in her best chant-like tones."[62] Such was her way of maintaining an authoritative presence in

61. "The Abbey Theatre / Mrs. Patrick Campbell as 'Deirdre,'" *Freeman's Journal*, November 10, 1908, 10. In "The Irish Helen" the critic for the *Irish Independent* reported that "her emotional intensity was stupendous and her voice took unwonted variety of tone from whimper to wail" (November 10, 1908, 4).

62. This passage was deleted from the entry in *JHAT* 121–2.

the company and of affirming her role as instructor and performer when needed in future productions of Yeats's romantic plays.

The next night, after the concluding performance, Yeats went on stage to thank the audience "for the manner in which you have received my play" and to express his gratitude to Mrs. Campbell:

> She has shown me my work in a way I should never have thought to have seen it. She has put into it qualities which I never dreamed of possessing. She has given us to-night one of the most noble and beautiful performances that I have ever seen, one which moved me, because, after all, they are my own words. Nothing ever moved me like it and I am glad to find that others were moved also (applause).[63]

The Dublin papers were uniformly impressed by the import of the production, and in a generous editorial the *Daily Express* stated that "This obviously genuine tribute from a great actress has greatly gratified the following of the Abbey Theatre, and drawn to it many to whom it was terra incognito."[64] The paper went on to praise the impact of the Abbey on the Dublin dramatic scene and to weigh its importance as a counterbalance to an oppressive "theatre of commerce." By the end of the week Yeats had been lifted into his rapture seat: "Deirdre has been played with triumphant success," he wrote to Quinn, "great audiences and great enthusiasm . . . There has not been one hostile voice here & I am now accepted as a dramatist in Dublin. Mrs. Campbell was magnificent."[65]

She was also magnanimous, offering to take Sara Allgood to London as First Musician in *Deirdre* and as Chrysothemis in *Electra*. After the first of several matinees opened at the New Theatre on November 27, she was singled out for praise as the Irish actress "who, besides declaiming beautifully as the First Musician, also helps in the musical rendering of Arthur Darley's setting of the lyrics, her comrades in alternate chanting and reciting, that recall the work of the Chorus in recent representations of Greek drama."[66]

63. *Daily Express* (Dublin), November 12, 1908, 4.

64. Ibid.

65. Letter of [October 30–November 15, 1908], *CL InteLex* 980.

66. "The New," *The Stage*, December 3, 1908, 13. There were further matinee performances on December 8, 10, and 11. Farr's settings were still not used. As Yeats had explained in notes dated March 1908, "I have not yet put Miss Farr's *Deirdre* music to the test of performances, but, as she and I have worked out all this art of spoken song together, I have little doubt but I shall find it all I would have it. Mr. Darley's music was used at the first production of the play and at its revival last spring, and was dramaticallly effective. I could hear the words perfectly . . . They had not, however, the full animation of speech, as one heard it in the dirge at the end of the play set by Miss Allgood herself, who played the principal musician. It is very difficult for a musician who is not a speaker to do exactly what I want. Mr. Darley has

Another critic observed that the sense of coming doom in the play "is kept before us largely by means of the three strange wandering minstrel women who crouch over the fire. . . . Miss Sara Allgood, who appears in London too seldom, gave great significance and a compelling charm to the figure of the singing woman."[67] She was further praised for her acting of Chrysothemis: "In this part Miss Allgood, by the simplicity and emotional sincerity of her performance, further shows her merits as an actress in poetic drama and hence gives admirable support to Mrs. Patrick Campbell, whose embodiment of Electra . . . is as powerful, moving, and truly tragic an embodiment as she has given for years." Yeats, exhilarated by the opening performances, was again called to the stage. If he was to be criticized for bringing English actresses to the Abbey stage, he could take delight in Allgood's commanding presence on the English stage, chanting his lyrics and demonstrating with Farr the impact of the new art on dramatic and choral speech. "Yeats has been over in high feather," Farr wrote to Quinn on December 5, herself the object of favorable reviews. "Miss Florence Farr's Clytemnestra," declared the *Times*, "is the most powerful thing we have seen her do."[68]

On that day, as Farr wrote her letter to Quinn, Yeats was called on by Reginald Hine, a young lawyer who hoped that Yeats would read his first book, *Anima Celtica*, a study of Irish literature and culture. As Yeats's eyes were too bad to read, he insisted on showing Hine some of his books, including his Ballantyne Club edition (1827) of Gavin Douglas's *Palice of Honour* (1553), Gérard de Nerval's *Le Rêve et la Vie* (1855), and a first edition of Baudelaire's *Fleurs du Mal* (1857), telling colorful stories about each author. "When it grew time to go," wrote Hine,

> I begged a parting favour. Catching sight of his *Cathleen ni Houlihan* I asked, would he sit by the fire and croon over the lyrics *I will go cry with the woman,*

written for singers not for speakers. . . . I have not had sufficient opportunity to experiment with the play to find out the exact distance from ordinary speech necessary in the first two lyrics, which must prolong the mood of the dialogue while being a rest from its passions. Miss Farr's music will be used at the next revival of the play" (*CW3* 223). Yeats included Farr's settings for all three Musicians' songs and Sara Allgood's for the third song in the *Collected Works* (*CW3* 228–30), omitting Darley's music for the play. When he reprinted this note in *Plays in Prose and Verse* (London: Macmillan, 1922) he remarked that "I have never found but three people, Miss Farr, a certain Miss [Hilda] Taylor . . . and Miss Sara Allgood who could chant or sing modern poetry," reprinting the music of Farr and Allgood because "it is part of an attempt, which seemed to me important, to recover an art once common and now lost" (435).

67. "New Theatre," *The Times*, November 28, 1908, 13.

68. Ibid.

> *Do not make a great keening,* and *They shall be remembered for ever,* following the musical notes as printed in the play? To this he smilingly consented, and added to my delight by showing me the original, preserved with the rest of his manuscripts and his tarot cards and his astrological calculations in a long chest. In years to come I was to listen to him reading or rather chaunting from his own poems at the Poetry Society and in many a London hall, but it was never the same; never again did the lines come hauntingly home with the intimacy, the secret private pleasure, the ineffaceable impression of that first fireside reading; 'they *shall* be remembered for ever.'[69]

Maud Gonne meanwhile had come to London for the production of *Deirdre*, and as soon as he could get away he followed her back to Paris until the end of December. There he worked on *The Player Queen* for Mrs. Campbell and on "No Second Troy" for Maud Gonne. "Why should I blame her that she filled my days | With misery" he asks himself of his noble, Helenized love, who would now receive him on the physical as once on the astral plane and address him as her "Dearest" and her "beloved"—previously only as her "friend" (*G-YL* 258). On the 9th, when Nevinson called on Farr, he heard incredulously "of Yeats & how in Paris lately Maud Gonne had at last given in & told him she had really loved him all these 15 years. That he has made his vain affection the chief string of his poetry, & now he is happy, the string snaps!"[70] Nonetheless, the potentially disastrous year that began with the departure of the Fays had ended in a triumph at the Abbey and at the New, in the complete publication of the *Collected Works*, and in the intimate embrace of Maud Gonne. If he was indeed now the established poet, accepted dramatist, and welcomed lover, he was in all of these roles no less the champion of the living voice.

To further establish the presence and influence of the new art, Farr printed a new circular, "Chanting & Speaking to the Music of a Psaltery," and on December 10 set out upon another provincial tour to Glasgow, Edinburgh, Dundee, Liverpool, and Leeds, concluding in Chesterfield on December 21. "Miss Farr's voice is full and soft, and infinitely varied in expression," wrote the Chesterfield critic; "such a voice is found only once or twice in a generation." Farr included among the lyrics and choruses a passage from Swinburne's "Tristram of Lyonesse," Nietzsche's "Song of Life," a "wonderfully dramatic" poem from the *Zarathustra Rhapsodies*,

69. Reginald Hine, *Confessions of an Un-Common Attorney* (London: J. M. Dent & Sons, 1945), 153.
70. Nevinson diary, Bodleian.

and an unidentified poem by the Chesterfield poet Edward Carpenter. Carpenter, who had been her colleague at the *New Age*, was himself in the audience and afterwards stood to propose the vote of thanks, "testifying warmly to the value and beauty of her method and the genius of her dramatic rendering. This rarest art," he declared, "suggests new possibilities of a rational union between music and drama, but at present its one and all-sufficient exponent is Miss Florence Farr."[71] The new art, introduced to Great Britain, North America, and Southern France, was now in full swing. In the past eight years Yeats and Farr had made the new art the most visible poetic movement in Great Britain, but the art of chanting was about to find itself face to face with a major counter-movement in modern poetry.

71. "Lyrical Recital at Chesterfield," *Derbyshire Courier*, December 26, 1908, 8. The democratic socialist poet and novelist Edward Carpenter (1844–1929) had settled in 1891 on a nearby farm—Millthorpe, Holmesfield—near Chesterfield and Sheffield. Notices and reviews of Farr's recitals on this tour appeared in *The Dundee Courier and Argus*, December 16, 1908, 1, which announced the program for her lecture in the Lower West Foresters' Hall; in *The Scotsman* (Edinburgh), December 15, 1908, 1, which reported that "her performance was loudly applauded by the large audience" at the Edinburgh Theosophical Society; and in the *Yorkshire Daily Observer*, December 21, 1908, 7, which reported that in her lecture entitled "The Theatre and the Arts" before the Leeds Arts Club "There was chanting, declamation, and what she would call ordinary speech . . . bringing in to use the psaltery with considerable effect. At the conclusion of the lecture a discussion took place, and Miss Farr answered several questions."

8

"As Regarding Rhythm": Minstrels and Imagists

Soon after Florence Farr returned from her American tour and began writing dramatic criticism for the *New Age*, she found herself in the company of T. E. Hulme and a group of poets who were soon to form what Ezra Pound called "the forgotten school of 1909."[1] Hulme, a brilliant student of maths, Bergson, and French *vers libre*, had been sent down from Cambridge for prankish behavior and had left the University of London in 1906 without graduating. After a maturing year of travel, hard labor, and philosophical reflection in Canada and a short period of teaching English and perfecting his French in Brussels, he returned to London intent upon making an impact on English poetry with his developing Imagist aesthetic. He was soon asked to help organize the Poets' Club, and following a successful subscription of members he was elected Honorary Secretary. In that capacity he set about arranging activities and drawing up a set of rules that stipulated monthly dinner meetings at the United Arts Club in St. James's Street, followed by "a paper on a subject connected with poetry by a member or guest of the Club."[2] What has not been recorded is that Farr, who met Hulme through A. R. Orage and their work as contributors to *The New Age*, was one of the club's first speakers. She wrote to Quinn on June 18, 1908, that she was going to dinner at the United Arts Club "and am to speak and read my translation of Nietzsche's dance

1. Pound so named Hulme's group in his "Prefatory Note" to "The Complete Poetical Works of T. E. Hulme," which he appended to *Ripostes of Ezra Pound* (London: Stephen Swift, 1912), 59.
2. For the rules and objectives drawn up by Hulme for the Poets' Club, see Alun R. Jones, *The Life and Opinions of T. E. Hulme* (Boston: Beacon Press, 1960), 29–30; also in Robert Ferguson, *The Short Sharp Life of T. E. Hulme* (London: Allen Lane, 2002), 44.

song."[3] Most members of the Poets' Club had witnessed and indeed had for several years been indoctrinated in the Yeats–Farr chanting movement, particularly Joseph Campbell, "the mountainy singer," an avid proponent and practitioner of poetry as a spoken art, and Lady Margaret Sackville, who had been an advocate of chanted verse since she first attended one of Yeats's Monday evenings in 1902.[4] Farr's illustrated discussion of chanting before the Poets' Club and the enthusiastic endorsement it surely received actually sparked the first stage of the Imagist movement—by provoking Hulme into formulating his own ideas about counterdirections in modern poetry. The confrontation of Farr's chanting and Hulme's Imagism set off a dialogue on prosody that was to energize the development of *vers libre* and *imagisme* for the next five years. More dramatically, as the recovered activities of the forgotten school reveal, Farr and Yeats set about battling the visual paradigm of the Imagists with their auditory poetics, successfully reshaping their "devil's metres," as Yeats called them,[5] into the third proposition of the Imagist manifesto—"As regarding rhythm: to compose in sequence of the musical phrase, not in sequence of a metronome" (*EPPP1* 119).

The Poets' Club did not hold summer meetings, but when activity resumed in the autumn of 1908 Hulme had put together his "A Lecture

3. NYPL. Farr's translations of passages from *Thus Spake Zarathustra* included "A Dance Song" ("Pray you unlearn the hornblowing of affliction") from "On the Higher Man," first chanted at the opening meeting of the Dancers' Society on December 5, 1903, and subsequently made a familiar part of her repertoire.

4. Yeats had written to Violet Hunt [February 20, 1902]: "The 'chanting' is at my rooms on Monday.... Of course if you can bring Lady Margaret Sackville I shall be delighted" (*CL3* 155). Campbell, originally from Belfast, had collaborated with Herbert Hughes (Padraig Mac Aodh O Neill) in *Songs of Uladh* (1904), a collection of airs and songs with words provided by Campbell, who wrote the epigraph: "These songs we gathered from the Folk, | Who caught them from the Sidhe, | Who sing them in the mountainy airs | To world-old minstrelsie." In reviewing his *The Mountainy Singer* (1909), the critic for the *Irish Book Lover* of October 1909 described him as a poet who "sings in spirited cadences the legends, customs and superstitions that yet linger amongst his own folk" (28). As the organizer of the "Original Nights" for the Irish Literary Society, he would arrange on March 5, 1910, a centenary celebration of Sir Samuel Ferguson, with recitations by Farr, Anna Mather, and himself before a very large audience, as reported in the *Irish Book Lover* of April 1910: "Mr. Joseph Campbell recited Ferguson's translation from the Irish 'The Fair Hills of Ireland,' the Gaelic refrain 'Uileacan dubh O!' being chanted in chorus with excellent effect" (124).

5. "Is Mr. Yeats an Imagiste?" Ezra Pound asked in 1914. "No, Mr. Yeats is a symbolist, but he has written *des Images* as have many good poets before him; so that is nothing against him, and he has nothing against them (*les Imagistes*), at least so far as I know—except what he calls 'their devil's metres.' " See Pound's "The Later Yeats," *Poetry*, 4 (May 1914), 65; rpt. in *Literary Essays of Ezra Pound*, ed. T. S. Eliot (New York: New Directrions, 1968), 378–81; here, 378; also *EPPP1* 242.

on Modern Poetry."[6] Yeats's *Collected Works* had begun to appear at the end of the summer, and Hulme evidently felt that Yeats, whose poetics he implicitly addresses in the lecture, had duly shelved his career and opened the way for protomodernism. Hulme had not wholly escaped Yeats's influence, writing in a poem entitled "The Embankment" of "gold heels on the pavement grey," a direct borrowing of Yeats's "pavements grey" in "The Lake Isle of Innisfree,"[7] but he was opposed to Yeats's chanting and his attempt to bring "the infinite" into poetry. As he plotted his classical reaction to the Yeatsian scene, he jotted down in his "Notes on Language and Style" his opposition to "The popular idea of poet as in communion with the infinite, cf. account of Yeats walking in the woods, but remember Tennyson and his hair" (*CWTEH* 37).[8] Hulme had studied Yeats's poetry and prose carefully, particularly "The Symbolism of Poetry" (1899) and "Magic" (1901), setting him up as the romantic giant to be slain: "W. B. Yeats attempts to ennoble his craft by strenuously believing in supernatural world, race-memory, magic, and saying that symbols can recall these where prose couldn't. This is an attempt to bring in an infinity again" (*CWTEH* 43). Hulme had not yet met Pound, recently arrived in London, or Edward Storer, though he had read two recent reviews of Storer's *Mirrors of Illusion*, one by the poet-critic F. S. Flint. These unacquainted men, each moving independently toward visual, nonmetrical verse, were soon to become Imagist allies, but at the moment Hulme seemed a single voice.

6. Hulme's lecture is published in *The Collected Writings of T. E. Hulme* (*CWTEH* 49–56). The undated lecture has traditionally been dated "1908 or 1909," but internal evidence points to November 1908. In the opening paragraph Hulme refers to an article the previous week in *The Saturday Review*, where the author "spoke of poetry as the means by which it became merged into a higher kind of reality" (*CWTEH* 49). The reference appears to be to an unsigned review of five recent books of poetry, one of which is praised for springing "from a spirit most passionately bent upon the visible and invisible worlds, often both together, seeing them as one," while imagist poet Edward Storer's *Mirrors of Illusion* is criticized as "slag" that can only supply "a spiritual equivalent to the sucking of chocolate" (*Saturday Review*, November 14, 1908, 611–12).
7. The date of composition of "The Embankment" is uncertain, but it was first published in the Club's second volume, *The Book of the Poets' Club* (1909). When the poem was reprinted in the *New Age* in 1912, the wording was changed, evidently under Pound's influence, to "pavement hard," and when it appeared later that year in *Ripostes* (1912) it had been changed to "hard pavement."
8. Hulme evidently alludes to Cornelius Weygandt's interview with Yeats, "With Mr. W. B. Yeats in the Woods of Coole," first published in *Lippincott's Magazine*, 73 (April 1904), 484–7: "Strange visions had come to him, he said, after walking in these woods, visions of 'immortal, mild, proud shadows,' but always as dreams, and not as objective realities. At times, however, he had seen visions in waking dreams, and he felt the border of the unseen so near that no man should say that no man had crossed it.... The poet is now maker of magic and seer, as was in old time the priest" (487).

The principal feature of verse at the present time, he asserted in his lecture, in a public challenge to Yeats and Farr, "is this: that it is read and not chanted" (*CWTEH* 54). In contrasting the features of the outmoded poetry with the trends of the new, he noted the modern movement away from absolute toward relative truth, from heroic action to "momentary phases in the poet's mind," from regular meter to free verse, from hypnotic rhythms to an arresting and exhausting succession of visual images that "serve to suggest and evoke the state" that the poet feels (*CWTEH* 53–4). The character of poetry, he concluded, "has changed from the ancient art of chanting to the modern impressionist, but the mechanism of verse has remained the same. It can't go on doing so" (*CWTEH* 56). For Hulme, the image was to carry the burden of intellectual-emotional evocation, couched in a free-verse prosody that would allow the poet more delicately to arrange his pattern of images and fit the rhythm to the idea. Yeats and Farr, both of whom had often expressed their desire to adapt chanting to modern needs and common, "passionate" speech rhythms, held that the visual image finds its greatest evocative power in the auditory imagination and that the cadence of the living voice, which gives expression to the imagination, gives meter the semblance of freedom.

Shortly after Hulme's lecture, two splinter groups separated themselves from the Poets' Club—Hulme's "little Secessionist" group and an even more forgotten school of 1909, the Poetry Recital Society, founded in February 1909 by Lady Margaret Sackville in an effort to "encourage the intelligent reading of verse with due regard to emphasis and rhythm and the poet's meaning."[9] At the inaugural meeting Lady Margaret spoke on the topic "The Art of Speaking Verse," attacking the techniques of modern elocution and praising the Irish National Theatre Society for its "interesting attempt to break through the traditional methods and introduce a more vital and sincere way of speaking."[10] The Poetry Recital Society, independent of Yeats's involvement but heavily indebted to his inspiration, set out to create a verse-speaking renaissance, and, in a somewhat less democratic adaptation

9. The Society's Constitution was published in *The Poetical Gazette*, 16 (January 1912), [53]; officers included Lady Margaret Sackville, president; G. K. Chesterton, Wilfrid Blunt, F. R. Benson, Lt. E. Shackleton, and Sir Frank Marzials, vice presidents. With this issue, the "Official Journal" ot the society was incorporated with continuous paging into Harold Monro's *The Poetry Review*, 1 (January 1912), 41–56.

10. The lecture, read at the inaugural meeting of the Poetry Recital Society on February 24, 1909, was originally published in the first number of *The Poetical Gazette* (May 1909). It was reprinted in *The Poetry Review* for September 1912, 454–6.

of Yeats's "spiritual democracy," its constitution expressed the plan "to bind poetry readers and lovers together throughout the English-speaking world, forming a desirable freemasonry."[11] For the next two years the society served as an important counterpoise to the early Imagist movement.

When Hulme seceded from the Poets' Club, he was joined not only by Storer and Flint, who had written of their first anthology that "the Poets' Club is death,"[12] but also by Farr, who mischievously led the Imagists into a virtual chantry. What Flint left out of his "The History of Imagism" (1915), but preserved in manuscript, was the fact that many of the early Imagist meetings took place not only in Hulme's rooms but also at the Irish Literary Society, citadel of Yeats's theories in Hanover Square. Here Hulme carried the Imagist case to Joseph Campbell, secretary of the Society, and to Campbell's close friend Padraic Colum, who had been immersed in the chanting of AE and Yeats during his three years in the Irish theatre. To this Irish setting Farr brought two former Rhymers, Ernest Radford and Ernest Rhys, and by late March this incongruous group of poets, some writing for the eye, some for the ear, had grown into the forgotten school of 1909. Just out was Storer's book, in which he says in an appended essay, "If we wish to write music, let us use notes, not words: they are provedly superior."[13] Campbell's *The Mountainy Singer* and Flint's *In the Net of Stars* (modeled on Yeats's *The Wind Among the Reeds*) were in proof. "We proposed at various times," wrote F. S. Flint,

> to replace [English poetry] by pure *vers libre*; we all wrote dozens of the latter as an amusement; by poems in a sacred Hebrew form, of which 'This is the house that Jack Built' is a perfect model. Joseph Campbell produced two good specimens of this, one of which, 'The Dark,' is printed in 'the Mountainy Singer'; by rhymeless poems like Hulme's 'Autumn,' and so on.[14]

Farr's membership in Hulme's Imagist group prompted her into publishing *The Music of Speech*, dedicated to Yeats and Dolmetsch; it had a bold and imposing subtitle: *Containing the Words of Some Poets, Thinkers and Music-Makers Regarding the Practice of the Bardic Art Together with Fragments of Verse*

11. *The Poetical Gazette*, 16 (January 1912), [53].
12. "Recent Verse," a review of *For Christmas MDCCCCVIII* by members of the Poets' Club, *The New Age*, February 11, 1909, 327. The contributors to this first anthology were Selwyn Image, Lady Margaret Sackville, Miriam Cram, Henry Simpson, F. W. Tancred, T. E. Hulme, and Dermot Freyer.
13. Edward Stores, *Mirrors of Illusion* (London: Sisley's, 1909 [1908]), 112.
14. "The History of Imagism," *The Egoist*, 2 (May 1, 1915), 71.

Set to Its Own Melody.[15] For seven years Yeats had tried unsuccessfully to get her to bring out the book, but now she was motivated less by the competitive spirit than by the urgent need for an authoritative record of their achievements in musical speech. The book was a defense of chanting before the Imagists, a testimonial to the place of their auditory poetics in the newly emerging mainstream of modern poetry.

Farr's maverick presence in Hulme's group was, not surprisingly, welcomed and valued, particularly by those who knew the critical respect she commanded from Yeats. Following the initial meeting at the Café Tour d'Eiffel on March 25, 1909, Hulme told Flint that he was delaying a second meeting until Farr could arrange to join them. "I showed your poem to Miss Farr," he added in a postscript, referring to Flint's "The Mask of Gold." "She liked the line about poppies" ["Red poppies wanton in the golden corn"].[16] And while the Imagists looked to her critical opinion of their work, which she judged in relation to both image and cadence, she redoubled her lectures to make herself more visibly and unmistakably the center of discussions on music and poetry and chanted verse. On April 5 she wrote to Quinn: "I've been frightfully active this year, giving recitals all over the place" (NYPL). Her efforts had the desired effect, for Flint became more familiar with and sympathetic to her chanting. As he later wrote, "I have never yet heard verse read in any way pleasing to me except perhaps Miss Florence Farr's speaking to Psaltery of W. B. Yeats's verse."[17] Indeed, Farr appears to stand behind the radical change that took place in Flint's verse the following year, when in a group of poems called "Moods" he began the free-verse experiments that he called "unrhymed cadence."[18] The graft of the Yeatsian bell branch on the Imagist tree had begun to take.

Pound had been introduced to the Poets' Club on Februrary 23 by his publisher, Elkin Mathews. Although he had already put Dorothy Shakespear into swoons of rapture, he was himself charmed into the verse-speaking company of Lady Margaret, writing to William Carlos Williams that her verse was among several recent discoveries that showed

15. *The Music of Speech* was published in 1909 by Elkin Mathews, Yeats's friend and publisher, who introduced Pound to the Poets' Club.

16. Upublished letter, March 31, 1909 (HRHRC).

17. Quoted in J. B. Harmer, *Victory in Limbo: Imagism 1908–17* (London: Secker and Warburg, 1975), 25, from a typescript of Flint's unpublished lecture in 1940, "The Appreciation of Poetry" (HRHRC).

18. Ibid. 57. Flint subsequently published *Cadences* (London: Poetry Bookshop, 1915), inscribing a copy "To William Butler Yeats, homage of F. S. Flint" (*YL* 685), and *Otherworld: Cadences* (London: Poetry Bookshop, 1920).

"what people of the second rank can do, and what damn good work it is."[19] He later admitted that "Margaret Sackville was my despair when I first got to England."[20] On April 22 he found his way to Hulme's secessionist group, introduced, Flint recalled, "by Miss Farr and my friend T. D. Fitzgerald."[21] Flint, himself an evangelizing student of contemporary French poetry, found that Pound "could not be made to believe that there was any French poetry after Ronsard. He was very full of his *troubadours*; but I do not remember that he did more than attempt to illustrate (or refute) our theories occasionally with their example." Pound likely did both, for as an Imagist who would come to believe strongly that poetry should be read aloud, he soon became liaison between the two poetries. On his first meeting at the Café Tour d'Eiffel, Pound as troubadour disrupted the restaurant with his impassioned and sonorous *chanting* of "Sestina: Altaforte." It was clearly time for him to meet Yeats.

Meeting Yeats had been Pound's primary ambition since arriving in London. He had steeped himself in Yeats's work, echoes of which filled his new book, *A Lume Spento* (1908), and he even affected a semblance of Yeats's voice. As Dorothy Shakespear describes his first visit in her notebook entry of February 16, 1909, "At first he was shy—he spoke quickly, (with a strong, odd, accent, half American, half Irish) . . . He talked of Yeats, as one of the Twenty of the world who have added to the world's poetic matter—He read a short piece of Yeats, in a voice dropping with emotion, in a voice like Yeats's own" (*EP/DS* 3).

Yeats had spent the winter of 1909 in Dublin, enmeshed in burdensome theatre business. He had planned to meet Maud Gonne and lecture in London during the first week of March, but he suddenly delayed the trip due to her detainment in Paris and Synge's illness. Farr had been preparing the new group of Imagist poets for his arrival, and on March 9 Desmond Fitzgerald wrote to F. S. Flint about a possible misconnection: "I hear a vague rumour that Yeats was in London on Sunday—If he were—It was very badly managed though when you think of it he might have been a[t]

19. Ezra Pound, *The Letters of Ezra Pound 1907–1941*, ed. D. D. Paige (New York: Harcourt Brace, 1950), 8.
20. BBC Sound Archives, T26074.
21. "The History of Imagism," 71. Flint's manuscript notebook, containing the original draft of this essay, is in the HRHRC. T. D. Fitzgerald was Desmond Fitzgerald (1889–1947), an Irishman who was born and brought up in London, lived in Paris from 1911–13, returned to Ireland, and was imprisoned for his part in the Easter Rebellion. After his release in 1918 he visited his friends in London, as described by Pound in Canto 7: "The live man, out of lands and prisons, / shakes the dry pods, / Probes for old wills and friendships."

13. Close-up photograph of Yeats chanting

14. Rabindranath Tagore and William Rothenstein

15. The Poets' Party for Wilfrid Scawen Blunt. Left to right: Victor Plarr, Sturge Moore, Yeats, Wilfrid Scawen Blunt, Pound, Richard Aldington, F. S. Flint

16. Yeats at his first broadcast in September 1931

17. Harry Partch with the Adapted Viola

NO. 2 (NEW SERIES) FEBRUARY, 1935.

A BROADSIDE

EDITORS: W. B. YEATS AND F. R. HIGGINS; MUSICAL EDITOR, ARTHUR DUFF. PUBLISHED MONTHLY AT THE CUALA PRESS, ONE HUNDRED AND THIRTY THREE LOWER BAGGOT STREET, DUBLIN.

THE WICKED HAWTHORN TREE.

O, but I saw a solemn sight;
Said the rambling, shambling travelling-man;
Castle Dargan's ruin all lit,
Lovely ladies dancing in it.

What though they dance; those days are gone;
Said the wicked, crooked, hawthorn tree;
Lovely lady and gallant man
Are blown cold dust or a bit of bone.

300 copies only.

18. Arthur Duff's music for Yeats's "The Wicked Hawthorne Tree"

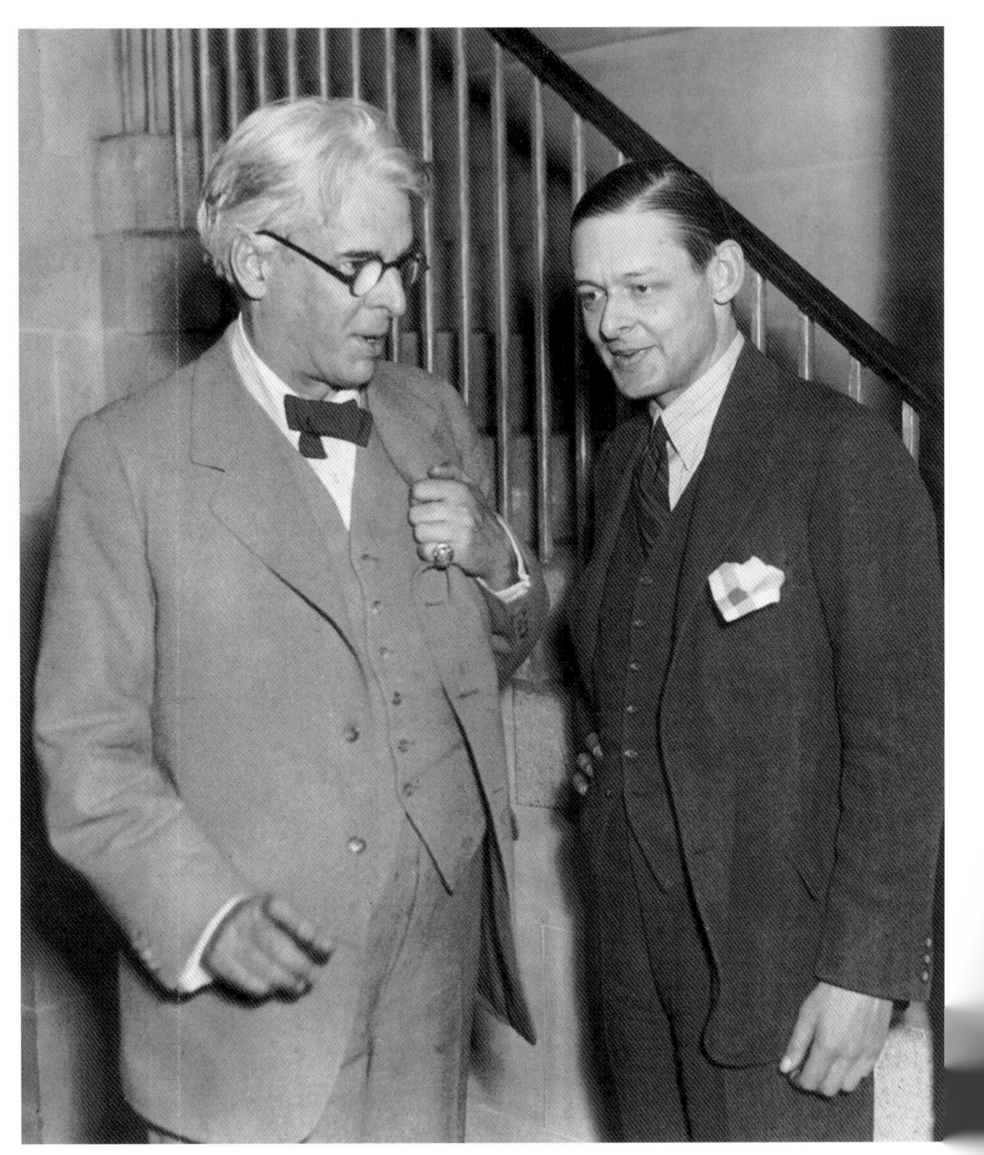

19. Yeats and Eliot at Harvard

A GROUP at last night's meeting of the Oxford University English Club, when Mr. W B. Yeats read and spoke about his poems: Mr. Derek Palmer, the Rev. Montague Summers, Mr. J. G. Greenlees, Mr. W. B. Yeats, Miss Allison-Brown, and Mr. W. R. Rumbold.

20. Yeats with members of the English Club, Oxford

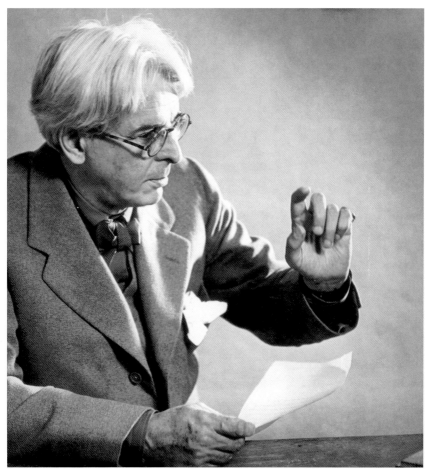

21. Yeats chanting at a broadcast rehearsal

HENRY NEWBOLT. DRAKE'S DRUM DRUM

(Henry Newbolt)

Drake he's in his hammock an' a thousand mile away,
  (Capten, art tha sleepin' there below?),
Slung atween the round shot in Nombre Dios Bay,
  An' dreamin' arl the time o' Plymouth Hoe.
Yarnder lumes the Island, yarnder lie the ships,
  Wi' sailor lads a-dancin' heel-an'-toe,
An' the shore-lights flashin', an' the night-tide dashin',
  He sees et arl so plainly as he saw et long ago.

DRUM roll

Drake he was a Devon man, an' ruled the Devon seas,
  (Capten, art tha sleepin' there below?),
Rovin' tho' his death fell, he went wi' heart at ease,
  An' dreamin' arl the time o' Plymouth Hoe.
"Take my drum to England, hang et by the shore,
  Strike et when your powder's runnin' low;
If the Dons sight Devon, I'll quit the port o' Heaven,
  An' drum them up the Channel as we drummed them long ago."

DRUM roll

Drake he's in his hammock till the great Armadas come,
  (Capten, art tha sleepin' there below?),
Slung atween the round shot, listenin' for the drum,
  An' dreamin' arl the time o' Plymouth Hoe.
Call him on the deep sea, call him up the Sound,
  Call him when ye sail to meet the foe;
Where the old trade's plyin' an' the old flag flyin'
  They shall find him ware an' wakin', as they found
                    him long ago!

timpani

Cymbal roll

22. Music and drum-roll for Henry Newbolt's "Drake's Drum"

23. Margot Ruddock

24. Yeats and Dorothy Wellesley

25. Yeats and Edmund Dulac

(a)

[MUSIC] (harp)

No 2

AN IRISH AIRMAN FORESEES HIS DEATH

VCCB
Read by Clinton Baddeley

I know that I shall meet my fate
Somewhere among the clouds above;
Those that I fight I do not hate,
Those that I guard I do not love;
My country is Kiltartan Cross,
My countrymen Kiltartan's poor,
No likely end could bring them loss
Or leave them happier than before.
Nor law, nor duty bade me fight,
Nor public men, nor cheering crowds,
A lonely impulse of delight
Drove to this tumult in the clouds;
I balanced all, brought all to mind,
The years to come seemed waste of breath,
A waste of breath the years behind
In balance with this life, this death.

quicker

Ecstasy

(b)

SAILING TO BYZANTIUM

VCCB
Spoken by Clinton-Baddeley

Old men should quit a country where ~~That is no country for old men.~~ The young
In one another's arms, birds in the trees,
- Those dying generations - at their song,
The salmon-falls, the mackerel-crowded seas,
Fish, flesh, or fowl, commend all summer long
Whatever is begotten, born, and dies.
Caught in that sensual music all neglect
Monuments of unageing intellect.

II

An aged man is but a paltry thing,
A tattered coat upon a stick, unless
Soul clap its hands and sing, and louder sing
For every tatter in its mortal dress,
Nor is there singing school but studying
Monuments of its own magnificence;
And therefore I have sailed the seas and come
To the holy city of Byzantium.

III

O sages standing in God's holy fire
As in the gold mosaic of a wall,
Come from the holy fire, perne in a gyre,
And be the singing-masters of my soul.
Consume my heart away; sick with desire
And fastened to a dying animal
It knows not what it is; and gather me
Into the artifice of eternity.

26. Notations for Victor Clinton-Baddeley's broadcast recitations

27. Jack Yeats, *The Ballad Singer*

Florence Farr's affair."[22] He finally made a week-long trip to London in April, primarily to see Mrs. Patrick Campbell about his play, *The Player Queen*, but he made time to see Farr and hear of her new activities and acquaintances. When he returned to Woburn Buildings in early May he wrote promptly to Pound, to whom he had been introduced by Olivia Shakespear, inviting him to join "Florence Farr with a Psaltery and some other friends" at his next Monday evening.[23] Their mutual interests in troubadours sparked an immediate friendship, and by the end of the year Yeats and Pound had talked through their independent theories on the ancient relation of music and poetry, agreeing, in Pound's words, that in Greece and in Provence poetry "attained its highest rhythmic and metrical brilliance at times when the arts of verse and music were most closely knit together, when each thing done by the poet had some definite musical urge or necessity bound up within it."[24] But the two poets also sparred with each other over rhythm and cadence: Pound later recalled that

> Yeats was struggling with my rhythms and saying they wouldn't do. I got him to read a little Burns aloud, telling him he cd. read no cadence but his own, or some verse like Sturge Moore's that had not any real characteristics strong enough to prohibit W.B.Y. reading it to his own rhythm. I had a half hour of unmitigated glee in hearing 'Say ye bonnie Alexander' and 'The Birks o Averfeldy' *keened*, wailed with infinite difficulty and many pauses and restarts to *The Wind Among the Reeds*.[25]

Pound was perhaps unaware, however, of how increasingly imitative of Yeats his own voice was to become; their friend Wilfrid Blunt would testify to the fact that Pound "makes himself a sort of understudy of Yeats, repeating Yeats's voice with Yeats's brogue."[26]

22. Unpublished postcard, Flint papers (HRHRC).
23. Unpublished letter, May 8, 1909, Beineck Library, Yale University.
24. *Literary Essays of Ezra Pound*, 91; *EPPP1* 210.
25. Pound, *The Letters of Ezra Pound*, 180. An earlier version of this story appeared in Pound's review of T. S. Eliot's *Prufrock and Other Observations* in *Poetry*, 10 (August 1917), 271; *EPPP2* 250.
26. See Elizabeth Longford, *A Pilgrimage of Passion: The Life of Wilfrid Scawen Blunt* (London: Weidenfeld and Nicolson, 1979), 397. Pound later carried his imitation of Yeats to parody in Canto 82, *The Pisan Cantos*, where he mimicked his chanting of "The Peacock" ("What's riches to him | that had made a great peacock | With the pride of his eye?"), composed on November 23, 1913. What Pound supposed to be wind in the chimney "was in reality Uncle William | downstairs composing | that had made a great Peeeeacock | in the proide ov his oiye | had made a great peeeeeeecock in the ... | made a great peacock | in the proide of his oyyee | proide ov his oy-ee ... " (*The Cantos of Ezra Pound* [London: Faber and Faber, 1964], 569).

Pound continued to meet with the Imagists and the Poets' Club through the year, and at Yeats's Monday evenings he began to espouse the dogmatic principles of prosody that inform *The Spirit of Romance* (1910), where he finds in his troubadours the needs of modern poetry, and where he argues, after Yeats, that all fine poetry "can be well judged only when heard spoken, or sung to its own measure."[27] On at least one occasion, Pound boldly "took over" Yeats's familiar circle, as illustrated in Douglas Goldring's account of accompanying him to one of Yeats's Mondays late in 1909:

> I shall never forget my surprise . . . at the way in which he dominated the room, distributed Yeat's [*sic*] cigarettes and Chianti, and laid down the law about poetry. Poor golden-bearded Sturge Moore, who sat in a corner with a large musical instrument by his side (on which he was never given a chance of performing) endeavoured to join in the discussion on prosody, a subject on which he believed himself not entirely ignorant, but Ezra reduced him to a glum silence.[28]

Much of Pound's prosody was absorbed from Yeats, but Pound had his own way with Yeats, too, illustrating his own chanting techniques with some persuasiveness. On December 10, Yeats wrote to Lady Gregory:

> Which reminds me that that queer creature Ezra Pound, who has become really a great authority on the troubadours has I think got closer to the right sort of music for poetry than Mrs Emery—it is more definitely music with strongly marked time & yet it is effective speech. However he can't sing as he has no voice. It is like something on a very bad phonograph.[29]

A week later, on December 18, Yeats, Farr, and Pound were guests at Ernest Rhys's notorious "tulip-eating" party.[30] Rhys had begun to have the Imagists in for supper gatherings, "resuming the nights at the old Cheshire Cheese of the Rhymers' Club." As the original nucleus of the forgotten school began to break up in the autumn, the evenings were now infiltrated by poets who would form the second Imagist group in 1912. One critic asserts that "there is no evidence that discussion at Rhys's evenings ever

27. Ezra Pound, *The Spirit of Romance* (Norfolk, CT: New Directions, 1952), 26. The book is based on twenty-one lectures that Pound contracted to give at the Regent Street Polytechnic beginning in the autumn of 1909.
28. Douglas Goldring, *South Lodge: Reminiscences of Violet Hunt, Ford Madox Ford and the English Review Circle* (London: Constable, 1943), 49. Douglas Goldring served as Ford's assistant editor on *The English Review*.
29. Letter of [December 10, 1909], *CL InteLex* 1239.
30. This date is satisfactorily established in Kim Herzinger, "The Night Pound Ate the Tulips: An Evening at the Ernest Rhys's," *Journal of Modern Literature*, 8 (1980), 153–5.

took the more urgent tone it seems to have had for Hulme and some of his colleagues,"[31] but it was at Rhys's instigation that Pound undertook *The Spirit of Romance*, and by now the urgent tone had switched from Hulme's image to Yeats's cadence. On this particular night Ford Madox Hueffer brought one of his unknown discoveries from *The English Review*, D. H. Lawrence. The familiar retellings and exaggerations of the amusing evening focus on Pound, who, forced to contain himself while Yeats held forth in unbroken discourse during supper, impatiently seized a tulip from the table "and proceeded to munch it up. As Yeats, absorbed in his monologue, did not observe this strange behavior, and the rest of us were too well-bred to take any notice, Ezra, having found the tulip to his taste, did likewise with a second flower."[32] If Rhys can trust his memory, by the end of the meal Pound had consumed all the tulips.

Pound's tulip-eating has become such a favorite anecdote of the early movement that the significance of the bizarre evening has become obscured. In the month before Rhys's party, Yeats and Farr had been in Ireland and had given a hugely successful lecture–recital on "Literature and the Living Voice" before the Cork Literary and Scientific Society in the Assembly Rooms. "The lecture was listened to with rapt attention," wrote the reporter for the *Constitution* in his lengthy coverage, "and the illustrations of the subject in prose and verse spoken to the psaltery, by Miss Florence Farr, were greatly appreciated . . . and there was a very large attendance."[33] Yeats had spoken passionately about reviving the new art and an oral culture, stating that "If literature was to go amongst the mass of the people they should get back again to the old words of vocal literature," and in asking "how could they get the culture that came from the living voice?" he said that he wanted the poets "to go back to the age of the minstrel, to the songs composed to be sung aloud or spoken aloud, and he knew quite well that in doing so they would create something new—something that would express their age and no other." Farr's illustrations on the psaltery "were deeply appreciated" by the receptive audience, and the two minstrels returned to London with a new enthusiasm for spreading the new art. What is not surprising, but what has been ignored, is the fact that at Rhys's party Yeats "held forth at length on this new art of bringing music and poetry

31. Harmer, *Victory in Limbo*, 23.
32. Ernest Rhys, *Everyman Remembers* (London: J. M. Dent & Sons, 1931), 244.
33. "Literary and Scientific Society. / 'Literature and the Living Voice,'" *Cork Constitution*, November 5, 1909, 8.

together."[34] Here, on one clear evening in the historical haze of 1909, Yeats directly transmitted his theories to the fluctuating Imagist circle, lending his full authority to the continuous pressure exerted by Farr and Pound. The monologue on music and poetry led to after-dinner recitations by Yeats, Radford, Hueffer, Lawrence, and Pound. Farr then brought out the psaltery, chanting in a "haunting wail" Yeats's "The Man Who Dreamed of Faeryland," her reading "suggestive of a priestess intoning a litany." Yeats, Rhys confirmed, was still "bent on using the psaltery as a means of giving poetry a new musical vogue," and he suggested that she chant another. Farr then surprised and delighted Rhys by chanting his own "Sir Dinadan and La Belle Isoud."[35] As the evening attests, by the end of 1909 Hulme's assertion that poetry "is read and not chanted" had been overruled. The nature of rhythm and the musical properties of prosody had become a primary topic of the group, and much of what Yeats now conveyed to them came from his recent discovery of Coventry Patmore's temporal prosody.

Yeats had come upon Patmore's work early in 1909, and on March 4 he wrote to Lady Gregory: "Patmore is I find most exciting—no poetry has excited me so much for ever so long."[36] His excitement increased when he came upon the odes a few days later: " 'The Angel of the House' is nothing like as fine as 'The Odes,' " he declared: "Vol 2 of his poetic works. That is really very great poetry."[37] In that volume he came across Patmore's "Essay on English Metrical Law" and wrote with equal excitement to Farr to add to her weaponry: "I find in Patmore's book of Odes an appendix in which he states our theory of music and speech very clearly."[38] To Yeats,

34. *Everyman Remembers*, 244.
35. Ibid. 248. Rhys's poem had been listed among those on a sample program for Farr's 1907 tour of America.
36. Letter of [March 4, 1909], *CL InteLex* 1102. See also *Mem* 170, 189–90. When Thomas MacDonagh began his masters' thesis at University College, Dublin, on song-verse and speech-verse, later published as *Thomas Campion and the Art of English Poetry* (Dublin: Hodges, Figgis, 1913), Yeats read for him "in a chanting voice some of Coventry Patmore's poems from *The Unknown Eros*" (5). "It is this chanting quality in his verse," observed MacDonagh, "joined to a wandering rhythm caught from Irish traditional music, that has informed a new species of verse. It is chant-verse, overflowing both song-verse and speech-verse. For not only does something of the word reverence of chanted speech unstress the lyric beat of this poetry, but something of the musical quality of chant lightens and changes the weight of its speech-verse" (52).
37. Letter [March 8, 1909], *CL InteLex* 1106.
38. Letter of [March 17, 1909], *CL InteLex* 1111.Yeats continued: "In the 3.6 edition (Poetical Works Vol II) you will find a long passage starting on page 232 which will interest you and at any rate give you the support of a great authority." In its final form, the "Essay on English Metrical Law" was appended to the second volume of Patmore's *Poems*, second collected

Patmore provided "the support of a great authority," for in his discussion of the relation of music to language he had arrived at a strongly emphasized conclusion: "*Perfect poetry and song are, in fact, nothing more than perfect speech upon high and moving subjects.*" Yeats pointed out the essay to members of his circle, and Sturge Moore thereafter quoted from it in his own lectures on chanting to the Poetry Recital Society.[39] Yeats used Patmore's scholarly discussion of English prosody to support his own theory of cadence, by showing that in English meter "those qualities which, singly, or in various combination, have hitherto been declared to *be* accent, are indeed only the *conditions of accent.*" Patmore pointed out that in modern prosody accentual division has unfortunately become "the *sole*, instead of merely the *main*, source of metre." To him, the true rhythm of a verse line arose not from accentual stress on certain syllables but from patterns of sound in time, units of sound and silence. For Patmore, this was time-rhythm, for Yeats, cadence. Patmore's discussion of monotone also supported Yeats's belief that "all art is, indeed, a monotony in external things for the sake of an interior variety, a sacrifice of gross effects to subtle effects, an asceticism of the imagination" (*E&I* 18). "There is no charm in the rhythm of monotones," Patmore explains, "unless the notion of monotone can be overcome; and, when that is the case, it is not rhythm, but rhythmical melody, whereby we are pleased." The rhythmical value of monotones, as Yeats well knew, is that they admit of "imagined variations," allowing the voice to express (in quarter-tones) what the mind imagines.[40]

edition (London: George Bell, 1886), 218–67; subsequent page references below are to the 1906 edition in Yeats's library (*YL* 1540) of Patmore's *Poems*.

39. Sturge Moore's lecture on "The Reading of Poetry" on April 29, 1912, was reported in *The Poetical Gazette*, incorporated in *The Poetry Review* for June 1912, 287–8. After quoting Patmore's statement, "*Perfect poetry and song are in fact nothing more than perfect speech on high and moving subjects,*" he went on to affirm his modified Yeatsian view of reading: "The essentials are a pronunciation raised to an ideal standard of sonority and the movement proper to impassioned enunciation. Vulgar singers make speech subserve music till they denaturalize it, vulgar reciters underline the prose accents and make the meaning painfully clear at the expense of the melody." Afterwards he read the poems of several poets, including Yeats, "repeating wherever he failed at first to produce the intended effect." In "Hark to Sturge Moore," an appreciative assessment of Moore's work, Pound stated that "Sturge Moore is more master of cadence than any of his English contemporaries. If Mr. Yeats has perfect mastery in *Red Hanrahan's Song About Ireland*, and in the verse of *The Wind Among the Reeds*, even his most fervent admirers must grant that Moore has the greater variety of cadences in his quiver, and that he excels his friend in onomatopoeic aptness; in varying and fitting the cadence to its subject emotions" (*Poetry: A Magazine of Verse*, 6 [June 1915], 141; *EPPP2 90*.)

40. Patmore, *Poems*, 231–3, 236.

Members of Pound's circle heard all of this from Yeats, who was to Pound the recognized master of rhythm, and he was discussing with the master the definitions of rhythm that appeared during the next two years, particularly "absolute rhythm" and the "inner form" of the poetic line: "it is this 'inner form,' I think, which must be preserved in music; it is only by mastery of this inner form that the great masters of rhythm—Milton, Yeats, whoever you like—are masters of it."[41]

In late December the activities of 1909 came to a close at the Poets' Club, where Joseph Campbell, attired in bardic robes, chanted Pound's "Ballad of the Goodly Fere" and Pound, who envied Campbell's rich voice, gave a lecture, "Arnaut Daniel, finest of the trouadours." Pound's and Hulme's poems appeared together in *The Book of the Poets' Club* for 1909, but thereafter, says Pound, "Hulme stopped writing poetry."[42] Pound left England for America in the early summer of 1910, leaving Hulme studying Bergson, Yeats and Farr chanting in the provinces, and the Poetry Recital Society flourishing.

In America, meanwhile, Dolmetsch had come on hard times at Chickerings, which, following a deep trade recession, had informed him that they could not renew his contract. To the delight of his London friends, he suddenly appeared in the city for three weeks in October, stopping on his way to France for an interview with Maison Gaveau and other Parisian manufacturers, hoping to find new employment at the age of 52. He met Selwyn Image, the architect Arthur MacMurdo, and other old friends at the Art Workers' Guild, where he was greatly pleased to discover that he had been kept on the list of members. During his stay he played in private houses, and before his departure gave a packed-house concert at Clifford's Inn. "The concert is finished," he wrote to his wife, Mabel, on October 18. "Success of the first order. . . . All the friends were there." His long list included Todhunter, Yeats, Farr, and Roger Fry, who was now preparing his great exhibition, "Manet and the Post-Impressionists."

41. Ezra Pound, *The New Age* (February 8, 1912), 344; rpt. in *Ezra Pound and Music*, ed. R. Murray Schafer (New York: New Directions, 1977), 471. Pound had begun to define "absolute rhythm" as early as 1910 in his Cavalcanti translations and most precisely in the essay "Prologomena" in *The Poetry Review* of February 1912: "I believe in an 'absolute rhythm,' a rhythm, that is, in poetry which corresponds exactly to the emotion or shade of emotion to be expressed. A man's rhythm must be interpretative, it will be, therefore, in the end, his own, uncounterfeiting, uncounterfeitable" (*EPPP1* 60).

42. "This Hulme Business," *Townsman*, 2 (January 1939), 15. For *Canzoni* (1911), Pound wrote "for the cenacle of 1909" a poem, "To Hulme (T. E.) and Fitzgerald," affirming his own decision to continue writing poetry, but he canceled the poem in page proof and published it later in *Des Imagistes* (1914).

The subsequent journey to Paris resulted in an offer from Gaveau, and after a brief return to Boston and a final lecture series on "Early Music and its Instruments" at Harvard, Dolmetsch made the move in March 1911, settling near the factory in the village of Fontenay-sous-Bois. There he renewed his old friendship with Gabriele d'Annunzio and began to concentrate on his book, *The Interpretation of the Music of the XVIIth and XVIIIth Centuries,* a book that would seize the interest of Ezra Pound when it appeared in 1915. In Maison Gaveau he began to produce and restore harpsichords, clavichords, and virginals and to take on new pupils and concert engagements in Paris. Even so, during the next two years he would make periodic returns to England for London concerts and extended tours, eventually capturing the notice of J. F. Runciman, who informed the readers of the *Saturday Review* that Dolmetsch "has come back, and is lecturing in the provinces to audiences of two and three thousand; and the small hall at Clifford's Inn is full at each of his concerts."[43] Gradually Dolmetch began to entertain the risks of returning to London, where he knew that no pianoforte-makers had a workshop for early keyboard instruments.

When Pound resettled in London in August 1911, poetry, he said, underwent "retirement to Church Walk,"[44] where "*Les Imagistes,* the descendants of the forgotten school of 1909" were to develop and practice the principles of Imagism.[45] Accounted present in Pound's new school were Richard Aldington, Farr, John Gould Fletcher, Flint, H. D., Hueffer, D. H. Lawrence, and Brigit Patmore. Lawrence, nicknamed "Lorenzo" by Brigit Patmore, loved to parody Farr's chanting of Yeats's poems to the psaltery. "Did any of you hear Florence Farr do her ping-wanging?" he asked the coterie. Patmore recounts Lawrence's performance of the opening lines of Yeats's *The Wanderings of Oisin*:

> Lorenzo began chanting monotonously, "You who are bent and bald and blind...." Paused, then stretched his thin hands over his knees delicately, as if an instrument lay there, plucked an imaginary string and whined: "Ping...wa...n...ng." Then, three semitones lower: "Ping...pi...iing, wang." Deepening his voice, "With heavy heart, staccato ping-wang and a

43. John F. Runciman, "Three Hundred Years," *Saturday Review*, 117 (December 13, 1913), 743. Runciman refers to Dolmetsch's performances of "The Original Music of Shakespeare's Plays" to huge audiences in Bristol, Newcastle, Aberdeen, and Dundee between November 20 and December 12.

44. See Christopher Middleton, "Documents on Imagism from the Papers of F. S. Flint," *The Review*, no. 15 (April 1965), 50.

45. *Ripostes of Ezra Pound*, 59.

> wandering mind." And he pinged so violently to show the state of his mind that our hoots of laughter swept him with us and he couldn't look holy any longer.[46]

Despite Lawrence's devastating mimicries, Yeats, Farr, and a growing number of allies kept the pressure on the Imagists, determined never to let them substitute a visual for an aural paradigm. They had recently found an energetic proselytizer in Harold Monro, who had joined the Poetry Recital Society in March 1910 and who incorporated the society's publication, *The Poetical Gazette*, into *The Poetry Review*, where he published Pound's credo on absolute rhythm in February 1912. Yeats had taken an interest in Monro and his new periodical, and after a few numbers had appeared Monro wrote that "Yeats, Newbolt, Sturge Moore and some others have now all been expressing strong approval, which delights me."[47] But even as Monro joined the struggle against visual poetry, one of the most startling figures in Yeats's life appeared before the Imagist circle—the Bengali poet Rabindranath Tagore.

Tagore's host and sponsor for his English tour was William Rothenstein, whom he had met in Calcutta the previous year. Tagore sailed on May 27, using the long journey to make prose translations in English of some of his poems before arriving in London on June 16. Rothenstein, deeply impressed by the poems, sent copies to Yeats, inviting him, Lady Gregory, and Sturge Moore to dinner with Tagore on June 27. Yeats promptly invited Tagore to his next Monday evening on July 1. A week later Rothenstein held a larger gathering of guests in his drawing room to introduce Tagore, accompanied by his son and daughter-in-law, to more literary friends, including Pound, Rhys, Nevinson, Alice Meynell, and others. Nevinson described Tagore in his diary that evening as "a tall, thin, very mild Hindu, with hair & beard going grey, very attractive, though too gentle." For most of the evening, according to Nevinson,

> he sat silent, & would not give the Bengali of any of his poems because his memory is bad. Yeats read a lot of them in Tagore's own English prose translation, very beautifully done. Short glimpses of spiritual moods, many in the spirit of the Imitation, full of surrender of self & adoration of God.

46. Brigit Patmore, *My Friends When Young* (London: Heinemann, 1968), 81.
47. Quoted in John Drinkwater, *Discovery*: Being the Second Book of an Autobiography 1897–1913 (Boston and New York: Houghton Mifflin, 1933), 224. On June 12, 1912 Dorothy Shakespear informed Pound that Yeats had not only come to tea and read "with due music" Pound's new poems, "The Return" and "Apparuit," but that Yeats had "been induced to take an interest... in Munro [*sic*] & the P. Review" (*EP/DS* 110–11).

> Some beautiful as pictures of nature & mind, but all too passive & moody for me. Yeats has gone grey at last & looks heavier & less fairylike, but what a superb head & face it is! And how genuine & generous his enthusiasm! May Sinclair, Miss Yeats, Sturge Moore, [J. L.] Hammond, Rolleston & some whom I didn't know there ... Mrs. Emery came late in large show hat & white & scarlet things.[48]

Sturge Moore, tired of Yeats's dominance and mannerisms, was initially impatient with Tagore's lyrics, writing to his wife about the scene at Rothenstein's: "Yeats read them abominably as usual so that it was very difficult to hear the last word of each retch of his parson's haw."[49] In his summary of the evening for Robert Trevelyan, he wrote that Tagore's "unique subject is 'the love of God'. When I told Yeats I found his poetry preposterously optimistic, he said 'Ah, you see, he is absorbed in God.'"[50]

After chanting Tagore's poems for the first time at Rothenstein's, Yeats arranged for Farr to chant them to the Imagists at Church Walk. Then, on July 12, he presided over a dinner sponsored by the India Society and *The Nation* at the Trocadero Restaurant for Tagore and seventy guests. He opened the event by proposing a toast, "Our Guest" ("I know of no man in my time who has done anything in the English language to equal these lyrics"[51]). In his introductory remarks he compared Tagore to the medieval troubadours and chanted three of his poems, an action that led Arthur Fox Strangways, a member of the Society and recently named music critic of the *Times*, to write amusedly to Rothenstein about the spectacle of Yeats's "mystic waving of arms over the victim of the evening."[52] Yeats was utterly

48. Nevinson's diary entry for July 7, 1912 (Bodleian).
49. Undated letter [July 1912], Sturge Moore Papers, Box 35/221.
50. Sturge Moore Papers, Box 16; quoted in *YA4* (1986), 178, and in Foster, *Life 1* 470.
51. "Dinner to Mr. Rabindra Nath Tagore," *Times*, July 13, 1912, 5. "Even as I read them in this literal prose translation," Yeats continued, "they are as exquisite in style as in thought. The style was familiar in Europe several hundred years ago. Mr. Rabindra Nath Tagore is also a great musician; he sets his poems to music; then he teaches poem and music to some one, and so together they go from mouth to mouth, sung by his people, very much as poetry was sung in Europe three of four centuries ago. In all his poems there is one single theme: the love of God." The *Times* quoted two of the three lyrics chanted by Yeats, beginning "I was not aware of the moment when I first crossed the threshold of this life" and "In the deep shadows of the rainy July," poems numbered 95 and 22 respectively in Tagore's *Gitanjali* (London: Macmillan, 1913), 87, 18.
52. Quoted in *Imperfect Encounter: Letters of William Rothenstein and Rabindranath Tagore 1911–1941*, ed. Mary M. Lago (Cambridge, MA: Harvard University Press, 1972), 40. Strangways subsequently attempted to intervene in Yeats's editing of *Gitanjali*, leading Yeats to protest vigorously to Rothenstein on September 7: "I have had an interminable letter from a man called Strangways suggesting alterations in Tagore's translation. He is the sort of man societies

enthralled by the person and poetry of this saint-like visitant from another world. Nevinson wrote that Yeats "spoke admirably" and that "Tagore himself was brief & excellent."

Within a week Yeats was working with Tagore to select, edit, and arrange the 103 prose translations that would make up *Gitanjali*. He had copies of poems typed for Farr to chant and began learning several off by heart himself.[53] He postponed his departure for Coole to spend more time in Tagore's company, asking questions about his life as a poet in his distant culture, about his school in Bhawalpur, the Shantiniketan ("The Abode of Peace"), in which he sought to revive the ideals of Indian culture and philosophy. In Tagore, Yeats and Pound found the living examplar of the modern troubadour, his lyrics displaying for Yeats, as he would write in his preface to *Gitanjali*, "in their thought a world I have dreamed of all my life long" (*E&I* 390). Tagore stirred Yeats's Chaucerian imagination once again, leading him to divine the present unity of Bengal culture by analogy to one fragmented since Chaucer's fragile time: "When there was but one mind in England Chaucer wrote his *Troilus and Cressida*, and though he had written to be read, or to be read out—for our time was coming on apace—he was sung by minstrels for a while" (*E&I* 390–1). Yeats subsequently told an interviewer that

> as far as literature is concerned he [Tagore] is still living in the fourteenth century, for the conditions for creating and holding an audience are very much like those that existed in Chaucer's time. His poetry is spoken and sung by everybody and he writes the music for his words.... from time to time the minstrels go to visit him and learn his new poetry. They, in turn, teach them to other minstrels, and so the songs are passed on in an unbroken chain from village to village. His songs are hummed by travelers on the highway and caught up by those going down the rivers, until the whole country is echoing with his songs.[54]

like the India Society fatten. He is a manifest goose. I want you [to] get the society to understand that I am to edit this book & that they are to send me proofs as any other publishers would. I cannot argue with a man who thinks that 'the ripples are rampant in the river' should be changed because 'rampant suggests' to his goose brain 'opposition to something'... I have replied politely saying I would go carefully through the text in proof but do please see that he goes back to his pond" (*CL* InteLex 1972).

53. Tagore was evidently not impressed with Farr's chanting of his lyrics. Sturge Moore remarked in a letter of October 14, 1912, to his wife that "in the matter of recitation" he and Tagore "seem to agree perfectly. He doesn't like Miss Farr at all, & can't understand Yeats recommending her" (Sturge Moore Papers; quoted in Foster, *Life 1* 616).

54. See Elsie F. Weil, "William Butler Yeats and the New Ireland," *Inter-Ocean* (Chicago), March 1, 1914, Magazine, 1.

To Yeats, this was the manifestation of a "supreme culture" still extant in the modern world (*E&I* 390), a true spiritual democracy wherein the prince and the ploughman alike murmur the cadences of the poet, who resides at the center of culture. Tagore made him believe anew that the dream was possible.

In August, as he prepared to write his preface, Yeats took Tagore's poems to France, where he spent several days at Les Mouettes with Maud and Iseult Gonne, and Gretta and James Cousins, who described Yeats as being "on fire with the fullness in them that told that the renaissance of poetry had appeared in India.... From poem to poem Yeats went from hour to hour, annotating, expatiating, rejoicing, till we were all afire with a new revelation of spiritual beauty."[55] The day following this rhapsodic evening, the two being left alone, Cousins observed Yeats in poetic composition, and of all the accounts of those who have heard Yeats's eerie poetic murmuring, Cousins' description is the most revealing, for it dramatizes the relation of organic rhythm to metrical rhythm and cadence:

> After a while I became aware of a queer monotonous murmur somewhere in the house. It was Yeats' voice ... and I concluded he was engaged in some private ceremonial of worship and enchantment. The utterance ... was not spontaneous, as it had some kind of vague architecture and design. Its constant repetition of the same sounds in similar order had the eeriness of the inaudible made audible.... Ultimately I got an angular and meagre glimpse through an almost closed door; ... Yeats was sitting on a chair in a corner of the kitchen with his head bent close into the corner. For three hours the sound went on, and during the time I neither heard nor wrote [i.e., saw written] a word.[56]

55. James H. Cousins and M. E. Cousins, *We Two Together* (Madras: Ganesh, 1950), 161.
56. Ibid. 160. The poem would have been one of two composed at Les Mouettes in August 1912: "The Mountain Tomb" and "A Memory of Youth." Anne Gregory records a similar experience in *Me and Nu: Childhood at Coole* (Gerrards Cross: Colin Smythe, 1978): Yeats had written "Yellow Hair" ("For Anne Gregory") and "proceeded to read it in his 'humming voice.' We used to hear his voice 'humming' away for hours while he wrote his verse. He used to hum the rhythms of a verse before he wrote the words, Grandma told us, and that was why his poems are so good to read aloud" (29). In *W.B. Yeats: A Memoir* (Dublin: Dolmen, 1963), Oliver St. John Gogarty recounts how "He composed with what appeared to be great mental agony. With his hands behind his back, his head down, or suddenly looking up, he would pace the floor humming and murmuring to himself until the poem arose from the rich darkness. I observed him at work in my house when he was composing 'What finger first began,' one of the songs in a late play of his [*The Dreaming of the Bones*, 1919]. It comes from a Chinese legend that they who hear aerial music are listening to the music of a lost kingdom. It took him several minutes of humming to get the second line: 'What finger first began | Music of a lost kingdom?' As the rhythm-wedded words came up, he wrote them in pencil on odd pieces of paper.I found many such pieces in my study when he had finished the poem" (23).

When Maud and Iseult Gonne and Gretta Cousins returned from church, Yeats emerged, Cousins continues, "muttering in an undertone the same sound as I had heard all morning. 'How did you get on, Willy?' Madame queried. 'I finished it.' Then I began to understand and later ascertained that such was the Yeats method of composing verse, making a sound-scheme into which words were fitted after much trial and alteration."

Years later, Cousins, reflecting on the significance of Yeats's "after-dinner chantings" of Tagore's poems for guests gathered before a rainy-night fire at Les Mouettes, remembered the chantings as being "like the ritual of a new era":

> The prose-poems in the Indian's manuscript book were ostensibly translations from the Bengali, but appeared to me to be no more alien to English than our own poems that were our translations, if not of the Irish language, certainly of the ancient Celtic imagination in its sensitive reaction to the phenomena of nature and the mystery of human nature. Their wave-lengths, long and short and always eloquent, like Yeats' waving hand synchronising with his distinguished throaty cathedral voice, and their figurativeness, so rich yet never merely dressy, evocative of inner sight, had an authenticity that gave them the rank of originals. Their simple profundities and exaltations reached depths and heights beyond the bearings of race and country and language. . . . We were one in spirit, we pioneers of the new Irish movement in poetry, and the poet from India.[57]

Yeats returned to London inspired by Tagore to re-energize his dream of reviving the oral tradition by training reciters to chant and carry poetry to the people once again. By November 1912, when the India Society's limited edition of *Gitanjali* appeared, Yeats's plans had been taken up by Monro, who wrote enthusiastically to John Drinkwater to invite him to a must-attend meeting at the Poetry Bookshop:

> We've something tremendous on the carpet. Roughly the project is to read poetry in villages without formality, payment, pose, condescension, propaganda, or parson. You just give it them like the Eastern story-tellers, who gather people together at street corners. . . . When you hear the whole plan I am sure you will help, later. . . . It does not sound very much like this, but you should hear me explain it![58]

57. James H. Cousins, "Introduction," to Abinash Chandra Bose, *Three Mystic Poets: A Study of W. B. Yeats, A. E. and Rabindranath Tagore* (Kolhapur: School and College Bookstall, 1946), pp. v–vi.
58. Drinkwater, *Discovery*, 224–5.

Yeats's desire to turn the London imagists into minstrels in the provinces did not take hold, but in January 1913 Monro announced the Poetry Bookshop readings, which had their origins and found their momentum in Yeats's theory of spoken verse.[59] Ironically, when W. W. Gibson inaugurated the readings in February with a recitation of Yeats's poems, Hulme had taken rooms above the Poetry Bookshop at 35 Devonshire Street.

On July 15 at Clifford's Inn, as part of a lecture series sponsored by Monro's *Poetry Review*, Hulme had stepped boldly before a Poetry Bookshop audience to address them on "The New Philosophy of Art as Illustrated in Poetry," an early title for his "Romanticism and Classicism," in which he rejects the "spilt religion" of romanticism and prophesies "that a period of dry, hard, classical verse is coming" (*CWTEH* 69).[60] It was meant to be, as posthumously it would become in *Speculations* (1924), his new clarion call for the end of a Yeatsian romanticism, of "dragging in the infinite," and the beginning of a modern classicism based on the reality of Original Sin. Though he did not publish in *The Second Book of the Poets' Club* (Christmas, 1911), he had remained an active member,

59. Monro wrote of the Poetry Bookshop readings in *Poetry and Drama*, 1 (December 1913): "We are absolutely certain that the proper values of poetry can only be conveyed through its vocal interpretation by a sympathetic and qualified reader. Indeed so obvious does this appear that we regard the books on sale in the shop merely as printed scores for the convenience of refreshing the memory in hours of study or of indolence.... The transplantation of poetry out of the common ways of life into the study is an abuse not to be tolerated. We refuse to consider poetry as pure literature: it is the supreme form of verbal expression, and, as such, is of no signification in the dusty shelves of libraries, of no specific value until brought out into the active ways of life" (387). Yeats first read his poems at the Poetry Bookshop on July 3, 1913, with a hundred people present and forty turned away for lack of room. Arundel Del Re recounts how Yeats "began softly, almost chanting, 'The Hosting of the Sidhe', his silvery voice swelling up to the solemn finale. No one moved, waiting for him to continue. I cannot remember how long he read—all lyrics... varying the pitch and tone of his voice to suit the mood, weaving a spell over his listeners. And when he concluded with the Faery Child's song from *The Land of Heart's Desire,* we were drawn back with a start into ourselves, as if we too had been wandering with Yeats in that land" (Quoted in Joy Grant, *Harold Monro and the Poetry Bookshop* [London: Routledge and Kegan Paul, 1967], 78). Yeats did not read for the Bookshop again until April 11, 1916, when the expected crowd required a change of venue (335 turned up at the Passmore Edwards Settlement, the largest crowd in the history of the readings), but in the interim other readers read his poems and plays on several occasions. See BL Add. MS 57756. Henry Newbolt, who formally opened the Poetry Bookshop readings as a member of the Poetry Recital Society, later wrote: "The new movement for the better speaking of English verse did not in the end keep to Yeats's method, which was a method of chanting rather than of reciting; but it was I believe the origin of the organised competitions and societies which now hold the field" (*The Later Life and Letters of Sir Henry Newbolt*, ed. Margaret Newbolt [London: Faber and Faber, 1942], 5).

60. Hulme's editor Karen Csengeri states that "Romanticism and Classicism," written in late 1911 or early 1912, was "very possibly the lecture Hulme delivered on 15 July 1912 at Clifford's Inn Hall, London. No other text for that lecture has yet been identified" (*CWTEH* 59).

serving on the selection committee that awarded Rupert Brooke a prize of £30 for the best poem, "Old Vicarge, Grantchester," published in the *Poetry Review* in 1912.[61] Although Hulme's interests had already shifted from poetry to philosophy and art, leading him to overwhelm his friends with the philosophy of Bergson, Hulme was still an important intellectual presence for Pound, who wrote to Dorothy on August 13, "Hulme & I discussed the metaphysics of art until 11.30" (*EP/DS* 142).[62] Indeed, Pound was still a champion of Hulme's poems; he had included "The Complete Poetical Works of T. E. Hulme" as an addendum to his *Ripostes*, which would appear in October.[63] But by the time Yeats completed his preface and made the manuscript of *Gitanjali* available to Pound in September, Tagore had wholly displaced Hulme in Pound's mind.

Rothenstein recorded that of the poets who gathered at Tagore's feet none did so more "assiduously" than Pound.[64] During the last week of September, Pound spent a successive evening and afternoon with Tagore to discuss in detail the poetry whose importance to English verse he would try to convey in his essay for the *Fortnightly Review*. Pound had begun a book on the troubadours of Provence coincident with Tagore's arrival, and so he was also eager to draw from Tagore the Provençal parallels with his Bengali "jongleurs."[65] To recreate the flavor of their sessions, Pound worked snippets of their conversation and Tagore's singing into his informal narrative. "It is a little over a month," he began, "since I went to Mr. Yeats' rooms and found him much excited over the advent of a great poet, someone 'greater than any of us.' "[66] "What is it you find in these poems (translated)?" asked Tagore. "I did not know that they would interest a European." While Rothenstein painted Tagore's portrait, Pound and Tagore

61. *Poetry and Drama*, 1 (1913), 7. In addition to Hulme, the committee included old and new members of the Poets' Club, which had become the Poetry Society: Henry Newbolt, Ernest Rhys, Victor Plarr, Harold Monro, Edward Thomas, and Edward Marsh.

62. Hulme's translation of Henri Bergson's *An Introduction to Metaphysics* was published in America in November 1912, in England in March 1913.

63. Hulme's "Complete Poetical Works" had appeared independently earlier in the year in *The New Age*, 10 (January 25, 1912), 297–9.

64. William Rothenstein, *Men and Memories* (London: Faber and Faber, 1932), 264.

65. The abandoned manuscript fragments of this study, entitled "Gironde," is in the Beinecke Library, Yale University. Richard Sieburth includes two "Fragments from *Gironde*" in his edition of Pound's *A Walking Tour in Southern France* (New York: New Directions, 1992), 81–4, indicating in a note that "The remainder of the typescript consists of cut-up snippets of twenty-one troubadour *vidas* and *razos*—in all likelihood the textual debris left over from the series of biographical summaries that were recycled into the published version of 'Troubadours: Their Sorts and Conditions' [1913]" (123).

66. "Rabindranath Tagore," *Fortnightly Review*, 93 n.s. (March 1, 1913), 571–9, here 571.

discussed "meetres" and prosody, and Pound listened to Tagore reading and singing: "He can boast with the best of the troubadours, 'I made it, the words and the notes.' Also he sings them himself, I know, for I have heard him." Pound was particularly impressed with the "Golden Bengal," which he heard "with its music, and it is wholly Eastern, yet it has a curious power, a power to move the crowd."[67] While he crafted the review he informed Dorothy that he had invited the pianist-composer Walter Morse Rummel, whom Pound was assisting with English adaptations of troubadour songs for voice and piano, "to come play before King Rabindra, so we may have some real soirées artistique during October. . . . You have seen the eagle [Yeats] in a state of exhultation over this matter and you may readily judge the condition of my lighter & more volatile spirits" (*EP/DS* 163).[68] Pound confessed to Dorothy that in the midst of the Tagore fever he had "done nothing else"; Dorothy replied that "W.B.Y. is here . . . We have been told many tales of Tagore père going up the Ganges & fleeing from Goorkah regiments etc:" (*EP/DS* 164). Yeats was in such "exhultation" that he could hardly attend to the demands of his own work, but his excitement over and envy of Tagore's "song offerings" enabled him to dash off a one-sentence preface for the Tauchnitz edition of his poems:

> If I had but music enough to make settings that had but enough music to adorn the words yet leave them natural and audible, I should have written lyrics to be sung, for it is speaking or singing before an audience that makes us tell our stories well, and put our thoughts into some lasting order and set our emotions clambering to some arduous climax, but as it is, lacking music but that of words I have chosen the lyrics not out of singer's mouths but from little books published at Stratford-on-Avon, or in London, or by my sisters at the hand-press worked by the village of Dundrum, in Ireland.[69]

67. Tagore's song, "Amar Sonar Bangla" ("My Golden Bengal"), became the national anthem of Bangladesh.
68. Walter Morse Rummel (1887–1953) was a member of Debussy's inner circle and greatly interested in the revival of old music, especially of the troubadours. His *Walter Morse Rummel / Hesternae Rosae / Serta II* (London: Augener, 1913) contained nine French songs of the 17th century and nine troubadour songs of the 12th and 13th centuries. Rummel wrote in acknowledgment of Pound's contribution: "The writer with the help of Mr. Ezra Pound, an ardent proclaimer of the artistic side of mediaeval poetry, has given these melodies the rhythm and ligature, the character which from an artistic point of view, seems the most descriptive of the mediaeval spirit." Rummel would later compose the music for Yeats's "The Dreaming of the Bones" (1919).
69. *A Selection of the Poetry of W. B. Yeats* (Leipzig: Bernhard Tauchnitz, 1913), 6. The preface is dated "October, 1912."

Pound himself took every opportunity to write and lecture on Tagore's work, including a commentary for six poems taken from *Gitanjali* and published in the December issue of *Poetry* (Chicago). He had heard in the poetry a musical quality that heralded their appearance as "an event in the history of English poetry and of world poetry," and he created an amalgam of comparisons to describe the subtle metrical and rhythmical structure: "If you refine the art of the troubadours, combine it with that of the Pleiade, and add to that the sound-unit principle of the most advanced artists in *vers libre*, you would get something like the system of Bengali verse."[70] He prepared three interrelated lectures on Provençal troubadours, Tagore's poetry, and *vers libre* and systems of metric, all of which informed the review that awaited publication of the trade edition of *Gitanjali* in March. In that review Pound urged Tagore's readers to read the poems aloud, explaining that "this apparently simple translation has been made by a great musician, by a great artist who is familiar with a music subtler than our own."[71] He drew analogies between Tagore's Bengali culture and that of twelfth-century Provence, between Tagore's poems and Provençal canzoni, between his meters and "the latest development of *vers libre*." He noted "the occasional brilliant phrases, now like some pure Hellenic, in 'Morning with the golden basket in her right hand,' now like the last sophistication of De Gourmont or Baudelaire" (573).[72] More importantly for modern poetry, he asserted that Tagore's language

> has already found that sort of metric which we awhile back predicted or hoped for in English, where all the sorts of recurrence shall be weighed and balanced and coordinated. I do not mean to say that the ultimate English metre will be in the least like the Bengali, but it will be equally fluid and equally able to rely on various properties . . . there will be new melodies and new modulations.[73]

Tagore had confirmed for Pound the truth of what Pound had learned from Yeats and Farr and his own troubadour studies, that the new English metric would be achieved by poets composing "in the sequence of the musical phrase, not in sequence of a metronome." And thus, as Pound's "Rabindranath Tagore" appeared in the March issue of the *Fortnightly*

70. "Tagore's Poems," *Poetry* (Chicago), 1 (December 1912), 92.
71. "Rabindranath Tagore," 571.
72. Ibid. 573. Pound refers to Tagore's prose translation number 67 in *Gitanjali*, p. 63: "There comes the morning with the golden basket in her right hand bearing the wreath of beauty, silently to crown the earth."
73. "Rabindranath Tagore," 578.

Review, his "A Few Don'ts by an Imagiste" appeared in the March issue of *Poetry.* The latter was immediately preceded by the three cardinal principles of *Imagisme*, Pound's long-considered directives for a modern poetry: "To begin with, consider the three propositions [direct treatment, economy of words, sequence of the musical phrase], not as dogma . . . but as the result of long contemplation, which, even if it is some one else's contemplation, may be worth consideration."[74]

Yeats was in Dublin for the launch of *Gitanjali,* lecturing on "The Poetry of Rabindranath Tagore" on March 23, his second lecture in connection with the Gordon Craig exhibition of scenery and stage designs in the Central Lecture Hall. "Yeats was in great form and spoke most interestingly," Holloway recorded in his journal. The several accounts of the lecture show Yeats not only conveying his enthusiasm for Tagore but grappling with parallel problems in India and Ireland of nationalism, politics, and poetry that he labored to articulate (and that his reporters labored to describe).

Yeats began by telling his Dublin audience that when Rothenstein introduced Tagore's poems to him he "was at once intoxicated by them, and so greatly moved that he feared to read them in any public place, lest he should betray his emotion."[75] He went on to praise the spontaneity and sanctity of Tagore's religious lyrics, revealing that Tagore had recently written to him about "some words having souls & some not having any or never would be born to have any, or words to that effect" (Holloway). He described how the poems were known and sung all over Bengal, and, following Pound, how "the poetry was in very different metres, which were something like the metres of the Provençal poets, whose work had been sung to music by the Troubadours." In these regards he outlined what he conceived to be some "remarkable parallels," between the India and the Ireland of today,

74. A Few Don'ts by an Imagiste" (*EPPP1* 120). Pound's article was preceded by a "note" by F. S. Flint entitled "Imagisme" (*EPPP1* 119), which set forth the three principles of the *imagistes* for the first time. Flint says that he had "sought out an *imagiste*" [Pound] to get them firsthand: "1. Direct treatment of the 'thing,' whether subjective or objective. 2. To use absolutely no word that did not contribute to the presentation. 3. As regarding rhythm: to compose in sequence of the musical phrase, not in sequence of a metronome" (199). In "The History of Imagism" (*Egoist*, May 1, 1915, 71), however, Flint confirms that this note was an "interview"; although it was printed over his signature for effect, it was actually by Pound, who changed the title from "Imagisme" to "A Retrospect," freely revised the note, and dropped Flint's name when he reprinted it as his own in *Pavannes and Divisions* (1918). From a distance of five years, Pound remembers in "A Retrospect" that the three principles were formulated with Richard Aldington in "the spring or early summer of 1912," but it is evident that they were written late in 1912 or early 1913 for publication in the March 1913 issue of *Poetry.*

75. *Irish Times* (March 24, 1913), 11.

stating that "a great Indian had called Ireland the India of the West."[76] He said that he had gleaned much about India from Tagore and from his talks with young Indians in London:

> In India, as in Ireland, English was made the vehicle of teaching in the schools, with strange effects upon the boys. Then, too, there was a great political movement in India, and just as they had a political movement with its good and its bad side in Ireland—and in this he spoke as an Irish Nationalist—so the Indian movement had its good and bad side.

As he drew the India/Ireland resemblances, he remarked that someone had rightly described nationalism as "service," a service that is due to the place of our birth. "Tagore was a great force in his country," Yeats declared. "He wrote for his people!" (Holloway). And thus Yeats began to inquire into the leading motive of Tagore's poetry and the manner in which he turned aside from Indian politics in the service of art and the souls of his people. "It was something of the same motive," he said, reflecting on the 1890s, "that led them in the Irish movement to turn away from politics." "I saw that when you are attempting to speak high things and sincere things, and at the same time carry on a political life, that, sooner or later, you give up the sincere things and the high things and you speak expedient things." Tagore's poetry had made him realize again that "those whose business it is to express the soul in art, religion or philosophy . . . must have no other pre-occupation." Years ago he had written *The Countess Cathleen* to make this point, that people (and poets) in Ireland "sell their opinions—their souls—in self-sacrifice for the good of others without attaining their ends."

Yeats's lecture reflected an extraordinary moment of self-examination for a poet who would, like Tagore, escape political pressures and write for the people. But he seemed to realize that for the past ten years he had not been free, that he had become caught up in an irrevocable modern plight that Tagore's minstrel presence had underscored. On the one hand he would justify the necessity of turning aside from politics, and on the other lament the impossibility of doing so, as the compositon of "September 1913" several months later would confirm. He concluded by reading several of Tagore's poems in translation, "in his chant-like monotonous method of reading," observed Holloway, "that robs, as a rule, the poem he reads of

76. "Mr. Yeats's Ideals," *Freeman's Journal*, March 24, 1913, 2.

any meaning it may have & replaces it by voice sounds of a melodious if formless kind."[77]

Tagore's *Gitanjali* won him the Nobel Prize for literature in 1913. After he returned to India in October of that year, he wrote an account of Yeats and English poetry for the press. Most of the modern English poets, he wrote, "have become experts—specialists," devoting themselves to "word-workmanship" and feeling no impulse to write from "the innermost chambers of their hearts." Their literary modernism, he declared, "is not a new thing; but it is threadbare, it is worn out.... It does not shake the whole being."[78] In contrast, he praised Yeats's imaginative, anti-modern vitality, declaring that his muse had "defiantly refused to follow the hollow voice of the time," and that he had remained a true, universal poet by evading the current fashions in literature and by singing from the deep heart's core: "Yeats reveals the soul of Ireland through his individual soul. He sees this world not with his eyes; he embraces this world not with his intellect; but he does both with his life and soul."

The enthusiasm of Yeats and Pound for Tagore's poetry began to wane in the post-*Gitanjali* period, and Tagore became wary of further translations of his work.[79] Even so, Yeats's interest in exploring Tagore's minstrel culture

77. Holloway went on to characterize Yeats's mannerisms as a lecturer and reader: "He continually uses his hands in angular fashion & all his gestures are modelled on Japanese attitudes seen in prints.... Yeats is a fascinating talker—one which is good to listen to, even if one did not grasp all he said. He always invites questions at end of his lectures for fear some would go away without understanding him! His answers, as a rule, are more mystifying than his original statements! He is so full of musical words that his sentences form themselves with rapsodies [*sic*] of speech rather than clear explanations of base fact!... He couldn't say 'yes' or 'no' to anything—a flood of words comes forth as sure as he opens his mouth to form the simple yea or nay! He is a wonder truly. What would Dublin be without its Yeats! Why, empty of distinction."

78. Tagore's article originally appeared in *Prakashi* (Calcutta) and was translated by Basanta Koomar Roy as "A Hindu on the Celtic Spirit" for *The American Review of Reviews*, 49 (January–June 1914), 101–2.

79. On May 8, 1913, Pound, on holiday in Italy, wrote to Dorothy from Venice, "I'm fed up with Tagore. I wish he'd get thru' lecturing before I get back. I don't want to be any more evangelized than I am already—which is too dam' much. And I much prefer the eagle's [Yeats's] gods to any oriental beetle with 46 arms" (*EP/DS* 224). This letter is misdated 1912 in James Longenbach's *Stone Cottage* (New York and Oxford: Oxford University Press, 1988), 26.

Even as Pound was losing interest, Tagore was encountering and having an impact on T. S. Eliot, as yet unknown to Pound and Yeats. In 1913 Tagore visited and lectured at Harvard University, invited by Professor James Woods, professor of Indian philosophy. As Tagore's friend R. F. Rattray, recounts, "Professor Woods invited some of us to meet Tagore at his house and the latter chanted for us passages from the Upanishads, sang some of his own songs, and read 'The Post Office,' still in manuscript. A fellow student present was T. S. Eliot. In connexion with Tagore's 80th birthday I wrote an article and sent him a copy. In his reply

was slow to subside; he considered taking Tagore to Ireland in 1913, and when that did not work out he made plans to go to India himself. On September 12, 1914, Yeats wrote to Tagore, regretful that the outbreak of war had disrupted his plans: "I had planned to go to India this winter. I had wanted to hear some minstrels sing your poems and to study the world out of which you have made them."[80] Less than a year later, Yeats strongly encouraged Tagore to complete his *Reminiscences* in the belief that they would help him with the revival of Irish culture.[81] As Yeats wrote to Rothenstein, "Perhaps I am biassed because I believe it to point a moral that would be valuable to me in Ireland."[82] On March 5, 1916, Tagore wrote that nothing would please him more "than to have a part, however, remote, in the revival of Irish national culture," but he feared that the pace of translation and the personal nature of the memoirs, which extended only to his twenty-fifth year, would not meet Yeats's plans. Tagore agreed to "send you the Memoirs as they near completion and then leave you to judge for yourself. My anxiety is that I may not give you any false expectations. If you think that a delay would be fatal to the plan altogether then would you let me know" (*LTWBY2* 322–3).[83] Inevitably, the war dealt a decisive blow to Yeats's dream of establishing a minstrel culture in Ireland, just as it sundered many another dream: on September 28, 1917, in a trench at Nieuport, near Flanders, a shell explosion killed in action the first Imagist, T. E. Hulme.

Hulme had given his "A Lecture on Modern Poetry" a second time at the Kensington Town Hall in April 1914, a few months before he joined the Honourable Artillery Company and left for France. By then the new climate for spoken, cadenced verse may have contributed to the abstracted and mumbled delivery that few could hear. To Yeats, as the war approached, the imagists still wrote "devil's metres" (Fletcher recalls Yeats's attempt "to change a line in my 'Irradiations' into something 'more

of May 2, 1940, he wrote: 'I am interested to read what you say about Mr. T. S. Eliot—some of his poetry have [*sic*] moved me by their evocative power and consummate craftsmanship. I have translated—that was some time ago—one of his lyrics called "The Journey of the Magi"'" (Letter to the editor, *TLS* [August 23, 1941], 409).

80. Yeats's letter to Tagore is printed in Naresh Guha, *W. B. Yeats: An Indian Approach* (Calcutta: Jadavpur University, 1968), 153–4.
81. Ibid. 154–5. The letter is dated "July 31 [1915?]."
82. Undated letter, Houghton; the letter is dated [August? 1915] by Mary Lago and printed in *Imperfect Encounter*, 226.
83. Tagore's *My Reminiscences* was translated by his nephew, Surendranath Tagore (London, 1917).

Yeatsian' "[84]) but they had at least redefined *vers libre* as "a verse-form based upon cadence."[85] As the Imagist poets who gathered at Church Walk split up into Georgians, Vorticists, and "Amygists," they carried with them the rhythmic principles and the auditory poetics of Yeats, Farr, Patmore, and Tagore.[86] Ahead lay a decade of historic readings at the Poetry Bookshop, followed in the 1920s by John Masefield's Oxford Recitations (founded explicitly on the principles of Yeats's chanting[87]), and in the 1930s by Elsie Fogerty's English Verse Speaking Association. But the ultimate forestalling of Hulme's prophecy (at least until T. S. Eliot took up Hulme's classical banner), appeared in the second volume of *Some Imagist Poets* (1916), where Amy Lowell, whom Yeats had met in August 1913, got the Church Walk imagists—Aldington, Fletcher, Flint, H.D., and Lawrence—collectively to reexplain the principles of Imagism. In their preface they felt compelled to focus on "this very fact of 'cadence' which has misled so many reviewers, until some have been betrayed into saying that the Imagists discard rhythm, when rhythm is the most important quality in their technique."[88] As though Yeats and Farr were looking over their shoulders, they concluded that "one thing must be borne in mind: a cadenced poem is written to be read aloud, in this way only will its rhythm be felt. Poetry is a spoken and not a written art."[89]

84. John Gould Fletcher, *Life Is My Song* (New York: Farrar and Rhinehart, 1937), 78. *Irradiations: Sand and Spray* was published in 1915.
85. *Some Imagist Poets* (Boston: Houghton Mifflin, 1916), p. ix.
86. When the anthology *Georgian Poetry, 1911–1912* appeared in December 1912, Pound wrote to Dorothy that "The eagle [Yeats] groans that 'no one' could read the georgian anthology with pleasure, & yet he forbids me to remove [it] from W.blds. [Woburn Buildings] as he 'ought to know something about these people' " (*EP/DS* 167–8).
87. See John Masefield, *So Long to Learn* (New York: Macmillan, 1952), 128–37.
88. *Some Imagist Poets*, pp. viii–ix.
89. Ibid., p. x.

9

Minstrels and Moderns

I

During the Yeats–Farr engagement with the Imagists, Yeats became increasingly caught up in theatre business and saw the Abbey Theatre weather some momentous events—the death of Synge, the fight with Dublin Castle over censorship, the withdrawal and arbitration of Annie Horniman's subsidy, and the necessity of securing a new Patent. By the end of 1910, as these distracting events approached resolution, Yeats had become fascinated with Gordon Craig's new system of screens and lighting, proclaiming the importance of the new decorative effects to the press before he employed them in productions of *The Hour Glass* and Lady Gregory's *The Deliverer* on January 12, 1911.[1] At the close of these performances, in anticipation of the revival of his *Deirdre*, Yeats lamented privately that his new director, Lennox Robinson, had no pictorial sense of the stage, but he expressed no concern about how ineffectual the verse-speaking had become. In his new preoccupation with Craig's screens and lighting, he had found a new metaphor: a play should be staged like a missal, the text framed

1. In his journal, Holloway quoted from Yeats's interview in the *Evening Telegraph* of January 11, 1911: "The scenery differs entirely from the old style of scenery, and consists chiefly of portable screens, by means of which beautiful decorative effects can be obtained, the working of the screens being based on certain mathematical proportions of which the stage manager can make walls, pillars, etc—a palace almost in a moment. . . . One enters into a world of decorative effects which give the actor a renewed importance. There is less to compete against him, for there is less detail, though there is more beauty." This was followed by his own negative view: "With a great flourish of egotistical trumpets on the part of the management and Yeats in dress clothes with crush opera hat in hand, the Gordon Craig freak scenery and lighting were tried at the Abbey in Lady Gregory's Hiberno-Egyptian one-act tragic comedy *The Deliverer*, and also in Yeats's morality *The Hour Glass*. And while most voted the innovation an affected failure with possibilities for effective stage pictures, none considered it in any way an improvement on the old methods. . . . The dresses designed or carried out from sketches supplied by Craig were most unsightly and ungainly, especially in *The Deliverer*" (*JHAT* 148).

and enhanced by decorative effects. Curiously unmindful of the verse, Yeats made a casting decision for *Deirdre* that signaled not only a major shift of emphasis in his dramaturgy but a diminution of the psaltery for the effects of screens and lighting. As he wrote figuratively of the new stage effects in the preface to *Plays for an Irish Theatre* (1911), "I am very greatful [to Mr. Gordon Craig] for he has banished a whole world that wearied me and was undignified and given me forms and lights upon which I can play as upon some stringed instrument."

Yeats was so pleased with Maire O'Neill's (Molly Allgood's) performance as the Angel in *The Hour-Glass* that he decided to cast her as Deirdre for the new Dublin and Manchester productions in place of her sister Sara, who had played Deirdre to Molly's First Musician the previous year and fully expected the role. "This was the last straw," wrote Holloway. "Sara Allgood had reached her Waterloo at the Abbey!" Infuriated by the rebuff, she walked out of the green room and was found sobbing and directing her anger at her sister more than at Yeats and the other directors. She spitefully refused to step down and play the First Musician, which she had played to the Deirdres of Letitia Darragh, Mona Limerick, and Mrs. Patrick Campbell (and to Molly's Second Musician) in earlier Abbey productions. Yeats seemed unfazed by the row and confident in his decision, believing that Molly had matured into a fine tragic actress since her haunting performance in Synge's *Deirdre of the Sorrows* a year earlier. "I should be very happy now that I have what may well be the ideal Dierdre," he wrote to Mabel Dickinson on January 28, 1911, "for Miss O Neill has just the youthful wildness & innocence I have longed for, but I find always less & less in Dublin to give me pleasure."[2] To solve the First Musician problem, Yeats followed his old recourse: "I am bringing over Mrs Emery to play 1 Musician," he informed Lady Gregory, "as this will save rehearsals for Manchester. She comes for expenses & will teach the others her music for chorus."[3] Not unaware of the company's resentment over the decision, he wrote to Mabel Dickinson that there would soon be stories to fill a letter: "Next week I shall have plenty to tell for Mrs Emery is almost on hand to manage for Miss Allgood. She has started off by objecting to her dress & demanding an increase of pay because of the watchfulness she will have to keep up at Euston & Holyhead to keep the railway porters from

2. Letter of January 28, 1911, *CL InteLex* 1522.
3. Letter of January 25, 1911, *CL InteLex* 1518.

breaking the psaltery."[4] To complicate matters, Farr brought Mrs. Patrick Campbell's daughter Stella with her to play Second Musician.

Yeats was delighted to have Farr on the Abbey stage as his First Musician at last. "The lyrics when Mrs Emery does them are most living & bea[u]tiful and seem to make the play more bea[u]tiful," he wrote to Lady Gregory.[5] His only disappointment was in Stella Campbell, who had no voice and tended to sing the lyrics emptily, but when he substituted a new member, Eithne Magee, for Campbell's first lyric, he found that she "was no good in it either," too given to singing. "The lyrics are far finer chanted than when sung," he wrote in frustration, but otherwise all seemed nearly perfect: "But for Miss Campbell I should have the best cast I could hope for." Impressed by Molly's performance in rehearsals, Yeats informed Lady Gregory that the scenes between her and Farr "are wonderful things—everyone else on the stage is blotted out."[6] With Farr herself confirming that Molly's "natural emotion" made her even finer that Mrs. Campbell in the role, Yeats was ready for a great revival.

How could it have been otherwise? How could it have been the most embarrassing and ruinous opening night in five years of staging *Deirdre*? How could Florence Farr inexplicably fail Molly and Yeats so utterly on this long-awaited occasion? Holloway, still upset over Sara's unjust removal, acknowledged nonetheless that Molly "gave a picturesque & dramatic rendering of Deirdre—superficial, perhaps, but pleasing." Nonetheless, he continued, "It is more than could be said for Florence Farr's 1st Musician." As he described it, without exaggeration, Farr's performance was unbelievably disastrous. Her voice "seemed hard & unmusical & her style of delivery unduly tragic and affected":

> She had not off her lines & made a slip in the text on the first words she had to utter. She seemed in distress & worried from the very first & appealed to the prompter piteously frequently. She was a fiasco & that's a fact. Outsiders don't harmonise with the Abbey company. The grouping of the wandering musicians was not as charmingly beautiful as heretofore—one missed the sweetly sad chanting of Miss Allgood.

The new Abbey actor Brinsley MacNamara joined the loud chorus of criticism over Farr's performance, exclaiming in dismay, "And this is the lady Yeats dedicated one of his books to as the only lady who had the art

4. Letter of January 28, 1911, *CL InteLex* 1522.
5. Letter of January 31, 1911, *CL InteLex* 1526.
6. Letter of February 1, 1911, *CL InteLex* 1530.

of speaking verse beautifully!"[7] MacNamara shook his head sadly, wrote Holloway,

> and Yeats's critical judgment in his estimation fell rapidly below zero. And who could wonder hearing her declaim her lines with all the self-consciousness of a tragedy Queen at a penny-gaff! The soft sweet voices of the other players made the contrast even more strongly marked. Their style was easy & natural, less loaded with affectation.

Farr's ill-advised and ill-prepared visitation stirred bitter feelings among members of the company once again; they were tired of visiting English actresses and strongly voiced their opinion, as Holloway recorded, that "any of the talented actresses of the company would have interpreted quite as artistically & quite as successfully." No one was more devastated than Yeats by the total collapse of Farr's performance, which ruined Molly's Deirdre in the first half of the play. "Miss Farr lost her head & was exceedingly bad," he wrote to Lady Gregory in disbelief:

> Over acted when she acted at all lost control of her voice & spoke wrong notes. If she had been playing with inexperienced players the curtain would probably have had to come down. She has no sense of having done as badly as she did—talks as if she had made but one slip that mattered (forgetting all of her second lyric except two lines & then stopping dead) yet she was magnificent in rehearsal.[8]

Perhaps Yeats could not as yet see that this flawed revival of *Deirdre* was a dark omen for the chanting movement on the Abbey stage, though he must have sensed that Farr had forfeited her professional authority and welcome in the company, which had in any case developed a style of speech and chanting distinct from her own. The American professor Cornelius Weygandt, who had heard Farr "half chant" the lyrics from *Deirdre* at Bryn Mawr in 1907, and who had come to witness the new Abbey performances while writing his book on the Irish theatre, observed the change:

> It was noticeable, when she played one of the musicians in his "Deirdre" on its later presentations, that her method of intoning the verses differed a great deal from their delivery by the regular members of the company. If Mr. Yeats has not changed his views somewhat in regard to the speaking of dramatic verse, he no longer insists on the half chant as it was practiced by Miss Farr,

7. MacNamara alludes to Yeats's earlier dedication of *In the Seven Woods* 'TO FLORENCE FARR | The only reciter of lyric poetry | who is always a delight, because | of the beauty of her voice and | the rightness of her method' (*VP* 850).

8. Letter of February 3, 1911, *CL InteLex* 1534.

but is content if the actors reproduce its rhythm in "the beautiful speaking" that is characteristic of their art.[9]

Immediately after the performances Yeats and Farr collected themselves and their friendship and crossed over to London for a scheduled engagement at the Little Theatre on February 16. After ten years of public and private appearances with the psaltery on platforms and stages, the wandering minstrels gave what would prove to be their final lecture–recital, together with a new actress-singer whom Yeats had invited to join them, Hilda Taylor. Since 1905 Taylor had been giving concerts with her own settings of Yeats's poems and had recently set the lyrics of *The Countess Cathleen.*[10] Farr cannot have welcomed this arrangement but was evidently silent about it; she had previously encountered Hilda Taylor as a disagreeable, even "truculent" member of the Chorus for the productions of the *Hippolytus* in May and October 1904.[11] Yeats had become quite taken with her, however, writing to Lady Gregory in advance of the lecture:

> Mrs Emery & Miss Hilda Taylor illustrate it by songs & speaking to the Psaltery. You would delight in Hilda Taylors [*sic*] singing of "Sally Garden" & "we who are old & gay". It [is] a most subtle thing & yet full of the spirit of folk. They chant very finely in two voice poems & would be magnificent in the Deirdre choruses. I shall get them to do the last at any rate. I think you would prefer Hilda Taylor even to Mrs Emery. I have offered to write a preface to her music to my poems if she publishes it.[12]

In an interview with the *Irish Times* about the forthcoming causerie in London, Yeats explained that it was an attempt to return to the original aims of the Abbey Theatre. "I had intended," he said,

9. Cornelius Weygandt, *Irish Plays and Playwrights* (London: Constable, 1913), 25–6.
10. On October 18, 1905, Miss Hilda Taylor's program of "Songs and Readings," including "Verses by W. B. Yeats . . . to music of her own composition" was performed at the Art School, 3 Logan Place, Pembroke Road. She sent a copy of the program to Yeats, inscribed "Do Come!" (NLI MS 12146).
11. Miss Taylor, having "embellished" some of Farr's music for the Chorus, claimed authorship, and expected to be paid for use of the music in subsequent productions. Murray wrote her a strong letter to put down her claims, and on September 14, 1904, before the October revival, Farr informed him, "I have rewritten Miss Taylor's music & I think improved it so that she shant be able to make herself disagreeable as she seemed inclined to do. I should have been quite glad about her if she'd not been so truculent, but perhaps you've not heard all that history & I haven't time to explain." Murray had indeed heard the history and evidently insisted that Farr take further steps, for on September 22 she wrote to assure him that she had "eliminated all traces of Miss Hilda Taylor so there will be no uncomfortableness about authorship."
12. Letter of January 22, 1911, *CL InteLex* 1508.

> side by side with these Irish plays, to try and reach the Irish people by a revival of the art of the Minstrel. The three great forms of poetry—narrative, dramatic, and lyric—have arisen and taken their shape from the reciter, the player, and the singer. Why should we not bring these three artists back once more to the science of literature?

Regretful that he had been unable to achieve this aim to the degree he had wished, he still thought that it "should not be more difficult to find singers who will have the beauty of the words for their pre-occupation; perhaps it may not be impossible to create what no longer exists, to the accompaniment of very simple notes, played upon some stringed instrument—narrative verse."[13] Toward his aim of bringing singers, too, back to "the science of literature," he explained his curious attraction to Hilda Taylor, a singer of his verse who had dissolved his resistance to musical settings of his poems:

> I shall introduce to my audience not merely Miss Florence Farr, whose art of speaking to the psaltery many of them know, but Miss Hilda Taylor, whose art is nearer to singing. She sings lyrics of my own, and of other people, as some country woman sings some old folk song, and yet without losing what they have of modern and subjective feeling. At least, so it seems to my ears, which are always delighted by her.

Thus, in a program entitled "Ireland and the Arts of Speech," Yeats reiterated his dream of reestablishing an imaginative culture on platform, stage, and street. "In England," he regretted, "pre-eminently the land of that miserable thing the printed book, merchants of a class now perfectly satisfied with a brass band and a gramophone had once had their lyric competitions in which the words were the important thing." In contrast, he pointed out, "in the West of Ireland there still survived a remnant of popular culture, founded on sung or spoken traditional literature, once existing all over the world," and this was the culture he would revive. The Abbey Theatre had found excellent players in becoming primarily a folk theatre that described the imaginative life of the people, "but without the minstrel and singer they could not give back to literature its old power over men's hearts."[14]

13. "Mr. W. B. Yeats on the Art of the Minstrel," *Irish Times*, February 6, 1911, 7.
14. "Spoken Literature," *Times*, February 17, 1911, 10. " 'Musical settings,' Yeats continued, 'should be greatly simplified and subordinated to the mainly literary effect of beautiful words.' " The lecture was "illustrated by Miss Florence Farr, who spoke or chanted to the accompaniment of a psaltery designed by Mr. Arnold Dolmetsch."

Even as he described the importance of training actors, reciters, and singers, however, he knew that without someone like Frank Fay to do the job the power of verse-speaking in the Abbey could no longer meet his expectations. He returned from London immediately to attend the last night of the Abbey's first production of *The Land of Heart's Desire*, which he had long wished to make part of the Abbey repertoire with *The Countess Cathleen*, but he had not been present for rehearsals. Holloway thought it an abysmal production: with the exception of Sara Allgood as Maire Bruin, the cast "made less than nothing out of the other roles & robbed the poet's lines of all the poetry they possess. They recited the lines with very little conviction." Holloway knew that Yeats was painfully aware that the verse speaking had been woefully neglected; he made a point of noting that Yeats "walked restlessly about during the interval following his play."

During these Dublin–London events of January–February 1911, Yeats had been in contact with a protégé of William Poel, the actor-director Nugent Monck, who had begun producing medieval morality and mystery plays in Norwich. Monck had since written to inform Yeats that he had been asked to produce *The Countess Cathleen*. Yeats replied on February 9: 'I am delighted that they have chosen you to produce the Countess Cathleen. . . . I have never produced it myself and doubt if I could lay hands on the music we used, though I think I could get you music for the song about Fergus in Act II. Miss Hilda Taylor has done a very beautiful setting."[15] Yeats was excited by the revival and made plans to travel to Norwich for the one evening performance on February 21 (there was a matinee the following afternoon), writing from Holyhead on crossing from Ireland that he had just seen *The Land of Heart's Desire* "produced for the first time by my own people & did not like it it [*sic*] much."[16] He had given Monck the freedom to cut and produce *The Countess Cathleen* as he wished, but he was surely unaware of how irrelevant was the offer of getting music from Farr and how thoroughly amateurish the production would prove to be. The play was advertised in Norwich as the first production in England: "It was first produced in Dublin in 1899," reported a local paper, "when it attracted considerable attention, and very hard things indeed were said of the author." It was performed before a large audience in the Assembly rooms of the Theatre-plain by the Dramatic Society of the Norwich High

15. Letter of February 9, 1911, *CL InteLex* 1539.
16. Letter of February 19, 1911, *CL InteLex* 1550.

School Old Girls' Association, all proceeds to benefit the Norfolk and Norwich Hospital. "Whatever may be said of the theme of it," wrote the reporter, "there was no question as to the merit of the performance," and full credit was extended to Monck, who took no part in the play, for his staging and lighting effects and for overcoming the many obstacles of production "so well as they were." Yeats responded to loud calls for the author "with a few words of warm approval of the manner in which the play had been presented."[17]

Yeats could not have approved of the verse-speaking, but he was pleased with Monck's medieval staging, writing to Edith Lister that the play was staged "like a page out [of] a missal. I was delighted with what I saw & shall now produce the play myself."[18] The effect of the February productions of *The Land of Heart's Desire* and *The Countess Cathleen* was to throw him into a revising mood yet again, and by mid-July he was hard at work on new versions of the two plays. When he informed Maud Gonne of this activity, she wrote in reproach, "as for the rewriting of your Abbey plays, you have not IMPROVED them at all & I hate to think of 'Countess Kathleen' being re-written" (*G-YL* 301).

Yeats's revisions were now influenced by his recent success with Gordon Craig's screens and stage decoration in *The Hour-Glass*, and by the immediate prospect of opening an Abbey School of Acting that would train a second company to perform plays while the permanent company was on tour. As he revised, and as the Abbey's first American tour materialized, Yeats wrote to Monck on 22 July that he wanted him to direct the new School: "You will take charge of pupils & if they mature produce some plays & help me with some work with Craig screens. It is all rather vague but we may be able to do some interesting work," adding in postscript, "I am still at work on the new 'Countess Cathleen.' "[19]

By September all arrangements for the tour and school had been made. On the 10th, three days before sailing to Boston to help launch the tour, Yeats wrote to Monck in anticipation of his arrival in Dublin:

> I shall send you a complete script of the new Countess Cathleen and you will find not only the big Craig screens but the little model screens in Dublin when you get there.... I want you to begin the work for a production of the Countess Cathleen either during the absence of the main company (Miss

17. *Norfolk Chronicle and Norwich Gazette*, February 25, 1911, 10.
18. Letter of February 23, 1911, Spencer Research Library, University of Kansas.
19. Letter of July 22, [1911], *CL InteLex* 1685.

O'Neill will be available) or after its return. Make yourself familiar with the effect of the big screens on the stage.[20]

Yeats then turned all his energy to the first American tour of the Abbey Players. After arriving in Boston on September 21, he devoted the next three weeks to rehearsing the company, giving lectures and interviews, attending performances, and defending the Abbey against the first American attacks on *The Playboy*. On October 10 he left Boston for five days in New York, where he would visit his father at the Petipas boarding house on West 29th, and be feted as the guest of the recently founded Poetry Society of America. Nearly two hundred members gathered for the luncheon held in the National Arts Club, Gramercy Park. One of the welcoming speakers on the program was the Reverend Merle St. Croix Wright, a Unitarian clergyman and orator who petrified the audience by taking Yeats to task on "the negative character of Irish poetry and its baleful reaction upon Irish life," pleading for a more constructive modern literature in Ireland. Jessie Rittenhouse, Secretary of the Society, recalled their apprehension over the way Yeats might respond,

> but at the end of the clergyman's pyrotechnics the poet arose, as if in a dream, and stretched forth what George Moore has called his "long, Buddhistic hands." A hush fell upon us. He agreed with what Dr. Wright had said, judged from the obvious side, but began to interpret poetry from the mystical side, declaring it had nothing to do with polemics, nor nationalities, save as it disclosed to Ireland its own soul; that it was altogether a thing of the spirit, a search for the beauty at the heart of the universe.

In this extraordinary reply, Yeats gave the impression that he was "detached from time" and that he moved in "a charmed orbit of the eternal," but the spellbinding effect of his chanting was yet to come:

> Again he stretched out his hands and began to chant "The Dream of Wandering Aengus," that most magical lyric whose symbolism it is unnecessary to know, so beautiful is the mere music and phrasing. Yeats's voice in this poem will chant forever in my ears and I shall always see him standing with lifted hands, the visible embodiment of the poet.[21]

20. Letter of September 10, [1911], *CL InteLex* 1727.
21. Jessie B. Rittenhouse, *My House of Life* (Boston and New York: Houghton Mifflin, 1934), 231–2. Not every American listener was so impressed with Yeats's method of chanting, as the journalist Burton Rascoe revealed of his encounters with Yeats in 1912 and 1914: "Like most poets, Yeats reads his own incomparably beautiful verses badly; indeed, he mangles them by reciting them in a dreary monotone, with care only for the beat of a measure." Rascoe further delighted in recounting a chanting incident that he witnessed: "And at a dinner given

Within the week he would sail for England, meet Craig in London to secure rights to use the screens in his plays, and return to Dublin at the end of October to help Monck with the Acting School. Monck began producing a combination of medieval morality plays and Irish dramas with the pupils in November, leading up to the production of *The Second Shepherd's Play* and the revised version of *The Countess Cathleen* from December 14 to 16. Yeats attended all the performances, sitting in the balcony next to the limelight operator, calling the cues for lighting changes. Monck, seemingly uninstructed in the requirements of the role, had decided to cast himself as Aleel to Molly Allgood's Cathleen. "I must candidly confess," wrote Holloway, "that I could not get interested in *The Countess Cathleen* as revised & presented at the Abbey":

> The mediaeval treatment suggestive of tapestry robbed the play of its drama & gave only occasional prettiness instead. . . . My recollection of its first performance some twelve years ago is of a beautiful poetic play beautifully enacted without distracting elements, save the occasional noise of the students who had a crow to pluck with Yeats over his slighting comments on Thomas Davis.
>
> (Holloway)

Holloway was greatly put off by the scenery and the use of limelights, which he felt were "more distracting than helpful to the spoken words—the play vanished in the strange setting and the erratic lighting." The unfamiliar and unwelcome stage experiments, however, upset Holloway no more than Monck's portrayal of Aleel. Monck had not mastered his lines in rehearsal and fluffed several in the opening. Even worse, thought Holloway, Monck brought to Aleel's lines "a hardness of voice I had not noticed before, scarcely in keeping with the role." The extent to which the symbolic effect of the verse-speaking had been lost in twelve years, however, was best measured by the realistic theatre critic of the *Irish Independent*, "Jacques," who thought Monck "a very impressive Aleel, but he might have dispensed with the mandoline-shaped instrument. It served no useful purpose."[22]

If the chanting had disappeared and the psaltery was now antiquated, so might the lyrics dependent on their effects have to go. After the

for him, he so far forgot where he was as to begin chanting some verse while a brother poet was paying an eloquent and thoughtful tribute to him, and continued so audibly and monotonously that the other poet forgot the conclusion to his talk and had to sit down in great confusion." See *W. B. Yeats Interviews and Recollections*, ed. E. H. Mikhail (London: Macmillan, 1977), i. 118–19.

22. *Irish Independent*, December 15, 1911, 4. "Jacques" was the pen name of John J. Ryce.

performances, Yeats continued to revise the play for a separate edition (June 1912) and for inclusion in his new edition of *Poems* (September 1912). In the process he discarded the original chanted lyric, "Who will go drive with Fergus now?" and gave it a new home, placing it in *The Rose* (composed of the lyrics from *The Countess Kathleen and Various Legends and Lyrics,* 1892) for the 1912 edition of *Poems*, but he kept "Impetuous Heart" in its old place in Scene 2. After the verse-speaking fiascoes of the previous year, Yeats began to revise the two verse plays on a new principle. Whereas earlier versions depended on the mood and chanting of the players, he now rewrote them so that they would, he explained to his readers, depend "less upon the players and more upon the producer, both having been imagined more for variety of stage-picture than variety of mood in the player. It was, indeed, the first performance of 'The Countess Cathleen' . . . that set me writing plays where all would depend upon the player" (*VPl* 1291). When the new editions of *The Countess Cathleen* and *The Land of Heart's Desire* appeared simultaneously in June 1912 as the first two volumes of "Dublin Plays," they reflected the dramatic shift of emphasis in Yeats's dramaturgy from players and verse speakers to stage producers and decorative scenery.[23]

Late in June, just after the new edition of *The Countess Cathleen* appeared, Farr began writing to Quinn, Shaw, and other friends to inform them of her plans to leave London for a position as headmistress of a Tamil school for girls in Ceylon, Ramanathan College, founded by Sir Ponnambalam Ramanathan, her recruiter, whom she had met in London with his English wife in 1902. "I plan to end my days in the 'society of the wise' as the Vedanta books say one should," she wrote to Quinn,[24] subsequently informing him that she had returned to Cheltenham Ladies College to learn the latest Western educational ideas, "& I find they consist of an elaborate thing called 'The Montessori System' . . . It is exactly what I

23. When Monck restaged *The Land of Heart's Desire* for Yeats on February 22, 1912, Holloway recorded that the staging "was pretty and fanciful—Monck has a knack for pretty effective fantastical plays of the kind. . . . Nugent Monck as Father Hart was effective & the others were in the picture—it was more a picture than a play. . . . Of all the pieces produced by Nugent Monck *The Land of Heart's Desire* has been the most picturesque in its setting and lighting—he has an eye for the picturesque & fantastical & in this fanciful little play he gave his bent full play with charming effectiveness." On the success of this picturesque production Yeats completed his revisions of the play, writing in his preface, dated March 1912: "Till lately it was not part of the repertory of the Abbey Theatre, for I had grown to dislike it without knowing what I disliked in it. This winter, however, I have made many revisions and now it plays well enough to give me pleasure." (*The Land of Heart's Desire* [London: T. Fisher Unwin, 1912], 47).

24. Unpublished letter of June 18, 1912, NYPL.

have always thought ought to be done. So I am looking forward with tremendous interest to my educational experiments."[25] A few days later, she informed Shaw that she would be away "for five years certain" and that, as he had subsidized the publication of her new novel, *The Solemnization of Jacklin* (1912), she had arranged for all royalties to be paid to him.[26] Dorothy Shakespear wrote to Pound on June 30 to inform him that "Mrs. Emery was here the other day: she is going in August to Ceylon—to be head of some college, or something queer.... She says she is leaving the psaltery with W. B. Y. and out there can get a lovely instrument with quarter-tones to play & sing with" (*EP/DS* 127). Dorothy wrote to him again the following week to say that she had finished Farr's novel, describing it as "Such a Sargasso Sea muddle":

> Every body divorced several times, & in the end going back to their originals: & a young man called 'Dorus Callando' who lay among lilies all night & is Oscar [Wilde], without the bittersweetness.
>
> (*EP/DS* 127)

Pound adapted Dorothy's descriptive phrase for the first line of his own tribute to Farr, "Portrait d'une Femme." "Your mind and you are our Sargasso Sea," he began, "one comes to you | And takes strange gain away":

> These are your riches, your great store; and yet
> For all this sea hoard of deciduous things,
> Strange woods half sodden, and new brighter stuff:
> In the slow float of differing light and deep,
> No! there is nothing! In the whole and all,
> Nothing that's quite your own.
> Yet this is you.

"As for F.F. Ceylon ought to suit her," wrote Dorothy somewhat cattily, evidently receiving a copy of the poem from Pound, who was including the poem in *Ripostes*, currently in press: "I wonder if she'll see her portrait before she goes. Of course she always did dress in towling made loose—chez elle, that is—or remnants of stage properties & improprieties."[27]

25. Unpublished letter of August 9, 1912, NYPL. In a letter about Farr from S. H. Perinbanayagam of Ceylon, Shaw was informed that the school "was brought into being by its founder for the specific purpose of keeping away the nice Hindu girls of this part of the world from the demoralizing influence of Christian missionary education" (Letter of August 14, 1948, BL Add. MS 50533, vol. xxvi).
26. Letter of June 22, 1912, BL Add. MS 50533, vol. xxvi.
27. Letter of July 5, 1912 (*EP/DS* 130). Unless Pound sent it to her, Farr may not have seen the poem before she departed, as *Ripostes* did not appear until October.

Farr had invited Yeats to come to her rooms to tell him personally of her decision, but he had to put her off for several days due to the "usual theatre distractions" and Lady Gregory's dinner on the arrival of Tagore (Bax 84–5). He was evidently disconsolate at the news, but he did not let his unrecorded disappointment keep him from pressing her into chanting for Tagore. At some point, however, in a disillusioned moment, knowing that her departure spelled the end of the new art, he muttered to Sturge Moore that she was " 'a chalk egg' he had been sitting on for years."[28]

Farr began her leavetaking with a final solo performance on the psaltery to a sympathetic audience at the Clavier Hall on July 18, 1912. Nevinson was there as witness, once again enraptured by her recitation of Rossetti's "Sister Helen" and Ronsard's "Sur le Mort de Marie," the latter "the most beautiful." "When the last sound of that beautiful voice died away," he wrote in his diary, "never to sound again, it was very sad."[29] In September, Harold Monro wrote London's farewell to the mistress of chanting in the *Poetry Review*:

> We can but regret our loss of so fine an artist, and hope that there are others who may have learnt something from her, and who have sufficient restraint and self-surrender to submit themselves, after her manner, to the cadence and rhythms of poetry, becoming for the time being, a sensitive medium for their conveyance to an audience, rhapsodist rather than exponent, instrument rather than representative.[30]

Farr's last act before embarking was to place in Yeats's hands the Dolmetsch psaltery, like returning a ring, the object most symbolic of their twenty-two-year collaboration. On September 5 she sailed on the SS *Leicestershire*, just as the new edition of Yeats's *Poems* appeared, just as Monck was preparing a second production of *The Countess Cathleen* with the Abbey's main company. After breaking her journey with a fortnight stopover in

28. See T. Sturge Moore, "Yeats," *English*, 2 (Summer 1939), 277. Yeats's impatience over her inopportune departure later surfaced in the preface to *The King of the Great Clock Tower* (1934): "When I had enough knowledge to discover some dramatic form to give her the opportunity she lacked," he wrote, "Florence Farr had accepted a post in a Cingalese girls' school that she might hide her ageing beauty" (*VPl* 1009).
29. Nevinson's journal, July 18, 1912, Bodleian (MS Eng.misc.e. 617). "Spoke to her on the stage," Nevinson continued. "Met the Housmans, Mrs. Havelock Ellis, Clifford Bax, & others there." To Bax, to whom she entrusted a "Black Box" of letters from Yeats, Shaw, and others on July 28, "she was still beautiful and no one who saw her could forget her starry eyes. She was, in fact, one of the four or five genuinely poetic women I have known" (Bax [i]).
30. *Poetry Review*, I (September 1912), 424.

Cairo, Yeats's first Aleel wrote to Shaw from her second ship, in the middle of the Indian Ocean:

> In the first boat I made friends, played bridge, recited Verlaine's verse as an imitation of Sarah Bernhardt which was the nearest I could get to the Music Hall spirit. In this boat I am remaining quite obscure & just speak to a few people who wonder what the eccentric person in a Chinese robe & spectacles is. I feel as if something real is going to happen over this college at Jaffna—everyting seems to be falling right for it.[31]

Writing to Yeats shortly after arriving in Ceylon, she described her temporary rooms in a garden bungalo of the Ramanathan residence in Colombo, where she would reside, meditate, and study Tamil while construction of a college building in Jaffna was being completed. "Beautiful creatures walk about the streets like exquisite mahogany statues come to life," she wrote of her new world, "everyone, even the crooked and old, has the air of being an extraordinary work of art. . . . At the currey meals Ramanathan appears, & we have great talks about the nature of the soul."[32]

When *The Countess Cathleen* opened at the Abbey Theatre on September 26, Holloway and several of his friends agreed that the pupils in the Acting School had put on a better performance the previous season. "The staging is of the Gordon Craigish up-to-date unreal kind," complained Holloway,

> with the stage lighted from the front of the house, footlights done away with & the apron on the stage thrust out well beyond the proscenium arch. . . . All this may be arty, but I am hanged if it makes for drama . . . Yeats & Co may like this sort of thing, but the playgoing public think a little of it goes a long way & go elsewhere to be entertained when a freak show is on at the Abbey.

The actress Maire Walker told Holloway that Monck's voice "was very hard & grating—he was a bad actor—a good producer," but Holloway was even harsher: "The poet 'Aleel' of Nugent Monck replaced the glamour of poetic fire by a touch of Bunthornish wriggling & unmusical affected delivery. There was a dash of Uriah Heep humility about him that betrayed insincerity . . . A poet inspired by the love of such a woman as the Countess should have more of the man in him!"[33]

31. Undated letter [late September 1912], BL Ashley MS 50533, Vol. xxvi.
32. Letter of October 26, 1912. For Farr's letters to Yeats from Ceylon, see Josephine Johnson, "Florence Farr: Letters to W. B. Yeats, 1912–17," *YA9* 216–54; here, 225.
33. Bunthorne is a character in Gilbert and Sullivan's *Patience*, Uriah Heep in Dickens's *David Copperfield*.

Whatever pleasure Yeats received from the Craig screens and lighting used in this latest production, he knew that a price had been paid for the poor verse-speaking. Monck's second performance of Aleel finally convinced him that "Impetuous Heart" could no longer sustain its position and effect without a player trained to chant the lyrics. Thus, in December he took a copy of the 1912 edition of *The Countess Cathleen* and made his final revisions of the play for *Poems* (1913). He began by pasting the typed copy of a new lyric, "Were I but crazy for love's sake," over "Impetuous Heart." He could not, however, bring himself to remove the old lyric from the play, and so he pasted it unobtrusively to the end of scene four, thereby sacrificing the foreboding sense of terror that had moved him so deeply since Farr's first performance.[34] "Impetuous Heart" was finally still.

Within a year of Farr's departure for Ceylon both Sara and Molly Allgood would leave the Abbey. Without the Fays and Allgoods to train new members in chanting, and in musical speech without singing, there was no hope that the verse-speaking could meet his expectations or that he could mount productions of his verse that would give him pleasure. Thus, his early verse plays began to lose their place in the Abbey repertory. "*The King's Threshold* and *Deirdre* and *Baile's Strand* want each one player of genius," he wrote to Allan Wade a decade later, "and that is out of reach probably henceforth for ever."[35]

II

"I gave up the fight," Yeats later wrote of his verse-speaking experiments at this time, "began writing little dance plays, founded upon a Japanese model . . . Whenever I produced one of these plays I asked my singers for no new method did not even talk to them upon the subject" (*VPl* 1009). Four years would pass, however, before the first of these plays, *At the Hawk's Well*, appeared with the characteristic chorus of Three Musicians, no longer speaking to the psaltery but to a variety of musical instruments. During these transitional years, however, Farr kept Yeats informed of her musical

34. The manuscripts related to these revisions are in the collections of the late Anne Yeats and the Berg Collection and are described in *The Countess Cathleen: Manuscript Materials* as ABY (B), Berg (C), and Berg (D), pp. xiii–xiv.
35. Letter of October 18, [1912], *L* 674.

discoveries in Ceylon: "you'd delight in the place," she wrote on January 7, 1913, describing the music and rules of poetic recitation:

> the music is planned out like a Dutch garden you chose [*sic*] your mode your rhythm & your time & then you may not use any notes that are not in that mode otherwise you can sing as you please. You cannot change the key but you may change the note you stop on. I think you would be excited about the verse if you could hear it with the proper pronunciation.
>
> (*YA9* 227)

She gave examples and translations of Tamil verses—"it means 'Hurts my heart, hurts my heart' "—and described for him existing elements of his ideal culture. In Jaffna, which means, she wrote, "The land of the lute player," her college employed a man to tell stories with songs in them to the students: "He plays the violin holding it between his chest & his knee. He twangs a long stringed instrument in such a way as to make it buzz all the time." Knowing how much it would appeal to him, she closed her letter by telling him that in this culture the sounds of a poet's verse-songs are crucial to his reputation and greatness: "The thing one wants to know about a great poet is the sort of sounds his verse made One doesn't particularly want to know anything else about him that cannot be put into prose."

Yeats was of course "very deeply" intrigued by her descriptions and wished that he had the musical knowledge to better understand the relation of native music to poetry as she portrayed it. "I wish you would write a short essay on the subject & get it published somewhere," he urged her. "You have probably found the thing we have all been looking for. Tagore writes all his poems to music & is said to be a great musician."[36] Within a month Farr had acquired a vina, a seven-string Indian lyre: Yeats wanted to know if she had learned to play it or whether she longed for the psaltery. "I have a Vina in the corner of my room," she replied, "& the other day got an excellent book about it so now I tune it properly & try all kinds of experiments. It is an instrument which has as many varieties of timbre as Dolmetsches harpsichords" (*YA9* 233). By the end of the year she had become sufficiently proficient with the vina to describe some of her experiments with old Tamil poetry, and she delighted in telling him about cultural events that illuminated their own experiments. She had witnessed a biweekly performance in a nearby college, where the priest

36. Letter of February 18, [1913], quoted in Sothebys auction catalogue, July 15–16, 1998, lot 158; *CL InteLex* 2092.

tells old stories of the Gods in a chanting voice, breaking into a sort of song full of shakes and quivers quaverings and modulations which he sings to the accompaniment of silver cymbals, violins, and a strange instrument called "the thamban," which though stringed makes a buzzing sound like a long drawn out organ note. He is singing to perhaps a 100 of our girls who know some of the less difficult songs or hymns by heart and join in when they can. The whole language is made for its own peculiar song-speech which goes something like this

ahhahhah ~ ah ah ah ~
ooo thum bum ooo thum bum

ah
A ey ey
oooaou (*YA9* 240)

As much as Yeats enjoyed hearing about her discoveries, experiments, and experiences in the oral culture of Ceylon, he was, in the aftermath of her departure and Tagore's, looking for new directions in his work. In January 1914, as he prepared to write the first of his memoirs, the nature of his thoughts on the state of his own career became evident at a signal literary event—a gathering of writers to honor the poetic achievement of Wilfrid Blunt at his home in Newbuildings, Sussex, where he was presented with a marble reliquary carved by Gaudier-Brzeska and filled with recent poems by the participants. Called upon to speak on behalf of the assembled Imagists (Pound, Flint, Aldington) and writers of other modern schools (Sturge Moore, Masefield, Victor Plarr, Frederic Manning), writers whom Pound described as "representative of the present vitality of English verse,"[37] Yeats paid homage in terms of his own twenty-year campaign against Victorian abstraction and impersonality, expressing his victorious mood at the end of a conflict. "When you published your first work, sir," Yeats began, "it was at the very height of the Victorian period":

> The abstract poet was in a state of glory. One no longer wrote as a human being with an address, living in a London street, having a definite income, and a definite tradition, but one wrote as an abstract personality.... This abstraction was the result of the unreal culture of Victorian romance. Now, sir, instead of abstract poetry, you wrote verses which were good poetry because they were first of all fine things to have thought and said in some real situation

37. Ezra Pound, "Homage to Wilfrid Blunt," *Poetry*, 3 (March 1914), 222; *EPPP1* 225. Pound regretted the unavoidable absence of D. H. Lawrence, Padraic Colum, James Joyce, and Rupert Brooke: "Still it was a fairly complete sort of tribute, representing no one clique or style but a genuine admiration for the power behind all expression, for the spirit behind the writing." See Plate 15.

> of life. They had behind them the drama of actual life. We are now at the end of Victorian romance—completely at an end. One may admire Tennyson but one cannot read him. The whole movement is over, but the work that survives is this work which does not speak out of the life of an impossible abstract poet, but out of the life of a man who is simply giving the thoughts which he had in some definite situation in life, or persuades us that he had; so that behind his work we find some definite impulse of life itself.[38]

In this new paean to the power and triumph of personal utterance, Yeats turned to his own need for renewal:

> If I take up to-day some of the things that interested me in the past, I find that I can no longer use them. They bore me. Every year some part of my poetical machinery suddenly becomes of no use. As the tide of romance recedes I am driven back simply on myself and my thoughts in actual life, and my work becomes more and more like your earlier work, which seems fascinating and wonderful to me. A great many of us feel the same. Just as the Victorian time recedes, your work becomes younger and more fascinating to us. I say that for myself.

Left unstated, of course, was the fact that Yeats had already encountered the new "machinery" with which he would remake himself as poet and dramatist. Fortuitously, Pound had recently received into his care from Mary Fenollosa, who had read and liked his poems in *Poetry*, the papers of her late husband, Ernest Fenollosa, a remarkable scholar of Japanese Noh and former Imperial Commissioner of Arts in Tokyo. His wife, in London after his death there, had pressed his notes and Noh manuscripts on Pound, whom she believed would edit and publish the papers as her husband, who disliked academics, would have wanted them done.[39] "By one of the more unexpected turns of chance," wrote Pound, "there has come into my possession a most interesting and . . . unique set of documents relating to one of the greatest and least-known arts of the world, the art of the classical Japanese drama, generally called *Noh*." Yeats had been introduced to Noh as early as 1907 by the Japanese scholar Yone Noguchi, who had traced the affinity of Yeats's plays with Noh and proposed in print that Yeats study

38. Quoted in Richard Aldington, "Presentation to Mr. W. S. Blunt," *Egoist*, 1 (February 2, 1914), 57. In his renewed poetic correspondence with Robert Bridges, Yeats replied to his question about punctuation in his poems: "I chiefly remember you asked me about my stops & commas. Do what you will. I do not understand stops. I write my work so completely for the ear that I feel helpless when I have to measure pauses by stops & commas" (Letter of [July 13, 1915], *CL InteLex* 2708).

39. See Yoko Chiba, "Ezra Pound's Versions of Fenollosa's Noh Manuscripts and Yeats's Unpublished 'Suggestions & Corrections,'" *YA* 4 (1986), 121.

the form.[40] With the arrival of the Fenollosa papers in December 1913, that study began in earnest at Stone Cottage, the Sussex retreat where for the next two winters Yeats and Pound both immersed themselves in the notes and plays. As Noguchi had suggested, Yeats found in the Noh a more concentrated form of his own total theatre—a drama of masks with symbolic stage, subtle gestures and movements of body, chanted or intoned verse, a chorus of musicians, suggestive music, and pantomimic dance. He also found an extraordinary grasp of the supernatural and preternatural worlds, of ghosts operating under spiritual forces rendered through masks, and he sensed at once the parallels with Irish folklore and his magical studies.

In his depiction of the two poets writing and translating together at Stone Cottage, James Longenbach indicates how they influenced each other in their shared study of the Noh. When Pound began working on passages of *Nishikigi*, Yeats's chanting of the composition of "The Peacock" and other poems in the adjacent room had its effect on Pound's translation of a long speech. "Pound's version of the passage," writes Longenbach,

> reveals the influence of Yeats chanting his poetry in the next room: "Times out of mind am I here setting up this bright branch, this silky wood with the charms painted in it as fine as the web you'd get in the grass cloth of Shinobu, that they'd be still selling you in this mountain." The Irish lilt of the prose in Pound's translations, which has often been noticed, is not merely the casual result of his proximity to Yeats: the effect is calculated to express the similarity that both poets sensed between Noh drama, Irish folklore, and the literature of the occult.[41]

"It is, of course, impossible to give much idea of the whole of this art on paper," wrote Pound in introducing Fenollosa's work on the Noh. "One can only trace out the words of the text and say that they are spoken, or half-sung and chanted, to a fitting and traditional accompaniment of movement and colour, and that they are themselves but half shadows."[42] He wrote with privileged awareness of the enormous effect the dramatic

40. "Mr. Yeats and the Nō," *Japan Times*, November 3, 1907, 6. For a recent, full account of Yeats's literary relationship with Noguchi (1875–1947), see Edward Marx, "Nō Dancing: Yone Noguchi in Yeats's Japan," *YA17* (2007), 51–93. See also Shotaro Oshima, *W. B. Yeats and Japan* (Tokyo: Hokuseidō, 1965).

41. James Longenbach, *Stone Cottage: Pound, Yeats, and Modernism* (New York and Oxford: Oxford University Press, 1988), 46–7.

42. Ernest Fenollosa and Ezra Pound, *'Noh' or Accomplishment: A Study of the Classical Stage of Japan* (London: Macmillan, 1916), 6.

form had had on Yeats, who was contemplating the first of his Noh-based "dance plays," *At the Hawk's Well*, and assisting Pound with the language of his Noh translations: "It is a theatre of which Mr. Yeats and Mr. Craig may approve."

The Imagists who had gathered at Blunt's Newbuildings in January 1914 had eagerly awaited the publication of the movement's first anthology, *Des Imagistes*, which appeared in America in February and England in March. Edited by Pound, it proved to be a badly mismanaged collection: readers and reviewers were put off by the affected title, the lack of an explanatory preface or manifesto, and the inclusion of some authors who were at best only Imagists in tendency, friends whose work Pound admired. The bona fide Imagists were Pound, Flint, Aldington, H.D., Amy Lowell, and William Carlos Williams. To flesh out the slim volume, Pound included poems by Skipwith Cannell, John Cournos, James Joyce, Ford Madox Hueffer, and Allen Upward.[43] Pound was of course dismayed and defensive about the critical reception. Moreover, the arrival from America of Amy Lowell as the aggressive new manageress and promoter of the movement, the principles of which she sought to broaden in anthologies entitled *Some Imagist Poets*, further frustrated him. The diffusive effect of what he termed "Amy-gism" led him to incorporate his stricter form of Imagism into Wyndham Lewis's Vorticism, a movement based on the "primary pigment" of each of the several arts—painting, sculpture, music, poetry—the primary pigment of poetry being the image. In "Vortex," published in the inaugural issue of *Blast* (June 1914), and in "Vorticism," which followed in the *Fortnightly Review*, Pound labored to define the broader movement in the arts, writing there and elsewhere of the vorticist principles manifest in the work of Wyndam Lewis, Edward Wadsworth, Gaudier-Brzeska, and Jacob Epstein. Altering his initial terminology from "primary pigment" to "pattern-unit" or "unit of design," his focus was on the emotional energy and intensity that generated the pattern-unit in the artist's mind and work. In "As for Imagisme," he thus defined the place of the image in the larger

43. In an interview in *The Daily News and Leader* (London) on March 18, 1914, Pound replied defensively when asked about the inclusion of Upward and Hueffer, "The anthology does not represent the personalities of those included, nor does it represent their differences, but the line where they come together, their agreement that the cake-icing on the top of poetry—the useless adjectives and the unnecessary similes which burden verse like cumbrous ornaments—should be avoided" (14). In a subsequent review of Hueffer's *Collected Poems*, Pound added a note in response to criticism of the anthology: "Mr. Hueffer is not an *imagiste*, but an impressionist. Confusion has arisen because of my inclusion of one of his poems in the *Anthologie des Imagistes*" (*Poetry*, 4 [June 1914], 120; *EPPP1* 248).

vorticist concept: "Not only does emotion create the 'pattern-unit' and the 'arrangement of forms,' it creates also the Image":

> Emotion seizing up some external scene or action carries it [the Image] to the mind; and that vortex purges it of all save the essential or dominant or dramatic qualities, and it emerges like the external original. . . . It is a vortex or cluster of fused ideas and is endowed with energy . . . By "direct treatment," one means simply that having got the Image one refrains from hanging it with festoons.[44]

By late summer of 1914 he had found the pattern-unit in all but a vorticist musician, which coincidence would soon provide.

In February 1914, just as *Des Imagistes* appeared, Dolmetsch decided to leave Gaveau and Paris, determined to re-establish himself in London, which he regarded as his spiritual home. He took a house at 4 Tanza Road in Hampstead, and while the rooms were being fitted for his family's musical life he found a country retreat in Kent to complete the draft of his book, *The Interpretation of the Music of the XVIIth and XVIIIth Centuries*. The Dolmetsches were welcomed back to London with a dinner party hosted by the Sturge Moores, with Yeats in attendance, at nearby 40 Well Walk. After talk that ranged from the suffragette movement to the financial plight of the Abbey Theatre, Yeats, on the invitation of the Dolmetsches, "turned to lilting some of his own poetry. That is to say," recalled Mabel, "he thought he was lilting it; but, as Arnold remarked to me afterwards, he was really only droning it on one note. Strange to say, despite his acute rhythmic sensitiveness, his ear for music was dreamily monotonous."[45] More than his wife, Dolmetsch understood from his sessions with Yeats years earlier how the seemingly monotonous speaking or "droning" to a note could express the subtlest variety of emotion or dreaminess through quarter-tones, like Aherne asking Robartes to sing the changes of the moon once more: "True song, though speech" (*VP* 373). After Dolmetsch's return and reestablishment, Yeats would resume his support of the concerts. In October 1915 he would write in disappointment to his spiritualist friend and mistress Alick Schepeler: "I find that wretched Dolmetsch has not a concert until December."[46]

44. "As for Imagisme," *New Age* (January 28, 1915), 349; *EPPP2* 8.
45. Mabel Dolmetsch, *Personal Recollections of Arnold Dolmetsch* (New York: Macmillan, 1958), 111.
46. Letter of October 24, 1915, Huntington (HM28366).

Yeats would also lend needed support to Dolmetsch's workshop. When Ezra Pound and Dorothy Shakespear married on April 20, 1914, shortly after the Sturge Moore dinner party, Yeats gave them a gift of money toward the purchase of a Dolmetsch clavichord. Dorothy wrote for Ezra with thanks for "your wedding present which is being sent to Dolmitsch. We hope it will flower into deathless music—at least into an image of more gracious & stately times."[47] At the end of the summer, when he was settled into his new workshop and schedule of concerts, Dolmetsch was visited by Alvin Langdon Coburn, who began a series of photographic portraits of the Dolmetsch family. On one of these occasions, Coburn was accompanied by Pound. Though he had anticipated a meeting with Dolmetsch for years, especially after ordering the clavichord, Pound was not prepared for the immediate and lasting fascination that the meeting would hold for him. "I found myself in a reconstructed century—," he wrote,

> in a century of music, back before Mozart or Purcell, listening to clear music, to tones clear as brown amber. And this music came indifferently out of the harpsichord or the clavichord or out of virginals or out of odd-shaped viols, or whatever they may be . . . one steps into a past era when one sees all the other Dolmetsches dancing quaint, ancient steps of sixteenth-century dancing. One feels that the dance would go on even if there were no audience.[48]

Swept away by the scene, and in the midst of preparing his prospectus for a proposed "College of Arts," he immediately recruited Dolmetsch for "Ancient Music" and Mabel Dolmetsch for "XVI. Century Dances." They would join a faculty that included Coburn, Lewis, Wadsworth, Cournos, Gaudier-Brzeska, Edmund Dulac, William P. Robins, and other "artists of established position, creative minds, men for the most part who have already suffered in the cause of their art."[49] Dolmetsch was singled out for special notice: "M. Arnold Dolmetsch's position in the world of music is unique,"

47. Letter of April 30, 1914, "Ezra Pound Letters to William Butler Yeats," ed. C. F. Terrell, *Antaeus*, 21/22 (Spring / Summer 1976), 34. When an unidentified lady subsequently wrote to Yeats about acquiring and using a psaltery to accompany her recitations, he replied: "I dare say Dolmetsch would make you a Psaltery, but I think you had better experiment with some stringed instruments. I have known no one but Florence Farr to use the Psaltery with success as yet. I think that Dolmetsch charged about £8. I am without musical knowledge and so can throw no light on the matter except to say the [*sic*] Florence Farr almost always delighted me" (Letter of June 8, [?1915], *CL InteLex* 2660.

48. Ezra Pound, "Affirmations. I. Arnold Dolmetsch," *New Age*, 16 (January 7, 1915), 246; *EPPP2* 2.

49. "Preliminary Announcement of the College of Arts," *Egoist*, I (November 2, 1914), 413; *EPPP1* 316.

Pound wrote in the preliminary announcement, "and all music lovers are so well aware of it that one need not here pause to proclaim it." When proof for the prospectus arrived, he wrote to Harriet Monroe, describing how attractive the College would be to American students and explaining that "while the vorticists are well-represented, the College does not bind itself to a school. Vide Dolmetsch, Robins and in less degree Dulac and Coburn."[50] He strategically suggested to her that in a future issue of *Poetry* "Dolmetsch's forthcoming book ought to be good for a column."

Shortly after the announcement, Pound informed Monroe's associate editor, Alice Corbin Henderson, that "Coburn and, I believe, Dolmetsch have each a perspiring apprentice already. The demand for positions *on* the faculty is most brisk."[51] However brisk the demand and promising the future, Pound's vorticist College of Arts never rose out of the ground, but his enthusiasm for Dolmetsch's work nonetheless materialized in the first of numerous essays and reviews over the next three years. "I have seen the Great God Pan," he wrote of his Dolmetsch adventure in initiating his series of "Affirmations" in the *New Age*, "and it was in this manner: I heard a bewildering and pervasive music moving from precision to precision within itself."[52] In Dolmetsch's performance of early music with early instruments he had discerned the vorticist pattern-unit that set his music apart and above impressionist music: "the early music starts with the mystery of pattern; if you like, with the vortex of pattern; with something which is, first of all, music, and which is capable of being, after that, many things." To Pound, Dolmetsch's genius lay not only in discerning that the great and various beauty of early music was untranslatable with modern instruments, but also in remaking and playing with precision the virginals, clavichords, harpsichords, viols, and viola da gambas that made the recovery of pattern music possible. Pound was quick to see the vorticist analogy of Dolmetsch's music to painting and other arts. "As I believe that a certain movement in painting is capable of revitalising the instinct of design," he wrote, "so I believe that a return, an awakening to the possibilities, not necessarily of 'Old' music, but of pattern music played upon ancient instruments, is, perhaps, able to make music again a part of life, not merely a part of theatricals." Pound had not written with such intellectual excitement or

50. *The Letters of Ezra Pound,* 1907–1941, ed. D. D. Paige (New York: Harcourt Brace, 1950) 47.
51. Letter of December 21, 1914, *The Letters of Ezra Pound to Alice Corbin Henderson*, ed. Ira B. Nadel (Austin: University of Texas Press, 1993), 90.
52. Ezra Pound, "Affirmations. I. Arnold Dolmetsch," *New Age* (January 7, 1915), 246; *EPPP2* 2.

with a greater stimulation of his renaissance spirit since his discovery of Tagore: "are we," he asked in conclusion, "as one likes to suppose, on the brink of another really great awakening, when the creative or art vortices shall be strong enough, when the people who care will be well enough organised to set the fine fashion, to impose it, to make the great age?" Dolmetsch was immensely pleased and encouraged by the article: "The very depth of my ideas and feelings is reflected in it," he wrote to Pound, "and they were felicitously expressed. Such an article ought to do much good to a cause, the ultimate success of which I am convinced of, but which, at times, I almost despair of carrying through."

Within a fortnight of meeting Dolmetsch, Pound met T. S. Eliot, who, having safely arrived in London from the University of Marburg after the declaration of war in Germany, went up to Merton College, Oxford, in October to redirect and salvage his traveling fellowship from Harvard. Eliot wrote to Conrad Aiken on September 30 that there was a possibility of meeting Yeats at a Chinese restaurant with the Pounds, but this expectation evidently evaporated. When the Michaelmas term ended, however, Pound made definite arrangements for Eliot to meet not only Yeats but Dolmetsch and his family in Hampstead during the holiday period.[53] On January 7, in the letter thanking Pound for his article, Dolmetsch further thanked him for sending Eliot: "I saw Mr Elliot yesterday; he is very sympathetic and intelligent. If I did not occasionally meet people of that kind, I should not have the courage to go on." Eliot, too, was transported by the meeting. After returning to Oxford, he wrote to Pound, expressing his hope that Yeats would still be in London when he next came down in March:

> I must thank you again for your introduction to the Dolmetsch family—I passed one of the most delightful afternoons I have ever spent, in one of the most delightful households I have ever visited. You were quite right—there was no difficulty about the conversation, and I made friends with the extraordinary children in no time, and am wild to see them again. As for the dancing, they all danced (expect the head of the family) for about an hour, I think, while I sat rapt.[54]

53. Eliot's first meeting with Yeats was probably delayed until January 1915; he wrote to Mrs. Jack Gardner on April 4, 1915 that when he was last in London in January "I had the pleasure of meeting Yeats: he is now in Ireland, I believe because a play of Lady Gregory's is coming on at the Abbey. I am hoping for his return—he is a very agreeable talker" (*The Letters of T. S. Eliot*, Vol. i, 1898–1922 [London: Faber and Faber, 1988], 95.

54. Ibid. 86.

Pound was eagerly awaiting Dolmetsch's book, so much so that when it was delayed he got Dolmetsch to give him a set of galleys. To placate him further, Dolmetsch finally delivered the clavichord, leading Pound to write parenthetically to Joyce after reading the final installment of *Portrait of the Artist*, "(so here I am with a clavichord—beside me, which I cant afford, and cant reasonably play on)."[55] For his patience, Pound received from Dolmetsch one of the first copies of the book, inscribed "To EP with kindest regards, Nov. 26, 1915." Over the next eighteen months he studied and heavily marked his copy, exhilarated by the discovery of its implications for modern poetry, especially for the fading *vers libre* movement. He first revealed his primary observation in a review of Thomas MacDonagh's *Literature in Ireland* (1916), a continuation of his earlier study of word-music and chant-verse: "It is, however, interesting to find Dolmetsch 'justifying *vers libre*' in his book on the history of the seventeenth and eighteenth-century music, and MacDonagh . . . analyzing the breaking from false shackles in a quite different manner. Perhaps all metric has grown in a lengthening of the bar or foot or unit."[56] Pound was finally ready to include Dolmetsch's book as part of an omnibus review of six extraordinary volumes (including *Passages from the Letters of John Butler Yeats*, Joyce's *Portrait*, Fenollosa's *Certain Noble Plays of Japan* and *Noh, or Accomplishment,* and Eliot's *Prufrock* [the one-sentence review: "The book-buyer can not do better"]).[57] Acknowledging that Dolmetsch's book "has been out for some time," he declares that while no intelligent musician should be without it, the book "is more than a technical guide to musicians. It is not merely 'full of suggestions' for the thorough artist of any sort, but it shows a way whereby the musician and the 'intelligent' can once more be brought into touch." Pound tells his readers that the book is too important for a brief review, that he is writing of Dolmetsch at greater length in the *Egoist,* but he affords them a taste of his excitement: Dolmetsch's "citations from Couperin show the existence of

55. *Pound / Joyce: The Letters of Ezra Pound to James Joyce*, ed. Forrest Read (New York: New Directions, 1967), 46. Pound's Dolmetsch clavichord, which would later accompany him to Rapallo and Brunnenburg, is number 25.

56. "Thomas MacDonagh as Critic," *Poetry*, 8 (September 1916), 309–12; *EPPP2* 174. In discussing the syllabic measure of Yeats's verse, MacDonagh declares, "Indeed I should say that the effects of our more deliberate Irish speech on our verse are these two: first, a prose intonation . . . and second, a tendency to give, in certain poems, generally of short rhyming lines, almost equal stress value to all the syllables, a tendency to make the line the metrical unit": (*Literature in Ireland: Studies Irish and Anglo-Irish* [New York: Frederick A. Stokes, 1916], 72–3).

57. The reviews appeared under the title "List of Books: Comment by Ezra Pound," in *The Little Review*, 4 (August 1917), 6–11; *EPPP2* 237–41, here 241.

vers libre in early eighteenth-century music. I do not however care unduly to stir up the rather uninteresting discussion as to the archaeology of 'free' verse" (*EPPP2* 241).

He had, however, already duly stirred it up in "Vers Libre and Arnold Dolmetsch," which had just appeared in the *Egoist*. "One art interprets the other," he had written in his first essay on Dolmetsch's music, and now he set out to show how some of Dolmetsch's dicta from early musicians "are susceptible of a sort of transposition into terms of the sister arts, still others have a direct bearing on poetry, or at least on versification."[58] As though he were quoting poets on *vers libre*, Pound quoted numerous passages from seventeenth- and early-eighteenth-century musicians—from Thomas Mace's *Musick's Monument* (1613), Jean Rousseau's *Maître de Musique et de Viole* (1687), and especially François Couperin's *L'Art de toucher le Clavecin* (1717): "I find that we confuse Time, or Measure, with what is called Cadence or Movement. Measure defines the quantity and equality of beats; Cadence is properly the spirit, the soul that must be added."[59] In Dolmetsch's book Pound had found the musical justification for irregularity and the expression of "absolute rhythm" in *vers libre*. "No one but an imbecile can require much further proof for the recognition of vers libre in music," he concludes, "and this during the 'classical' period":

> Dolmetsch's wisdom is not confined to the demonstration of a single point of topical interest to the poet.... The serious writer of verse will not rest content until he has gone to the source. I do not wish to give the erroneous impression that old music was all vers libre. I state simply that vers libre exists in old music. Quantzens, 1752, in so far as he is quoted by Dolmetsch, only cautions the player to give the shorter notes 'inequality.' Christopher Simpson, 1655, is much concerned with physical means of getting a regular beat. His date is interesting. The movement toward regularity in verse during the seventeenth century seems condemnable if one compare only Dryden and Shakespeare, but read a little bad Elizabethan poetry and the reason for it appears.... On the other hand, Couperin's feeling for irregularity underlying "classical" forms may give us the clue to a wider unexpressed feeling for a fundamental irregularity which would have made eighteenth-century classicism, classicism of surface, tolerable to those who felt the underlying variety *as strongly as the first regularizers* may have felt it.
>
> (*EPPP2* 222–3)

58. "Vers Libre and Arnold Dolmetsch," *Egoist*, 4 (July 1917), 90–1; *EPPP2* 222.
59. Arnold Dolmetsch, *The Interpretation of the Music of the XVIIth and XVIIIth Centuries* (London: Novello, 1915), 20.

Pound had not yet had his full say: "Vers Libre and Arnold Dolmetsch" was followed in the next issue by his "Arnold Dolmetsch." In revealing the misinterpretations of the old musical notation, Pound argues, Dolmetsch successfully removes the elements that obscure the major structure of a piece of music. "It seems to me that in music, as in the other arts," writes the vituperative vers librist, "beginning in the eighteenth century, and growing a poison from which we are not yet free, greater rigidity in matters of minutiae has forced a break-up of the large forms; has destroyed the sense of its main form." Within the major form, the artist must maintain the freedom to fight against the mechanics of regularity. In his study of major form and notation in old music, Pound declares, pressing the cause of *vers libre*, "Dolmetsch has also made a fine diagnosis":

> He has incidentally thrown a side-light on metric, he has said suggestive things about *silence d'articulation*, about the freedoms of the old music. When I say suggestive, I do not mean that we are to get a jargon out of these things, to use for artistic controversy; but there is enough in them to prevent fools from interfering with, or carping at, rhythms achieved by the artist in his own way.[60]

What Pound found in such musical qualities as articulation, pause, rest, and cadence—all crucial qualities of a musician's independent expression within a structural form—were analogies that applied more to the poet's "own way" of spoken or chanted verse than to the metrical form of that verse. After hearing a recording by Yeats, for instance, Igor Stravinsky ironically used Yeats's chanting as a way of explaining the musical "*silence d'articulation*":

60. Ezra Pound, "Arnold Dolmetsch," *Egoist*, 4 (August 1917), 105; *EPPP2* 236. Pound wrote "metric" and heavily marked the margin next to Dolmetsch's quotation from an eighteenth-century treatise on *silence d'articulation*: "All the notes in execution . . . are partly in *hold* and partly in *silence*, which united make the whole value of the note. These *silences* at the end of each note fix its articulation and are as necessary as the holds themselves, without which they could not be detached from one another; . . . A little attention in the pronunciation given to the articulation of the syllables [in speech] which show that, to produce the effect of nearly all consonants, the sound of the vowel is stopped either by bringing the lips together or by pressing the tongue against the palate, the teeth, &c. All these stoppages of the vowel's sound are as many short silences which detach the syllables from one another to form the articulation of speech. It is the same in the articulation of music, with the only difference that the sound of an instrument being everywhere the same, and producing so to speak only one vowel, the *silences d'articulation* must be more varied than in speech, if a kind of intelligent and interesting articulation is to be produced" (*Interpretation of the Music of the XVIIth and XVIIIth Centuries*, 282–3). I am grateful to Omar Pound for permission to read Pound's copy.

> Articulation is mainly separation, and I can give no better example of what I mean by it than to refer the reader to W. B. Yeats's recording of three of his poems. Yeats pauses at the end of each line, he dwells a precise time on and in between each word—one could as easily notate his verses in musical rhythm as scan them in poetic meters.[61]

No metrical scansion, however, could alone ever reveal the absolute or inner rhythm of Yeats's or Pound's chanting of a poem; this was why Yeats and Dolmetsch had worked together on the notation of regulated declamation fifteen years earlier.

Eliot, who had become assistant editor of the *Egoist*, not only followed Pound's essays on Dolmetsch; he underscored their importance in *Ezra Pound: His Metric and Poetry* (1917). "The Provençal canzon, like the Elizabethan lyric," Eliot observes,

> was written for music. Mr. Pound has more recently insisted, in a series of articles on the work of Arnold Dolmetsch, in the *Egoist*, on the importance of a study of music for the poet.... As to the "freedom" of his verse, Pound has made several statements in his articles on Dolmetsch which are to the point.

To illustrate the point, Eliot quoted approvingly from "Arnold Dolmetsch" an interpretive passage in which Pound applies Dolmetsch's principles to their experiments in *vers libre*:

> Any work of art is a compound of freedom and order. It is perfectly obvious that art hangs between chaos on the one side and mechanics on the other. A pedantic insistence upon detail tends to drive out "major form". A firm hold on major form makes for a freedom of detail. In painting men intent on minutiae gradually lost the sense of form and form-combination. An attempt to restore this sense is branded as "revolution". It is revolution in the philological sense of the term... Art is a departure from fixed positions; felicitous departure from a norm.[62]

Pound's essays greatly complemented Eliot's own "Reflections on *Vers Libre,*" published four months earlier, by providing Dolmetsch as a musical and historical authority to support Eliot's description of the "constant evasion and recognition of regularity" in *vers libre*. There can be little doubt that Dolmetsch influenced Eliot's ideas on the relation of music

61. Igor Stravinsky, *Conversations with Igor Stravinsky* (Garden City, NY: Doubleday, 1959), 136. Stravinsky refers to the extant recordings of "The Lake Isle of Innisfree," "The Song of the Old Mother," and the third and fourth stanzas of "Coole Park and Ballylee, 1931."

62. T. S. Eliot, *To Criticize the Critic* (London: Faber and Faber, 1965), 171–2.

and poetry, or that Eliot was impressed by the importance of Pound's discoveries in Dolmetsch's work. He made a point of keeping Pound's essays on Dolmetsch current in his periodic editing of Pound's poems and prose. In his introduction to Pound's *Selected Poems* (1928), Eliot refers to "a note on 'Dolmetsch and Vers Libre' " as essential to Pound's point of view during the war,[63] and he later included both "Arnold Dolmetsch" and "Vers Libre and Arnold Dolmetsch" as exceptions to his exclusion of Pound's essays on music, painting, and sculpture from his *Literary Essays of Ezra Pound* (1954).[64] Eliot would himself carry into the far future his belief that "poetry must be written to be spoken," revealing implicitly in "The Spoken Word" (1951) how the Dolmetsch–Pound discoveries of *vers libre* in early English music had liberated the personal expression of poetic rhythm in modern poetry. "What is now called 'modern verse,' " he wrote,

> is partly a return to older forms of English versification—to the stress, to "sprung rhythm", to alliteration—the apparent irregularity and lawlessness of which is due to its being based on the musical bar instead of the foot, and to its refusal to admit that some syllables of the English language are *always* long and others *always* short, instead of their being longer or shorter according to their position.[65]

As Pound sought and found in Dolmetsch's book authoritative theoretical energy for the flagging Imagist and *vers libre* movements, so he found additional support in the Noh, which further illuminated his sense of their future in modern poetry. If the Noh has its unity in emotion, he observed, it also has "what we may call Unity of Image. At least, the better plays are all built into the intensification of a single Image."[66] All the elements of Noh—verse, voice, costume, motion, music, dance—unite to produce that Image. Thinking of the Noh and its image in vorticist terms, he suddenly

63. Introduction to Ezra Pound, *Selected Poems* (London: Faber and Gwyer, 1928), p. xiv.

64. Eliot later became a strong supporter of the Dolmetsch Foundation, incorporated under the presidency of poet laureate Robert Bridges. "Arnold Dolmetsch has the gratitude and admiration of everyone who cares for music," Eliot wrote in the *Criterion*, 8 (July 1929). "His work in discovering and interpreting old music, in the technique of copying the old instruments and in the technique of playing them, is known throughout the world. But it is not realized that Mr. Dolmetsch has not yet communicated any share of his learning and accomplishment to more than a very few persons; and the Foundation is to serve the purpose of carrying on his work. . . . This is a society which deserves and needs the support of everyone" (577–8).

65. T. S. Eliot, "The Spoken Word," *Festival of Britain 1951: London Season of the Arts*, Official Souvenir Programme (London: Lund Humphries, published for the Arts Council of Great Britain, May–June 1951), 7–8.

66. *"Noh" or Accomplishment*, 45–6.

realized the answer to a nagging poetic question. "This intensification of the Image," he noted,

> this manner of construction, is very interesting to me personally, as an Imagiste, for we Imagistes knew nothing of these plays when we set out in our own manner. These plays are also an answer to a question that has several times been put to me: "Could one do a long Imagiste poem, or even a long poem in vers libre?"[67]

Pound also found in Fenollosa's instructions regarding the singing, speaking, and intoning of verse "suggestions for comparison with sapphics and with some of the troubadour measures."[68] These were crucial structural and technical discoveries for Pound as he turned to the long poem in "Three Cantos" (1917)[69]—declaring in the second that "Dolmetsch will build our age in witching music. | Viols da Gamba, tabors, tympanons." Imagism, *vers libre*, vorticism, Dolmetsch's early music, and the Noh had given rise not only to his maturing aesthetic but to the finely honed criteria for his judgment of modern verse—the hard, gaunt, direct qualities that now informed his reviews.

Yeats's verse, too, he asserted in his first review ("The Later Yeats") of *Responsibilities* (Cuala, 1914), had struck "a manifestly new note" since the publication of *The Green Helmet and Other Poems* (1910): "one has felt his work becoming gaunter, seeking greater hardness of outline" (*EPPP1 242*). Pound's admiration for Yeats—for his intensity and capacity for renewal, for his ability to change his tonality and manner without losing any of his evocative or descriptive power—was now at its highest. "It is perhaps the highest function of art," he continued, "that it should fill the mind with a noble profusion of sounds and images, that it should furnish the life of the mind with such accompaniment and surrounding. At any rate Mr. Yeats's work has done this in the past and still continues to do so." When the expanded trade edition appeared in 1916, Pound reiterated his recognition of significant artistic transformation within a permanent self:

> He is the only poet of his decade who has not gradually faded into mediocrity, who has not resigned himself to gradually weaker echoes of an

67. Ibid. 45.
68. Ibid. 56.
69. Cantos I, II, and III, originally published in *Poetry* from June to August 1917, were reprinted in *Future* in 1918 with titles to emphasize the form and technique: "Passages from the Opening Address in a Long Poem"; " 'Images from the Second Canto of a Long Poem'; and "An Interpolation Taken from the Third Canto of a Long Poem."

> earlier outburst. . . . Mr. Yeats is a romanticist, symbolist, occultist, for better or worse, now and for always. That does not matter. What does matter is that he is the only one left who has sufficient intensity of temperament to turn these modes into art.[70]

Much of Yeats's transformation occurred in the company of Pound and their discussions of Imagism, *vers libre*, and the Noh during the previous two winters at Stone Cottage. But both poets had now come to share the genius and generosity of Dolmetsch, who had appeared at precisely the right time to help each work out the relation of metrics, rhythm, and cadence for their chanted and spoken verse. As Pound listened to Yeats chanting his poems in their Sussex retreat, and as he measured the importance of Dolmetsch's musical studies for his own and modern verse, he came fully to understand what it meant "to compose in the sequence of the musical phrase, not in sequence of a metronome." And yet, ironically, it was the rationale of *vers libre* that Pound found in Dolmetsch that would lead the two poets to turn from each other in sharply different directions.

III

Yeats had not begun the actual writing of *At the Hawk's Well* until January 1916, but by March it was ready for staging. The composition and rehearsing of the play had been preceded and influenced by the appearance in November 1915 of another exotic personage in Yeats's life, Mrs. Maud Mann, a mystic and musician whom he described to Lady Gregory as "emaciated with ascetism."[71] He explained that she had been an accomplished violinist until she lost the use of her arms and went to India to study Oriental religion, folk-singing, and Indian musical instruments. Having recuperated her arm strength, she had recently returned to London with a passion for these pursuits, introduced herself to a susceptible Yeats, and charmed him by offering to set some of his poems to music. "I will bring some verses & we can talk over the setting," he wrote to her on November 23. "I have a curious tale to tell you. A friend [William Horton] who gets telepathic communiation from me has taken to hearing music."[72] On the following Sunday he spent an entire afternoon chanting his poems to Mann and her friend the musician John Foulds while they sat rapt on

70. "Mr. Yeats' New Book," *Poetry*, 9 (December 1916), 150–1; *EPPP2* 185.
71. Letter of December 1, 1915, *CL InteLex* 2821.
72. Letter of [November 23, 1915], *CL InteLex* 2819.

the ground and listened. "They discovered all kinds of strange qualities in the lilts or tunes or whatever they are that I make up when I am writing verse," he reported with surprise to Lady Gregory:

> The musician kept saying "beautiful beautiful" and taking them down. I have been examining my verse since by this new light and I find that practically everything except the blank verse—until I had been writing for the theatre for a few years—goes to these lilts or tunes. I think it may account for the fact that people in Ireland don't care for my later work the folk quality goes out of it when the tune goes out.
>
> (*CL InteLex* 2821)

There should have been no surprise. Mann and Foulds had only reconfirmed what Martyn, Dolmetsch, MacDonagh, and other musicians had been telling him for fifteen years. If he met each instance with amazement, however, each new confirmation that folk tunes permeated his verse was to ensure his eventual attempt to act upon the mystery of it all.

Yeats thus invited Mann and Foulds to his Monday evening to meet Horton, Dulac, and other friends, and during the following months, much to Dulac's dismay, Yeats allowed her to insinuate herself and Foulds into the production of *At the Hawk's Well*. Dulac indulged Yeats by allowing her to write the music (which she agreed to make more Greek than Indian), but she infuriated Dulac with random intrusions of her improvisations, arguing, as Yeats reported to Lady Gregory, that "in the big London theatres the action is stopped from time to time to give the musician his turn."[73] Feuding with her at every rehearsal, Dulac demanded that Yeats keep her from interfering with the dance, dancer, costumes, and make-up. Adding insult to injury in a play of the heroic age, Foulds insisted on playing the music with a guitar, which Dulac insisted on disguising in cardboard. Thus, with very limited rehearsals, and with a long lute-like instrument from India and a disguised guitar, Mann and Foulds joined Dulac in the Chorus of Three Musicians for the private premiere of *At the Hawk's Well*. Dulac was so distressed by her "ululations" that he made her perform behind a back-cloth.[74] Yeats admitted before the opening that he had bought more than he bargained for. "The play goes well," he informed Lady Gregory, "but the musician gives more & more trouble & will have to be eliminated

73. Letter of March 26, [1916], *CL InteLex* 2913.
74. As will be seen, Dulac would summon his sour memory of Mrs Fould's "ululations" in a vitriolic letter of July 4, 1937, to Yeats after receiving his complaints about the broadcast rehearsals for several performers reciting his poems.

when we are through our first performances."[75] Agreeing with Dulac that the music of Mann and Foulds was out of control, Yeats even considered removing the music and chanting the musicians' lyrics himself in future productions, until Dulac expeditiously wrote his own primitive music for gong, drum, zither, and flute.

While final preparations for the first performance were being made, Yeats's imagination was greatly excited by Dulac's designs for the masks, costumes, and sets. In response, he immediately began writing "Certain Noble Plays of Japan," his introduction to the Cuala Press edition by that title of three of Fenollosa's translations, "Chosen and Finished by Ezra Pound."[76] Expressing his debt to the Noh plays, Yeats announced that he had "invented a form of drama, distinguished, indirect, and symbolic, and having no need of mob or Press to pay its way—an aristocratic form" (*E&I* 222). Aware that the Noh itself had grown out of an aristocratic culture over several centuries, Yeats, in adapting the aristocratic form for his own plays, was in no way contradicting the spiritual democracy he continually envisioned for Ireland. Indeed, he told Yone Noguchi that he was delighted at the way the Noh incorporated "the folk element," affirming his belief that "the true literature should be a folk literature invigorated, not weakened, by the cultured elements."[77] In his attempt to absorb Irish folklore and musical speech into the Noh, he declared in his introduction: "I love all the arts that can still remind me of their origin among the common people, and my ears are only comfortable when the singer sings as if mere speech had taken fire, when he appears to have passed into song almost imperceptibly" (*E&I* 223). Yeats was tired not only of a provincial Mob and Press for whom his muses were unwelcome and that attacked his theatrical arts; he had grown no less tired of more cultured audiences for whom his muses were but half-welcome, "those who prefer light amusement or have no ear for verse, and fortunately they are all very polite." Now, in transposing his dramaturgy into a Noh-based drama, he desired a small audience, one "for whom one need not build all on observation and sympathy, because they read poetry for their pleasure and understand the traditional language of passion" (*E&I* 255). And yet

75. Letter of March 28, [1916], *CL InteLex* 2917.

76. *Certain Noble Plays of Japan: From the Manuscripts of Ernest Fenollosa, Chosen and Finished by Ezra Pound, with an Introduction by William Butler Yeats* (Churchtown, Dundrum: Cuala Presss, 1916). Yeats's Introduction is dated "April 1916."

77. Yone Noguchi, "A Japanese Poet on W. B. Yeats," *Bookman* (New York), 43 (June 1916), 431–3. See Marx, "Nō Dancing: Yone Noguchi in W. B. Yeats's Japan," 65.

in writing for such an audience—an intellectual aristocracy of verse-lovers who can perceive the poet's symbolic mysteries—his ultimate aim was to enrich the imaginative life of Ireland. Even though *At the Hawk's Well* was being rehearsed for production in London, he longed for the day when his new plays might belong to a people's theatre in Dublin, concluding his introductory essay by saying that

> it pleases me to think that I am working for my own country. Perhaps some day a play in the form I am adapting for European purposes may excite once more, whether in Gaelic or in English, under the slope of Slieve-na-mon or Croagh Patrick, ancient memories; for this form has no need of scenery that runs away with money nor of a theatre-building.[78]

On April 2, three weeks before the Easter Rising, Pound, who had helped rehearse the play in the absence of a chief actor, took Eliot to the first performance of *At the Hawk's Well* in Lady Cunard's drawing room, where "only those who cared for poetry had been invited" (*VPl* 415).[79] It was a bonus occasion for Eliot, for Pound introduced him to Dulac, who subsequently helped Eliot with his French poems.[80] Edward Marsh described how the play began with "some very atmospheric 'keening' behind the screen and a man in black solemnly pacing to the front."[81] This was the Japanese dancer Michio Itow, playing the Guardian of the Well. In the natural light of the drawing room, as Yeats described Itow's movement,

> did I see him as the tragic image that has stirred my imagination. There, where no studied lighting, no stage-picture made an artificial world, he was able, as

78. In the note for his second dance play, *The Only Jealousy of Emer*, Yeats said that his plays "should be written for some country where all classes share in a half-mythological, half-philosophical folk-belief which the writer and his small audience lift into a new subtlety. All my life I have longed for such a country, and always found it quite impossible to write without having as much belief in its real existence as a child has in that of wooden birds, beasts, and persons of his toy Noah's Ark" (*Four Plays for Dancers* [London: Macmillan, 1921], 106).
79. For the second performance a few days later, played in Lady Islington's larger drawing room at Chesterfield Gardens, there was a different, less desirable, more aristocratic audience: "And round the platform upon three sides were three hundred fashionable people including Queen Alexandra, and once more my muses were but half welcome." On this occasion, Yeats delighted in the removal of a newspaper photographer: "What a relief after directing a theatre for so many years . . . to think no more of pictures unless Mr. Dulac or some other distinguished man has made them, nor all of those paragraphs written by young men, perhaps themselves intelligent, who must applaud the common taste or starve!"(*VPl* 416).
80. See "The Art of Poetry, I: T. S. Eliot," *Paris Review*, 21 (Spring/Summer 1959), 56.
81. See B. L. Reid, *The Man from New York: John Quinn and His Friends* (New York: Oxford University Press, 1968), 242–3. Eliot subsequently reviewed the Fenollosa–Pound edition in "The Noh and the Image," *Egoist*, 4 (August 1917), 102–3.

> he rose from the floor, where he had been sitting cross-legged, or as he threw out an arm, to recede from us into some more powerful life. . . . One realised anew, at every separating strangeness, that the measure of all arts' greatness can be but in their intimacy.
>
> (*E&I* 224)

This recovered intimacy between audience and actors was, to Yeats, of even greater importance than the economy and simplicity of the staging—the closeness allowed the audience to see the masks changing with the light that fell upon them, to sense the deep feeling expressed by subtle movements of the whole body, to hear every inflection of the voice. Indeed, the primary effect of the new dramatic form had been the full liberation of the living voice from competition with the distancing, intimacy-destroying conventions of proscenium stage, realistic scenery, powerful lighting, and loud music. "With every simplification," he wrote, "the voice has recovered something of its importance," and the simplicity and intimacy of his new play gave him the confidence to affirm an old belief: "It should be again possible for a few poets to write as all did once, not for the printed page but to be sung" (*E&I* 223). The three musicians of the chorus were again conceived as wandering minstrels, "whose seeming sunburned faces will, I hope, suggest that they have wandered from village to village in some country of our dreams" (*E&I* 221). The minstrels would describe the scenery, use the drum and gong to enhance the expressiveness of movement, the zither and flute to deepen the emotion of the words. With these simple, unobtrusive instruments, Yeats had found for his minstrel chorus an acceptable replacement for the psaltery; he was particularly pleased by their "great pictorial effect."[82] The dramaturgy for all the dance plays was now in place: "the music, the beauty of form and voice all come to climax in pantomimic dance" (*E&I* 221).

Whether or not, as he said, Yeats gave no direct instructions in speaking and chanting his verse to the actors of his dance plays, he certainly did to the directors and musicians who composed the music for them. Recalling the primary principle that Dolmetsch had laid down twenty years earlier, Yeats dictated that the plays "must be played to the accompaniment of drum and zither and flute, but on no account must the words be spoken 'through music' in the fashionable way."[83] In his note on the instruments and their

82. *Four Plays for Dancers*, p. vii (*VPl* 1305).

83. Ibid., p. v. In his report of the press rehearsal for the first public performance of "Speaking to Musical Notes" in June 1902, William Archer described a point "emphasised by Mr. Dolmetsch: namely that the system of 'speaking through music' (known in Germany as

distribution for *At the Hawk's Well*, Dulac was careful to emphasize that the music must remain subservient to the words: "one musician plays the drum and gong, one the flute, the singer takes the harp [zither]. The drum and the gong must be used at times during the performance to emphasize the spoken word; no definite notation of this can be given, and it is left to the imagination and taste of the musician." In presenting his music for *The Dreaming of the Bones* (1919), Walter Morse Rummel was even more direct in representing Yeats's intentions. "*Music of tone and music of speech are distinct from each other*," he began his note on the music:

> *Here my sole object has been to find some tone formula which will enhance and bring out a music underlying the words. The process is therefore directly opposed to that of tone-music creation, which from the formless directly creates its tone form, whereas I seek to derive a formless overflow from the already formed.*

For the First Musician, he prescribed "*A medium voice*, more chanting than singing, not letting the musical value of the sound predominate too greatly the spoken value," and he further underscored the general principle governing the role of music in the play: "*All instrumental music, especially during the speaking parts, must always leave the voice in the foreground.*"[84]

A week after the first performance of *At the Hawk's Well*, Yeats gave a packed-house reading of his poems for the Poetry Bookshop.[85] Eliot probably went out of his way to attend this large poetic event, for the power and modernity of the play had greatly altered his view of Yeats. "And thereafter," he later wrote, "one saw Yeats rather as a more eminent contemporary than an elder from whom one could learn."[86] Longing to find his own way toward a modern poetic drama, he was much intrigued by Yeats's adaptation of an ancient form, an interest that would lead him to review *Noh, or Accomplishment*, focusing on the nature of the image and the ghosts in relation to Greek and Shakespearean drama—especially on the "phantom-psychology" that he would later incorporate into his own plays.[87] But it is also evident that Yeats's chanted verse had begun to grow on him.

melodrame) led to horrible dissonances and was wholly inartistic" ("Study and Stage," *The Morning Leader*, June 7, 1902, 4). See p. 61. Yeats often repeated Dolmetsch's caveat, later giving a specific example in his 1937 broadcast, "In the Poet's Pub": "There must be no speaking through music, nothing like Mendelssohn's accompaniment to the *Mid-Summer Night's Dream*" (*LAR* 267).

84. Ibid. 108.
85. Advertised as "His Own Poems: W. B. Yeats," the reading on April 11 required a change of venue from the Poetry Bookshop to the Passmore Edwards Settlement: 335 persons attended. BL Add. MS 57756.
86. T. S. Eliot, "Ezra Pound," *New English Weekly*, October 31, 1946, 27.
87. Eliot, "The Noh and the Image," 102.

Over the years of their ensuing friendship, Eliot heard Yeats chanting his poems on numerous occasions. "I shall always remember the impression of W. B. Yeats reading poetry aloud," he wrote in "The Music of Poetry" (1942). "To hear him read his own works was to be made to recognize how much the Irish way of speech is needed to bring out the beauties of Irish poetry: to hear Yeats reading William Blake was an experience of a different kind, more astonishing than satisfying."[88] The extent to which Yeats and Pound influenced Eliot in the recitation of verse is unclear, but Virginia and Leonard Woolf and others have preserved accounts of Eliot chanting his poems. In June 1922, when Eliot read *The Waste Land* to them after dinner, Virginia recorded in her diary how "He sang it & chanted it rhythmed it. It has great beauty & force of phrase: symmetry; & tensity . . . One was left . . . with some strong emotion."[89] Leonard later described another evening of readings in Eliot's flat: "We all sat solemly on chairs round the room and Tom began the proceedings by reading the poem [*Ash-Wednesday*] aloud in that curious monotonous sing-song in which all poets from Homer downwards have recited their poetry."[90] Eliot's own chanting was not as pronounced as that of Yeats and Pound, but in answer to an interviewer's question, "Why is it your instinct to chant verse in a monotone?", he replied (with an oblique reference to Yeats's hieratic movements),

> As for chanting verse, for me the incantatory element is very important. So far as possible, the reciter should not dramatize. It is the words that matter, not the feeling about them. When I read poetry myself I put myself in a kind of trance and move in rhythm to rhythm of the piece in question.[91]

Eliot had addressed the importance of the incantatory element—the ritual recitation of words, phrases, and sounds to produce a magical effect or spell—in "Note sur Mallarmé et Poe" (1926), affirming the importance

88. T. S. Eliot, *On Poetry and Poets* (London: Faber and Faber, 1957), 24. Eliot reiterated this view twenty years later when he expressed his admiration for Yeats's later poems: "I admire his later poems very much indeed. And he read them well; but when he read aloud from English poets, in the chant and brogue that suited his own—well, Blake sounded rather odd" ("T. S. Eliot . . . An Interview," *Grantite Review*, 24 [Election 1962], 18).
89. *Diary of Virginia Woolf*, ed. Anne Olivier Bell (New York: Harcourt Brace Jovanovich, 1978), ii. 178. She added, "Mary Hutch[inson], who has heard it more quietly, interprets it to be Tom's autobiography—a melancholy one."
90. Leonard Woolf, *Downhill All the Way: An Autobiography of the Years 1919–1939* (London: Hogarth Press, 1967), 109.
91. Ranjee Shahani, "T. S. Eliot Answers Questions," *John O'London's Weekly*, 58 (August 19, 1949), 497–8; here, 497.

of incantation in restoring the primitive power of the word to modern poetry.[92] He would return to Mallarmé's "M'introduire dans ton histoire" in his Turnbull lectures (1933), finding in the poem's fourteen lines "four or five images which it is quite impossible to imagine or conceive simultaneously, and at least one ["Tonnerre et rubis aux moyeux"] which cannot be visualised at all." In using such images, Eliot explains, the poet must know what effects he intends to produce in the auditory imagination; he had taken a leaf from Yeats's book:

> There is the element of rationality, the element of precision, and there is also the element of vagueness which may be used; and we must remember that one distinction between poetry and prose is this, that in poetry the word, each word by itself, though only being fully itself in context, has absolute value. Poetry is *incantation* as well as imagery. "Thunder and rubies" cannot be seen, heard or thought together, but their collocation here brings out the connotation of each word.
>
> (*VMP* 271–2)

Intrigued by Mallarmé's example, Eliot later adapted "Thunder and rubies up to the wheel hub" (his translation), to begin an incantatory passage in *Burnt Norton* (1934): "Garlic and sapphires in the mud | Clot the bedded axle tree."

IV

In March 1916 Farr suddenly resigned the principalship of Ramanathan College, agreeing to serve temporarily as Hon. Treasurer. At a ceremony honoring her contribution to the school, her friend Ramanathan

92. "Note sur Mallarmé et Poe," *La Nouvelle Revue Française,* 14 (November 1, 1926), [524]–526 (English text not published). Trans: "In the works of Poe and Mallarmé philosophy is in part replaced by an element *of incantation.* In 'Ulalume' for example, and in 'Un Coup de Des,' this incantation, which insists on the primitive power of the Word ('Fatum'), is manifest. In this sense the verse of Mallarmé, applied if good in itself, constitutes a brilliant critique of Poe: *to give a sense more pure to the words of the tribe.* The effort to restore the power of the Word, which inspires the syntax of both and makes them discard the pure sound or pure melody (that they can both, if they wish, exploit so well), this effort which hinders the reader *from following the flow* of their phrase or verse, is one of the qualities which reconciles the best of the two poets. There is also the firmness of their step when they pass from the tangible world to the world of phantoms." Eliot was later to reiterate Poe's "power of incantation" in "Ulalume": "The strange names he invents take on meaning, and the repetitions . . . have their hypnotic effect." See " 'A Dream within a Dream,' " *The Listener,* 29 (February 25, 1943), 244. "What cannot be translated," he wrote in "Goethe as the Sage," "is the incantation, the music of the words, and that part of the meaning which is in the music" (*On Poetry and Poets,* 216).

announced that her resignation was due to the strain of heavy work during the past three years, and as the girls were all distressed at her leaving, he offered her the hospitality of his home in Colombo as long as she wanted to remain in Ceylon. Writing to Shaw of these developments, Farr confessed that she had

> spent my years here getting rid of many barriers between me and liberation—all my little disagreeableness & the things I never noticed about myself as bonds have got loosened. Also my recent horror of death. I mean of the death-bed scene—I have been through with it once or twice & it is nothing after all.

In August, while staying with Maud Gonne in Normandy, Yeats wrote to inform Farr of the aftermath of the Easter Rising—the execution of MacBride, Gonne's reception of the news, and the need to put the Abbey back in order. He revealed that though his income had been halved by the World War, he hoped to visit India and Ceylon after the armistice. But his abiding desire to visit Tagore and Farr and study their minstrel cultures would not be fulfilled. In November, as she confided to Shaw, Farr felt a twinge in her left breast "and became aware of a 'dead place'—I said to myself 'cancer' & felt the force of doom, but I didn't let anyone see & went & lunched & laughed & talked with the English Principal."[93] It was, she had learned, "galloping cancer with a vengeance." While recovering from a radical mastectomy, she wrote to Yeats about her operation and recovery, withholding from him any dire prognosis, cheerfully turning to her new experiments in translating poetry by a sound system:

> Now I am loafing & enlarging my soul & the last night I, having learned a verse of High Tamil poetry, thought of a new way of translating poetry. You don't worry about the subject at all only the mood & then translate each series of vowel sounds into words which have the same kind of vowel sounds and if possible consonant sounds.
>
> (*YA9* 250)

Yeats was "greatly distressed" to hear of her illness, writing on March 5, 1917, that he trusted she was on the mend. Telling her about their mutual friends, he informed her that "old Todhunter," whose *A Sicilian Idyll* had prompted their collaboration in minstrelsy twenty-seven years earlier, had died. Seven weeks later, on April 29, her last lay sung, Florence Farr died of heart failure in Colombo. She was cremated on the grounds

93. Letter of December 7, 1916, BL Add. MS 50533, fols. 111–12.

of Ramanathan's home. Shaw did not learn of her death and its immediate cause until he received a letter two months later from Farr's sister, Henrietta Paget. When Nevinson heard the news, he remembered his dear friend as possessing "one of the most poetic natures among women."[94] Yeats's immediate reaction to her death is unrecorded, but for three years he would hold in reserve for her the two elegiac stanzas in "All Souls' Night." Summoning his last image of her when she departed for Ceylon, and drawing on letters that recounted her discussions of Indian philosophy with Ramanathan, he invoked her as one

> Who finding the first wrinkles on a face
> Admired and beautiful,
> And knowing that the future would be vexed
> With 'minished beauty, multiplied commonplace,
> Preferred to teach a school
> Away from neighbour or friend,
> Among dark skins, and there
> Permit foul years to wear
> Hidden from eyesight to the unnoticed end.
>
> Before that end much had she ravelled out
> From a discourse in figurative speech
> By some learned Indian
> On the soul's journey. How it is whirled about,
> Wherever the orbit of the moon can reach,
> Until it plunge into the sun;
> And there, free and yet fast,
> Being both Chance and Choice,
> Forget its broken toys
> And sink into its own delight at last. (*VP* 472–3)[95]

In the months following the Easter Rising, marked by rejected proposals of marriage to Maud and Iseult and by the death of Florence, Yeats's darkening state of mind, as reflected not only in Cuala edition of *The Wild Swans at Coole* (1917) but in his chanting of the poems, was observed by St. John Ervine, the Ulster playwright whom Yeats had appointed manager of

94. Henry Woodd Nevinson, *Last Changes, Last Chances* (New York: Harcourt Brace, 1929), 121.
95. In the dedication to *A Vision* (London: T. Werner Laurie, 1925), Yeats described how "Florence Farr coming to her fiftieth year, dreading old age and fading beauty, had made a decision we all dreamt of at one time or another, and accepted a position as English teacher in a native school in Ceylon that she might study oriental thought, and had died there" (p. xi).

the Abbey Theatre in October 1915. "I do not know of anyone who can speak verse so beautifully and yet so depressingly as he can," wrote Ervine.

> The very great beauty that is in all his work does not stir you: it saddens you. There is no sunrise in his writing: there is only sunset. In his lyrics, there is the cadence of fatigue and of the lethargy that comes partly from disappointment, partly from loneliness, partly from doubt, and partly from inertia.[96]

Even so, his marriage to Georgie Hyde-Lees in October 1917, enveloped as it initially was in Yeats's morose guilt and melancholy, would be followed within days by an astonishing rejuvenation of spirit and a return to visionary life, where, in the words of his persona Tom O'Roughley, liberated from the hawk of thought and free to follow the butterfly of vision, "An aimless joy is a pure joy... And wisdom is a butterfly | And not a gloomy bird of prey" (*VP* 338).[97] It was among the earliest of eighteen new poems that would transform the character of the trade edition of *The Wild Swans at Coole* (1919).[98]

The mounting dangers of the endless war now worked to hasten the disbanding of the last minstrels. When the Zeppelin raids and blackouts intensified in the summer of 1917, Dolmetsch, concerned for the safety of his family and unable to work in Hampstead, took a friend's cottage in Surrey prior to buying a permanent home, "Jesses," in Haslemere, where he would conduct his family's musical life and consort until his death in 1940. After their October marriage, Yeats and George made several moves to cottages outside London to escape the air raids, with plans to move to Dublin, but the World War, followed in Ireland by the Anglo-Irish war, set them on nomadic pathways, with many short-term stays and circular returns to London, Oxford, Thoor Ballylee, Coole, Galway, Dublin, small English and Irish towns—inhabiting twenty houses in one twelve-month period, all before going on a six-month American tour and seriously entertaining a two-year professorship in Japan.

In the midst of these removals and dislocations, on February 26, 1919, Anne Yeats was born in a private nursing home in Dublin. When mother

96. St. John Ervine, *Some Impressions of My Elders* (New York: MacMillan, 1922), 271–2.

97. On September 26, 1934, Yeats wrote to William Force Stead about the ring that Dulac had made for him: "The Butterfly is the main symbol on my ring—the ring I always wear—the other symbol is the hawk. The hawk is the straight road of logic, the butterfly the crooked road of intuition—the hawk pounces, the butterfly flutters" (*CL InteLex* 6102).

98. For the visionary transformation that takes place between the two volumes, see my "Hawk and Butterfly: The Double Vision of *The Wild Swans at Coole* (1917, 1919)," *YA10* (1993), 111–34.

and daughter were discharged, the new family and their cat took a furnished house in Dundrum, where Yeats began writing "A Prayer for My Daughter." "In that nondescript furnished room," wrote Ernest Boyd of his visit there, "amid the distracting rustling of the cat's perambulations, I heard him intone [the poem], with an intensity of emotion characteristically at variance with the elaborate formality of the verses, which he read carefully from the manuscript in his small difficult writing."[99] The expenses of a family and costs of restoring Thoor Ballylee now necessitated giving up the luxury of 18 Woburn Buildings, for twenty-three years the headquarters and recruiting center of the chanting movement, but he would not let the psaltery go with it. On June 15, ten days before giving up the lease, he replied to Gwen John's inquiry about the availability of the psaltery that he did not wish to relinquish the object of a legacy that he still hoped to pass on and keep alive, if only in his family: "I have the psaltery but I want to keep it myself. It is the only thing of Florence Farrs that I have . . . I hope some day my daughter may use it."[100] Gwen John might have looked elsewhere for abandoned psalteries: in March 1920 Dolmetsch bought back, for £1.10.0 each, three in the possession of Annie Horniman, for use in teaching music at Bedales School in Hampshire.[101]

Pound remained in London through the war, gradually drifting apart from his mentor and directing his poetic energy into the Cantos. Under the continued inspiration of Dolmetsch, he developed his alter ego as the pseudonymous music critic William Atheling, determined to explore further the relation between music and poetry, which in his view had received scarce development since the death of John Jenkins in 1678.[102]

99. Ernest Boyd, *Portraits: Real and Imaginary* (London: Jonathan Cape, 1924), 244. Yeats had known the critic Boyd since 1915, when Boyd was writing *Ireland's Literary Renaissance* (1916).

100. Letter of June 15, 1919, *CL InteLex* 3618.

101. Dolmetsch diary, Haslemere. Sturge Moore, who was also affiliated with Bedales, had Yeats down on December 2, 1925, to lecture on "My Own Poetry." As he described the visit to A. H. Fisher, "We had Yeats here for two days last week. He gave Bedales a lecture which was very successful in spite of the hall being horribly cold. He is very delightful and has finished his philosophy, or at least all that he could get from the Spirits but the most important and fundamental idea remains unrevealed and now he is reading other philosophers to find out to what degree the Spirits agree with them, and is much smitten with an Italian Gentile who is Musolini's Minister of Education" (Letter of December 13, 1925, Sturge Moore Papers, University of London).

102. In the *Pisan Cantos* (1948), canto 81, Pound invokes the seventeenth-century golden age of music and poetry, alluding to the love songs of Edmund Waller (1606–87), the lutesongs of John Dowland (1563–1626), the lutenists William Lawes (1602–45), John Jenkins (1591–1678), and their successor Arnold Dolmetsch ("*Lawes and Jenkins guard thy rest /*

Indeed, he described his literary and musical desires to Margaret Anderson of the *Little Review* at the expense of Yeats, the first hint that he was breaking away from the master: "And I desire also to resurrect the art of the lyric, I mean words to be sung, for Yeats' only wail and submit to keening and ch*au*nting (with a *u*), and Swinburne's only rhapsodify."[103] It did not please him that Yeats readily made light of *vers libre*, which he had always associated negatively with Tyndall and Huxley (*Aut* 121).[104] Yeats had not liked the first canto, later admitting that after reading it and its successors the best he could do was attempt to "suspend judgement" (*OBMV* p. xxv). After Yeats sent him copies of "The Phases of the Moon" and "The Double Vision of Michael Robartes," Pound began to mock Yeats's new visionary mode, writing to Quinn: "You will be glad to hear that Yeats has finally decided against Japan. Bit queer in his head about 'moon'; whole new metaphysics about 'moon', very very very bug-house." And he was no less mocking of Yeats's restoration of Thoor Ballylee, his "phallic symbol on the Bogs," his "Bally phallus or whatever he calls it with the river on the first floor."[105] In his newfound irreverence, he had turned his attention and allegiance to the work, intellectual energy, and publications of his nearer contemporaries: Eliot, Joyce, Lewis, Brzeska, all the young moderns. "Might listen to my wife," he wrote to Quinn, "who has assured me that the *energy* in Joyce, W[yndham]. L[ewis]. & myself is what upsets people."[106]

At the same time that Eliot discovered Yeats's *At the Hawk's Well* in 1916, he discovered the verse and prose of T. E. Hulme, teaching the poems in adult extension classes as sterling examples of free verse and Imagism, underscoring Hulme's assertion that the turn to dry, hard, classical verse was indeed at hand, teaching and reviewing the prose to emphasize a

Dolmetsch ever be thy guest"), lamenting that "for 180 years almost nothing." The implication is that between the death of Jenkins in 1678 and the birth of Dolmetsch 180 years later in 1858 there was no measureable advancement in the relation of poetry and music.

103. Letter of [?January 1918], *The Letters of Ezra Pound*, 128.

104. As Yeats later described his position to William Rothenstein, "the upholders of free verse claimed that its form was, without restriction, accommodated to the matter. He took the opposite view: the essence of poetry is the outpouring of the personal into a static form (this he compared with the metaphysical antinomy of the individual and the infinite—the many and the one) although the form could of course be changed and adapted." See William Rothenstein, *Since Fifty: Men and Memories, 1922–1938* (London: Faber and Faber, 1939), 251.

105. *The Selected Letters of Ezra Pound to John Quinn, 1915–1924*, ed. Timothy Materer (Durham and London: Duke University Press, 1991), 181, 188.

106. Ibid. 176.

classicism founded on the reality of Original Sin.[107] In his respectful but anti-romantic review of Yeats's *Per Amica Silentia Lunae* (1918), he declared himself "lost" in the theory of Anima Mundi, "or Mr. Yeats is lost to me, in some delicious soft mist as that in which Venus enwrapt her son," allowing that "there is no one else living whom one would endure on the subject of gnomes, hobgoblins, and astral bodies."[108] In a review entitled "A Foreign Mind," Eliot was even more severe in his criticism of the romantic and esoteric underpinnings of Yeats's work in *The Cutting of an Agate* (1919). "When we engage Yeats's mind in this book," he declared,

> we are confirmed... in a baffling and disturbing conviction—that its author, as much in his prose as in his verse, is not "of this world"... It is a mind in which perceptions of fact, and feeling and thinking are all a little different from ours.... His remoteness is not an escape from the world, for he is innocent of any world to escape from; his procedure is blameless, but he does not start where we do.[109]

The camaraderie, admiration, and shared interests of the past three years could not hold together their rapidly diverging intellectual assumptions and aesthetic temperaments. By the end of the war, the gap between classical and romantic philosophies had been sharply widened by the wedge of modernism. As Eliot would soon define the thrust of the new movement, a refined poetic sensibility "must produce various and complex results. The poet must become more and more comprehensive, more allusive, more indirect, in order to force, to dislocate if necessary, language into his meaning."[110] To Yeats, the younger generation of poets had lost the music and passion of poetry, and, like the realists in the theatre before them, had stepped out of the great processional order of symbolist writers.

Pound and Dorothy moved between London and France, as travel restrictions allowed, until they finally left London in December 1920 for a three-year residence in Paris. His departure was marked by the publication of "Five Troubadour Songs," prefaced by a "Proem" signed jointly by

107. For a full account of Hulme's influence on Eliot in and after 1916, see my *Eliot's Dark Angel* (New York and Oxford: Oxford University Press, 1999), and "Did Eliot Know Hulme? Final Answer," *Journal of Modern Literature*, 27 (Fall 2003), 63–9.
108. T. S. Eliot, "Shorter Notices" (unsigned), *Egoist*, 5 (June/July 1918), 87.
109. T. S. Eliot, "A Foreign Mind," *Athenaeum*, 4653 (July 4, 1919), 552–3.
110. T. S. Eliot, "The Metaphysical Poets" (1921), in *Selected Essays*, new edn. (New York: Harcourt Brace, 1950), 248.

Pound and Atheling, his musical alter ego,[111] and with that he left his troubadours behind, displacing the spirit of romance with the machinery of modernism. Except for a week that he spent with the Yeatses in November 1921, their encounters would be few until they were together again in Rapallo for short periods in 1928 and 1929. When Pound later reflected on his early relationship with Yeats for the BBC, he described, with voice illustration, how Yeats's "means of getting or seeing his rhythm was pulling out the vowels" in his chanting. "My reading shows more interest in the meaning of what I got on the the page," he added, but as for Yeats, "I have no idea how he read after 1920."[112] Yeats may still have thought that Pound's chanting sounded like a bad phonograph recording.

V

In September 1920 Yeats was back at 4 Broad Street in Oxford and working on "All Souls' Night." He had just finished the first version when a tonsillitis infection required him to return to Dublin for a tonsillectomy, thereby making him miss a literary event and meeting that he had fostered six years earlier on his second American tour—the arrival in Oxford for a reading by the American poet Vachel Lindsay. When Harriet Monroe, editor of *Poetry* (Chicago), planned a banquet in Yeats's honor on March 1, 1914, she invited the impecunious Lindsay to attend and read a poem. Yeats and Lindsay had both received cash awards from *Poetry* the previous November for "The Grey Rock" and "General William Booth Enters into Heaven," respectively, and Monroe was keen to bring them together. As Yeats was Monroe's house guest, she placed a copy of "General Booth" on his bedside table before he arrived. When at the banquet he stood to give his after-dinner talk on "Contemporary Poetry" to the distinguished audience, Yeats singled out Lindsay and announced not only that he was addressing his remarks to him as "a fellow craftsman" but praised "General Booth," which he had read several times, for its "strange beauty." When Yeats concluded his address, Lindsay rose in reply, electrifying the audience

111. *Four Troubadour Songs with the Original Provençal Words* (London: Boosey, 1920). The songs were adapted by Pound, with English words from Chaucer, and arranged for voice and piano accompaniment by Agnes Bedford.

112. Ezra Pound, "Readings and Recollections." recorded by the BBC (T26074) at Brunnenberg, July 1, 1959.

with the chanting of his new poem, "The Congo" ("Fat black bucks in a wine-barrel room"), shaking the room with his resounding "Boom, boom, BOOM!" As he chanted the poem, rocking on the balls of his feet, "his eyes blazing, his arms pumping like pistons," he transported the audience, which burst into thunderous applause at the end. "The Negro waiters against the walls applauded," wrote his biographer. "The guest of honor, jerked from the misty kingdom of his Celtic imaginings, must have felt like one who pats a kitten and sees it turn into a lion, and there were bravos from Lindsay's fellow midwesterners, persuading him into reciting *General Booth*."[113]

After Lindsay's powerful performance, Yeats, deeply impressed, was moved to ask him, "What are we going to do to restore the primitive singing of poetry?" Their full dialogue is unrecorded, but Lindsay would describe the banquet experience and his conversation with Yeats that night as "the literary transformation scene of my life."[114] He carried Yeats's question back to his desk, where he was drafting "The Santa Fé Trail," and began to infuse the poem with modes of primitive singing. He then sent "The Congo," "The Santa Fé Trail," and other poems to Monroe for publication in *Poetry* under the general title "Poems to Be Chanted," complete with marginal voice instructions on how to chant, intone, and sing the various sections. The issue also contained his short explanatory article, "Mr. Lindsay on 'Primitive Singing,'" in which he recounted his meeting with Yeats and described his Yeatsian intentions. Working out of the American vaudeville tradition, he introduced the poems as "an experiment in which I endeavor to carry this vaudeville form back towards the old Greek precedent of the half-chanted lyric."[115] As he described the essential points of chanting each poem, he suggested that parts "could be intoned in a semi-priestly manner.... It is the hope of the writer that, after two or three readings, each line will suggest its own separate touch of melody to the performer who has become accustomed to the cadences." Later in the year Lindsay brought out *The Congo and Other Poems*, entitling the first section "Poems intended to be read aloud, or chanted." In her introduction, where she describes Lindsay as "the young Illinois troubadour," Monroe emphasized "his plea for poetry as a song art, an art appealing to the ear

113. Eleanor Ruggles, *The West-Going Heart: A Life of Vachel Lindsay* (New York: Norton, 1959), 218.

114. Quoted in Foster, *Life 1* 515.

115. *Poetry: A Magazine of Verse*, 4 (July 1914). "Poems to Be Chanted," 123–40, "Mr. Lindsay On 'Primitive Singing,'" 161–2, here 161.

rather than the eye," and his belief that poetry "can be restored to the people only through a renewal of its appeal to the ear."[116] She identified Lindsay's poems as an American manifestation of Yeats's modern movement—of returning "to primitive sympathies between artist and audience, which may make possible once more the assertion of primitive creative power"—and she saw the possibility of Lindsay's art revitalizing that tradition abroad: "If Mr. Lindsay's poetry should cross the ocean, it would not be the first time that our most indigenous art has reacted upon the art of older nations."

Due to the outbreak of war, Lindsay was unable to cross the ocean with his poetry until August 1920, when he arrived for readings in London, Oxford, and Cambridge. He had been sorely disappointed that he and Yeats had not been able to carry on their dialogue of a shared vision, and when he went up to Oxford on October 15 he must have greatly anticipated a reunion. His reading was organized by Robert Graves, with Sir Walter Raleigh, Oxford's first professor of poetry, in the chair. Yeats's friends Robert Bridges and John Masefield were there to greet him and take him afterward to Boar's Hill. Lindsay, his chanting voice now in full power, gave them a sensational reading. "Sir Walter led the cheers after each recitation," wrote Mrs. Lindsay, "and I never saw such an ovation! Nor did I ever hear Vachel read so well. Enthusiasm went wild in staid old Oxford, the heart of all educational interests in the English speaking world."[117] "Lindsay was a most staggering success!" wrote Graves, who recorded the audience's minute-by-minute reaction:

> By two minutes he had the respectable and intellectual and cynical audience listening. By ten, intensely excited; by twenty, elated and losing self-control; by half an hour completely under his influence; by forty minutes roaring like a bonfire. At the end they lifted off the roof and refused to disperse, and Raleigh in returning thanks said he had never been so moved by a recitation in his life—quite like the pictures.[118]

The undergraduate poet Richard Hughes recalled that Lindsay "left the audience spellbound with his hypnotic sibilants." He and other Oxford poets afterward kept Lindsay "jailed in their rooms at Oriel until he taught them by heart every intonation and rhythm of his recited verse."[119]

116. Vachel Lindsay, *The Congo and Other Poems* (New York: Macmillan, 1914), p. vi.
117. Quoted in Ruggles, *The West-Going Heart*, 274.
118. Ibid. 274–5.
119. "Vachel Lindsay: 'The Congo' and 'The Daniel Jazz' " BBC broadcast introduced and read by Richard Hughes, July 26, 1968, Caversham Written Archives (MT32039).

The visit to Oxford was for Yeats's American protégé the second literary transformation scene of his life—too cruel the irony that after six years of waiting, the master, convalescing, missed it by a few days—all possibility of fruitful collaboration initially foiled by war now ended by tonsils.[120]

VI

After the publication of *Four Plays for Dancers* (1921), Yeats declared that he was "tired of the theatre," certain on completion of *Calvary* that the singers and composers of his choruses, "when the time came for performance, would certainly make it impossible for the audience to know what the words were."[121] He wished to create for himself "an unpopular theatre and an audience like a secret society," one of fifty people who "read poetry for their pleasure and understand the traditional language of passion" (*Expl* 254–5). More of his time and strength were now husbanded for the automatic writing and construction of *A Vision*, but for three days in April 1921 his recurrent brooding upon personal utterance resurfaced once again. In a cottage in Shillingford, outside Oxford, he wrote in a notebook an entry that begins, "I have been wondering why I like a lyric that sings, rather than talks, to go to an old rhythm, to sound as if men might sing it when half asleep, or when riding on a journey."[122] That morning, far from musicians and singers, he felt that after months of wondering he had hit upon the answer:

> If a poem talks, a good sonnet (say Blunt, that begins "When I hear laughter at the tavern door") we have the passionate syntax, the impression of the man who speaks, the active man no abstract poet, the dreamer; but if it sings we want the impression of a man either actually singing, or at least murmuring it over, and not as a show, a performer, but at some moment of emotion. We cannot do this if the poet does not call up the image of sailors, of horsemen or unhappy lovers, a multitude out of other days. I want therefore, when I

120. Yeats, who never forgot the impact of Lindsay's chanting, later planned to include "The Congo" and "General Booth" in his 1937 BBC broadcast, "In the Poet's Parlour," but they were canceled when the time allotted was too short to include them.

121. *Four Plays for Dancers*, 135 (*VPl* 789).

122. W. B. Yeats, Notebook, NLI MS 13576. The three separate entries in the notebook, on April 7, 24, and 26, were conflated into an undivided essay by Richard Fallis and published as "Language and Rhythm in Poetry: A Previously Unpublished Essay by W. B. Yeats," *Shenandoah*, 26 (Summer 1975), 77–9; however, much of the manuscript is erroneously transcribed and unannotated.

> cannot get the syntax of common passionate life (& I seldom can in a song,) a measure that seems a part of that life.

His revisitation here of "passionate syntax," the natural speech order of passionate life lifted into lyric or song, is accompanied by a reflection on the defective syntax of Tennyson, his lack of "good speech" and passion: " 'In Memoriam' is detestable because of its syntax. It is not that of any mans speech when moved [sic]." A fortnight later, in a second sitting, he went after Browning: "He wrote a language which he studied from outside as if it were a dialect... Only at rare moments do we get a passionate rhythmical syntax, & often when he is most poetical as in that song about the 'aloe balls' in Paracelsus he is further from the natural order of words."[123]

Yeats had focused on Tennyson and Browning to clarify and specify his long objection to Victorian rhetoric and moral fervour—ever the antinomies of his symbolist enterprise—that the poets brought to the end of the nineteenth century. But as he thought about the problem over the next two days, he began to see them as late manifestations of a process that had begun to accelerate in the seventeenth century—the gradual dissociation of the bardic mind. His reflections are remarkably parallel, from a different point of view and emphasis, to those that Eliot, using Dante as his model of a unified sensibility, had begun to make regarding the seventeenth-century dissociation of thought and feeling in English poets, first evident to Eliot in Donne. On April 26 Yeats began his entry with a confident assertion: "We tolerate, or enjoy an artificial syntax & a rhythm which is neither speech nor anything suggesting a song because our thought is artificial." Against the artificiality of syntax and thought that he traces from Milton to Tennyson, he places Dante's personal dramatization of emotion and vision:

> Milton began it by bring[ing] into English literature a mass of thought "to justify the ways of God" which was believed to have value apart from its value as dramatization. In Dante when he is not dramatizing some lost or suffering soul [he] gives one an emotion of personal ecstasy. His Paradise is a mystic vision, an exaltation. He writes it all for that ecstasy's sake, not for the edification of others. Milton brought the mischief from Rome which systematized what had been natural impulse in Greece, & he thought more of the state than of paradise, & in Dryden & Pope the mischief is there unmixed—sheer dry lines. Burns and Blake are a revolt, but Wordsworth &

123. Browning's "Song from 'Paracelsus' " begins: "Heap cassia, sandal-buds and stripes | Of labdanum, and aloe-balls, | Smear'd with dull nard an Indian wipes | From her hair:"

even Coleridge and Shelley in much of their work follow Dryden and Milton. So too did Tennyson.

Parallel to the development of this tradition of "impersonal eloquence" in literature, Yeats observed, was the tradition of impersonal form in painting and sculpture. Both traditions went wrong in attempting to substitute character for beauty, for beauty is passion and "character is obstruction of passion." In Yeats's view, the revolt against this impersonal tradition and its "classical morality" by Blake accounted for his violence of opinion—by Burns, Verlaine, and "the poets of the 90's" for the disorder in their lives. "Blake alone saw that it was classical, not Christian, morality in origin. It is Christian now because it no longer derives itself from the old pride—'lonely to the lone I go divine to the divinity'—but is imposed by 'the sense of duty'[,] duty that is to others."[124]

The three notebook entries over three weeks represent his most sustained attempt to comprehend the passing of the lost bardic kingdom that he had heroically tried to restore for the past twenty years. In his analysis of a poetic tradition that had come to place ideas before images, eloquence before passion, character before beauty, and, implicitly, the self before the mask, he knew that the only escape from that tradition was through personal utterance, dramatization of emotion, passionate syntax, visionary ecstasy, and achieved mask. And he also knew, as he concluded his assertions, that personal expression "must not become characterization nor in poetry can drama itself become chiefly characterization. In personal expression characterization is egotism." It was a necessary critical coda for the romantic aesthetic with which he would soon encounter the publication of *The Waste Land*. As he wrote in the letter-preface addressed to Lady Gregory for *The Cat and the Moon and Certain Poems* (1924), "the other day when I read that strange 'Waste Land' by Mr. T. C. Eliot [*sic*] I thought of your work and of Synge's; and he . . . writes but of his own mind. That is the kind of insoluble problem that makes the best conversation, and if you will come and visit me, I will call the Dublin poets together, and we will discuss it until midnight" (*VPl* 854). Musing on Eliot's poem, and on the nature of personal expression, Yeats had come to the conclusion, borne of *Per Amica* and *A Vision*, that Eliot had sought his self rather than his opposite, that

124. Yeats quotes from the two concluding lines of Lionel Johnson's "The Dark Angel": "Lonely, unto the Lone I go; | Divine, to the Divinity."

ironically he had failed to achieve, in Eliot's word, impersonality, in Yeats's, the mask.

In April 1922, following the ratification of the Anglo-Irish treaty and the onset of the Civil War, the Yeatses had taken refuge in Ballylee, where he began to write one of his greatest poems, "Meditations in Time of Civil War." As he worked on successive sections, he continued to revisit the psaltery experiments, preserving their import in memoirs, prefaces, and revisions. On May 1 he turned to his 1908 note on "The Music for Use in the Performance of these Plays," revising it to note that he prints Farr's music for *Deirdre* "because now that she is dead it cannot be amended, and it is part of an attempt, which seemed to me important, to recover an art once common and now lost."[125] That summer, in "Four Years," he wrote again of his long friendship with Farr—"an enduring friendship that was an enduring exasperation"—seemingly resigned to the perception that their minstrel art was destined to be "an unfashionable art, an art that has scarce existed since the seventeenth century," one that for her "could only earn unimportant occasional praise" (*Aut* 119). In September, before "Meditations" was quite completed, the blowing up of the Ballylee bridge and flooding of the ground floor of the tower forced the family to take residence at 82 Merrion Square, a Dublin home at last. In December, almost twenty years after the composition of *The King's Threshold*, in which Seanchan the Chief Poet of Ireland asserts the poet's right to sit in "the great council of the State" with "Makers of the Law" (*VPl* 259), Yeats was appointed to the Irish Senate by the Free State government. The prophetic poet and playwright, assuming his new political office and about to be named a Nobel laureate, was in his relished public oratory as yet unaware of the advent of broadcasting, which would inspire a last attempt to stem the tide of artificial syntax with impassioned lyrics, lyrics sounding more like poems singing than poems thinking.

125. W. B. Yeats, *Plays in Prose and Verse* (London: Macmillan, 1922), 435.

10

The Last Minstrel

I

Immersed as he was in Senate affairs, the writing and revisions of *A Vision*, the struggle to reclaim the Hugh Lane pictures for Ireland, and his many literary and theatrical activities, Yeats was not attentive to the development of wireless broadcasting in the 1920s as a wondrous medium for taking the living voice of the poet to the people. Although the BBC began broadcasting in October 1922, its programs were not relayed to Belfast until September 1924, and the Dublin Broadcasting Station (Radio Telefis Éireann) did not broadcast its first program until New Year's Day 1926. His prominence as winner of the Nobel Prize, however, attracted the rapidly expanding BBC to his poetry and plays in July 1926, and for the next four years his early poems, ballads, and plays were broadcast out of Yeats's hearing, since he had little interest and no wireless.[1] It was not until 1930 that the new Poet Laureate, John Masefield, who on Yeats's inspiration became a lifelong proponent of spoken verse and founded the verse-speaking competitions known as the Oxford Recitations (1923–9), urged poets to recover through the radio the "Homeric Dream" of placing their voices in the public domain once again.[2] No one more than Masefield

1. The BBC had contacted the Incorporated Society of Authors as early as July 1924 requesting permission to broadcast *Cathleen ni Houlihan* from Manchester, and though agreement was reached there is no evidence that the transmission occurred. A chronological listing of the actual broadcasts of Yeats's work for this period, which began with *The Hour-Glass* on July 4, 1926 and ended with Sara Allgood's reading of Yeats's poems on November 27, 1930, is provided by Jeremy Silver, "W. B. Yeats and the BBC: A Reassessment," *YA5* (1987), 181–5. Douglas Hyde formally opened the Dublin Broadcasting Station ("2RN"), speaking mainly in Irish Gaelic while expressing his interest in the broadcasting service as a means for the dissemination of culture. The opening program of band music, songs, and musical solos included Herbert Hughes's rendition of Yeats's "Down by the Salley Gardens."
2. Masefield's cross-Atlantic broadcast from London to America was quoted extensively in an article entitled "Poets on the Air," *Literary Digest*, 107 (October 4, 1930), 107, and the responses

wanted to hear Yeats's voice on the air. Indeed, so indebted was Masefield to Yeats for the impact on him of the chanting recital given before the Fellowship of the Three Kings in February 1901, that on November 5, 1930, he held a verse festival at Boar's Hill, outside Oxford, to celebrate the thirtieth anniversary of their meeting and to pay public tribute to Yeats for his influence on verse-speaking in the modern literary world. "It was he," said Masefield, "now thirty years ago, who first made public experiments in new methods of the speaking of verse, who roused up a ferment not yet dead, and set before us ideals not yet realised."[3] Within a year of Masefield's praise and prodding, Yeats, who had evaded all previous attempts to be placed in front of a microphone, would begin the gradual resurrection of his dormant ideals by giving his first public broadcast from the Belfast studio of the BBC.

Yeats's pessimism regarding the theatre generally and the Abbey particularly had increased during the 1920s, heightened by the rise of what he called the "slum plays" of Sean O'Casey, Lennox Robinson, and others. Resigned to the impracticality of staging the chorus of his *Sophocles' King*

of several US papers were reported. In expressing the hope "that broadcasting may make listening to poetry a pleasure again," Masefield echoed Yeats's views throughout his address: "In times past, poetry was the delight of every member of the community. The Community was small . . . and all ranks and classes of men met together in the King's Palace . . . and the poet sang or spoke to all and was listened to with rapture by all. . . . Then there came the printing-press . . . a detriment to the poetical art. It has had this result—that it has put away the poet from his public . . . Since the printing-press came into being poetry has ceased to be the delight of the whole community of man; it has become the amusement and delight of a limited few. . . . The minstrel has ceased to be. He no longer goes about singing, chanting his verse." Shortly after founding the Oxford Recitations, Masefield addressed the first general meeting of the Scottish Association for the Speaking of Verse on October 24, 1924, embodying his absorption of Yeats's ideas into his own in *With the Living Voice: An Address* (Cambridge: Cambridge University Press, 1924).

3. John Masefield, "Words Spoken at the Music Room, Boars Hill, Nov. 5, 1930, at a Festival designed in the honour of Wm. Butler Yeats, Poet," BL MS. Eng. Misc.d.657. "Poetry is seldom heard upon the modern English stage," Masefield continued, "but when it is heard, it is largely due to Mr. Yeats that it is heard with any pleasure. . . . The best poetry comes like life itself from a high state of the soul. It comes as a living image, upon a rhythm, out of eternity, into the minds of men and women, who are thereby touched into generosities. . . . Thirty years ago, hardly any living man had perceived this fact. Mr. Yeats perceived it, and saw, too, that an all pervading commonness had advanct slowly upon the world and usurpt all sorts of authority once held by artists, and poets . . . His perception of the badness of speech was a perception of a bluntedness of mind to all fineness and delicacy and beauty of thought: an indifference to good work, that now rules, as the ruthless intellect wrenches itself further and further apart from any complete humanity." The edited and shortened script was privately printed as *Words Spoken at the Music Room Boars's Hill in the afternoon of November 5th, 1930 at a Festival designed in the honour of William Butler Yeats, Poet* (not for sale); rpt. in the 1932 revised English edition of *Recent Prose*.

Oedipus (1928) on the choral principles developed by Farr, he told his producer Robinson to ignore that method and to go ahead with a chorus of liturgical singers, with whatever "comes to hand."[4] Throughout the decade he repeated grudgingly that one could not rely on the theatre paying any attention to verse, and his experience in the Senate led him to deplore equally the decline of oratory in public life.[5] A rare exception was his pleasure in hearing the dramatic music composed by the American musician George Antheil for his last dance play, *Fighting the Waves* (1929).[6] Although his choral and verse-speaking ideals had been in abeyance for a over a decade, he continued to reflect upon his "unfashionable art" in his prose writings. On his sixty-fifty birthday, recovering from Malta fever contracted in Rapallo, he reminisced in "Pages from a Diary in 1930" how in the most creative years of his life his efforts for poetry and poetic drama were driven by the desire to make those arts public, recalling yet again how he "disliked the isolation of the work of art. I wished through the drama, through a commingling of verse and dance, through singing that was also speech, through what I called the applied arts of literature, to plunge it back into social life" (*Expl* 300). This was a nostalgic reflection, however, no longer an active dream.

In the aftermath of the Civil War and the Nobel Prize, Yeats did enjoy taking his poetry into the new social life of Dublin, where huge audiences

4. W. B. Yeats, *Sophocles' King Oedipus: A Version for the Modern Stage* (New York: Macmillan 1928), p. vi.

5. See "Mr. W. B. Yeats on Decline of Modern Oratory," *Irish Times*, August 10, 1925, on the occasion of thanking the government for an endowment that made the Abbey Theatre the first State-endowed theatre in any English-speaking country: "The Irish oratory of the period of the Old Irish Parliament had been among the greatest of modern times. Their own Oireachtas was far more representative of the people, but the day of oratory was past, not only there, but everywhere in the modern world" (12). On a less public occasion he was more vehement, holding forth, before Holloway and other friends at Gogarty's house on October 2, 1931, "on this age's lack of appreciation of great declamatory oratory" and on his belief "that no one living appreciated the beauty of speech." See *Joseph Holloway's Irish Theatre*, vol 1, *1926–1931*, ed. Robert Hogan and Michael J. O'Neill (Dixon, CA: Proscenium Press, 1968), 79.

6. A rewriting of *The Only Jealously of Emer* (1919), *Fighting the Waves* was first produced with Antheil's music in August 1929 but not published until it appeared (with Antheil's music) in *Wheels and Butterflies* (London: Macmillan, 1934). As Yeats wrote to Sturge Moore on March 24, 1929, Yeats agreed to let Antheil write the music after learning that he was "a man whose theories about the relations between words and music seem to be exactly my own. In my moments of personal hopefulness . . . I begin to think that what my friends call my lack of ear is but an instinct for the music of the twelfth century" (*CL InteLex* 5229). After hearing the music, Yeats wrote to Lennox Robinson: "What he played to me seemed to me the only dramatic music I have ever heard, a powerful beat, strangeness, something hard & heroic. When you selected Antheil I think it was a <piece of> divination" (Letter of [late April 1929], *CL InteLex* 5240).

and glowing receptions accompanied his public readings and commentary. He was in his element on such occasions, as in the Examination Hall of the Royal College of Surgeons, where he "faced an audience which was close-seated from his feet to the far end of the long hall, and flanked by rows of people glad to stand if they might be within the hall, and a gallery also was closely packed."[7] The reporter was astonished by the fact that for the hour that Yeats chanted and talked "he had no notes. He held one volume of his poems, but seldom looked at it, even when nominally 'reading' his poems." The colourful account named the poems read and the commentary given, from "The Lake Isle of Innisfree" to "An Irish Airman Foresees His Death": "With these, then, lightly introduced, Mr. Yeats ended his lecture, which had been a masterpiece of sequence, variety and charm of delivery." In these high, intimate moments with his Dublin audience in his hand, he was exalted; no microphone could replace the quality of poetic intimacy cultivated and achieved.

Nonetheless, if he was to open himself to the new broadcasting adventure, he would assert his own ideals of poetry and recitation with a passion and vehemence that required a new persona. In the days before his first broadcast, the members of Yeats's fictional phantasmagoria—John Aherne, John Duddon, Denise de L'Isle Adam, Michael Robartes, and others—admitted a new member to their company. "My name is Daniel O'Leary," says the angry romantic intruder who comes to tell his story in the preface to *Stories of Michael Robartes and His Friends*:

> my great interest is the speaking of verse, and the establishment some day or other of a small theatre for plays in verse. You will remember that a few years before the Great War the realists drove the last remnants of rhythmical speech out of the theatre. I thought common sense might have returned while I was at war or in the starvation afterwards.... The realists turn our words into gravel, but the musicians and the singers turn them into honey and oil. I have always had the idea that some day a musician would do me an injury.... You at any rate cannot sympathise with a horrible generation that in childhood

7. " 'My Own Poetry.' / Mr. Yeats's Reading," *Irish Times* (January 26, 1924), 6. A similar reading in the Town Hall, Rathmines, was reported in the *Irish Times* of February 25, 1926, when he spoke eloquently about the importance of folk poetry in Ireland: "Whatever they got out of 'folk,' said Mr. Yeats, went straight to the human heart, because there was no complication of speculation or thought, or any of the things that made us unhappy: it was pure emotion. He thought that the almost overwhelming patriotism of our people and our Gaelic Catholic peasantry had been influenced by thoughts of the other world, and that the thought of Ireland in the folk-mind had got penetrated with emotion that arose originally from what was, perhaps, the paradise of pagan Ireland, and was gradually changing into the paradise of Christian Ireland" (" 'My Own Poetry.' Mr. Yeats Talks and Recites," 6).

> sucked Ibsen from [William] Archer's bottle. You can understand even better than Robartes why that protest must always seem the great event of my life.[8]

In O'Leary, Yeats had brought forth a persona whose protesting voice would direct his broadcasts and fight his battles with a new generation of dramatic realists, modern poets, diatonic musicians, and trained singers Thus, when the BBC contacted Yeats in August 1931 about broadcasting his version of Sophocles' *Oedipus* on September 15, to be preceded a week earlier by a talk about the play and a reading of his poems, he accepted with sudden alacrity. George insisted that he have a studio rehearsal in a standing, stationary position, writing to him that "as you haven't broadcasted before I think a try out might be an advantage—you won't be able to tiger up and down the room as you usually do when you speak!"[9]

> YEATS'S "HELLO TO EVERYBODY!"
>
> *
>
> FAMOUS IRISH POET "ON THE AIR" FOR FIRST TIME.
>
> *
>
> BELFAST STATION DEBUT.
>
> *
>
> Describing his feelings at approaching the microphone for the first time, Mr. Yeats said he was not experiencing any sensation of "stage fright." "The only thing about it," he said, "is that instead of speaking to a great many people altogether I shall be speaking to a great many people who will be separated. What it feels like to listen to a man speaking over the radio I do not know, for although I have heard music broadcast I have never listened to anyone speaking over the wireless.[10]

For the first quarter-hour of the broadcast, Yeats read from a prepared script on the history of his conception and composition of the play,

8. W. B. Yeats, *Stories of Michael Robartes and His Friends* (Dublin: Cuala Press, 1931), [1]–3; rpt. in second edn of *A Vision* (London: Macmillan, 1937), 33–5. O'Leary's appearance was preceded by an untitled, three-stanza poem that begins, "Huddon, Duddon and Daniel O'Leary | Delighted me as a child; | But where that roaring, ranting crew | Danced, laughed, loved, fought through | Their brief lives I never knew." Yeats evidently took and adapted the names from a Celtic fairy tale, "Hudden and Dudden and Donald O'Neary," a tale included in *Celtic Fairy Tales*, ed. Joseph Jacobs (London: David Nutt, 1892), 47–56.
9. Letter of "Friday" [August 1931], quoted in Foster, *Life 2* 427.
10. *The Northern Whig and Belfast Post*, September 9, 1931, 3. Yeats did not actually hear the broadcast of a speech until October 8, when he listened to Gerald Heard speaking on "This Surprising World."

provided a summary of the dramatic scenario, and described the difference between ancient and modern staging, but his main concern was to prepare his listening audience for the chorus. "Probably the first thing that will seem to you very strange," he said, "as very unlike anything seen on the English stage, is that every few minutes a number of persons who are citizens of Thebes sing their comments upon the actors."[11] He wanted his listeners to understand his own discovery about the function of the chorus, how it preserves the mood while resting the mind with a change of focus: "the chorus is there so that we may sit back and relax our strained attention. Not that we must cease to listen, for the chorus is beautiful, past ages are called up before us, vast emotions are aroused, but our attention is no longer concentrated upon a single spot, a single man." The chorus would not be conducted as he liked in the broadcast, but his preoccupation with its function in drama had moved into the composition of his poems: during the past year he had begun to find an analogy between the choral lyrics of the plays and the communal refrains of the Crazy Jane poems that were soon to appear in *Words for Music Perhaps* (1932), an experiment that would be expanded in the ballads written for future broadcasts.

Yeats then turned from the play to the chanting of some early poems, stating emphatically at the beginning, "I am going to read my poems with great emphasis on their rhythm. That may sound strange if you are not used to it." Justifying his method, he described his favorite anecdote of William Morris coming in a rage out of a lecture hall where someone had badly recited a passage from his *Sigard the Volsung*: " 'It gave me a devil of a lot of trouble,' said Morris, 'to get that thing into verse.' It gave *me* the devil of a lot of trouble to get into verse the poems that I am going to read and that is why I will not read them as if they were prose."[12]

11. The BBC provided the complete text of Yeats's talk about the play for exclusive publication in *The Irish News and Belfast Morning News*, September 9, 1931, 5. The BBC copy was subsequently destroyed during the war. Unaware of the earlier publication, Karen Dorn published a transcription of Yeats's copy (NLI MS 30,109) in *YA5* (1987), 195–9. Except for minor differences of punctuation, capitalization, and paragraph breaks in the *Irish News*, the two texts are essentially the same. It was re-edited and included in *LAR* 219–33.

12. The broadcast script appears in *LAR* 224–9, here 224 (italics mine, to show Yeats's emphasis on the broadcast, which was recorded by the BBC (Sound Archives, Cat. No. LP22145). It was later reproduced on the Siobhan McKenna and Michael MacLiammoir recording of *The Poems of William Butler Yeats*, Spoken Arts 753 (1959). When David Greene reviewed the recording, quoting Yeats's remark on Morris, he remarked: "To Yeats, and to all Irish poets of his time at least, this meant reading with the same tonality I thought was bogus when I heard it from James Stephens twenty-five years ago but which I have since come to learn is the heritage of a rich and perfectly valid tradition" ("Recordings of William Butler Yeats," *Evergreen Review*, 2 [Spring 1959], 200–1).

And with that dramatic forewarning he chanted, with commentary, "The Lake Isle of Innisfree," "The Fiddler of Dooney," "The Song of Wandering Aengus," "In Memory of Eva Gore-Booth and Con Markiewicz," and "For Anne Gregory." Aware of the audience's natural curiosity about his unusual chanting, he closed his first broadcast with an anecdote about an American woman, a professional elocutionist, who had asked him why he read his poetry in that strange chant-like manner. "All poets from Homer up to date have read their poetry exactly as I read mine," he replied passionately, to which she countered, "What is your authority for saying Homer read his poetry in that manner?" "The only authority I can give you," he said, "is the authority that the Scotchman gave when he claimed Shakespeare for his own country. The ability of the man warrants the presumption." The anecdote had become his standard technique for disarming in advance those members of an audience whose modern ears were skeptical of or objected to his bardic chanting.

Yeats's unfamiliar emphasis on the rhythm captured the attention of several journalists reporting the success of the broadcast. One Belfast reporter thought that Yeats "no doubt surprised many by the manner in which he read his own poems":

> The rather sing-song effect created by the way he raised his voice at the end of a line was disconcerting at first, but I am not sure that it was not the best way of emphasising the rhythm, concerning which he is most particular in all his works.[13]

"He imbued every word with colour and life," wrote another reviewer effusively, "and no one who heard him could fail to be thrilled with his delightful interpretations of his own poems."[14] The enthusiastic expressions of pleasure and satisfaction to the BBC by the large listening audience ensured that similar broadcasts would follow. Yeats was thus in a jocular mood the next day in responding to an interviewer's questions about his first experience. "Speaking in front of a microphone is like addressing the Senate in Dublin," he quipped, and when he was asked to explain the analogy replied, "You see, you are speaking to an audience which is

13. "Our London Letter," *The Northern Whig and Belfast Post*, September 10, 1931, 6. This observation was echoed in the *Belfast Telegraph* of September 10, 1931: "His peculiar sing-song quality, with the sudden raising of the voice at the end of the line, sometimes gives his reading the air of a well-trained schoolchild reciter. That is how it strikes one on first hearing, but I have heard Mr. Yeats read many times, and, though I disliked his reading at first, I have come to the conclusion that for his particular poems it is the one way to stress their rhythms" (9).
14. "A Poet Broadcasts," *Belfast News-Letter*, September 9, 1931, 6.

only just not there."[15] "It is a remarkable experience," he continued, taking playful delight in imagining the use of broadcasting by fellow senators, "to speak thus to a multitude, each member of it being alone. It would be wonderfully good for politicians. Such a lot of rhetoric could not be flung directly at one solitary man in the flesh. This broadcasting may change the oratory of the world." But even in the lighthearted afterglow of a successful beginning, he was strongly conscious of the lost intimacy with his disembodied audience, stating resolutely that "the microphone, a little oblong of paper like a visiting card, is a poor substitute for a crowded hall."

Six months passed before a second broadcast was scheduled in London for a BBC National Programme on April 10, 1932. "I am resting to day to be ready for my broadcast," he wrote to George from his London club, the Savile Club, conscious of conserving some of the energy that he was expending on founding the Irish Academy of Letters.[16] Following Olivia Shakespear's suggestion, and stating with certainty before the microphone that "she has had her portable wireless brought to her room, that she is at this moment listening to find out if I have taken her advice," he chanted with commentary eight poems about women, including "His Phoenix" and "The Folly of Being Comforted" (Maud Gonne), parts of "Upon a Dying Lady" (Mabel Beardsley), and "On a Political Prisoner" (Constance Gore-Booth Markiewicz).[17] "Think my broadcast was successful," he wrote to George. "Broadcast people like it & said they would always fit me in if they could if I suggested myself."[18]

If he refrained from putting himself forward to the BBC, the broadcasts had stimulated his minstrel imagination once again, especially when he found a chanting ally in a member of the younger generation, James Stephens. Returning to Manchester in October to give the Ludwig Mond Lectures on "The New Ireland" in the Whitworth Hall, the scene of his and Farr's first provincial success with the psaltery in 1903, he sang the

15. Ibid. Yeats's process of poetic composition, during which he would recite a single line hundreds of times, often interrupted his political conversations, which may have seemed distracting or disconcerting to fellow senators: "Even in the middle of a conversation with you—," said Frank O'Connor in a June 1949 broadcast, "he would be talking about politics perhaps, and quite suddenly he would lift the right hand and would begin to beat time and you would hear him recite a line a couple of times and then the hand would drop again and he'd go on with the conversation, just as though nothing had happened" (*Irish Literary Portraits*, ed. W. R. Rodgers [London: BBC, 1972], 15).

16. Letter of April 10, 1932, *CL InteLex* 5633.

17. The edited typescript, entitled "Poems About Women," is included in *LAR* 234–43, here 234.

18. Letter of April 15, 1932, *CL InteLex* 5637.

praises of Stephens as a new manifestation of the modern minstrel. "The poets live in the Middle Ages," he began:

> I would go back. We sing departed things. James Stephens is like a mediaeval minstrel. He sings and speaks his own poetry. I would point out to you that speech is the mainspring of all our literature. Nothing else seems to have any passion. We want to get behind the Renaissance.[19]

The old theme was re-energized with his championing of Stephens, from whose *Deirdre* (1923), quarried out the *Tain Bo Cuailgne,* he chanted for the audience before closing with Padraic Pearse's "The Wayfarer" ("The beauty of the world hath made me sad | This beauty that will pass)". The stirring lecture on "The New Ireland," in which he drew upon the literature of the country "to show the powers which had shaped it," accompanied him when he left for his last tour of America later that month. "Yeats did not read from his own poetry that evening," recalled a member of the audience at Bowdoin College, one of his first stops in Maine:

> He read mostly from James Stephens. I remember my own surprise when he first began with "Deirdre," for he chanted it, swaying slightly, his vibrant voice ritualizing the lines. The effect was impressive, but also—I found—embarrassing. Anyone but Yeats intoning that way would have made himself ridiculous. I preferred him speaking. His voice then had a hypnotic flow that bore one along with it.[20]

While most members of his contemporary audiences were "thrilled" by his otherworldly chanting, others found it unsettling to their cultivated emotional reserve, finding the public expression of intense emotion with quavering voice and bodily movement "embarrassing," unable to see an ancient poetic act as anything other than an outlandish performance that only the poet's achieved greatness made excusable. But Yeats was unfazed by and willfully unconscious of such discomfiture; he would never shrink into the expected decorum of ordinary speech, as most poets had, in the recitation of his or others' poems: the chanting voice was to lift the audience out of the ordinary. Indeed, when he returned from America to bring out his *Collected Poems* (1933), he added an introductory stanza to "The Old Age of Queen Maeve," one of the narrative poems written thirty years earlier to balance his lyrical and dramatic verse for musical speech. The addition was to emphasize that the ancient folk legend was told not

19. "W. B. Yeats in Manchester," *Manchester Guardian*, October 8, 1932, 15.
20. Francis Russell, "The Archpoet," *Horizon*, 3 (November 1960), 68.

by an ordinary reciter but by a mysterious, psaltery-playing minstrel from a distant place, Yeats's own persona, fully aware that his unconventional dress, speech, and instrument were essential to his public role as poet:

A certain poet in outlandish clothes
Gathered a crowd in some Byzantine lane,
Talked of his country and its people, sang
To some stringed instrument none there had seen,
A wall behind his back, over his head
A latticed window. His glance went up at times
As though one listened there, and his voice sank
Or let its meaning mix into the strings. (*VP* 180)

In the spring of 1933 Yeats learned that he was to receive an honorary degree from Cambridge in June, an event that allowed him to accept an invitation to recite his poems at Oxford a few days earlier. The invitation had come from an undergraduate at Christ Church, Richard Rumbold, who was currently enjoying a *succès de scandale* with his novel *Little Victims* (1933), which had offended dons, Roman Catholics, and good taste in describing the suicidal demise of a youth who became entangled with dissolute Oxonians. Rumbold, whom John Betjeman damned as a "ghastly and pretentious undergraduate," had successfully revived the English Club by arranging recent appearances by his friend Lord Alfred Douglas, Richard Aldington, and Frieda Lawrence at the Taylorian Institute, one of the largest halls in Oxford, chock full at 500, as it was for Yeats.[21] One member of the Club's welcoming party was Derek Patmore, great-grandson of Yeats's master metricist Coventry Patmore. Before the reading, Patmore observed that Yeats seemed exhausted and distracted, but as they approached the Institute, which was "packed with eager attentive undergraduates," he grew animated and seemed to be "filled with a secret force."[22] Formally dressed in an old-fashioned evening coat with tails and bow tie as in the performances of his younger days, Yeats stepped on the platform to a roar of applause, bowing graciously "like a king accepting his due." After a few introductory remarks about the aims and ideas behind his poems, he began

21. Rumbold's precocious notoriety earned international coverage in *Time*, June 19, 1933, 2.
22. Derek Patmore, *Private History* (London: Jonathan Cape, 1960), 217–18. Patmore incorrectly places the reading in the spring of 1935, but Rumbold, who was no longer at Oxford in 1935, records the event in his diary entry for June 6, 1933: "Yeats meeting a great success." See *A Message in Code: The Diary of Richard Rumbold 1932–1960*, ed. William Plomer (London: Weidenfeld & Nicolson, 1964), 32.

to chant them. "He had a particularly beautiful voice and used it with consummate skill," wrote Patmore:

> Almost intoning some of the passages, he made an elaborate orchestration out of the words and rhythms, and the quietened hall was filled with the lovely verbal music. Evocations of a far-off legendary Ireland, the bitter words of a disappointed patriot, the cries of a passionate lover, and the memory of friends: all lent their moods and sounds to this poetic symphony, and the audience listened in hushed silence.

Patmore did not know that he was witnessing Yeats's last great reading before a large public audience, but he did sense that he had been part of a privileged occasion, that something of value in the history and hearing of poetry was coming to an end.

> Standing there alone on the platform, now old and forced to wear spectacles but with an inner fire burning in him, W. B. Yeats had a majesty belonging to another world . . . and as his magnificent voice rolled out his verses he looked more like an ancient prophet than a man of today. At one moment . . . he talked of his friends, and especially of Lady Gregory and her house at Coole. I remember that he recited 'The Wild Swans at Coole' . . . Soon the recital was over, and we left the hall realizing that never again should we hear a modern poet read his own poems with such eloquence and expressiveness.[23]

Yeats had written to Sturge Moore that the Oxford and Cambridge outings were "legitimate forms of self-advertisement," and he would tell George that the Oxford experience, which included Rumbold's cocktail party for members of the English Club, was "pleasant,"[24] but his contact with undergraduates in both places had a sobering, disturbing effect on him: while they paid homage, they wanted to hear from him about the exciting poets whose poetry and criticism they were now reading—Eliot, Pound, Auden, and the younger generation of poets he had parted from at the end of the war. As will be seen, the evidence that this new modern school was displacing his own would preoccupy him for the next two years and determine the course of future decisions and advertisements.

23. Yeats, Rumbold, and other members of the English Club were photographed by the *Oxford Mail* and printed on the front page on 6 July (see Plate 20 and caption, where Derek Palmer should be Derek Patmore). A brief report of the reading appeared under the title "Mr. W. B. Yeats Reveals His Poet's Shrine | Readings and Reminiscences for the | Oxford University English Club" (6). Once again, Yeats told the anecdote of the American elocutionist asking him why he read his poems in such a strange manner. At Cambridge, Yeats was appropriately honoured with Marchese Gugliemo Marconi, inventor of the wireless. (*Cambridge Daily News*, June 8, 1933), 5.
24. Letters to Sturge Moore of June 4 and to George of [June 7, 1933], *CL InteLex* 5890, 5893.

After Oxford and Cambridge, Yeats's public readings would be almost exclusively before BBC microphones, and his next invitation was to participate in "St Patrick's Night" (March 17, 1934), an hour-long broadcast from the Belfast studios, announced as "A Programme of Irish Music and Humour, and Poetry by W. B. Yeats spoken by himself." Taking much of his content from the Oxford reading, he now began to shape his commentary and to choose poems that exemplified his reaction against Victorian rhetoric and his lifelong effort to write passionate verse with simple emotions, emphasizing his ready formula, "natural words in their natural order." "When I was a young man poetry had become eloquent and elaborate," he began. "Swinburne was the reigning influence and he was very eloquent. A generation came that wanted to be simple, I think I wanted that more than anybody else."[25] From poem to chanted poem Yeats traced his poetic and dramatic aims and the increasing opposition to them, stating that he had to make his thoughts "modern" in order to overcome that opposition:

> Modern thought is not simple; I became argumentative, passionate, bitter; when I was very bitter I used to say to myself, "I do not write for these people who attack everything that I value, not for those others who are lukewarm friends, I am writing for a man I have never seen."

Out of his frustrated desire to write "for my own race | And the reality," and in scorn of his attackers, he imagined into being another figure for his phantasmagoria, a simple, unnamed fisherman from Connemara: "I said to myself, 'I do not know whether he is born yet, but born or unborn it is for him I write.' " Yeats thus closed the broadcast by chanting "The Fisherman" (1914), the first angry expression of his now fully developed poetic, crying out his determination to write for him "one | Poem maybe as cold | And passionate as the dawn."[26]

Behind the scene of this third broadcast, a sequence of persons had begun making their way into Yeats's life, as if arranged by fate, all contemporary

25. The edited script of Yeats's contribution to the broadcast was published in *The Listener* of April 4, 1934, as "The Growth of a Poet," 591–2, and is included in *Later Articles and Reviews*, 249–53, here 249.

26. Yeats would later find the private despair that seeks internal strength through the creative will analogous to the public despair that seeks an external form of strength through the will. "When there is despair, public or private," he wrote to Dorothy Wellesley in 1935, "when settled order seems lost, people look for strength within or without. The lasting expression of our time is not this obvious choice [Marxian socialism or Major Douglas' social credit] but in a sense of something steel-like & cold within the will, something passionate and cold" (Letter of July 6, 1935, *CL InteLex* 6274).

counterparts of the musicians, actresses, poets, and friends that had helped him initiate his early experiments in speaking to the psaltery. A young California musician struggling to find a musical life in New York, Harry Partch, had written to Yeats in October 1933, requesting permission to write a musical score for *Sophocles' King Oedipus* according to a new system of intonation that he was developing for the speaking voice. Yeats mislaid the letter for two months before sending permission in January and expressing his "complete sympathy" with Partch's "exceedingly interesting" theory of a music rooted in the spoken word.[27] When Partch received a timely Carnegie Fellowship to study intonation in London that autumn, he notified Yeats of his plans to visit him. Partch had been inspired by Yeats's description of the degeneration of words in modern music and of his search for a poet's musician. "I have but one art," Yeats had written, "that of speech, and my feeling for music dissociated from speech is very slight, and listening as I do to the words with the better part of my attention, there is no modern song sung in the modern way that is not to my taste 'ludicrous' and 'impossible.' " Partch loved Yeats's declaration in that passage, "I hear with older ears than the musician," and felt that Yeats was speaking directly to him in concluding the note:

> I have to find men with more music than I have, who will develop to a finer subtilty the singing of the cottage and the forecastle, and develop it more on the side of speech than that of music, until it has become intellectual and nervous enough to be the vehicle of a Shelley or a Keats. For some purposes it will be necessary to divine the lineaments of a still older art, and re-create the regulated declamations that died out when music fell into its earliest elaborations.

When Partch thus asked him about the employment of his vocal theories in the production of *Sophocles' King Oedipus,* Yeats replied that he had made no attempt to carry out his theories in the play, "nor have I done so since Florence Farr died. We used, I think singers from the Cathedral."[28] And though Yeats insisted that with his unmusical mind he could be of little help to Partch, seemingly reluctant to entertain an abandoned cause, he agreed to receive him in November.

In the midst of his correspondence with Partch, Yeats received a letter of admiration from a beautiful, recently married (for the second time, now

27. Yeats answered Partch's letter of October 27, 1933 on January 6, 1934, *CL InteLex* 5992.
28. Letter of mid-July 1934, *CL InteLex* 6070. Yeats had allowed Lennox Robinson to use singers from the Palestrina Choir in St. Patrick's Cathedral, Dublin, for the production.

with an infant) actress, Margot Collis, the acting name of twenty-seven-year-old Margot Ruddock Lovell, who, seeking work on the London stage, praised his work and asked if they might meet when he was next in London. Replying that he would "try not to lose" her letter so that he could contact her, he was readily seeking an infatuation in the aftermath of his Steinach procedure (essentially a vasectomy) the previous April. On September 24, her letter in hand, he wrote that one word of hers, describing the "trueness" of his work, had brought him out of his artistic solitude, and, moreover, that he would be in London on October 3 and would reserve his time for their meeting on the 4th: "perhaps I shall put a book in your hand to ask you to read out some poems, that too one of the ways to knowledge."[29]

Their first brief meeting took place as planned, with the reading of poems evidently mixed in with the lively prospect of discussing and founding a new Poets' Theatre in a fortnight's time. Yeats and George were passing through London on their way to a theatre conference in Rome with Ashley Dukes, the playwright, critic, and proponent of little theatre companies who had broached the idea of a Poets' Theatre to Yeats. For the week following his return to London on October 17, when George would go on to Dublin alone, Yeats had taken a furnished flat in Seymour Street, eschewing the lack of privacy in his usual rooms at the Savile Club. Enamored of Margot and pleased that she agreed to meet him at the flat upon his return, he assured her by letter the day after their brief meeting that she was "bound to nothing; not even to come & look at me."[30] Before departure, he sent her a copy of Bhagwan Shri Hamsa's *The Holy Mountain*, introduced by Yeats and translated by his friend Shri Purohit Swami, through whom he was exploring Tantric sexual arousal and sublimation, and to whom he promised her an introduction.[31] Feeding

29. Letter of September 24, 1934, *CL InteLex* 6100.
30. Letter of October 5, [1934], *CL InteLex* 6106.
31. In his introduction, Yeats had begun to discuss the transformation of sexual into spiritual desire through meditation in which "all passion aroused in his present life" is offered to the divine object (*E&I* 463); his specific focus on Tantric sublimation of sexual desire actually begins in "The Mandukya Upanishad," first published in Eliot's *Criterion* (July 1935) under the title "*Māndookya Upanishad* with an Introduction by William Butler Yeats": "An Indian devotee may recognise that he approaches the Self through a transfiguration of sexual desire; he repeats thousands of times a day words of adoration, calls before his eyes a thousand times the divine image. He is not always solitary, there is another method, that of the Tantric philosophy, where a man and woman, when in sexual union, transfigure each others's images into the masculine and feminine characters of God, but the man must not finish, vitality must not pass beyond his body, beyond his being. There are married people who, though they do not forbid passage of the seed, practice, not necessarily at the moment of union, a meditation,

his fantasy in Rome, he informed her that he was rewriting *The King of the Great Clock Tower* to give the silent Queen a speaking part for her to act. He had already begun to imagine her as his new mistress of chanted verse, a successor to Florence Farr: "O my dear," he wrote, "my mind is so busy with your future & perhaps you will reject all my plans—my calculation is that, as you are a trained actress, a lovely sense of rhythm will make you a noble speaker of verse—a singer and sayer. You will read certain poems to me, I have no doubts of the result, & <on Wednesday> October 19 I begin the practical work."[32]

The work at hand during the week of his return to Margot was to meet with Ashley Dukes, who owned the small Mercury Theatre at Notting Hill. Dukes offered to support a season of poetic plays to be performed by Rupert Doone's Group Theatre company at the Mercury. Dismayed by the predominance of realistic drama at the Abbey, Yeats eagerly sought a new outlet for his dance plays in London and envisaged Margot as the singer and sayer whom he would train for that enterprise. He formed a committee of Dukes, Doone, Dulac, Frederick Ashton, T. S. Eliot (who had already been working with the Group toward a production of *Sweeney Agonistes*), Margot, and himself to proceed with plans, delaying his return to Dublin until the last day of the month with every excuse to George. The initial plan was to open with a triptych of Yeats's plays: *A Full Moon in March, The Player Queen*, and *The Resurrection*, to be followed by a double-bill of Auden's *The Dance of Death* and Eliot's *Sweeney Agonistes*. After having lunch with Yeats, Eliot wrote to Ottoline Morrell of his immense liking and admiration of him and of having agreed to collaborate in "Yeats's theatre season."[33] Although some members of the committee objected to Yeats working with Auden and Eliot on the grounds that "comparison with rival schools prevents proper understanding," Yeats was keen to stage his plays against the younger "radical" poets and playwrights whose "disillusioned" work had come into challenging prominence.

Back home in Rathfarnham, Yeats fixed his imagination on Margot and her future with him. Informing the Dulacs of her talents, he had Helen Beauclerk cast her horoscope. Evidently unhappy with the results, and

wherein the man seeks the divine Self as present in his wife, the wife the divine Self as present in the man" (*E&I* 484).

32. Letter of [October 11, 1934], *CL InteLex* 6110.

33. Letter of October 29, 1934, to Ottoline Morrell; quoted in Michael Sidnell, *Dances of Death: The Group Theatre of London in the Thirties* (London: Faber and Faber, 1984), 267.

perhaps sensing an underlying instability, he had her recast it with corrected dates and times: "It makes the horoscope stronger & more stable so far as the general life is concerned."[34] When he wrote to her on November 13 she was "My dearest": he planned to write two poems for her, and he asked her to practice the recitation of five or six of his poems in preparation for his return to London with the zither used for Dulac's music. Hard at work on *A Full Moon in March* (the verse version of *King of the Great Clock Tower*) for the new theatre project, he envisaged Margot as the Queen, telling her of his plans "to introduce you as a 'sayer' of my verse before the play begins."[35] The following day, in the heat of these plans, Harry Partch arrived in Dublin and made his way to Yeats.

Partch had been developing a unique system of intonation. Avoiding the twelve notes of the diatonic scale as he studied theories of tonality abandoned in the seventeenth century, he used mathematical ratios to divide an octave into forty-three distinct microtones, all of which he had marked on the expanded fingerboard of the custom-made viola he brought with him. Partch sensed that Yeats awaited the exposition of his method with "guarded worry and disbelief," that is, until Partch spoke to the tones of his viola the 137th Psalm, "By the Rivers of Babylon," the *pièce de resistance* of Florence Farr. "Now, in the flood of comment that followed my playing, the feeling of disbelief was entirely dispelled."[36] Yeats was fascinated by his explanation of how voice and instrument worked in the ancient manner to preserve the inherent rhythm and tone of individual words. Partch knew their views were in perfect accord when, in a statement he would never forget, Yeats declared, "No word shall have an intonation or accentuation it could not have in passionate speech." Partch illustrated his method of intonation further with translations of the Chinese poet Li Po; in turn, he sought Yeats's assistance in interpreting his *Oedipus*. Although Yeats continued to insist that his ignorance of music prevented any help, he was easily persuaded to chant the choruses. "I can still hear his reading," wrote Partch, "of the line: *For Death is all the fashion now, till even Death be dead*. I made diagrams of his inflections, but my memory of his vibrant tones is more accurate than my marks."[37] Yeats wrote twice to

34. Letter of November 6, [1934], *CL InteLex* 6120.
35. Letter of November 13, 1934, *CL InteLex* 6124.
36. Harry Partch, *Bitter Music: Collected Journals, Essays, Introductions, and Librettos*, ed. Thomas McGeary (University of Illinois Press, 2000), 166.
37. Ibid. 167. The quoted line (124) is from the Chorus of *Sophocles' King Oedipus* (*VPl* 814).

inform Margot of Partch's striking way of wedding words and music and to describe techniques that she could adopt for her own recitations. He was particularly impressed by the manner in which Partch achieved variety by breaking up his vocal monotone with the singing of nonsense words. "He only introduces melody when he sings vowels without any relation to words."[38] This was exactly the effect that Yeats had sought in adding "*Fol de rol, fol de rol*" as a nonsense refrain between the stanzas of "Crazy Jane Reproved":

> I think when you find words like that in an old ballad, they are meant to be sung to a melody, as Partch . . . sings his "meaningless words" . . . I put "fol de rol" at the end of the stanzas in this poem to make it less didactic, gayer, more clearly a song. If you feel inclined to you may put such words at the end of any stanza of any poem where there is not already a burden.[39]

Yeats met with Partch on at least four of the seven days he was in Dublin, inviting friends in to hear him, including AE, who on hearing that Partch planned to set Yeats's play to music informed him as a matter of course that Yeats was tone deaf, had no feeling for music, could not distinguish one note from another, and could not carry a tune.[40] Partch prodded Yeats into arranging meetings with Abbey actors, too, for the primary aim of his visit to Dublin was to hear both Yeats and his actors speaking the lines of the play; he would make graphs and notations of their speech inflections and use them as the basis for a setting. He showed them a cardboard model of a chromatic organ he was designing, with a keyboard of forty-three tones arranged like a typewriter, and described at least two other instruments that he would devise for a score and production. Yeats agreed in principle with his plans, and in the exciting thought of seeing *Sophocles' King Oedipus* produced according to his own dramatic and choral principles, he spoke to Partch of seeking chanters for an eventual performance, even of the possibility of him writing music for one of Yeats's or Eliot's poetic plays at their new theatre. Exhilarated by the visit, Yeats sent him off to London with letters of introduction to Dulac and Dolmetsch,

38. Letter of [November 17, 1934], *CL InteLex* 6126.
39. Letter of November 23, [1924], *CL InteLex* 6134.
40. Partch defended Yeats against such "calumnies" of observation, describing them as "commonplace utterances": " 'No feeling for music' . . . as an idea is literally an impossibility in the human animal. And the inability to carry a tune is more like hypersensitivity to tone. Such a person hears all the tones in the gamut, instead of the seven or eight or twelve our musical fathers have insisted must be our limit. In answer to such critics I like to quote Yeats's own words: 'I hear with older ears than the musician' " (*Bitter Music*, 166).

seeking their confirmation of the validity of Partch's theory of music and words. Promising to meet Partch in London and to introduce him to more friends, he said more in anticipation than farewell, "You are one of those young men with ideas, the development of which is impossible to foretell, just as I was thirty years ago."[41]

Yeats wrote immediately to Dulac, alerting him to Partch's impending visit. "His whole system is based upon a series of notes within the range of the speaking voice," he reported excitedly:

> within that range he has found a series of minute intervals more minute than quarter tones. He believes that he has rediscovered the foundation of Greek & Chinese music. He never sings or even chants to his viola but always speaks, and every inflexion and tone of his voice is recorded in the score. He is, in fact, working out what Florence Farr and I attempted but with a science and a knowledge of music beyond Florence Farr's reach. I want you to hear him.[42]

Dulac was also charmed by the "tall big-boned youth," as Yeats had described Partch. Yeats had informed Dulac that he did not think Partch's method of speaking to musical notes was sufficiently developed to help them with the London theatre project just yet, but that he expected it would in future. When Dulac and Partch discussed Yeats's dance plays, Dulac confirmed what Yeats had told Partch in Dublin, that the music was ineffective—an admission that they had not made previously to each other. Partch later explained that "although the scores show syllables allotted exact tones, in the actual rendition the spoken tones and the music were generally not integrated, except by accident." He noted further:

> I gathered that a complete understanding as to purpose, as between poet and composers and executants, was lacking; also, it was evident that the *sine qua non* of any such effort—persistence in the face of apparent failure—was not a party to the adventure."[43]

Although Dulac was not prepared to endorse Partch's theory without a full exhibition, he "guaranteed" his music to Yeats, as did George Antheil, whose music for Yeats's last dance play had had just been published.[44]

41. Ibid. 167. 42. Letter of November 21, 1934, *CL InteLex* 6130.

43. Harry Partch, *Genesis of a Music* (Madison: University of Wisconsin Press, 1949), 39.

44. In his preface to *Wheels and Butterflies*, Yeats wrote that all his dance plays had been revived at the Abbey except *Fighting the Waves*, "which drew large audiences, not at all, because Mr. George Antheil's most strange, most dramatic music requires a large expensive orchestra. A memory of that orchestra has indeed roused a distinguished Irish lyric poet to begin a dance play which he assures me requires but a tin whistle and a large expensive concertina" (p. vi).

Yeats had written a similar letter that same day to Dolmetsch, regretting their long lack of contact and expressing "the most admiring memories of those old days." "He is working on the problem you and I and Florence Farr worked on many years ago," he wrote of Partch, "music for, and a notation of the speaking voice. . . . Should he present to you the formal note of introduction which I have given him please ask him to come and see you, to bring his viola (made according to his own principles) and to expound his discovery."[45] Dolmetsch received Partch in Haselmere as requested, but it was an inauspicious meeting: Partch did not take his viola, only the cardboard keyboard, and he did not stand up well to Dolmetsch's intensive interrogation about his music and instrument making. "I don't think he had ever met any one who could do that," Dolmetsch wrote to Yeats. "He could not (why?) use one of my instruments." Dolmetsch assured Yeats that he was quite willing to hear Partch demonstrate his method and give him an opinion, but that Partch, evidently intimidated by Dolmetsch's overbearing authority and inquisition, departed "rather suddenly" and never returned.[46]

Aside from this disappointing report, however, Dolmetsch expressed the "thrill of pleasure" that Yeats's letter brought him. He too was transported by memories of their early friendship, making him wish that they could meet again "and revive some of the joys of the old days":

> The experiments we made together are fresh in my mind. We achieved success. We had not found the best solution of the problem, but even then the art of reciting to fixed tones would have progressed had we found a few people endowed with poetic feeling and really musical, that is having a quick and accurate ear and fingers sufficiently responsible.[47]

And yet his memory of Farr's performances was not so complimentary, in part because, as a musician, he found her insufficiently skilled with the psaltery, in part because he seems to have been disappointed by the quality of her performance at his concert in Boston in 1907. "Florence Farr had the poetic feeling," he continued. "All went well when I played for her—but

45. Letter of November 21, 1934, *CL InteLex* 6131.

46. Partch's account of the meeting, from which he left "very happy," is contradictory. "In Partch's version of the meeting," writes his biographer, "Dolmetsch, talking effusively about ancient writings on music, refers to Marin Mersenne's *Harmonie universelle* and is astonished when Partch asks him which edition of the book he is referring to, stammering out: 'For *twenty* years I have been talking about Mersenne, and nobody even knows who I am talking about. And now you—you ask me which edition!" See Bob Gilmore, *Harry Partch* (New Haven: Yale University Press, 1998), 107.

47. Letter of December 17, 1934 (*LTWBY2* 568–9).

she could not follow her own voice with her instrument, specially when performing in public!"[48]

Shortly after receiving Dolmetsch's letter, Yeats fell seriously ill with lung congestion and was bedridden in Dublin until mid-March, preventing any further meeting with Partch, for whom Yeats now apologized, aggrieved to learn that he did not take his viola to Dolmetsch as requested: "He could not, or would not play on your instruments, I suppose, because his intervals are different. He is in Germany now as far as I know."[49] With news of Partch's European travels and impending return to America, Yeats realized that this promising episode with a poet's musician had been a pipe dream. He longed to bring Dolmetsch back into his company, especially after reading his description of the "Bardic Music" that he had recently deciphered from an ancient Welsh manuscript. "Those who have heard this music on the little harps I have made for it, with the crwth, are moved to an incredible degree."[50] In writing his last wistful sentence to Dolmetsch, Yeats knew that any renewed collaboration was impossible: "I wish I saw some chance of our meeting again," he wrote; "I have the particularly fine psaltery you made for Mrs. Emery she gave it me when she went to Ceylon."

48. When Dolmetsch responded to Joseph Hone's request for his reminiscences about Yeats, Farr, and the psaltery for his biography of Yeats, he replied: "In my own room, with nobody but Yeats and myself present, it was delightful. But I got engagements for her in America and it came out that in public, she raised the pitch of her voice and was not capable of following it with the Psaltery, as I did myself. Result, the whole thing was discordant; she did not know it and it ended in failure. I never found a reciter with a sufficiently musical ear to *listen* to the instrument and make the voice and the instrument fit together. The art of listening is almost extinct among the present day Singers, as witness the way they get out of tune with their accompaniments. Listeners have become hardened to this" (NLI MS 5919; partially quoted in Joseph Hone, *W. B. Yeats 1865–1939* [London: Macmillan, 1942], 191).

49. Letter of March 18, 1935, *CL InteLex* 6204. Partch had actually gone to Rapallo, where he briefly met with Pound, to work on his book, *Genesis of a Music*, which he unsuccessfully asked Yeats to introduce. It did not appear until 1949.

50. Dolmetsch had recently written about the Welsh manuscript (British Library, Add. MS 14905) in *The Consort*, Special Number (June 1934). Dolmetch's article, "Concerning My Recent Discoveries," followed by his "Analysis of the Harmonies and Forms of the Bardic Music," had been transcribed "from a manuscript of William Penllyn, a celebrated minstrel . . . and is stated to comprise 'The Music of Britain, as settled by a congress of chief musicians . . . about A.D. 1040, with some of the most ancient pieces of the Britons, supposed to be music itself, which is utterly unlike any music previously known to us. I doubt if it could have originated at any date later than the eighth century" (7). When Dolmetsch with his six-string crwth and his wife with her two harps performed the music in Bangor, the response, she wrote, "was electrifying; and during the 'death song of Ivan the Smith' (*Caniad Marwnad Ivan y Gov*), a deep groan ran through the assembly in the most poignant stanza" (Mabel Dolmetsch, *Personal Recollections of Arnold Dolmetsch* [New York: Macmillan, 1958], 153).

Yeats would never see Dolmetsch or Partch again. Partch left for the United States in March on a freighter, arriving to find himself in a jobless economic Depression that pushed him into an eight-year period of hobo wandering; moreover, seventeen years would pass before he wrote and produced his setting of Yeats's *King Oedipus*.[51] In the travel-journal of his days with Yeats, he captured succinctly the essence of their brief encounter: "Yeats was too early for me, and I was too late for Yeats."[52] Nonetheless, the timely association with Partch and Margot, the renewed contact with Dolmetsch, the promise of the Poets' Theatre, and the broadcasting experiences had fully reactivated his long deferred dream. He had already begun to bring new poets and musicians into his company to make it real.

II

The autumn of 1934 had been for Yeats an extraordinarily productive period that saw not only the publication of *Wheels and Butterflies*, *The Collected Plays,* and *The King of the Great Clock Tower*, but the near-completion of a new autobiographical chapter *Dramatis Personae*, the undertaking of a new edition of *A Vision,* and commitments to produce *The Oxford Book of Modern Verse* and to assist Shri Purohit Swami with his translation of *The Ten Principal Upanishads*. A principal preoccupation, nonetheless, was the preparation of the first issue of a new series of monthly broadsides to begin in January 1935. Edited in collaboration with the poet and folk-musician F. R. Higgins, the poems were to be accompanied by tunes arranged by the Abbey musician and master of Irish airs Arthur Duff, color illustrations by Irish artists, Jack Yeats prominent among them, and published by his sister Lolly at the Cuala Press.[53] Yeats's plan was to retrieve old poems, ballads, and songs from eighteenth-century Ireland and mix them with new ones by modern Irish poets to show the vitality and persistence of the ballad tradition in which he had immersed himself in the 1880s and 1890s. He had already cast his mind back to that period of the literary

51. The first performances took place at Mills College in Oakland, California, in November 1951. When Partch subsequently sought to issue a recording of one of the performances, having had Yeats's verbal permission to write the score in 1934, he was denied permission by Yeats's agent in accordance with Yeats's general policy against musical settings of his work.
52. Partch, *Bitter Music*, 167.
53. Yeats was inspired to revive Jack Yeats's illustrations of ballads and poems in *A Broadside* (1908–15), adding musical accompaniments.

revival in writing *Dramatis Personae,* and in the introduction to *The King of the Great Clock Tower* he had summarized the history of the psaltery experiments on platform and stage with Dolmetsch and Farr up to his abandoned emphasis on rhythmical speech in the production of his plays. "The orchestra brings more elaborate music and I have gone over to the enemy," he declared sardonically, saying that the audience "can find my words in the book if they are curious, but we will not thrust our secret upon them" (*VPl* 1009–10). But in revisiting the early revival, he perceived that the ideals he asserted and fostered there had to be recaptured as the basis for any new revival. He thus returned to writing ballads once again, with every expectation now of their public performance. When he was writing the poems in *Words for Music Perhaps*, the title was merely a fantasy: " 'For Music' is only a name," he lamented to Olivia Shakespear, "nobody will sing them."[54] Now, however, the old and new ballads might be sung both on the Abbey stage and on the wireless. "Yeats had heard the ballad singers in fairs and markets," Duff recalled of their conversations, "crying out their pointed words in dramatic passion to catch and hold the ears of the passing crowd. And he wanted the songs of Irish poets sung among Irish people and at convivial meetings of the Irish Academy of Letters."[55]

Thus, the new broadsides were to constitute, in effect, a monthly updating and living renewal of his *A Book of Irish Verse*, with the addition of music from an adapted Irish air or tune and a colored illustration for each work. In the months ahead he would return to Halliday Sparling's *Irish Minstrelsy* and to his editions of *A Book of Irish Verse* for broadside material, including the anonymous street ballads "Johnnie I Hardly Knew Ye," "The Croppy Boy," "The Boyne Water," "Famine Song," and Thomas Moore's "At the Mid Hour of Night" among others.[56] Where he had included his early contemporaries (Hyde, Tynan, AE) in *A Book of Irish Verse*, he would now extend the tradition by including in the broadsides poets of the succeeding

54. Letter of September 13, 1929, *L* 769; *CL InteLex* 5285.
55. Arthur Duff, broadcast of May 5, 1953, on his meeting with Higgins and Lennox Robinson; reproduced on Evin O'Meara's Arthur Duff website: http://homepage.eircom.net/~arthurduff/Broadcasts.htm#Broadcasthiggins.
56. In the preface, "Anglo-Irish Ballads," to the bound volume of *Broadsides* (Dublin: Cuala Press, 1935), Yeats characterized or justified many of his choices of old ballads, saying of the inclusion of Moore's poem, which he had included in BIV_1 11–12, "This poem, and perhaps one other, are the only poems of Moore that have the poet's rhythm; his musician Stephenson made Irish tunes conform to modern notation, and Moore, a man without background, tradition, felt himself free to invent or copy mechanical, facile rhythm" (*P&I* 178).

generation (Stephens, Colum), whose work, he believed, had since entered the popular mind, and contemporary poets (himself, Higgins, Gogarty, and the Gaelic translations of Frank O'Connor), whose lyrics also spoke to the common man. Together with his *Oxford Book of Modern Verse*, the volumes would be set against and serve as a counter to the modern school of Eliot, Pound, and Auden.

The immediate inspiration for the broadsides had come from his collaboration with Arthur Duff on the music or "tunes" for "Three Songs to the Same Tune," and for songs in *The King of the Great Clock Tower*, including "The Wicked Hawthorn Tree," "Three Songs to the Same Tune," and "Alternative Song for the Severed Head." Duff, director of the Abbey orchestra, recounted their several sessions in the theatre, remembering what pleasure Yeats got from the combination of acting, speaking, and music as long as the words kept their natural rhythm when they rose into song:

> Rhythm was his strong point and I had a lively respect for his judgment. Every tune, he always used the word "tune", had to be played over to him many times. As if he were testing it, sampling it and sizing its character. He would sit in the darkened theatre with only very little orchestral light over the upright piano. I at the piano, Yeats a few feet behind me in the front row of the stalls. I would strum out the tune and I could hear the low voice of the poet speaking the words and testing if the speed of his speech fitted the speed of my notes. Sometimes he would move on too quickly for me or slow up and I would have to adjust my tune to suit his speech rhythm.[57]

For Yeats, struggling patiently to see that Duff's musical notation was as close as possible to the "tune" to which he wrote the poem, the arduous process was analogous to his sessions of regulated declamation with Dolmetsch. "But we would usually hit it off pretty well," Duff continued,

> because I worked him as hard as he worked me. I never attempted to write a note of music for a line of his until I had made him recite every line about a dozen times. A thing he was only too delighted to do and hearing him chant in that monotone of his I rarely left him without some line, some tune coming into my head. Maybe having played a new tune for him he would be silent and I would be afraid to ask him what he thought because I knew his silence meant he was not satisfied. But when I detected a certain suppressed excitement and a quick movement of his head I knew he was pleased and

57. Transcribed from Duff's notes for his 1939 broadcast on Yeats (HRHRC, W. R. Rogers Papers, 26). An edited version appears on Evin O'Meara's Arthur Duff website: http://homepage.eircom.net/~arthurduff/Broadcasts.htm#Broadcastyeats

expectant, and we would break up the session, and he would take me off to the Kildare St. Club for a cup of tea and a crumpet.

From these cordial sessions came Duff's "tune" for "The Wicked Hawthorn Tree," Yeats's separate title for the song sung at the end of the play by the Queen's two attendants as she lays the Stroller's severed head upon her breast (*VPl* 1003–5). Illustrated by Victor Brown and accompanied by Duff's music (see Plate 18), the song appeared with Richard Alfred Milliken's "The Groves of Blarney" (*c*.1798) in the second issue of *A Broadside* (February 1935), the past and present connected in song.[58]

As the early issues of broadsides appeared, Yeats was working assiduously on selections for *The Oxford Book of Modern Verse*, reading widely in poetry written after the death of Tennyson, looking in every corner for authors and poems that he could place within the threatened tradition of passionate syntax. He had discovered and immersed himself in the poems of Margot, praising her potential genius, and to bring her into the theatre movement he had Ashton and Dulac work with her on rhythmical speech. He then took her to Ottoline Morrell and friends to recite and sing poems in preparation for reciting to Eliot, Auden, and other members of the committee on the stage of the Mercury Theatre. In discussing Eliot's poems and presence on the committee, Margot told Yeats that her husband said that many people could write "for fun" something better than what Eliot had done in *The Waste Land*. Yeats politely agreed but insisted on keeping him: "I want Eliot for the Mercury because he represents a movement that has grown all over the world and is strong at the Universities. It seeks modernness in language and metaphor and helps us to get rid of what Rossetti called 'soulless self-reflections of man's skill' but it does throw out the baby with the bath-water."[59] When she later pressed him about including Eliot in the

58. Yeats had included Milliken's ballad in *BIV1*; it appeared here with a note by Yeats, who was not averse to modernizing the diction, stating that of several extant versions of the ballad "the version published in this Broadside shows the touch of a more modern hand." Duff's music accompanied Yeats's "The Rose Tree" in no. 5 (May 1935) and "The Soldier Takes Pride" (part III of "Three Songs to the Same Tune") in no. 12 (December 1935).

59. Letter of [November 17, 1934], *CL InteLex* 6126. Yeats quotes from Dante Gabriel Rossetti's sonnet "St. Luke the Painter" (1849), in which Art, taught to pray by Luke the Evangelist, "turned in vain | To soulless self-reflections of man's skill". He would quote the line again in his introduction to the *OBMV*: "A modern writer is beset by what Rossetti called 'the soulless self-reflections of man's skill'; the more vivid his nature, the greater his boredom, a boredom no Greek, no Elizabethan, knew in like degree, if at all. He may escape to the classics with the writers I have just described, or with much loss of self-control and coherence force language against its will into a powerful, artificial vividness" (xviii).

Oxford anthology, he had become even more emphatic about his purpose in working out the dynamic of his choices: "I am trying to understand for the sake of my *Cambridge* [*sic*] *Book of Modern Verse* the Auden, Eliot school. I do not mean to give it a great deal of space, but must define my objections to it, and I cannot know this till I see clearly what quality it has [that has] made it delight young Cambridge and young Oxford. When you and I have argued it out my mind may clear."[60] He could only define the qualities that they lacked, however, and these he expressed freely in letters to friends, including the novelist and journalist Ethel Mannin, a new rival to Margot for his affections. "Nothing is poetry that does not run in one's head because of the sweetness or majesty of the sound," he wrote to her. "Owing to the struggle for new subject matter the younger poets to-day lack that sound."[61] By the time he wrote the introduction to the volume, which he approached in the belief that "*vers libre* lost much of its vogue some five years ago" (*OBMV* xli), the modern dilemma was clear to him. "I too have tried to be modern," he wrote of his own experience, aware of the visionary cost that his poetry had paid between the marriage of Maud Gonne in 1903 and his marriage to George in 1917. "They have pulled off the mask ... Here stands not this or that man but man's naked mind" (*OBMV* xxxvi).

As his seventieth birthday approached, Yeats signed a contract with the BBC in London for a celebratory broadcast, "W. B. Yeats reading his own poems." Although he wrote the script and chose the poems, he deferred to one of the BBC's own readers, Audrey Moran, evidently under pressure from family and friends to be present for a birthday event in Dublin. Whatever the reason, someone wrote on the contract, "No longer

60. Letter of February 25, [1935], *CL InteLex* 6189.

61. Letter of [June 8, 1935], *CL InteLex* 6250. In her memoir, *Privileged Spectator*, revised edition (London: Jarrolds, 1948), Mannin, too, declared that Yeats "was tone deaf" and that settings of his poems to music outraged him. When she attempted to play for him the records of Peter Warlock's settings for his "Curlew" poems (1924), which she admired, he refused to hear them all: "he hooted with laughter—the singer's voice rose when he contended that it should fall, and the whole thing seemed grotesque to him; it was terrible, he said, ridiculous, and proceeded to chant some of the lines in illustration of how they should be rendered to give them the meaning they were intended to convey" (64). Another of her lovers, Reginald Reynolds, whom she subsequently married, was introduced by her to Yeats at the Shelbourne, "where we began talking of oratory and acting ... [Yeats] spoke of that moment in drama or oratory where all gesture becomes worse than superfluous 'and you must hold your audience by your voice and your eyes alone.' ... He began presently to tell us of Irish orators whom he had heard in his youth ... He could recall long passages from their speeches" (*My Life and Crimes* [London: Jarrolds, 1956], 59).

reading these himself."[62] More broadcasts lay ahead, but, as recurring illness gradually weakened his voice, those of the poems would henceforth be arranged primarily for other reciters under his instruction.

Yeats's search for contemporary poets in his own tradition led him to poems by Dorothy Wellesley, the Duchess of Wellington. "I had never heard of her," he wrote. "My eyes filled with tears. I read in excitement that was the more delightful because it showed I had not lost my understanding of poetry" (*P&I* 182). He wrote to her at once, stating that he saw her poems as "an example of nobility of style—the noblest style I have met of late years."[63] He immediately prevailed upon Ottoline to arrange a meeting at Lady Wellesley's late-seventeenth-century country house, Penns in the Rocks, in East Sussex. With its pastoral landscape, ordered gardens, sophisticated company, baroque paintings, and rich library in leather bindings, Yeats wanted it to fill the need that Coole Park had provided until Lady Gregory's death three years earlier. And Yeats's praise of Wellesley's poetry filled a great need for her, too. As their friendship developed rapidly over the summer, with Yeats making extended visits to Penns, he would begin to take her into his confidence about the aims of his poetry and make her an advisor of the broadsides. In turn, she took on his poetic beliefs as her own, affirming them as she wrote new poems under his inspiration: "It seems to me that poetry is begotten of a tune," she wrote after a feverish period of creativity, the music of the poems pounding in her ears. "More and more deeply I feel this, have never really doubted it."[64] Yeats's characterizations of her verse were invariably expressions of his own aesthetic: "It is all speech carried to its highest by intensity of sound & meaning, all magnificent, yet modern and novel . . . a masterpiece of oritory."[65] In the aura of this poetic camaraderie, and with the illustrated broadsides coming off the Cuala Press, he summoned the remnants of his diminished energy to make a dramatic declaration: "I want to make another attempt to unite literature and music."[66] In his new Coole Park, the separate literary activities of the past three years had coalesced into a

62. Allan Wade, *A Bibliography of the Writings of W. B. Yeats* (London: Rupert Hart-Davis, 1958), 412.

63. Letter of May 30, [1935], *CL InteLex* 6236.

64. *Letters on Poetry from W. B. Yeats to Dorothy Wellesley* (London: Oxford University Press, 1940), 35. For a detailed examination of the creative relationship of Yeats and Wellesley, see Deborah Letizia Ferrelli, "W. B. Yeats–Dorothy Wellesley," *YA17* (2007), 273–352.

65. Letter of July 27, 1935. *CL InteLex* 6303.

66. Letter of September 25, [1935], *CL InteLex* 6363.

coherent vision of how he could rekindle the poetic movement that had lost its momentum after the departure of Farr and the rise of the modern school. A new singleness of purpose informed the broadsides, the Oxford anthology, the Poets' Theatre, and all future broadcasts. He need not give up the fight, he had determined, nor go over to the enemy.

The new attempt involved finding immediate musical endorsements for the current series of broadsides and setting the second series in motion. To that end he contacted the poet and music critic for the *New Statesman*, W. J. Turner, whom he had seen occasionally at the Savile Club, and expressed his desire to discuss with him "a project that has been in my head lately." Simultaneously requesting Wellesley's assistance for "a great project of mine," Yeats asked her to invite Turner to Penns to seek his support. Yeats had also discovered Turner's "strange philosophical poems" for the anthology and hoped that he might set one to a bamboo pipe or flute for a broadside. He could not have found a more spontaneously sympathetic critic. As Yeats informed Turner of the principles behind the broadsides and the battle lines to be drawn between lyrical and intellectual poetry, he lavished praise on Turner's philosophical poem, "The Seven Days of the Sun" (1925), and took it for the anthology. Turner responded with a prominent review-article in the *New Statesman*, describing the broadsides as "the most delightful and attractive things of their kind in existence, as far as my knowledge goes."[67] Enlivened by the "great refreshment" to be got from the subtlety of rhythm in the old folk songs and new ballads, he placed them against the aridity and "devastatingly intellectual" quality of most contemporary writing. "It is very likely that the decay of lyric poetry in recent times," he wrote on Yeats's behalf, "is largely due to its divorce from living song, for without the regenerative influence poets are apt to adopt an academic ready-made metrical scheme for their lyrical utterance." In sharp contrast, he declared, Yeats and Higgins "have shown themselves capable of writing songs understandable and singable by the people." Turner would replace Duff, who had moved to Belfast, as the music editor of the second series of broadsides and defend the validity of Yeats's musical aims and claims when Dulac and others rose to challenge them. After reading Turner's review, Yeats told Wellesley that Turner was "to some extent fighting all our battles."[68] As in the old days, when the music critics of

67. W. J. Turner, "Broadside Songs," *New Statesman and Nation*, 10 (December 7, 1935), 848.
68. Letter of December 21 [1935], *CL InteLex* 6490.

the *Manchester Guardian* gave credence to the new art, Turner served now and for the next three years as Yeats's necessary champion in an increasingly modern environment. Concluding his article by quoting Yeats's "The Rose Tree" from the May broadside, and declaring that it has "the simplicity and directness of the old folk songs," Turner boldly asked his English readers, "Is there a poet in England who could write such a political song devoid as it is of all banality and self consciousness?"

The next step was to issue all the broadsides together in a single volume with an introductory essay entitled "Anglo-Irish Ballads," authored jointly with Higgins but written mostly by Yeats, who described it to Wellesley as an essay "on tune & poetry . . . We show that even the poet who thinks himself ignorant of music will sometimes write unconsciously to tunes."[69] Asserting that folk and political ballads in Ireland were sung to Gaelic music at least from the eighteenth century, the larger aim of the introduction was to show how that tradition persists in modern Irish poetry, how the Irish ballad meters are distinct from the English, and how they include the use of quarter-tones, which "permit speech to rise imperceptibly into song," and the gapped scale, "the wide space left unmeasured by the mathematical ear where the voice can rise wavering, quivering, through its quarter-tones." If a singer tried to sing certain lines in "The Groves of Blarney" to a tune by a modern musician, argued Yeats, recalling MacDonagh's study, "he would be condemned for the imperfection of his ear, yet no rich-sounding two or three syllabled word can be spoken or sung without quarter-tones" (*P&I* 178). The superior subtlety of rhythm in Irish music reminded him of those modern listeners that were deaf to Farr's recitations: "When Florence Farr spoke or sang to her psaltery her mastery of the subtle rhythm of words made her out of tune to ears responsive alone to the modern rhythm of notes." It made him describe how Dolmetsch took down the tunes not only from himself but from recitations of his poems by Binyon and Bullen, each incapable of recognizing a modern tune when he heard it. In effect, the essay was an affirmation of the tradition of musical speech and chanting against the mechanical sounds of modern intellectual verse, "a bundle of dry sticks." The authors reached out to young Irish poets and lovers of verse, inviting them to turn away from the dry sticks to the lyrical rhythms of Irish poetry, to verse written to a tune. "A study of our music," the authors wrote, "might unite music and speech once more."

69. Letter of October 9, [1935], *CL InteLex* 6383.

III

The antithetical temperaments of Yeats and Eliot had been brought together again by the magnetic force of poetic drama, as both were in reaction against the crushing dominance of realistic plays and prosaic dialogue on the contemporary stage. Neither man, however, had allowed the poetic differences that divided them at the end of the war, and that led them to criticize each other's work with no abatement since, to affect their cordial relationship. Their criticism of each other took place in the public arena of literary politics, where they sought to foster and forward their separate romantic and classical traditions in creating a modern audience for them. Division never meant exclusion: each held a genuine respect for the force and poetic genius of the other. After Ottoline Morrell arranged the first lunch meeting between them in December 1922, Eliot wrote to her that he had "enjoyed seeing him immensely... He is really one of a very small number of people with whom one can talk profitably about poetry, and I found him altogether stimulating."[70] Since 1923 Eliot had frequently published Yeats's prose, plays, and poems (including "The Tower") in the *Criterion*. In *The Use of Poetry and the Use of Criticism* (1933) and in *After Strange Gods* (1934), he dealt severely with Yeats's romantic and esoteric tendencies, but he paid generous tribute to Yeats on his seventieth birthday, expressing in the *Criterion* his gratitude to him not only for keeping poetry in the theatre and maintaining high dramatic standards, but for the greatness of his poetry:

> it should be apparent... that Mr. Yeats has been and is the greatest poet of his time... I can think of no poet, not even among the very greatest, who has shown a longer period of development than Yeats.... Development to this extent is not merely genius, it is character; and it sets a standard which his juniors should seek to emulate, without hoping to equal.[71]

70. Letter of December 12, 1922, *The Letters of T.S. Eliot*, vol. i, *1898–1922*, ed. Valerie Eliot (London: Faber and Faber, 1988), 611.

71. "A Commentary," *Criterion*, 14 (July 1935), 612–13. When in December 1932 Yeats and Eliot arrived independently in Cambridge, Massachusetts, where they met and were photographed at Harvard (see Plate 19), an interviewer reported their answers to the same question: "Asked what modem writers appeal to him, [Yeats] said, 'I am not well read in contemporary literature. I read the literature of my own country mostly. When a man becomes as old as I am he has half a dozen or so writers he reads over and over again. But you can mention T. S. Eliot as one I admire greatly.' Two days before T. S. Eliot at an interview at Harvard had declined to name any modern poet except W. B Yeats, of whom he spoke flatteringly" (Karl Schriftgiesser, "W. B. Yeats, in Boston, Sees No End to Irish Censorship in Near Future," *Boston Evening Transcript*, December 9, 1932, 20).

Eliot now lunched frequently with Yeats to discuss the Poets' Theatre project, even as he commissioned Michael Roberts to edit, as a rival to Yeats's anthology, *The Faber Book of Modern Verse*, which Yeats described to Wellesley as "ultra-radical, its contents having been approved by Robert Graves and Laura Riding!"[72] Not to be out-manoeuvered, Yeats read Wellesley's poems to Eliot and boldly proposed that he publish them at his firm.[73] Nor did Yeats's long friendship with Pound keep his former protégé from participating in this extra-personal critical dynamic: he had condemned *The King of the Great Clock Tower* for Yeats's reactionary dislike of modern intellectual poetry, describing it in a word as "Putrid,"[74] thereby provoking Yeats to write "A Prayer for Old Age" ("God guard me from those thoughts men think | In the mind alone; | He that sings a lasting song | Thinks in a marrow-bone.") Thus, when Yeats read Pound's *Cantos* for the anthology, he found in them "a single strained attitude instead of passion, the sexless American professor for all his violence," a view that he extended in his formal introduction to the volume.[75]

To counter his radical intellectual friends, Yeats had a strategic purpose in placing the poems of Wellesley and Turner next to and in greater number than the poems of Eliot in the anthology. "You have the animation of spoken words & spoken syntax," he wrote to Wellesley. "The worst

72. Letter of October 24, 1935, *CL InteLex* 6411.

73. Eliot took the proposal under serious consideration, as Yeats had hoped, but eventually decided not to publish them. Yeats admitted to Wellesley that his scheme was "very definitely sending the wooden horse into Troy. T. S. Eliot was I know in favour of its acceptance . . . I think the reason which he gives in his letter, which I enclose, is probably quite sincere. They are concentrating on a certain type of poetry. This winter they are about to bring out a volume by MacNeice, an extreme radical; your book might interfere" (Letter of October 20, 1935, *CL InteLex* 6403).

74. See A. Norman Jeffares, *A Commentary on the Collected Poems of W. B. Yeats* (Palo Alto, CA: Stanford University Press, 1968), 423–4: "When I had written all but the last lyric [of the play] I went a considerable journey partly to get the advice of a poet not of my school [Ezra Pound] who would, as he did some years ago, say what he thought. . . . He took my manuscript and went away denouncing Dublin as 'a reactionary hole' because I had said that I was re-reading Shakespeare, would go on to Chaucer, and found all that I wanted of modern life in 'detection and the wild west.' Next day his judgment came and that in a single word 'Putrid.' "

75. Letter to Dorothy Wellesley of September 8, [1935], *CL InteLex* 6335. "When I consider his work as a whole I find more style than form," Yeats wrote in his introduction, "but it is constantly interrupted, broken, twisted into nothing by its direct opposite, nervous obsession, nightmare, stammering confusion; he is an economist, poet, politician, raging at malignants with inexplicable characters and motives, grotesque figures out of a child's book of beasts. . . . He has great influence, more perhaps than any contemporary except Eliot, is probably the source of that lack of form and consequent obscurity which is the main defect of Auden, Day Lewis, and their school" (*OBMV* xxiv–vi).

language is Elliot's in all his early poems—a level flatness of rhythm."[76] But if Yeats and Eliot were antagonists in verse they had become allies in poetic drama. Yeats recognized immediately and generously the dramatic force and poetic power of Eliot's *Murder in the Cathedral*, which, following the postponement of Yeats's plays and the Auden–Eliot double bill, had been proposed by Margot for production at the Mercury before the scheduled production in the Chapter House of Canterbury Cathedral in June.[77] Yeats went to hear Eliot's director E. Martin Browne lecture on—and the actor Robert Speaight read verse and choruses from—the play on the Abbey stage in September. After attending a performance of Ashley Duke's revived production at the Mercury in November, he wrote to George, "It is to my great surprise a powerful religious play," admitting that it would be a success at the Abbey. But what struck his interest most was the Chorus of Eliot's Women of Canterbury, directed by Elsie Fogerty, now like Yeats in her seventieth year. An early admirer of Farr's choruses for Greek drama, she had participated in choric performances for Masefield's Oxford Recitations, became a founding member of the English Verse Speaking Association when the former came to a close, and now worked out of the Central School of Speech and Drama. Yeats saw immediately what was right and wrong with the Chorus, drawing on his memory of Farr's choral experiments for Murray's translations of Euripides' plays at the Court thirty years earlier. "It needs however a chorus of women of five or six they have eight at the Mercury," he explained to George. "Miss Fogerty admired Florence Farr & no doubt learned this from her."[78] In his excitement about Eliot's chorus, he shared his observations with Martin Browne:

76. Letter of December 21, [1935], *CL InteLex* 6490.

77. On April 2, 1935, Elsie Fogerty wrote (private) to Eliot's director E. Martin Browne that she had received a letter from Margot Collis announcing that Eliot had given her permission to produce "Fear in the Way," the provisional title of *Murder in the Cathedral*, before the Canterbury production."Surely this cannot be," Fogerty exclaimed, "as it would be a great pity to have any anticipatory performance. She wants me to do the choric work for it, and will be pleased if I will produce the whole play !!! in Ashley Dukes's little Notting Hill Theatre." Browne sent Fogerty's letter to Eliot with a note: "I think you'll like to see this. I've advised her to give no encouragement." After receiving reassurance from Eliot, Fogerty wrote to explain to him that she had told Miss Collis "that I would do the Canterbury play, but that I could only undertake it at your explicit instruction, as in these cases I never hold myself responsible to anyone but my author." Although Margot's dubious proposal was stopped, Dukes did produce the first revival of *Murder in the Cathedral* at the Mercury in November 1935.

78. Letter of [November 6, 1935], *CL InteLex* 6436.

> My only criticism is that the chorus of women speaking in unison was too large by three. When Florence Farr adopted a similar method in a production of Euripedes [*sic*] play we found that a chorus of five could speak so that their words were distinct, but that a greater number could not. Florence Farr got great beauty by alternating voices which had a different quality of tone, but that would probably have interfered with your simple massed effects.[79]

Yeats had reason to be thrilled with the chorus of Eliot's play: he had witnessed the living legacy of Farr's choruses at the Court renewed at the Mercury and saw at once the prospect for the choruses of his own plays in London. As Fogerty described the difficulty of training the chorus, "few people have an ear keen enough to understand the difference between speaking in tune and chanting. The musical note must never be the dominant effect, and the group must work until they can *speak* with harmonious inflection, not chant."[80] As her biographer asserts, Fogerty's choruses for Eliot's *Murder in the Cathedral* represented "the crowing triumph" of a career that had brought the arts of choral speaking back into dramatic prominence, arts that originated with Yeats and Farr.[81]

However excited he was over Fogerty's chorus, Yeats had lost faith in Ashley Duke's promise to produce his plays in the Poets' Theatre. "Ashley Dukes says he will do 'The Player Queen' in September," he had written to Olivia Shakespear in June, "but I don't believe him—'false, fleeting perjured Ashley.' We were to have opened in March last."[82] As had happened so frequently in the past when Yeats tried to found or find London theatre societies for his plays—the Masquers, the Dancers, the Literary Theatre Club—societies which depended upon his personal organizing energy and visionary direction for survival, his absence from London at crucial moments similarly and inevitably led to the dissolution of the Poets'

79. Letter of [*c*. November 12, 1935], *CL InteLex* 6439. "*Murder in the Cathedral* is a powerful play," Yeats wrote, "because the actor, the monkish habit, certain repeated words, symbolize what we know not what the author knows" (*OBMV* xxii–xxiii).

80. Quoted in Marion Cole, *Fogie: The Life of Elsie Fogerty* (London: Peter Davies, 1967), 168.

81. Ibid. 169. Following the success of her Glasgow Musical Festival in 1922, which included choruses from Murray's translations, Marjorie Gullan had also become a significant contributor to the revival of verse and choral speaking. "In recent years," she wrote with co-author Clive Sansom in *The Poet Speaks: An Anthology for Choral Speaking* (London: Methuen, 1940), "there has been a revival of verse-speaking—not the 'elocution' in whose name so many crimes were committed in Victorian drawing-rooms, but the sincere speaking of poetry for the sake of the poem and not for self-display.... But perhaps the most remarkable development has been the growth of Choral Speaking... It has influenced the theatre, producing such plays as... T. S. Eliot's *Murder in the Cathedral*... and the plays of W. H. Auden and Christopher Isherwood" (vii–viii).

82. Letter of June 16, [1935], *CL InteLex* 6255.

Theatre. Eliot sensed this astutely after Yeats's plays were postponed over conflicts of production and acting between Doone and Dukes. "I am afraid the whole thing has been badly muddled," he wrote regretfully to Doone. "Whether the issue would have been more successful had Yeats been able to be in London I do not know."[83] Moreover, Dukes did not have the financial backing that he claimed to have and was still seeking guarantors. When there was no sign of a production in September, Yeats informed Margot that there was "no need to think any more about Ashley Dukes except as a swamp we got mired in."[84] In dismay, he gave *The Player Queen* to Margot, giving her permission to arrange for a production by Nancy Price's People's National Theatre Company, with the expectation that Margot would play the lead. But when Yeats attended a matinee performance on October 28, he was baffled to discover Margot in a minor role, the Player Queen having been given to Price's daughter for her stage debut. Yeats tried to console her in this, the first of several rebuffs to come: "You must hold on—," he wrote the next day, "you may become a great actress . . . You have passion and precision."[85] But Margot had already begun to lose her hold.

A fortnight after seeing *Murder in the Cathedral*, Yeats sailed from Liverpool with the Swami and Mrs. Gwyneth Foden, one of his disciples, to Majorca, where they had agreed to collaborate on a translation of the *Upanishads*. On the voyage out all three agreed to participate in a ship's concert, spontaneously arranged around the talents of passengers, with Yeats chanting three poems and Mrs. Foden, dressed in temple clothes for a sacred Indian dance, performing "badly but with contagious good humour."[86] Yeats was left in amazement, however, by the performance of the Swami, who "sang a passage from the upanishads announcing that India had sung it exactly as he did for 5000 years." Once in Majorca, Yeats began writing *The Herne's Egg* while working on the translation, an experience enhanced for him by the Swami's singing and chanting. By April he had begun his introduction to *The Ten Principal Upanishads* (which Eliot would publish at Faber and Faber), even there conveying the constant theme that music should be restored to literature, seizing the opportunity to complain that many modern poets—Eliot, Auden, Day Lewis, MacNeice—had thrown off "the sensuous tradition of the poets,"

83. Letter of March 20, 1935, quoted in Sidnell, *Dances of Death*, 269.
84. Letter of [September 8, 1935], *CL InteLex* 6334.
85. Letter of October 29, [1935], *CL InteLex* 6425.
86. Letter of [December 12, 1935], *CL InteLex* 6477.

had lost the quality of song found in a poetic tradition that extended from the ancient *Upanishads* to Dante and Shakespeare, from Shelley to Wellesley and Turner. In their collaboration on the *Upanishads*, wrote Yeats, he and the Swami offered to "some young man" who might be hungry for the "vast sentiments and generalisations" of that great and popular tradition, "the oldest philosophical compositions of the world, compositions, not writings, for they were sung long before they were written down."[87] As the translation neared completion, Yeats wrote to Eliot about the urgency of recording the Swami's beautiful chanting of the *Upanishads*, fearful otherwise that "we may lose altogether what is perhaps the most ancient music in the world."[88]

Within weeks of arrival in Majorca, Yeats became critically ill with lung, heart, and kidney problems that required months of convalescence, prolonging his stay until June. In May, as his own recovery seemed assured, Margot, having run away from husband, infant, and home, arrived on the verge of insanity, thrusting her ignored poems before him and demanding his opinion for book publication, an experience that he incorporated sympathetically into his introduction for the poems that he pushed into print as *The Lemon Tree* (1937). Leaving as abruptly as she arrived, she sailed to Barcelona, where in a possible suicide attempt she fell from a hotel window through a barber's roof, breaking her kneecap. Found in a ship's hold singing her poems, her dire physical and mental condition required Yeats and George to go to her from Majorca and provide financial support for her recovery, an investment that yielded "A Crazed Girl" ("Her soul in division from itself . . . in desperate music wound"). In the aftermath of these disturbing events, he would gradually shift much of his attention to Wellesley. "Blot out what I told you about Margot & myself," he wrote to her at summer's end:

> I cannot endure that moral torture chamber where hysteria manufactures thumb-screws daily of some new pattern. All I can do for her is get her poems published & find work for her if possible. If she works her mind into the light & into genius she will have passed through a worse ordeal than most of that tortured race.[89]

87. *The Ten Principal Upanishads* | Put into English by Shree Puroit Swami and W. B. Yeats (London: Faber and Faber, 1937), 10–11.
88. Letter of July 6, 1936, *CL InteLex* 6605. Eliot also accepted for publication at Faber and Faber Shree Purohit Swami's translation of Patanjali's *Aphorisms of Yoga* (1938), on condition that Yeats write the introduction.
89. Letter of [October 29, 1936], *CL InteLex* 6688.

Still, in coming months she would recover to become a public sayer and singer of his poems once again.

Yeats was eager to return to Penns and resurrect his "great project" from the setback of the Poets' Theatre. Within four days after arrival in London he was there, accompanied by Turner to plan the second series of broadsides. Rothenstein joined them as well, himself a connoisseur of English folk songs (proposing the old English ballad *Nottamun Town* for a broadside). The second series would include contemporary English poets (Belloc, Wellesley, Sitwell, Bottomley, De La Mare) as well as Irish poets (Gogarty, Stephens, Higgins, Colum, Yeats). Yeats originally planned to pair the contemporary poems with old English as well as old Irish ballads, drawing on the parallel traditions of Percy's *Reliques* and Sparling's *Irish Minstrelsy* that had shaped his early aesthetic; however, his idea was dropped in favor of pairing a contemporary English and Irish poet in each issue. At Penns, Rothenstein found Yeats making final selections of poems for the *Oxford Book* and holding forth on favorite themes, much like the vigorous young poet Rothenstein had known at Woburn Buildings in 1901, still the minstrel and magician, "dressed in crimson shirt, flowing coloured tie . . . his dark eyes aslant, broad-shouldered and ample of form—he once so pale and lanky":

> He read from the books before him with his musical lilting voice, accepting this poem, rejecting that. And after dinner Yeats would expand, talking as only the Irish can, of mystic experiences, deploring the loss of the ancient wisdom, praising the old secret knowledge handed on by word of mouth to the instructed. . . . But little of the old poetry still lingered among the people; in future he would write ballads to be sung in the streets, ballads set to new tunes, if musicians would make them. For poetry should be said to music again, as it was by the Troubadours, and the old Irish poets.[90]

As plans for the new series materialized, with Wellesley as co-editor, Dulac as musical editor, and a variety of illustrators and musicians, Yeats was moved to write the first of several new ballads, "Come Gather Round Me, Parnellites," written he told Wellesley for an old man who begged him for a piece that would "convince all Parnellites that Parnell had nothing to be ashamed of in her [Kitty O'Shea's] love."[91] The ballad would appear with music arranged by Dulac and a full-color illustration by Jack Yeats in

90. William Rothenstein, *Since Fifty: Men and Memories, 1922–1938* (London: Faber and Faber, 1939), 249–50.
91. Letter of [September 8, 1936], *CL InteLex* 6644.

January 1937. As succeeding numbers appeared monthly, with four more of Yeats's new ballads to Dulac's and Art O'Murnaghan's music, he wrote in the preface for the proposed Scribner edition of his work the rationale of his revived efforts to bring poetry and the arts back to the common man: "Then too I would have all the arts drawn together, recover their ancient association, the painter painting what the poet has written, the musician setting the poet's words to simple airs, that the horseman and the engine-driver may sing them at their work."[92] The restatement of this old theme from his 1930 diary was no longer motivated by passive reminiscence but by passionate commitment.

IV

If Yeats felt betrayed by Dukes and his Poets' Theatre, an even greater betrayal awaited him at the Abbey. Frank O'Connor, who had contributed Gaelic translations to the first volume of *Broadsides*, but who was known to Yeats as a "realist novelist," had become the director of the Abbey in October 1935. On the ill-advised recommendation of John Masefield, Yeats had appointed a twenty-four-year-old Englishman, Hugh Hunt, as manager and producer when the alcoholic Lennox Robinson suddenly had to be replaced. Hunt, a past president of the Oxford University Dramatic Society who had since produced plays at Nugent Monck's theatre in Norwich and at the Croydon Repertory Theatre, arrived in Ireland for the first time as a strong proponent of modern realistic drama. O'Connor, evidently considering the recent clerical controversy over the Abbey's production of O'Casey's *The Silver Tassie*, which Yeats had rejected in 1928 following riots over *The Plough and the Stars*, saw a need to revive some plays in the Abbey's "classical repertory." Yeats offered him *The Player Queen*, with the stipulation that Margot play the lead, but when O'Connor and Hunt refused to accept her, Yeats withdrew the offer. Instead, he gave them his *Deirdre*, which had not been produced at the Abbey since Farr's failed performance seventeen years earlier. It was a disastrous choice.

Ignorant of and irreverent toward Abbey traditions and battles won, Hunt not only wanted to revamp the repertoire but to include English

92. The Scribner edition was never published. The preface written in 1937 first appeared as the introduction to *Essays and Introductions* (1961), here p. ix. See also *LE* 218.

actresses in his productions. He thus persuaded O'Connor and the Abbey Board to bring over the London actress Jean Forbes-Robertson to play Deirdre to Micheál MacLiammóir's Naisi and Ria Mooney's First Musician. "Apart from the fact that we didn't like the play," wrote O'Connor, "it was quite unsuitable for Jean Forbes-Robertson," whose professional voice had a "fairylike coloratura quality."[93] O'Connor was actually sympathetic to what Yeats called the "Abbey Tradition" of chanting his verse plays, but Hunt considered that style "dead as the Dodo" and mounted a production that was seen as a deliberate denial of Yeats's theories of verse-speaking.[94]

When the revival opened on August 10, Yeats arrived in the vestibule of the Abbey for the first time since recovering from illnesses contracted in Majorca. Jean Forbes-Robertson acted with "dramatic emotionalism," thought Joseph Holloway, sole witness over the years to all the Abbey productions of *Deirdre,* but he was aware that the verse-speaking had suffered woefully: "The present interpretation of *Deirdre* emphasised its worth as a drama at the sacrifice of its verse."[95] Worse, Forbes-Robertson felt no obligation to follow the script. She informed O'Connor gaily that as she did not understand a word of the part she had "made up a little story of my own that covers it pretty well."[96] Ria Mooney as First Musician had been directed to speak her lines with a "clear articulation" that was "strictly followed" by the other musicians, who recited the lyrics to orchestral music composed by conductor Frank May. Holloway, speaking to her at the end of the week, recorded that she seemed "thoroughly disheartened" by the way the directors were wont to "cross her endeavours" in teaching verse-speaking to young members of the acting school. Inevitably, Yeats stormed out of the stalls at the curtain, clutching his head: " 'Terrible! Terrible! Terrible!' was all he could bring out," wrote O'Connor, giving new poignancy to lines written a few months later, that "actors lacking music | Do most excite my spleen, | They say it is more human | To shuffle, grunt and groan, | Not knowing what unearthly stuff | Rounds a mighty scene."[97] As Holloway sympathetically intuited, Yeats "missed the

93. Frank O'Connor, *My Father's Son* (London: Macmillan, 1968), 170–1.

94. Hugh Hunt, *The Abbey: Ireland's National Theatre 1904–1979* (New York: Columbia University Press, 1979), 155.

95. *Joseph Holloway's Irish Theatre, Vol. ii, 1932–1937*, ed. Robert Hogan and Michael J. O'Neill (Dixon, CA: Proscenium Press, 1969), 58.

96. O'Connor, *My Father's Son*, 171.

97. Ibid. 201; "The Old Stone Cross" (*VP* 599).

poetic diction and intoning of the earlier performances. He thinks in poetry rather than drama."[98] Yeats informed Hunt of his intense displeasure, and in his fury at the liberties taken with his verse and rhythms, he told Wellesley that though MacLiammóir's Naisi was noble and tragic, "all drama–all song," Miss Forbes-Robertson's Deirdre was "an Upper Tooting hen, a Camberwell canary, a Blackpool sparrow."[99]

The drama critic Andrew Malone, going off to write his review, said to Holloway immediately after the curtain, "Bearing vividly in mind previous performances, I think this is the best, on the whole, I have seen."[100] Taking notice of the "unduly prolonged period" since the last production of the play, Malone named the previous actresses who had played Deirdre, all of whom had spoken the verse "in the manner originally prescribed by Mr. Yeats himself," but he took pleasure in noting that Forbes-Robertson had broken with that tradition.[101] As though in conspiracy with Hunt, he believed that it was time to sound the death knell for chanted verse in the Abbey. "The old manner of speaking the verse," he wrote,

> is now probably interred in the tomb with Deirdre and Naoise, and the keening monotony of the past will be heard no more. Perhaps, there is some loss in this—loss to the beauty of speech and to the rhythm of the lovely lines. But what has been thus lost has been more than rectified in the enrichment of the play's dramatic value . . . This revival will not hearten the traditionalists of the Abbey, but it is surely time that another mode had its day. Death, Synge said, is a poor untidy thing, even if it's a queen that dies; but Mr. Hunt's death tableau achieved the tidiness of an authentic Old Master.

Yeats responded to Malone's review cynically as "a sign that the Abbey was now up to date & had got rid of Mr. Yeats's tradition of rhythmical speech."[102] The full-house audiences loved the new mode and the flashy Deirdre—the receipts were the largest previously taken at the Abbey—but Yeats, unable to bear the travesty of the production, exercised his author's right to withdraw the play at the end of the week. The expense of the production, however, forced the directors to continue after MacLiammóir left at week's end, requiring Hunt, with half the physical build and voice, to take his place. In this untoward situation, O'Connor observed, there was no hope of musical speech, "no use trying to explain to him how

98. Hogan and O'Neill (eds), *Joseph Holloway's Irish Theatre*, ii. 58.
99. Letter of August 13, 1936 to Dorothy Wellesley, *CL InteLex* 6636.
100. Hogan and O'Neill (eds), *Joseph Holloway's Irish Theatre*, ii. 58.
101. "A New Deirdre," *Irish Times*, August 11, 1936, 6.
102. Letter of August 13, 1936 to Dorothy Wellesley, *CL InteLex* 6636.

an actor . . . can build a tremendous climax merely by using fractions of semitones."[103] Yeats went before the Abbey board, vehemently protesting the production: "he gave us a sales talk on the traditions of the theatre," O'Connor recalled, "and how it differed from the naturalistic English theatre, all of which I could have repeated in my sleep. I replied that he might remember the tradition, but that nobody else did."[104] In compromise, Hunt was debarred from directing Yeats's plays; he resigned as manager to devote himself to producing new realistic plays, doing so until Yeats succeeded in having the board dismiss him two years later. Nonetheless, the "modern way," as Yeats described it, had prevailed; the tradition of rhythmical speech in the Abbey had been broken.

No one dared say as much to Yeats, who carried his fury over the verse-speaking in *Deirdre* to his broadcast on "Modern Poetry" for the BBC on October 11. Essentially a recasting of his preface to the Oxford anthology, he began with the poets of his youth—Dowson, Johnson, and others—leading his listeners to the third year of the Great War, when T. S. Eliot, "the most revolutionary man in poetry during my lifetime," wreaked havoc on the romantic tradition with his realism: "No romantic word or sound, nothing reminiscent," he said of Eliot's baleful influence: "Poetry must resemble prose . . . The past had deceived us: let us accept the worthless present." Again, he set Turner, Wellesley, Herbert Read, and Edith Sitwell against Eliot and his "racketeers." He explained to his Irish listeners that, though he had rather be discussing Synge or Stephens, he was focusing on the English rather than the Irish movement to show how they had given way to "an impersonal philosophical poetry." Because Irish poets have a living folk tradition, he explained, they "will be remembered by the common people. Instead of turning to impersonal philosophy, they have hardened and deepened their personalities" (*LE* 100). In his portrayal of the divided traditions, however, his final emphasis was on the proper speaking of poetry, whatever the tradition. "When I have tried to read you a poem," he told his listeners, "I have tried to read it rhythmically . . . there is no other method." Defining a poem as "an elaboration of the rhythms of common speech and their association with profound feeling," he now

103. O'Connor, *My Father's Son*, 171.

104. *The Abbey Theatre: Interviews and Recollections*, ed. E. H. Mikhail (London: Macmillan, 1988), 152–3. "I knew I was not being fair," O'Connor explained, "because I had already given Hunt exactly the same sales talk in private; but I felt that, if Yeats insisted on establishing a party with Higgins against Hunt, I must back up my man."

made an emotional appeal, letting the vehement voice of Daniel O'Leary, brought down from *Stories of Michael Robartes and His Friends* to a prominent place in the new edition of *A Vision,* speak out against prosaic readers:

> If anybody reads or recites poetry as if it were prose from some public platform, I ask you, speaking for poets, living dead or unborn, to protest in whatever way occurs to your perhaps youthful minds; if they recite or read by wireless, I ask you to express your indignation by letter.
>
> (*E&I* 508; *LE* 103)

Calling on William Morris once again to dramatize his point, he was cut off in mid-quotation by the BBC when he substituted "a lot of damned" for "a devil of a lot": "It cost me a lot of damned hard work to get that thing into verse."[105]

Immediately after the broadcast Yeats was motored back to Penns, where guests included David Cecil and his wife Rachel, who thought Yeats a "thundering egoist" but who wrote to her friend Lady Salisbury of the astonishing effect that his musical voice could still have on an unsuspecting stranger: "I have never anyhow heard anyone quite like him," she wrote in awe of the evening:

> and after dinner he read aloud some of the poems which he had just written. One was a long sort of ballad—and although again I couldn't quite follow it—yet the sound was too lovely. He reads in singing, chanting voice, which lulls one almost to sleep—but he does it beautifully. I enjoyed that part the most, and he is so unselfconscious and spontaneous about his poetry—and it is so imaginative, that it is very moving to hear him read it.[106]

V

Back in London from Penns, Yeats met with George Barnes and Hilda Matheson of the BBC to discuss ways of expanding the audience for broadcasts of poetry. As a result of that meeting, it was agreed that Yeats

105. Sturge Moore wrote to Yeats of the broadcast that he "was so shocked by its abrupt end that I imagined that you had been cut off in the middle of a sentence. I wrote to *The Times*, but they said they would only publish my letter after I had written to the B.B.C. My conviction was increased when Riette [his daughter] met *[a friend]* who told her that what had been cut off was 'It cost me a damned lot of hard work to put that into poetry *and the——has been and taken it all out.*' But the B.B.C. most politely persuaded me that this last phrase had not been in your MS" (*W. B. Yeats and T. Sturge Moore: Their Correspondence 1901–1937*, ed. Ursula Bridge [London: Routledge and Kegan Paul, 1953], 183).

106. Letter of October 16, [1936] to Lady Salisbury; quoted in Foster, *Life 2* 562–3.

could write the scripts, choose the poems, and have them spoken or sung as he liked, using a variety of musical instruments according to his directions and excluding professional singers, the BBC orchestra, and chamber music of any kind. In control of the format, Yeats now began the last major phase of his public project with a series of broadcasts that would give a wide communal life and sound to poems, ballads, and songs taken from the *Oxford Book*, the *Broadsides*, his plays, and newly written ballads. Material from these sources would also be brought to the Abbey stage for performance between plays. He also planned to use the Abbey for occasional public gatherings to hear modern Irish poetry spoken, chanted, and sung. As he explained to Edith Sitwell, whose poems he had discussed at length in his broadcast, "The broadsides are part of a scheme to get poetry sung here. We have already begun with poems sung from 'The Abbey Theatre' stage. The folk song is still a living thing in Ireland. Much of the National feeling in Ireland has been sustained by ballads."[107]

Yeats and Higgins had introduced the Abbey actors Ria Mooney and John Stephenson to the ballads and their tunes during three sessions at Yeats's house in Rathfarnham. His plan was to replace the one-act curtain-raisers that the Abbey used for short plays with the singing of ballads. "Yeats read them over to me in the queer rhythmic fashion peculiar to himself," Stephenson recalled of their meetings. "It was fascinating to watch him beat out the rhythm he wanted to use."[108] Yeats wanted the ballads spoken or sung unaccompanied, and they were to be sung not in ordinary dress but "in character," for he had also revived his old idea of the Black Jester as reciter and Irish minstrel. "I was to make up as a man of the roads. I was to wear the clothes of a man of roads. In this way, he said, they will get over." Yeats and Higgins drilled the two repeatedly, though Stephenson felt that Yeats, unlike Higgins, who was a stickler for accuracy, did not really care if he made mistakes with the tunes: "he was wholly concerned now with what lines or passages I could treat lightly, throw away in fact. And then of course with the bits that had to be highly dramatised. He spared neither time nor labour to get exactly what he wanted." Once they had perfected the method for the Abbey audience, it was time to bring broadcasting equipment to the Abbey stage.

107. Letter of December 13, 1936, *CL InteLex* 6753.

108. See W. R. Rodgers, "Broadcast: Poetry and the Seeing Ear," transcription dated June 19, 1950, 22 (HRHRC). See also John Stephenson, "Memories of W. B. Yeats at the Abbey Theatre," BBC LP15832, band 5, recorded June 22, 1950.

In anticipation of the London broadcasts, Yeats acquired his first wireless set through the BBC in January 1937. His imaginative delight in planning the programs stimulated a creative resurgence not experienced since he wrote in rapid succession the poems of *Words for Music Perhaps* while recovering from Malta fever a decade earlier, and he relished writing to friends of how happy he was writing ballads for music. "I write poem after poem," he wrote to Wellesley, "all intended for music, all very simple—as a modern Indian poet has said 'no longer the singer but the song.' "[109] More importantly, the prospect of expanding his listening audience beyond the platform and stage had fully restored his confidence in becoming a poet of the people. "I have recovered a power of moving the common man I had in my youth," he continued. "The poems I can write now will go into the general memory."

Margot, sufficiently recovered from her nervous breakdown, was brought back on the scene, for she was Yeats's only trained reciter in London. Turner, Barnes, and Matheson began to rehearse her and a professional actor, Ronald Watkins, for the first program, "At the Village Inn" (later changed to "In the Poet's Pub"), but in their shared confusion over Yeats's aims it was postponed until he could attend rehearsals in March. As Yeats wanted part of the program to originate from the Abbey stage in any event, he arranged a fifteen-minute broadcast on the Athlone band of Radio Éireann on February 1, recording the material for Barnes's later use. Stephenson began the program, briefly introduced and narrated by Yeats, by singing two ballads from the Oxford anthology—Higgins' "The Ballad of O'Bruadir" and James Stephens's translation of a Gaelic poem, "A Glass of Beer."[110] A violinist played traditional airs during the brief intervals between songs, just as Yeats had planned for Herbert Hughes to do in 1906 before that aspect of the Abbey dream was deferred.[111] Ria Mooney then sang Yeats's unpublished "Come on to the Hills of Mourne" ("I forgot who wrote it" he said in the introduction)[112] and

109. Letter of [January 21, 1937], *CL InteLex* 6785.

110. The edited scripts of this ["Abbey Theatre Broadcast"] and the four succeeding BBC broadcasts in 1937 are included in *LAR* 259–96, here 259–65.

111. As Yeats had written to Katherine Tynan Hinkson on September 1, 1906, "I have plans for improving our new poets myself. I want to get them to write songs to be sung between the acts. Herbert Hughs [*sic*] will set them & we have a fine singer in Miss Allgood... I am not quite sure that the time has come yet but I shall get one or two things set as a start. One has to go slowly, perfecting first one thing & then another" (*CL3* 490).

112. Yeats did not want to claim authorship publicly of the "He" and "She" dialogue poem, about a woman who "killed my husband last Saturday night | And tumbled him down the

Stephens' "The Rivals," both to music by Art O'Murnaghan. Stephenson concluded the program by speaking what Yeats described as "a beautiful, strange, mysterious poem" by Stephens ["In the Night"], and then singing Yeats's new ballads, "Come Gather Round Me, Parnellites" and "Roger Casement," his angry, accusative response to the forged Casement diaries. The performance at the Abbey seemed flawless, but when Yeats listened to the recorded broadcast on his new wireless, having alerted many friends to tune in, he was shocked by the dramatic contrast between stage performance and wireless broadcast. In utter disbelief, his high expectations for that and future broadcasts were simultaneously shattered. "Broadcast a fiasco," he wrote in furious humiliation to Barnes the next day:

> Every human sound turned into the groans, roars, bellows of a wild [beast]. I recognise that I am a fool & there shall be no more broad cast of verse from the Abbey stage if I can prevent it. Songs were at the Abbey itself a success—three curtains and so on. . . . I got Stephenson while singing "Come all old Parnellites" to clap his hands in time to the music, after every verse & Higgins added people in the wings clapping their hands. It was very stirring—on the wireless it was a school-boy knocking with the end of a pen-knife, or a spoon.[113]

Letters of self-deprecating apology went out to friends, who tried to console him, but it was the ingenuity of Higgins that saved the day. Aware that Yeats was inexperienced with his wireless, Higgins persuaded him that he had "mismanaged" the station setting: for local broadcasts he should have set the dial on Dublin, not Athlone, which was "too powerful." Admittedly, said Higgins, the broadcast was not as it should have been, due to the microphones being wrongly placed on the stage, but he assured Yeats that it was not nearly as bad as it sounded to him. The singers had since been

stair," composed on the verso of Gogarty's bawdy ballad, "Poem of Lancelot Switchback." In the second part of her autobiography, *Players and Painted Stage,* Ria Mooney recalled her reciting the poem, which she reproduces, with John Stephenson on the Abbey stage: "Once Higgins tried to lead [Yeats] back to writing ballads which Yeats used to favor as a young man. I have at this moment in my possession one of these experiments never before published because Yeats (understandably!) didn't like it." See *George Spelvin's Theatre Book*, I (Fall 1978), 65–121, here 112. It remained unpublished until the broadcast script was printed (*LAR* 261–2), and the manuscript appears in *New Poems: Manuscript Materials by W. B. Yeats*, ed. J. C. C. Mays and Stephen Parrish (Ithaca and London: Cornell University Press, 2000), 398–9. In a letter to Wellesley of [January 28, 1937], Yeats described it as a "comic song" which "might amuse you" (*CL InteLex* 6790).

113. Letter of February 8, [1937], *CL InteLex* 6798.

taken to the studio for a new recording, which was now "quite right." "I am to hear it on Wednesday morning," Yeats wrote to Turner about Higgins' completely satisfying explanation. "If I like it I shall ask Barnes to let me do In a poets garden from here—where I have enthusiastic helpers."[114]

Yeats returned to London in March as promised to attend rehearsals for the BBC's twenty-minute broadcast of "In the Poet's Pub" on April 2. During the postponement, however, Margot had taken a role with a provincial repertory company and could not participate as planned. When no satisfactory replacement could be found, Yeats wrote the script for a single new actor, Victor Clinton Clinton-Baddeley (to Yeats, "Baddeley"). Unrecognized by Yeats as a member of his new club (The Athenaeum) with whom he had dined, he was received at rehearsal with the admonition "not to read 'like an actor'—the word almost savagely spoken."[115] But Clinton-Baddeley would prove to be not only an ideal male reciter but an important recorder of Yeats's verse-speaking instructions. A BBC producer announced at the outset that Yeats had come "to illustrate his theory and conviction that poetry would be as popular in England, or anywhere else, as in a poet's pub of his imagination, if it were only delivered in the right way and in the right circumstances."[116] In his script, Yeats sought to educate fellow poets and his audience in the way that public readings should be conducted and heard, for as Clinton-Baddeley confirmed, "he was not so much interested in the art of song as in the art of the public presentation of poetry. He earnestly desired music, but solely as a support to the right speaking of verse: and that is another matter altogether."[117] Describing his own experience at a well-known verse-speaking society, where all the reciters "knew that lyric poetry must not be spoken as if it were dramatic dialogue," and "knew that every word was important and that the whole must be a form of music," Yeats expressed his frustration

114. Letter of February 21–2, [1937], *CL InteLex* 6817."In the Poet's Garden" was to be the title of the second broadcast, but a program of that title was delayed until March 1937, when it was rehearsed but never broadcast. Yeats inserted a list of poems for the program in one of his copies of *The Tower* (*YL* 2430a).

115. V. C. Clinton-Baddeley, "Reading Poetry with W. B. Yeats," *London Magazine*, 4 (December 1957), 47. The article is based on his BBC Bristol broadcast, "Broadcasting with W. B. Yeats," December 11, 1949, as described in Wade, *A Bibliography of the Writings of W. B. Yeats*, 417.

116. Library No. 14879–81, BBC Sound Archive, complete recording of "In the Poet's Pub," BBC National Programme, transmitted April 2, 1937, 9:20 to 9:40 p.m., with slight variations from the typescript in the BBC Written Archives, Caversham, as described in *LAR* 403–5.

117. V. C. Clinton-Baddeley, *Words for Music* (Cambridge: Cambridge University Press, 1941), 155.

at the "intolerable monotony" of one poem coming right after another: "While I was thinking of one poem, the next had begun. My mind could not move quickly enough" (*LAR* 276). Yeats urged poets to learn the tricks of folk singers, who break up the monotony or rest the mind between each verse or poem by clapping their hands, snapping their fingers, whistling, or singing a refrain. "Why not fill up the space between poem and poem with musical notes," he asked, "and so enable the mind to free itself from one group of ideas, while preparing for another group, and yet keep it receptive and dreaming?"[118]

Yeats maintained that such techniques were essential for resting and varying the listener's attention, the same function that he meant for the choruses of his plays to serve. His methods described, Yeats asked his audience to imagine themselves in a lively pub, surrounded by poets, musicians, farmers and workers—all drunk or in love—as Clinton-Baddeley prepared to recite three country poems appropriate for the setting: Belloc's "Tarantella" ("Do you remember an Inn, | Miranda?"), followed by "the first and more vigorous part" of Chesterton's "The Rolling English Road" ("Before the Roman came to Rye or out to Severn strode, | The rolling English drunkard made the rolling English road"), and De La Mare's "Three Jolly Farmers" ("Three jolly farmers | Once bet a pound | Each dance the others would | Off the ground").[119] Kettledrums, played by musicians under Turner's eye, were used for effective intervention with rolls and taps, such as improvising imagined tankards pounding the tables between stanzas and poems ("tăp tăp táp tăp tăp táp"), fading away at the end. So were

118. (*LAR* 266). Yeats canceled in the script his anecdote about substituting music in wireless broadcasts for body movement in live performance: "I have suggested to the B.B.C. that it should use some musical instrument to fill up pauses, whether in the middle of a verse or at the end of it, to vary and to rest the attention. When I first produced a play at the Abbey Theatre some thirty years ago I told an actor to pause to mark a change of mood, and the impression he gave me was that of a man who had forgotten his lines. Then I told him to fill up the pause with a significant movement of his body and all was well. But when you are reciting to the wireless and nobody can see your body it seems right to fill up the pauses with musical sounds" (*LAR* 404).

119. During rehearsals Clinton-Baddeley got through Belloc's poem with little comment from Yeats, "but when I started off on Chesterton's 'Rolling English Road', in a careful sort of voice which I devoutly hoped would be considered sufficiently untheatrical, I was rewarded with an agonized cry from the talk-back–'No! No! You must be a comedian here.' . . . Poets normally entreat their readers not to dramatize their poetry. I was used to that. But here was a man who wanted me not to read like an actor and yet to be a comedian. It was my first introduction to Yeats's apparent confusions and contradictions, but I began now to understand what he wanted. It was something perfectly reasonable, well worth doing, and extremely difficult." See V. C. Clinton-Baddeley, "Reading Poetry with W. B. Yeats," 47.

they used for the second part of the program, when Yeats described the arrival of two sailors talking about the sea, prompting someone in the pub to recite the first of three sea poems, Newbolt's "Drake's Drum" ("Drake he's in his hammock an' a thousand mile away"), with an impressive drum roll between the stanzas and a concluding cymbal roll (see Plate 22). "Then somebody else or is it the same man," Yeats says in bringing his poet's songfest to an end, "speaks Sylvia Townsend Warner's charming and amusing 'Sailor' ['I have a young love— | A landward lass is she—'], and then just before closing time, he sings to a folk tune 'The Lady and the Shark' ['There was a queen that fell in love with a jolly sailor bold'], translated from the French of Paul Fort by Frederick York Powell," with all drinkers and lovers joining in for the chorus at the end: "Now all you pretty maidens what love a sailor bold, | You'd better ship along with him before his love grows cold."[120] Yeats said in closing that his family's old friend from Bedford Park days, the scholar York Powell, a man of "incredible learning" but with a lighter side and a love of prize fights, "would have been at home in such a pub as I have imagined." Yeats himself had little experience in pubs, but he had imagined for himself, his friends, and his audience a poet's evening with and for the common man, inviting all to enter through the auditory imagination a pub of popular poems and folk songs with good lyrics made enjoyable and understandable by a combination of words and music. In its simplicity, it was meant to suggest the possibility of a new communality of poetry through the wireless—scholar, farmer, worker, and sailor sharing the poet's musical speech together. "The Broadcast was entirely delightful," George wrote to him approvingly the same day:

> I don't like most of the pomes, as you know, but the result of the performance seemed to me most exciting. You spoke in your natural unrestrained voice, a voice very unlike the artificial one of the "Modern Poetry", and whatever listeners thought of any portion of the twenty minutes a whole lot of people will have been glad to hear the real Yeats evidently enjoying himself. The

120. Yeats told Wellesley that he had chosen Powell's translation of Paul Fort's ballad, which he included in the *Oxford Book*, as "a song . . . which I delight in" (Letter of July 26, [1936], *CL InteLex* 6622), and he incorporated his discussion of Powell in the broadcast on "Modern Poetry" into the narrative of "In the Poet's Pub." "When we came to the last poem," Clinton-Baddeley wrote of the rehearsal, "I found to my alarm that I was expected to sing it. No one had written any music. I was just told to sing it—and sing it I did to some old tune I remembered, which happened to fit the shape" ("Reading Poetry with W. B. Yeats," 50).

> whole production during its twenty minutes sounded as if you and the speaker and the drums were really enjoying yourselves and that you had locked the door on the solemn portentous BBC and had no intention of unlocking the door until you had your final laugh—which we heard distinctly! . . . From certain intonations I believe you were the "chorus"??[121]

"It was something of an ordeal, that broadcast—," wrote Clinton-Baddeley, "but an exciting experiment had been made, and Yeats was all ready with a fresh lot of ideas for the second broadcast, three weeks later."[122]

Margot had in the meantime given up her part with the repertory company and was free to join Clinton-Baddeley for "In the Poet's Parlour," Yeats's imaginative recreation of many Monday evenings in Woburn Buildings. While the poems heard in the poet's pub were "written for everybody," Yeats said in his introduction, the parlour poems were written for poets: "Those present are his intimate friends and fellow students. There is a beautiful lady, or two or three beautiful ladies, four or five poets, a couple of musicians and all are devoted to poetry" (*LAR* 276). Exhilarated by the success of the previous program, Yeats felt in better health than he had for years and thoroughly enjoyed attending rehearsals, where Barnes heard Margot chant and sing for the first time. He observed quickly that she was Yeats's "chosen instrument" and confirmed that she "possessed one quality which [Yeats] valued beyond price—the ability to pass naturally and unselfconsciously from speech to song."[123] She began by speaking a poem that Yeats had written specially for the programme, "Sweet Dancer" ("The girl goes dancing there"), with a dance tune played by piper Eva Towns after each refrain line, "*Ah, dancer, ah, sweet dancer!*" Barnes remembered "the lilting way" in which Yeats taught her to speak the line, but he was not so struck by it as Clinton-Baddeley, who carried it in memory for years: the line "was not to be spoken in a smooth, caressing kind of voice (a pardonable supposition) but in the rhythm of a dance, and the way he

121. Quoted in Ann Saddlemyer, *Becoming George: The Life of Mrs W. B. Yeats* (Oxford: Oxford University Press, 2002), 521. The refrain of York Powell's translation was vigorously taken up by producers, studio attendants, and Yeats himself, whose intonations George correctly heard.

122. Clinton-Baddeley, "Reading Poetry with W. B. Yeats," 50.

123. George Barnes' typescript, "Account of Yeats at B.B.C." (NLI MS 5919; copy in BBC Written Archives, Caversham), prepared for Joseph Hone's biography of Yeats and dated May 23, 1940, has been edited and published with an introductory note by Jeremy Silver as "George Barnes's 'W. B. Yeats and Broadcasting' 1940," *YA5* (1987), 189–94; here, 192.

wanted it said is so firmly in my mind that I can still reproduce it in musical notation":

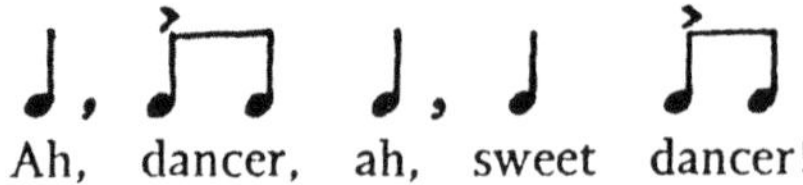
Ah, dancer, ah, sweet dancer!

Margot also spoke and sang the second of Yeats's poems, "I am of Ireland," introduced by Yeats as "an expansion of a mediaeval dance song." Clinton-Baddeley spoke the third, "The Wicked Hawthorne Tree" ("O, but I saw a solemn sight") which portrays what Yeats had heard Irish country people describe as "an apparition of dancers in an old ruin" ("Castle Dargan's ruin all lit, | Lovely ladies dancing in it"). Nonetheless, last-minute changes were made, as Clinton-Baddeley later described:

> In "I am of Ireland" I spoke the verses and the refrain was sung by Margot Ruddock: and she and I sang in alternate verses "The wicked, crooked, Hawthorn tree" with music from bamboo pipe. There is nothing in the book to say that Yeats wished these poems to be performed by two voices, and before it is forgotten I am glad to set the fact down in an Irish paper.[124]

For the second part of the program Yeats changed the parlour mood with love poems by other poets, beginning with Margot speaking James Elroy Fleckers's "Santorin (A Legend of the Aegean)," ["Who are you, Sea Lady, | And where in the seas are we?"], which describes, Yeats told his listeners, "a nymph mourning her lover Alexander, and is I think, the most beautiful of all Flecker's poems." Barnes would never forget "the majesty of fulfilment" with which she spoke "Alexander, Alexander, | The King of the World was he." Nor would Yeats forget her speaking and chanting of Lionel Johnson's only love poem, "To Morfydd," introduced by a pipe tune:

> A voice on the winds,
> A voice by the waters,
> Wanders and cries:
> *Oh! what are the winds?*
> *And what are the waters?*
> *Mine are your eyes!*

124. V. C. Clinton-Baddeley, "Reciting the Poems," *Irish Times* (June 10, 1965), *Yeats: A Centenary Tribute Supplement*, p. iv. He had earlier affirmed this program change in "Reading Poetry with W. B. Yeats," 51. Yeats informed Clinton-Baddeley that "I Am of Ireland" was "developed from three or four lines of an Irish fourteenth-century dance song somebody repeated to me a few years ago" (*Words for Music*, 157).

"That poem is a perfect speech order," Yeats had written of this favorite poem, recalling Johnson's own recitations in the 1890s, "but it is still more a perfect song."[125]

Yeats wrote into the script at this point a feigned interruption by a BBC producer with a message that some of the poets present were complaining that the program had become too melancholy and insisting that they take charge at the end of Johnson's poem: "(I will rustle paper)," Yeats writes: "O—O—I understand." Then came a loud interruption by drum and clatter-bones prefacing Clinton-Baddeley's recitation of Higgins's more lively "Song for the Clatter Bones" ("God rest that Jewy woman, | Queen Jezebel, the Witch | Who peeled the clothes from her shoulder-bones | Down to her spent tits"), a song that John Stephenson had earlier mastered with difficulty for the Abbey stage.[126] The program was to conclude with Clinton-Baddeley's reading of Yeats's new ballad, "The Pilgrim," as the script indicates, but it was replaced on the day by his nine-line "Imitated from the Japanese," which had been practiced in rehearsal. "A most astonishing thing— | Seventy years have I lived", the poem begins. "In the book there is nothing to show that the poem is intended for two voices," wrote Clinton-Baddeley, appalled by a critic's interpretation of the poem as an example of Yeats's love of Nature. "I want to set on record that...I spoke the main part of the poem in the voice of a pompous old curmudgeon...And Margot Ruddock, slightly in the background, sang out the third and fourth lines in an enchanting voice of youthful excitement": "(Hurrah for the flowers of Spring, | For Spring is here again)."[127] As the curmudgeon reciter affirmed elsewhere, Yeats wanted the voice of a girl "singing for joy as she passes the garden of the pretentious old bore, and performed in this way by two voices this small poem becomes an exquisite miniature comedy,"[128] exactly what the intervening poets commanded.

125. From Yeats's 1921 notebook, dated April 7, 1921 (NLI MS 13575); mistranscribed in Richard Fallis, "Language and Rhythm in Poetry: A Previously Unpublished Essay by W. B. Yeats," *Sherandoah*, 26 (summer 1975), 78.

126. Yeats changed Higgins' "teats" to "tits" on the script. "On one occasion I was to sing a ballad of Higgins called 'Jezebel,'" wrote Stephenson. "For this I was to make up as a beggar on the Dublin streets in the eighteenth century. But this wasn't enough for Yeats...I was to use clatter-bones, he said, rattled between my fingers as an accompaniment to the song. Well, I'd no knowledge of this particular instrument but after three or four weeks of almost ceaseless practice, during which time I developed blisters on all my fingers, I became quite a passable exponent of this art. And in the end I think I more than satisfied WB with my performance." See Rodgers, "Broadcast: Poetry and the Seeing Ear," 22.

127. Clinton-Baddeley, "Reading Poetry with W. B. Yeats," 50–1.

128. Clinton-Baddeley, "Reciting the Poems," p. iv.

Yeats wrote to Dorothy before the broadcast that he believed his recent ballads were "more poignant than anything I have written" but feeling a need to return to "poems of civilisation."[129] There was some guilt in justifying the ballads, for George did not approve of them and blamed Higgins for the diversion. As soon as the broadcast was over, he did devote himself to correcting the page-proofs of *A Vision* and to composing "The Gyres" and "The Old Stone Cross," but when the BBC requested more proposals for programs he returned to his ballads and to finding suitable poems and songs to fill the second *Broadsides*. There he would publish in sequence "The Three Bushes," The Curse of Cromwell," "The Pilgrim," and "Colonel Martin," confident that these and other poems in the two volumes "will become popular songs in the next generation."[130] Thousands of circulars were to be sent out for the next volume, and his publisher Macmillan had expressed interest in publishing a large trade edition of both. As Yeats had included seven of Tagore's poems in the Oxford anthology, Rothenstein evidently suggested a broadside by Tagore, a suggestion that brought an unexpected expletive: "Damn Tagore," Yeats replied, exasperated that after *Gitanjali* Tagore's attempts to write poetry in English had resulted in "sentimental rubbish." "I shall return to the question of Tagore," he promised Rothenstein, "but not yet—I shall return to it because he has published in recent & in English prose books of great beauty & these books have been ignored because of the eclipse of his reputation."[131]

Yeats also approached Dulac, not only about participating in a broadcast debate with him and writing the music for his next broadcast, but for a special collection of his poems: "Then (& this is near my heart) if I select six or seven of my poems . . . to be sung or chanted with you for my musician . . . it may turn out a model for a whole movement."[132] Yeats was now convinced that his movement for poetry and music had gained real momentum, and he wanted to create as many new venues for its development as possible. Turner agreed to write new articles about the movement and the broadsides in the *New Statesman*.[133] Barnes listened to Yeats's proposal for a broadcast in

129. Letter to Dorothy Wellesley of March 29, [1937], *CL InteLex* 6888.
130. Letter to Edith Shackleton Heald, May 18, [1937], *CL InteLex* 6934.
131. Letter of May 7, [1937], *CL InteLex* 6925.
132. Letter of May 4, [1937], *CL InteLex* 6921.
133. In "Music and Words," Turner boomed the second series of broadsides by praising Yeats's "revolt from virtuosity" and return to simplicity: "Now is it not significant that in his revolt from virtuosity Mr. Yeats has had a strong and persistent desire to wed poetry again to

which Margot would sing and chant poems from Blake's *Songs of Innocence and Experience*, introduced and interpreted by himself. As much as Barnes admired her voice, especially under Yeats's direct tutelage, he did not think that she was as effective on the air as in rehearsal, and he doubted that she had the professional presence of mind to speak and sing to Yeats's satisfaction in a solo program. When she herself balked at the idea, Yeats dropped the proposal, which was meant to show the movement's debt to his master. Nonetheless, he made arrangements for Stephenson to sing "The Three Bushes" and "The Curse of Cromwell" at the next meeting of the Irish Academy. They were sung so well, he informed Dulac, who wrote the music for the ballads, that "not a word, not a cadense [*sic*] I would or could have changed."[134] Indeed, the audience made Stephenson sing the latter ballad again. "I never saw an audience more moved," he wrote again to Dulac, "a good many joined in the chorus."[135] It was one of Yeats's happiest and most rewarding, long-awaited moments, such that he turned the waiters out and backed against the doors to keep them from returning and interrupting the singing. The musician Walter Starkie told him afterward just what he wanted to hear, that his method "unites poetry & music in the true original way & is the start of 'a new movement' & 'an art of infinite subtlety of rhythms with music faintly pencilling in the rhythms of the verse.'" His heart was now wholly in that movement, and it informed his announcement to the Academy that evening that he was retiring from public life to devote his declining energy to the creative work ahead, and that he would leave the Abbey and the Academy in the complete control of a new generation of leaders (or so he said).

Shortly after the Academy dinner, Dulac informed Yeats that Barnes was "enthusiastic about your methods of training people & your own delivery" (*LTWBY2* 589).The encouragement made him keen to chant in a program

music? . . . Mr. Yeats has written many lyrics which are really songs and should be sung, but who is to compose the music to them? Certainly not the expert modern musician using the diatonic scale . . . Mr. Yeats is haunted by the possibility of his lyrical songs being sung. He himself sings them in a sort of chant which is not unmusical, though it is not music as professional musicians understand it" (*New Statesman and Nation*, July 24, 1937, 146–7). He lent further support to Yeats's efforts in "Poets and Musicians," explaining "the difficulty, even impossibility, of putting the poet's rhythm into musical bars . . . In the original songs of poets there is only rhythm and melody, there is no harmony. It is the attempt to fix a harmony to the melodic line which ruins the folk-song, and it is the compulsion of harmony and the complex harmonic language of music as used by musicians which unfits them for writing the poets' songs" (*New Statesman and Nation*, September 3, 1938, 347–8).

134. Letter of July 15, [1937], *CL InteLex* 7014.

135. Letter of May 27, [1937], *CL InteLex* 6942.

devoted to his own poems if he felt that his voice was strong enough. He wrote to Barnes that he would be in London for rehearsals "in plenty of time to find out if I can read my own poems in full, and without putting the musician out. Not having an ear, I cannot know on what note I shall be."[136] In mid-June he took all his enthusiasm to Penns, where he was joined by Clinton-Baddeley and others, to plan and rehearse poems for "My Own Poetry." "I have talked poetry at every moment since I arrived," he wrote to Edith Shackelton Heald, "or life in relation to it & now I must lie down—guests are expected—they too will talk poetry."[137] Clinton-Baddeley found Yeats's vitality and eagerness to discuss the problems of poetry and music at Penns unbounded. Although he would try to rest, Yeats could not bear to be away from the discussion of tunes for poems and would return unexpectedly, "for his whole heart was set upon the solution of this problem."[138] In the event that Yeats could not recite any of his poems at the broadcast, however, he wanted Clinton-Baddeley to be fully instructed in the rhythms and cadences of those that were chosen. In these sessions Clinton-Baddeley came to understand what it meant to be trained by Yeats as a reciter of his poems:

> For Yeats was a master of hidden rhythms and much of what he wanted to hear is not obvious to the eye. He longed for a tongue to declare these perfections, to explain these intricacies, and his best hope of conveying them to future generations lay in the establishment of an oral tradition.... To Yeats the reader was the trained interpreter of his mysteries.[139]

> POET TELLS RADIO SECRET
>
> **Old Gaelic as Challenge to Yeats's Listeners**
>
> **W. B. Yeats, the Irish poet who came from Dublin to introduce the broadcast of seven of his poems on Saturday night, told me afterwards a secret he had left his listeners to guess.** The line in his poem 'The Curse of Cromwell,' which he challenged listeners to identify as 'the best though not his own,' is: 'My fathers served their fathers before Christ was crucified.' This he translated from the old Gaelic, and considers a fine example of the speech of the common people—a speech now rapidly disappearing.[140]

136. Letter of May 13, [1937], *CL InteLex* 6930.
137. Letter of June 16, [1937], *CL InteLex* 6967.
138. Clinton-Baddeley, *Words for Music*, 162.
139. Clinton-Baddeley, "Reading Poetry with W. B. Yeats," 48.
140. Louise Morgan, "Poet Tells Radio Secret," *News Chronicle* (London), July 5, 1937, 3.

Yeats wanted a public theme for the new two-part broadcast, including poems that portrayed tragic Ireland in the first set—"The Rose Tree," "An Irish Airman Foresees His Death," The Curse of Cromwell"—the dream of Ireland in the second: "Mad as the Mist and Snow" (requested by Barnes), "Running to Paradise," "Sailing to Byzantium," and "He and She" (requested by George as "a perfect song"). Clinton-Baddeley woud speak the first two and "Sailing to Byzantium," Margot the rest to music by Dulac. Yeats then began his intensive training of Clinton-Baddeley, starting with line endings, rhythmic suspensions, stresses and pauses, the value given to syllables and small words. Of first importance to Yeats was the reciter's strict observance of the poet's line: "To speak strictly according to the line is to create music," Clinton-Baddeley was told, "to chase the grammar round the edge is to create prose." Yeats was appalled by the indifference of poets and reciters to the ancient skill of marking line endings, and it increased his contempt for "the modern debility of writing for the eye." Thus, the first rule to observe was that "whenever a Yeats line ends in the middle of a grammatical construction he always intended a rhythmic pause to be held." Yeats used the technique to produce exquisite effects in certain lines in "Sailing to Byzantium" ("Caught in that sensual music all neglect," "Soul clap its hands and sing, and louder sing") and especially in "Mad as the Mist and Snow":

> I shudder and I sigh to think
> That even Cicero
> And many-minded Homer were
> *Mad as the mist and snow.*

The first three lines, Clinton-Baddeley attests, provide "a remarkable example of three successive rhythmic pauses, something like tied notes in music: and the reader must achieve precisely that effect or the poem is nothing." He remembered from "The Rose Tree" the "heraldic swing" that Yeats gave to "Said Pearse to Connolly," the sharp sound of the double consonants in words like "bitter" ("Across the bitter sea"), and the "clarion note" that he liked to hear resounding in a name like Connolly, the "ly" at the end "as important to him as any other syllable. It is not that the 'ly' is drawn out—but rather that it carries a sort of rest with it which gives it equality as a syllable."[141] The most unforgettable line, however, was Yeats's chanting

141. Another example of unexpected syllabic value is the value of "a" in "A Terrible beauty is born" ("Easter 1916"), described by Clinton-Baddeley as "an eminent example of a

of "A tattered coat upon a stick, unless" in the second stanza of "Sailing to Byzantium":

> It was essential to him that the kick of that line should not be ironed out by any voice of gentle sympathy. But the full extent of Yeats's bitterness against old age is not apparent on the printed page. The defiant rhythm that he wanted can only be hammered out by the human voice.
>
> 
>
>
> 'Tattered' was separated by a hair from 'coat'; 'coat upon a stick' was one phrase, with a jabbing accent at each end.

After instructing Clinton-Baddeley in his rhythmical principles and regulating the declamation according to his expectations, Yeats, believing that Clinton-Baddeley was reciting beautifully, generously decided to withdraw from chanting any of the poems himself, "for fear it might seem a reflection on his skill."[142] In rehearsals at the BBC, however, he did not hesitate to intervene impulsively to get his desired effects. When Clinton-Baddeley built up to the dramatic lines of "An Irish Airman" ("A lonely impulse of delight | Drove to this tumult in the clouds"), Yeats cried out from the talk-back booth, "Ecstasy, Baddeley, Ecstasy!" chanting the lines repeatedly until Clinton-Baddeley too read them as if experiencing mentally and physically a soaring sensation of flight. As if there were any likelihood of forgetting this correction, Clinton-Baddeley wrote next to the bracketed lines on his script, "to self—but Ecstasy." And when he had difficulty reciting the opening line of "Sailing to Byzantium" ("That is no country for old men. The young"), telling Yeats that it was easier on the page than on the tongue, hard to read aloud and retain the sense, Yeats replied disingenuously that it was "the worst piece of syntax I ever wrote." Before the formal broadcast that evening Yeats handed him a substitute line, "Old men should quit a country where the young". Clinton-Baddeley was much impressed by Yeats's willingness to alter a line in a major poem and often re-told

concealed Yeats rhythm. Elide, or skip over the 'a', and the line falls to pieces. Dwell on the 'a' and the reader will necessarily dwell on the 'terrible', as well, and after that he cannot fail to speak the rest of the line in the impressively slow pace which Yeats wanted" ("Reading Poetry with W. B. Yeats," 52).

142. Letter to George Yeats of June 28, 1936, *CL InteLex* 6995.

the well-known story. But Yeats made the change on the day solely to accommodate the rhythmical difficulty of his English reciter for a one-off program; he had no difficulty with the line himself and never considered making that change permanent. "What was inspiring," Clinton-Baddeley reflected on his rehearsal and broadcast experience with Yeats, "was the mighty confidence that he conveyed that what we were creating was of enormous importance."[143]

Margot's separate rehearsals with Dulac were not so happy. In the previous fortnight he had finally responded to Yeats's repeated requests by writing music for four poems: "The Curse of Cromwell," "Mad as the Mist and Snow," "Running to Paradise," and "He and She." He had reminded Yeats in complying that he had written music for no other poet; that he had not invented a new style of singing poetry as Yeats claimed; that to invent such a style and train performers would be the work of years; and that he would write music for poems to be sung, not chanted. Strongly convinced that the singing of poetry must be modal and not tonal, he complained that in rehearsal Margot kept falling into tonal drift.[144] Deeply frustrated by her inability to follow his music, he took "Running to Paradise" and "He and She" away from her, leaving her only "The Curse of Cromwell" to speak with Clinton-Baddeley and sending her a cheque for her troubles, lest she lose her BBC fee. Yeats agreed to this only because he did not want to rehearse her "with that equal measuring out of her voice" that the music required and that affected the rhythm of the poems. On Dulac's emergency request, the BBC allowed him to bring in two professional musicians, singer Olive Groves and harpist Marie Goosens, to play his settings of the poems and provide transitional music between them. This decision was a recipe for the violent quarrel that erupted when Yeats heard the singer and harpist at the next rehearsal. He was first distressed by the harp notes behind the reading of "Mad as the Mist and Snow" and "The Curse of Cromwell," but his anger became uncontrollable when he heard Dulac's "singing wench," as he called her, the embodiment of everything he disliked about trained

143. Clinton-Baddeley, "Reciting the Poems," p. iv.

144. As Dulac explained in a letter of July 16, 1937, to Yeats, "The only firm conviction I hold about the singing of poetry is that it must be *modal* and not *tonal*. I can give reasons for this. The modern musician thinks *naturally* of a tune in a *key*. There are very few musicians today who can get into the modal mood. Even in Ireland they may use what you call the 'gapped' scale but they produce with it *tonal* melodies. Duff's music for the Broadside is entirely tonal" (Included in Diana Poteat Hobby, "William Butler Yeats and Edmund Dulac, A Correspondence," PhD Dissertation, Rice University, 1981; Ann Arbor, MI: University Microfilms International [Order 8116967], 1983. 238).

singers for the past thirty years. He told Dulac that her words were "scandalous and ridiculous," that the music distorted the shape of the poems, and that he wanted to give the two songs to Clinton-Baddeley. When Dulac threatened to take his music and leave, Yeats relinquished furiously, "Damn everybody, your music will be done." That evening he wrote to George: "Stormy rehearsal today. Dulac's professional singer has an extreme distaste for the English language. BBC said they had engaged her. I said I was quite ready to pay her to stay away."[145] In compromise, Yeats agreed to allow Groves to sing if the BBC producer announced beforehand that she was produced by Dulac, not by him. This was done.[146]

The row was followed by mutual recriminations for the next fortnight. As for the performance itself, Dulac told Yeats that only the two songs by Groves had gone smoothly: he thought Margot "incredibly bad—she murdered your poem and was 'plummy,'" Clinton-Baddeley "throaty and nervous." In his anger over Yeats's insults and behavior in doing everything he could to "queer my pitch," Dulac vented in a long letter twenty years of pent-up frustration, pulling out all the stops in giving Yeats a frank and brutal opinion of his "amateurish" theory and practice of reciting poetry to music:

> You have no knowledge of music and no feeling for it. You say that in Dublin they do what you want; what you want seems to be the theosophical lady's ululations to the Hawk's Well, twenty years ago, Margot's crooning, and the music for your other recitals, all of which is amateurish village green, arty, and would make any one with the slightest taste for good stuff shiver down his back. . . . Had you definite ideas it would have been a different matter. I would have known from the start where I stood. As things are, for the sake of some nebulous conception that you can only test by the amateurish taste of a few people in Ireland, everybody has had far more trouble and worry that the occasion warranted.[147]

In provoking Dulac, Yeats in O'Leary's vehement voice came as close as possible to having a musician "do him an injury." He knew that he had let his anger get the best of him and asked Dulac's pardon before directing

145. Letter of July 1, [1937], *CL InteLex* 6996.

146. The announcer stated: "My Own Poetry: A programme selected and introduced by W. B. Yeats with music composed by Edmund Dulac. The poems are spoken by Margot Ruddock and V. C. Clinton-Baddeley and have been produced by Mr. Yeats in accordance with his own ideas. The two songs are produced by Mr. Edmund Dulac and are sung by Miss Olive Groves" (*LAR* 310).

147. Letter of July 4, [1937], in Hobby, *William Butler Yeats and Edmund Dulac, A Correspondence*, 229–32.

his own fury over the quarrel into his public "manifesto" for the second volume of *Broadsides,* "Music and Poetry," describing it to George as "a fiery denunciation of the treatment of poetry by modern musicians."[148] Wellesley, his co-signatory, advised him to make it even more furious after she read the draft. "We fix a quarrel upon the concert platform," it begins. "We must win if poetry is to get back its public." Arguing that "there must be some right balance between sound and word," Yeats accuses modern musicians of ignoring the ancient art of song and of wronging poets on the concert platform "by masticating their well-made words and turning them into spittle." In combating the arrogance, those who consider song "a natural expression of life" must continue to sing "traditional songs, or songs by new poets set in the traditional way," eschewing musical accompaniment and professional singers: "We reject all professional singers because no mouth trained to the modern scale can articulate poetry."[149]

Turner weighed in on the program as well. Even as he sympathized with Yeats, he was not hesitant to say that, though the harp music did not fulfill its purpose, Groves' performance of "He and She" "was well sung & musically a very good effort for an amateur composer." Nor was he reluctant to assert that Margot's performance of "The Curse of Cromwell" was "downright bad; in fact horrible—a mere whining." He thought Clinton-Baddeley's "Mad as the Mist & Snow" not much better, but that he spoke his other poems well, especially "Sailing to Byzantium" (*LTWBY2* 591). Yeats thanked him for shedding light on what he admitted was "my chief obsession," and he wrote to Dulac that since both of them were the objects of Turner's criticism, "We may as well make friends for we are both rats in the water."[150]

148. Letter of [*c.* July 10, 1937], *CL InteLex* 7005.

149. W. B. Yeats and Dorothy Wellesley (eds), *Broadsides* (Dublin: Cuala Press, 1937). Perhaps for Dulac's benefit, Yeats gave his Noh-based dance plays as an example of seeking the balance between sound and word: "contemplative emotion left to singers who can satisfy the poet's ear, exposition of plot to actors, climax of the whole to dancers . . . He does not say that he has succeeded, but that his experiment should be repeated." He believed that an achieved balance was to be found in Tagore's and Shri Purohit Swami's India: "Tagore sings to men he 'keeps near him for the purpose'; then come the minstrels, and then to these other minstrels. The broadcasts sent out from Delhi, in the vernacular tongues of India, are almost altogether sung or spoken poetry; and everywhere throughout the East, competent authority assures us, the harlots sing as we would have them sing."

150. Letter of [July 10, 1937], *CL InteLex* 7007. On July 26 Yeats reported to Wellesley that Higgins had appeared with a late opinion: "said my broadcast was a failure, and blamed Dulac in the main, thought his music good but—, said no singer trained on the diatonic scale can sing poetry; said all respectable people in Ireland sang according to that scale, but that he and all disreputables sang in the ancient 'modes' " (*CL InteLex* 7026).

When Turner asked Dulac to spell out his views on the singing of poetry, he complied by typing out his "purely theoretical" thoughts and sent a copy to Yeats, saying that though he thought Turner's views prejudiced and his knowledge of non-Western music limited, he was "glad we have all simmered down. Some obscure grievance in you must have wanted an outlet. It found it in these discords let us rejoice it is over" (*LTWBY2* 592). In seeking to explain that grievance to Dulac, Yeats described how his earlier experiments with Farr's pupils and others "had taught me that no singer, who is not first and foremost a speaker can speak or sing a line of poetry with poetical vitality," and he dragged up for illustration his experience in 1903 with Mary Price Owen, his prototype of Olive Groves: "I quite literally rehersed [*sic*] for weeks 'a trained singer,' & an able & willing woman, a friend of Miss Hornimans. At the end her words were not flesh & blood but veal. They had been drained before I began my work."[151] The thought that in the rehearsal with Groves he had come full circle to his experience with Owen, that there had been no advance in the singing of his poetry, had led to the explosive déjà vu outburst, the worst of his career. His rage over musicians was soon to spread in *On the Boiler* to the ills of a coarsening culture

In his own untitled typescript on music and poetry, Dulac sought to recognize the division and separate paths of poets and musicians in Western culture during the past three hundred years and to outline a straightforward plan for their reunification in terms of Yeats's desires. He readily admitted that "it is the music that must give way," keeping the accompaniment to the poem simple and not allowing the melodic line to assume a complex quality of its own. "That is what I humbly tried to do," he addressed Yeats directly, "and that you mistook for *organised* music. My object was to dissociate you and your poems from amateurish efforts at *the same kind of thing*, to substitute some sort of efficiency for inefficient improvisation."[152] After absorbing Dulac's criticism, Yeats sent him a chastened reply of self-justification, a heartfelt summary of his lifelong effort to keep an ancient tradition alive by combating the effects on poetry of Victorian rhetoric and modern subjectivity:

151. Letter of July 17, [1937], *CL InteLex* 7016.

152. Dulac's typescript, later revised and expanded as "Music and Poetry" (see Appendix 3), has been printed as an appendix, "The 'Neuchâtel Document,'" in Wayne McKenna's "W. B. Yeats, W. J. Turner and Edmund Dulac: The *Broadsides* and Poetry Broadcasts," *YA8* (1991), 232–3.

> You say this poetry cannot be changed but all my life I have tried to change it. Goethe said that all our modern poetry is wrong because subjective, & in the past in the *Battle of the Books* connected with the fable of the bee & the spider Swift has said the same. All my life I have tried to get rid of modern subjectivity by insisting on construction & contemporary words & syntax. It was to force myself to this that I used to insist that all poems should be spoken (hence my plays) or sung. Unfortunately it was only about a year ago that I discovered that for sung poetry (though not for poetry chanted as Florence Farr chanted) a certain type of stress was essential. (I would like to discuss this with you). It was by mastering this "stress" that I have written my most recent poems which have I think, for me, a new poignancy.
>
> I want to get back to simplicity & can best do it—I believe by working for our Irish unaccompanied singing. Every change I make to help the singer seems to improve the form. A man of my ignorance learns from action.[153]

The friendship had survived the row, but neither had a stomach to stage the proposed broadcast debate on the subject, which was canceled, and Dulac would arrange no more music for Yeats's poems.

Barnes still pressed Yeats for more programs, however, and in arranging what would be his last broadcast, "My Own Poetry Again," Yeats dramatically altered the format, removing all music and musical interludes for unaccompanied chanting and singing by himself and Margot, the two on their own, like he and Farr began. In his introduction to the broadcast on October 29, he provided the autobiographical background for the composition of the first two poems, "The Lake Isle of Innisfree" and "The Fiddler of Dooney." For the first time in many years he the chose "The Happy Townland," chanting the lyrics to Margot's sung refrain, ("*The little red fox he murmured, | 'O what of the world's bane?'* "), made so popular to earlier audiences by Farr, Pixie Smith, and other pupils. Barnes thought unforgettable "those wonderful refrains which he made Margot sing and which he longed to sing in some way himself." Yeats introduced her with warmth and affection, affirming the "great pleasure"

153. Letter of July 15, [1937], *CL InteLex* 7014. Yeats first described this "certain type of stress" to W. J. Turner in a letter of mid-December 1935: "I am writing four stress lines but I doubt if it will grow into 'sprung verse'. I dislike the uncertainty of accent" (*CL InteLex* 6483); he wrote further to Wellesley on December 21: "I am writing in short lines but think that I shall not use 'sprung verse'—now that I am close to it I dislike the constant uncertainty as to where the accent falls; it seems to make the verse vague & week [*sic*]. I like a strong driving force. If there should be a subtle hesitating rhythm I can make it. I do not want it as part of the metrical scheme" (*CL InteLex* 6490).

that her chanting and singing gave him. "She is not Irish," he said, "but she sings as we sing without accompaniment. If you listen, as a trained musician listens, for the notes only, you will miss the pleasure you are accustomed to and find no other. Her notes cannot be separated from the words." He had her begin with "Into the Twilight" ("Out-worn heart, in a time out-worn"), an early poem of "longing for the West of Ireland" when some love affair "had gone wrong." Barnes's most vivid memory of Margot in all the broadcasts was her "use of her lovely contralto voice to speak the climax of "Into the Twilight" ("And God stands winding His lonely horn").

The BBC script for the broadcast was destroyed in the following war, and some of the poems in Yeats's incomplete copy were changed beforehand. Margot's second song was to be taken from *The Countess Cathleen*, "The Countess Cathleen in Paradise," but it was replaced by "The Old Men Admiring Themselves in the Water," with which she may have concluded the program. However, Yeats's surviving script ends abruptly after he introduces and chants "Coole Park and Ballylee, 1931," which he described, self-critically invoking Arnold, as "typical of most of my recent poems, intricate in metaphor, the swan and water both symbols of the soul, not at all a dream, like my earlier poems, but a criticism of life." (*LAR* 295).[154] But it appears that he may have ended more appropriately with "Sailing to Byzantium," which he had introduced in the previous broadcast and which members of the broadcast team had heard him chant passionately and memorably on several occasions. One of his listeners, Francis Berry, wrote that "those who heard Yeats broadcast his later poems in the thirties will recall the quavering impassioned chaunting of his delivery of the Byzantine poems":

> They will also remember his vocal realization of the poem with a refrain, the care and force with which he distinguished the refrains (dry and high-pitched) from the stanzas to which they subscribed. If, previous to Yeats' own rendering, some of us had failed, depending on the printed signs alone, to hear him, then we can admit that memories of his broadcasts have enabled us to apply the memory of his voice to the printed signs so that they are no longer mute.[155]

154. At the rehearsal the day before, October 28, the introduction to the program, Yeats's reading of "The Lake Isle of Innisfree" and the third and fourth stanzas of "Coole and Ballylee, 1931" were recorded on a BBC disc (no. 22145). Barnes told Mrs. Yeats that the program on October 29 was not recorded.

155. Francis Berry, *Poetry and the Physical Voice* (London: Routledge and Kegan Paul, 1962), 181–2.

"It was very moving," Barnes wrote of the broadcast, "and Yeats read with great feeling." Afterward, Yeats took Margot and Barnes to celebrate over a late-night meal at an Italian restaurant that he particularly liked, only to have their spirits deflated by the discovery that it had changed management. In the ultimate anticlimax to a momentous evening, Barnes recalled, "a stern Scottish waitress denied us drink and eventually brought Margot a white coffee and Yeats a hard boiled egg." Even though Yeats was extremely tired, Barnes took advantage of his heightened post-broadcast mood to suggest three more programs before Yeats went off in January for two months in Monte Carlo, Menton, and finally at the Hotel Idéal-Séjour, Cap-Martin, in the south of France. The strategy worked, for Yeats formally agreed to a revival on January 3 of "In the Poet's Pub" with a theme of "Poems of Love and War"; a new broadcast with Professor Walter Starkie playing his fiddle for Yeats's reading of ballads; and another as part of a BBC series entitled "I Became an Author," on how he began his writing life and the obstacles he had to overcome. Then, five days after the boiled-egg dinner, he received an invitation from Vyvyan Adams of BBC television to take part in a televised reading of his poems, bringing too late another new public medium to his doorstep.[156] But his enthusiasm and energy for these exhausting programs had begun to wane, and in mid-December he postponed them all until April. On his return from France in March, he took steps to reduce his obligation to Barnes: "I have refused to do the Yeats Starkie broadcast," he wrote to Heald, "& I wish I could get out of the other two." On March 31 Barnes arranged for Yeats to hear a phonograph recording of the original "In the Poet's Pub," but as his ear for the music had been soured by the conflict with Dulac, he listened to it with "amused disgust."[157] The new version was scheduled for April 8, but problems arose. Yeats had lost contact with Margot, unaware that she had collapsed after the previous broadcast and had been placed in a mental institution, and when Clinton-Baddeley became ill Yeats readily postponed it on the grounds that he knew no one who could take his place. Attempts were made to reschedule, but further illness undermined his spirit for further broadcasts. "I see no chance of being able to fix dates ahead," he wrote to Barnes, struggling with fatigue and losing his voice in

156. Letter of November 2, 1937, NLI MS 30,160. Yeats's reply is missing, but he never took part in a televised program. On April 25 and May 4, however, the BBC televised a production of *The Shadowy Waters*.

157. Letter to Edmund Dulac of July 17, [1937], *CL InteLex* 7216.

the evenings. "My broadcasting is finished. I am sorry considering all the trouble you have taken with me."[158]

VI

To shore up his public project, Yeats decided to bring out a third series of broadsides, probably to include the old English ballads. He placed it in the hands of Higgins, under whose neglect it eventually collapsed. Yeats knew, however, that leaving the broadcasts turned him toward a larger leave-taking of body and soul, evident in the meditative poems that followed. The essential drama of withdrawal is embodied in "The Spirit Medium," where ghostly, medium-summoned images of the dead come into his soul. "Poetry, music, I have loved," his agèd persona begins, for the music of poetry has long sustained him against the reality of death and the abstraction of the supernatural. But when an old ghost beckons him anew to the "lightning" to be found with him, he knows not only that "To follow is to die" but that his defense is down: "Poetry and music I have banished," he cries in his new vulnerability, but being vulnerable he mounts his defense against the lightning-lure of the soul in the "stupidity" of the natural world and its clay, in the cyclical regeneration of root, shoot, and blossom, content to dig his grave with the spade of tragic joy, groping toward the dark "*with a dirty hand*," a final affirmation of the blind human self that echoes earlier dialogues of self and soul.[159]

His farewell to the stage was yet to come, heralded by the Abbey's late-summer "Festival" representing the work of thirty-five years, a fortnight of seventeen plays concluding with Yeats's *Purgatory* and *On Baile's Strand*. The general quality of the productions and acting had not been good, he heard, a failure attributed to Hugh Hunt, who had stayed on through the festival, and new players, but he was pleased with the acting of his own plays and sensed a genuine excitement in the audience. Going on the Abbey stage

158. Letter of June 16, 1938, *CL InteLex* 7243. Although Yeats did not broadcast "I Became an Author," it was published in *The Listener* on August 4, 1938, his last periodical publication (*LAR* 297–300).

159. "I am content to live it all again," the Self affirms in "A Dialogue of Self and Soul" (1929), "And yet again, if it be life to pitch | Into the frog-spawn of a blind man's ditch, | A blind man battering blind men" (*VP* 479). "Seek out reality, leave things that seem," the Soul urges in "Vacillation." "What, be a singer born and lack a theme?" the Heart replies.

> *The Soul.* "Look on that fire, salvation walks within."
> *The Heart.* What theme had Homer but original sin?" (*VP* 502)

for the last time, he said of *Purgatory*, no longer concerned with pictorial effect, "I have put nothing into the play because it seemed picturesque; I have put there my own convictions about this world and the next."[160] The revival of *On Baile's Strand*, with a "magnificent 'Cuchulain,'" could not have been more timely or inspiring: "I have not seen it for years & it seemed to me entirely right," he told Wellesley. "Cuchulain seemed to me a heroic figure because he was creative joy separated from fear."[161] The revived identification with Cuchulain's mind and death as he races out to fight the waves turned him toward the completion of his Cuchulain cycle with *The Death of Cuchulain.* His creative excitement, however, was not sufficient to offset his reflection in *On the Boiler* on the misdirection of the Abbey and the reception of his verse plays. He accepts the fact that at the close of his career "the theatre has not . . . gone my way or in any way I wanted it to go," but even in recognizing the Abbey's preference for realistic plays he asserts a great personal fulfillment: "I have written for tragic ecstasy, and here and there in my own work . . . I have seen it greatly played. What matter if the people prefer another art, I have had my fill" (*Expl* 415–16).

And yet, Yeats's final withdrawal from public life into the meditative self was not a withdrawal from the public, even in light of his scorn in "Under Ben Bulben" for "the sort now growing up" and his views of cultural degeneration in *On the Boiler.* Just before canceling his broadcasts, he read in the *Yale Review* an article by the American poet Archibald MacLeish on the "public speech" of his poetry, "the only article on the subject which has not bored me for years," he wrote to Wellesley. "It commends me above the other modern poets because my language is 'public.'" That word which I had not thought of myself is a word I want."[162] Indeed, MacLeish portrays Yeats as the sole leader of a needed poetic revolution to bring to modern poetry the public speech of which it has long been deprived, a "human, living, natural, and unformalized speech, capable of the public communication of common experience, which . . . cannot be confined . . . to those intimate whisperings in the personal ear which pass for purest poetry in periods of decline."[163] Yeats's later poetry, he argues,

160. Letter to Dorothy Wellesley of August 15, [1938], *CL InteLex* 7290.
161. Letter of August 15, [1938], *CL InteLex* 7290.
162. Letter to Wellesley of May 24, [1938], *CL InteLex* 7243. Yeats refers to Archibald MacLeish's "Public Speech and Private Speech in Poetry," *Yale Review*, 27 (March 1938), 536–47.
163. MacLeish, "Public Speech and Private Speech in Poetry," 537.

like that of all the great ages of poetry, is "of the world. It is the first English poetry in a century which has dared to re-enter the world. It is the first poetry in English in more than a century in which the poem is again an act upon the world." MacLeish places Yeats in contrast to the younger Eliot and Auden, who, while "consciously employing the methods of the revolution in their art, seem for some inexplicable reason to be doubling back on their tracks":

> Or more exactly they seem to be engaged in pushing the use of idioms of living speech inherited from their predecessors on beyond the true limits of those idioms into the artificiality of a new closet poetry. Instead of the live phrases of passionate utterance to be found in Yeats—the human rhythms . . . there is an inversion of naturalness which uses natural utterance for satiric and subjective ends. Auden and his imitators have chosen for their poetic language the living language of the time but the living language in its most banal and deadened phrases. They have created from this stereotyped language a satiric, and sometimes a lyric, poetry of great power. But the meanings of this poetry are not outward towards the world but inward towards the private references of the poet.[164]

MacLeish's passionate analysis of public and private voices in modern poetry was Yeats's own; it articulated for him his quarrel with the Eliot–Auden school and gave him the self-image he sought to fashion all his career, "public poet."

Yeats's desire to be known and remembered as a poet of the people writing in a passionate public language for the world began to permeate his last poems. It was fitting that he closed *On the Boiler* with "A Statesman's Holiday" (untitled at the time), a late-life rewriting of "King Goll" (1884). Yeats's statesman persona retreats like Goll from the mad affairs of state to take up the "better trade" of a wandering street-singer, singing "an old foul tune," not with Goll's tympan but with a one-string "Montenegrin lute," the one that Lady Gregory brought him for his earliest chanting experiments in 1901: "And its old sole string | Makes me sweet music | And I delight to sing: | *Tall dames go walking in grass-green Avalon.*" In imagining his permanent holiday in poetry, the statesman gladly dons the poor Irish singer's outlandish garb, much like his brother's painting of *The Ballad Singer* (*c.*1915, Plate 27), taking to the streets and roads to be among the people:

164. Ibid. 547.

With boys and girls about him,
With any sort of clothes,
With a hat out of fashion,
With old patched shoes,
With a ragged bandit cloak,
With an eye like a hawk,
With a stiff straight back,
With a strutting turkey walk,
With a bag full of pennies,
With a monkey on a chain,
With a great cock's feather,
With an old foul tune. (*VP* 627)

Moreover, in "The Municipal Gallery Revisited," where a succession of familiar portraits leads him to an emotional reflection on a lifetime of friendships, his memory turns to the "sole test" which he, with the support of Synge and Lady Gregory, applied to the aims and ideals of the Abbey Theatre—that everything done, said, or sung "come from contact with the soil," that the performance of all plays, songs, and poems contribute to the dream of a spiritual democracy:

We three alone in modern times had brought
Everything down to that sole test again,
Dream of the noble and the beggar-man. (*VP* 603)[165]

At the end of November 1938, Yeats left London for a return visit to Cap-Martin in southern France, leaving in his wake several other "poems of civilisation"—"The Statues," "Long-Legged Fly," "His Convictions," "Man and the Echo," "The Circus Animals' Desertion." At their last meeting, Barnes asked him what he wanted done with his broadcasts for the BBC; Baddeley would know what to do with them, he replied. After settling into his room at the Hôtel Idéal-Séjour, he wrote to Clinton-Baddeley, who had recently given three of his own broadcasts on "Words for Music," chapters of a book he was writing by that title. Reading the chapters with much interest and some disagreement, he now asked Clinton-Baddeley to let him and two or three others, probably Higgins, Turner, and Dulac, add essays to his for a separate book. "What I am hoping for," he wrote, "is a small book dealing with the relations between speech & song." While Clinton-Baddeley mulled the request, reluctant to

165. Yeats's "sole test" finally replaced "ancient test" in late drafts of the poem. See *New Poems: Manuscript Materials by W. B. Yeats*, 337–43.

relinquish his own direction, Yeats made enquiries on the Swami's behalf about the whereabouts of Margot. "She was put into an Asylum a year ago," he reported of his discoveries, "ceased to recognize anybody husband or child."[166] Her estranged husband had departed. "She was a tragic beautiful creature," he told the Swami of his last sayer and singer. She died in the asylum twelve years later.

Yeats was now working hard to complete *The Death of Cuchulain*, which itself gave rise to a dream-inspired poem, "Cuchulain Comforted." "I think my play is strange & the most moving I have written for some years," he wrote to Heald on New Year's Day, 1939. "I am making the prose sketch for a poem—a kind of sequel—strange, too, something new."[167] George and their son Michael, now seventeen and on holiday from school, were with him. Wellesley and Matheson visited frequently from the former's nearby villa in Beaulieu-sur-Mer, and they were joined in early January by Heald and the Turners, a gathering like many others at Penns. Wellesley thought he seemed as lively and excited as ever, full of his theories of words and music, but he confided his awareness of approaching death to Lady Elizabeth Pelham, yet another mystical friend met in the Swami's retinue: "I know for certain that my time will not be long," he wrote on January 4. "I am happy and I think full of an energy, of an energy I had despaired of."[168] During the next three weeks he drew on that energy for a final creative surge, composing in the mornings in his room on the third floor. "Then in the afternoon," Michael recalled, "he would come out on the lawn and sit in a chair with a rug over him . . . He'd make a low tuneless hum and his hand would start beating time . . . He was oblivious to everything else."[169] Alone there, all reciters and musicians away, his right arm rising, the last keeper of the bardic flame began conducting an inner music into rhythmical speech, chanting the emerging lines over and over. For Yeats, the composing and chanting were not an expenditure but a storing of energy for a proud and exultant face-to-face with death, a storing begun over forty years earlier, bundling poems away "That the night come," an "increasing Night | That opens her mystery and fright," testing every work to make him worthy of joining "such men as come | Proud, open-eyed

166. Letter of December 22, [1938], *CL InteLex* 7335.
167. Letter of January 1, [1939], *CL InteLex* 7360.
168. Letter of January 4, [1939], *CL InteLex* 7362.
169. See Steward Kellerman, "Yeats at the End: Still Writing," based on an interview with Michael Yeats, *New York Times*, April 6, 1989, C17, 21.

and laughing to the tomb."[170] He had always believed what he had the oldest pupil say on the death of Seanchan in *The King's Threshold*, "Not what it leaves behind in the light | But what it carries with it to the dark | Exalts the soul" (*VPl* 312). On the 13th he finished "Cuchulain Comforted," a week later "The Black Tower," his last poem, which he chanted to Wellesley and Matheson on the 21st. "He asked Hilda to make a tune for it," Wellesley reported to Rothenstein. "She walked out of the hotel and she and I walked up and down in the darkness trying the tune. When we came back she sang the air, he seemed pleased. His last projective thought seems to me to be this wish for 'words for melody.' "[171] Two days later, his "chief obsession" rising up again, he wrote to Clinton-Baddeley to press him for a decision about the book on speech and song, asking further if he had not read one of his poems in a broadcast: "I forgot its title ["The Wild Old Wicked Man"] but it has for its chorus 'Daybreak and a candle end.' It must have been well done for people keep writing to me about it."[172]

When Wellesley and Matheson visited him on the morning of the 26th, they saw that he was dying and stayed only a few minutes. Returning that afternoon on George's invitation to "Come back and light the flame!", Wellesley found him "murmuring poetry" to himself,[173] not unlike Blake on his deathbed. That evening, he rallied to dictate to George corrections for his last poems, changing the title of "His Convictions" to "Under Ben Bulben," a final touch before his right arm came down for the last time. The next day, Friday, after receiving morphia for heart pain, Yeats, overtaken while drafting a list of contents for a new volume, slipped into a coma in his corner room at the Hôtel Idéal-Séjour. Clinton-Baddeley, writing on Sunday morning to say that he agreed to the book on speech and song as

170. Successively, "That the Night Come" (*VP* 317); "The Apparitions" (*VP* 624); "Vacillation" (*VP* 501);

171. Undated letter to William Rothenstein, quoted in Rothenstein's *Since Fifty*, 306. "He read aloud his last poem" she said in the letter. Later that year she wrote an almost verbatim account in the "Last Days" section of *Letters on Poetry*, specifying that "his last poem" was "The Black Tower" (213); however, when she wrote about Yeats's death thirteen years later, she stated that she had taken to his bedside a poem that she had written for the Cuala broadsides, "Golden Helen," and that Yeats asked Matheson to make a tune for that poem. See her *Far Have I Travelled* (London: James Barrie, 1952), 167. Ann Saddlemyer thinks Wellesley's later version in 1952 "more probable" (*Becoming George*, 777, n. 146, from 560), but this author believes that Wellesley's original accounts in 1939 must stand.

172. Letter of January 23, 1939, *CL InteLex* 7375. Clinton-Baddeley had given his three broadcasts on "Words for Music" in September 1938, the third on the eve of the Munich Conference.

173. Wellesley, *Letters on Poetry*, 215.

Yeats wished, was stopped by a wireless report that the last minstrel was gone, that on the previous afternoon the last strains of a lost kingdom were suddenly stilled.[174] Yeats had long before chanted an epitaph, not for a headstone, but for the historic moment of this bardic passing, given to a poet's musicians in *The Dreaming of the Bones:*

At the grey round of the hill
Music of a lost kingdom
Runs, runs and is suddenly still.
The winds out of Clare-Galway
Carry it: suddenly it is still.

I have heard in the night air
A wandering airy music;
And moidered in that snare
A man is lost of a sudden,
In that sweet wandering snare.

What finger first began
Music of a lost kingdom?
They dream that laughed in the sun.

174. Clinton-Baddeley proceeded with his original plan for his book, *Words for Music* (Cambridge: Cambridge University Press, 1941), including only a final chapter on Yeats ("W. B. Yeats and the Art of Song," 151–61). On February 4, 1939, less than a week after Yeats's death, Clinton-Baddeley broadcast a "Farewell to Yeats" for a BBC National Programme. Reading and commenting on several poems, he told the audience that Yeats "considered it essential that certain poetry should be sung, but it had to be sung in the ancient tradition of song—unaccompanied and to a tune designed only to express the words, not to embroider them." He described Yeats's equally strong views of reading poetry: how he demanded that a reciter's whole execution be dedicated to the service of the words; how he was at war with those who thought rhyme and rhythm were things to be avoided, with those who read with false beauty in their voices. "Any reading which dodged the implications of a line of verse he would call 'Trivial!' " (BBC catalogue 13849).

Clinton-Baddeley later produced with Jill Balcon and Marjorie Westbury a 331/3 rpm recording, *Poems by W. B. Yeats / Spoken According to His Own Directions* (Jupiter Recording, Jur OOB2, 1958), writing a preface on the sleeve: "In 1937 the B.B.C. invited W. B. Yeats to arrange four broadcasts of poetry . . . I was a reader in the first three of these programmes, and remember very clearly the way Margot Ruddock . . . and I were expected to speak—and to sing . . . Included in this disc are all the Yeats poems that I rehearsed and broadcast for him . . . and those which I did in duet with Margot Ruddock; and the tunes to which two of them are sung are the tunes which were used in 1937. In between the poems Yeats tried various instrumental effects—the knucklebones for a poem by F. R. Higgins, a bamboo pipe for some of his own. These effects are not attempted on this disc . . . In the 1937 broadcast Margot Ruddock read 'The Curse of Cromwell'. On this record I have not given this poem to a woman—partly because . . . the poem so plainly speaks in the voice of Yeats himself."

Dry bones that dream are bitter,
They dream and darken our sun.

Those crazy fingers play
A wandering airy music;
Our luck is withered away,
And wheat in the wheat-ear withered,
And the wind blows it away. (*VPl* 775–6)

Appendix 1

The Chanting of Poems

To the Editor of *The Outlook*

Sir,—After Mr. Baughan's very interesting article on the chanting of poems, your readers may care to hear exactly what the mechanism of my method is. Some years ago Mr. Arnold Dolmetsch invented a musical instrument for my use. It has thirteen open strings, and a compass from G below the middle C, of the piano to the G above. My speaking voice is rather low, and when Mrs. Patrick Campbell ordered a psaltery like mine, the compass of hers was to be from the B♭ to the B♭'. This appears to suit most people better than the compass of my instrument. The Greek lyre was a far simpler thing, as it probably did not include the semitones, and had from four to seven strings at different periods of time.

Within the limits of an octave of semitones I set to work to discover and write down the inherent melody of a number of poems. I reduced everything connected with the art to the simplest possible terms, and used letters to indicate the notes of my scale,

G A♭ A B♭ B C D♭ D E♭ E F G♭ G'

G indicating below and G' above the central C. I then spoke the first line of a poem in the most impressive way that occurred to me, and immediately after sang and wrote down the notes I found I had used as starting points for the spoken words. It was impossible to record the inherent melody of each spoken word. I will give a few examples from my collection.

E♭ C D E♭ D C
"We Are the music makers."

A simple minor phrase.

G' F♯ E C B
"As ye came from the Holy Land of Walsingham."

A descending melodic phrase

A♭ B E♭
"The heavy clouds are threatening,
E E♭
And it's little but they'll take the roof off the house."

An ascending phrase.

G B♭ D G♭ G'
"The flame will catch thy floating veil
F E♭ D
If thou dancest round the fire."

Naturally many poems are accompanied by chords (shown by letters enclosed in brackets), and some spoken in harmony to the notes played on the psaltery. For instance:—

E E♭ D♭ A A♭
"By the waters of Babylon we sat down and
A♯ (E D♭ A) (E♭ C A♭)
Wept when we remembered thee, O Zion."

I will now give an example from Franz, transposed for a contralto voice:—

D♯ F♯ B' A'♯ G'♯ F♯ G'♯ F♯ E D♯
"Weil' auf mir du dunk-les Auge"—

a beautiful song, which seems very difficult to speak naturally, because of the interval of one tone on the portament. In speaking, one naturally varies one's voice in a word either a semitone or a minor 3rd, hardly ever a tone. This is a famous song by Richard Strauss:—

A A' A A' A' D' F♯ G' A'
"Awake, awake, my love, softly rise"—

which could certainly be cried out, but could not possibly be spoken over so large a range of notes. I find very few people who can speak naturally on more than five full tones, let alone on more than an octave, as in this case, where I have indicated all notes above G' on the second line of the treble clef by a stroke over the note.

No one knows better than I do that chanting in the sense of making a monotonous singing sound on notes robs the voice of its beautiful sense-inflections. For the difference between speech and singing is just this—that in speech each word has a melody of its own, which starts from a certain keynote on which it is uttered, while in singing the melody of the separate word is sacrificed to the melody of the phrase. I do not chant myself or use the singing voice except for refrains, as in the case of "Sister Helen." I simply speak as I would without music, and having discovered the drift of my voice in the phrase, indicate that on the psaltery.—Yours faithfully,

FLORENCE FARR.

The Outlook, February 18, 1905, 220–1; edited with deletions in *The Music of Speech* (London: Elkin Mathews, 1909), 16–17. Farr's letter was written in response to E. A. Baughan's criticism of Yeats's claims and Farr's chanting in "The Chanting of Poems," *The Outlook*, January 21, 1905, 89–90. In declaring that the kind of chanting that may have appealed to ancients is "a form of music that can never be resuscitated with success now that we know the full powers of the art," Baughan went on to state that in Farr's performances "the chanting itself robs the voice of its beautiful sense-inflections, that music of speech which has a curious magic of its own. Nor is this elementary attempt to express the hidden song of poetry required. When Mr. Yeats says that 'to-day the poet, fanatic that he is, watches the singer go up on the platform, wondering and expecting every moment that he will punch himself as if he were a bag,' I feel that his knowledge of modern music and modern singing must be very limited. Composers of to-day, from Robert Franz to Richard Strauss, have written songs so that the accompaniment shall express the emotional content of the poems, and the vocal part be arranged so that its music does not obscure the poetry, and there are many singers (although I admit there are others who view the verse as of no account) who are quite capable of singing these songs so that you can hear every syllable of the poems. In short, the medium of modern music is much more plastic to the expression of fine shades of meaning than the monotonous chanting which Miss Farr has recently brought to the notice of the public."

Appendix 2

Music in Words

by Florence Farr

Anyone that has questioned the traditions that remain to us, and has seen them afar off, emerging from a mist—stark, obsolete, sometimes absurd—may find that, on further questioning, their dead lips will utter a subtle benediction, awakening in him that enthusiasm which is said to arise when the parts of the soul are united in the state called Faith. When the faithful soul is at peace and listens for the voices of tradition, sometimes it understands those voices, and sometimes can repeat their meanings to others who have voices, and sometimes can repeat their meanings to others who have been too bewildered by the clamour and the storms of their own clashing thoughts to understand them for themselves.

Such a tradition, dead to many of us, is found in many legends of the Word of the Creator that made heaven and earth, of the magic words that cast glamour, of "words of power" that opened doors, of the spoken spell of the witch, of the curse of the bard. In remote places, where faith in the power of words is still alive, we find the power is supposed to lie in the rhythm and rhyme of what may be mere doggerel verse and refrains. Mediaeval spells, too, there are in plenty, very similar to that used by Shakspere for the witches in Macbeth; and we can but wonder what compelling quality there should be about such sounds.

The solution is partly to be found in the vocal methods employed. The oral traditions current among priests, for the recitation of religious ceremonies, show that there are three distinct ways of using the voice—illustrated by Gregorian chant, the intoning of prayers, and the oratorical pulpit style. These exemplify the singing, the chanting, and the speaking voices, and we may divine that there were many ways of uttering "words of power" in order to create moods of the soul or set in operation formative forces.

The questioning part of the soul is instructed in an oratorical style, which conveys thoughts from one mind to another. But in prayer it is the emotional part of the soul which should seek to annihilate itself before its ideal, and for this the sound of the intoned chant is efficacious. In the East, choirs of priests repeat for hours together short formulas, phrases called *mantrams*, while the people sit chatting together—until the spell begins to work. Then their bodies sway to the rhythm and melody of the words, their souls melt under the breath of the inspiring spirit, the sound of the words enters their inmost beings. As in a dream, so they pass away from the life of actuality into the more real ideal, the life as they would have it be! Mayhap in this state they first catch a glimpse of the great truth that heaven and hell, and God, can be with us here and now. This is the magic wrought by the refrain, the repetition of phrase, the secret power in such words as "Hallelujah!" "Amen!" or "Kyrie Eleison!" Beyond this magic of chanting is the magic of praise or of wailing wrought by the singing voice.

In the absolute singing voice the little melody of an individual word is abandoned, the melody of the phrase along being considered. Sometimes in the songs of musicians devoid of feeling for the music of poetry, all relation to the words is deliberately ignored, in favour of the meaning of the thought or emotion behind the words; and when the poetry is not great poetry this disregard may be quite excusable. I ought to explain exactly what I mean by the melody of words; and the best way I can do so is to give a few practical examples:—

Thus I say the word "*melody*" on three notes; *mel* on F, *o* sinking to C sharp, and *dy* rising to D.

In "*melodious*" I rise from F to A, then sink to C sharp and D.

The two words *sarcophagus* and *simplicity* I say on the same notes, D, C, B flat, A, with the falling inflection.

In *municipal* and *orchestration* I first rise from E to G, then fall to F, E.

Cumulative falls from G, G, F, to E.

Some words of one syllable are spoken on the tonic and its semitone or minor third, and back again to the tonic, so that they appear to a careless listener to be spoken on one note; but it may readily be discovered that every letter of the alphabet has its natural relation to every other letter.

The Hindu names for the notes of the scale reduce some sounds to a relative formula, and a native told me that the relation between the natural pitch of these consonants was indicated by the pitch of the note, *sa* being movable in pitch, *ra* a tone higher, *ma, pa, ni*, each a tone higher than the last. We can see for ourselves that it is natural to pitch the vowel sounds *ou*, *o*, *ah*, *ee*, on rising notes of the musical scale.

It is only by listening very carefully to the little tunes contained in every word that one comes to divine something of the real meaning of the tradition of magic words. There is a magic about all arts, for all the arts can be traced back to old religions, or magical formularies. The oldest rituals are elaborate dramas of a soul's adventures in time; the oldest pictures were talismans, the oldest buildings were temples for the mysteries; and music was the most powerful of all the magical arts. Modern concert music, from the delicate tracery of Bach's Fugues on through the elemental sounds of Beethoven, awaken in us great moods more than human, splendid and more cold than those familiar to us in ordinary consciousness. Coming to the great masters of human emotion, Chopin and Wagner touch our intensest human possibilities, and bathe us in the raptures of love and death.

So on to Richard Strauss, who gives music an intricacy of characterisation it has never had before. In him we feel the music of the individual soul in relation to itself and to other individuals. We get away from all generalities, and want to know every detail of his music before we can tell what our judgment really is. It is impossible to know what you feel about Strauss's music until you study it, just as it is impossible to know what you feel about an accomplished and varied personality until you have studied all its possible modifications.

But if this be what modern concert music gives us—and these are great gifts—we must not forget the old music of magic, which it does not give us. A really magical effect is very simple and slow; it cannot be hurried, it cannot be carried through if the attention be distracted. All the conditions of modern life and modern music are death to a creative magical operation. The attention must not wander; the subject must be simple, and not overlaid by ornament or irrelevances. An eight-barred folk-melody has more power to create a lasting impression on the sources of emotion, if it be repeated often enough, than elaborate orchestral effects;—although the orchestra might be used by a musician who wrote with the intention of using its magical possibilities, with more effect than the strings, wood-wind, brass, or drums could have separately. We have noticed again and again that a play decorated in three colours, a dress in which very few perfectly harmonised colours are combined, will give delight to the onlookers, far greater than more varied and less carefully chosen effects can produce. So it might be with modern concert music. Simplicity of orchestration, and the determination that the audience should not be hurried and wearied by violent transitions, but should absorb each phrase, and feel that each changed phrase was building up a great cumulative effect—this would have a really magical power. That is to say, it would chain and concentrate the attention of the audience until a unity of mood had been established among them.

In the meantime, apart from the music of instruments and the singing voice, we have the music of the poets, with its rhythm, pitch, time, and tone. And we have the music of the beautiful speaking voice, which can be used either in chanting, recitative, or speech. As I have already suggested, a word is beautiful because the relation of its natural melody is a beautiful relation, and a great speaker does all that is possible to fit the right melody or harshness to each work as he speaks it.

This effort, again, makes for elaboration in place of the straight-forward utterance of the conscientious newspaper reader, whose endeavour is merely to convey sense. For he need not strive in any way to give value to the style of the writer whose work he is interpreting. People read the newspapers so much more than they read literature, that they are inclined to resent the idea that the sound in words, or the relation of words to each other, is of any account. Yet they ought to know that "style" is the only thing that endures; the matter concerns us for a little time, but our style concerns us for all time. And style is the appreciation of words as *sounds*, not merely as symbols for conveying ideas; style is the appreciation of phrases as *melodies*, not merely as the expression of thought. The Vedantists tell us that sound is the elemental correspondence of etheric spaces, the root of measurable things. And our hearing and our speech, the part of the mind that feels the relationship between the inner and the outer life, the part of the mind that receives impression, can all be resolved into the element of sound—the strange grey world of sound, flashing or detonating; imperceptibly subduing and mastering, or roaring maledictions upon us; grasping in ecstasy or choking in death, thousand-tongued.

The mystery of sound is made manifest in words and in music. In music we know and feel it; but we are forgetting that it lives also in words, in poetry, and noble prose; we are overwhelmed by the chatter of those who profane it, and the din of the traffic of the restless disturbs the peace of those who are listening for the old magic, and watching till the new creation is heralded by the sound of the new word.

Originally printed in *Musical World*, 5 (September 15, 1906), 67–8; rpt. in *The Music of Speech* (London: Elkin Mathews, 1909), 17–21.

Appendix 3

Music and Poetry

by Edmund Dulac

In our Western world the Poet and the Musician parted company some 300 years ago. Everywhere else they are still on the best of terms. In fact they are still inseparable all over the East, Africa, and in some parts of Europe wherever the musical side of the partnership has been lucky enough to escape the attentions of the academic musician or the folk-lorist.

Eastern, ancient, and "folk" poetry consists mostly in story-telling or lyric poems with *direct* symbol-images, part of a *common* psychological background. The musical expression is *modal* and in both poems and music the emphasis is on the *universal value of already classified modes and themes.*

Our Western, post-Renaissance poetry is an entirely *personal* affair with an *indirect* appeal. At the same time Western music also sets up a claim for *individual* expression, discarding the symbolism of the mode, keeping only two amorphous scales from which the "composer" can, with imaginary freedom, extract his material. The musical expression is *tonal*. The emphasis is on the *individual value of particular, invented themes*. Both poetry and music having assumed a new character are thus competing to satisfy the same need; hence the gradual drifting apart.

In consequence, "composers"—especially in the nineteenth century—are primarily concerned with music and the noise quality of the singer's voice. The poem set hardly counts; the singer eventually takes care that it does not count at all; the limit of contempt on the part of both composer and singer being reached in Opera.

Well-meaning but misguided "artistic" souls have, at times, endeavoured to improve relations between poetry and music by devices such as:

Intoning of the neo-parsonic variety;

Improvised chanting by gifted amateurs "with no musical training but a natural melodic instinct";

Irish and other "folk" tune adaptations;

Recitations to existing works of defunct or living composers. Etc.

Taking it for granted that none of these can be considered as acceptable solutions by sensitive and respectable persons, is it possible to revive the old poet-musician association with any sort of success?

The obvious answer is that it is, provided those concerned are willing to reform entirely on ancient and Eastern lines our musical system as applied to poetry. Which would mean:

Making a distinction between poetry that need not be recited with music: versified prose, verse where *meaning* is the first consideration, plays—except for occasional lyrical passages—etc., and: poetry that need be sung: story-telling, lyrical poems, etc., and of course songs;

Dividing these into categories and inventing musical modes to suit them;

Training the poet to become a musician and the musician to master the poetic categories.

As the poetry-loving public could not be expected to undergo in time the necessary training, publication of poetry in book form, even with the music, would have to be suspended and replaced by public or private recitals by the poets. While adding to the joys of life this last aspect of an otherwise ideal scheme, might, however, be enough to spoil its chances from the start.

Nevertheless efforts should not be abandoned. A number of modern composers have very successfully collaborated with poets. I cannot mention them all. Some will say Debussy. With Debussy, the man is willing, the musician is weak. We only get "composers'" songs with pseudo-modal settings Sauce Paris—1905. But Stravinski has done it again and again: "Noces," "Symphonie des Psaumes," etc. Perhaps the best is "Reynard the Fox" and "Persephone," if one forgets Miss Ida Rubinstein. Walton's "Façade" was also a good, though more specialized, attempt. Which shows that intimate collaboration can be achieved provided the musician shows respect and intelligence and, when not a genius, is willing:

To restrict his melodic compass in most cases;

To vary the bar-extent of his tune according to the character of the poem from a mere musical emphasis of rhythm to the more coloured pattern suggested by the "song";

To concentrate not necessarily on the metre but on the rhythm;

To disregard the usual harmonic and tonic constructions, and also, perhaps, to consider the possibility of establishing a new system of notation, keeping staff, notes, and stress points, but doing away with keys, bars, and the necessity for "endings."

In the absence of a fixed musico-poetical system, the results will depend entirely on the musician. The Stravinski brand will adapt themselves naturally, the others should be encouraged to stick for the moment to the quiet, rhythmic noise-accompaniment.

Musicians, especially those at the training stage, might benefit from a closer acquaintance with ancient and non-European music. Gramophone records exist that are relatively easy to procure. I would recommend those from the Balkans—Bulgaria, Serbia, Greek songs that are not too Arabic in character, those from South and Eastern Russia—as published by the Research Department of the Soviets, those from India—avoiding the "virtuosi"—and from Java and Bali.

(Unsigned typescript with autograph emendations in Dulac's hand; a revision and expansion of the "Neuchatel Document"; copy in HRHRC; printed in Diana Poteat Hobby, 'William Butler Yeats and Edmund Dulac: A Correspondence,' PhD Dissertation, Rice University, 1981, 256–9; Ann Arbor, MI: University Microfilms International (Order 8116967), 1983.

Selected Bibliography

(Additional bibliography on Abbreviations pages)

BOOKS

Allingham, William, *William Allingham: A Diary*, ed. H. Allingham and D. Kradford (London: Macmillan, 1907).

Archer, Charles, *William Archer: Life, Work and Friendships* (London: Allen and Unwin, 1931).

Bauerle, Ruth (ed.), *The James Joyce Songbook* (New York and London: Garland, 1982).

Beerbohm, Max, *More Theatres* (London: Rupert Hart-Davis, 1969).

Berry, Francis, *Poetry and the Physical Voice* (London: Routledge and Kegan Paul, 1962).

Blake, William, *The Works of William Blake*, vol. i, ed. Edwin J. Ellis and W. B. Yeats (London: Bernard Quaritch, 1893).

——, *The Poems of William Blake* (London: George Routledge and Sons, 1905).

——, *The Complete Poetry and Prose of William Blake*, newly rev. edn, ed. David V. Erdman (New York: Doubleday, 1988).

Blunt, Wilfrid Scawen, *My Diaries, Part Two* (New York: Knopf, 1923).

Bose, Abinash Chandra, *Three Mystic Poets: A Study of W. B. Yeats, A.E. and Rabindranath Tagore* (Kolhapur: Second and College Bookstall, 1946).

Bowen, Zach, *Musical Allusions in the Works of James Joyce* (Dublin: Gill and Macmillan, 1975).

Boyd, Ernest, *Portraits: Real and Imaginary* (London: Jonathan Cape, 1924).

Campbell, Margaret, *Dolmetsch: The Man and His Work* (London: Hamish Hamilton, 1975).

Chappell, William, *The History of Music*, vol. i (London: Chappell, 1874).

Clinton-Baddeley, Victor C., *Words for Music* (Cambridge: Cambridge Univ. Press, 1941).

Coburn, Alvin Langdon, *Alvin Langdon Coburn Photographer: An Autobiography*, ed. Helmut and Alison Gernshein (London: Faber and Faber, 1969).

——, *Men of Mark* (London: Duckworth, 1913).

Cole, Marion, *Fogie: The Life of Elsie Fogerty* (London: Peter Davies, 1967).

Cousins, James, *We Two Together* (Madras: Ganesh, 1950).

Craig, Edward Gordon, *Index to the Story of My Days* (New York, Viking Press, 1957).

Devine, Brian, *Yeats, the Master of Sound* (Gerrards Cross: Colin Smythe, 2006).

DiBattista, Maria, and Lucy McDiarmid (eds), *High and Low Moderns* (New York and Oxford: Oxford Univ. Press, 1996).

Dolmetsch, Arnold, *The Interpretation of the Music of the XVIIth and XVIIIth Centuries* (London: Novello, 1915).

Dolmetsch, Mabel, *Personal Recollections of Arnold Dolmetsch* (New York: Macmillan, 1958).

Douglas, Lord Alfred, *Without Apology* (London: Martin Secker, 1938).

Drinkwater, John, *Discovery: Being the Second Book of an Autobiography 1897–1913* (Boston and New York: Houghton Mifflin, 1933).

Dyce, Alexander, *The Reminiscences of Alexander Dyce*, ed. Richard J. Schrader (Columbus: Ohio State Univ. Press, 1972).

Eglinton, John, *Irish Literary Portraits* (London: Macmillan, 1935).

Eliot, T. S., *The Letters of T. S. Eliot*. vol. i, 1898–1922, ed. Valerie Eliot (London: Faber and Faber, 1988).

——, *Selected Essays*, new edn. (New York: Harcourt Brace and World, 1950).

Ellmann, Richard, *James Joyce* (New York: Oxford Univ. Press, 1957).

——, *Yeats: The Man and the Masks* (Oxford: Oxford Univ. Press, 1979).

Elton, Oliver, *Frederick York Powell: A Life*, vol. i (Oxford: Clarendon Press, 1906).

Erdman, David V., *Blake: Prophet Against Empire*. rev. edn. (Princeton: Princeton Univ. Press, 1969).

Ervine, St. John, *Some Impressions of My Elders* (New York: Macmillan, 1922).

Farr, Florence, *The Music of Speech* (London: Elkin Mathews, 1909).

——, *The Mystery of Time: A Masque* (London: Theosophical Publishing Society, 1905).

Fay, Frank, *Towards a National Theatre*, ed. Robert Hogan (Dublin: Dolmen Press, 1970).

Fay, Gerard, *The Abbey Theatre: Cradle of Genius* (New York: Macmillan, 1958).

Ferguson, Robert, *The Short Sharp Life of T. E. Hulme* (London: Allen Lane, 2002).

Fink, Henry T. (ed.), *Fifty Mastersongs by Twenty Composers*, vol. ii (Boston: Oliver Ditson, 1902).

Flannery, James W., *Miss Annie Horniman and the Abbey Theatre* (Dublin: Dolmen Press, 1970).

—— *W. B. Yeats and the Idea of a Theatre* (New Haven and London: Yale Univ. Press, 1976).

Field, Michael [pseud. Katherine Bradley and Edith Cooper], *Works and Days*, ed. T. & D. C. Sturge Moore (London: John Murray, 1953).

Gawthorpe, Mary, *Uphill to Holloway* (Penobscot, ME: Traversity Press, 1962).

Gibbon, Monk, *The Masterpiece and the Man: Yeats As I Knew Him* (London: Rupert Hart-Davis, 1959).

Gilchrist, Alexander, *Life of William Blake*, vol. i, 1880 (New York: Phaeton Press, 1969).

Gilmore, Bob, *Harry Partch* (New Haven: Yale Univ. Press, 1998).

Gogarty, Oliver St. John, *Many Lines to Thee: Letters to GKA Bell from Martello Tower . . . 1904–1907*, ed. James F. Carens (Dublin: Dolmen Press, 1971).

Goldring, Douglas, *South Lodge: Reminiscences of Violet Hunt, Ford Madox Ford and the English Review Circle* (London: Constable, 1943).

Gosse, Edmund, *The Life of Algernon Charles Swinburne* (London: Macmillan, 1917).

Grant, Joy, *Harold Monro and the Poetry Bookshop* (London: Routledge and Kegan Paul, 1967).

Gregory, Anne, *Me and Nu: Childhood at Coole* (Gerrards Cross: Colin Smythe, 1978).

Gregory, Augusta, *Lady Gregory's Journals*, ed. Lennox Robinson (London: Putnam and Company, 1946).

——, *Our Irish Theatre* (New York: Capricorn Books, 1965).

Guha, Naresh, *W. B. Yeats: An Indian Approach* (Calcutta: Jadavpur Univ., 1968).

Gwynn, Stephen, *Experiences of a Literary Man* (London: Thornton Butterworth, 1926).

Hackett, Francis, *American Rainbow* (New York: Liveright, 1971).

Hapgood, Norman, *The Changing Years* (New York: Farrar and Rinehart, 1930).

Harmer, J. B., *Victory in Limbo: Imagism 1908–17* (London: Secker and Warburg, 1975).

Hazlitt, William, *The Complete Prose of William Hazlitt, vol. 17*, ed. P. P. Howe (London and Toronto: J. M. Dent and Sons, 1932).

Hine, Reginald, *Confessions of an Un-Common Attorney* (London: J. M. Dent and Sons, 1945).

Hobby, Diana Poteat, "William Butler Yeats and Edmund Dulac: A Correspondence," PhD Dissertation, Rice University, 1981; Ann Arbor, MI: University Microfilms International (Order 8116967), 1983.

Hogan, Robert, and James Kilroy (eds), *Lost Plays of the Irish Renaissance* (Dixon, CA: Proscenium Press, 1970).

Holloway, Joseph, *Joseph Holloway's Abbey Theatre: A Selection from his Unpublished Journal*, ed. Robert Hogan and Michael J. O'Neill (Carbondale and Edwardsville: Southern Illinois Univ. Press, 1967).

——, *Joseph Holloway's Irish Theatre*, vol. ii, *1932–1937*, ed. Robert Hogan and Michael J. O'Neill (Dixon, CA: Proscenium Press, 1969).

Hone, Joseph, *W. B. Yeats 1865–1939* (London: Macmillan, 1942).

Hunt, Hugh, *The Abbey: Ireland's National Theatre 1904–1979* (New York: Columbia Univ. Press, 1979).

Jeffares, A. Norman, *A Commentary on the Collected Poems of W. B. Yeats* (Palo Alto, CA: Stanford Univ. Press, 1968).

Jepson, Edgar, *Memories of a Victorian*, vol. i (London: Victor Gollancz, 1933).

Johnson, Josephine, *Florence Farr: Bernard Shaw's "New Woman"* (Gerrards Cross: Colin Smythe, 1975).

Johnston. Kenneth R., *The Hidden Wordsworth* (New York and London: W. W. Norton, 1998).

Jones, Alun R., *The Life and Opinions of T. E. Hulme* (Boston: Beacon Press, 1960).

Joyce, James, *Dubliners* (New York: Penguin, 1992).

——, *Letters of James Joyce*, ed. Stuart Gilbert (New York: Viking Press, 1957).

——, *Portrait of the Artist as a Young Man*, ed. Seamus Deane (New York: Penguin Books, 1992).

——, *Ulysses* (New York: Vintage, 1990).

Joyce, Stanislaus, *My Brother's Keeper*, ed. Richard Ellmann (New York: Oxford Univ. Press, 1982).

Kavanagh, Peter, *The Story of the Abbey Theatre* (New York: Devin-Adair, 1950).

Kelly, John, *A W. B. Yeats Chronology* (London: Palgrave, 2003).

King, Francis, *Ritual Magic in England* (London: Neville Spearman, 1970).

Lhombreaud, Roger, *Arthur Symons: A Critical Biography* (London: Unicorn Press, 1963).

Longenbach, James, *Stone Cottage: Pound, Yeats, and Modernism* (New York and Oxford: Oxford Univ. Press, 1988).

Longford, Elizabeth, *A Pilgrimage of Passion: the Life of Wilfrid Scawen Blunt* (London: Weidenfeld and Nicolson, 1979).

Lowell, Amy (ed.), *Some Imagist Poets* (Boston: Houghton Mifflin, 1916).

MacDonagh, Thomas, *Thomas Campion and the Art of English Poetry* (Dublin: Talbot Press, 1913).

——, *Literature in Ireland: Studies Irish and Anglo-Irish* (New York: Frederick A. Stokes, 1916).

MacCarthy, Desmond, *The Court Theatre, 1904–1907* (London: A. H. Bullen, 1907).

MacManus, Francis, *The Yeats We Knew* (Cork: Mercier Press, 1965).

McCarthy, Lillah, *Myself and My Friends* (London: Thornton Butterworth, 1933).

McHugh, Roger (ed.), *Davis, Mangan, Ferguson: Tradition and the Irish Writer* (Chester, PA: Dufour Editions, 1970).

Mannin, Ethel, *Privileged Spectator*, rev. edn. (London: Jarrolds, 1948).

Masefield, John, *Some Memories of W. B. Yeats* (Dublin: Cuala Press, 1940).

——, *So Long to Learn* (New York: Macmillan, 1952).

——, *With the Living Voice: An Address* (Cambridge: Cambridge Univ. Press, 1924).

——, *Words Spoken at the Music Room Boar's Hill in the Afternoon of November 5th, 1930 at a Festival Designed in the Honour of William Butler Yeats, Poet*, privately printed, not for sale; rpt. in *Recent Prose*, 2nd Eng. edn. (London: William Heinnemann, 1932).

Massé, H. H. L. J., *The Art-Workers' Guild, 1883–1934* (Oxford: Shakespeare Head Press, 1935).

Mikhail, E. H. (ed.), *The Abbey Theatre: Interviews and Recollections* (London: Macmillan, 1988).

Moore, George, *Hail and Farewell*, vol i, ed. Richard Cave (Washington, DC: Catholic Univ. of America Press, 1985).

Murray, Gilbert, *An Unfinished Autobiography*, ed. Jean Smith and Arnold Toynbee (London: George Allen and Unwin, 1960).

Nevinson, Henry Woodd, *Changes and Chances* (New York: Harcourt, Brace, 1923).

——, *More Changes, More Chances* (London: Nisbet and Company, 1925).

Newbolt, Margaret (ed.), *The Later Life and Letters of Sir Henry Newbolt* (London: Faber and Faber, 1942).

O'Connor, Frank, *My Father's Son* (London: Macmillan, 1968).

O'Grady, Standish, *The Coming of Cuchulain* (Dublin: Talbot Press, 1920).

O'Sullivan, Seamus, *The Rose and Bottle* (Dublin: Talbot Press, 1946).

Oshima, Shotaro, *W. B. Yeats and Japan* (Tokyo: Hokuseidō, 1965).

Partch, Harry, *Bitter Music: Collected Journals, Essays, Introductions, and Librettos*, ed. Thomas McGeary (Champaign: Univ. of Illinois Press, 2000).

——, *Genesis of a Music* (Madison: Univ. of Wisconsin Press, 1949).

Patmore, Brigit, *My Friends When Young* (London: Heinemann, 1968).

Patmore, Derek, *Private History* (London: Jonathan Cape, 1960).

Patmore, Coventry, *Poems*, 2nd collected edn. (London: George Bell, 1886).

Payne, Ben Iden, *Life in a Wooden O: Memoirs of the Theatre* (New Haven and London: Yale Univ. Press, 1977).

Percy, Thomas, *Reliques of Ancient English Poetry*, vol. i. ed. Henry B. Wheatley (London: George Allen and Unwin, 1885; rpt. 1927).

Plarr, Victor, *Ernest Dowson 1888–1897* (London: Elkin Mathews, 1914).

Pound, Ezra, *The Cantos of Ezra Pound* (London: Faber and Faber, 1964).

——, *Certain Noble Plays of Japan* (Churchtown, Dundrum: Cuala Press, 1916).

——, *The Letters of Ezra Pound 1907–1941*, ed. D. D. Paige (New York: Harcourt Brace, 1950).

——, *The Letters of Ezra Pound to Alice Corbin Henderson*, ed. Ira B. Nadel (Austin: Univ. of Texas Press, 1993).

——, *Literary Essays of Ezra Pound*, ed. T. S. Eliot (New York: New Directions, 1968).

——, *Pound/Joyce: The Letters of Ezra Pound to James Joyce*, ed. Forrest Read (New York: New Directions, 1967).

——, *Ripostes of Ezra Pound* (London: Stephen Swift and Company, 1912).

——, *Selected Letters of Ezra Pound to John Quinn, 1915–1924*, ed. Timothy Materer (Durham and London: Duke Univ. Press, 1991).

——, *Selected Poems*, introduction by T. S. Eliot (London: Faber and Gwyer, 1928).

——, *The Spirit of Romance* (Norfolk, CT: New Directions, 1952).

Purdom, C. B., *Harley Granville Barker* (London: A. H. Bullen, 1907).

Putnam, Nina Wilcox, *Laughing Through: Being the Autobiographical Story of a Girl Who Made Her Way* (New York: Sears, 1930).

Quinn, John, *The Letters of John Quinn to W. B. Yeats*, ed. Alan Himber (Ann Arbor: UMI Research Press, 1983).

Reid, B. L., *John Quinn and His Friends* (New York: Oxford Univ. Press, 1968).

Rhys, Ernest, *Everyman Remembers* (London: J. M. Dent and Sons, 1931).

——, *Letters from Limbo* (London: J. M. Dent and Sons, 1936).

——, *Wales England Wed* (London: J. M. Dent and Sons, 1940).

Ricketts, Charles, *Self Portrait: Taken from the Letters and Journals of Charles Ricketts, R.A.*, comp. T. Sturge Moore, ed. Cecil Lewis (London: Peter Davies, 1939).

——, *Letters from Charles Ricketts to "Michel Field" (1903–1913)*, ed. J. G. Paul Delaney (Edinburgh: Tragara Press, 1981).

Rittenhouse, Jessie B., *My House of Life* (Boston and New York: Houghton Mifflin, 1934).

Robinson, Lennox (ed.), *The Arrow: W. B. Yeats Commemoration Number* (Dublin: Abbey Theatre, 1939).

Rodgers, W. R. (ed.), *Irish Literary Portraits* (London: BBC, 1972).

Rothenstein, William, *Men and Memories* (London: Faber and Faber, 1932).

——, *Since Fifty: Men and Memories, 1922–1938* (London: Faber and Faber, 1939).

——, and Rabindranath Tagore. *Letters of William Rothenstein and Rabindranath Tagore 1911–1941*, ed. Mary M. Lago (Cambridge, MA: Harvard Univ. Press, 1972).

Ruddock, Margot, *The Lemon Tree*, introduction by W. B. Yeats (London: J. M. Dent and Sons, 1937).

Ruggles, Eleanor, *The West-Going Heart: A Life of Vachel Lindsay* (New York: W. W. Norton, 1959).

Rumbold, Richard, *A Message in Code: The Diary of Richard Rumbold 1932–1960*, ed. William Plomer (London: Weidenfeld and Nicolson, 1964).

Russell, George, *Letters from AE*, ed. Alan Denson (London: Abelard-Schuman, 1961).

——, *Passages from the Letters of AE to W. B. Yeats* (Dublin: Cuala Press, 1936).

——, *Some Irish Essays* (Dublin: Maunsel, 1906).

Saddlemyer, Ann, *Becoming George: The Life of Mrs W. B. Yeats* (Oxford: Oxford Univ. Press, 2002).

Schafer, R. Murray (ed.), *Ezra Pound and Music* (New York: New Directions, 1977).

Scott, W. Dixon, *The Leters of W. Dixon Scott*, ed. Mary McCrossan (London: Herbert Joseph, 1932).

Shaw, George Bernard, *Music in London 1890–94*, vol. ii (New York: Vienna House, 1973).

Shaw, Martin, *Up to Now* (London: Oxford Univ. Press, 1929).

Shiubhlaigh, Maire nic, *The Splendid Years* (Dublin: James Duffy, 1955).

Sidnell, Michael, *Dances of Death: The Group Theatre of London in the Thirties* (London: Faber and Faber, 1984).

Sieburth, Richard, *A Walking Tour of Southern France* (New York: New Directions, 1992).

Smith, Constance Babington, *John Masefield: A Life* (New York: Macmillan, 1978).
Sparling, Henry Halliday (ed.), *Irish Minstrelsy* (London: Walter Scott, 1888).
Speaight, Robert, *William Poel and the Elizabethan Revival* (London: Heinemann, 1954).
Stravinsky, Igor, *Conversations with Igor Stravinsky* (Garden City, NY: Doubleday, 1959).
Symons, Arthur, *Images of Good and Evil* (London: Heinemann, 1899).
——, *Plays, Acting, and Music* (London: Duckworth, 1903).
Tagore, Rabindranath, *Gitanjali* (London: Macmillan, 1913).
——, *My Reminiscences*, trans. Surendranath Tagore (London, 1917).
Tynan, Katherine, *Twenty-Five Years* (London: Smith, Elder, 1913).
Walkley, A. B., *Drama and Life* (London: Methuen, 1907).
Watts-Dunton, Clara, *The Home Life of Swinburne* (London: A. M. Philpot, 1922).
Wellesley, Dorothy, *Far Have I Travelled* (London: James Barrie, 1952).
Weygandt, Cornelius, *Irish Plays and Playwrights* (London: Constable, 1913).
——, *Tuesdays at Ten* (Philadelphia: Univ. of Philadelphia Press, 1928).
Wilson, Duncan, *Gilbert Murray OM* (Oxford: Clarendon Press, 1987).
Woolf, Leonard, *Downhill All the Way: An Autobiography of the Years 1919–1939* (London: Hogarth Press, 1967).
Woolf, Virginia, *Diary of Virginia Woolf*, vol ii, ed. Anne Olivier Bell (New York: Harcourt, Brace, Jovanovich, 1978).
Yeats, W. B., *A Selection of the Poems of W. B. Yeats* (Leipzig: Bernhard Tauchnitz, 1913).
——, *A Vision* (London: T. Werner Laurie, 1925).
—— (ed.), *Beltaine: The Organ of the Irish Literary Theatre, Number One to Number Three (May 1899–April 1900)* (London: Frank Cass, 1970).
—— (ed.), *Samhain: An Occasional Review* (Dublin: Sealy Bryers and Walker, 1901–6; Maunsel, 1908).
—— (ed.), *The Arrow*, numbers 1–5 (Dublin, 1906–9).
—— and F. R. Higgins (eds), *Broadsides* (Dublin: Cuala Press, 1935).
—— and Dorothy Wellesley (eds), *Broadsides* (Dublin: Cuala Press, 1937).
——, *The Countess Cathleen: Manuscript Materials*, ed. Michael J. Sidnell and Wayne K. Chapman (Ithaca, NY: Cornell Univ. Press, 1999).
——, *The Death of Cuchulain: Manuscript Materials*, ed. Phillip L. Marcus (Ithaca, NY and London: Cornell Univ. Press, 1982).
——, *Four Plays for Dancers* (London: Macmillan, 1921).
——, *Interviews and Recollections*, ed. E. H. Mikhail, vol. i (New York: Barnes and Noble, 1977).
——, *The King's Threshold: Manuscript Materials*, ed. Declan Kiely (Ithaca, NY and London: Cornell Univ. Press, 2005).
——, *The Land of Heart's Desire* (London: T. Fisher Unwin, 1912).
——, *Letters on Poetry from W. B. Yeats to Dorothy Wellesley* (London: Oxford Univ. Press, 1940).

Yeats, W. B., *New Poems: Manuscript Materials*, ed. J. C. C. Mays and Stephen Parrish (Ithaca, NY and London: Cornell Univ. Press, 2000).

——, *Plays in Prose and Verse* (London: Macmillan, 1922).

——, *The Poetical Works of William B. Yeats in Two Volumes, volume ii, Dramatical Poems* (New York: Macmillan, 1907).

——, *The Shadowy Waters* (London: Hodder and Stoughton, 1900).

——, *Sophocles' King Oedipus: A Version for the Modern Stage* (New York: Macmillan, 1928).

——, *Stories of Michael Robartes and His Friends* (Dublin: Cuala Press, 1931).

——, *W. B. Yeats and T. Sturge Moore: Their Correspondence 1901–1937*, ed. Ursula Bridge (London: Routledge and Kegan Paul, 1953).

——, *Wheels and Butterflies* (London: Macmillan, 1934).

Young, Ella, *Flowering Dusk* (New York and Toronto: Longmans, Green, 1945).

ARTICLES

Aldington, Richard, "Presentation to Mr. W. S. Blunt," *Egoist*, 1 (February 2, 1914), 57.

Ashby-Sterry, J., "The Bystander," *The Graphic*, June 14, 1902, 794.

——, "Tramping Troubadours," *Truth*, July 3, 1902, 6.

Binyon, Lawrence, "Mr. Bridges' 'Prometheus' and Poetic Drama," *The Dome*, 2 (March 1899), 199–206.

Chiba, Yoko, "Ezra Pound's Versions of Fenollosa's Noh Manuscripts and Yeats's Unpublished 'Suggestions & Corrections.'" *Yeats Annual No. 4*, ed. Warwick Gould (London: Macmillan, 1986), 121–44.

Clinton-Baddeley, Victor C., "Reciting the Poems," *Irish Times* (June 10, 1965), *Yeats: A Centenary Tribute Supplement*, iv.

——, "Reading Poetry with W. B. Yeats," *London Magazine*, 4 (December 1957), 47–53.

——, "The Written and the Spoken Word," *Essays and Studies*, 18 (1965), 73–82.

Corbin, John, "Lilting to the Psaltery," *The Saturday Evening Post*, 179 (April 20, 1907), 22–3.

Eliot, T. S., "A Commentary," *Criterion*, 14 (July 1935), 610–13.

——, "A Foreign Mind." *Athenaeum*, 4653 (4 July 1919), 552–3.

——, "The Noh and the Image," *Egoist*, 4 (August 1917), 102–3.

——, "The Spoken Word," *Festival of Britain 1951: London Season of the Arts*, Official Souvenir Programme (London: Lund Humphries, 1951), 7–8.

——, "Note sur Mallarmé et Poe," *La Nouvelle Revue Française*, 14 (November 1, 1926), 524-6.

Fallis, Richard, "Language and Rhythm in Poetry: A Previously Unpublished Essay by W. B. Yeats," *Shenandoah*, 26 (Summer 1975), 77–9.

Farr, Florence, "The Rites of Astaroth," *New Age* (September 5, 1907), 294–5.

Flint, F. S., "The History of Imagism," *Egoist*, 2 (May 1, 1915), 71.

Herbst, Oswald [pseud. James Gostick], "Letter from England," *Tait's Edinburgh Magazine,* n.s. 11 (August and October, 1844), 521–4, 641–5.

Herzinger, Kim, "The Night Pound Ate the Tulips: An Evening at Ernest Rhys's," *Journal of Modern Literature*, 8 (1980), 153–5.

Johnson, Colton, "Yeats's Wireless," *Wilson Quarterly*, 24 (Spring 2000), 24–30.

Johnson, Josephine, "Florence Farr: Letters to W. B. Yeats, 1912–17," *Yeats Annual No. 9*, ed. Warwick Gould (London: Macmillan, 1992), 216–54.

Kellerman, Steward, "Yeats at the End: Still Writing," *New York Times* (April 6, 1989), C17, 21.

Litz, A. Walton, "Florence Farr: A 'Transitional' Woman," in *High and Low Moderns: Literature and Culture 1889–1939*, ed. Maria DeBattista and Lucy McDiarmid (New York and Oxford: Oxford Univ. Press, 1996), 85–106.

Londraville, Richard (ed.), "Four Lectures by W. B. Yeats, 1902–4," *Yeats Annual No. 8*, ed. Warwick Gould (London: Macmillan, 1991), 78–122.

MacLeish, Archibald, "Public Speech and Private Speech in Poetry," *Yale Review*, 27 (March 1938), 536–47.

Marx, Edward, "Nō Dancing: Yone Noguchi in Yeats's Japan," *Yeats Annual No. 17* (London: Palgrave, 2007), 51–93.

Masefield, John, "Poets on the Air," *Literary Digest*, 107 (October 4, 1930), 107.

McKenna, Wayne, "W. B. Yeats, W. J. Turner and Edmund Dulac: The *Broadsides* and Poetry Broadcasts," *Yeats Annual No. 8*, ed. Warwick Gould (London: Macmillan, 1991), 225–34.

Middleton, Christopher, "Documents on Imagism from the Papers of F. S. Flint," *The Review*, no. 15 (April 1965), 35–51.

Moore, T. Sturge, "The Renovation of the Theatre," *Monthly Review*, 7 (April 1902), 102–16.

——, "Yeats." *English*, 2 (Summer 1939), 273–8.

Morgan, Louise, "Poet Tells Radio Secret," *News Chronicle* (July 5, 1937), 3.

Noguchi, Yone, "A Japanese Poet on W. B. Yeats," *Bookman* (New York), 43 (June 1916), 431–3.

Quinn, John, "Lady Gregory and the Abbey Theatre," *The Outlook* [NY], 99 (December 16, 1911), 916–19.

Runciman, J. R., "At the Alhambra and Elsewhere," *Saturday Review*, 91 (February 23, 1901), 236–7.

Russell, Francis, "The Archpoet," *Horizon* [NY], 3 (November 1960), 66–9.

Silver, Jeremy, "W. B. Yeats and the BBC: A Reassessment," *Yeats Annual No. 5*, ed. Warwick Gould (London: Macmillan, 1987), 181–5.

—— (ed.), "George Barnes's 'W. B. Yeats and Broadcasting,' 1940," *Yeats Annual No. 5*, ed. Warwick Gould (London: Macmillan, 1987), 189–94.

Tagore, Rabindranath, "A Hindu on the Celtic Spirit," *The American Review of Reviews*, 49 (January–June 1914), 101–2.

Toomey, Deirdre, "Bards of the Gael and Gall: An Uncollected Review by Yeats in *The Illustrated London News*," *Yeats Annual No.* 5, ed. Warwick Gould (London: Macmillan, 1987), 203–11.

Turner, W. J., "Broadside Songs," *New Statesman and Nation*, 10 (December 7, 1935), 848–50.

——, "Music and Words," *New Statesman and Nation*, 14 (July 24, 1937), 146–7.

——, "Poets and Musicians," *New Statesman and Nation*, 16 (September 3, 1938), 347–8.

Weygandt, Cornelius, "With Mr. W. B. Yeats in the Woods of Coole," *Lippincott's Magazine*, 73 (April 1904), 484–7.

Index